ANNALS OF THE NEW YORK ACADEMY OF SCIENCES

VOLUME 163, ART. 2 PAGES 589–1029

October 3, 1969

BIOLOGICAL EFFECTS OF ALKYLATING AGENTS*

Consulting Editor
BENJAMIN L. VAN DUUREN

Conference Cochairmen
BENJAMIN L. VAN DUUREN AND HANS L. FALK

CONTENTS

Introductory Remarks. *By* HANS L. FALK 591

Part I. Chemistry of Alkylating Agents

Mechanism of Action of Alkylating Agents. *By* CHARLES C. PRICE, G. M. GAUCHER, P. KONERU, R. SHIBAKAWA, J. R. SOWA AND M. YAMAGUCHI 593

New Methods of Formation of Carbon-Nitrogen Bonds. *By* DANIEL SWERN 601

Reactions with Purines and Pyrimidines. *By* ROBERT SHAPIRO 624

Part II. Chemical Carcinogenesis

Carcinogenic Epoxides, Lactones, and Halo-Ethers and Their Mode of Action. *By* B. L. VAN DUUREN 633

Comparison of the Mode of Action by which some Alkylating Agents and Ionizing Radiations Kill Mammalian Cells. *By* PETER ALEXANDER 652

N-Nitroso Compounds in Organotropic and Transplacental Carcinogenesis. *By* H. DRUCKREY, R. PREUSSMANN AND S. IVANKOVIC 676

Chemical Structure and Carcinogenicity of Aliphatic Hydrazo, Azo, and Azoxy Compounds and of Triazenes, Potential *In Vivo* Alkylating Agents. *By* R. PREUSSMANN, H. DRUCKREY, S. IVANKOVIC AND A. V. HODENBERG 697

*This series of papers is the result of a conference entitled Biological Effects of Alkylating Agents, held by The New York Academy of Sciences on September 16, 17, and 18, 1968.

In Vivo Reactions of Nitroso Compounds. *By* P. N. MAGEE 717

Studies on the Mechanism of Activation of Aromatic Amine and Amide Carcinogens to Ultimate Carcinogenic Electrophilic Reactants. *By* ELIZABETH C. MILLER AND JAMES A. MILLER 731

In Vivo Reactions of β-Propiolactone. *By* R. K. BOUTWELL, NANCY H. COLBURN AND CAROLYN C. MUCKERMAN 751

Part III. Mutagenesis and Teratogenesis

Consequences of Alkylation for the Behavior of DNA. *By* B. STRAUSS, M. COYLE AND M. ROBBINS 765

Mutagenicity of Alkylating Carcinogens. *By* H. V. MALLING AND F. J. DE SERRES 788

Teratogenic Agents: Mammalian Test Systems and Chemicals. *By* JOSEPH A. DIPAOLO 801

Transplacental Carcinogenesis in Mice by ethyl-1-Nitrosourea. *By* JERRY M. RICE 813

The Mutagenicity and Initiating Activity of some Aromatic Amine Metabolites. *By* FRANK MUKAI AND WALTER TROLL 828

Part IV. Environmental Alkylating Agents

Pyrrolizidine Alkaloids as Alkylating and Antimitotic Agents. *By* C. C. J. CULVENOR, D. T. DOWNING AND J. A. EDGAR 837

Toxic and Carcinogenic Alkylating Agents from Cycads. *By* MARIA SPATZ 848

Alkylating Agents as Insect Chemosterilants. *By* ALEXEJ B. BOŘKOVEC 860

Degradation and Residues of Alkylating Agents. *By* LAWRENCE FISHBEIN 869

Analysis of Alkylating Agents: Applications to Air Pollution. *By* E. SAWICKI AND C. R. SAWICKI ... 895

Part V. Chemotherapy by Alkylating Agents

Alkylating Agents in Clinical Cancer Chemotherapy. *By* MANUEL OCHOA, JR. 921

Some Effects of Alkylating Agents on Epithelia in Man and in an Experimental System in the Rat. *By* LEOPOLD G. KOSS 931

Properties of L5178Y Lymphoblasts Highly Resistant to Nitrogen Mustard. *By* GERALD J. GOLDENBERG 936

Preclinical Investigation of Alkylating Agents in Cancer Chemotherapy. *By* ABRAHAM GOLDIN AND HARRY B. WOOD, JR. 954

Structure-Activity Relationships of Alkylating Agents in Cancer Chemotherapy. *By* T. J. BARDOS, Z. F. CHMIELEWICZ AND P. HEBBORN 1006

Carcinogenesis: Frontiers in Inner Space. *By* MICHAEL B. SHIMKIN 1026

INTRODUCTORY REMARKS

Hans L. Falk

National Environmental Health Sciences Center
Research Triangle Park, N. C.

It is a great privilege for me to give an introduction to the very important problem of the biological effects of alkylating agents, particularly since these agents have grown in diversity and usefulness as well as in hazard.

Following the original use of mustard gas as a vesicant, its biological properties were further explored, until a large number of chemotherapeutic agents, specifically designed for the treatment of cancer, were synthesized. Other groups of chemicals possessing alkylating properties were brought on the market for chemotherapeutic trials or for insect sterilization, for which several aziridine compounds were found to be most effective. Solvents, intermediates for rocket fuels, fumigants, sterilants for biological fluids, and surgical plastics and instruments were developed and have been used extensively, even though problems of toxicity due to residues have been encountered.

It should be stressed, however, that not all alkylating agents have been produced by the chemical and pharmaceutical industries, nature having provided various types of these agents in natural products, which are also discussed in this monograph.

A third aspect, which arose as the result of man's activity in his daily life, must be mentioned. This group represents unplanned and unexpected production of alkylating agents in various familiar products that I should like to discuss specifically.

The most harmful effects of alkylating agents, which represent the main topic of this monograph, can be classified as cytotoxic, teratogenic, mutagenic, and carcinogenic properties. They have been observed for certain members of each of the groups in laboratory experiments. Among natural products, alkylating groups have been detected and toxic reactions have been described following ingestion of the constituent with the food. The properties of cycasin and its aglycone, a constituent of cycad meal and of other components of members of that family, will be discussed in detail in the monograph. From moldy hay and corn, interesting epoxy compounds have been isolated and characterized as the toxic principles. They were named nivalenols and scirpenols, respectively.

Interesting properties were found in cedarwood oil, which showed prophylactic properties against infection by *Schistosoma mansoni*. This could be attributed to an epoxide: 14,15-epoxygeranylgeraniol. This interesting activity may be related to juvenile hormone activity possessed by another natural epoxide: methyl-10,11-epoxyfarnesoate. Some of the important synthetic and natural flavors also possess epoxy groupings in the molecule.

Other interesting fungal metabolites were searched for in efforts to detect new chemotherapeutic agents against cancer. Streptozotocin, a promising fungal metabolite, possesses the nitrosamine grouping in the molecule, and carcinogenic properties can be predicted for this compound. Alkylating properties are also possessed by many naturally occurring, unsaturated, gamma lactones of higher or lower plant origin, for which structural requirements for carcinogenic properties are still not completely clear.

The third topic on alkylating agents is the most difficult to evaluate. Evidence for the presence of nitrosamines in herring meal, which was toxic to sheep, was attributed to the treatment of the meal with sodium nitrite as preservative. Nitrosamines were also found in other foods treated with nitrite, but a different problem existed in the case of wheat flour, where further study established the presence of nitrosamines already in the green plant. Heating to 170° C increased the content of nitrosamines considerably. Further research established that nitrosamines can be formed on heating aminoacids, such as L-alanine with D-glucose, in the presence of starch at an alkaline pH between 8 and 9.6. It can also be expected that the nitrosamines detected in tobacco and tobacco smoke, and still presenting topics for discussion, may indeed be present. These compounds have also been detected in incense smoke and artificial charcoal flavor.

Fatty acid epoxides and lactones have been found to result from prolonged heating of fats. They may possess undesirable properties besides potential carcinogenicity. Epoxides have also been detected in air pollution samples, but their significance has not been evaluated.

With this large variety of hazards and potential hazards in our environment, it is particularly urgent to better understand the mode of action of these alkylating agents, their retention in certain species and tissues, and the nature of the residues. This will allow a better assessment of benefit versus risk. I am therefore grateful to Executive Director E. S. Schanze and the members of The New York Academy of Sciences, to Dr. Van Duuren, and to the participating scientists for making possible this exchange of knowledge on the biological action of alkylating agents.

Part I. Chemistry of Alkylating Agents

MECHANISM OF ACTION OF ALKYLATING AGENTS

Charles C. Price, G. M. Gaucher, P. Koneru, R. Shibakawa, J. R. Sowa, and M. Yamaguchi

Department of Chemistry, University of Pennsylvania Philadelphia, Pa.

In the last decade, since a summary on this topic was presented at an earlier symposium,[1] an impressive array of data has accumulated on the importance and nature of attack of alkylating agents on DNA, RNA, and their constituents.[2–33] Most of the alkylating agents responsible for the biological interest in this class of chemical reagents proceed through a common mechanism, involving second-order nucleophilic substitution (S_{N2}):

$$X: + R{-}Y \longrightarrow \overset{\oplus}{X{-}R} + Y:^{\ominus}$$

X: = amine, sulfide, phenolate, carboxylate, phosphate (1)

$Y:^{\ominus}$ = halide, sulfonate

In addition to simple S_{N2} reactions as above, an important modification in the biological alkylating agents involves cyclic compounds, where Y is an oxygen, nitrogen, or sulfur in a three-membered ring:

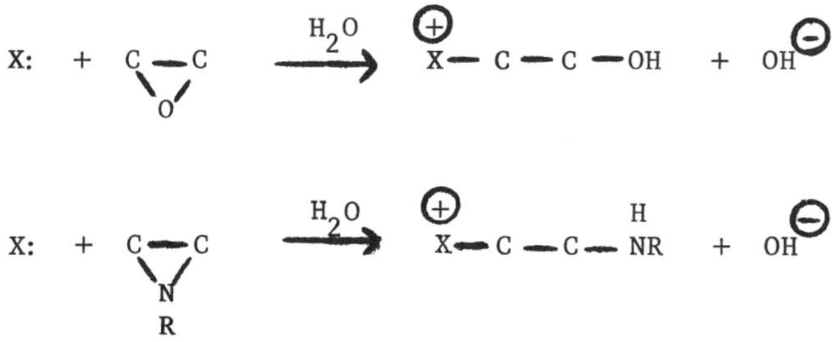

(2)

The sulfur and nitrogen mustards constitute classes that involve as a first step in alkylation the formation of such a cyclic alkylating agent.

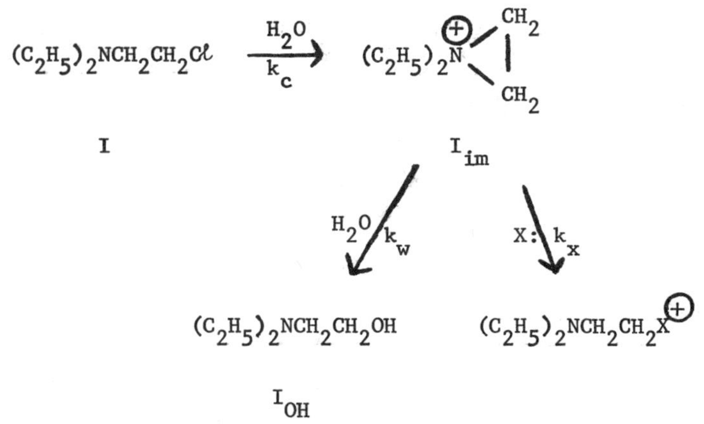

(3)

The overall kinetics of this type of alkylation (Scheme 3) is influenced substantially by the relative rates of the reactions involved. If the rate of first-order cyclization is very fast and of the bimolecular nucleophilic ring opening by water, or nucleophile X: is very slow, then the latter step will be rate-controlling and the reaction kinetics will be second-order. This has been observed for the specific case outlined in Scheme 3.[34–36] In this case, k_w is so slow compared to k_c that solutions of the imonium ion (I_{im}) can be used as reasonably stable reagents, the hydrolysis having a half-life of over one week at 37° C and pH 7. The fast formation and slow reaction of the cyclic imonium ion in this case can be supported not only by conventional analysis,[35,36] but is clearly shown by NMR (nuclear magnetic resonance) data.[36] In D_2O at pH 10.5, I shows initially a triplet (6H) at $\delta = -3.63$ ppm (with respect to H_2O), J = 7 cps, a quadruplet (4H) at −2.00 ppm, J = 7 cps, a triplet (2H) at −1.80 ppm, J = 5.6 cps, and a triplet (CH_2Cl) at −1.10 ppm, J = 5.6 cps. Even at 0° C, this spectrum changed in a few minutes to that of I_{im}: $\delta = -3.38$ ppm, J = 6.0 cps (6H, triplet), $\delta = -1.50$ ppm, J = 6.0 cps (4H, quadruplet), and $\delta = -1.69$ ppm (4H, singlet). At pH 10.5 and 0° C, the I_{im} disappeared with a half-life of 6 hr, yielding I_{OH}: $\delta = -3.78$ ppm, J = 7cps (6H, triplet), $\delta = -2.18$ ppm, J = 7 cps (4H, quadruplet), $\delta = -1.44$ ppm, J = 7 cps (2H, triplet), and $\delta = -1.03$ ppm, J = 7 cps (2H, triplet).

If the rate of the cyclization (k_c) is very slow compared to ring opening (k_w), then there will be no accumulation of the cyclic intermediate, the rate-determining step will become the first-order cyclization (k_c), and the reaction will *superficially* resemble an S_{N1} nucleophilic substitution. It should be strongly emphasized that this resemblance is only superficial, and contrary to the views expressed even fairly recently by some authors, these cases *do not* proceed through a mechanism involving carbonium ion intermediates. Thus this easily explained and expected change in kinetics from a strongly basic nitrogen mustard (such as I) to a sulfur mustard, an aromatic mustard, or a β-chloroethylamide does *not* connote any change in mechanism for the alkylation step, which remains the attack of the nucleophile X: (or water) on the cyclic intermediate.

The significance of this point lies in the fact that for all alkylation reactions proceeding through the S_{N2} mechanism (Schemes 1, 2, and 3), the relative reactivity of nucleophiles as compared to water is surprisingly constant. This can

TABLE 1

COMPETITION FACTORS FOR THE REACTION OF ADENINE AND ITS 9-SUBSTITUTED DERIVATIVES WITH THE N,N-DIETHYLETHYLENIMONIUM ION AT pH 7 AND 37° C

Compound Alkylated*	Site Alkylated	Competition Factor
Adenine	N_3	7,530 (7,570)†
	N_9	1,620 (1,630)
	N_1‡	2,210 (1,530)
Adenosine	N_1	850
2′-Deoxyadenosine	N_1	840 (900)
5′-Adenylic acid	N_1	810
	5′-phosphate	11,400
Poly(adenylic acid)	N_1	1,960
	phosphodiester	12,700

*The pK_a values of adenine (4.2, 9.8) and the adenine moiety in adenosine (3.5) and 5′-adenylic acid (3.3) indicate that 99.9% of the base is in the nonionic or free base form at pH 7, while pK_a values for the phosphate moiety of 5′-adenylic acid (1, 6.1) and poly-(adenylic acid) (~6) indicate that the phosphate groups are at least 90% in the reactive anionic forms at pH 7.

†The results in parenthesis were for alkylation with II_{im},[35] corrected for the extensive competing dimerization of the morpholine mustard.[35] The values for N_1, N_3, and N_9 alkylation in adenine are in good agreement with the relative amounts of ethylation by ethyl methane sulfonate at pH 7 and 40° C; N_1, 19.7%; N_3, 60%; and N_9, 20.6%.[13]

‡All products assigned to N_1 alkylation were isolated as 6-alkylaminopurines, the initial alkylation being followed by rearrangement.[6,39]

be seen by comparing k_x/k_w for reactions of methyl bromide with those for the cyclic sulfonium ion from sulfur mustard (see, e.g., TABLES 1 and 3 in reference 1) as well as comparing data for I_{im} and II_{im} with ethyl methanesulfonate (TABLE 1).

Our recent efforts[37,38] have involved a quantitative study of the alkylation of DNA and its components by two monofunctional nitrogen mustards, diethyl-β-chloroethylamine (I) and β-chloroethylmorpholine (II).

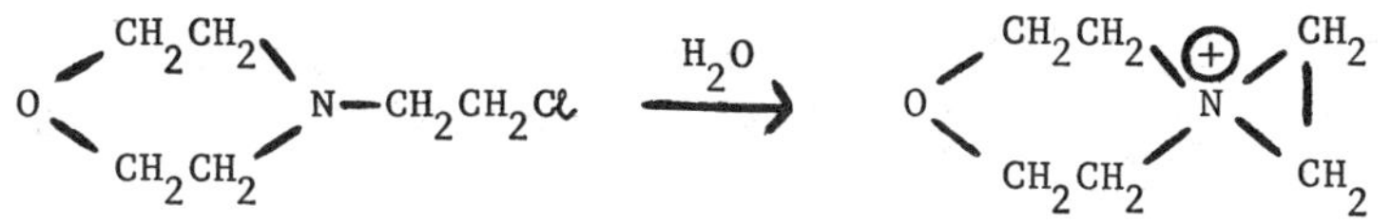

II II_{im}

The nucleic acid bases, nucleosides, and nucleotides were alkylated by I_{im} and II_{im} in dilute aqueous solution at pH 7 and 37–40° C. The products were separated by chromatography on ion-exchange columns with 2–6 N hydrochloric acid. The separate products were identified and measured quantitatively by UV absorption spectroscopy. The results, summarized in TABLES 1, 2, and 3, have been expressed in terms of competition factors.

In the case of N_7 alkylation of the nucleosides and nucleotides related to guanine, the products isolated after hydrolysis and chromatography involved not only cleavage of the sugar moiety at N_7 but opening of the imidazole ring. We suggest that this latter reaction proceeds by the following steps:

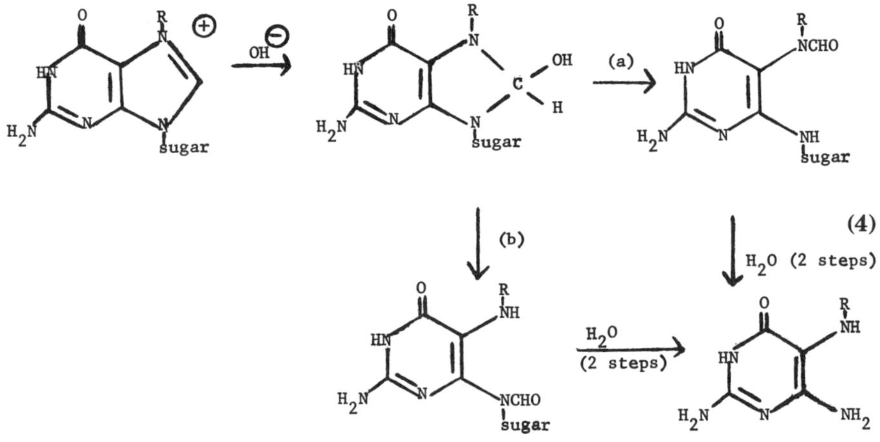

(4)

The relative amounts of cleavage by mode (a) vs. mode (b) seem to depend on the nature of the sugar (ribose or deoxyribose) and of the group R (β-diethylaminoethyl or β-morpholinoethyl).

TABLE 2

COMPETITION FACTORS FOR THE ALKYLATION OF GUANINE AND SOME 9-DERIVATIVES BY I_{im} AT pH 7 AND 37° C

Compound	Site	Competition Factor*
Guanine	N_1	– (950)
	N_7	– (4,000)
Guanosine	N_7	3,500 (2,700)
Deoxyguanosine	N_7	2,400 (3,000)
Guanylic acid	N_7	2,800
	PO_4^-	9,300
Deoxyguanylic acid	N_7	2,600
	PO_4^-	9,000

* Values in parentheses are for alkylation by II_{im}.

TABLE 3

COMPETITION FACTORS FOR THE ALKYLATION OF THYMINE, THYMIDINE, AND DEOXYCYTIDINE

Compound	Site	Competition Factor
Thymine	N_1	40
	N_3	30
	O_4	40
Thymidine	N_3	40
Deoxycytidine	N_3	~500

When native DNA was alkylated by I_{im} in dilute aqueous solution for 2 hr at pH 7 and 37° C, the only identified product after hydrolysis and chromatography was 7-alkylated guanine. Calculation of the competition factor for this experiment gave a value of 150,000, a remarkable enhancement of about fiftyfold over any of the monomeric guanine nucleosides or nucleotides. A similar markedly enhanced reactivity for native DNA has been observed by Professor R. R. Rutman of the Department of Chemistry at the University of Pennsylvania, using radio-labeled HN-2 at a thousandth the concentrations we used. We also found no products corresponding to cleavage of the imidazole ring, so prevalent in the products of alkylation of monomeric guanine nucleosides and nucleotides.[34]

We propose that the enhanced reactivity to alkylation, as well as the enhanced stability of the imidazole ring in the alkylated product, may be ascribed to the same unique feature of the purine ring system in the double helix structure. In the now commonly accepted arrangement of the units, each base is not only bound by hydrogen bonding to a matching unit on the second chain, but the bases are so stacked along the central axis of the helix that there is strong π bonding between the π-molecular orbitals of bases in adjacent units of the same chain. This proximity of filled π-molecular orbitals above and below a guanine unit about to be alkylated would provide a source of electrons to partially neutralize the positive charge being added to the imidazole ring in the course of alkylation at N_7. By distributing this charge over several ring systems, the potential energy of the transition state will be lowered and thus the rate of the reaction enhanced. Furthermore, by diminishing the charge in this ring in this way, the energy for attraction of an hydroxyl ion to attack C_8 (Scheme 4) will be decreased, offering an explanation for the failure to observe the imidazole ring cleavage products so prevalent for the monomeric guanine nucleosides and nucleotides.

While we and others have found no adenine alkylation products from native DNA, denatured DNA produces almost equal amounts of N_7-guanine and N_1-adenine products. The competition factors calculated for denatured DNA are about 2×10^4 for both alkylations. This indicates that even in denatured DNA, some enhancement by adjacent base interactions persists. In the native DNA, the N_1 position in adenine is, of course, blocked by hydrogen bonding.

In addition to nucleophilic alkylation by the reagents summarized by Schemes 1, 2, and 3, there is a class of unsaturated compounds containing double bonds with electron-withdrawing groups, which also attack the same types of nucleophiles X: with about the same relative reactivities:

$$X: + C{=}C{-}Z \xrightarrow{H_2O} \overset{\oplus}{X}{-}C{-}\overset{H}{C}{-}Z + OH^-$$

$$Z = CN, \quad CO_2R, \quad COR, \quad NO_2, \quad SO_2R$$

The case of alkylation by diazomethane (and its analogs) deserves some mention, as this seems to be one example of an alkylation reaction proceeding by a significantly different mechanism with a resulting significant difference in selectivity. Thus, whereas all the "conventional" alkylating agents attack the more basic nucleosides and nucleotides preferentially (guanine $>$ adenine $>$ cytosine $>>$ thymine and uracil), the reverse order seems to be the preference with diazomethane.[28] Presumably this process involves acid-catalyzed decomposition of the diazomethane to a methyl carbonium ion followed by rapid collapse to the methylated product:

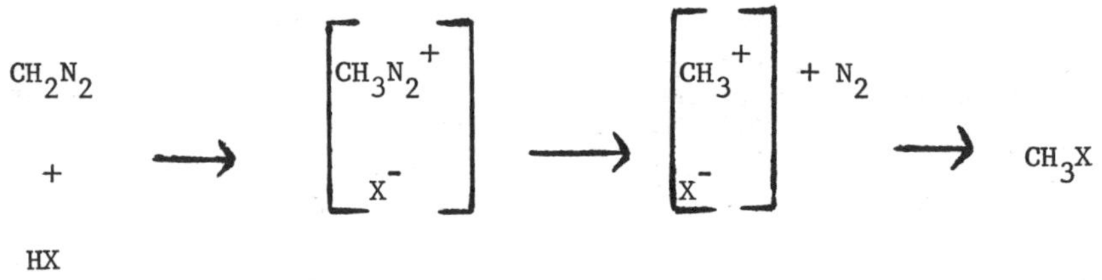

References

1. Price, C. C. 1958. Fundamental mechanisms of alkylation. Ann. N. Y. Acad. Sci. **68:** 663.
2. Wheeler, G. P., J. S. Morrow & H. E. Skipper. 1955. Arch. Biochem. **57:** 124.
3. Reiner, B. & S. J. Zamenhof. 1957. J. Biol. Chem. **228:** 475.
4. Lawley, P. D. & C. A. Wallick. 1957. Chem. Industr. : 633.
5. Wacker, A. & M. Ebert. 1959. Z. Naturforsch. **146:** 7.
6. Brookes, P. & P. D. Lawley. 1960. J. Chem. Soc. : 539.
7. Brookes, P. & P. D. Lawley. 1960. Biochem. J. **77:** 478.
8. Windmueller, H. G. & N. O. Kaplan. 1961. J. Biol. Chem. **236:** 2716.
9. Brookes, P. & P. D. Lawley. 1961. Biochem. J. **78:** 2P.
10. Brookes, P. & P. D. Lawley. 1961. Biochem. J. **80:** 496.
11. Wheeler, G. P. 1962. Cancer Res. **22:** 651.
12. Ross, W. C. J. 1962. Biological Alkylating Agents. Butterworth and Co. London, England.
13. Pal, B. C. 1962. Biochemistry **1:** 558.
14. Codington, A. 1962. Biochim. Biophys. Acta **59:** 472.
15. Jones, J. W. & R. K. Robins. 1962. J. Amer. Chem. Soc. **84:** 1914.
16. Griffin, B. E. & C. B. Reese. 1963. Biochim. Biophys. Acta **68:** 185.
17. Jones, J. W. & R. K. Robins. 1963. J. Amer. Chem. Soc. **85:** 193.
18. Lawley, P. D. & P. Brookes. 1963. Biochem. J. **89:** 127.
19. Kriek, E. & P. Emmelot. 1963. Biochemistry **2:** 733.
20. Kriek, E. & P. Emmelot. 1964. Biochim. Biophys. Acta **91:** 59.
21. Brookes, P. & P. D. Lawley. 1964. J. Cell. Comp. Physiol. **64:** Sup. 1, 111.
22. Brookes, P. 1964. Proc. Int. Symp. Cancer Chemotherapy **32.** Lugano, Switzerland.
23. Pal, B. C. & C. A. Horton. 1964. J. Chem. Soc. **71:** 400.
24. Broom, A. D., L. B. Townsend, J. W. Jones & R. K. Robins. 1964. Biochemistry **3:** 494.
25. Montgomery, J. A. & H. J. Thomas. 1964. J. Heterocyclic Chem. **1:** 115.
26. Lawley, P. D. & P. Brookes. 1964. Biochem. J. **92:** 19c.
27. Ludlum, D. B., R. C. Warner & A. J. Wahba. 1964. Science **145:** 397.
28. Haines, J. A., C. B. Reese & Lord Todd. 1964. J. Chem. Soc.: 1406.
29. Bollack, C., G. Kieth & J. P. Ebel. 1965. Bull. Soc. Chim. Biol. **47:** 765.
30. Ludlum, D. B. 1965. Biochim. Biophys. Acta **95:** 674.
31. Chen, J. H. & F. F. Davis. 1965. Biochem. Biophys. Res. Commun. **20:** 124.
32. Friedman, O. M., G. N. Mahaptra, B. Dash & R. Stevenson. 1965. Biochim. Biophys. Acta **103:** 286.
33. Brookes, P. & P. D. Lawley. 1967. J. Molec. Biol. **25:** 143.
34. Price, C. C., G. M. Gaucher, P. Koneru, R. Shibakawa, J. R. Sowa & M. Yamaguchi. 1968. Biochim. Biophys. Acta **166:** 327.
35. Koneru, P. 1964. Ph.D. Thesis. University of Pennsylvania. Philadelphia, Pa.
36. Sowa, J. R. 1964. Ph.D. Thesis. University of Pennsylvania. Philadelphia, Pa.
37. Gaucher, G. M. 1963. Ph.D. Thesis. University of Pennsylvania. Philadelphia, Pa.
38. Shibakawa, R. 1966. Ph.D. Thesis. University of Pennsylvania. Philadelphia, Pa.
39. Elion, G. B. 1962. J. Org. Chem. **27:** 2478.

DISCUSSION OF THE PAPER

ROBERT SHAPIRO (*New York University*, New York, N. Y.): In explaining the high reactivity of the N-7 position of guanine in DNA, you said that this was due to a stacking factor in the double helix. Many ORD studies have shown that the same stacking factors also occur in single stranded nucleic acids, RNA's, denatured DNA's, and even in dinucleotide monophosphates. If your explanation were correct, we would expect to see the same enhancement in denatured DNA and in simple dinucleotide monophosphates. How do you account for that?

DR. PRICE: I think the reason is that the stacking is probably much less perfect in these single-stranded or denatured DNA's. There is one thing I forgot to mention that I think bears on this point. We did study polyadenylic acid. In polyadenylic acid, we found that the N-1 competition factor was enhanced approximately threefold. The competition factors in all the monomeric adenines are around 800. That number for polyadenylic acid is 1,960. There have been studies that indicate that polyadenylic acid is, as you say, partially organized into segments of three to five units by some kind of stacking or pi-orientation of adjacent units. It therefore seems to me that what you say is correct. We see a small amount of enhanced reactivity, a threefold increase in polyadenylic acid, while in denatured DNA, the competition factor for guanine units goes from 3,000 to 20,000, which is a factor of about a sevenfold increase in reactivity. However, when you go to the double helix, where you have a completely organized and oriented structure, it goes up fiftyfold. Therefore, I can say that I agree with you, that these less perfect organizations do some of this activation, but not as much as in the DNA double helix.

UNIDENTIFIED SPEAKER: I think your rather high value of k_x/k_y for guanine also includes some reaction at the phosphate. You analyzed only for 7-alkyl guanine, but you did not include, for example, any reactions taking place at phosphate, which would not give you small molecules, but rather, alkylated DNA. Is that the case?

DR. PRICE: The procedure that we used is that we alkylated, then hydrolyzed and then fractionated the bases themselves. This was true whether we alkylated guanosine or deoxyguanosine or guanylic acid or DNA. We alkylate at pH 7 at 37° C, usually for 48 hours. The only exception was DNA, because of denaturation, which we did for two hours. We then hydrolyzed in acid in order to free the bases from the sugar, and then we fractionated the free bases. We would thus isolate any bases that were alkylated directly by the alkylating agent or any that might have been alkylated indirectly by first alkylating at phosphate sites. Certainly, I would not be able to tell you what fraction of 7-alkylguanine that we obtained came from direct alkylation or via phosphate transfer.

As a matter of fact, the other explanation that we considered for the polyadenylic acid data that I just gave you is that the extra threefold enhancement could come from primary alkylation of phosphate groups in polyadenylic acid followed by transfer. This is a perfectly feasible and reasonable suggestion, because the phosphate groups alkylate about five to ten times as rapidly as the adenine nitrogen does, so that you could envisage a rapid alkylation of the phosphate and a transfer of the alkyl group from phosphate to nitrogen. However, if the phosphate group alkylates only with the competition factor of 10,000, it is impossible to use this explanation for the alkylation in DNA, which is going by a competition factor of 150,000. Some transfer may occur, and in my opinion I am convinced that some does occur. Dr. Rutman at the University of Pennsylvania has some evidence that, if you alkylate at 0° C, you can get cross-linking of DNA with difunctional mustards that can be labilized by thiosulfate. But if you let that mustard reaction stand at room temperature, this becomes a permanent cross-link that can no longer be destroyed by thiosulfate. This is in accord with the view that some of the ultimate nitrogen alkylation may occur by first alkylating phosphate, but I don't think that that is a tenable explanation for the 150,000 number. At least that is what I can say at this time.

UNIDENTIFIED SPEAKER: Your denaturation—how do you explain that?

DR. PRICE: I believe that does occur largely by alkylation of phosphate.

UNIDENTIFIED SPEAKER: You might then be inclined to have cleavage?

DR. PRICE: Alkylation would promote cleavage, which would lead to denaturation. We have no data to support this; however, we have not yet done a complete quantitative following of the disappearance of the alkylating agent with DNA. As you noticed, I did not give you a competition factor for the phosphate in DNA, because we have not done that.

UNIDENTIFIED SPEAKER: May I comment on this a little? We have done experiments in our laboratories with oligothymidylic acid. At low concentrations of the alkylating agent, it does not react to a great extent. We definitely found phosphate alkylation and cleavage of the intranucleosidic linkage after product formation.

DR. PRICE: Very good. I am delighted to hear that you have evidence for this. We are reasonably sure that it must have occurred, but we ourselves have no evidence for this except the indirect evidence that we are losing alkylating agent far faster than we can explain by the formation of nitrogen alkylated products. We assume that this must have gone to phosphate. By our technique, we could not isolate and identify the phosphate ester, so I am delighted to hear that you have some evidence in support of that. Phosphate alkylation would, of course, be especially important for oligothymidylic acid because of the low reactivity of the thymine nucleus.

DR. P. ALEXANDER (*Chester Beatty Research Institute, London, England*): Bearing on that same point, when you react DNA and measure the hydrolyzed product, this is not the right way to express the primary reaction that occurred. I know that phosphate esterification is difficult to measure, but one way of approaching this problem is to break down the reacted DNA, not by hydrolysis, which is bound to break down any triphosphate ester and almost certain to make that triphosphate ester react with the N-7, but to do an enzyme hydrolysis of the reacted DNA. This is not easy, because as a result of the reaction, the DNA resists the phosphate diesterase. With reasonable precautions, one can see that with some of the alkylating agents, particularly methanesulfonates and so on, there is virtually no reaction with the N-7 under those conditions, that all the N-7 one sees does appear after hydrolysis, when the esters are broken down. One can see this rather indirectly by means of the UV-spectral changes earlier, but using esterase, one can see the enzyme breakdown of the alkylated DNA. I think this reaction, which is, of course, probably not the most important one, can be the principle one giving rise to the N-7 product. The N-7 is, from the biological point of view, not a very good reaction; it is one that occurs during the course of the analysis.

DR. PRICE: Do you mean by rearrangement from the phosphate?

DR. ALEXANDER: It is not really a rearrangement. Triphosphate alkyl is a perfectly good alkylating agent, which is going to alkylate with a reasonable competition.

NEW METHODS OF FORMATION OF CARBON-NITROGEN BONDS*

Daniel Swern

Fels Research Institute, Department of Chemistry
Temple University, Philadelphia, Pa.

Synthetic organic chemistry was born in 1828 with the preparation of a nitrogen-containing compound (urea) from ammonium cyanate. The growth of organic nitrogen chemistry has been rapid, and it not only shows no signs of abatement, but the literature has been proliferating at an increasing rate.

At first, attention was directed to the synthesis of many classes of compounds and determination of their chemical and physical properties to provide libraries of data. But as chemists and chemistry became more sophisticated, notably since World War II with the availability of spectral instruments, more effort has been directed to the mechanisms of formation and reactions of organic nitrogen compounds and to the synthesis of highly complex molecules with known and controlled stereochemistry. A field that has grown especially rapidly as synthetic methods and characterization techniques improve is heterocyclic organic nitrogen chemistry, of which more will be said later.

Aside from the intellectual challenge involved in preparing novel organic nitrogen compounds of the most amazing complexity and structural ramifications, organic chemists should be deeply concerned with nitrogen compounds because of their widespread use and intrinsic importance. Of the large number of organic compounds with useful biological activity, for example, organic nitrogen compounds are among the most prominent.[1]

Since 1964, studies have been in progress in the author's laboratory to devise and improve methods of formation of carbon-nitrogen bonds of known and controlled stereochemistry in acyclic, alicyclic, and heterocyclic systems. The main portion of this paper will be devoted to a summary of the methods we have used in preparing and determining the structure of (see below) β-halocarbamates (1), aziridines (2), 2-oxazolidones (3), vicinal diamines (4), and nitrosoacyloxy compounds (5):

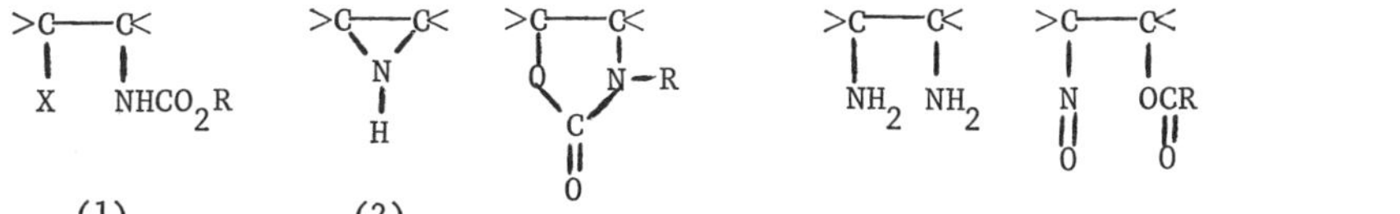

(1) (2) (4) (5) (R=H,alkyl or aryl)

(X = Cl or I)

(3) (R=H,alkyl or aryl)

* Support for this work was received from the U.S. Public Health Service under Research Grants CA-07803, CA-10439, and CA-07174 of the National Cancer Institute.

The major theme in this paper will be the reactions of pseudohalogens (halogenoids) with olefinic compounds to elaborate the carbon-nitrogen bond directly; the minor theme will be the use of oxiranes and aziridines as intermediates for further synthetic and mechanistic applications in forming carbon-nitrogen bonds.

β-Halocarbamates, 2-Oxazolidones and Aziridines

Iodine isocyanate (INCO) is a highly reactive useful pseudohalogen. First prepared by Birckenbach and Linhard[2] by reaction of iodine with silver cyanate, it was also shown by them[3] to add to olefinic double bonds to form β-iodoisocyanates. In the early 1960's, Drefahl and Ponsold[4,5] showed that the isocyanate

$$AgOCN + I_2 \longrightarrow INCO + AgI$$

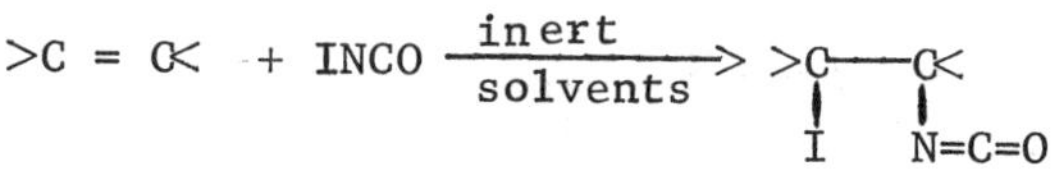

group becomes attached to the more alkyl or aryl-substituted olefinic carbon in substituted cyclohexenes, and Hassner and Heathcock[6] obtained a similar result in acyclic systems. Both groups demonstrated that addition occurs in a stereospecific *trans*-manner and suggested an iodonium ion intermediate.

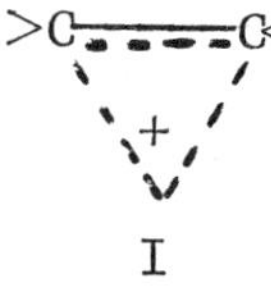

Although these and other studies[7] suggest that INCO is an electrophilic reagent, the investigations of Gebelein and Swern[8,9] and of Gebelein, Rosen, and Swern[10] on the relative rates of addition of INCO to unsaturated compounds of widely varying structure (and nucleophilicity) confirm that conclusion. Table 1 summarizes these relative rate data.

Relative reactivities under heterogeneous conditions are determined by dissolving olefin and iodine in anhydrous ether, adding silver cyanate, thus generating INCO *in situ,* and periodically following the disappearance of olefin at constant temperature by GLPC (gas-liquid phase chromatography).[9] Relative reactivities in homogeneous solution are determined by first preforming INCO in ether or tetrahydrofuran,[11] then adding pairs of olefins in large molar excess,[10] and following disappearance of both olefins by GLPC. Reaction of INCO with olefins in homogeneous solution is considerably more rapid and is a simpler reaction than that in heterogeneous media. Reactions in homogeneous solution are recommended with unsaturated compounds that add INCO slowly, whereas the *in situ* heterogeneous solution method is satisfactory with olefins that react rapidly.

Although the relative reactivities of unsaturated compounds under heterogeneous conditions are complicated by the problem of iodine complexation with the double bond, both sets of data in Table 1 are unmistakably clear: INCO is an effective electrophilic reagent. Electron-donating alkyl groups attached to the double bond accelerate the rate of addition, while the electron-withdrawing

TABLE 1

RELATIVE REACTIVITIES OF UNSATURATED COMPOUNDS WITH IODINE ISOCYANATE

Compound	Relative Reactivity	
	Heterogeneous*	Homogeneous†
2,3-Dimethyl-2-butene	3,800	>3,200
Isopropenyl acetate	3,700	–
Vinyl acetate	1,950	–
2-Methyl-2-pentene	–	>1,400
2-Methyl-1-pentene	1,250	–
Methyl oleate	570	–
Trans-3-hexene	570	180
Methyl elaidate	500	–
Cyclopentene	220	>1,000
Cyclohexene‡	100	100
2,3-Dimethyl-1-butene	–	140
1-Hexene	50	–
1-Octene	–	44
Methyl vinyl ketone	0	–
Vinylidene chloride	0	–
Methyl methacrylate	0	–
Ethyl crotonate	0	–

*Gebelein and Swern, 1968.[9]
†Gebelein, Rosen and Swern, 1968.[10] Rosen and Swern, 1966.[11]
‡Arbitrarily assigned a value of 100.

carbonyl, chlorine, and ester groups markedly retard it. The results obtained parallel the expected stabilizing or destabilizing effect of substituents on the positive charge in an intermediate iodonium ion.

Vinyl acetate reacts extremely rapidly, a surprising result in view of its low rate of reaction with other electrophiles.[12,13] Isopropenyl acetate is about twice as reactive as vinyl acetate. It must be concluded that the acetoxy group is able to stabilize a positive charge effectively in the reaction of these two enol esters with INCO.

Owing to their reactivity, β-iodoisocyanates are useful intermediates in the preparation of β-iodocarbamates, β-iodoureas, and β-iodoamine hydrohalides by reaction with alcohols, ammonia, or halogen acids, respectively:[7,9]

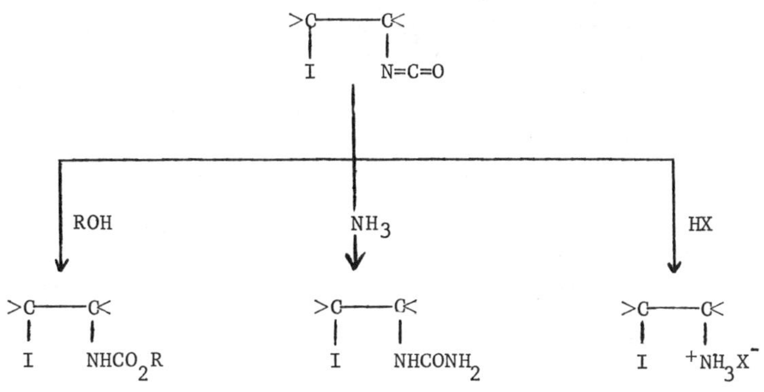

β-Iodocarbamates are readily converted to 2-oxazolidones by pyrolysis[14] and to aziridines by reaction with base.[7,9] Possible reaction pathways for these two reactions are shown below:

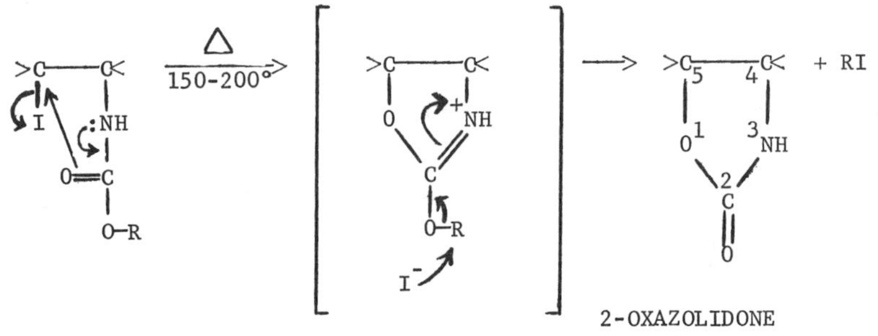

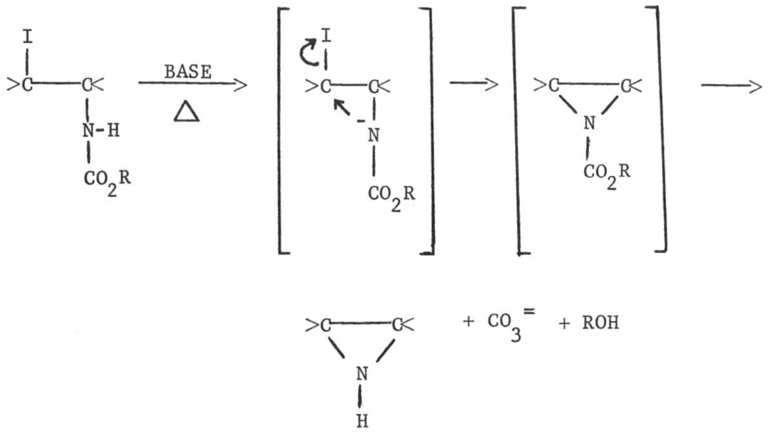

Pyrolysis of β-iodocarbamates gives good yields of 2-oxazolidones, and the ring closure is stereospecific when the oxazolidone ring is fused to another ring, as in cyclohexane and indane derivatives.[14] When the iodocarbamate is derived from an internal acyclic olefin, however, ring closure is not stereospecific and mixtures of *cis*- and *trans*-2-oxazolidones are formed.[15]

In contrast, the formation of aziridines from olefins is stereospecific. If INCO is added to *cis*-olefins, only *threo*-iodoisocyanates are obtained by *trans*-addition. These are converted to carbamates with no change in stereochemistry, and then they undergo ring closure with base to aziridines with clean inversion by internal nucleophilic displacement. Thus, *cis*-olefins yield *cis*-aziridines. The analogous situation applies in starting with *trans*-olefins; these yield *erythro*-iodoisocyanates by *trans*-addition of INCO. The *erythro* iodocarbamates derived from them are converted to *trans*-aziridines by reaction with base.

The stereochemical transformations in converting olefins to aziridines are shown:

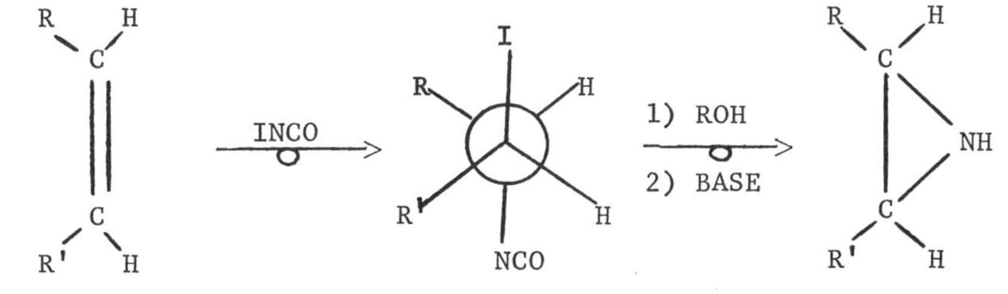

cis threo cis

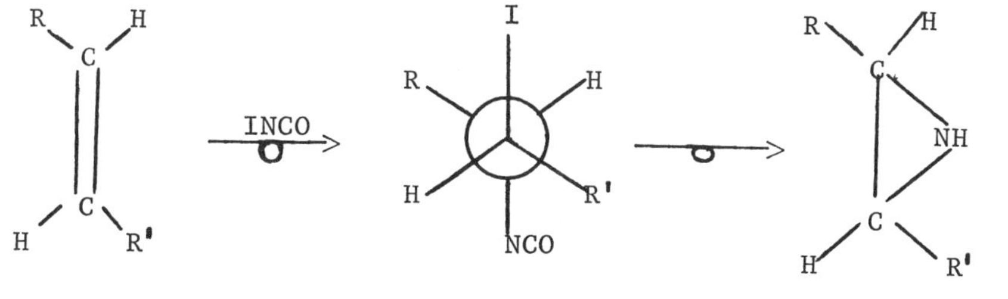

trans erythro trans

Threo-iodocarbamates are readily converted in high yield to aziridines on reaction with methanolic potassium hydroxide, the usual reaction system for effecting ring closure, but *erythro*-iodocarbamates give lower yields. A reason for this apparently anomalous situation has been offered by Gebelein and colleagues[16] based on conformational considerations and will not be repeated here. It is possible, however, to overcome the difficulty and obtain satisfactory yields of *trans*-aziridines from *erythro*-iodocarbamates by reducing the nucleophilicity of the methanolic potassium hydroxide by addition of water.

Another pseudohalogen of considerable versatility is N,N-dichlorourethan (DCU) prepared in good yield by reaction of chlorine with urethan in buffered aqueous solution:

$$H_2N-\overset{\displaystyle O}{\overset{\|}{C}}-OC_2H_5 + 2Cl_2 \xrightarrow[\text{HOAc}]{\text{NaOAc}} Cl-\overset{\displaystyle Cl}{\overset{|}{N}}-\overset{\displaystyle O}{\overset{\|}{C}}-OC_2H_5 + 2HCl$$

(DCU)

DCU is unusual in being highly reactive in adding to double bonds, yet it is readily distilled and can be stored in the dark at low temperatures with little or no loss of positive chlorine. DCU adds to many unsaturated compounds to give N-chloro adducts in excellent yield in many cases; washing with aqueous sodium bisulfite solution yields β-chlorocarbamates. The addition reaction is illustrated below with styrene, but the reaction proceeds well with terminal olefins, the usual vinyl monomers, and cyclic olefins.[17,18] These compounds are listed in TABLE 2 with yields of analytically pure β-chlorocarbamates obtained.

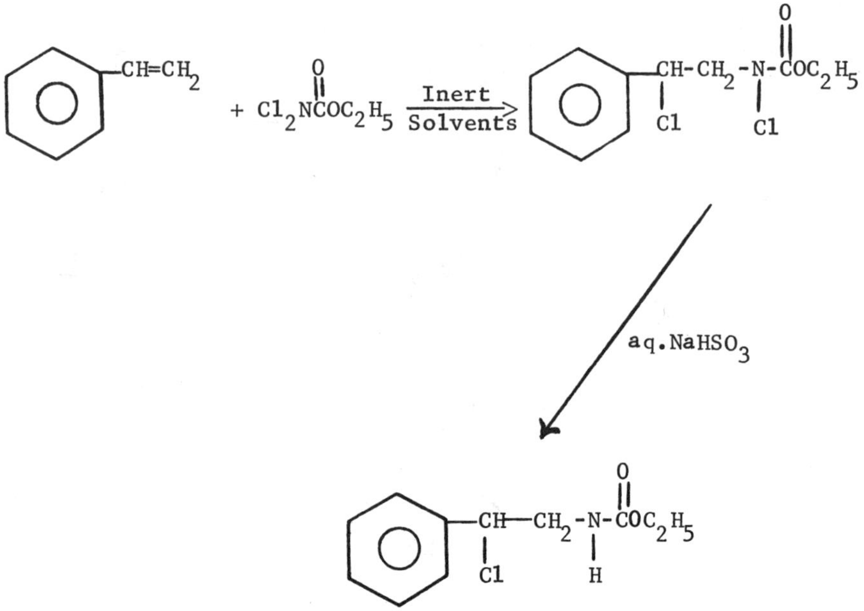

TABLE 2

UNSATURATED COMPOUNDS CONVERTED TO β-CHLOROCARBAMATES BY ADDITION OF DCU*

Unsaturated Compound	Yield of β-Chlorocarbamate†
Styrene	80
Trans-stilbene	65
Cyclohexene	30
1-Octene	65
1-Decene	65
1-Dodecene	61
1-Octadecene	53
2-Methyl-1-pentene	60
Trans-3-hexene	40
t-Butylethylene	80
2,3-Dimethyl-1-butene	40
Ethyl cinnamate	60
Acrylonitrile	60
Methyl acrylate	55
Vinylidene chloride	75
Vinyl acetate	100‡
Methyl vinyl ketone	35

* Foglia & Swern, 1966[17] and 1968.[18]

† Analytically pure products.

‡ Crude product; unstable and could not be distilled, but spectral properties confirm structure.

With terminal olefins and vinyl monomers, addition proceeds in an anti-Markownikow fashion. With internal olefins, allylic chlorination competes with double bond addition and yields of adducts are usually only low to fair, and mixtures of *threo* and *erythro* adducts are formed. Structures of all reaction products have been demonstrated unequivocally by NMR (nuclear magnetic resonance), IR (infrared), and chemical methods.[18,19]

The addition reaction has numerous characteristics of a free radical chain reaction: (a) an induction period is sometimes observed followed by rapid exothermic reaction; (b) light causes a rate enhancement and free radical inhibitors slow it down; (c) double bond addition is anti-Markownikow and, with internal olefins, nonstereospecific; (d) yields of double bond adducts decrease as the number of allylic hydrogen atoms increases and especially if a tertiary, allylic hydrogen atom is present; and (e) the yield of by-product urethan increases as the number and activity of allylic hydrogen atoms increase. A reaction sequence that accounts for these facts is shown below:

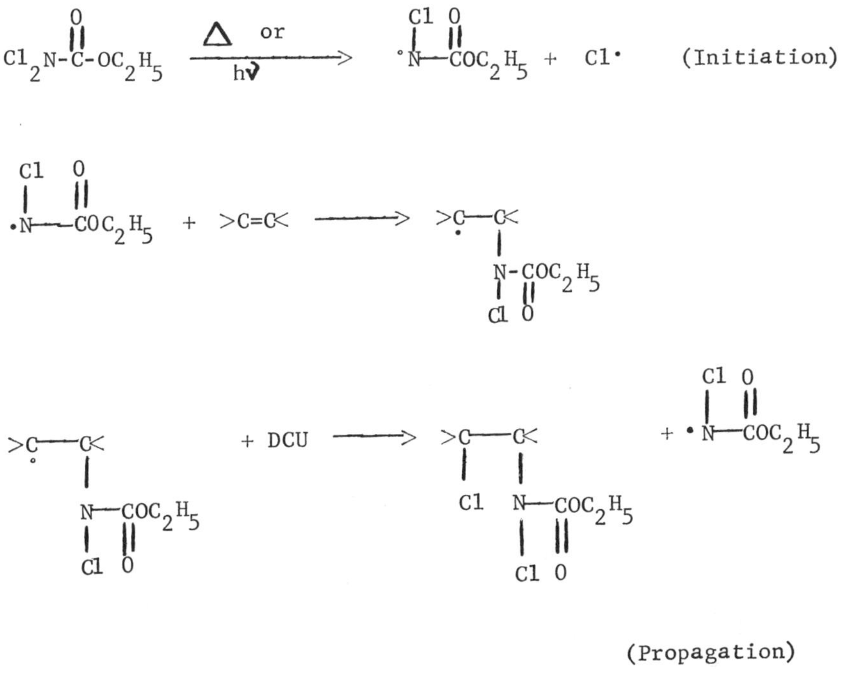

Allylic attack occurs with internal olefins because the radicals formed in the initiation step have the option of adding either to the double bond or of abstracting a hydrogen atom to form a stable allylic radical, which then propagates the chain.

Although DCU addition is nonstereospecific with internal olefins, its reaction with the other types of olefins mentioned is efficient and rapid. Noteworthy is the formation of β-chlorocarbamates with a C—N bond at the terminal carbon atom of a vinyl compound, in contrast with the β-iodocarbamates (C—N formed nonterminally) obtained by INCO addition followed by reaction with an alcohol:

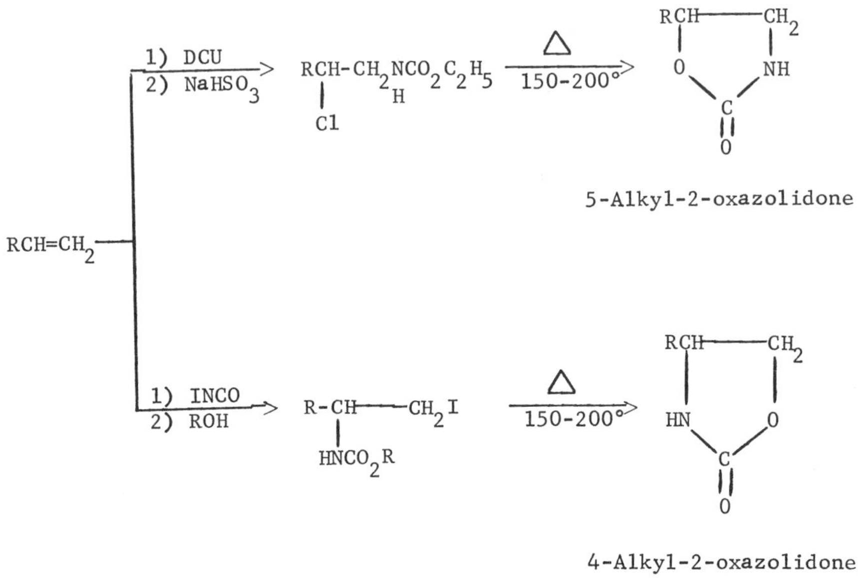

On pyrolysis, both types of β-halocarbamates are converted to 2-oxazolidones, the first (via DCU) yielding 5-alkyl and the second (via INCO) yielding 4-alkyl isomers. The two routes thus complement each other and permit the preparation of isomeric 2-oxazolidones in good yield.[19]

Reaction with base yields aziridines from β-iodocarbamates or β-chlorocarbamates in essentially the same yield. Although the displaced chlorine is secondary in the DCU adducts, it is quite labile. β-Chlorocarbamates have the advantage over β-iodocarbamates in that they are stable for long periods and are relatively insensitive to ordinary laboratory illumination. β-Iodocarbamates, on the other hand, should be used promptly owing to their instability.

The DCU and INCO routes are two of the best procedures for obtaining aziridines and 2-oxazolidones from unsaturated compounds. Reaction conditions are mild, overall yields are usually high, and the wide range of olefins and olefin derivatives readily available makes many types of 2-oxazolidones and aziridines easily accessible. Especially noteworthy is that those unsaturated compounds that react slowly or not at all with INCO (olefins with electron-withdrawing functions near the double bond) react exceedingly rapidly with DCU. Internal olefins, in contrast, that react nonstereospecifically with DCU and also undergo allylic attack react rapidly and stereospecifically *trans* with INCO without allylic attack.

A third route we have explored for preparing 2-oxazolidones uses epoxides as starting materials.[20] Reaction of epoxides derived from straight-chain 1-olefins with potassium cyanate, a relatively weak nucleophile, in dimethyl formamide suspension containing a controlled quantity of water and a nucleophilic initiating species (tetraethylammonium halide) yields 2-oxazolidones in fair yields (40–65%). In the absence of catalyst, reaction does not occur. A reaction scheme that rationalizes the function of the catalyst and the water is shown:

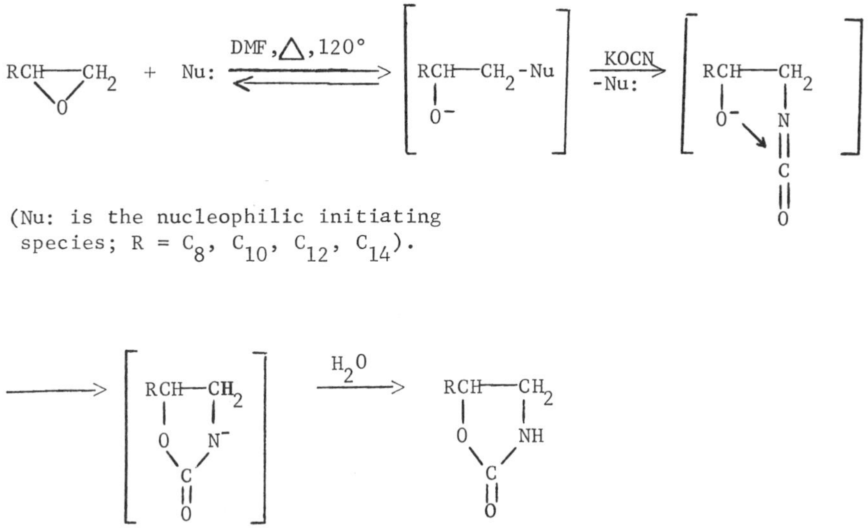

(Nu: is the nucleophilic initiating species; R = C_8, C_{10}, C_{12}, C_{14}).

5-Alkyl-2-oxazolidones

Water is the terminating species to convert the highly basic and nucleophilic nitrogen anion to the final product. In the absence of water, the anion attacks another molecule of epoxide and the anticipated monomeric 2-oxazolidones are not obtained. If too much water is present, however, the potassium cyanate is destroyed by hydrolysis.

The potassium cyanate-epoxide reaction does not have general applicability. Internal epoxides, such as *cis*- and *trans*-9,10-epoxyoctadecane and epoxycyclohexane, do not react with potassium cyanate at 120° C. Styrene oxide and 1,2-epoxy-2-methylpentane react rapidly but do not form 2-oxazolidones.

The epoxide ring of terminal epoxides is attacked predominantly at the terminal carbon atom, and the products are 5-alkyl-2-oxazolidones as shown above. This was proven by independent unequivocal synthesis of isomeric 5- and 4-alkyl-2-oxazolidones, and by NMR spectroscopy.

Reaction of potassium cyanate with terminal epoxides yields 5-alkyl-2-oxazolidones unsubstituted on nitrogen. N-substituted 5-alkyl-2-oxazolidones are obtained in good yield by reaction of the epoxides with aryl or alkyl isocyanates in dimethyl formamide solution at 150° C, using tetramethylammonium iodide or lithium chloride as the nucleophilic initiating species, a reaction previously described in the literature, but one we have expanded in scope.[21,22] A reaction scheme is shown:

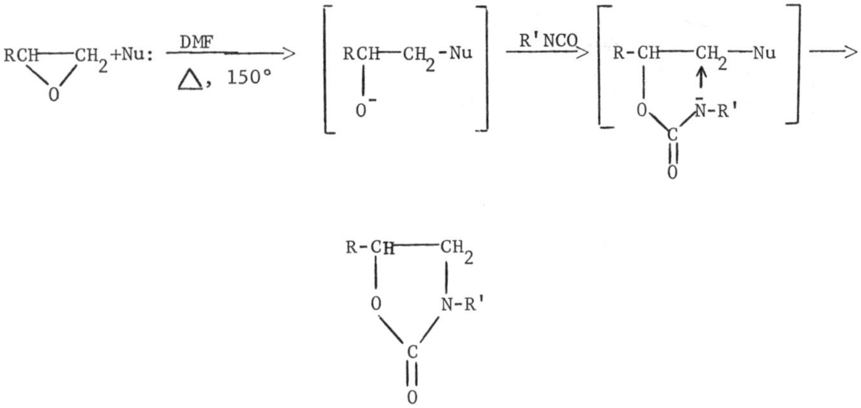

3,5-Disubstituted-2-oxazolidones

Vicinal Diamines

Although a variety of 1,2-diamines had been prepared when we became interested in them in 1964, stereospecific syntheses had not been described. Our interest developed because nitrogen-containing fatty acid derivatives are widespread in animal and vegetable lipids, but their functions are unknown. Prior to attempting the synthesis of certain complex nitrogen-containing lipids, we studied the preparation of simpler compounds, starting with model olefins and unsaturated fatty acids.[23,24] Illustrated below are the synthetic routes employed to prepare (a) the *cis*- and *trans*-1,2-diaminocyclohexanes and intermediate diazide, aziridine, and aminoazide from cyclohexene (Scheme I), (b) *erythro* and *threo*-1,2-diamines and intermediate diazides, aziridines, and aminoazides from *cis*-olefins and unsaturated fatty acids (Scheme II), and (c) *erythro* and *threo*-1,2-diamines and the corresponding intermediates from *trans*-olefins and unsaturated fatty acids (Scheme III). In these schemes an inversion is shown by the symbol

.

Scheme I

Cyclohexene (1) is converted to the *cis* epoxide (2) by epoxidation with peroxyacetic acid. The epoxide (2) is ring-opened, with inversion, to the *trans*-azido alcohol (3; 70–75% yield) by reaction with sodium azide in ethanol, followed by mesylation with methanesulfonyl chloride in pyridine to yield (80%) *trans*-2-azidocyclohexyl methanesulfonate. It is then treated with sodium azide in dimethylformamide to displace the methanesulfonate function, with inversion, to yield (73%) *cis*-1,2-diazidocyclohexane (4), a readily distillable liquid. Caution must be exercised at this point. The vicinal diazide (4) is then hydrogenated at room temperature over Adams' catalyst to yield (79%) *cis*-1,2-diaminocyclohexane, isolated by distillation. It reacts so readily with carbon dioxide that it

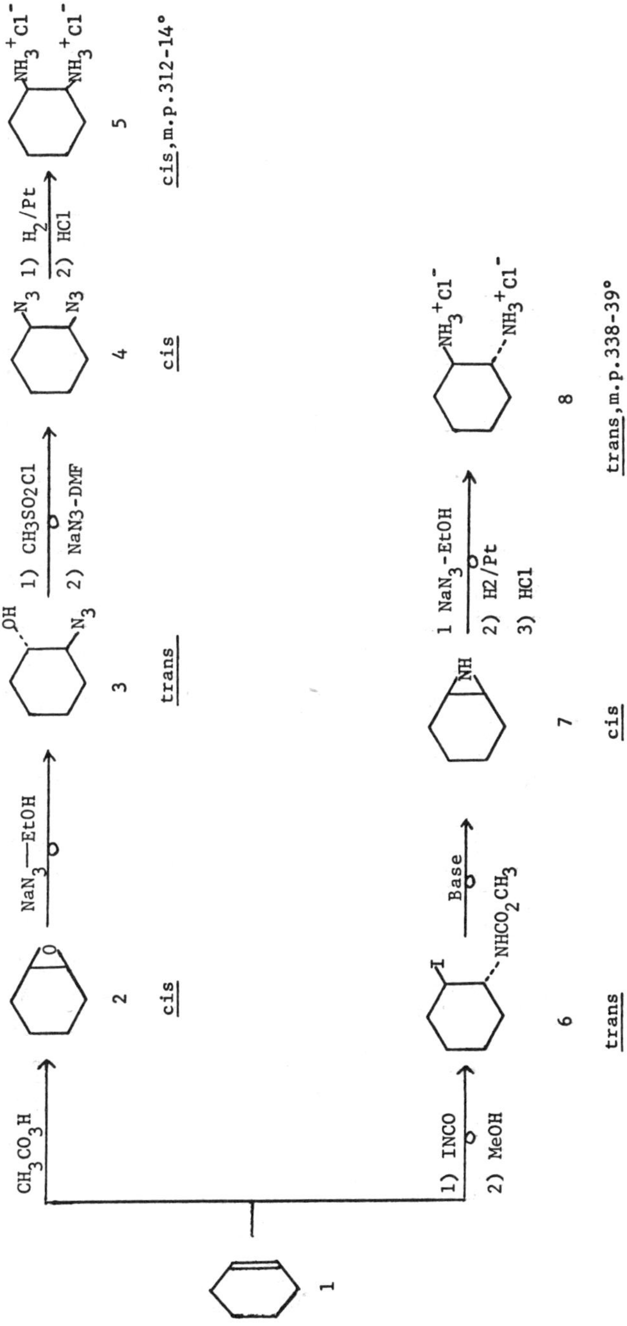
CH3CO3H
1) INCO
2) MeOH
NaN3—EtOH
Base
NHCO2CH3
1) CH3SO2Cl
2) NaN3-DMF
1) H2/Pt
2) HCl
1 NaN3-EtOH
2) H2/Pt
3) HCl
1
2
3
4
5
6
7
8
cis
trans
cis
cis,m.p.312-14°
trans
cis
trans,m.p.338-39°

Scheme I

is immediately converted (97% yield) to the dihydrochloride (5), m.p. (melting point) 312–314° C.

The *trans* isomer is prepared by a sequence involving three inversions, in contrast with the preparation of the *cis* isomer that involves only two. Iodine isocyanate, generated *in situ* from silver cyanate and iodine, is added to cyclohexene (1), and the crude vicinal *trans*-iodoisocyanate is immediately converted to methyl *trans*-1,2-iodocyclohexylcarbamate (88%; 6). Reaction of 6 with methanolic potassium hydroxide converts it, with inversion, to 7-azabicyclo [4.1.0]-heptane (7; 60% yield). The aziridine (7) is converted to the *trans*-diamine by ring opening with sodium azide in ethanol followed by hydrogenation over Adams' catalyst at room temperature. The diamine is immediately converted to the crystalline *trans*-dihydrochloride (8; 60% overall from aziridine), m.p. 338–339° C. A mixture melting point determination of approximately equal weights of 5 and 8 shows considerable depression, m.p. 290–296° C.

The two-step sequence (azide ring opening and hydrogenation) for converting an aziridine to a vicinal diamine is preferred to the usual literature method of one-step reaction with ammonia. Work-up is easier, overall yields are higher, and gummy polymeric products are not obtained.

Schemes II and III

The successful reaction sequences shown in Scheme I have been applied to the preparation of vicinal diamines from *cis*- and *trans*-4-methyl-2-pentene and methyl oleate and elaidate (methyl *cis*- and *trans*-9-octadecenoate, respectively) (Schemes II and III). Since both isomers (9 and 18a) in each case are available in pure form, both sequences of Scheme I have been applied to them. In this way an internal check can be obtained on the cleanness of the chemical operations and separations, and at the final stage, we can compare the properties of the purified dihydrochlorides of the *erythro*- and *threo*-4-methyl-2,3-diaminopentanes obtained from both olefinic isomers and the corresponding dihydrochlorides. Without discussing the procedures again in detail, the dihydrochlorides of the *erythro* isomers (17 or 22a), obtained from either *cis*- or *trans* unsaturated compounds, are identical in every respect—IR spectra, m.p., and m.m.p. (mixture melting point). Likewise, the dihydrochlorides of the *threo* isomer (13 or 26a), prepared from either *cis*- or *trans*-unsaturated compound, are also identical (m.p. and m.m.p.).

As a further check on the generality of the methods, *trans*-3-hexene has also been converted to the dihydrochlorides of *meso*-3,4 diaminohexane (22b; m.p. 263–266° C) and its *threo* isomer (26b; m.p. 298–300° C) (Scheme III).

Although the sequences shown in Schemes I, II, and III are multistep, most of the steps are rapid and yields are high. The sequences are stereospecific, as has been demonstrated unequivocally.[23,24] With the information obtained in the author's laboratory on the properties of the final products, it is now possible to go back to the older literature and, in some cases, utilize less elaborate reaction routes to obtain 1,2-diamines and their salts.

Nitrosoacyloxy Compounds

Nitrosyl chloride addition represents one of the simplest ways of elaborating a carbon-nitrogen bond directly from unsaturated compounds, but the reaction

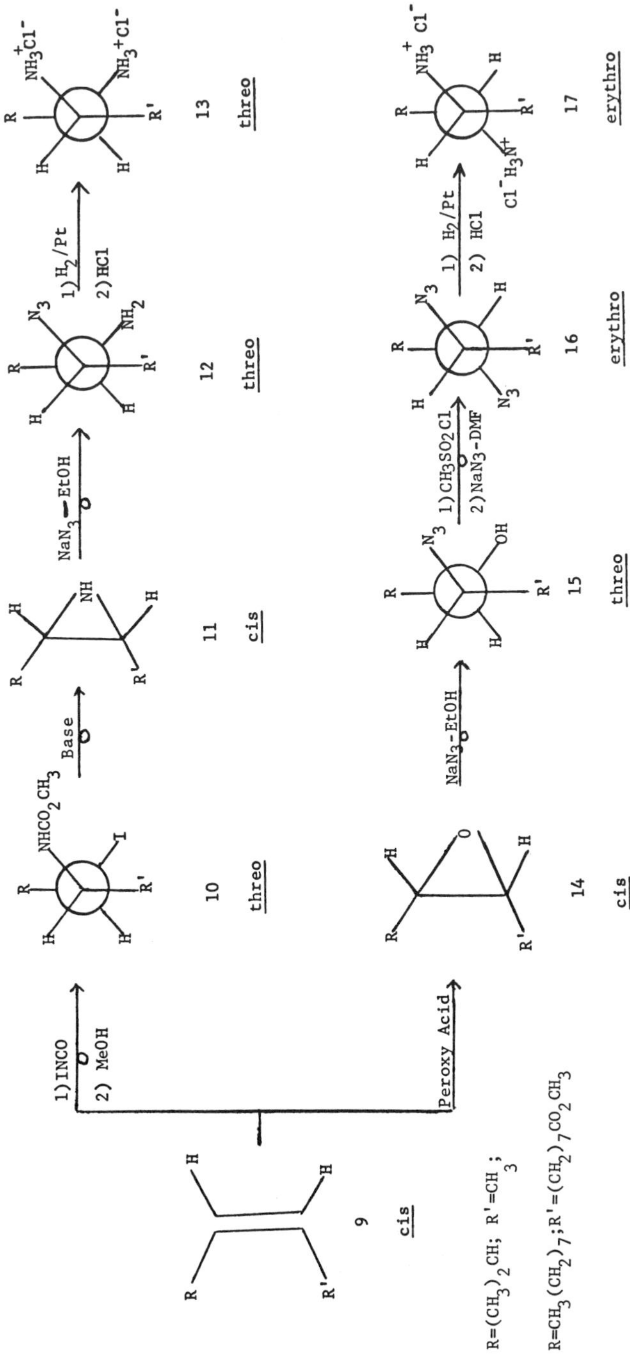

1) INCO
2) MeOH
Peroxy Acid
Base
NaN_3-EtOH
1) H_2/Pt
2) HCl
1) CH_3SO_2Cl
2) NaN_3-DMF
9 cis
10 threo
11 cis
12 threo
13 threo
14 cis
15 threo
16 erythro
17 erythro
R=$(CH_3)_2CH$; R'=CH_3;
R=$CH_3(CH_2)_7$; R'=$(CH_2)_7CO_2CH_3$

Scheme II

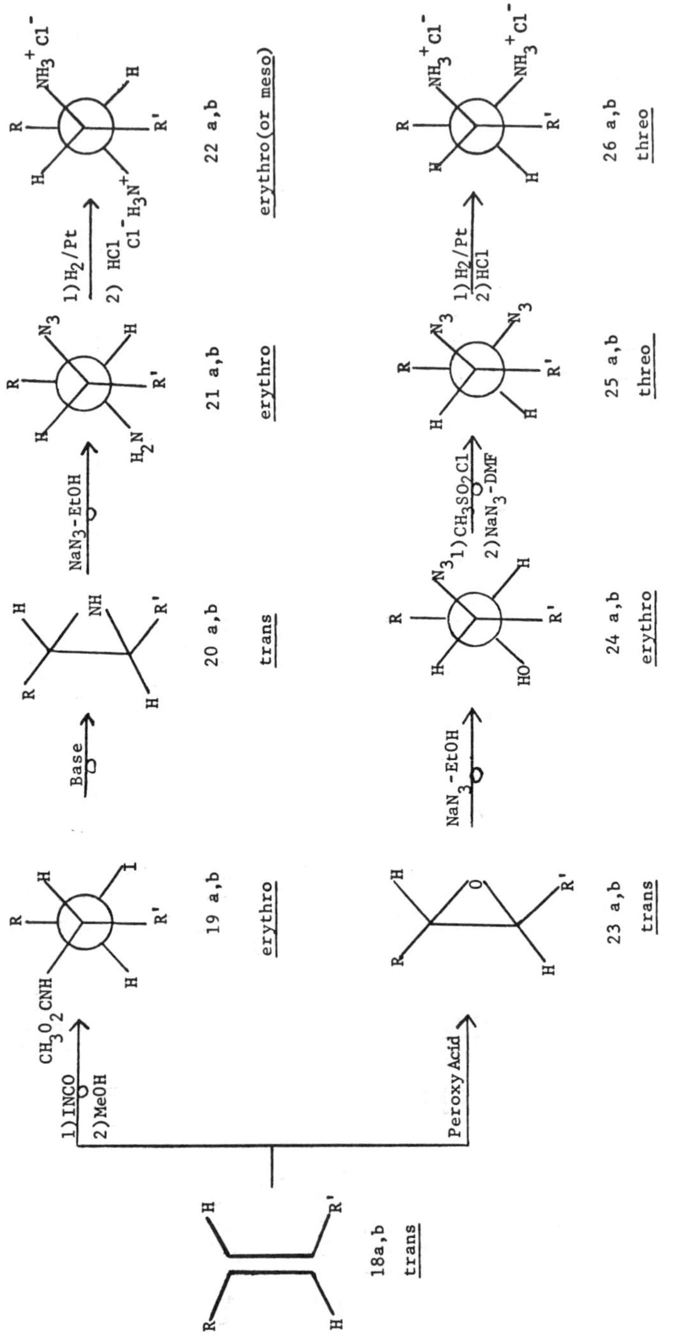

Scheme III

a: $R = (CH_3)_2CH-$; $R' = CH_3$ b: $R = R' = C_2H_5$

$R = CH_3(CH_2)_7$; $R' = (CH_2)_7CO_2CH_3$

products are frequently unstable and not readily amenable to further reaction except in special cases.

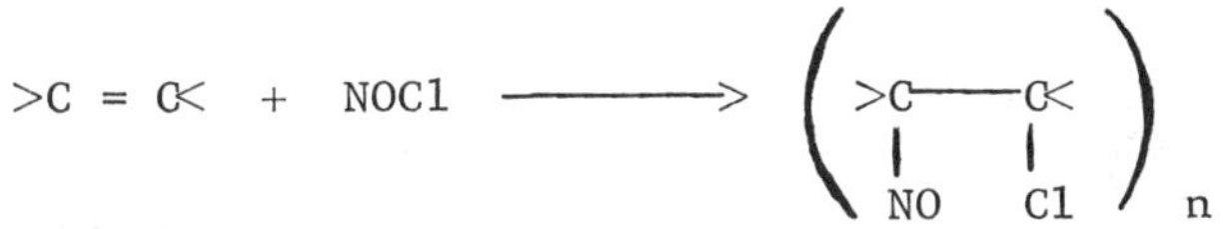

n = 1 or 2

Nitrosyl chloride may be regarded as the mixed anhydride of nitrous and hydrochloric acids. Mixed anhydrides of nitrous acid with carboxylic acids (the so-called acyl nitrites or nitrosyl acylates) were prepared many years ago by the reaction of nitrosyl chloride with silver salts of carboxylic acids,[25] but no information has been published on their synthetic utility, if any. Reasoning by analogy, we assumed that acyl nitrites would probably add readily to double bonds, as does nitrosyl chloride, but the resulting products would also be amenable to further chemical manipulation—a hope that has been realized in many cases. Besides defining the scope and limitations of the synthetic reactions, we have also explored the stereochemistry, mechanism, and orientation of addition of acyl nitrites to unsaturated compounds.

Briefly then, in the concluding portion of this paper, we wish to describe our work[25a] on (a) the *in situ* formation and consumption of nitrosyl formate† in the presence of suitable olefins, (b) properties and reactions of some of the resulting formoxynitroso adducts, (c) nitrosyl acetate and benzoate additions, and (d) tentative conclusions concerning the stereochemistry and mechanism of some of the reactions.

Formic acid is a relatively strong acid and causes alkyl nitrites to decompose readily, whereas acetic acid without a strong acid catalyst does not. Nitrosyl formate may be assumed to form *in situ* by the following sequence:

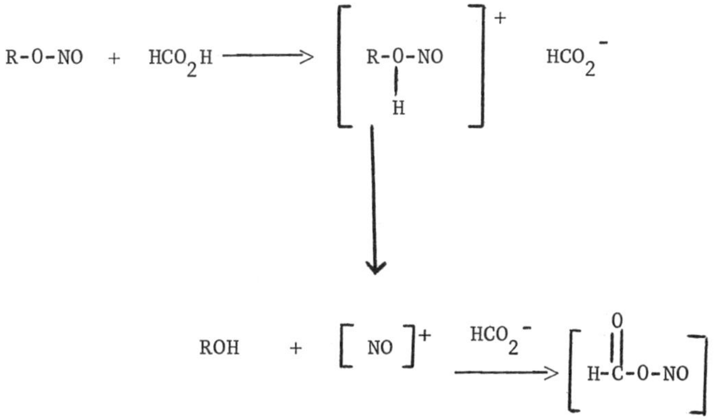

An alternative reaction may be written in which the protonated alkyl nitrite undergoes direct bimolecular reaction with formic acid to yield protonated nitrosyl formate:

†Nitrosyl formate is reported to be explosive and was studied by us only by the *in situ* method.

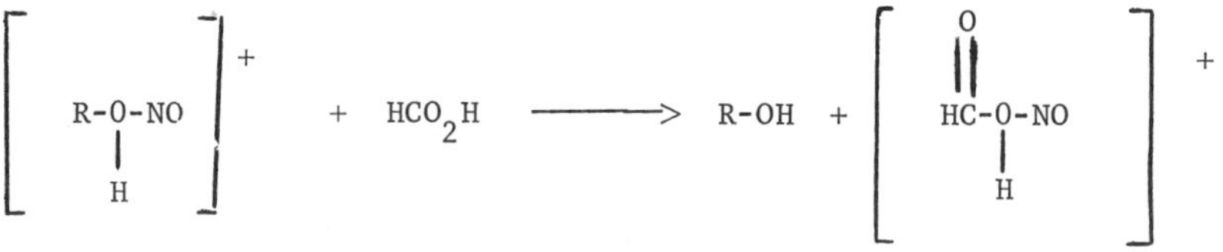

The product is analogous to protonated acetyl nitrate postulated by Bordwell and Garbisch[26] as the reactive intermediate in the addition of acetyl nitrate to olefins. If nitrosyl formate is able to add to a double bond, its formation (existence) could be deduced by trapping it as it is formed by a suitable unsaturated compound.

Addition of a solution of excess isoamyl nitrite and cyclohexene to cold formic acid gives an excellent yield of crystalline *trans*-1-formoxy-2-nitrosocyclohexane dimer (27), a stable compound. Infrared and ultraviolet spectroscopy as well as elemental analysis and molecular weight confirm the *trans*-nitroso dimer structure:

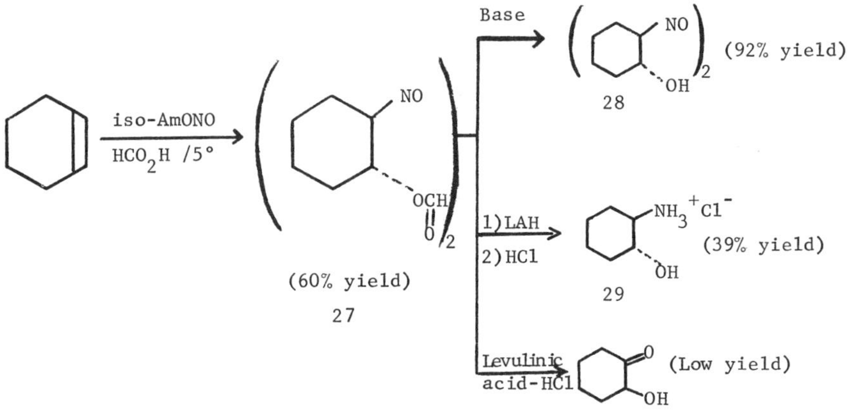

Trans-addition of nitrosyl formate to the double bond of cyclohexene is shown by lithium aluminum hydride (LAH) reduction of 27 to 29, *trans*-1-hydroxy-2-aminocyclohexane hydrochloride, a known compound. Number 27 is readily converted in almost quantitative yield to the corresponding alcohol (28), also a dimer. Adipoin (30) is obtained from 27 by transoximination-hydrolysis with levulinic and hydrochloric acids, but yields are low.

Addition of nitrosyl formate to styrene, α-methylstyrene, and β-methylstyrene gives excellent yields of dimeric adducts (31, 32, and 33, respectively) as stable crystalline solids:

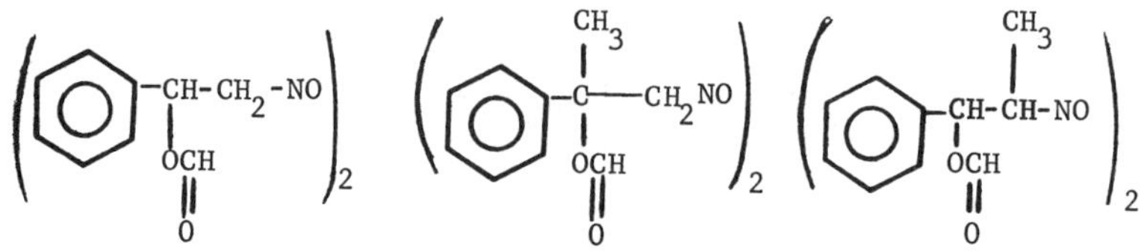

31 32 33

Their structures have been proven unequivocally by IR, UV(ultraviolet), and NMR spectroscopy as well as by elemental analysis and molecular weight. Addition occurs in Markownikow fashion, with the formate portion adding to the carbon atom best able to accommodate positive charge.

Addition of nitrosyl formate to unsaturated compounds which have no hydrogen atoms on the double bond yields deep blue monomeric, not dimeric, adducts. Addition to 2,3-dimethyl-2-butene and Δ^9-octalin yields 2,3-dimethyl-2-formoxy-3-nitrosobutane (34) and a mixture of *cis*- and *trans*-9-formoxy-10-nitrosodecalins (35), respectively. Spectral data, elemental analysis, and molecular weight confirm the structures:

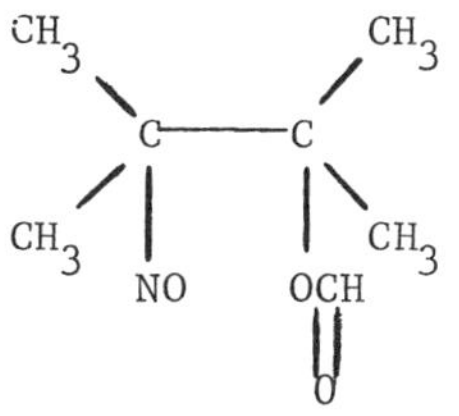

34

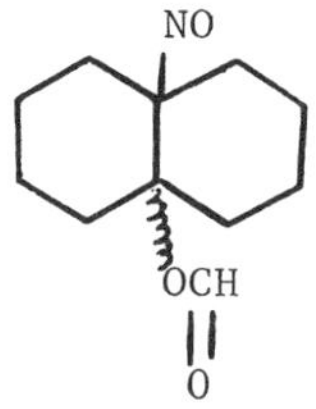

35

The electron spin resonance (ESR) spectrum of 34 clearly demonstrates its free radical character. At a field strength of 3.225 kilogauss and a sweep width of 500 gauss, 34 shows a triplet centered at 54 gauss downfield with a splitting of 11 gauss ($g = 1.97956$). Its ESR spectrum is similar to that of the nitrosyl chloride adduct of 2,3-dimethyl-2-butene.[27]

Addition of nitrosyl formate to norbornene proceeds without rearrangement and yields dimeric *exo-cis*-2-formoxy-3-nitrosonorbornane (36):

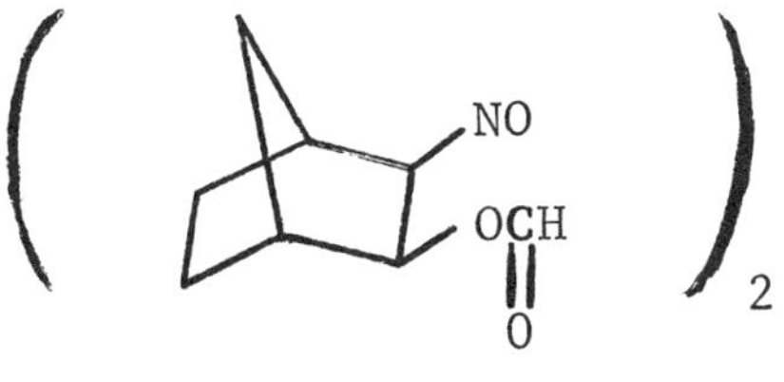

36

Absence of rearrangement was deduced from the nuclear magnetic resonance spectrum of 36 and also by comparison of its spectrum with those of related 2,3-disubstituted norbornanes.[28]

Occurrence of nitrosyl formate addition without rearrangement of the norbornene skeleton and in a *cis* manner has precedent in the addition of nitrosyl chloride to norbornene.[29,30] We conclude that nitrosyl formate adds to norbornene in an *exo-cis* manner by either a four-center or a six-center addition mechanism:

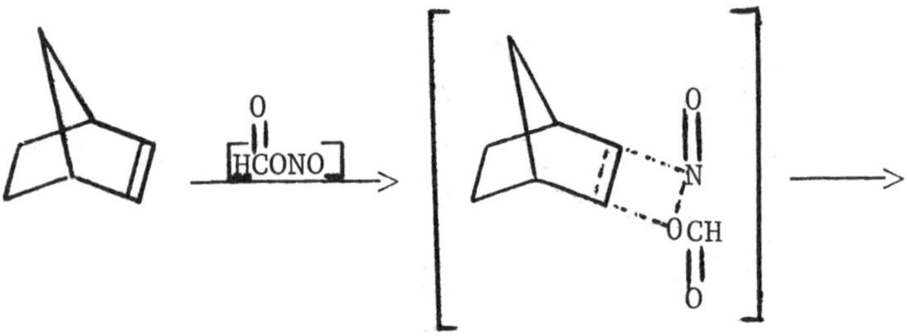

36

Four-Center Mechanism

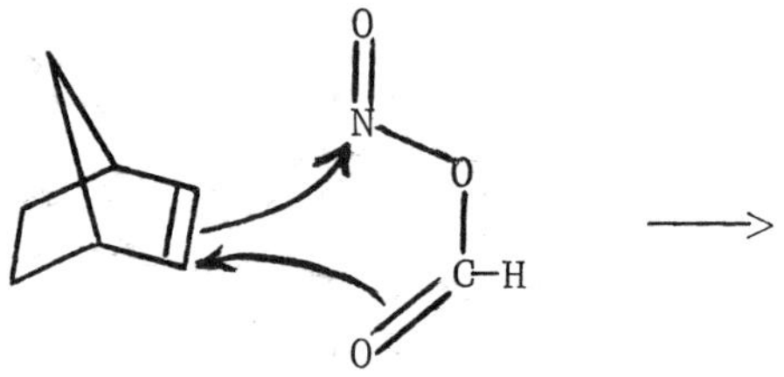

36

Six-Center Mechanism

Addition of nitrosyl formate to norbornadiene, however, gives an interesting and unusual result. Although addition of nitrosyl chloride to norbornadiene is reported to proceed without rearrangement,[29] and we anticipated the same result in view of the literature and our results with norbornene, the only crystalline product isolated in 13% yield is 37, a dimeric adduct in which one of the norbornyl skeletons is rearranged to a tricyclene and one is unrearranged. Number 37 was shown to be homogeneous by thin-layer chromatography, and it has a sharp melting point and correct elemental analysis and molecular weight.

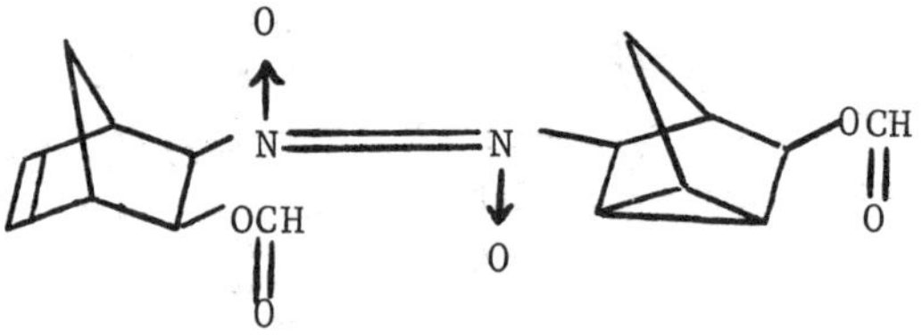

37

The structure of 37 is based on IR evidence (prominent absorption at 822 cm^{-1}, characteristic of a tricyclene structure)[31] and the NMR spectrum, which shows two slightly different chemical shifts for the aldehydic protons. The remainder of the NMR spectrum is consistent with the proposed nitroso dimer structure, in which each half of the dimer is different. Since there are three possible dimer structures, the isolation of 37 in low yield does not preclude the presence of the other products in the initial, crude reaction product.

In some cases (*trans*-3-hexene and 2-methyl-2-butene) it is not possible to obtain the nitrosyl formate adduct free of the isomeric oximinoformate (formed by prototropy). These reaction products are converted directly to the α-hydroxyketones in low yield by alkaline hydrolysis and transoximination with levulinic acid. In the case of 2-methyl-2-butene, illustrated below, the hydroxyketone isolated is 2-hydroxy-2-methyl-3-butanone (38), demonstrating that the nitroso or oximino group had been on the less substituted and the formate group on the more substituted carbon atom (Markownikow addition).

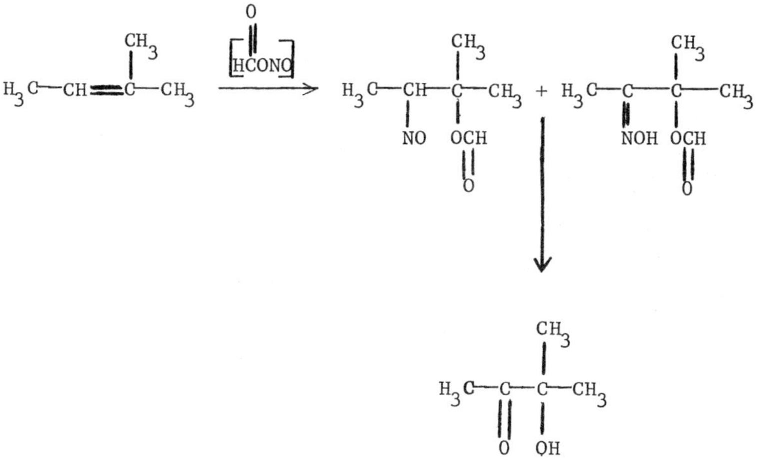

38

It has been suggested that nitrosyl formate does not have an independent existence but that the reaction proceeds by addition of a positive species, NO^+, to the double bond, followed by termination by the most populous nucleophile present, formic acid. Addition of nitrosyl chloride to cyclohexene in a large molar excess of formic acid (approximately 15:1) yields only the nitrosyl chloride adduct, dimeric *trans*-2-chloronitrosocyclohexane, in good yield; no formic acid addition is observed. We conclude tentatively that nitrosyl formate must have a finite lifetime, albeit short, but until the compound is prepared and added to double bonds we cannot be positive.

Formic acid is a relatively strong acid and is therefore able to decompose isoamyl nitrite, a reaction that does not occur with acetic acid unless a strong acid catalyst, such as perchloric acid, is present to protonate the alkyl nitrite. Perchloric acid was chosen because the perchlorate ion is a poor nucleophile and should not react with intermediate nitrosonium ions or ion pairs derived from the olefins. When a solution of 2,3-dimethyl-2-butene in isoamyl nitrite is added to a cold acetic acid solution containing a catalytic quantity of 70% perchloric acid, an immediate blue color develops indicative of a monomeric nitroso compound (tertiary nitroso group), and workup yields the expected product, 2,3-dimethyl-2-acetoxy-3-nitrosobutane (39) a royal blue liquid.

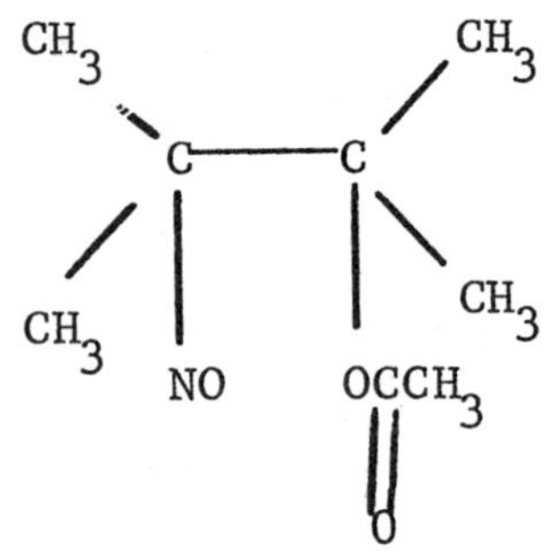

39

Alternatively, reaction of an olefin with a stable nitrosonium salt in which the anion is not a nucleophile, for example, nitrosonium tetrafluoroborate, should yield a nitrosonium intermediate ion pair capable of reaction with a nucleophile, such as acetic acid or acetate ion. Reaction of 2,3-dimethyl-2-butene with nitrosyl tetrafluoroborate and sodium acetate-acetic acid yields the expected 2,3-dimethyl-2-acetoxy-3-nitrosobutane (39), identical in every respect with the product from the olefin and isoamyl nitrite-acetic acid-perchloric acid.

Finally, to ascertain whether preformed nitrosyl acylates can, in fact, add to double bonds, nitrosyl benzoate was prepared.[32] Its addition to 2,3-dimethyl-2-butene is a facile reaction at 0° C, and a single product, 2,3-dimethyl-2-benzoyloxy-3-nitrosobutane (40), is obtained in essentially quantitative yield:

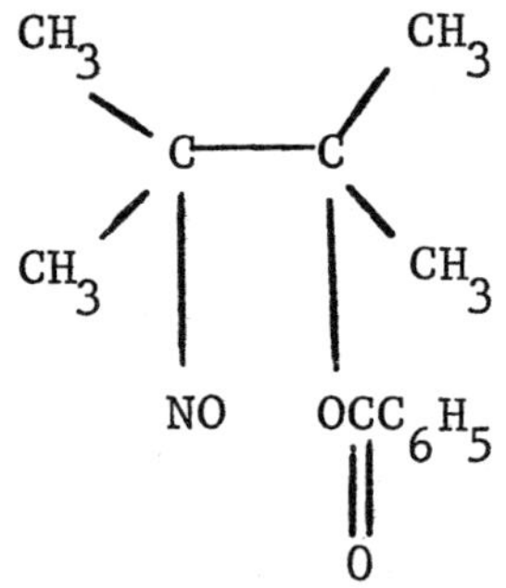

40

This product is a royal blue liquid that is readily hydrolyzed, even on exposure to moist air. Its IR, UV, visible, and NMR spectra are consistent with the proposed structure. It has the correct elemental analysis also.

Summary

A variety of newer methods for the formation of carbon-nitrogen bonds in organic compounds is described.

β-Halocarbamates are obtained in excellent yield by the addition of iodine isocyanate (followed by reaction with methanol) or N,N-dichlorourethan to unsaturated compounds of a wide range of structures. Pyrolysis of β-halocarbamates yields 2-oxazolidones, and reaction with base yields aziridines. Iodine isocyanate adds stereospecifically in a *trans*-manner by an electrophilic mechanism; dichlorourethan adds nonstereospecifically by a free radical mechanism.

Reaction of terminal aliphatic epoxides with potassium cyanate or organic isocyanates in dimethyl formamide yields 5-alkyl-2-oxazolidones unsubstituted or substituted on nitrogen, respectively.

Stereospecific syntheses of 1,2-diamines from cyclohexene, *cis*- and *trans*-olefins, and unsaturated fatty acids by multistep routes are described.

Nitrosyl formate, the lowest homologue of the nitrosyl acylate series and heretofore unknown, was prepared *in situ* and added to a number of acyclic, alicyclic, and aryl substituted unsaturated compounds to yield novel, reactive formoxynitroso compounds. Addition proceeds best with olefins activated electronically or sterically toward electrophilic addition to yield Markownikow addition products. Preliminary results are given on the addition of nitrosyl acetate and nitrosyl benzoate to 2,3-dimethyl-2-butene.

Acknowledgments

The work reported in this paper from the author's laboratory could not have been carried out without the collaboration and devotion of students and postdoctoral colleagues. It is a genuine pleasure to express thanks to Martin E. Dyen, Thomas A. Foglia, Charles G. Gebelein, Herman C. Hamann, Samuel M. Rosen, and Graham Swift.

References

1. Sexton, W. A. 1963. Chemical Constitution and Biological Activity. D. Van Nostrand Co., Inc. Princeton, N. J.
2. Birckenbach, L. & M. Linhard. 1930. Über Pseudohalogene. XI. Über Jodoxycyan, Dijoddioxycyan und Trijodcyanursäure. Ber. **63:** 2544–2558.
3. Birckenbach, L. & M. Linhard. 1931. Pseudohalogene. XIII. Über die Anlagerung von Jodoxycyan an Olefine. Ber. **64:** 961–968.
4. Drefahl, G. & K. Ponsold. 1960. Addition von Jodisocyanat an unsymmetrische Olefine. Chem. Ber. **93:** 519–523.
5. Drefahl, G., K. Ponsold & G. Köllner. 1964. Addition von Jodisocyanat an Substituierte Cyclohexene. J. Prakt. Chem. **23:** 136–142.
6. Hassner, A. & C. C. Heathcock. 1964. Stereospecific additions to olefins. The iodonium ion. Tetrahedron Lett. : 1125–1130.
7. Hassner, A., M. E. Lorber & C. Heathcock. 1967. Addition of iodine isocyanate to olefins. Scope and synthetic utility. J. Org. Chem. **32:** 540–549.
8. Gebelein, C. G. & D. Swern. 1965. Pseudohalogens. I. Relative electrophilicity of iodine isocyanate, dibromocarbene and bromine. Chem. Industr. (London) : 1462.
9. Gebelein, C. G. & D. Swern. 1968. Pseudohalogens. II. Relative rates of addition of iodine isocyanate to unsaturated compounds. J. Org. Chem. **33:** 2758–2762.
10. Gebelein, C. G., S. M. Rosen & D. Swern. 1968. Pseudohalogens. VI. Mechanism of addition of iodine isocyanate to unsaturated compounds. Submitted to J. Org. Chem.

11. ROSEN, S. M. & D. SWERN. 1966. Pseudohalogens. III. Preparation, stability and use of preformed solutions of iodine isocyanate. Anal. Chem. **38:** 1392–1397.
12. HANNA, J. G. & S. SIGGIA. 1965. Relationship Between Addition of Bromine to Unsaturated Compounds and Dielectric Constant of Solvent. Anal. Chem. **37:** 690–692.
13. SWERN, D. & E. F. JORDAN. 1948. Preparation of some polymerizable esters of long-chain saturated aliphatic acids. J. Amer. Chem. Soc. **70:** 2334–2339.
14. HEATHCOCK, C. & A. HASSNER. 1963. Formation of 2-oxazolidones from β-iodourethanes. Angew. Chem. [Eng.] **2:** 213–214.
15. FOGLIA, T. A. & D. SWERN. 1968. Accepted by J. Org. Chem. for publication.
16. GEBELEIN, C. G., G. SWIFT & D. SWERN. 1967. Synthesis of fatty acid derivatives containing an internal aziridine group (Pseudohalogens. IV). J. Org. Chem. **32:** 3314–3317.
17. FOGLIA, T. A. & D. SWERN. 1966. Pseudohalogens. VII. Scope and mechanism of addition of N,N-dichlorourethan to monoolefinic compounds. J. Org. Chem. **31:** 3625–3631.
18. FOGLIA, T. A. & D. SWERN. 1968. Pseudohalogens. X. Effect of some electronic or steric factors on the addition of N,N-dichlorourethan to unsaturated compounds. J. Org. Chem. **33:** 766–771.
19. FOGLIA, T. A. & D. SWERN. 1967. Pseudohalogens. VIII. New synthesis of aziridines and oxazolidones. J. Org. Chem. **32:** 75–78.
20. DYEN, M. E. & D. SWERN. 1968. Chemistry of epoxy compounds. XXI. Reaction of potassium cyanate with epoxides. J. Org. Chem. **33:** 379–384.
21. DYEN, M. E. & D. SWERN. 1967. 2-Oxazolidones. Chem. Rev. **67:** 197–246.
22. DYEN, M. E. & D. SWERN. 1968. Preparation of some long-chain 2-oxazolidones. J. Amer. Oil Chem. Soc. **45:** 325–330.
23. SWIFT, G. & D. SWERN. 1966. Stereospecific synthesis of *erythro-* and *threo-*9,10-diaminooctadecanoic acids. J. Org. Chem. **31:** 4226–4229.
24. SWIFT, G. & D. SWERN. 1967. Stereospecific synthesis of *cis-* and *trans-*1,2-diaminocyclohexanes and aliphatic vicinal diamines. J. Org. Chem. **32:** 511–517.
25. FRANCESCONI, L. & M. CIALDEA. 1904. Mixed organic-inorganic anhydrides. Gazz. Chim. Ital. **34:** 435–446.
25a. HAMANN, H. C. & D. SWERN. 1968. Pseudohalogens. XI. *In situ* addition of nitrosyl formate to olefins. J. Amer. Chem. Soc. **90:** 6481–6486.
26. BORDWELL, F. G. & E. W. GARBISCH. 1960. Nitrations with acetyl nitrate. I. The nature of the nitrating agent and the mechanism of reaction with simple alkenes. J. Amer. Chem. Soc. **82:** 3588–3598.
27. CLOSS, G. L. & S. J. BROIS. 1960. A new synthesis of aziridines. J. Amer. Chem. Soc. **82:** 6068–6070.
28. SUBRAMIAN, P. M., M. T. EMERSON & N. A. LEBEL. 1965. Nuclear magnetic resonance studies of 5,6-dihalo-2-norbornenes and 2,3-dihalonorbornanes. J. Org. Chem. **30:** 2624–2634.
29. MEINWALD, J., Y. MEINWALD & T. N. BAKER. 1964. The addition of nitrosyl halide to olefins. Dependence of steric course on olefin structure. J. Amer. Chem. Soc. **86:** 4074–4080.
30. MILLER, J. B.. 1961. Reaction of nitrosyl chloride with norbornene and norbornadiene. J. Org. Chem. **26:** 4905–4907.
31. YOUNGBLOOD, G. T., V. D. TRIVETTE & P. WELDER. 1958. Studies in the bicyclo-[2.2.1]heptane series. V. Reactions of bicyclo[2.2.1]heptadiene. J. Org. Chem. **23:** 684–686.
32. PRITZKOW, W. & H. NITZER. 1964. Über die Pyrolyse von Acylnitriten. J. Prakt. Chem. **25:** 69–78.

DISCUSSION OF THE PAPER

B. L. VAN DUUREN (*New York University, New York, N.Y.*): I should like to compliment you on some very fine organic chemistry. I know that Dr. Swern and Dr. Shimkin at the Fels Research Institute have a collaborative program, and I was wondering whether you would know if any of these very interesting compounds, the nitroso compounds and other electrophilic compounds you mentioned, are being tested for carcinogenic activity?

DR. KIRBY: I believe that these are being screened by the National Cancer Institute. I don't know if the nitroso products are, but I think they are.

C. C. PRICE (*University of Pennsylvania, Philadelphia, Pa.*): I notice that one of the compounds for which you made a chlorocarbamate addition product was t-butylethylene. I wonder whether you converted this to the aziridine? The reason I ask this question is that we have just completed a study of t-butylethylene oxide, and it is really quite remarkable how different some of the chemical properties of t-butylethylene oxide are from simple oxides like propylene oxide. We have been interested in this from an entirely different point of view. We found in our polymerization research that t-butylethylene oxide is less readily polymerized by base. It is much more difficult to attack by nucleophiles, but it is attacked stereoselectively. It is the first example of syntatic stereospecific polymerization of an epoxide. It seems to me that it might be very interesting, if you could synthesize the t-butyl aziridine, to see whether its biological properties might also be very much more selective than other aziridines.

DR. KIRBY: t-Butyl aziridine is prepared in fair yield (60%) by treating the chlorocarbamate adduct with base. The ring closure is much slower than with unhindered compounds. The oxazolidone could not be obtained by the usual pyrolysis.

T. BARDOS (*State University of New York, Buffalo, N.Y.*): In answer to Dr. Price, we have made some nitrosoaziridines. I shall discuss the relationship of chemical structure and pharmacological activity of these compounds in my paper.

REACTIONS WITH PURINES AND PYRIMIDINES*

Robert Shapiro

Department of Chemistry, New York University, New York, N. Y.

The purine and pyrimidine components of the nucleic acids offer a variety of functional groups to an attacking chemical reagent. A number of factors operate in determining the site of attack of a particular reagent. In this paper, we will first discuss the situation with regard to alkylating agents. We will then consider another type of reaction, which, while not related to alkylation in its mechanism, is akin to alkylation in its potential for the modification of nucleic acids.

Alkylation is perhaps the most studied chemical reaction of the nucleic acids and their components. A variety of alkylators have been used, which include alkyl halides, sulfates, and sulfonates, nitrogen and sulfur mustards, diazo compounds, small ring lactones, epoxides, and aziridines. The purines and pyrimidines have been allowed to react as free bases, and in nucleosides, nucleotides, nucleic acids, and entire organisms. A vast body of information, sometimes contradictory and confusing, has been compiled.[1,2] In attempting to organize this into a readily comprehensible pattern, two important variables must be kept in mind. These are the chemical environment of the purine or pyrimidine (whether it is the free base or in a nucleotide or DNA, et cetera) and its charged state (whether it is neutral or anionic). The reactions of free bases with alkylating agents present the simplest situation chemically, but results obtained here cannot always be extended to more complex environments. Adenine, for example, can

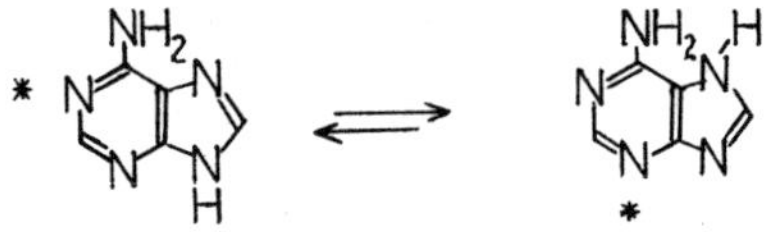

I II

exist as a mixture of the 9-H tautomer (I) and the 7-H tautomer (I). Tautomer I resembles a nucleotide in that the 7-position is available for alkylation, but this is not so for II, which instead offers the 9-position. These differences in reactivity extend to the pyrimidine ring of adenine as well. It is known that 7-substituted adenines direct alkylation to the 3-position (indicated by an asterisk in II), whereas 9-substituted adenines direct the attacking reagent to the 1-position (indicated by an asterisk in I).[3] One might expect considerably more of the 3-substituted product from the alkylation of adenine than from adenosine, in which the substitution in the imidazole ring is fixed in the 9-position.

The second environment for the purine or pyrimidine to be considered covers the cases where the heterocycle is substituted "normally" (for a purine, in the 9-position; for a pyrimidine, in the 1-position) and where no specific hydrogen-bonding schemes come into play. This includes nucleosides, nucleotides, and

* Supported in part by grant no. GM-11437 from the U. S. Public Health Service.

single-stranded nucleic acids. While differences in reactivity exist between these different levels due to effects such as base stacking, and sugar to base hydrogen bonding, some simple generalizations can be drawn. Alkylation occurs predominantly at the pyridine-type nitrogens (those indicated by numbers in the diagram below).

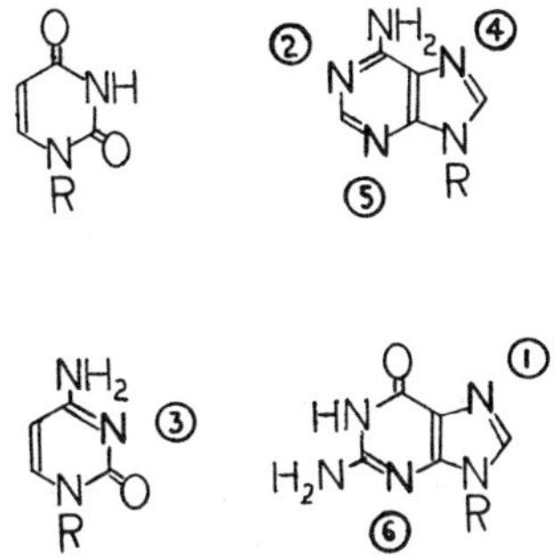

The sites are numbered in order of decreasing reactivity. Thus, N-7 of guanine is the most reactive site, followed by N-1 of adenine and N-3 of cytosine. The preference for attack at this type of position can be rationalized in the following way: Alkylation is irreversible, and kinetic factors, rather than the stability of the products, control the product distribution. Each pyridine-type nitrogen possesses an unshared pair of electrons, which is in the plane of the ring and plays no part in the conjugated system of electrons of the heterocyclic ring. Bond formation by this pair of electrons involves no disruption of the conjugated electron system, and little loss of resonance energy. This is not the case for attack by an alkylating agent on an imino nitrogen (such as N-1 or N-9 of guanine) or carbon atom. No simple verbal explanation can be offered to explain the observed order of reactivity among the various pyridine-type nitrogens, although arguments based upon molecular-orbital calculations have been advanced to justify this.[4] Adenine, cytosine, and guanine derivatives protonate in acid solution on the same sites that are most reactive to alkylation. The most basic site, however, is N-3 of cytosine, followed by N-1 of adenine and N-7 of guanine, the reverse of the order observed for alkylation. However, protonation, unlike alkylation, is a reversible, equilibrium-controlled process. The pyridine-type nitrogen least reactive to alkylation is undoubtedly N-3 of guanine. No product derived from attack at this point has been observed in alkylation studies on nucleic acids. This position does react in nucleosides under favorable circumstances, however, as when the alkylating agent is held in a nearby position in the sugar moiety of a nucleoside:[5]

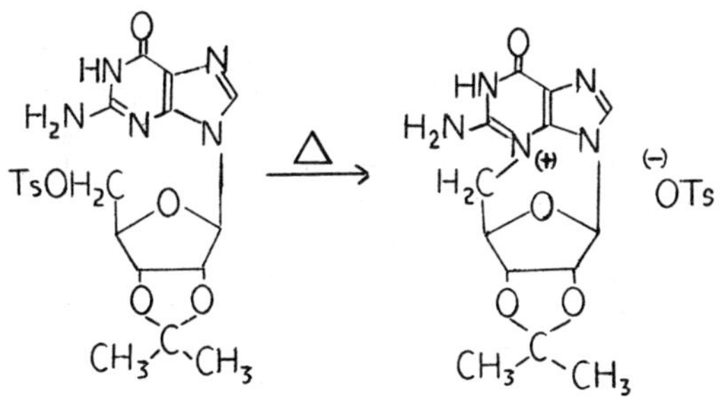

The general picture of reactivity is altered when the purines and pyrimidines are held within the hydrogen-bonded structure of a double-stranded DNA. This is summarized in the next diagram.

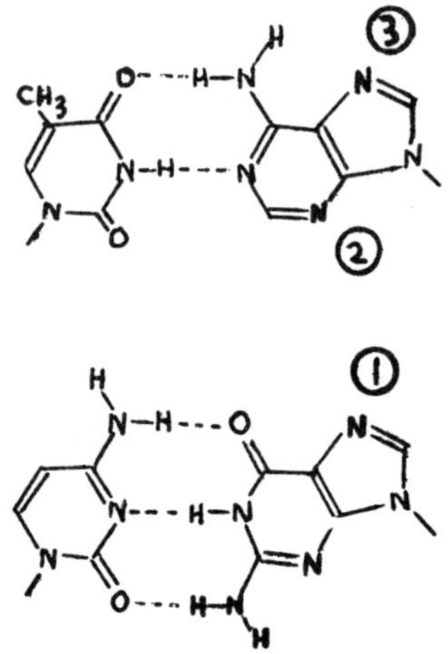

The reactivity has been suppressed at those sites involved in Watson-Crick hydrogen bonding. The N-7 position of guanine is now by far the most reactive site, followed by the N-3 and N-7 positions of adenine. The existence of the hydrogen bonding undoubtedly has some effect upon the distribution of electrons, and hence the chemical reactivity, of the heterocyclic ring systems. The observed results, however, can be explained reasonably well on steric factors alone, which deny the alkylating agent access to the hydrogen-bonded sites. A similar effect has been observed in a simpler situation. Whereas a 9-alkyladenine would be expected to react primarily at the 1-position, 6-diethylamino-9-methylpurine (III) gives the 3-substituted product, IV, with methyl iodine.[6] The bulky diethylamino group has hindered access to the 1-position.

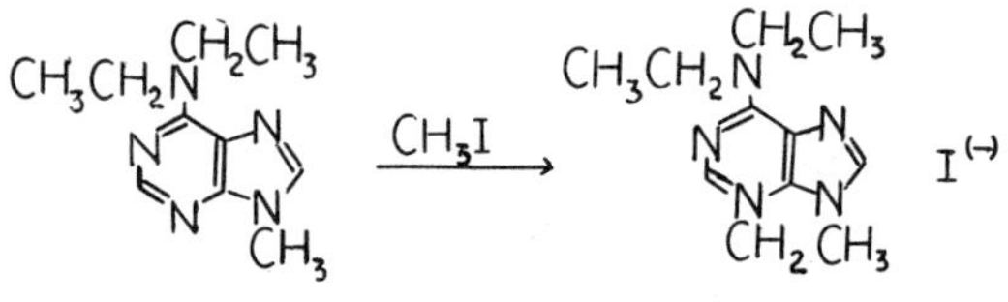

III IV

More complex environments for the purines and pyrimidines than that of DNA do exist, such as in a nucleic acid bound to a protein. Not enough data exists on reactivities in such situations, however, to allow generalizations.

The foregoing discussion refers to situations in which the heterocycles are in their uncharged forms. When they are converted to cations or anions, the overall picture changes. Few studies have been conducted upon alkylation of the protonated heterocycles, because their reactivity to electrophilic attack in general is diminished by the positive charges. Two of the bases, uracil (or thymine) and guanine, can form anions in mildly alkaline solution (pH < 10). The situation with respect to alkylation under these conditions is indicated in the next diagram.

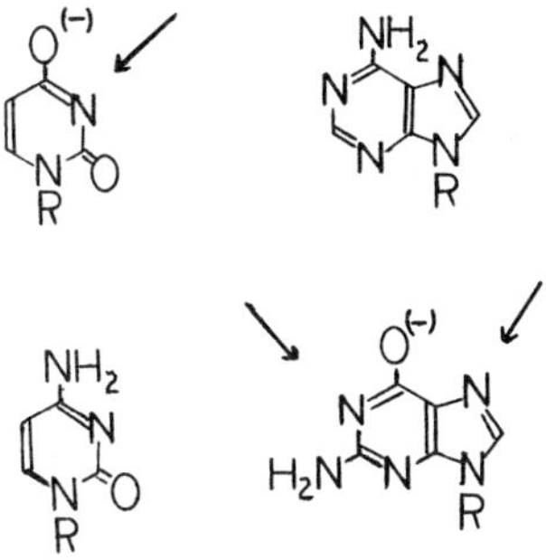

The resonance forms depicted for the uracil and guanine anions show the negative charge on oxygen, but it is, of course, distributed among the ring nitrogens as well. Two new sites capable of alkylation have been created: N-1 of guanine and N-3 of uracil. These sites, together with N-7 of guanine, appear to be the most reactive ones. As comparative data is not available, these positions are merely indicated by arrows in the above diagram.

The preceding generalizations hold reasonably well for a number of alkylating agents, but there is one notable exception: diazoalkanes. This is an important class of reactant, because several types of carcinogens, such as dialkylnitrosamines[7] and azoxy compounds,[8] may exert their effect by being metabolized to diazoalkanes *in vivo*. Even when the reaction is run in neutral solution, the pattern of substitution produced by diazoalkanes tends to resemble that of the other alkylating agents in alkali. This is because of the mechanism of action of diazoalkanes. Before reacting, they first accept a proton from the solvent or substrate to form a reactive methyldiazonium ion:

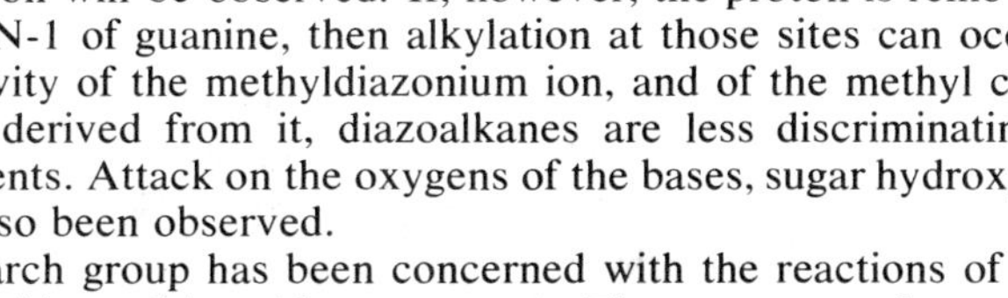

If the proton is taken from the solvent, the normal pattern for alkylation in neutral solution will be observed. If, however, the proton is removed from N-3 of uracil or N-1 of guanine, then alkylation at those sites can occur.[9] Because of the reactivity of the methyldiazonium ion, and of the methyl carbonium ion that can be derived from it, diazoalkanes are less discriminating than other alkylating agents. Attack on the oxygens of the bases, sugar hydroxyls, and phosphates has also been observed.

Our research group has been concerned with the reactions of polycarbonyl compounds with nucleic acid components. These compounds react at different sites than do alkylating agents, and are capable of much greater specificity. Glyoxal derivatives, for example, can react exclusively at the 1-position and amino group of guanine, under the proper conditions, to produce the product V. The reactions are fully reversible, and the product reverts completely to the starting materials under alkaline conditions.[10] This reversibility is the key to the specificity of the reaction. The reagent may react at a number of sites, but eventually it ends up in the most stable position, in which both carbonyl groups are involved in a cyclic structure. We have studied this reaction with glyoxal,

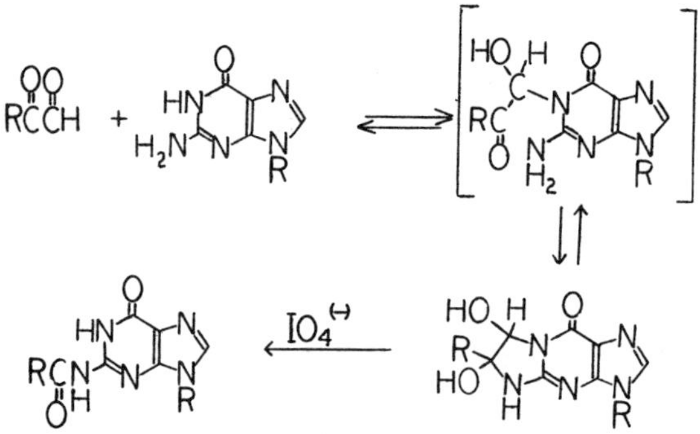

VI V

pyruvaldehyde, and α-keto-β-ethoxybutyraldehyde (Kethoxal®†). The last two reagents are unsymmetrical, and an alternative mode of addition is possible with guanine derivatives. The indicated structure (V), however, is the only one formed. This can be rationalized in terms of the intermediate indicated above for the reaction. The more reactive carbonyl group (the aldehyde) combines first with the more reactive site on the heterocycle, the imino group[11] (or, more likely, the anion derived from it). The ketone and amino group then combine in a slower step. The method used to demonstrate the structures of the adducts with pyruvaldehyde and Kethoxal was periodate cleavage to the acylguanines (VI).[12] Although this might have been expected to leave a formyl group attached to the 1-position, it was not detected. The structures of the acylguanines were in turn established by reduction with lithium aluminum hydride to the corresponding alkylguanines.[12]

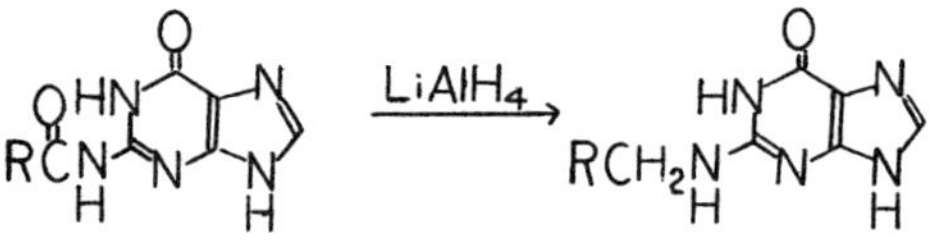

While the glyoxal reaction is selective for guanine derivatives at pH 7, an interaction with adenine derivatives takes place at pH 5. Although no adduct can be isolated or demonstrated by chromatography, oxidation by periodate *in situ* gives an N-formyladenine.

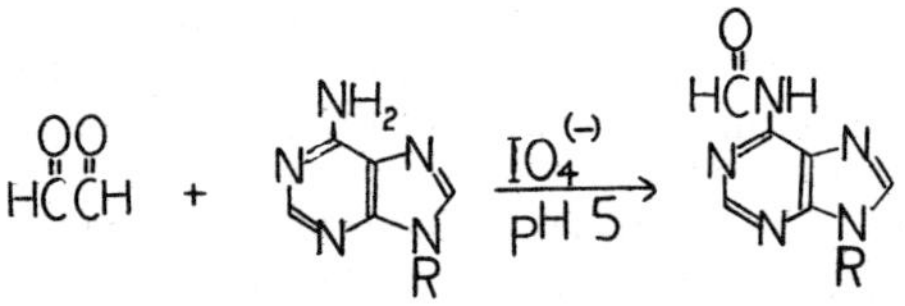

A reaction related both to the above ones and to alkylation has been reported recently.[13] Glycidaldehyde (VII), which contains both an aldehyde and an alkylating function, reacts with guanine derivatives at weakly alkaline pH. The product, VIII or IX, again contains a new ring formed at the N-1 and amino

† Upjohn Co., Kalamazoo, Mich.

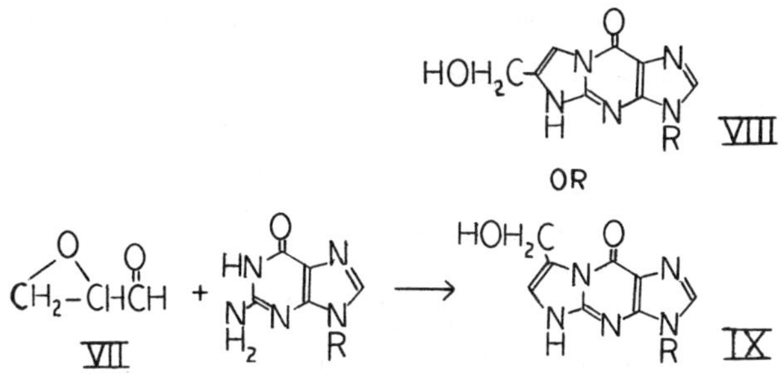

groups of guanine, but its structure is somewhat different.

Ninhydrin furnishes another interesting variation upon this theme. It reacts with guanine in a manner analogous to glyoxal,[10] but it also combines readily with cytosine derivatives.[14] While the guanine reaction is reversible, the one

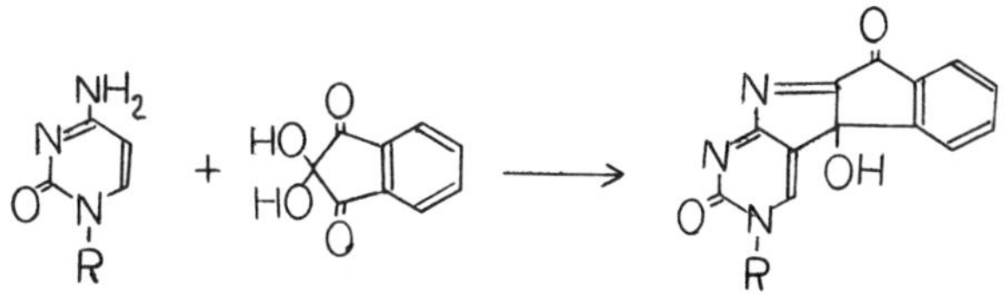

with cytosine, which involves a novel carbon-carbon bond formation at C-5 of cytosine, is not. Ninhydrin can thus be used as a specific reagent for cytosine derivatives. The orientation of the adduct with cytosine is in accord with the postulate that the more reactive carbonyl of ninhydrin (the central one, present in hydrated form) first attacks the more reactive position of the heterocycle (the amino group in this case).

Alkylating agents have been prominent both as potential hazards to genetic material and as agents for chemotherapy. It appears likely that the polycarbonyl compounds as a class will also possess these properties. Glyoxal is toxic to human cells in culture, and it has been suggested that this is due to a large extent to its inhitition of DNA synthesis by combination with DNA.[15] Pyruvaldehyde displays carcinostatic properties.[16] Kethoxal, and other α-ketoaldehydes, are antiviral agents.[17] Retine, a bacterial growth inhibitor, is believed to be a glyoxal derivative.[18] As additional reactions of related compounds with nucleic acids are discovered, the biological importance of this class of compounds will undoubtedly grow.

Acknowledgments

I wish to emphasize the contribution of my collaborators, Dr. Agarwal and Dr. Claggett, and Mr. Cohen, Mr. Hachmann, and Mr. Shiuey to this research.

References

1. Lawley, P. D. 1966. Progr. Nucl. Acid Res. **5:** 89.
2. Brookes, P. 1966. Cancer Res. **26:** 994.

3. Broom, A. D., L. B. Townsend, J. W. Jones & R. K. Robins. 1966. Biochemistry **3:** 494.
4. Pullman, B. & A. Pullman. 1963. Quantum Biochemistry : 234. Interscience Publishers. New York, N. Y.
5. Holmes, R. E. & R. K. Robins. 1963. J. Org. Chem. **28:** 3483.
6. Marsico, J. M. & L. Goldman. 1965. J. Org. Chem. **30:** 3597.
7. Magee, P. N. & E. Farber. 1962. Biochem. J. **83:** 114.
8. Laqueur, G. L. 1964. Fed. Proc. **23:** 1386.
9. Kriek, E. & P. Emmelot. 1963. Biochemistry **2:** 733.
10. Shapiro, R. & J. Hachmann. 1966. Biochemistry **5:** 2799.
11. Eyring, E. J. & J. Ofengand. 1967. Biochemistry **6:** 2500.
12. Shapiro, R., B. I. Cohen, S.-J. Shiuey & H. Maurer. 1969. Biochemistry **8:** 238.
13. Goldschmidt, B. M., T. P. Blazej & B. L. Van Duuren. 1968. Tetrahedron Lett. : 1583.
14. Shapiro, R. & S. C. Agarwal. 1968. J. Amer. Chem. Soc. **90:** 474.
15. Klamerth, O. L. 1968. Biochim. Biophys. Acta **155:** 271.
16. Együd, L. G. & A. Szent-Györgi. 1968. Science **160:** 1140.
17. Tiffany, B. D., J. B. Wright, R. B. Moffett, R. V. Heintzelman, R. E. Strube, B. D. Aspergen, E. H. Lincoln & J. L. White. 1957. J. Amer. Chem. Soc. **79:** 1682.
18. Szent-Györgi, A., L. G. Együd & J. A. McLaughlin. 1967. Science **155:** 539.

DISCUSSION OF THE PAPER

Unidentified Speaker: The amino group is susceptible to alkylation in ordinary amines, and of course, the hydroxyl group in alcohol is susceptible to alkylation, and you have indicated that the enolic form of the pyrimidine hydroxyl group was formed under alkaline conditions. Why do you say we do not have alkylation of these amino groups and of the potential hydroxy groups in these purines and pyrimidines?

Dr. Shapiro: I would like to say that this touches a concept that I believe has been abused frequently in biological circles over the past decade, that is, the mistaking of the amines of heterocyclic compounds for the amino groups of such compounds as anilines. There are very important chemical differences between them, enough so that the heterocyclic amines deserve to be considered separately. One important difference, which was brought out during my talk, is that these heterocyclics do not protonate on the amino groups, even though aniline of course does protonate on the amino group. I think we can simplify this situation just by talking about a simple amino-heterocyclic such as 4-aminopyridine. Of course, the discussion applies just as well to the amino groups on the purines and pyrimidines of the nucleic acids. One important interaction in 4-aminopyridine that does not occur in ordinary aromatic amines is a resonance interaction between the amino group and the ring nitrogen. That is, there can be a contribution of electrons from the amino group into the heterocyclic ring with a resulting localization of them on the heterocyclic ring nitrogen. This makes it advantageous for 4-aminopyridine to protonate on the ring nitrogen. Because 4-aminopyridine does protonate on the ring nitrogen, the charge can be shared between these two nitrogens. Each one of them carries half the charge, which greatly adds to the stability of this particular cation.

On the other hand, if 4-aminopyrimidine were to protonate on the exocyclic amino group, this would force this amino group to bear the full brunt of the positive charge. It would not be able to share it by any resonance effect with the ring nitrogen. Furthermore, this would even eliminate any interaction of this amino group with the heterocyclic ring. What I said about protonation would also apply to some extent to the transition state leading to alkylation. That is, if one is alkylating on the ring nitrogen, there can be some distribution of the charge between the amino group and the ring nitrogen. However, alkylation on the amino group bears the full brunt of the positive charge that is forming, and the same delocalization does not occur. I think that for this reason ring nitrogens are much better sites for alkylation than amino groups are. I do not know, at least as far as the nucleic acid heterocycles are concerned, whether any really authenticated illustrations of alkylation directly on the amino group have been reported. This is not to say that these amino groups cannot react with any chemical reagent. If attack occurs by a reagent that is more reversible, it may try a variety of sites on the heterocycles, and it may eventually settle on the amino group. This occurs when the amino group is the most stable site of attachment. For example, nitrous acid probably nitrosates first at the N-7 of guanine, just as in alkylation, but the attachment of a nitroso group at that position is unstable. The nitroso group comes right off again, and eventually it hits the amino group. This involves higher energy, but once it occurs, a diazonium ion is formed that then leaves with loss of nitrogen. As far as alkylation on oxygen is concerned, I think there is some reactivity. It goes up, of course, when the anion is formed. Alkylation upon neutral carbonyl groups can occur, but empirically they are not as reactive to alkylation as the nitrogens of the pyridine type are.

C. C. PRICE (*University of Pennsylvania, Philadelphia, Pa.*): I might just comment that the competition factor for the hydroxyl group is extremely low in its neutral form. Glucose is reported at zero competition factor, even less than water. So the nucleophilicity of the neutral oxygen atom in a hydroxyl group is very low. The only way one can really alkylate these hydroxyl groups is if there are conditions basic enough to get the anion, and that, of course, requires a very strong base.

UNIDENTIFIED SPEAKER: Do any of your reagents react with native or denatured DNA?

DR. SHAPIRO: We have not done extensive work with native or denatured DNA ourselves. Reactions of DNA with glyoxal, which is toxic to human cells in culture, may have been demonstrated. Apparently, glyoxal reacts with denatured DNA and not with native DNA. Investigators are going ahead on the assumption that glyoxal does not react with hydrogen-bonded sections of nucleic acids and are using various keto-aldehydes as modifying agents for transfer RNA. My impression is that the reagents would react with denatured DNA but not with native DNA unless their concentration was such that, like formaldehyde, they denatured the native DNA.

UNIDENTIFIED SPEAKER: It occurs to me in listening to this interesting discussion on the difference in the ease of alkylating aromatic and heterocyclic amino groups that there is one explanation for the nucleophilicity of the guanine 7-nitrogen in the nucleic acids. In the hydrogen bonding in DNA, guanine participates as a hydrogen bond donor. It donates two bonds and accepts only one, so there is an increase of electron density over the guanine ring system, which then expresses itself in the greater activity of the N-7 nitrogen in being alkylated.

DR. SHAPIRO: This is certainly possible, and it was to effects of this type that I referred when I mentioned that you no longer have the same electronic system when you have a hydrogen-bonded moiety in DNA. I think that Pullman intended to calculate what the adjusted electron densities would be after this hydrogen bonding occurs. I do not think it was enough to account for the magnitude of the effect that Dr. Price has demonstrated in his particular studies.

UNIDENTIFIED SPEAKER: When Pullman gets this data, he will no doubt be able to do the calculation. But, certainly, I think that Dr. Bardos pointed out a fact that should be considered; to whatever extent there is a net loss of the proton from the guanine moiety and hydrogen bonding of cytosine, it would enhance the reactivity of the guanine moiety, and if there is, indeed, a transfer of the proton, this could be at least a part of the enhancing effect that we have observed.

UNIDENTIFIED SPEAKER: How was the acylated guanine obtained back in 1893?

DR. SHAPIRO: Acetylguanine was made in 1893 by the simple expedient of refluxing guanine with acetic anhydride. This is good for making acetyl guanine, but it would not be very good for putting an acetyl group on to the guanine of the nucleic acid, because you would not have the nucleic acid left after you finished refluxing it with acetic anhydride.

PART II. CHEMICAL CARCINOGENESIS

CARCINOGENIC EPOXIDES, LACTONES, AND HALO-ETHERS AND THEIR MODE OF ACTION*

B. L. Van Duuren

Laboratory of Organic Chemistry and Carcinogenesis
Institute of Environmental Medicine
New York University Medical Center
New York, N. Y.

INTRODUCTION

Alkylating agents are being introduced into our environment with increasing frequency. Some of them are used in chemotherapy; others are used as industrial intermediates in organic synthesis, as organic solvents for various chemical processes, as cross-linking agents in manufacturing processes, and as antibacterial and fungistatic agents. Coupled with this increase in possible environmental or occupational exposure is the occurrence of alkylating agents as plant natural products, some aspects of which are discussed in other sections of this monograph. The known biological properties of these compounds—i.e., their mutagenic, carcinogenic, and cytotoxic properties—have, therefore, received increasing attention. Biochemical studies have focused on their possible modes of interaction with tissue constituents: proteins, purines, pyrimidines, nucleic acids, et cetera. In addition, organic chemists have studied the reactivity of these compounds with a variety of nucleophilic agents.

Alkylating agents cover a broad range of chemical compounds, and the present report will be concerned mainly with those types that have been investigated in this laboratory; the carcinogenicity, structure-activity relationships, and mode of action of these compounds have been the main concern in our work. The compound types that were explored are epoxides (mono-, di-, and polyfunctional), β- and γ-lactones, and halo-ethers.[1-9]

This report will be concerned only with selected aspects of this subject. The compounds of interest, their carcinogenicity or lack thereof, and various routes of administration used in mice and rats are listed in TABLE 1. The structures for these compounds are shown in FIGURES 1, 2, and 3. The compounds were usually tested at highest tolerable doses for the lifespans of the animals. Thirty to fifty animals were usually included per group; in the gastric feeding experiments, smaller groups were used; this is discussed below. The details of these experiments have appeared in our earlier reports.[1-6]

It is clear from TABLE 1 that compounds that were active or inactive when applied on mouse skin showed, with one exception, the same activity or were

* Supported by grant CA 08944 (Mode of Action of Alkylating Epoxides and Lactones) and contract PH43-66-962 (Carcinogenicity of Halo-ethers), from the National Cancer Institute, and ES-00260 from the Bureau of State Services.

TABLE 1

BIOASSAY OF EPOXIDES, LACTONES AND HALO-ETHERS*

Compounds†	Mouse Skin	Routes of Administration and Carcinogenicity‡ Subcutaneous Injection Mice	Rats	Feeding Rats
Monoepoxides				
Ethylene oxide (1)	–			
Glycidaldehyde (2)	+	+	+	–
Glycidol (3)	–			
Epibromohydrin (4)	–			
Ethylglycidyl ether (5)	–			
1,2-Epoxybutene-3 (6)	+			
1,2-Epoxybutane (7)	–			
1,2-Epoxydodecane (8)	–			
1,2-Epoxyhexadecane (9)	+			
9,10-Epoxystearic acid (10)	–	–	–	
Epoxycyclooctane (11)	–			
1-Ethyl-3,4-epoxycyclohexane (12)	–			
Styrene oxide (13)	+			
Indan epoxide (14)	–			
1,2-Epoxycyclohexane (15)	–		–	
1-Vinyl-3,4-epoxycyclohexane (16)	–			
Limonene monoxide (17)	–			
Ethyleneoxycyclohexane (18)	–			
Diepoxides				
d,l-1,2,3,4-Diepoxybutane (19)	+	+	+	–
meso-1,2,3,4-Diepoxybutane (20)	+			
1,2,4,5-Diepoxypentane (21)	+			
1,2,5,6-Diepoxyhexane (22)	+	+	+	
1,2,6,7-Diepoxyheptane (23)	+			
1,2,7,8-Diepoxyoctane (24)	+			
1,2,3,4-Diepoxycyclohexane (25)	–			
1,2,5,6-Diepoxycyclooctane (26)	–			
1-Ethyleneoxy-3,4-epoxycyclohexane (27)	+			–
9,10,12,13-Diepoxystearic acid (28)	–			
3,4-Epoxy-6-methyl-cyclohexyl-methyl-3,4-epoxy-6-methyl-cyclohexanecarboxylate (29)	+			
Resorcinoldiglycidyl ether (30)	–			
Hexaepoxysqualene (31)	–			
Lactones				
β-Propiolactone (32)	+	+	+	+
β-Butyrolactone (33)	+	+	+	+
4,5-Epoxy-3-hydroxyvaleric acid-*β*-lactone (34)	–			
Diketene (35)	–	–	–	

TABLE 1 *(Continued)*

Compounds†	Mouse Skin	Routes of Administration and Carcinogenicity‡		
		Subcutaneous Injection		Feeding
		Mice	Rats	Rats
3-Hydroxy-2,2-dimethylbutyric acid-β-lactone (36)	−			
3-Hydroxy-2,2-dimethyl-4,4,4-trichlorobutyric acid-β-lactone (37)	−			
2,2,4-Trimethyl-3-hydroxy-3-pentenoic acid-β-lactone (38)	−	−	+	
3-Hydroxy-2,2,4-trimethyl-heptanoic acid-β-lactone (39)	−			
γ-Butyrolactone (40)	−			
β-Angelicalactone (41)	−		−	
α-Angelicalactone (42)	−		−	
Halo-Ethers				
Chloromethyl methyl ether (43)	−		−	
Bis(chloromethyl)ether (44)	+		+	
Octachlorodi-n-propyl ether (45)§	−			
α,α-Dichloromethyl methyl ether (46)§	−			
Monochloro acetaldehyde diethyl acetal (47)§	−			

* These results are taken from earlier reports from this laboratory,[1–6] except where noted.

† The number in parentheses after the name refers to the structure numbers shown in FIGURES 1–3.

‡ Only compounds that gave malignant tumors in long-term tests were considered carcinogenic (+). Compounds which gave no tumors at the site of application or a few papillomas in the mouse skin experiments are indicated as noncarcinogenic (−).

§ Unpublished data.

inactive when given by subcutaneous (s.c.) injection in mice and in rats. The one exception was a β-lactone, structure 38, which gave one adenocarcinoma when given by s.c. injection in a group of 50 rats. It was inactive by mouse skin application and by s.c. injection in mice.

The inability of carcinogenic epoxides to induce gastric tumors in rats is ascribed to the rapid acid-catalyzed hydrolysis of epoxides. Since animals subjected to gastric feeding were starved for 24 hours prior to feeding, the pH of the rat stomach was estimated to be about 1.[10,11] Both β-lactones tested induced squamous carcinomas of the stomach in rats; the hydrolysis of β-lactones is not acid-catalyzed.

Subcutaneous injection in rats and in mice were, in these experiments, as reliable as skin application in mice for the establishment of carcinogenicity,[3,4] contrary to the views expressed in other reports.[12] Our findings with new experiments in this area will be described elsewhere.

The first reported carcinogenic epoxide was diepoxybutane[13] (stereochemically undefined), structures 19 and/or 20; β-propiolactone, structure 32, was the

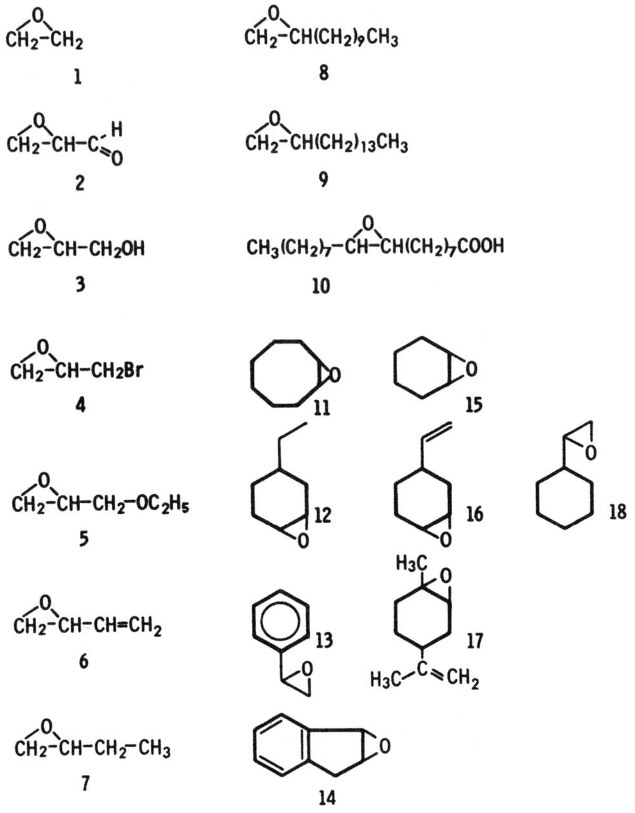

FIGURE 1. Monofunctional epoxides. Numbers refer to chemical names given in TABLE 1.

first reported carcinogenic β-lactone.[14] Since that time, a large series of these compounds has been tested for carcinogenicity,[1–6,15] so that it is now possible to consider structure-activity relationships and its relevance to possible modes of action. In recent work from this laboratory,[6] α-halo-ethers were shown to possess carcinogenic activity. The mutagenicity, tumor-inhibitory activity, and other radiomimetic properties of these compounds have been under examination for many years, and the relationship of these properties to carcinogenic and initiating activity will be discussed below. A number of epoxides, β-lactones, and α-halo-ethers have also shown initiating activity in two-stage carcinogenesis with the phorbol esters derived from croton oil as promoting agents.[2,6]

Structure-Activity Relationships of Epoxides

The series of mono- and difunctional epoxides that have been tested for carcinogenic activity is now sufficiently large to conclude that diepoxides are more frequently carcinogenic than monofunctional epoxides. Thus, of 18 monoepox-

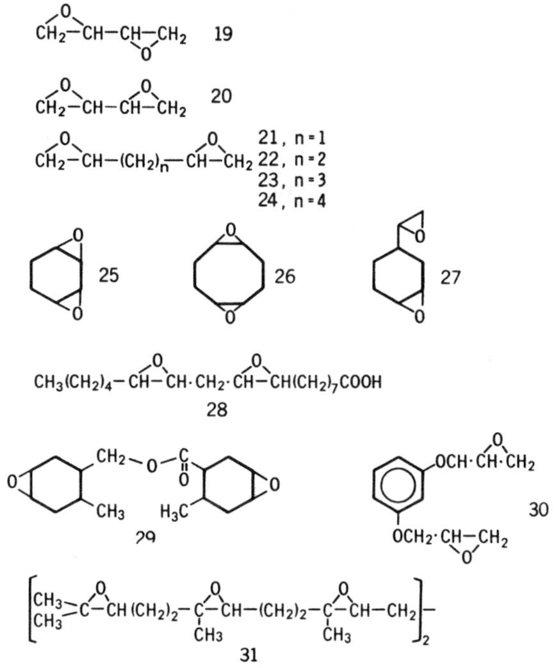

FIGURE 2. Bifunctional epoxides. Numbers refer to chemical names given in TABLE 1.

ides tested in our laboratory, only four showed activity. They are glycidaldehyde, structure 2; 1,2-epoxybutene-3, structure 6; styrene oxide, structure 13; and 1,2-epoxyhexadecane, structure nine. Weil[15] tested 11 monoepoxides by mouse skin application and did not observe skin tumors with any of them. On the other hand, 8 of 12 diepoxides tested by us by one or more routes in mice and rats were carcinogenic,[1–6] and in Weil's work,[15] 5 of 17 diepoxides were carcinogenic. In general, the tumor yield is lower with monoepoxides than with their difunctional analogs. In the monoepoxide series, compounds closely related to glycidaldehyde, structure 2, e.g., glycidol, structure 3, or ethyl glycidyl ether, structure 5, were inactive. It is possible that the aldehyde function of glycidaldehyde plays a role, so that glycidaldehyde behaves like a difunctional agent. Its reaction with guanosine is relevant in this respect and will be discussed below. Similarly, monoepoxides with an adjacent center of unsaturation such as 1,2-epoxybutene-3, structure 6, and styrene oxide, structure 13, are weakly carcinogenic; their saturated analogs 1,2-epoxybutane, structure 7, and ethyleneoxycyclohexane, structure 18, are inactive. It is possible that such epoxides are converted *in vivo* into biologically active bifunctional agents. Similar findings were reported by Roe,[16] who studied the initiating activity of methanesulfonic acid esters in initiation-promotion experiments with croton oil as promoting agent. Saturated monofunctional sulfonic esters e.g. butylmethane sulfonate were usually inactive; on the other hand, closely related unsaturated materials e.g. allylmethane sulfonate were active.

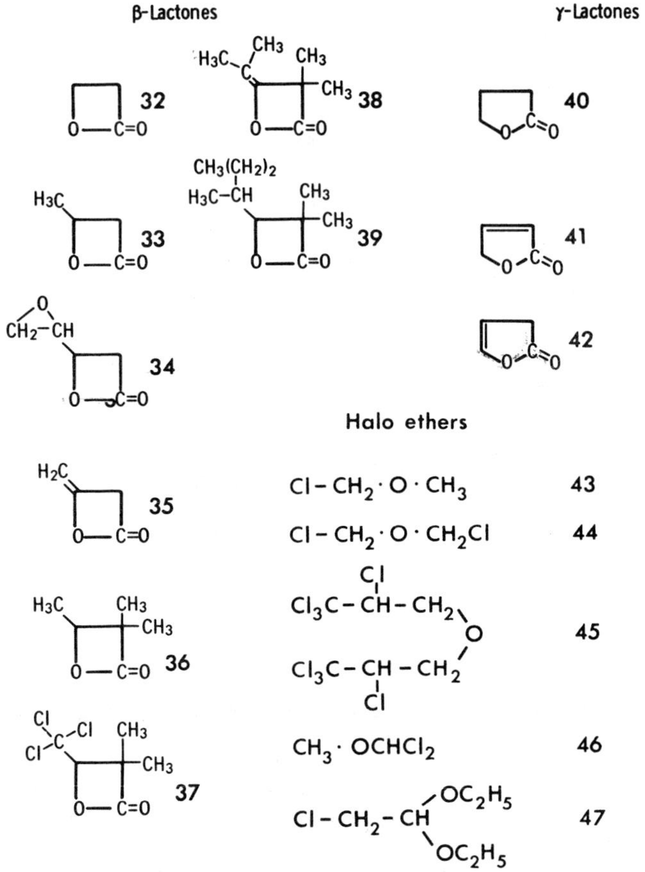

FIGURE 3. β- and γ-Lactones and halo-ethers. Numbers refer to chemical names given in TABLE 1.

In the difunctional epoxides there are several factors that were given attention in our work on carcinogenic activity and molecular structure. One concerns the interatomic distance between the epoxide functions, which was considered in an earlier report from this laboratory.[8] Although much has been speculated about cross-linking between strands of the DNA helix by alkylating agents, these interatomic distances were usually not considered. Such consideration renders a number of the suggested modes of crosslinking in native DNA unlikely, if not impossible, unless one assumes extensive distortion of the helix. The interatomic distances for a number of diepoxides were measured with Dreiding scale models; some of these are listed in TABLE 2.[8] The distances of greatest separation in flexible diepoxides that are carcinogenic range from 4.0–9.9 Å. It has been proposed[17] that difunctional alkylating agents cross-link the strands of the double helix of DNA at the N-7 position of two adjacent guanine moieties, and that this

TABLE 2

INTERATOMIC DISTANCES IN DIEPOXIDES*

Compound†	Interatomic Distances (Å) Closest Approach	Interatomic Distances (Å) Greatest Separation
1,2,3,4-Diepoxycyclohexane (25)	3.0‡	
d,l-Diepoxybutane (19)	2.5	4.0
meso-Diepoxybutane (20)	2.5	4.0
1,2,5,6-Diepoxycyclooctane (26)	1.6	4.3
1,2,4,5-Diepoxypentane (21)	1.5	5.2
1-Ethyleneoxy-3,4-epoxycyclohexane (27)	4.6	5.4
1,2,5,6-Diepoxyhexane (22)	0.0	6.6
1,2,6,7-Diepoxyheptane (23)	Overlap	7.7
1,2,7,8-Diepoxyoctane (24)	Overlap	8.9
3,4-Epoxy-6-methylcyclohexylmethyl-3,4-epoxy-6-methyl-cyclohexane-carboxylate (29)	Overlap	9.9
Resorcinoldiglycidyl ether (30)	Overlap	12.1

* As measured on Dreiding scale models.[8]

† Numbers in parentheses refer to structure numbers in FIGURES 1–3.

‡ Chair conformation.

linking may then result in incomplete duplication of genetic material, possibly resulting in carcinogenesis. The relatively short distances between reactive functions in such compounds as bis(chloromethyl)ether, discussed below, and diepoxybutane render cross-linking between the reactive sites of adjacent bases unlikely or impossible. On the other hand, resorcinol diglycidyl ether, structure 30, in which there are 11 carbon atoms between the terminal, epoxide-bearing carbon atoms is inactive as a carcinogen.[2]

In a recent report, Lawley and Brookes[18] point out that in the Watson-Crick model for DNA the reactive functions of a difunctional alkylating agent should be able to reach across ~8 Å. They report the identification of a product in which two guanine moieties are linked by reaction with diepoxybutane based on paper chromatography and elution of the product. Nevertheless, they attribute the occurrence of the product to intramolecular cross-linking in DNA as proposed by them earlier;[17] no explanation was given for this apparent anomaly.

There is little, if any, direct experimental evidence as yet to support the contention that cross-linking in DNA by these agents is related to the carcinogenic process. In examining this concept, which is a reasonable pursuit, it will be important to examine other possible types of cross-linking and interactions in addition to the ones so frequently cited.[17,18] Some of these have been enumerated in an earlier report from this laboratory[5] and by other earlier workers;[19,20] they include: (a) a cross-linking reaction by esterification at adjacent phosphate sites (intramolecular), possibly followed by disruption of the polymer chain; (b) cross-linking between adjacent nucleic acid molecules (intermolecular) (this can be at phosphate sites or at purine or pyrimidine bases); (c) cross-linking between DNA and surrounding nucleohistones. Our studies suggest that cross-linking may be important for carcinogenicity, and it is likely that the types of cross-linking (b) and (c) enumerated above may be most significant.

Another aspect of cross-linking that deserves consideration deals with molecular flexibility and carcinogenicity of diepoxides. A comparison was made of open-chain flexible diepoxides and their cyclic analogs in which the epoxides are held in rigid configurations. Thus, 1,2,3,4-diepoxycyclohexane, structure 25, is not carcinogenic; its open-chain flexible analogs, meso- and d,l-diepoxybutane, structures 19 and 20, are both carcinogenic. The cyclic compound 1,2,3,4-diepoxycyclohexane can be viewed as a diepoxybutane molecule in which the epoxides are held in relatively rigid configurations as a result of the attachment of an ethylene bridge. The same applies for 1,2,5,6-diepoxycyclooctane, structure 26, which is inactive; its open-chain analog, 1,2,5,6-diepoxyhexane, structure 22, is carcinogenic. 1-Ethyleneoxy-3,4-epoxycyclohexane, structure 27, which has flexible epoxide centers, is also carcinogenic. These findings suggest that flexibility of the reactive centers is important for carcinogenicity. It should be noted that in this series of compounds there is very little difference in other properties such as chemical reactivity,[7,8] which may be important for carcinogenicity. The apparent importance of molecular flexibility for carcinogenic activity in these diepoxides is in accord with the other evidence enumerated above, which suggests that difunctionality and, hence, the possibility to cross-link, apparently enhances the possibility of carcinogenicity for these agents.

It must, however, be borne in mind that there are a number of carcinogenic and monofunctional epoxides and β-lactones. The classical example is β-propiolactone,[14] to which may be added β-butyrolactone[2] and a substantial number of alkylating agents other than epoxides and lactones, such as the nitrosamines.[21] Thus, bifunctionality is not a prerequisite for carcinogenic activity.

These carcinogenic monofunctional agents would, by alkylation of nucleic acids, give rise to what has been called point mutations;[17] hence the difference between point mutations in DNA (caused by monofunctional agents) and large deletions (proposed to be caused by difunctional agents)[17] becomes irrelevant with respect to carcinogenesis.

The Carcinogenicity of β- and γ-Lactones

A series of 8 β-lactones that included a variety of structural features (FIGURE 3) was tested for carcinogenic activity by one or more routes of administration; of these, only three were active (TABLE 1). They are: β-propiolactone, β-butyrolactone, and 2,2,4-trimethyl-3-hydroxy-3-pentenoic acid-β-lactone. Substitution on carbon atoms-2 or -3 results in a decrease or loss in activity. Diketene, for example, which bears a methylene function on carbon atom-3, is inactive as a carcinogen in spite of its high chemical activity with nucleophilic and electrophilic reagents such as alcohols, aldehydes, amines, and ketones.[22] This compound, which can be thought of as the anhydride of acetoacetic acid, hydrolyzes in water to this acid. In the presence of catalysts, this hydrolysis is rapid;[22] this factor, combined with its chemical reactivity, may preclude its reaction at *in vivo* sites important for carcinogenesis. The compound was tested by life-time skin application in Swiss female mice in both acetone[1] and in tricaprylin[23] (30 mice/group) at 10% concentration, 0.1 ml of solution, three times weekly. In view of this surprising lack of carcinogenic activity, the compound was also tested by s.c. injection in mice with tricaprylin as vehicle, once weekly, 1.1 mg/injection. Subcutaneous implantation of gelatin capsules containing 1.1 mg diketene in 10 mg of trilaurin-tricaprylin (4:1) were made in the left axillary region in rats. Forty female Sprague-Dawley rats were used in these experiments. The purpose of these pellet implantations was to allow slow seepage of the diketene into the surrounding tissue. No local tumors were observed in these tests after 20 months.[23]

In TABLE 3, the rates of hydrolysis of some of these β-lactones are given.[8] β-Propiolactone is very rapidly hydrolyzed, and β-butyrolactone is hydrolyzed much more slowly. In spite of this difference in rate of hydrolysis, they have similar tumor responses in several test systems, as will be discussed below.

TABLE 3
RATE OF HYDROLYSIS OF β-LACTONES[8]

Compound	Carcinogenicity[1–5]	Hydrolysis rate constant, k $min^{-1} \times 10^3$, 37° C
β-Propiolactone	+	11.3
β-Butyrolactone	+	3.0
4,5-Epoxy-3-hydroxy-valeric acid-β-lactone	+*	0.02
Diketene	−	120
2,2,4-Trimethyl-3-hydroxypentenoic acid-β-lactone	+†	$\sim 2 \times 10^{-4}$

*Gave benign tumors only on mouse skin.[2]

†Gave 1 fibrosarcoma by subcutaneous injection in 50 rats;[3] this result is probably not statistically significant (see reference 3).

γ-Lactones are not reactive alkylating agents, but were included in these tests in view of the reports of the carcinogenicity of β-angelicalactone.[24] The γ-lactones show no reaction with potent nucleophiles such as the thiosulfate ion,[8] and they undergo acyl-oxygen cleavage in base-catalyzed hydrolysis. Only three of these compounds were tested, and they were all inactive; they were tested by skin application as well as by s.c. injection in mice and in rats.[1–4] Dickens[24] reported one of six rats with a tumor when β-angelicalactone was given subcutaneously. In the Dickens[24] experiment, a total dose of 260 mg of material was given. In our experiment with 20 rats, the cumulative dose was 1.56 g, and no local tumors were observed in an experiment that lasted for 546 days.[4] In addition, this compound was inactive when applied in life-time skin application in mice.[2]

α,β-Unsaturated lactone moieties occur in the aflatoxins B_1 and B_2,[25] and these compounds are carcinogenic;[26] lactone moieties (cyclic diesters) occur also in some of the pyrrolizidine alkaloids that have been reported to be carcinogenic,[27] but it is not known what role these moieties play in contributing to the carcinogenicity of these materials. Culvenor and co-workers[28] have suggested a mechanism whereby these materials may function as alkylating agents, and more recent findings confirming this suggestion appear elsewhere in this monograph.[29]

Reactions with Purines, Pyrimidines, and Nucleic Acids

It has been shown by *in vitro* reactions that epoxides such as diepoxybutane and β-lactones e.g. β-propiolactone react with guanosine at the N-7 position. Many other alkylating agents, carcinogenic, mutagenic, and particularly noteworthy noncarcinogenic agents such as ethylene oxide[30] also react at the N-7 of guanine, and it is, therefore, difficult to equate reaction of any of these agents at the N-7 of guanine with carcinogenesis and/or mutagenesis. Nevertheless, a surprisingly extensive series of studies has been carried out in which the reaction at this site is explored and is considered important for biological activity. It is worth while, in this context, to remember that reaction of some of these agents occurs also on other bases, particularly adenine.[31] The extent of reaction at other bases of DNA or RNA is less than in the case of guanine if alkylating agents are allowed to react with the nucleic acids.[32] However, this quantitative difference in degree of alkylation does not exclude the possibility that alkylation of bases other than guanine are of biological significance.

It should also be borne in mind that not all alkylating agents and, particularly significant, not all carcinogens react at the N-7 of guanine. N-acetoxy-N-2-fluorenylacetamide reacts at the C-8 position of guanine.[33] Glycidaldehyde has been shown in our *in vitro* work to react at the N-1 and C_2-amino group to give a Δ^4-imidazoline ring fused to the pyrimidine ring of guanosine.[9] Either of two structures is possible for this product: structures 48 or 49, shown in FIGURE 4. Of these, structure 48 is preferred, for reasons given earlier.[9] This reaction of guanosine and glycidaldehyde occurs at pH 7 in aqueous medium;[9] the reaction occurs considerably faster above pH 7. Studies on the reaction of glycidaldehyde with DNA are currently under way.

Some *in vivo* studies on the position of alkylation of guanine in nucleic acids have been carried out. Colburn and Boutwell[34] have shown that tritiated β-propiolactone binds covalently to DNA, RNA, and protein of mouse skin. It was shown that in the case of RNA the major binding product was 7-(2-carboxyethyl) guanine, which is the same as that formed in the reaction between β-propiolactone and guanosine.[35]

Some evidence has been obtained to indicate that epoxides alkylate nucleoprotein and DNA at phosphate groups with the formation of esters,[19] and it was in fact suggested that phosphate sites in DNA are the sites most available for alkylation. This and related aspects are discussed elsewhere in this monograph.[36]

It is therefore unwise to attach too much significance to any one type of reaction.

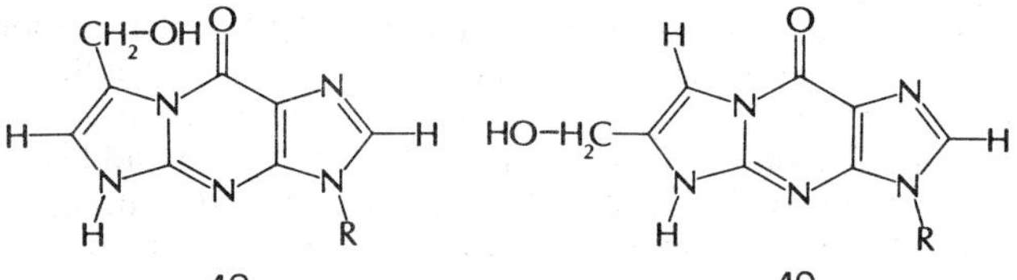

48 49

FIGURE 4. Reaction product of guanosine or deoxyguanosine with glycidaldehyde. R = sugar.

Epoxides of Aromatic Hydrocarbon Carcinogens

Attempts have been made to correlate the carcinogenicity of aromatic hydrocarbons with intercalation between purine-pyrimidine base pairs of nucleic acids based on solubilization and spectroscopic studies;[37] yet, very little evidence exists to support this and other hypotheses. This problem of physical interactions between carcinogens, mutagens, and nucleic acids has been discussed in other reports from this laboratory.[38–40]

It is much more likely that aromatic hydrocarbons must be metabolized to proximal carcinogens, and that one or more enzymes are involved in this process. The earliest isolable metabolites of aromatic hydrocarbons are their K-region dihydrodiols, as is shown in FIGURE 5 for dibenz(a,h)anthracene.[41] It is very likely that an epoxide, structure 50, is the precursor of this dihydrodiol. Several of the known metabolites of this hydrocarbon shown in FIGURE 5 can arise from such an epoxide through hydrolysis followed by oxidation, dehydration, or carbon-carbon bond cleavage. The metabolites shown in FIGURE 5 were isolated from the rat lung metabolism of dibenz(a,h)anthracene.[41] None of these metabolites has shown notable carcinogenic activity[42] or activity as initiating agents in initia-

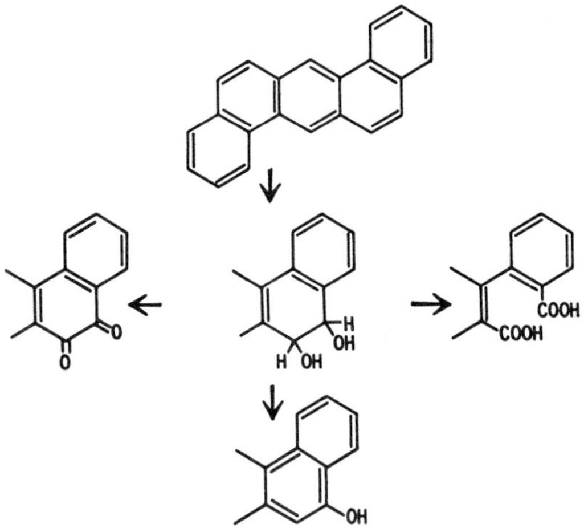

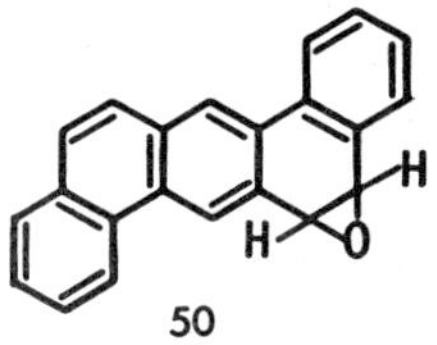

50

FIGURE 5. Metabolism of dibenz(a, h)anthracene: possible formation of 5,6-epoxy-5,6-dihydrodibenz(a, h)anthracene (structure 50).

TABLE 4
INITIATING ACTIVITY OF AROMATIC HYDROCARBON EPOXIDES*
(MOUSE SKIN)

Treatment: Primary† and dose (μg/0.1 ml solvent)	Treatment: Secondary	Number of Mice per Group with Tumors: Papillomas§	Number of Mice per Group with Tumors: Cancer	Days to First Papilloma
Test Data				
5,6-Epoxy-5,6-dihydrodibenz-(a,h)anthracene, 150	CR‡	10/20(14)	2/20	139
5,6-Epoxy-5,6-dihydro-7-methylbenz(a)anthracene, 300	CR‡	4/20(8)	1/20	126
5,6-Epoxy-5,6-dihydro-7-methylbenz(a)anthracene, 322¶	Croton oil‖	10/26(25)	3/26	–
Control Data				
Dibenz(a,h)anthracene, 150	CR‡	18/20(144)	10/20	93
5,6-Epoxy-5,6-dihydrodibenz-(a,h)anthracene, 150	None	0/20	0/20	–
Dibenz(a,h)anthracene, 150	None	3/20(7)	0/20	316
5,6-Epoxy-5,6-dihydro-7-methylbenz(a)anthracene, 300, III	None	0/15	0/15	–
None	None	0/30	0/30	–
None	CR‡	20/258	4/258	150–430**

*Reference 5 except where noted. Results at 330 days.
†Single dose.
‡100 mg/application of phorbol esters, A–D (CR) 3 times weekly beginning 14 days after initiation, as 0.025% solution in acetone (25 μg/application).
§Total number of papillomas given in parentheses.
¶Results reported by Miller and Miller;[43] results are at 203–245 days.
‖Twice-weekly application of 0.05 ml of a 0.3% solution of croton oil in acetone starting 10 days after initiating dose.
**Results of 12 experiments.[45]

tion-promotion experiments on mouse skin.[42] The epoxide, structure 50, was recently shown to possess notable initiating activity in initiation-promotion experiments on mouse skin;[5] another aromatic hydrocarbon epoxide, 5,6-epoxy-5,6-dihydro-7-methylbenz(a)anthracene, also showed initiating activity in two-stage carcinogenesis. The results of these experiments are summarized in TABLE 4. Miller and Miller[43] tested one of these compounds for initiating activity with croton oil as promoter, and observed 10 of 26 mice with benign tumors after 29 weeks and 3 of 26 mice with skin carcinomas after 38 weeks (TABLE 4). They also induced sarcomas at the injection site with this compound in mice and rats.[43] They concluded from their work that epoxides are probably not the proximal carcinogens, because of the low potency compared with the parent compounds; this was also observed in our work (TABLE 4). However, it must be remembered that these compounds are unstable, and that there are probably remarkable differences between skin application and *in situ* formation of the epoxide at a target site vital for carcinogenesis. In fact, as will be discussed below, epoxides are considered to be, in general, weak carcinogens because of the high doses used and the usual occurrence of local tumors only. From our results and the above considerations, we conclude that an epoxide or other proximal carcinogen is probably involved in aromatic hydrocarbon carcinogenesis.

Carcinogenic Halo-Ethers

The halo-ethers such as chloromethyl methyl ether, structure 43, and bis(chloromethyl)ether, structure 44, are potent alkylating agents that have found wide use in the chemical industry. The extraordinary reactivity of these ethers and their wide industrial use, coupled with the highly noxious nature of their hydrolysis products, prompted the examination of this class of alkylating agents as potential carcinogens in a series of animal test systems.[6] It was also of importance to determine whether any specific structural features of these alkylating agents can be correlated with their carcinogenic activity. The compounds in this series that have been tested are listed in TABLE 1, structures 43–47, FIGURE 3. Of these compounds, only bis(chloromethyl)ether, structure 44, FIGURE 3, has shown carcinogenic activity both by skin application in mice and by s.c. injection in rats. The order of carcinogenic activity of this compound is the same as that of β-propiolactone, as is shown in TABLE 5. The cytotoxic and irritant monofunc-

TABLE 5

POTENCY OF CARCINOGENIC ALKYLATING AGENTS ON MOUSE SKIN[6] *

Compound	Dose in mg (3 times weekly in 0.1 ml solvent)	Days to First Tumor	Mice with Carcinoma / Mice Tested	Median Survival Time (Days)
Bis(chloromethyl)-ether	2.0	161	12/20	313
β-Butyrolactone	10.0	252	15/30	438
β-Propiolactone†	2.5	—	9/30†	200
Glycidaldehyde	3.0	212	8/30	496
d, 1-Diepoxybutane‡	3.0	326	6/30	475

* Female Swiss ICR/Ha mice, except where noted.
† Male Swiss mice.
‡ Acetone as solvent; all others in benzene.

tional α-halo ether, chloromethyl methyl ether, structure 43, was not carcinogenic on mouse skin or by s.c. injection in rats.[6] β-Halo ethers such as structures 45 are much less reactive than α-halo ethers. The lack of carcinogenic activity of monofunctional α-halo ethers, as compared with the potent carcinogen bis(chloromethyl)ether, again points to the significance of cross-linking ability for carcinogenic activity. Both chloromethyl methyl ether and bis(chloromethyl)ether readily react with 4-(p-nitrobenzyl)pyridine to give the products shown in FIGURE 6.

It is noteworthy, however, that although not carcinogenic, chloromethyl methyl ether and α,α-dichloromethyl methyl ether did exhibit initiating activity

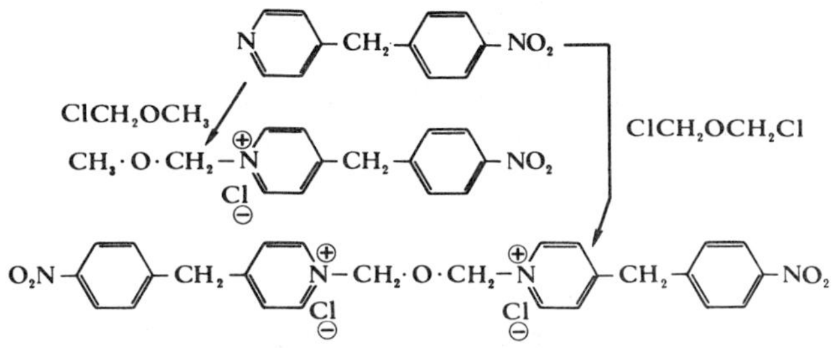

FIGURE 6. Reaction products of chloromethyl methyl ether and bis(chloromethyl)ether with 4-(p-nitrobenzyl)pyridine.

in two-stage carcinogenesis with phorbol esters as promoting agent. This aspect will be discussed below.

Initiating Activity of Alkylating Agents in Two-Stage Carcinogenesis

Roe and Salaman[44] reported on the initiating activity of β-propiolactone in two-stage carcinogenesis with croton oil as promoter. Significant also is that triethylenemelamine, which is not carcinogenic for mouse skin, showed initiating activity in their work.[44] In our work, seven alkylating agents were tested for initiating activity. Five of these are carcinogenic; the two other compounds tested were not. All seven showed initiating activity with phorbol ester as the promoting agent. The results are shown in TABLE 6. These compounds are less potent than 7,12-dimethylbenz(a)anthracene, as initiating agents. On the other hand, tumors appear earlier in initiation-promotion experiments than in the long-term application of the agent alone.

The finding that the two noncarcinogenic α-halo ethers, chloromethyl methyl ether, structure 43, and α,α-dichloromethyl methyl ether, structure 46, show initiating activity is not surprising. Similar findings were made for other agents that are not carcinogenic for mouse skin, such as urethane,[46] triethylenemelamine[44] and several borderline or noncarcinogenic aromatic hydrocarbons.[47]

Weak Carcinogenicity of Epoxides and Lactones

With all of the compounds discussed here, high doses must usually be employed in order to get a significant tumor response. The doses and tumor yields for some of the most potent alkylating agents in this series are shown for mouse skin application in TABLE 5. Corresponding data for s.c. injection in mice and rats are shown in TABLE 7. These experiments represented life-time tests, once-weekly s.c. injections, and survival, except for the positive control groups, was good. Only local tumors were usually observed, except with s.c. injection in mice or rats, where breast tumors were at times observed. However, the frequency of occurrence of these tumors was within the normal background level of breast tumors observed in no-treatment groups. It is possible that because of the high reactivity of these compounds, they are rapidly degraded *in vivo* and do not reach target sites in organs remote from the site of treatment even when given in high doses.

TABLE 6

INITIATING ACTIVITY OF EPOXIDES, LACTONES AND HALO-ETHERS IN TWO-STAGE CARCINOGENESIS* (MOUSE SKIN)

Treatment: Primary†	Treatment: Secondary‡	Cumulative No. of Mice with: Papilloma	Cumulative No. of Mice with: Carcinoma	Days to First Papilloma
Test Data				
Glycidaldehyde[2]	phorbol esters, A–D	4	1	133
d,1-Diepoxybutane[2]	same	7	2	137
meso-Diepoxybutane[2]	same	4	0	163
β-Butyrolactone[2]	same	3	1	110
Chloromethyl methyl ether	same	7	4	259
Bis(chloromethyl)ether	same	5	2	76
α,α-Dichloromethyl methyl ether	same	3	2	187
Control Data				
7,12-Dimethylbenz(a)-anthracene (DMBA)	phorbol esters, A–D	19	8	51
Benzo(a)pyrene	same	20	8	70
DMBA	none	0	0	–
DMBA	acetone	0	0	–
Benzo(a)pyrene	none	0	0	–
d,1-Diepoxybutane[2]	none	0	0	–
meso-Diepoxybutane[2]	none	0	0	–
β-Butyrolactone[2]	none	0	0	–
Chloromethyl methyl ether	acetone	0	0	–
Bis(chloromethyl)ether	acetone	0	0	–
α,α-Dichloromethyl methyl ether	acetone	0	0	–
None	phorbol esters§ A–D	20/258	4/258	150–428

*20 + Swiss mice per group; unpublished data, except where noted. Preliminary data on some of the other compounds were published recently.[6]

†DMBA and benzo(a)pyrene 150 μg in 0.1 ml acetone; chloromethyl methyl ether 100 μg in 0.1 ml acetone; all others 1,000 μg in 0.1 ml acetone or benzene. All initiating applications were single treatments.

‡Three times weekly beginning 14 days after primary treatment; phorbol esters A–D 25 μg in 0.1 ml acetone per application; lifetime application.

§Average of 12 experiments.[45]

Carcinogenicity and Mutagenicity of Alkylating Agents

In an earlier report, the carcinogenicity of a number of epoxides and β-lactones was compared with their radiomimetic properties, including mutagenicity.[2] The carcinogenic epoxides and lactones also exhibited mutagenicity; however, many of the compounds that were not carcinogenic showed mutagenicity in one or more test systems.

In another comparative study,[48] carcinogenicity, mutagenicity, and tumor-

TABLE 7

DOSE AND TUMORIGENICITY OF EPOXIDES AND LACTONES BY SUBCUTANEOUS INJECTION IN MICE AND RATS[3,4,6]

	Dose in mg	Number of Malignant Tumors at Injection Site / Number of Animals
Subcutaneous injection in mice*		
β-Butyrolactone	10	18/30
Glycidaldehyde	3.3	7/30
d,l-Diepoxybutane	1.1	5/30
β-Propiolactone	0.73	18/30
7,12-Dimethylbenz(a)anthracene†	0.01	21/30
	0.001	9/30
Subcutaneous injection in rats‡		
d,l-Diepoxybutane	1	10/50
Glycidaldehyde	33	5/20
β-Butyrolactone	100	9/20
β-Propiolactone	4	13/20
Bis(chloromethyl)ether	3	5/20
7,12-Dimethylbenz(a)anthracene†	1	30/50

*0.05 ml Tricaprylin as vehicle.
†Positive control.
‡0.1 ml Tricaprylin as vehicle.

initiating activity of 22 compounds were compared. These compounds included alkylating agents, aromatic hydrocarbons, and acridine dyes. As in the earlier comparison,[2] there was no clearcut correlation between these biological properties.

ACKNOWLEDGMENTS

The work described in this report was carried out in collaboration with B.M. Goldschmidt, C. Katz, S. Melchionne, and A. Sivak. L. Orris participated in many phases of this work. Pathological diagnoses were provided by M. Baden, M. Kuschner, D. Roth, and G. Teebor. (Department of Pathology, New York University Medical Center, New York, N.Y.).

REFERENCES

1. VAN DUUREN, B. L., N. NELSON, L. ORRIS, E. D. PALMES & F. L. SCHMITT. 1963. Carcinogenicity of epoxides, lactones, and peroxy compounds. J. Nat. Cancer Inst. **31:** 41–55.
2. VAN DUUREN, B. L., L. ORRIS & N. NELSON. 1965. Carcinogenicity of epoxides, lactones, and peroxy compounds. II. J. Nat. Cancer Inst. **35:** 707–717.

3. Van Duuren, B. L., L. Langseth, L. Orris, G. Teebor, N. Nelson & M. Kuschner. 1966. Carcinogenicity of epoxides, lactones, and peroxy compounds. IV. Tumor response in epithelial and connective tissue in mice and rats. J. Nat. Cancer Inst. **37:** 825–838.
4. Van Duuren, B. L., L. Langseth, L. Orris, M. Baden & M. Kuschner. 1967. Carcinogenicity of epoxides, lactones, and peroxy compounds. V. Subcutaneous injection in rats. J. Nat. Cancer Inst. **39:** 1213–1216.
5. Van Duuren, B. L., L. Langseth, B. M. Goldschmidt & L. Orris. 1967. Carcinogenicity of epoxides, lactones, and peroxy compounds. VI. Structure and carcinogenic activity. J. Nat. Cancer Inst. **39:** 1217–1228.
6. Van Duuren, B. L., B. M. Goldschmidt, C. Katz, L. Langseth, C. Mercado & A. Sivak. 1968. Alpha-haloethers: A new type of alkylating carcinogen. A.M.A. Arch. Environ. Health (Chicago) **16:** 472–476.
7. Van Duuren, B. L. 1965. Carcinogenic epoxides, lactones, and hydroperoxides. *In* Mycotoxins in Foodstuffs. Gerald N. Wogan, Ed. : 275–285. The M.I.T. Press. Cambridge, Mass.
8. Van Duuren, B. L. & B. M. Goldschmidt. 1966. Carcinogenicity of epoxides, lactones, and peroxy compounds. III. Biological activity and chemical reactivity. J. Med. Chem. **9:** 77–79.
9. Goldschmidt, B. M., T. P. Blazej & B. L. Van Duuren. 1968. The reaction of guanosine and deoxyguanosine with glycidaldehyde. Tetrahedron Lett. **13:** 1583–1586.
10. Roe, J. H. & H. M. Dyer. 1939. Relation of nutrition to gastric function. I. An experimental method. Proc. Soc. Exp. Biol. Med. **41:** 603–606.
11. Friedman, M. H. F. 1943. Histamine ineffective in the rat as a gastric secretory stimulant. Proc. Soc. Exp. Biol. Med. **54:** 42–44.
12. Food Protection Committee. 1960. Problems in the Evaluation of Carcinogenic Hazard from Use of Food Additives. Nat. Acad. Sci. (Wash.) Pub. No. 749.
13. Hendry, J. A., F. L. Rose, R. F. Homer, & A. L. Walpole. 1951. Cytotoxic agents. II. Bisepoxides and related compounds. Brit. J. Pharmacol. **6:** 235–255.
14. Roe, F. J. C. & O. M. Glendenning. 1956. The carcinogenicity of β-propiolactone for mouse skin. Brit. J. Cancer. **10:** 357–362.
15. Weil, C. S., N. Condra, C. Haun & J. A. Striegel. 1963. Experimental carcinogenicity and acute toxicity of representative epoxides. Amer. Industr. Hyg. Ass. J. 305–325.
16. Roe, F. J. C. 1957. Tumor initiation in mouse skin by certain esters of methanesulfonic acid. Cancer Res. **17:** 64–69.
17. Brookes, P. & P. D. Lawley. 1964. Alkylating agents. Brit. Med. Bull. **20:** 91–95.
18. Lawley, P. D. & P. Brookes. 1967. Interstrand cross-linking of DNA by difunctional alkylating agents. J. Molec. Biol. **25:** 143–160.
19. Stacey, K. A., M. Cobb, S. F. Cousens & P. Alexander. 1958. The reactions of the "radiomimetic" alkylating agents with macromolecules *in vitro.* Ann. N. Y. Acad. Sci. **68:** 682–701.
20. Trams, E. G., M. V. Nadkarni & P. K. Smith. 1961. On the mechanism of action of the alkylating agents. I. Interaction of alkylating agents with nucleic acids. Cancer Res. **21:** 560–566.
21. Magee, P. N. & R. Schoental. 1964. Carcinogenesis by nitroso compounds. Brit. Med. Bull. **20:** 102–106.
22. Boese, A. B., Jr. 1940. Diketene. A new industrial chemical. Ind. Eng. Chem. **32:** 16–22.
23. Van Duuren, B. L., C. Katz & S. Melchionne. (Unpublished data.)
24. Dickens, F. & H. E. H. Jones. 1963. Further studies on the carcinogenic and growth-inhibitory activity of lactones and related substances. Brit. J. Cancer. **17:** 100–108.
25. Asao, T., G. Büchi, M. M. Abdel-Kader, S. B. Chang, E. L. Wick & G. N. Wogan. 1965. The structures of aflatoxin B_1 and G_1. J. Amer. Chem. Soc. **87:** 882–886.
26. Lancaster, M. C., F. P. Jenkins & J. M. Philp. 1961. Toxicity associated with

certain samples of groundnuts. Nature (London) **192:** 1095–1097.
27. Schoental, R., M. A. Head & P. R. Peacock. 1954. Senecio alkaloids: Primary liver tumours in rats as a result of treatment with (1) a mixture of alkaloids from *S. Jacobaea Lin.;* (2) retrorsine; (3) isatidine. Brit. J. Cancer. **8:** 458.
28. Culvenor, C. C. J., A. T. Dann & A. T. Dick. 1962. Alkylation as the mechanism by which the hepatotoxic pyrrolizidine alkaloids act on cell nuclei. Nature (London) **195:** 570–573.
29. Culvenor, C. C. J., D. T. Downing & J. A. Edgar. 1969. Pyrrolizidine Alkaloids as Alkylating and Antimitotic Agents. This monograph.
30. Lawley, P. D. & C. A. Wallick. 1957. The action of alkylating agents on deoxyribonucleic acid and guanylic acid. Chem. Industr.: 633.
31. Montgomery, J. A. & J. H. Thomas. 1964. On the alkylation of adenine (1). J. Heter. Chem. **1:** 115–120.
32. Brookes, P. & P. D. Lawley. 1964. Reaction of some mutagenic and carcinogenic compounds with nucleic acids. J. Cell. Comp. Physiol (Suppl. no. 1) **64:** 111–127.
33. Kriek, E., J. A. Miller, U. Juhl & E. C. Miller. 1967. 8-(N-2-Fluorenylacetamido) guanosine, an arylamidation reaction product of guanosine and the carcinogen N-acetoxy-N-2-flourenylacetamide in neutral solution. Biochemistry (Wash.) **6:** 177–182.
34. Colburn, N. H. & R. K. Boutwell. 1968. The *in vivo* binding of β-propiolactone to mouse skin DNA, RNA, and protein. Cancer Res. **28:** 642–652.
35. Roberts, J. J. & G. P. Warwick. 1963. The reaction of some compounds of biological interest with nucleic acids. Biochem. J. **87:** 14P.
36. Alexander, P. 1969. Comparison of alkylating agents and ionizing radiation at the cellular level. This monograph.
37. Boyland, E. & B. Green. 1962. The interaction of polycyclic hydrocarbons and nucleic Acids. Brit. J. Cancer. **16:** 507–517.
38. Van Duuren, B. L. 1966. Complex formation and carcinogenicity of aromatic compounds. Nature (London) **210:** 622–623.
39. Van Duuren, B. L. & F. Irani. 1966. The fluorescence of colloidal suspensions of aromatic hydrocarbons. Proc. Int. Conf. Luminescence (Budapest, Hungary) **1B:** 29–32.
40. Van Duuren, B. L., B. M. Goldschmidt & H. H. Seltzman. 1969. The interaction of acridine orange dyes with nucleic acids: Spectroscopic studies. Ann. N. Y. Acad. Sci. **153**(3)**:** 744–757.
41. Van Duuren, B. L. 1963. The metabolism of dibenz(a, h)anthracene. Acta Un. Int. Cancr. **19:** 524–527.
42. Heidelberger, C., M. E. Baumann, L. Griesbach, A. Ghobar & T. M. Vaughan. 1962. The carcinogenic activities of various derivatives of dibenzanthracene. Cancer Res. **22:** 78–83.
43. Miller, E. C. & J. A. Miller. 1967. Low carcinogenicity of the K-region epoxides of 7-methylbenz(a)anthracene in the mouse and rat. Proc. Soc. Exp. Biol. Med. **124:** 915–919.
44. Roe, F. J. C. & M. H. Salaman. 1955. Further studies on incomplete carcinogenesis: triethylene melamine (T.E.M.), 1,2-benzanthracene and β-propiolactone as initiators of skin tumor formation in the mouse. Brit. J. Cancer **9:** 177–203.
45. Van Duuren, B. L. 1968. Tumor-promoting agents in two-stage carcinogenesis. Prog. Exp. Tumor Res. **11:** 31–68.
46. Salaman, M. H. & F. J. C. Roe. 1953. Incomplete carcinogens. Ethylcarbamate (urethane) as an initiator of skin tumor formation in the mouse. Brit. J. Cancer. **7:** 472–481.
47. Van Duuren, B. L., A. Sivak, L. Langseth, B. M. Goldschmidt & A. Segal. 1968. Initiators and promoters in tobacco carcinogenesis. Nat. Cancer Inst. Mono. **28:** 173–180.
48. Van Duuren, B. L. & A. Sivak. 1968. Tumor promoting agents from *Croton tiglium L.* and their mode of action. Cancer Res. **28:** 2349–2356.

DISCUSSION OF THE PAPER

E. C. MILLER (*University of Wisconsin Medical School, Madison, Wis.*): In relation to the carcinogenicity of the hydrocarbon epoxides that you mentioned, we tested the epoxide of 10-methyl-1,2-benzanthracene, whereas you tested the epoxide of 1,2,5,6-dibenzanthracene.

DR. VAN DUUREN: In addition to 5,6-epoxy-5,6-dihydrodibenz(a,h)anthracene, we also tested the one that you mentioned, i.e., 5,6-epoxy-5,6-dihydro-7-methylbenz(a)anthracene, and got results very similar to what I showed for the 5,6-epoxide of dibenzanthracene.*

C. C. PRICE (*University of Pennsylvania, Philadelphia, Pa.*): Several times today, questions were raised about whether cross-linked DNA, in fact, forms during alkylation. Recent work showed conclusively that at doses that are the same as those used in chemotherapy of tumors, DNA in tumors is cross-linked. Has any kind of similar experiment been done with some of these agents that you are studying for carcinogenicity?

DR. VAN DUUREN: Whether such cross-linking occurs with these epoxides *in vivo* has not been established.

* Van Duuren, B. L., L. Langseth, B. M. Goldschmidt & L. Orris. 1967. J. Nat. Cancer Inst. **39:** 1217.

COMPARISON OF THE MODE OF ACTION BY WHICH SOME ALKYLATING AGENTS AND IONIZING RADIATIONS KILL MAMMALIAN CELLS

Peter Alexander

Chester Beatty Research Institute, Institute of Cancer Research, Belmont, Sutton, Surrey, England

Introduction

At the first conference organized in 1958 by The New York Academy of Sciences on alkylating agents, I reviewed the possibility that the striking similarity in biological end-effects produced by the alkylating agents and by ionizing radiations arose from the fact that the chemical reactions that initiate the sequence of events leading to the final biological changes are of the same type. Now, as ten years ago, we are still ignorant of the precise nature of these "primary chemical lesions," both for alkylation and for ionizing radiations. While many reactions with a large variety of cell constitutents have been recognized, their relevance to the primary chemical lesions remains to be determined.

In reviewing this problem again, it is clear that generalizations are not possible; different primary lesions are involved in the different end effects, and for a comparison to be meaningful it must be limited to a precise end point. In this paper this is the killing of mammalian cells, since this is the factor on which the usefulness of these agents in cancer therapy depends. Both chemicals and ionizing radiation kill cells in a number of different ways, and it is necessary to specify rather precisely the type of cell-death that is being considered. My contribution will be confined to what has been called mitotic death; namely, the loss by rapidly dividing tumor or stem cells of the capacity for indefinite reproduction—in *in vitro* terms this is the loss of the ability to form a clone. Whether the cells that have been "sterilized" are viable in physiological terms of metabolism and membrane integrity is irrelevant from this point of view.

I must also restrict the comparison with x rays to the mustard and the myleran class of alkylating agents, since there are many indications that differences between different classes of alkylating agents that are so apparent when studied in the intact animal may also be found at the subcellular level. This applies particularly to the mitomycins and the nitroso compounds that are converted by metabolic processes into substances capable of alkylation. While they alkylate the same groups as the "classical" biological alkylating agents (i.e., the mustards, epoxides, ethylene imines, and mylerans) they are much more reactive and tend to be "consumed" by the first target they encounter. They are effective in low doses because their *in situ* formation makes it possible for them to gain access to biologically significant sites.

The Dose-Response Curve

An aspect of cell death in which both the mustards (nitrogen as well as sulphur) and the methane sulphonate esters (myleran-type compounds) mimic x rays in a striking way is the characteristic dose-response relationship[1-5] shown in FIGURE 1. After an initial shoulder, there is a semilogarithmic relationship between dose and the fraction of mammalian cells killed (i.e., loss of ability to form clones). This, as first demonstrated by Puck and Marcus,[6] is the same type of dose-response relationship found for ionizing radiations.* The linear portion of these dose-response curves is usually designated by a value "Do" that is

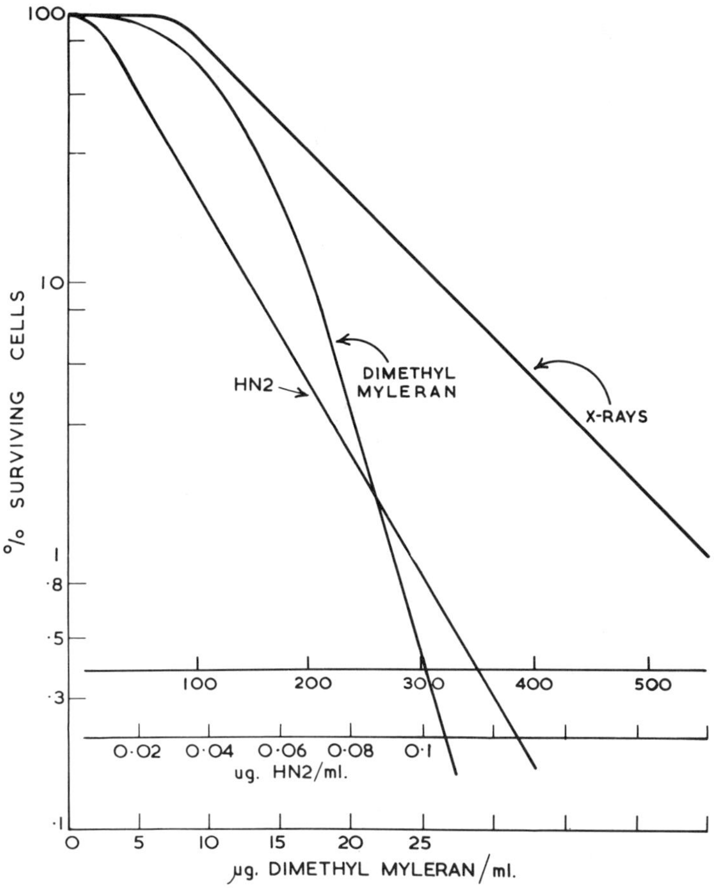

FIGURE 1. Relationship between dose of x rays (in r), HN2 and dimethyl myleran, respectively, and the fraction of cells retaining capacity for indefinite multiplication of the radioresistant diploid line of L5178Y murine lymphoma. (Adapted from reference 1.)

*This behavior is not confined to cells irradiated *in vitro*, but was shown for radiation and by the Skipper group for chemical agents to apply also *in vivo*.

inversely proportional to the slope of the line and corresponds to the dose necessary to reduce survival by the factor 1/e.

Unless the rate of reaction of the alkylating agents is rapid, such dose-survival curves become difficult to interpret, and for this reason we[1,3] have worked with dimethyl myleran ($CH_3SO_2 \cdot O \cdot CH \cdot (CH_3) \cdot CH_2 \cdot CH_2 \cdot CH(CH_3) \cdot O \cdot SO_2CH_3$) and NH2, both of which have a "half-reaction time" of approximately 30 minutes in culture. Myleran could not be used, because its "half-life" is of the order of 10 hours. Sulphur mustard, as used by Mauro and Elkind,[4] is even more suitable from this point of view, since its reaction is complete within a few minutes.

In the example illustrated in FIGURE 1, HN2 shows only a small shoulder, whereas the curve for dimethyl myleran has a relatively large shoulder. Monofunctional compounds are characterized by extremely large shoulders.[†3,5] For x rays, the size of the shoulder is variable and depends both on the type of cells used and on experimental conditions. In the case of radiation, the shoulder is a measure of "sublethal injury." In other words, before a radiation-induced chemical change can be lethal, other radiation effects must be produced first. The sublethal events are readily restored within a few hours.[7,8] As a result, those cells in a culture that have survived a dose of x rays behave as if they had not been exposed at all and exhibit a shoulder in the dose response similar to that of the original untreated culture.

In the case of the alkylating agents, the situation is more complex; recovery of the shoulder has been recorded with dimethyl myleran, but not with HN2,[9] nor with the monofunctional component methyl methane sulphonate.[10] With mustard gas, recovery of the shoulder has been found in cells that originated from hamster fibroblasts,[11] but not in those from mouse fibroblasts.[12] While it is tempting to interpret the shoulder in the dose-response curve of alkylating agents in the same way as in x rays, this may, in fact, not be valid, because with the alkylating agents, a factor other than sublethal injury could cause a shoulder. There is good evidence that there are reactive centers (e.g. glutathione SH groups) in cells that scavenge the alkylating agents as they diffuse into the cell, and until these "protective substances" have been removed, lethal reactions cannot occur. Analogies between x rays and the alkylating agents concerning recovery between fractionated doses cannot, therefore, be taken too far.

Factors Modifying Sensitivity of Cells

The sensitivity of cells to radiation varies in different parts of the cell cycle, and Walker and Hellsteiner,[13] with mouse fibroblasts, found that response to mustard gas paralleled that of radiation, the greatest resistance occurring in the G_2 stage. Hamster cells again are somewhat different;[14] while maximum resistance to both x rays and mustard gas was in the "S" period, it did not occur at the identical point in time.

In both mammalian and microbial cells there are enzyme-mediated systems that restore lesions that would otherwise be lethal. This phenomenon is quite

†The monofunctional compounds are approximately 100 times less active in causing mitotic death than the bifunctional compounds, but this by itself need not imply a large shoulder.

distinct from repair of sublethal injury, which is revealed by the difference in lethality of a given dose when administered all at one time and when given in several fractions. Repair of lethal radiation damage was revealed by experiments in which the fraction of cells killed by a given dose of x rays was altered by changing postirradiation conditions. Guided by the experience with microorganisms,[15] we observed[16] that murine lymphoma cells showed greater radioresistance if cultured in enriched media (see FIGURE 2) or maintained for some time after irradiation at a temperature lower than that required for optimal growth (see FIGURE 3). With dimethyl myleran, but not with HN2,[3] recovery of lymphoma cells was promoted by storing the cells for 24 hours after treatment at 30° C (TABLE 1). A posttreatment effect was found in hamster cells,[17] but not in mouse

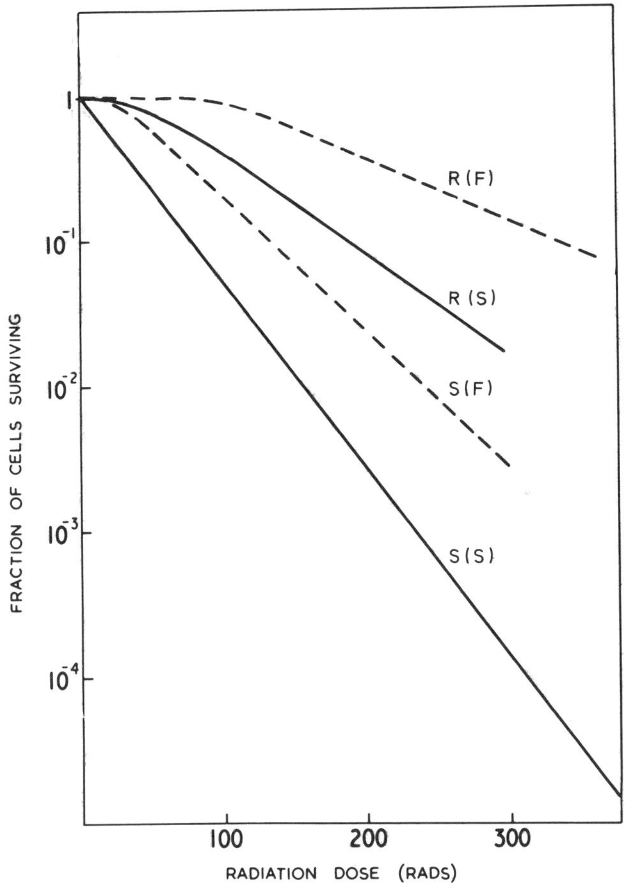

FIGURE 2. Influence of medium in which cells are grown after irradiation on radiosensitivity. The medium (F) contained whole horse serum, while the medium (S) contained three specific serum protein fractions only. The effect of medium is seen both with the radioresistant (R) and the radiosensitive (S) L5178Y lymphoma. (Adapted from reference 16.)

TABLE 1

EFFECT OF POSTTREATMENT STORAGE AT 30° C ON SENSITIVITY TO DMM AND HN2 EXPRESSED AS CHANGE IN THE Do*

	Do for Cells Allowed to "Recover" at 30° C (Do under normal conditions) for resistant line	for sensitive line
HN2	1.08	0.96
DMM	1.22	1.33

* From reference 3.

fibroblasts[12] exposed to mustard gas.‡ While the chemicals are radiomimetic in the sense that lethality can be modified by postirradiation treatments, there are very significant differences in detail, and the parallelism cannot be taken to imply a similarity of the biochemical lesions.

The differences are even more marked when considering preirradiation treatments that protect and sensitize against radiation. While all mammalian cells, though not all bacterial cells, become much more resistant when oxygen is removed, anoxia does not affect the action of HN2 or dimethyl myleran. The same applies to the effect of substituting bromouridine for thymidine in the DNA of cells, which sensitizes to radiation (FIGURE 4) but does not affect the response to dimethyl myleran or HN2,[18] or the response to a monofunctional compound.[19]

At first sight, the fact that pretreatment with thiols such as cysteine, cysteamine, or AET protects both against x rays and HN2 might indicate a similarity in action; detailed investigations (see review by Connors[20]) have shown that the chemical reactions involved are different. This becomes apparent when different thiols are compared. With the alkylating agents, protection is directly related to the increase in the concentration of free SH groups in the cell, and there is convincing evidence that the protection is the direct result of the reaction of the alkylating agents with these SH groups, thereby reducing the reaction with other cell components such as DNA. Protection against radiation in metabolizing mammalian cells—although this does not apply to simpler systems—occurs as a result of changes produced at quite a different level.[21] The magnitude of the primary radiochemical changes in DNA, for example, are the same in SH-protected as in unprotected systems.[22]

COMPARISON OF MUTANTS OF DIFFERENT SENSITIVITIES

TABLE 2 illustrates the complexities we[3] encountered with a series of mutants isolated from a murine lymphoma. By comparison with two diploid mutants, the parallelism between the alkylating agents and x rays is striking. However, the relative sensitivity of another mutant, a tetraploid line, was anomalous; it had the

‡ With hamster cells, the Elkind group[4,17] encountered an additional complication in that the serum used on the medium was toxic to mustard-treated cells, and the effectiveness of procedures promoting recovery, therefore, depended on whether serum was present or absent immediately after irradiation.

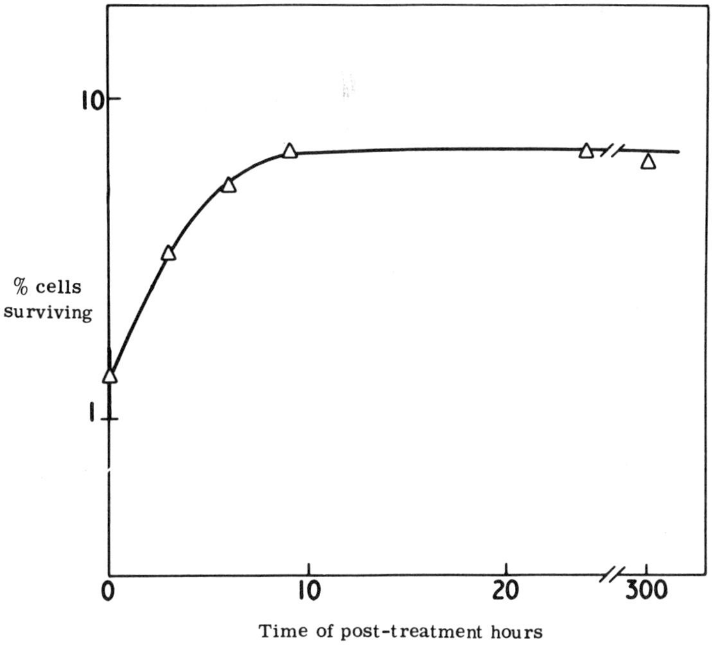

FIGURE 3. Restoration of radiation damage by maintaining cells for various times immediately after irradiation at 34° C and then returning them to the normal growth conditions at 37° C. This experiment shows increase in survival after 150 r of x rays by incubation at 34° C. of the radiosensitive L5178Y lymphoma. (Adapted from reference 16.)

same radiosensitivity as the parent line but was much more resistant to HN2 and less resistant to dimethyl myleran. An association of a change in the chromosome number in the cells from diploid to tetraploid with a marked increase in resistance to HN2 without a significant increase in resistance to x rays has also been observed by Goldenberg (this monograph). Two Yoshida rat sarcoma lines that differed widely in sensitivity to mustard had the same response to x rays,[23] and *in vivo* this situation has been encountered by Wheeler and co-workers.[24]

TABLE 2
RELATIVE SENSITIVITY OF DIFFERENT LYMPHOMA LINES TO X RAYS, DMM AND HN2*

Cell line	Sensitivity (Do) relative to radiosensitive diploid line X Rays	DMM	HN2
Radiosensitive Diploid (S63)	1	1	1
Radioresistant Diploid (R)	1·8	1·9	2·0
Tetraploid	1·9	1·0	7·8

* From reference 3.

Several reasons for changes in the sensitivity of different cell lines to alkylating agents can be envisaged:

1. The number of actual alkylating reactions required to cause lethal injury to a target molecule (or the inherent sensitivity of the target) may alter.
2. The proportion of the agent lost by biologically unimportant reactions will be determined by the concentration of highly reactive centers such as SH groups, and these are known to be different in different cells.
3. Differences in penetration of the drug into the cell so that a given dose will lead to different extents of reaction within the cells.
4. Variations in the capacity to restore alkylated macromolecules by enzymatic repair processes.

Both mechanisms 2 and 3 would result in a difference in the amount of alkylation of intracellular macromolecules that must result in a change in sensitivity to the alkylating agents. Yet for some cells, other processes leading to resistance are involved.

A comparison of the reaction of alkylating agents with macromolecular cell components in a sensitive and resistant line of tumor cells has been made.[24,25] The extent of alkylation was found to be the same in both these cases (TABLE 3), and the difference in sensitivity cannot, therefore, be attributed to mechanisms 2 and 3.

For x rays, it is becoming clear that differences in the extent of repair are the principal factors responsible for changes in sensitivity to mitotic death, since the inherent susceptibility of DNA to radiation damage is very similar for all cells.[22,26]

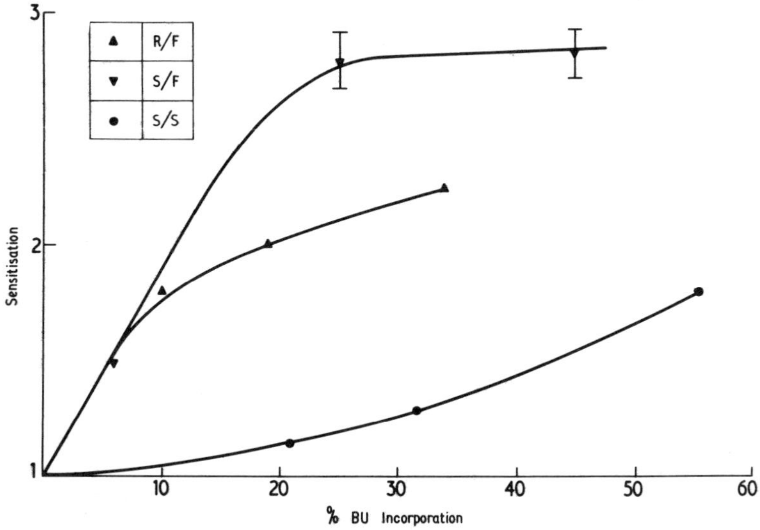

FIGURE 4. Effect on sensitivity to x rays of substituting increasing amounts of bromouracil for thymine in the DNA of lymphoma cells. Sensitization is greatest for the most radioresistant line (R/F) and least for the most radiosensitive line (S/S). The line S/F is intermediate in both respects. The three cell lines become approximately equally radiosensitive when grown in such a way that in the DNA of each 20% of the thymine is replaced by bromouracil. (Adapted from reference 32.)

TABLE 3

COMBINATION OF RADIOACTIVE ANILINE MUSTARD WITH DNA IN SENSITIVE AND RESISTANT LYMPHOMAS *in Vivo**

	cpm/mg DNA	
Time After Injection	Sensitive (PC6A)	Resistant LKA
1 hour	906	1,025
6 hours	1,180	1,800
24 hours	1,335	1,950
	Antitumor action on established tumor expressed as weight % control	
Dose Injected		
80 mg/kg	0%	40%
40 mg/kg	0%	60%
20 mg/kg	0%	100%
1·2 mg/kg	0%	100%
0·6 mg/kg	54%	100%

* From T. A. Connors (private communication).

TABLE 4

X-RAY DOSE NEEDED TO PRODUCE A SINGLE BREAK IN THE MAIN CHAIN OF DNA IN CELLS OF DIFFERENT RADIOSENSITIVITY (IRRADIATION CARRIED OUT IN PRESENCE OF OXYGEN)*

Cell	Dose Needed to Kill 90% of the Cells *In Vitro*	Dose (in ev/break) to Produce Main-Chain Scission
Diploid Lymphoma (sensitive)	120 r	65 ev
Diploid Lymphoma (resistant)	340 r	60 ev
Micrococcus radiodurans	800,000 r	45 ev

* From reference 26.

We[22] have studied the production of double breaks in native double-stranded DNA by a rather unsatisfactory technique, and, more recently,[26] the formation of single-strand breaks in DNA by the elegant method developed by McGrath and Williams. TABLE 4 shows that the energy needed to produce a break is the same for two cell lines of different radiosensitivity. Even more striking is the fact that the sensitivity of the DNA in the exceptionally radioresistant bacterium *micrococcus radiodurans* is closely similar to that in mammalian cells. The dose needed to produce breaks in the DNA of viruses or of isolated DNA in the solid state§ is in the same range as that found for the bacterial and mammalian cells.[27,28] As

§ When DNA is irradiated in dilute aqueous solution, the dose needed to produce a break depends on its concentration because the effect is brought about almost entirely by the highly reactive radiolysis products formed in water. This so-called "indirect" action of radiation contributes little or nothing to the radiochemical damage of DNA when irradiated within cells.[26]

a first approximation, the inherent susceptibility of DNA to damage by x rays appears to be unaffected by the nature of the cellular environment (i.e., by the type of cell in which it finds itself) and by the base composition, at least in the range encountered in cells.

Even if there is a close relationship between the capacity to repair radiation and alkylation lesions, one would not expect the sensitivity of different cells to alkylating agents and to x rays to run strictly parallel, because additional factors (e.g. competitive removal by SH compounds or penetration problems) that do not effect x-ray sensitivity will influence the response of different cells to alkylating agents.

Evidence for Repair at the Biochemical Level

Following exposure to x rays, there are immediate alterations in the biological properties of membranes, but these are rapidly repaired. This has been demonstrated by physiological techniques with membranes of nerve and muscle cells[29] and by biochemical techniques for red-cell membranes[30] and for the membrane in *Micrococcus radiodurans*.[31] While there are many indications that alkylating agents also affect the function of membranes, I do not know of any experiments that demonstrate restoration.

The repair process that has been studied in greatest detail is the rejoining of radiation-induced breaks by measuring the sedimentation properties of DNA released from cells. In the bacterial chromosome, the DNA is almost certainly present as one continuous molecule corresponding to a molecule weight for the single strand of $0.5–2 \times 10^9$ daltons. Such enormously long molecules are very susceptible to shear, and to avoid this the cells are lysed and deproteinized *in situ* without agitation on top of the gradient used for sedimentation. The number of breaks produced by x rays can be determined directly from the sedimentation rate of the DNA of irradiated cells. In *Micrococcus radiodurans*, which has been studied in great detail, the single breaks are rejoined by the ligase enzyme system extremely rapidly; i.e., 80% are rejoined within five minutes.[31] With bacteria that require a few minutes to lyse, some rejoining occurs when the cells are prepared for analysis, and the true number of breaks produced by radiation can only be determined if the ligases are inhibited (the values shown in TABLE 4 were obtained in this way). This difficulty is not encountered with mammalian cells that lyse instantly, but they present a different problem.[26] The molecular weight of the DNA is greater than that found in bacteria, and the technique breaks down probably because of interaction between the molecules. As a result, we found that we were able to measure the DNA in mammalian cells only after these had received a dose of 500 r, which reduced the molecular weight to 4×10^9 (single-stranded). At smaller doses or with unirradiated cells, reproducable values for the molecular weight could not be obtained. However, from the relationship between molecular weight and radiation dose, the energy to produce a break can be calculated, and the data shown in TABLE 3 was derived in this way. In theory, extrapolation back to zero radiation dose should give the molecular weight of the DNA in unirradiated cells. In practice, experimental error only allows the conclusion that the molecular weight (single-stranded) must be greater than 10^{10} daltons; if each chromosome consisted of one molecule of DNA, then its molecular weight would be 10^{11} daltons.

The radiation-induced breaks in mammalian cells are rapidly rejoined, presumably by ligase action.[26] The technique we have used, however, does not allow us to conclude that the rejoining is complete, because one can follow the increase in molecular weight only back to the 5×10^9 dalton level and not all the way to the original size. Also, the possibility that there is faulty rejoining cannot be excluded. Within these limitations, we have not observed any differences in rejoining capacity between the radiosensitive and the radioresistant mutants, and the difference in radiosensitivity would not appear to be due to a deficit in ligase activity. From this, however, it would not be justifiable to conclude that the primary lesion responsible for mitotic death is not a DNA lesion that escaped repair, since there are clearly many factors other than ligase activity involved. For example, lesions other than breaks may be produced, or there may be different types of breaks characterized by the production of different end-groups.

Strong support for the view that repair-capacity for DNA may determine radiosensitivity came from experiments on the sensitizing effect of replacing thymidine for bromouracil in the DNA by growing the cells prior to irradiation in desoxybromouridine. This replacement does not alter the sensitivity of the DNA when expressed as the energy needed to give a break.[32,33] Yet the presence of bromouracil in the DNA sensitizes the resistant strains to a much greater extent than the sensitive ones (see FIGURE 4).

While the actual cause of mitotic death may be an unrestituted or incorrectly rejoined break, the occurrence of such a lesion may be made possible by radiation damage of the repair system. In other words, we speculate[22] that there are two parallel actions of radiation: a) damage to DNA and b) damage to repair system. The radiosensitivity of the cell is determined by the damage to the repair system; so long as this system remains intact, radiochemical damage to the DNA is not lethal as it is restituted. Support for this concept is provided by studies in bacteria in which a number of radiosensitizors have been shown either to inhibit the repair system or to render it more vulnerable to inactivation by radiation. Radiation is unlikely to interfere with repair by inactivation of the enzymes involved, but may do so by affecting the membranes to which the repair system and the DNA are attached. In bacteria, the close association between plasma-membrane DNA and enzymes involved in DNA metabolism has been clearly demonstrated.

There is considerable evidence in bacteria for the existence of enzymatic processes that restitute DNA modified by reaction with alkylating agents. The evidence is strongest for the removal of interstrand crosslinks formed by HN2 that occurs in a resistant but not in a sensitive mutant of *E.coli*.[34] With sulphur mustard, enzymatically mediated elimination from the cell of some of the combined mustard was also demonstrated.[34,36]

In the case of bacteria, removal of damage from DNA is often associated with nuclease action that "cuts out" a considerable number of nucleotides from one of the strands. Before replication of DNA can start again, these gaps must be "patched" by what is essentially a type of DNA synthesis. By a variety of physicochemical techniques, this process, which is called "unscheduled DNA synthesis," can be distinguished from normal replication. The occurrence of unscheduled DNA synthesis is sometimes taken as an indication—and it is no more than that—that repair of a lesion had occurred. Following treatment with alkylating agents, unscheduled DNA synthesis occurs in bacteria. This test has also been applied to mammalian cells, exposed to x rays,[37] and to sulphur mustard,[38] but the results after both treatments are inconclusive, since unscheduled

DNA synthesis is seen only after doses that are greatly in excess of the lethal dose (e.g. after 10^5 r, which is 300 times the LD_{90} dose, or 5 μg/ml of sulphur mustard, 25 times the LD_{90} dose). In bacteria, the phenomenon occurs at doses well below the LD_{90} dose.

M. G. Ormerod and I are currently attempting to study whether DNA lesions produced by HN2 in mammalian cells are capable of repair by using the McGrath and Williams technique. As already mentioned,[26] the size of the DNA obtained from untreated cells is too large to be handled by the techniques we use. As expected, this situation is not altered by treatment with HN2, since this reagent does not cause extensive main-chain scission. However, by exposing the cells to x rays immediately after treatment with nitrogen mustard, the formation of crosslinks was demonstrated. FIGURE 5 shows that the molecular weight after 10,000 r of x rays was much greater in cells that had been pretreated with HN2. Since exposure to strong alkali (so as to dissociate the DNA into single strands) is an essential feature of this procedure, the cross-links formed must have been stable to strong alkali at 20° C for one hour. This makes it most unlikely that the links responsible for this effect involved quarternization of the 7 N groups of purines. The interchain cross-links produced by HN2 in *E.coli*[34] were also resistant to strong alkali. Experiments are now in progress to test if, on incubation

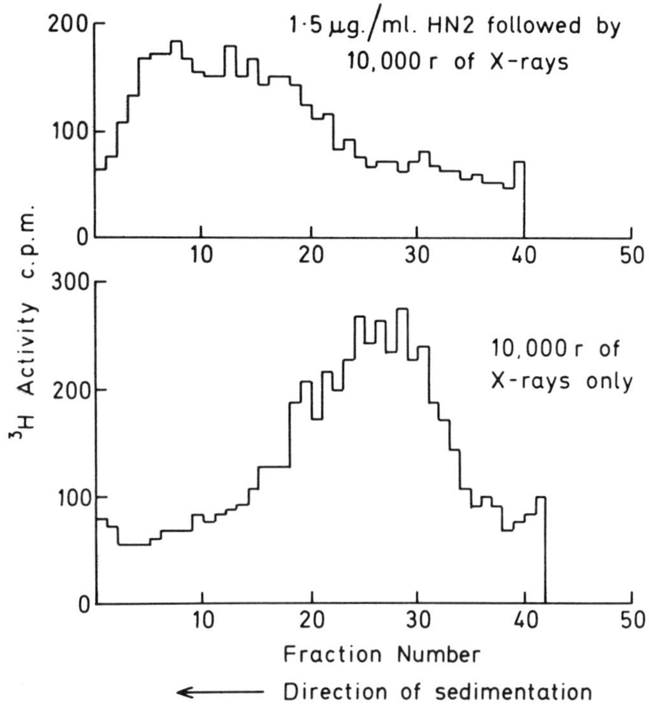

FIGURE 5. Sedimentation pattern on an alkaline sucrose gradient (cf. 26) of the DNA from lymphoma cells treated with HN2 and then to x rays. (Material on the left is of highest molecular weight; 4×10^4 rpm for 50 minutes.) (G. M. Ormerod, unpublished data.)

after treatment with HN2, mammalian cells possess the capacity to excise these cross-links.

The Metabolism of Cells after Sustaining Lethal Damage—The Absence of a DNA Synthetic Lesion

One of the most characteristic properties of mammalian cells exposed in culture to doses of x rays in the LD_{90} range is that cell division continues nearly normally until the cells in culture have divided once and not, infrequently, twice. Except for a very short period¶ soon after irradiation, the numbers of cells in the irradiated culture does not differ from that in the unirradiated control culture until a cycle of division has been completed. Even when cell division has ceased, in the irradiated culture, the cells remain physiologically alive, continue to metabolize, and grow into giants. With the murine lymphoma cells that we have used in all our studies, the growth pattern after treatment with dimethyl myleran is exactly the same as that of x rays.[1] In this respect, there is no significant difference between the various mutants showing different sensitivities.[3] HN2, however, is characteristically different; the cells that have lost the ability to form clones stop dividing almost immediately, but metabolism does not cease. These cells grow in size, and the amount of DNA, RNA, and protein increases progressively. The majority of cells stop growing when they have doubled in size (and nucleic acid content) but a minority go on to form giants of 30 times the normal volume. Figure 6 shows that 18 hours after treatment (i.e., in the second cycle of cell division following treatment, the cycle time of these cells being 12 hours), all the HN2-treated cells are double the normal volume, while those treated with dimethyl myleran are only just beginning to increase in size, since they have undergone one "normal" division before enlarging. Twelve hours after giving dimethyl myleran, the cells sizes are all in the normal size range.

Given this posttreatment growth pattern, it is very surprising to note the repeated claims[9,12,35,39] that interference with the machinery of DNA synthesis is the biochemical lesion responsible for cell death. The suggestion that the DNA synthesis is the primary site of action is irreconcilable with the fact that the cells in the case of x rays and dimethyl myleran divide at least once, giving daughter cells of normal DNA content. A qualitative defect in the DNA made would be consistent with the posttreatment growth pattern, but not a quantitative interference with DNA synthesis.

Most of the experiments from which it is deduced that impairment of DNA synthesis is responsible for cell death suffer from one or both of the following defects:

1. The dose given is greatly in excess of that needed to kill (in the sense of loss of cloning ability) the vast majority of the cells. The phenomenon need not, therefore, be related to cell death.

2. The rate of DNA synthesis has been deduced from the rate of incorporation of radioactive precursors and, in particular, thymidine. This may be misleading, because under normal conditions the thymine incorporated into DNA is not de-

¶ A temporary effect of radiation is to block for a time the entry of cells into mitosis causing a temporary reduction in the mitotic index followed by a period in which there is an increase over the normal.

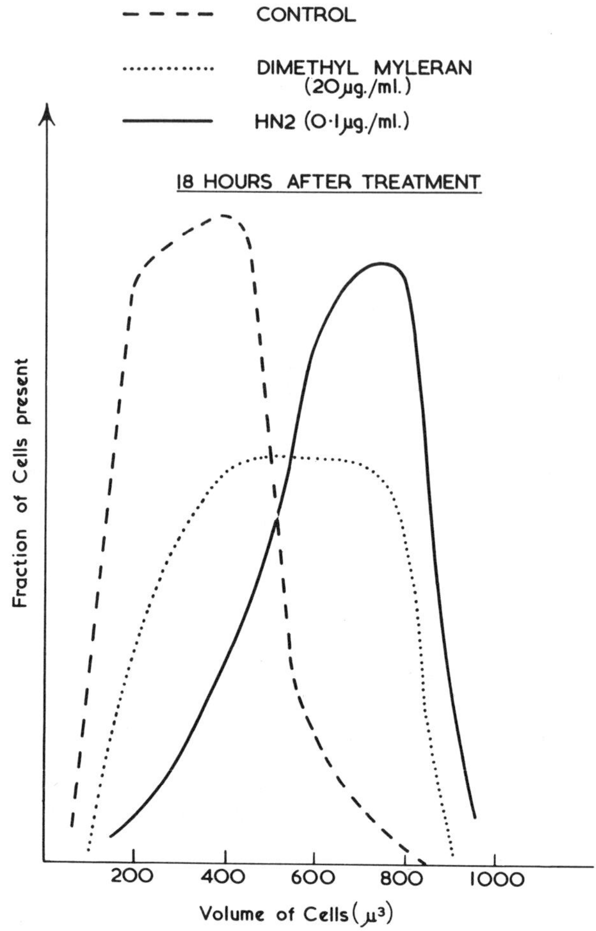

FIGURE 6. Changes in the volume (as measured in a Coulter counter) of lymphoma cells 18 hours after treatment with HN2 and dimethyl myleran.

rived from thymidine. A more important source of error is that treatment with radiation and cytotoxic agents leads to changes in the size of intracellular precursor pools. For example, exposure to x rays leads to an immediate increase in the amount of intracellular thymidine triphosphate and, consequently, the amount of radioactive thymidine that is incorporated into the DNA must decrease, even when the total amount of DNA made remains normal. This is exactly what happens after doses of x rays in the LD_{90} range.[40]

When DNA synthesis is determined by direct measurement of the increase in the total amount of DNA in the system (i.e., per ml of culture) no significant lesion in synthesis is observed. This is shown for x rays in FIGURE 7, and the pattern is the same with lymphoma cells treated with dimethyl myleran. Our results with HN2 agree completely with those of Brewer and colleagues,[41] who treated mouse fibroblasts. Levis and co-workers[42] also point out that one of the characteristics of HN2 damage is that cells go through several cycles of DNA replication after treatment. The resistance of the cells' DNA synthesing system is fully consistent with *in vitro* studies that showed that DNA obtained from cells treated with alkylating agents retains its template activity.[43]

Because cross-links are formed in the DNA of treated cells, the continuation of DNA synthesis appears to require that such crosslinks be eliminated. What, then, causes the death of the cell? Probably not crosslinks of DNA, since these are removed. Yet the much greater toxicity of bifunctional, as opposed to monofunctional, components can be adequately explained only on the hypothesis that crosslinking reaction is in some way involved in causing cell death. The hypothesis I should like to advance is that the lethal lesion arises from injuries

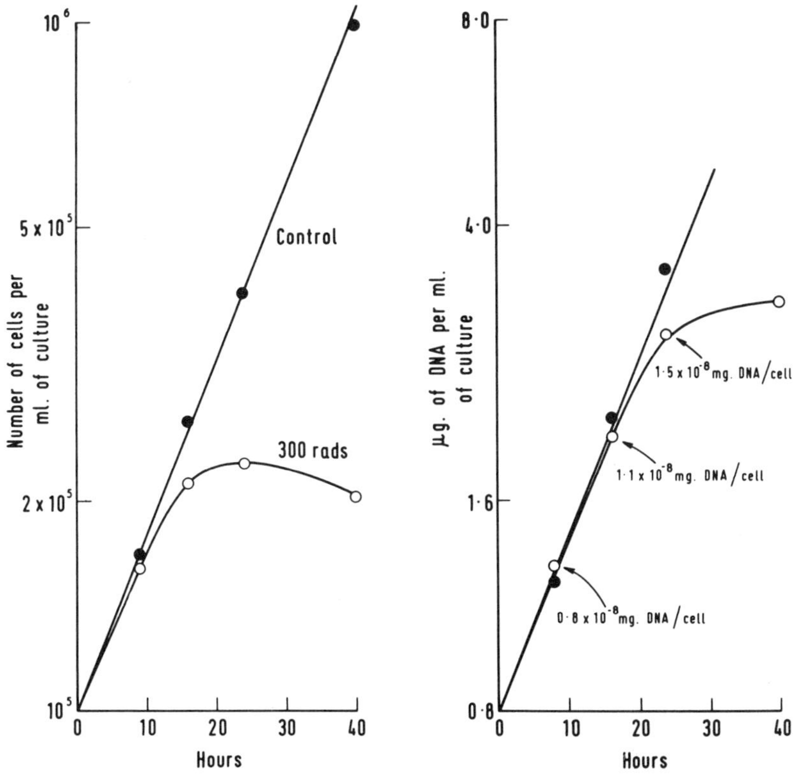

FIGURE 7. Effect of 300 r of x rays in cell proliferation and DNA synthesis in a culture of lymphoma cells (radioresistant L5178Y). After 300 r, 10% of the cells retain the capacity for indefinite cell growth.

produced during the enzymatic removal of the cross-links introduced by the alkylating agents.

Cross-Linking of DNA

Treating DNA, either in solution or within cells, with polyfunctional alkylating agents gives rise to three types of cross-links.

Linking of Two Twin Helices. Since we now know that DNA in cells is present as extremely large molecules, it is difficult to distinguish between cross-links between discrete twin helicese and between sections of the same "molecule" folded back in itself. Polyfunctional mustards, ethylene imines, epoxides, and methane suphonoxy esters (i.e., myleran-type compounds) were shown by physicochemical technique to produce interhelical cross-links in sperm heads.[44] In this very simple system, where effectively the only material that is alkylated is DNA, more than 60% of bifunctional nitrogen mustards could be shown to be involved in the formation of cross-links. Because of the rather crude techniques that had to be used at the time these experiments were done, crosslinking of this type could be demonstrated only in intact mammalian cells[44] with doses vastly in excess of those needed to kill. We now know this to be due to the fact that the DNA was degraded during isolation, thereby masking the effects produced by small numbers of cross-links. The stability of the cross-links formed in the DNA of sperm-heads depends on the nature of the alkylating group; those derived from mustard and myleran-type compounds are very stable, while the cross-links following treatment with bis-epoxides break down spontaneously.[44]

Intrahelical Cross-links. The finding by Geiduschek,[45] confirmed by others,[34] that HN2 prevents the irreversible denaturation of DNA suggests that intrahelical cross-links are formed that prevent complete strand separation. It is not clear if the procedures used distinguish unambiguously between inter- and intrahelical cross-links.

Reaction Between Adjacent Groups on the Same Chain. A reaction of this type is equivalent to forming a ring, and requires flexibility of the polyfunctional alkylating agent so that the necessary configuration can be attained. Differences in the properties of DNA cross-linked by $:CH_2{\cdot}CH_2{\cdot}CH_2{\cdot}CH_2{\cdot}$, which could form such rings, and by $:CH_2{\cdot}C\vdots C{\cdot}CH_2:$, which for steric reasons cannot form such rings, led me[46] to suggest that this reaction might occur and play a biologically significant role.

At first sight, cross-linking might be considered an important reaction that is shared by alkylating agents and ionizing radiations, since exposure of sperm heads[47] and of isolated DNA[27] (either dry or in the form of a gel, but not in dilute solution) to sparsely ionizing radiations like X and γ-rays leads to the production of interhelical cross-links. However, cross-linking of DNA by ionizing radiations is observed only if oxygen is absent during irradiation, and is also not produced by densely ionizing radiation like those from polonium α-rays.[48] But densely ionizing radiations are biologically more effective than sparsely ionizing radiations, and the lethal effect of radiation is less in the absence of oxygen than in its presence, so that there is no parallelism between cross-linking and radiation lethality. The view that cross-linking of DNA is not involved in radiation-induced cell death received direct support from investigations using the McGrath and Williams technique, which failed to reveal any evidence that cross-links were formed in the DNA of mammalian or microbial cells that were exposed to x rays.[26]

The Chemical Nature of the Reaction with DNA

The principal reaction that occurs in the DNA of cells exposed to ionizing radiations is the introduction of breaks in the main polynucleotide chain. Since 90% of these are restituted very rapidly, it seems probable that the end groups at the breaks are mainly 3′OH and 5′P, respectively, inasmuch as ligases capable of rejoining this type of group are present in all cells. The possibility that a small minority of breaks with different end-groups are also formed cannot be neglected, and it may be that such breaks are biologically much more harmful than those of the 3′OH, 5′P type. Changes involving groups other than the phosphodiester links must also occur, but little is known about these.

The various classes of alkylating agents differ in their site of reaction with DNA. Using electrometric titration techniques, we showed[44] that more than 90% of the reaction with DNA occurred by a reaction that consumed acid (i.e., with nitrogen mustards and myleran-type compounds, no acid was formed, and with epoxides alkali appeared). Alkylation of DNA associated with H^+ consumption must be either: (1) Esterification of phosphate groups or (2) quaternization of amino groups of the purine or pyrimidine bases.

With certain of the alkylating agents, initial esterification of the phosphate group is followed under physiological conditions by a transalkylation reaction in which the phosphate ester group interacts with an aromatic tertiary amine to give the quaternary nitrogen product. Andrews and co-workers[49] first observed intramolecular quaternization of a pyridine residue by the methyl group of a phosphate triester under very mild conditions (FIGURE 8). With an ethyl ester this reaction was, however, much more sluggish.[||]

With DNA, evidence for this type of reaction was found under physiological conditions for the monofunctional nitrogen mustard $(CH_3)_2N{\cdot}CH_2CH_2{\cdot}Cl$.[50,51] After the reaction was complete, the absorption spectrum of the DNA was virtually unaltered, but on standing, a new chromophore at 280 mμ—typical of 7-N alkylation of guanine—slowly appeared (FIGURE 9). As the transalkylation proceeds, slow release of free alkylated bases occurs, and this is followed by a progressive reduction in molecular weight due to breaks formed in the main polynucleotide chain.[51,52] With this mustard, the main sequence of reactions appears to be (FIGURE 10) the following:

(1) esterification of the phosphate group;
(2) transfer of some of the alkyl ester groups to form a quaternary base;
(3) elimination of the base as a result of hydrolysis of sugar-base link; and
(4) hydrolysis of phosphate diester bond (main-chain scission) as a result of instability introduced by elimination of purine.

With ethyl methane sulphonate[51] and its bifunctional derivative, myleran, no alkylation of the bases could be detected, and there was no evidence for transalkylation under physiological conditions, though under the conditions used to hydrolyze DNA with strong acid, this would occur.

At the other extreme, there are the epoxides that do not appear to react

[||] Attempts to establish the site of alkylation have frequently involved the study of the products obtained by acid hydrolysis of alkylated DNA. The condition used for hydrolysis favor transalkylation and lead to the breakdown of phosphate esters. It is not surprising, therefore, that reaction products found by such procedures consisted solely of alkylated bases.

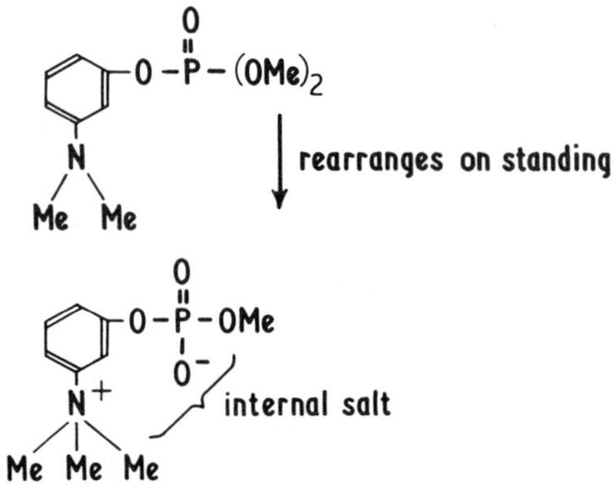

FIGURE 8. Transalkylation as demonstrated by Andrews and co-workers.[49]

significantly with the phosphate groups but alkylate the bases directly. The fact that bifunctional epoxides do not give rise to stable cross-links is consistent with the finding that these reagents alkylate the bases directly and do not detectably esterify phosphate groups, since cross-links formed between bases will be elimi-

TABLE 5

REACTIONS OF DIFFERENT ALKYLATING AGENTS WITH DNA*

Alkylating Agent	Main initial Reaction	Posttreatment changes: Trans-Alkylation	Loss of Alkylated Purine	Main-chain Scission	Stability of Crosslinks Formed by Equivalent Bifunctional Compound
Epoxide	purine	no	yes	marked	unstable
Nitrogen mustard	phosphate	yes	yes	slight	stable
Ethyl methane sulphonate	phosphate	no	no	none	stable
Methyl methane sulphonate	phosphate and purine	yes	yes	marked	(no corresponding compound)

*From references 44 and 51.

FIGURE 9. Changes in the UV absorption spectrum of DNA after reaction with monofunctional nitrogen mustard. After one hour, 97% of the mustard had reacted (with DNA and by hydrolysis). Changes in the spectrum seen after one hour must, therefore, be due to rearrangements (transalkylation) occurring in the alkylated DNA. Alkylation at the 7-N position of guanine leads to increased absorption at 280 mg. (Adapted from reference 51.) Left: Expressed as differences in the UV spectrum between the untreated DNA and the alkylated DNA at different times after the reaction. Right: Changes in the ratio of extinction at 280.260 mμ of DNA at different times after alkylation.

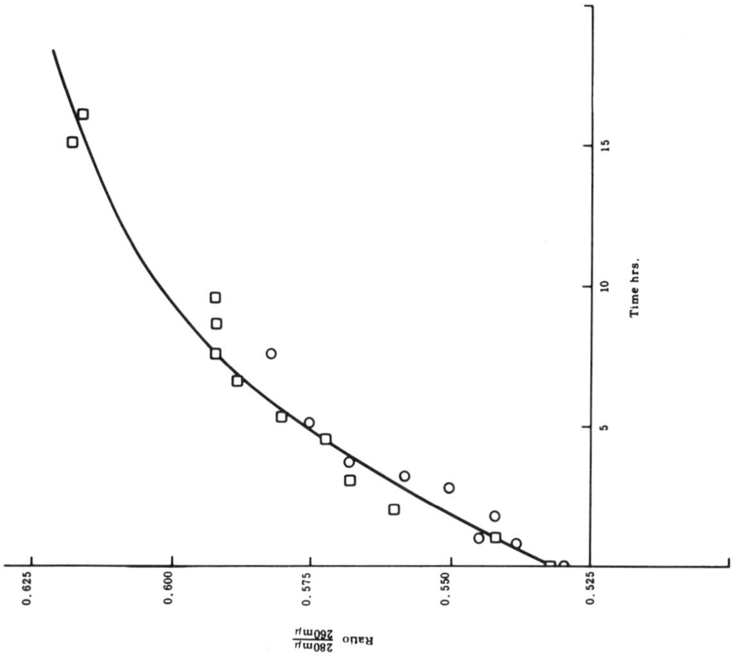
0.625
0.600
0.575
0.550
0.525
Ratio 280mμ/260mμ
5
10
15
Time hrs.

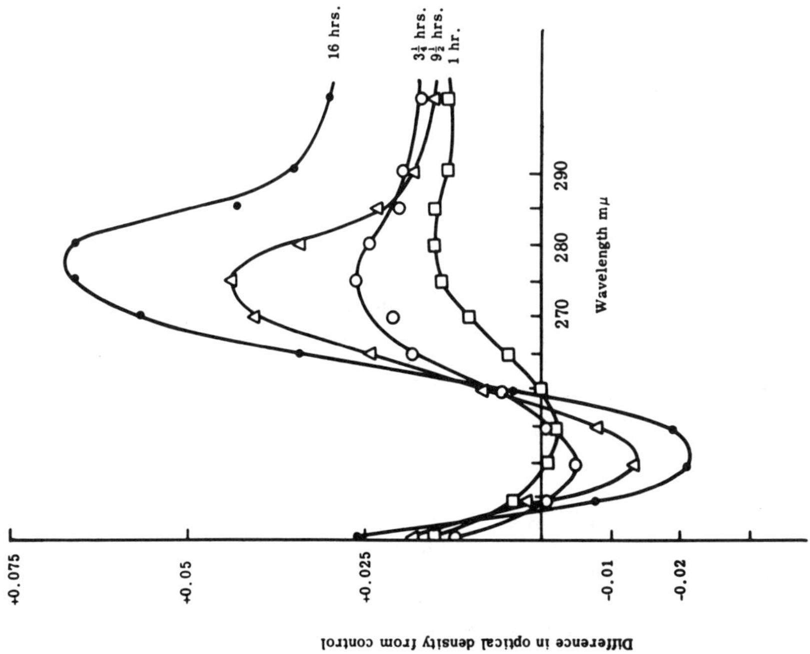
+0.075
+0.05
+0.025
-0.01
-0.02
Difference in optical density from control
270
280
290
Wavelength mμ
16 hrs.
3¼ hrs.
9½ hrs.
1 hr.

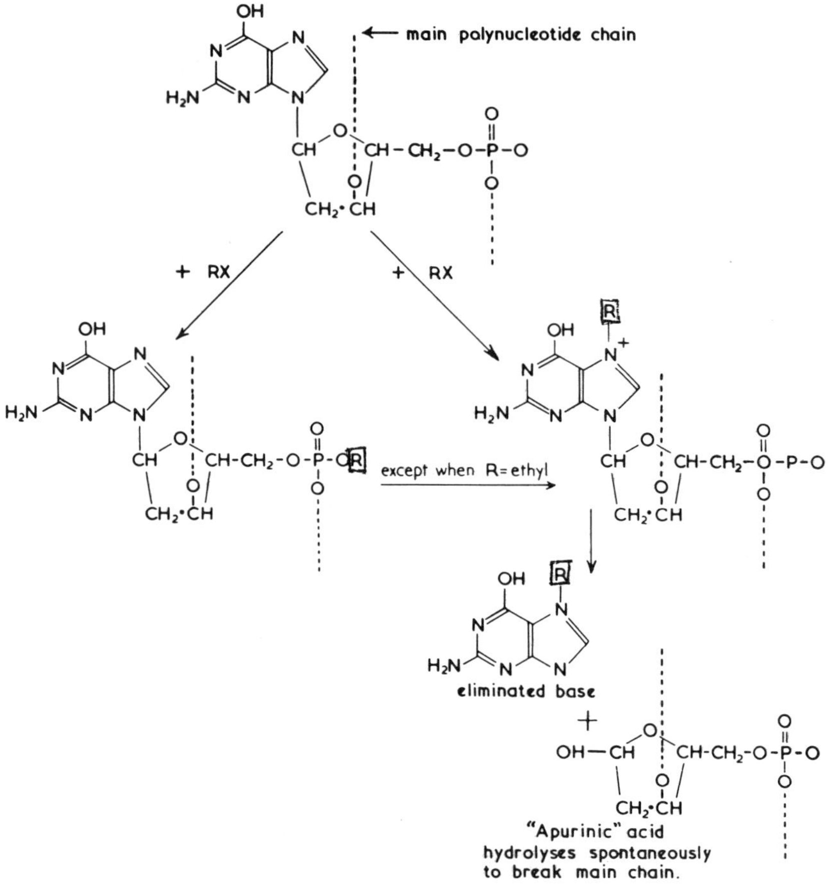

FIGURE 10. Direct alkylation and alkylation via triphosphate esters of purines in DNA.

nated by the splitting out of the alkylating bases, while those between phosphate groups are stable. Methyl methane suphonate appears to be intermediate in that both phosphate esterification (followed subsequently by transalkylation) and direct alkylation of the bases occur (TABLE 5).

CONCLUSIONS

From the preceeding two sections, it is clear that there are very profound differences between the primary chemical lesions produced by x rays and by the alkylating agents in the DNA of treated cells. Moreover, even the different classes of alkylating agents discussed in this paper—not to mention some like mitomycin, to which I have not referred—differ markedly in the nature of the chemical reac-

TABLE 6

COMPARISON OF THE ACTION OF HN2, DMM AND X RAYS ON LYMPHOMA CELLS

In Vitro

Posttreatment Effects		
Cell Division	DMM ≡ x rays	cells divide at least once before dying
	HN2	most cells enlarge but do not divide
DNA Synthesis	DMM ≡ HN2 ≡ x rays	one or more rounds of DNA replication occur
Recovery from Lethal Damage by Posttreatments	DMM ≡ x rays	recovery
	HN2	no recovery found
Recovery from Sublethal Damage	DMM ≡ x rays	recovery
	HN2	no recovery found
Pretreatment Effects		
Sensitization by O_2 and Bromouracil	None by DMM and HN2	(different from x rays)
Protection by SH Compounds	Relative effectiveness of different compounds different for HN2 and for x rays	
Relative Sensitivity of Mutants	DMM ≡ HN2 ≡ X-rays	for diploid mutants
	DMM ≡ X rays	for tetraploid mutants
	more resistant to HN2	

tion they undergo with DNA. Any common feature in the mode of action of alkylating agents and radiation must, therefore, be sought at a stage in the process of injury development beyond the primary chemical lesion. The realization that cells have the capacity to repair changes in their DNA raises the possibility that the critical site of action of all these agents involves the repair system in one of these ways: (1) Only when the repair system itself has been sufficiently damaged will cells die from a DNA lesion (i.e., the rate-determining step for cell death is the inactivation of the repair system). (2) The true lethal event may be misrepair, such as joining together of the wrong strands of broken DNA.

If errors introduced during repair were the true starting point of the injury process, then the same biological lesion could arise as the result of a number of chemically different changes in DNA. So long as DNA is damaged, the repair system will be brought into play, and with it the possibility of error leading to delayed death (e.g. via chromosome abnormalities).

In the system that Dr. Goldenberg and I have studied, namely, the killing by mitotic death of lymphoma cells *in vitro,* dimethyl myleran mimics x rays more closely than does HN2, but the concordance is far from complete (TABLE 6). I believe the time has come for abandoning the concept of radiomimetic behavior, which obscures one of the most characteristic features of all these agents—their great diversity.

REFERENCES

1. ALEXANDER, P. & Z. B. MIKULSKI. 1961. Differences in the response of leukaemia cells in tissue culture to nitrogen mustard and to dimethyl myleran. Biochem. Pharmacol. **5:** 275–282.
2. LEVIS, A. G., SPANIO, L. & DE NADAI, A. 1963. Radiomimetic effects of a nitrogen mustard on survival, growth, protein and nucleic acid synthesis of mammalian cells *in vitro.* Exp. Cell Res. **31:** 19–30.
3. GOLDENBERG, G. J. & P. ALEXANDER. 1965. The effects of nitrogen mustard and dimethyl myleran on murine leukaemia cell lines of different radiosensitivity. Cancer Res. **25:** 1401–1409.
4. MAURO, F. & M. M. ELKIND. 1967. Sulfur mustards and X-rays: differences in expression of lethal damage. Science **155:** 1561–1563.
5. FOX, M. & B. W. FOX. 1967. Effect of methyl methane-sulfonate on the growth of P.388 lymphoma cells *in vitro* and on their rate of progress through the cell cycle. Cancer Res. **27:** 1805–1812.
6. PUCK, T. T. & P. I. MARCUS. 1956. Action of X-rays on mammalian cells. J. Exp. Med. **103:** 653.
7. LAMARQUE, P. & G. BOBOJ. 1956. First UN Inter. Conf. on Peaceful Uses of Atomic Energy. Geneva, Switzerland. 1955. Vol. II. Publ. UN 1956.
8. ELKIND, M. M. & H. SUTTON. 1960. Radiation response of mammalian cells grown in culture, I. Repair of X-ray damage in surviving Chinese hamster cells. Radiat. Res. **13:** 556–593.
9. GOLDENBERG, G. J. 1968. Repair of sub-lethal damage of L.5178Y lymphoblasts *in vitro* treated with dimethyl myleran and nitrogen mustard. Biochem. Pharmacol. **17:** 820–824.
10. FOX, M. & A. H. W. NIAS. 1968. A modification of the sensitivity of mammalian cells surviving treatment with methyl methanesulphonate. Europ. J. Cancer **4:** 325–335.
11. MAURO, F. & M. M. ELKIND. 1968. Comparison of repair of sublethal damage in cultures Chinese hamster cells exposed to sulfur mustard and X-rays. Cancer Res. **28:** 1156–1161.

12. Walker, I. G. & C. J. Thatcher. 1968. Studies on the lethal effects of sulfur mustard on dividing mammalian cells. Radiat. Res. **34:** 110–127.
13. Walker, I. G. & C. W. Helleiner. 1963. The sensitivity of cultured mammalian cells in different stages of the division cycle to nitrogen and sulfur mustards. Cancer Res. **23:** 734–738.
14. Mauro, F. & M. M. Elkind. 1968. Differences in survival variations during the growth cycle of cultured Chinese hamster cells treated with sulfur mustard and X-rays. Cancer Res. **28:** 1150–1155.
15. Stapleton, G. E., D. Billen & A. Hollaender. 1953. Recovery of X-irradiated bacteria at suboptimal incubation temperatures. J. Cell. Com. Physiol. **41:** 345–357.
16. Beer, J. Z., J. Lett & P. Alexander. 1963. Influence of temperature and medium on the X-ray sensitivities of leukaemia cells *in vitro*. Nature (London) **199:** 193–194.
17. Mauro, F., M. M. Elkind & K. Sakamoto. 1968. Comparison of survival kinetics and modifications of lethal damage in cultured Chinese hamster cells exposed to sulfur mustard and X-rays. Cancer Res. **28:** 1143–1149.
18. Alexander, P. (Unpublished data.).
19. Fox M. 1968. The effect of halogenated nucleosides on the sensitivity of a mouse lymphoma P388F to X-rays and methyl methanesulphonate. Int. J. Cancer **3:** 382–389.
20. Connors, T. A. 1966. Protection against the toxicity of alkylating agents by thiols: the mechanism of protection and its relevance to cancer chemotherapy. Europ. J. Cancer **2:** 293–305.
21. Bacq, Z. M. & P. Alexander. 1964. Importance of Radioprotection of the reaction of cells to sulphydryl and disulphide compounds. Nature (London) **203:** 162–164.
22. Alexander, P., J. T. Lett & C. J. Dean. 1965. The role of post-irradiation repair processes in chemical protection and sensitization. Progr. Biochem. Pharmacol. **1:** 22–40.
23. Ball, C. R., T. A. Connors, J. A. Double, V. Ujhazy & M. E. Whisson. 1966. Comparison of nitrogen-mustard-sensitive and -resistant Yoshida sarcomas. Int. J. Cancer **1:** 319–327.
24. Wheeler, G. P., & J. A. Alexander. 1964. Studies with mustards. V. *in vivo* fixation of C^{14} of labeled alkylating agents by bilaterally grown sensitive and resistant tumors. Cancer Res. **24:** 1331–1337.
25. Connors, T. A. & C. R. Ball. 1968. Possible mechanisms of acquired resistance to alkylating agents. Gann. Monograph **3:** 13.
26. Lett, J. T., I. Caldwell, C. J. Dean & P. Alexander. 1967. Rejoining of X-ray induced breaks in the DNA of leukaemia cells. Nature **214:** 790–792.
27. Lett, J. T., K. A. Stacey & P. Alexander. 1961. Cross-linking of dry deoxyribonucleic acids by electrons. Radiation Res. **14:** 349–362.
28. Freifelder, D. 1965. Mechanism of inactivation of coliphage T7 by X-rays. Proc. Nat. Acad. Sci. **54:** 128–134.
29. Bacq, Z. M. & P. Alexander. 1961. Fundamentals of radiobiology. Pergamon Press. Oxford, England.
30. Sutherland, R. M. & A. Pihl. 1967. Repair of radiation damage to membrane sulfhydryl groups of human erythrocytes. Biochim. Biophys. Acta **135:** 568–570.
31. Dean, C. J. (In press.)
32. Lett, J. T., G. Parkins & M. G. Ormerod. 1964. Mechanisms of sensitization to X-rays of mammalian cells by 5-bromodeoxyuridine. Nature (London) **203:** 593–596.
33. Alexander, P., C. J. Dean, L. D. G. Hamilton, J. T. Lett & G. Parkins. 1965. Critical structures other than DNA as sites for primary lesions of cell death induced by ionizing radiations. *In* Cellular Radiation Biology : 241–263. 18th Annual Symposium on Fundamental Cancer Research. University of Texas. Austin, Tex.
34. Kohn, K. W., N. H. Steigbigel & C. L. Spears. 1965. Cross-linking and repair of DNA in sensitive and resistant strains of *E. Coli* treated with nitrogen mustard. Proc. Nat. Acad. Sci. USA **53:** 1154–1161.
35. Crathorn, A. R. & J. J. Roberts. 1966. Mechanism of the cytotoxic action of alkylat-

ing agents in mammalian cells and evidence for the removal of alkylated groups from deoxyribonucleic acid. Nature (London) **211:** 150–153.
36. Lawley, P. D. & P. Brooks. 1965. Molecular mechanism of the cytotoxic action of difunctional alkylating agents and of resistance to this action. Nature (London) **206:** 480–483.
37. Painter, R. B. & J. E. Cleaver. 1967. Repair replication in HeLa cells after large doses of X-irradiation. Nature (London) **216:** 369–370.
38. Roberts, J. J., A. R. Crathorn & T. P. Brent. 1968. Repair of alkylated DNA in mammalian cells. Nature (London) **218:** 970–972.
39. Fox, B. W. & M. Fox. 1967. Effect of methyl methanesulfonate on macromolecular biosynthesis in P388F cells. Cancer Res. **27:** 2134–2239.
40. Hamilton, L. D. G. & P. Alexander. (Unpublished data.)
41. Brewer, H. B., J. P. Comstock & L. Aronow. 1961. Effects of nitrogen mustard on protein and nucleic acid synthesis in mouse fibroblasts. Biochem. Pharmacol. **8:** 281–287.
42. Levis, A. G., G. A. Danieli & E. Piccinni. 1965. Nucleic acid synthesis and the mitotic cycle in mammalian cells treated with nitrogen mustard in culture. Nature (London) **207:** 608–610.
43. Ruddon, R. W. & J. M. Johnson. 1968. The Effects of nitrogen mustard on DNA template activity in purified DNA and RNA polymerase systems. Molec. Pharmacol **4:** 258–273.
44. Alexander, P., A. Swarcbort & K. A. Stacey. 1959. The reactivity of radiomimetic compounds—III Crosslinking of nucleoprotein. Biochem. Pharmacol. **2:** 133–145.
45. Geiduschek, E. P. 1961. "Reversible" DNA. Proc. Nat. Acad. Sci. USA **47:** 950–955.
46. Alexander, P. 1952. Interference with the formation of a nucleoprotein complex by radiomimetic compounds. Nature (London) **169:** 226.
47. Alexander, P. & K. A. Stacey. 1959. Cross-linking of deoxyribonucleic acid in sperm heads by ionizing radiations. Nature (London) **184:** 958–960.
48. Alexander, P., J. T. Lett, P. Kopp & R. Itzhaki. 1961. Degradation of dry deoxyribonucleic acid by polonium Alpha-particles. Radiat. Res. **14:** 363–373.
49. Andrews, K. J. M., F. R. Atherton, F. Bergel & A. L. Morrison. 1952. The synthesis of neurotropic and musculotropic stimulators and inhibitors. Part V. Derivatives of aminophenyl phosphates as anticholinesterases. J. Chem. Soc. 780–784.
50. Alexander, P., J. T. Lett & G. Parkins. 1961. Instability of alkylated deoxyribonucleic acid in relation to the mechanism of chemical mutagenesis. Biochim. Biophys. Acta **48:** 423–425.
51. Lett, J. T., G. M. Parkins & P. Alexander. 1962. Physicochemical changes produced in DNA after alkylation. Arch. Biochem. **97:** 80–93.
52. Alexander, P. & K. A. Stacey. 1958. Comparison of the changes produced by ionizing radiations and by the alkylating agents: evidence for a similar mechanism at the molecular level. Ann. N. Y. Acad. Sci. **68:** 1225–1237.

DISCUSSION OF THE PAPER

Unidentified Speaker: I would like to make several comments about Dr. Alexander's conclusion about repair mechanisms. The first and most important point is that there is evidence that there is more than one repair system. Repair in bifunctional alkylating agents is different from the repair systems for x rays and for monofunctional alkylating agents, so one finds cells that are unable to repair damage induced by bifunctional agents, but are nonetheless able to repair damage by x rays or monofunctional agents. I think that as soon as one understands that the repair as well as the sequence of the actions is different with different kinds of damage, some of the difficulties are removed.

UNIDENTIFIED SPEAKER: Could you elaborate on your thymidine incorporation experiments?

DR. ALEXANDER: When one measures thymidine incorporation using radioactive thymidine, one measures, of course, the thymidine in DNA and excludes acid-soluble material. But the factor that determines how much radioactive thymidine is incorporated into DNA is the thymidine phosphate pools in the cell. From changes in thymidine incorporation following a treatment of cells by radiation or chemicals, one cannot calculate directly the changes in DNA synthesis that have occurred unless one has also shown that the thymidine triphosphate pool in the cell, as well as the rate of conversion of thymidine from the medium into the triphosphate, is unaffected by the treatment being studied. There are many examples where treatments have raised thymidine triphosphate pools. As a result, the amount of thymidine incorporated (i.e., the radioactivity in the DNA) is decreased, because this depends on the level of activity of the thymidine in the pool inside, yet the total amount of DNA made may be exactly the same, and the treatment has, in fact, had no influences in DNA synthesis.

UNIDENTIFIED SPEAKER: I agree heartily with the difference between effects due to radioactive substances and the alkylating agent, partly because of the many different kinds of effects that radiation can produce. What about transmutation? Certainly, there is some of this going on in many substances, such as ribonucleic acids, proteins, and vitamins. Dr. Alexander, can you give any information on the influence or importance of the possibility of transmutation?

DR. ALEXANDER: One must make a very clear distinction between killing cells by exposing them to x rays, which I have been talking about, and killing cells by the decay of radioactive materials that will be a mixture of ionizing radiation effects and transmutation effects. It is difficult enough to compare x rays with other agents. I think that one could have a whole session devoted to comparing the difference between killing cells by means of x rays and killing cells by means of phosphorus disintegrations, sulfur disintegration, and carbon disintegration.

T. J. BARDOS (*State University of New York at Buffalo, Buffalo, N. Y.*): I should like to mention that we find a very sharp pH dependence in the reaction of DNA with various alkylating agents. At pH 5.3, for example, there was a much stronger effect on the change in the physicochemical properties of DNA, as well as on the decrease of its template activity for RNA polymerase, than there was at pH 7.0. This is quite understandable in connection with the aziridines which are activated by protonation, but not in the case of the nitrogen mustards which should be deactivated chemically by protonation. We attribute this to the effect of pH on DNA, causing a possible loosening up of the double strand and more exposure of the 7-nitrogen of guanine. However, according to Dr. Alexander, the primary reaction of the alkylating agent may be with the phosphate group. I wonder if Dr. Alexander has studied the rate of transactivation of the alkylating agent from the phosphate to the guanine nitrogen with respect to the pH.

DR. ALEXANDER: We have made no studies, but from the literature one can see that alkylation of a base by a triphosphate ester occurs more readily under acid conditions.

N-NITROSO COMPOUNDS IN ORGANOTROPIC AND TRANSPLACENTAL CARCINOGENESIS*

H. Druckrey, R. Preussmann, and S. Ivankovic

Forschergruppe Praeventiv-Medizin, Max Planck Institut für Immunbiologie, Freiburg, West Germany

Introduction

For a proper judgment of the potential role of chemical substances in human carcinogenesis, it is essential to know whether cancer can be induced in every organ of experimental animals, and whether these neoplasias are comparable to the corresponding tumors in man. The answer to these questions requires systematic studies, in which the problem of specificity is fundamental.

Organotropic effects (i.e., specific effects upon a certain organ) can best be attained with compounds that are inactive as such but that become activated by metabolic changes ("indirect" carcinogens). This applies to dimethylnitrosamine (Magee & Barnes, 1956), and similarly to the carcinogenic hydrazo-, azo-, or azoxyalkanes, and to 1-aryl-3,3-dialkyltriazenes. The first experiments of Dutton and Heath (1956) showed that dimethylnitrosamine becomes demethylated enzymatically mainly in the liver, and leads to diazomethane as the active alkylating carcinogen.

For biochemical reasons, however, we came to the conclusion that the first step of activation is an enzymatic hydroxylation on an (alpha) αC-atom (Druckrey *et al.*, 1961a). This should be possible in all dialkylnitrosamines possessing at least one disposable hydrogen atom in alpha position. The αC-hydroxyalkylnitrosamine then becomes dealkylated spontaneously to the corresponding monoalkylnitrosamine, which, by protonic change, yields the isomeric diazohydroxide, as explained in the formulas of Figure 1. Both these intermediates are extremely unstable and yield diazoalkane, diazotate, or alkyldiazonium, depending upon conditions. The latter is highly reactive. It can lead to diazotization, or decomposes rapidly to gaseous nitrogen and the respective alkyl-cation, which most probably is the ultimate "alkylating" carcinogen (Magee & Barnes, 1967). According to this "alkylation theory" of carcinogenesis, the activation of dialkylnitrosamines passes several steps, among which the initial αC-hydroxylation is the only enzymatic process. This, however, can lead to organospecific effects, as first shown with the liver carcinogen dimethylnitrosamine by Magee and Barnes (1956).

In contrast to dialkylnitrosamines, the acylalkylnitrosamides react by heterolysis. Therefore, many of them are widely used in chemistry for the production of diazoalkanes and for alkylations. After heterolysis, the further degradation pathways are the same as with dialkylnitrosamines. Both groups represent the class of N-nitroso compounds.

* The authors are indebted to the Deutsche Forschungsgemeinschaft for generous support.

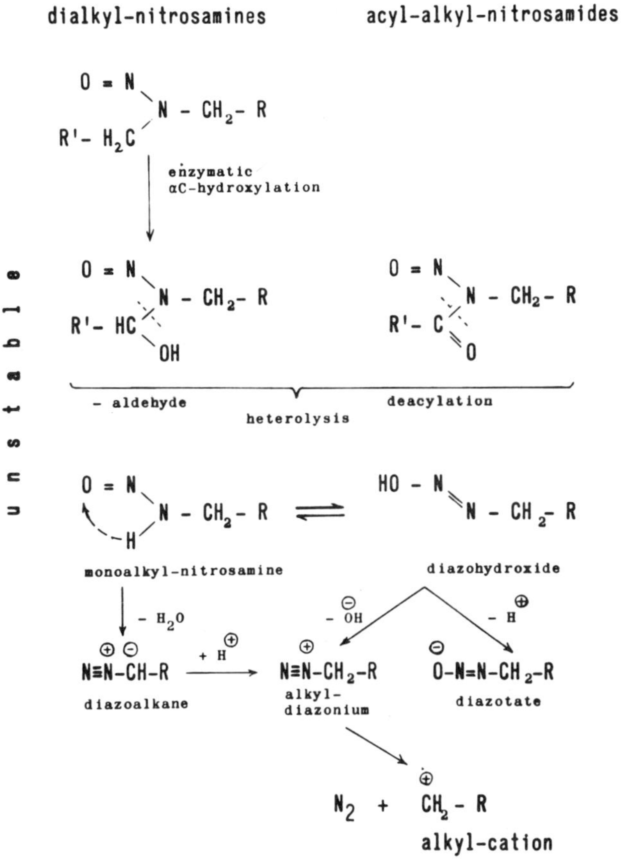

FIGURE 1. Scheme for the reactions of dialkylnitrosamines and acylalkylnitrosamides, eventually leading to alkylating intermediates.

ORGANOTROPIC CARCINOGENESIS IN ADULT ANIMALS

According to the formulas in FIGURE 1, carcinogenic activity was expected as a general feature of N-nitroso compounds. This could be shown in systematic studies with about 70 derivatives, synthesized in our institute by Preussmann. Most of them proved to be potent carcinogens with striking organospecific effects.

The experimental animals were mostly rats of our BD-inbred strains (Druckrey *et al.*, 1962a), but random-bred guinea pigs and golden hamsters have also been used. For chronic oral administration, soluble substances were given in the daily drinking water, insoluble ones in the diet, and single doses by stomach-tube. Subcutaneous (s.c.) injections were done under the dorsal skin, and intravenous (i.v.) into a vein of the rat's tail. As standard diet, Altromin (Brock & Wilk, 1961) has been used. The rate of spontaneous malignant tumors in our BD-rats is very low, one to two percent at the age of two years. All animals were observed over the whole life span, and after death, complete autopsies, including the nervous system, were performed. For the histological investigations, we are indebted to C. Thomas, Pathologisches Institut in Bonn, Germany, and Freiburg, and to K. J. Zülch, W. Wechsler and P. Kleihues, Max Planck Institut für Hirnforschung in Cologne, Germany. In the evaluation of the results, only malignant tumors will be considered.

Dialkylnitrosamines

Diethylnitrosamine proved to be a very potent liver carcinogen (Schmähl *et al.*, 1960). Extensive quantitative studies (Druckrey *et al.*, 1963d) revealed clear dose-response relationships down to a daily dosage of .075 mg/kg body weight. Even in guinea pigs, formerly considered resistant to carcinogens, hepatocellular carcinomas (FIGURE 2) have been produced with the same regularity as in rats (Druckrey & Steinhoff, 1962; Argus & Hoch-Ligeti, 1963). All other symmetrical dialkylnitrosamines up to the diamyl compound, after continuous oral administration to rats, produced liver cancer with decreasing potency. The only exception was di-n-butylnitrosamine, which, surprisingly, also produced carcinomas of the urinary bladder. Biochemical studies revealed that soluble metabolites are excreted in the urine in high concentration, probably coupled hydroxylated products. Therefore we prepared butanol(4)-butylnitrosamine. This proved to be a specific bladder carcinogen, even after oral administration (Druckrey *et al.*, 1964c).

Since hydroxylation occurs mainly in the liver, it was attempted to avoid the liver by s.c. injections. At the same time, this method allows one to decide whether the substance investigated is a direct, and therefore locally acting, carcinogen or an "indirect" one, producing cancer in remote organs. With dialkyl-

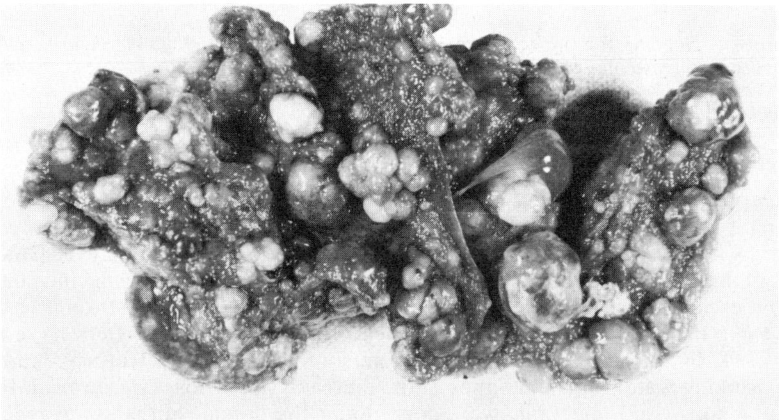

FIGURE 2. Hepatocellular carcinoma in a guinea pig, induced by diethylnitrosamine, 5 mg/kg b.w. in the daily drinking water. Death after 384 days.

nitrosamines, not one single local sarcoma at the site of injections was observed, during many experiments. This shows convincingly that dialkylnitrosamines are not carcinogenic *per se,* but become so only after metabolic activation. Subcutaneous injections of dibutylnitrosamine produced bladder cancer in all treated rats (FIGURE 3). With the diamyl compound, however, bladder cancer was never observed, but carcinomas of the lungs were seen instead (Druckrey & Preussmann, 1962a).

The nonsymmetric dialkylnitrosamines induced carcinomas of the esophagus with high regularity (Druckrey *et al.*, 1963b, 1963c). More than 200 cases were observed. Similar results were reported by Weisburger and colleagues (1966). In our experiments, the methylalkyl compounds were the most potent carcinogens in this group. The effect was completely independent of the route of administration. FIGURE 4 shows two cases of multiple esophageal cancers produced by s.c. injections of methylamylnitrosamine and by inhalation of methylbutylnitrosamine vapors, respectively (Druckrey *et al.*, 1968d). This proves convincingly the high organospecificity of these carcinogens. Methylphenylnitrosamine had the same effect, as confirmed by Boyland and co-workers (1964). Since the formation of phenyldiazonium is to be expected after demethylation, carcinogenesis may also be effectuated by arylation or diazotization, as will be discussed later. In this group, methylallylnitrosamine was the only exception, also leading to cancer of the kidney or liver.

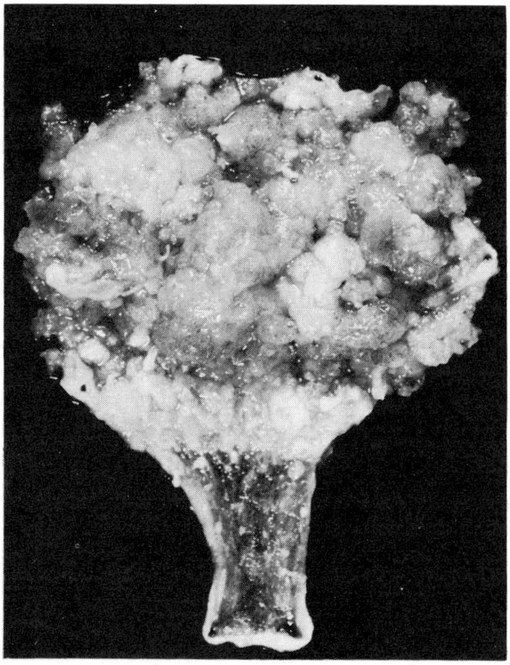

FIGURE 3. Carcinoma of the urinary bladder in a rat. Di-n-butylnitrosamine, 200 mg/kg once a week injected subcutaneously. Death after 369 days.

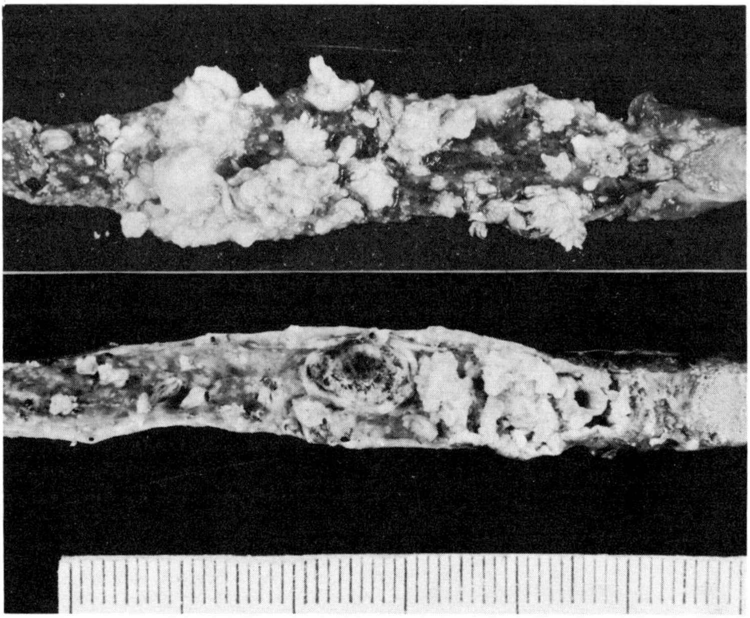

FIGURE 4. Squamous carcinomas of the esophagus in rats.
Above: methylamylnitrosamine 10 mg/kg injected subcutaneously once a week. Death after 262 days.
Below: methylbutylnitrosamine, inhalation of 25 ppm for one hour every week. Death after 257 days. Total dose: 69 mg/kg body weight.

With cyclic nitrosamines, again, organotropic effects were observed. After oral administration, N-nitrosopyrrolidine produced only liver cancer. The next higher homologues, nitrosopiperidine, as well as N,N′-dinitrosopiperazine, however, led to carcinomas of the esophagus. After s.c. injections in rats, both compounds produced carcinomas of the ethmoturbinalia and neuroesthesioepitheliomas of the olfactory nerve, as shown in FIGURE 5 (Druckrey *et al.,* 1964a). The same tumors have been observed by Herrold (1964) in golden hamsters after s.c. injections of diethylnitrosamine.

The dealkylation of dialkylnitrosamines is generally attributed to "drug-metabolizing enzymes" (Brodie *et al.,* 1958; McMahon, 1966), which are considered nonspecific. The surprising but nevertheless striking organospecific effects of dialkylnitrosamines, however, indicate that the oxidative dealkylation may be due to very specific hydroxylases, specific not only for the respective substrate, but also with regard to their activities in individual organs.

Acylalkylnitrosamides

Acylalkylnitrosamides become de-acylated by heterolysis and are unstable in alkaline solution. Accordingly, they should act as direct carcinogens. After

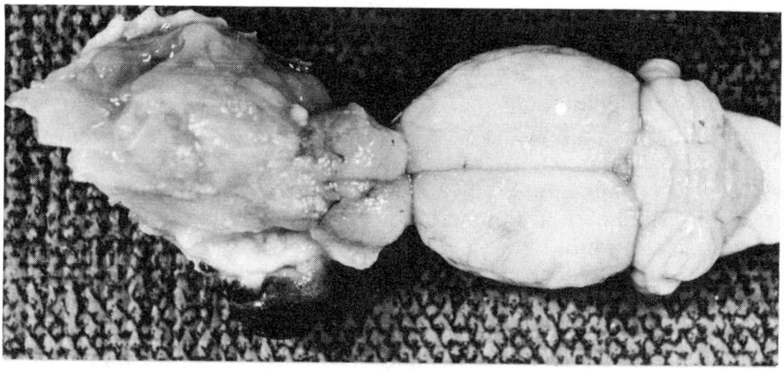

FIGURE 5. Neuroblastoma of the olfactory nerves in a rat, induced by s.c. injections of N,N′-dinitrosopiperazine, 10 mg/kg twice a week. Death after 564 days.

s.c. injections in rats, local sarcomas have been observed with several compounds of this group (Druckrey *et al.*, 1966b). Additionally, the very unstable phenylnitrosourea was active. Since phenyldiazonium is formed by de-acylation, as proved by chemical reactions, this indicates that the primary carcinogenic process can also be effectuated by diazotization or arylation (Preussmann *et al.*, 1968). Methylnitrosourea, painted on the skin of mice, rats, or hamsters, proved to be

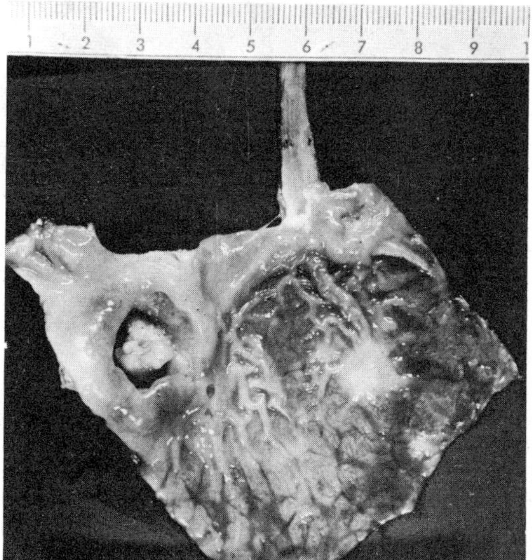

FIGURE 6. Clear-cell carcinoma on the pylorus of the stomach in a guinea pig. Methylnitrosourethane, 2 mg/kg b.w. in the daily drinking water up to a total dose of 274 mg/kg. Death after 642 days.

a strong topical carcinogen in experiments of Graffi *et al.* (1966, 67). When given by oral route, several acylalkylnitrosamides produced carcinomas of the forestomach in rats (Druckrey *et al.*, 1961b, 1967b; Schoental, 1963) and hamsters (Herrold, 1966). In guinea pigs, since the whole stomach is glandular, adenocarcinomas of the stomach and the pancreas have been produced in high yield with methylnitrosourea and methylnitrosourethane by Druckrey and colleagues (1968a). The gross appearance of a stomach cancer in a guinea pig is shown in FIGURE 6. The similarity to human stomach cancer is evident. This also applies to the histological picture.

In order to avoid local carcinogenic effects, experiments were performed with i.v. injections in rats. They revealed striking organotropic effects. Methylnitrosourethane, even at a dosage of 1 mg/kg body weight once every two weeks, regularly produced carcinomas of the lungs (Druckrey *et al.*, 1962b, 67b). Methylnitrosourea, by contrast, proved to be a carcinogen highly specific to the brain (FIGURE 7), and in some cases, also to the spinal cord (Druckrey *et al.*, 1964b,

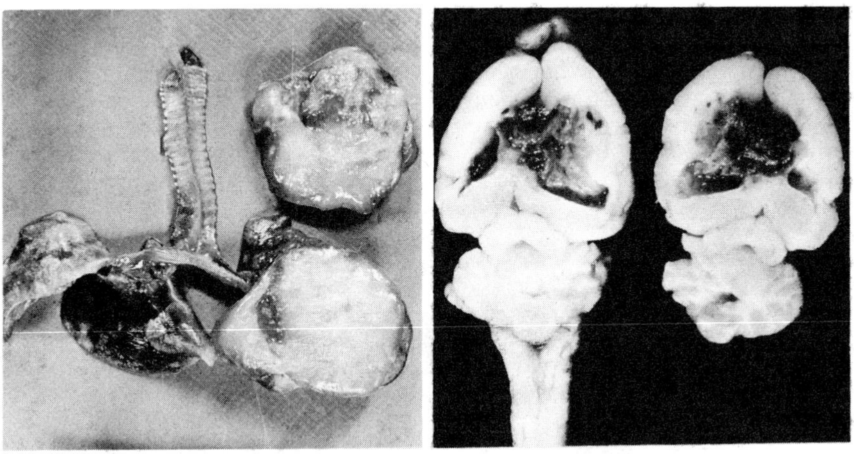

FIGURE 7. Organotropic carcinogenicity of acylalkylnitrosamides in rats.
Left: squamous carcinoma of the lung, induced by methylnitrosourethane, 1 mg/kg once every two weeks intravenously, total dose 22 mg/kilogram. Death after 374 days.
Right: polymorphic glioma of the brain, induced by methylnitrosourea, 5 mg/kg once a week intravenously, Death after 352 days.

65a, 67b). This result was confirmed by Thomas and co-workers (1967), and by Stroobandt and Brucher (1968), and in rabbits by Jänisch and Schreiber (1967).

Both compounds, methylnitrosourea and -urethane, after de-acylation yield the same "proximal carcinogen," namely, diazomethane and methyldiazonium. Therefore, the respective organospecific effects are to be attributed to the whole molecule as the "transport form." This has been shown also with other "indirect" carcinogens e.g. 1,2-dialkylhydrazines, azo- or azoxyalkanes, and 1-aryl-3,3-dialkyltriazenes. The striking difference in the organotropy of methylnitrosourea and -urethane furthermore leads to the conclusion that the activation cannot be due to a mere heterolysis, and that specific catalytic or enzymatic processes must be involved. Neurotropic effects have been likewise found with ethyl-, dimethyl- and trimethylnitrosourea, producing malignant neuroepithelial tumors of the brain, the spinal cord, and the peripheral nervous system (Ivankovic *et al.*, 1965). Corresponding biuret compounds were also active. Accordingly, the neurotropy depends on the urea group.

The histological findings were published by Thomas and Kersting (1964), and were recently reported in detail by Wechsler *et al.* (1969). Tumors of the brain or spinal cord were classified as iso- or pleomorphous oligodendrogliomas, astrocytomas, mixed gliomas, or medulloblastomas.

Ependymomas were relatively rare in these experiments with adult rats. In general, a high similarity to the corresponding tumors in man was established. Accordingly, the specific induction of malignant tumors of the brain and nervous system in experimental animals provides an useful model for further studies in neurooncological research.

Diazo Compounds

The results obtained with dialkylnitrosamines and acylalkylnitrosamides support the "alkylation theory" of their carcinogenic action. According to the formulas presented in FIGURE 1, the corresponding diazoalkanes and alkyldiazonium compounds probably may be considered "proximal carcinogens." With diazomethane, Schoental and Magee (1962) produced squamous carcinomas of the lung, the esophagus and the forestomach.

In our experiments, diazoacetic acid ethyl ester was used, which, by resonance of double bounds, is relatively stable and easier to handle. It is widely used in chemistry. Administration in the daily drinking water to rats produced carcinomas of the forestomach and occasionally on the base of the tongue (Druckrey *et al.*, 1963a). Surprisingly, no tumors of the esophagus were observed, although this organ is particularly susceptible to the carcinogenic action of N-nitroso compounds. This, however, is consistent with the fact that the reactivity of diazo compounds depends on acid conditions, which are present in the stomach. Accordingly, a direct and local effect is assumed.

In order to test the possibility of systemic effects, further experiments with repeated i.v. injections of diazoaceticethylester were conducted in rats. Twelve out of 15 animals developed squamous carcinomas and basaliomas of the skin (Druckrey *et al.*, 1965b). This organospecific effect is surprising, both because the skin of rats, in contrast with that of mice, is generally considered resistant to carcinogens, and because, on the other hand, it is a diazo compound that should act on every susceptible organ. As a probable explanation, it may be assumed that an enzymatic fission of the ester occurs in the skin. The diazoacetic acid then formed is extremely unstable and reactive. At least, this example shows that organospecific effects are possible even with diazo compounds.

In summary, all results obtained are consistent with the alkylation theory, as formulated by Magee and Barnes (1967) and by Druckrey *et al.* (1967b). The demonstration of the carcinogenicity of other compounds yielding alkyldiazonium, and particularly that of several direct alkylating substances such as alkylhalogenides, dialkylsulfates (Druckrey *et al.*, 1966d), or propane sultone (Druckrey *et al.*, 1968c) strongly support this theory. Many compounds of these groups have been shown to be potent mutagens (Pasternak, 1963; Marquardt *et al.*, 1964).

Prenatal Carcinogenesis

Extensive quantitative studies provided evidence that the primary carcinogenic effects are irreversible, and beyond this, grow on with time as an accelerated process to the eventual manifestation of cancer (Druckrey, 1967a). Accordingly, carcinogenesis by a single dose, even of short-living substances, was to be expected, and has been demonstrated in many examples by Magee and Barnes (1962), as well as by Druckrey and co-workers (1964d), particularly with the highly reactive methylnitrosourea. This knowledge made it possible to test the sensitivity to carcinogens during prenatal development. If their primary action, in fact, is based on reactions with genetic materials of somatic cells, a relatively high sensitivity should be expected in periods of great functional activity such as in embryonic or fetal development. At the same time, such studies promised to contribute to the elucidation of cancer in childhood, since, with regard to the long latent periods in carcinogenesis, origination in prenatal life must be considered.

The Production of Neurogenic Malignomas by Ethylnitrosourea

In children, cancer of the brain and nervous system is relatively frequent. For this reason we used the neurotropic ethylnitrosourea (ENU) in our first series of experiments. Pregnant BD IX-strain rats, on the fifteenth day of gestation, received one single i.v. injection of ENU in several dosage groups, ranging from 80 to 5 mg/kg body weight. The offspring have been carefully reared and observed over the whole lifespan. Practically all descendants later died of malignant neuroepithelial tumors of the brain, cranial nerves, spinal cord, and/or the peripheral nervous system (Ivankovic & co-workers, 1966, 1968; Druckrey *et al.*, 1966a, 67b). Up to now, more than 1,000 cases have been observed. For many histological diagnoses and for valuable information we are indebted to C. Thomas, K. J. Zülch, W. Wechsler and P. Kleihues. Histological pictures are not presented here because a detailed report, including the classification of the tumors, has been given by Wechsler *et al.* (1969).

Tumors of the brain were, for the most part, of considerable size, and occurred in both hemispheres and in the cerebellum (Figure 8). The vast majority of these tumors, however, were in the region of the ammons horns (hippocampus), often on both sides. On the other hand, not one tumor of the olfactory bulbs or nerves was found. This is remarkable, because such tumors can easily be produced in adult rats. Since the olfactory apparatus is not active during prenatal development, it is concluded that the sensitivity to the carcinogen depends on the functional activity, rather than on the size or the growth, of the respective organ.

The histological examinations of the brain tumors revealed oligodendrogliomas, astrocytomas, mixed gliomas, and a high proportion of ependymomas. This is of particular interest, because ependymomas are predominant in children and relatively rare in adults, as was also found in our experiments with rats.

In about a quarter of our cases we observed extensive tumors of the trigeminal nerve and the gasserian ganglion. Other cranial nerves were less affected, but some tumors of the vagus, facial, and in one case, of the hypoglossus have been found. The histological diagnoses were malignant neurinomas in all cases.

Tumors of the spinal cord occurred in all segments and were most often extended to considerable length. The histological pictures corresponded to those of the brain tumors.

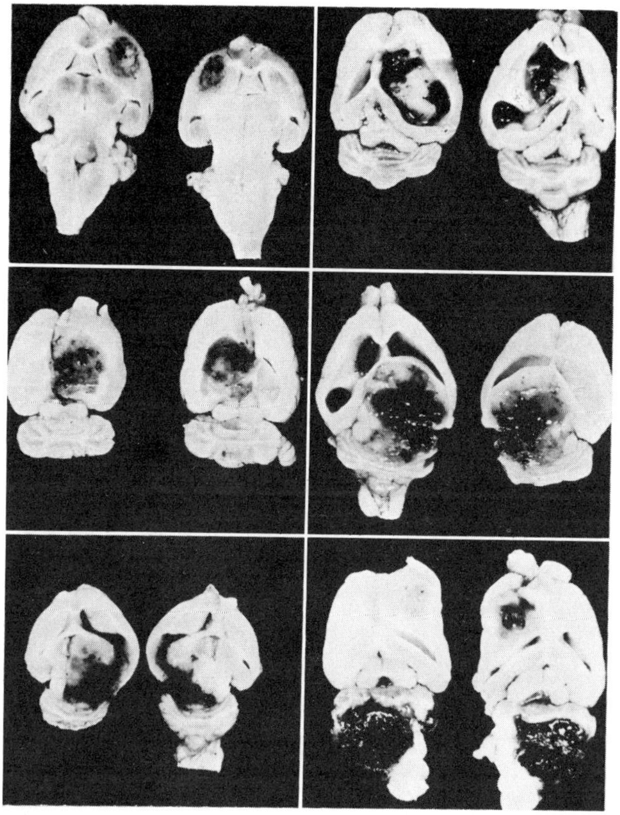

FIGURE 8. Prenatal carcinogenesis in rats. Brain tumors in descendants of rats treated on the fifteenth day of pregnancy with a single dose of ethylnitrosourea.

Malignant neurinomas of the peripheral nervous system were relatively frequent. They originated from the plexus brachiales or lumbosacrales, the sciatic or femoralis nerves, from motoric roots, and from the cauda equina. Most of them were of considerable size and were interspersed with hemorrhagic and serous cysts.

All tumors of the nervous system proved to be particularly malignant. Transplantations to other BD IX rats were regularly successful.

FIGURE 9 gives a synopsis of the length of the latent periods; i.e., the age at death of the individual rats in these experiments. Since the number of tumors is more than 820, each dot represents a group of five rats. A normal distribution is clearly recognizable with the tumors of the cranial nerves (mostly of the trigeminus), the peripheral nervous system, and the spinal cord. The brain tumors show a greater deviation, corresponding to the heterogenicity of this organ. Naturally, the time of death depended on the localization of the respective tumor.

Most rats died at the young age of 150–250 days. But in many cases the tumors, particularly those of the brain, developed only after 300–600 days. This shows that neurogenic tumors not only in "childhood" but also at a higher age level can be caused during prenatal development. Our results lead to a new interpretation of the Cohnheim-Ribbert theory. The essential point, however, is that the process is initiated by a very potent carcinogen.

The dose-response relationships are presented in FIGURE 10, comprising 205 rats with neurogenic malignomas, induced on the 15th day of prenatal development by a single dose of ethylnitrosourea. A clear normal distribution was obtained. Even 5 mg/kg (2% of the LD 50) still produced malignant tumors of the nervous system in 25 out of 40 descendants (63%). Accordingly, positive results were to be expected with smaller doses, and were observed. FIGURE 11 shows a malignant ependymoma of the brain in a descendant after 2 mg/kg was given on the fifteenth day of pregnancy.

For comparison, ENU has been tested in adult rats. Here a dose of 160 mg/kg was needed for a 50% yield of neurogenic malignancies, as shown in FIGURE 10. From this it follows that the sensitivity of the nervous system to the carcinogenic effect of ENU during prenatal development is about fiftyfold higher than in adults. Accordingly, special care must be given for the protection of females during the reproductive age. The results were confirmed in 10 different strains of BD-rats

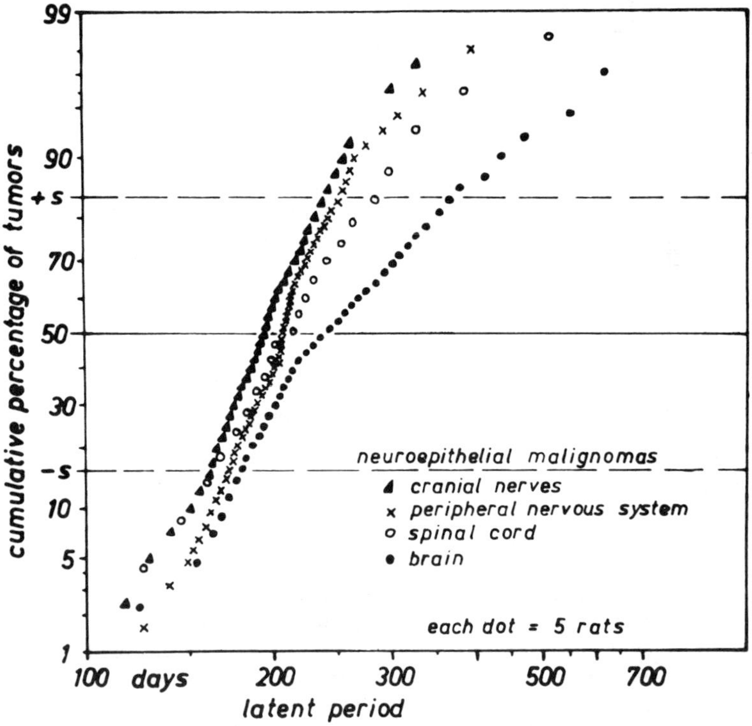

FIGURE 9. Latent periods till development of neurogenic malignomas in the progeny of rats treated on the fifteenth day of pregnancy with a single dose of ethylnitrosourea (827 cases).

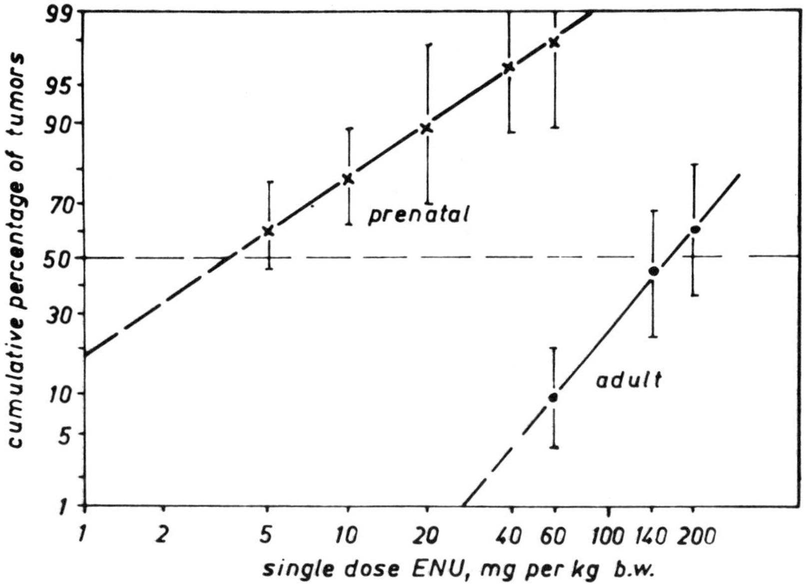

FIGURE 10. Dose-response relationships for the prenatal induction of malignant tumors of the nervous system as compared with that in adult rats. Single dose of ethylnitrosourea (205 and 106 rats, respectively).

(working with Christoph Landschütz), as well as with oral administration in rats and golden hamsters. Unfortunately, experiments with higher mammals, especially primates, are not possible for us. They can be performed easily, however, since all methodical details are now well known.

In order to test the sensitivity in the various phases of prenatal development, pregnant rats were treated with one single dose of ENU on each individual day of pregnancy, from the first to the last. The highest yield of neurogenic malignancies in the progeny was observed when ENU was given between the eighteenth day and shortly before birth, as shown in FIGURE 12. After treatment at that time with 5 mg/kg, all descendants, died of malignant tumors of the brain, the trigeminal nerve (FIGURE 13), the spinal cord, and the peripheral nervous system, respectively (FIGURE 14). Experiments with lower doses are under way.

When given before the twelfth day of pregnancy, ENU, even at a dose of 60 mg/kg, did not, surprisingly, produce any tumors in the offspring (FIGURE 12). This negative result cannot be due to an inability of the embryonic nervous system for tumor formation, since gliomas of the brain have been observed in the progeny of rats treated with cycas meal on days 2–5 of pregnancy, as reported by Spatz and Laqueur (1967). Therefore, we assume that the activation of ENU to the "ultimate" carcinogen occurs in rats only after the twelfth day of prenatal development. The striking neurotropism of alkylnitrosourea compounds had already indicated the importance of catalytic or enzymatic processes. The nature of these is still unknown.

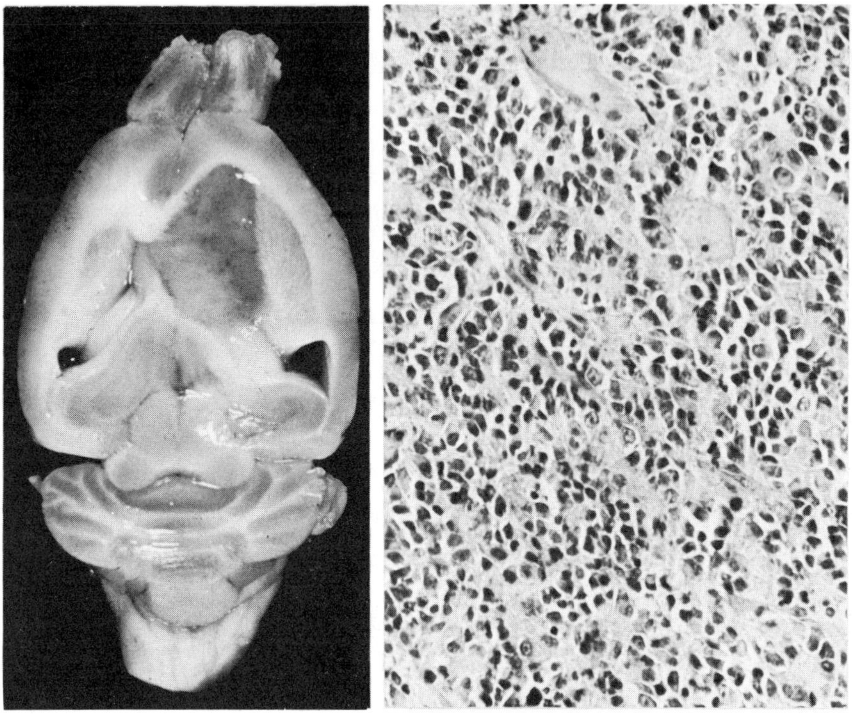

FIGURE 11. Malignant ependymoma of the brain in the descendant of a rat treated on the fifteenth day of pregnancy by a single dose of 2 mg ethylnitrosourea/kg body weight (0.8 percent of the LD 50).

Dialkylnitrosamines and Related Compounds

For comparison, several dialkylnitrosamines were tested in prenatal carcinogenesis. When given on the fifteenth day of pregnancy to rats, diethyl-, ethylvinyl-, methylbutylnitrosamine and N-nitrosopiperidine, even with 25% of the LD 50, completely failed to produce any cancer in the offspring. The negative outcome of these experiments is of special interest, because it indicates that the preactivated intermediates formed in the maternal organism are by far too unstable and short-lived to reach the fetus. Furthermore, it shows that the enzymatic system, necessary for the activation of dialkylnitrosamines, is not present in the fetus at that time. When given on the last (twenty-third) day of gestation, however, cancer of the kidney and liver has been observed in some descendants. Accordingly, the enzymatic system occasionally can develop shortly before birth, particularly in the kidneys (Lee & Spencer, 1964). The few positive cases—two and seven nephroblastomas, respectively, out of 186 descendants—reported by Pielsticker and co-workers (1967), Wrba *et al.* (1967), and Alexandrov (1968) may be similarly explained. In these experiments, the negative result in 95–99% of the animals certainly is more impressive. The strong carcinogenicity of dialkylnitrosamines in rats occurs only after birth.

Corresponding results have been obtained with 1-aryl-3,3-dimethyltriazenes, potent neurotropic carcinogens (Druckrey *et al.*, 1967a). Its activation again results from enzymatic oxidative demethylation, and eventually yields methyldiazonium, as shown by Preussmann. When given to rats on the fifteenth day of pregnancy, no tumors occurred in the offspring. After administration on the twenty-third day, however, the descendants died of malignant tumors of the nervous system. This again shows the dependence of the action of "indirect" carcinogens on the period of prenatal development.

Interesting results have been obtained with hydrazo-, azo-, and azoxyalkanes. 1,2-Dimethylhydrazine, as well as azoxymethane, powerful carcinogens in adult rats (Druckrey *et al.*, 1967c) were completely negative in prenatal carcinogenesis. Since the methylazoxymethanol glycoside cycasin has been shown to be active by Spatz and Laqueur (1967), it follows that the αC-hydroxylation is the decisive step in its activation to the proximal carcinogen. In contrast with the negative results with the methyl compounds, 1,2-diethylhydrazine, as well as azo- and azoxyethane, when given in very small doses on the fifteenth day of pregnancy, even by inhalation, induced malignant neuroepithelial tumors of the brain, cranial nerves, spinal cord, and the peripheral nervous system in almost all descendants (Druckrey *et al.*, 1968b). This striking difference indicates that the metabolic activation of the methyl and ethyl compounds is completely different, although an αC-hydroxylation probably is involved in both groups. Accordingly, prenatal carcinogenesis can be a useful model for the study of metabolic activation processcs, particularly at the time of their appearance in the ontological development.

The adult rats treated during pregnancy developed neurogenic malignomas in

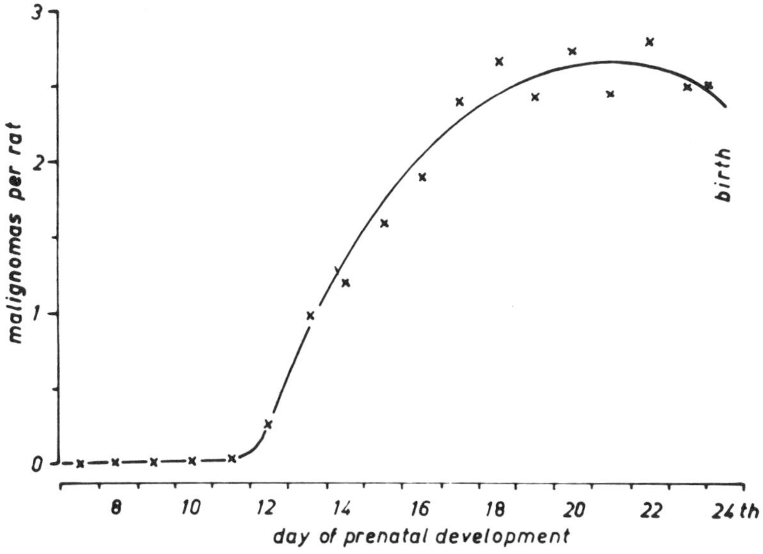

FIGURE 12. Sensitivity of rat-fetus to the carcinogen ethylnitrosourea on the individual days of prenatal development. Ordinate: average number of malignant tumors of the nervous system/rat. Single dose of 60 mg/kg injected intravenously on the respective days of pregnancy (445 rats).

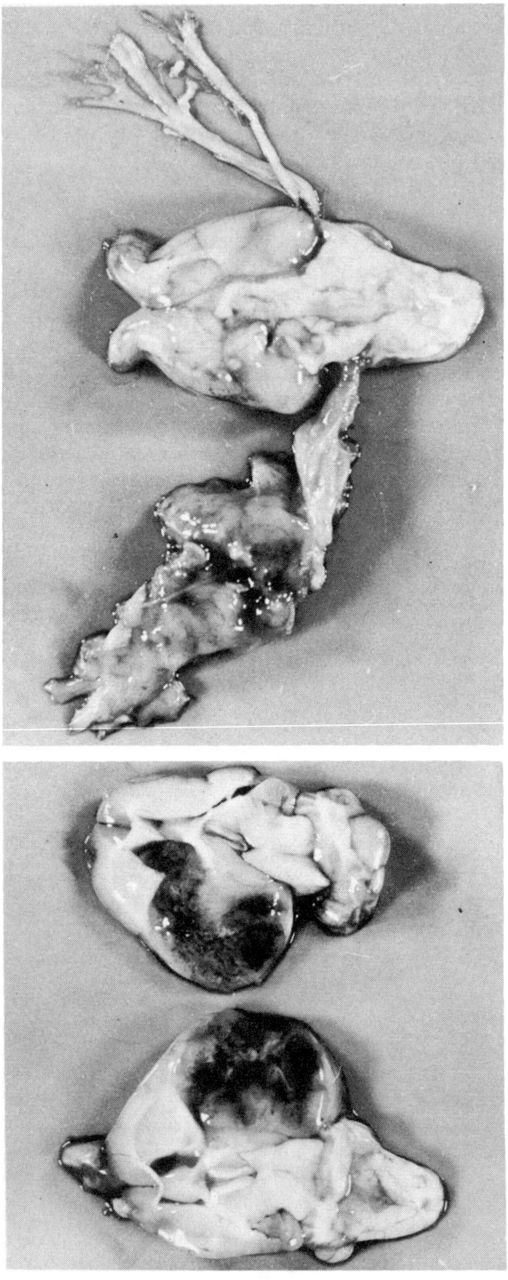

FIGURE 13. Neurogenic malignomas in descendants of rats treated on the twenty-third day of pregnancy with a single dose of 5 mg ethylnitrosourea/kg body weight.
Left: malignant ependymoma of the brain.
Right: malignant neurinoma of the trigeminal nerve.

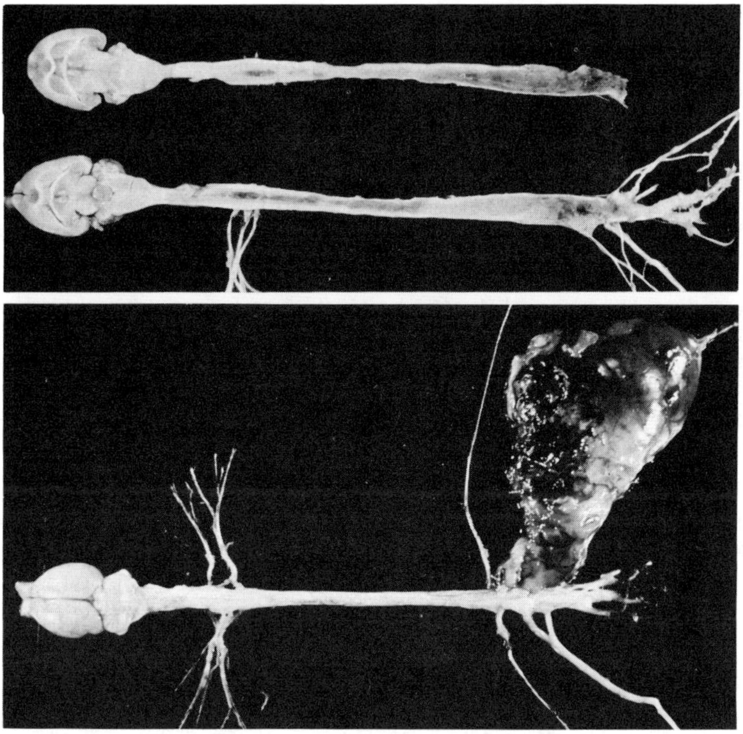

FIGURE 14. Neurogenic malignomas in descendants of rats treated on the twenty-third day of pregnancy with a single dose of 5 mg ethylnitrosourea/kilogram.
Above: malignant ependymoma of the spinal cord.
Below: malignant neurinoma of the right plexus lumbosacralis and the sciatic nerve.

only a few cases, and this only after a very high dose. The sensitivity of the adult nervous system to ENU and to the other carcinogens used is very much lower than in the fetus, as previously shown. About 50% of them, however, died later of clear-cell carcinomas of the ovaries. Since ovarian cancer never could be produced by any carcinogen with this regularity in nonpregnant rats, the sensitivity to carcinogenic changes apparently depends in high degree upon the functional activity. This has to be taken into account when organotropic effects are considered.

SUMMARY

About 70 N-nitroso compounds were tested for carcinogenic activity, mainly in rats and guinea pigs. Striking organospecific effects, dependent on chemical structure, were reported. Symmetrical dialkylnitrosamines produced liver cancer after continuous oral administration, and mostly nephroblastomas after single doses. When injected subcutaneously, di-n-butylnitrosamine proved to be a carcinogen specific to the urinary bladder, and diamylnitrosamine to the lungs. The unsymmetrical methylalkylnitrosamines selectively produced carcinomas of the esophagus independently of the route of administration, even after inhalation. Cyclic N-nitroso compounds led to cancer of the nasal cavity, mainly neuroblastomas of the olfactory nerves.

Acylalkylnitrosamides, after oral administration, produced cancer of the forestomach in rats, and adenocarcinomas of the glandular stomach and the pancreas in guinea pigs. Intravenous injection revealed striking organotropic effects. Methylnitrosourethane produced carcinomas of the lungs, in contrast to alkylnitrosourea compounds, which selectively led to malignant tumors of the brain and nervous system.

In transplacentar experiments, ethylnitrosourea, even in low doses, induced highly malignant neuroepithelial tumors of the brain, cranial nerves, spinal cord, and the peripheral nervous system, respectively, in almost all descendants. More than 1,000 cases were reported. The yield was highest when ENU was given on the last days of pregnancy, and zero before the twelfth day. After birth, the sensitivity of the nervous system decreased rapidly, and was 50 times higher in fetus than in adults. Dialkylnitrosamines, when given on the fifteenth day of pregnancy, were not carcinogenic to the offspring.

The mechanisms of action and some relationships to cancer prevention were discussed. All tumors observed showed striking similarity to the corresponding human tumors both in gross appearance and histologically.

References

1. Alexandrov, V. A. 1968. Blastomogenic effect of dimethylnitrosamine on pregnant rats and their offspring. Nature (London) **218:** 280–281.
2. Argus, M. F. & C. Hoch-Ligeti. 1963. Induction of malignant tumors in the guinea pig by oral administration of diethylnitrosamine. J. Nat. Cancer Inst. **30:** 533.
3. Boyland, E., F. J. C. Roe, J. W. Gorrod & B. C. V. Mitchley. 1964. The carcinogenicity of nitrosoanabasine, a possible constituent of tobacco smoke. Brit. J. Cancer **18:** 265–270.
4. Brock, N. & W. Wilk. 1961. Zur Ernährung der Laboratoriumstiere. 1. Altromin. Arzneimittelforschung **11:** 1071–1086.
5. Brodie, B. B., J. R. Gilette & B. N. Ladu. 1958. Enzymatic metabolism of drugs and other foreign compounds. Ann. Rev. Biochem. **27:** 427–454.
6. Druckrey, H. 1967. Quantitative aspects in chemical carcinogenesis. In Potential Carcinogenic Hazards from Drugs. UICC Monograph Series **7:** 60–77.
7. Druckrey, H., P. Danneberg, W. Dischler & D. Steinhoff. 1962a. Reinzucht von 10 Rattenstämmen (BD-Stämme) and Analyse des genetischen Pigmentierungssystems. Arzneimittelforschung **12:** 911–919.
8. Druckrey, H., S. Ivankovic, J. Bücheler &. R. Preussmann. 1968a. Erzeugung von Magen- und Pankreas-Krebs beim Meerschweinchen durch Methylnitrosoharnstoff und -urethan. Z. Krebsforsch. **72:** 167–182.
9. Druckrey, H., S. Ivankovic, H. D. Mennel & R. Preussmann. 1964a. Selektive Erzeugung von Carcinomen der Nasenhöhle bei Ratten durch N,N-Di-Nitrosopiperazin, Nitrosopiperidin, Nitrosomorpholin, Methyl-allyl-,Dimethyl- und Methylvinyl-nitrosamin. Z. Krebsforsch. **66:** 138–150.
10. Druckrey, H., S. Ivankovic & R. Preussmann. 1964b. Selektive Erzeugung von Hirntumoren bei Ratten durch Methylnitrosoharnstoff. Naturwissenschaften **51:** 144.
11. Druckrey, H., S. Ivankovic & R. Preussmann. 1965a. Selektive Erzeugung maligner Tumoren im Gehirn und Rückenmark von Ratten durch N-Methyl-N-nitroso-harnstoff. Z. Krebsforsch. **66:** 389–408.

12. DRUCKREY, H., S. IVANKOVIC & R. PREUSSMANN. 1966a. Teratogenic and carcinogenic effects in the offspring after single injection of ethyl-nitroso-urea to pregnant rats. Nature (London) **210:** 1378–1379.
13. DRUCKREY, H., S. IVANKOVIC & R. PREUSSMANN. 1967a. Neurotrope carcinogene Wirkung von Phenyl-dimethyl-triazen an Ratten. Naturwissenschaften **54:** 171.
14. DRUCKREY, H., S. IVANKOVIC, R. PREUSSMANN, C. LANDSCHÜTZ, J. STEKAR, U. BRUNNER & B. SCHAGEN. 1968b. Transplacentar induction of neurogenic malignomas by 1,2-diethyl-hydrazine, azo- and azoxy-ethane in rats. Experientia **24:** 561–562.
15. DRUCKREY, H., S. IVANKOVIC & B. T. SO. 1965b. Erzeugung von Carcinomen der Haut bei Ratten durch intravenose Injektion von Diazoessigester. Z. Krebsforsch. **66:** 523–525.
16. DRUCKREY, H., H. KRUSE & R. PREUSSMANN. 1968c. Propansultone, a potent carcinogen. Naturwissenschaften **55:** 449.
17. DRUCKREY, H., C. LANDSCHÜTZ & R. PREUSSMANN. 1968d. Oesophagus-Carcinome nach Inhalation von Methyl-butyl-nitrosamin (MBNA) an Ratten. Z. Krebsforsch. **71:** 135–139.
18. DRUCKREY, H. & R. PREUSSMANN. 1962a. Erzeugung von Lungenkrebs durch subcutane Injektion von N,N-Diamylnitrosamin an Ratten. Naturwissenschaften **49:** 111–112.
19. DRUCKREY, H. & R. PREUSSMANN. 1962b. N-Nitroso-N-methyl-urethane, a potent carcinogen. Nature (London) **195:** 1111.
20. DRUCKREY, H., R. PREUSSMANN, J. AFKHAM & G. BLUM. 1962b. Erzeugung von Lungenkrebs durch Methylnitrosourethan bei intravenöser Gabe an Ratten. Naturwissenschaften **49:** 451.
21. DRUCKREY, H., R. PREUSSMANN, G. BLUM & S. IVANKOVIC. 1963a. Carcinogene Wirkung von Diazoessigester und von N-Nitroso-Sarkosinester. Naturwissenschaften **50:** 99–101.
22. DRUCKREY, H., R. PREUSSMANN, G. BLUM, S. IVANKOVIC & J. AFKHAM. 1963b. Erzeugung von Karzinomen der Speiseröhre durch unsymmetrische Nitrosamine. Naturwissenschaften **50:** 100–101.
23. DRUCKREY, H., R. PREUSSMANN, S. IVANKOVIC & D. SCHMÄHL. 1967b. Organotrope carcinogene Wirkungen bei 65 verschiedenen N-Nitroso-Verbindungen an BD-Ratten. Z. Krebsforsch. **69:** 103–201.
24. DRUCKREY, H., R. PREUSSMANN, S. IVANKOVIC, C. H. SCHMIDT, H. D. MENNEL & K. W. STAHL. 1964c. Selektive Erzeugung von Blasenkrebs an Ratten durch Dibutyl- und N-Butyl-N-butanol (4)-nitrosamin. Z. Krebsforsch. **66:** 280–290.
25. DRUCKREY, H., R. PREUSSMANN, S. IVANKOVIC, B. T. SO, C. H. SCHMIDT & J. BÜCHELER. 1966b. Zur Erzeugung subcutaner Sarkome an Ratten. Z. Krebsforsch. **68:** 87–102.
26. DRUCKREY, H., R. PREUSSMANN, F. MATZKIES & S. IVANKOVIC. 1966c. Carcinogene Wirkung von 1,2-Diäthylhydrazin an Ratten. Naturwissenschaften **53:** 557–558.
27. DRUCKREY, H., R. PREUSSMANN, F. MATZKIES & S. IVANKOVIC. 1967c. Selektive Erzeugung von Darmkrebs bei Ratten durch 1,2-Dimethyl-hydrazin. Naturwissenschaften **54:** 285–286.
28. DRUCKREY, H., R. PREUSSMANN, N. NASHED & S. IVANKOVIC. 1966d. Carcinogene alkylierende Substanzen. I. Dimethylsulfat. Carcinogene Wirkung an Ratten und wahrscheinliche Ursache von Berufskrebs. Z. Krebsforsch. **68:** 103–111.
29. DRUCKREY, H., R. PREUSSMANN & D. SCHMÄHL. 1963c. Carcinogenicity and chemical structure of nitrosamines. Acta Un. Int. Cancr. **19:** 510–512.
30. DRUCKREY, H., R. PREUSSMANN, D. SCHMÄHL & M. MÜLLER. 1961a. Chemische Konstitution und carcinogene Wirkung bei Nitrosaminen. Naturwissenschaften **48:** 134.
31. DRUCKREY, H., R. PREUSSMANN, D. SCHMÄHL & M. MÜLLER. 1961b. Erzeugung von Magenkrebs durch Nitrosamide an Ratten. Naturwissenschaften **48:** 165.
32. DRUCKREY, H., A. SCHILDBACH, D. SCHMÄHL, R. PREUSSMANN & S. IVANKOVIC. 1963d. Quantitative Analyse der carcinogenen Wirkung von Diäthylnitrosamin.

Arzneimittelforschung. **13:** 841–851.
33. DRUCKREY, H. & D. STEINHOFF. 1962. Erzeugung von Leberkrebs an Meerschweinchen. Naturwissenschaften **49:**497–498.
34. DRUCKREY, H., D. STEINHOFF, R. PREUSSMANN & S. IVANKOVIC. 1964d. Erzeugung von Krebs durch eine einmalige Dosis von Methyl-nitroso-harnstoff und verschiedenen Dialkylnitrosaminen an Ratten. Z. Krebsforsch. **66:** 1–10.
35. DUTTON, A. H. & D. F. HEATH. 1956. Demethylation of dimethylnitrosamine in rats and mice. Nature (London) **178:** 644.
36. GRAFFI, A. & F. HOFFMANN. 1966. Starke cancerogene Wirkung von N-Methyl-N-nitroso-harnstoff auf die Hamster- und Rattenhaut im Tropfungsversuch. Arch. Geschwulstforsch. **28:** 234–248.
37. GRAFFI, A. F. HOFFMANN & M. SCHÜTT. 1967. N-Methyl-N-nitrosourea as a strong topical carcinogen when painted on skin of rodents. Nature (London) **214:** 611.
38. HERROLD, K. M. D. 1964. Induction of olfactory neuroepithelial tumors in Syrian hamsters by diethylnitrosamine. Cancer **17:** 114–121.
39. HERROLD, K. M. D. 1966. Epidermoid carcinomas of esophagus and forestomach induced in Syrian hamsters by N-Nitroso-N-methyl-urethane. J. Nat. Cancer Inst. **37:** 389–392.
40. IVANKOVIC, S. & H. DRUCKREY. 1968. Transplacentare Erzeugung maligner Tumoren des Nervensystems. I. Aethyl-nitroso-harnstoff an BD IX-Ratten. Z. Krebsforsch. **71:** 320–360.
41. IVANKOVIC, S., H. DRUCKREY & R. PREUSSMANN. 1965. Erzeugung von Tumoren im peripheren und zentralen Nervensystem durch Trimethyl-nitroso-harnstoff an Ratten. Z. Krebsforsch. **66:** 541–548.
42. IVANKOVIC, S., H. DRUCKREY & R. PREUSSMANN. 1966. Erzeugung neurogener Tumoren bei den Nachkommen nach einmaliger Injektion von Äthylnitrosoharnstoff an schwangere Ratten. Naturwissenschaften **53:** 410.
43. JÄNISCH, W. & D. SCHREIBER. 1967. Experimentelle Hirngeschwülste bei Kaninchen nach Injektion von Methylnitrosoharnstoff. Naturwissenschaften **54:** 171–172.
44. LEE, K. G. & K. SPENCER. 1964. Methylation of liver and kidney ribonucleic acids in newborn rats. J. Nat. Cancer Inst. **33:** 957–961.
45. MAGEE, P. N. & J. M. BARNES. 1956. The production of malignant primary hepatic tumours in the rat by feeding dimethylnitrosamine. Brit. J. Cancer **10:** 114–122.
46. MAGEE, P. N. & J. M. BARNES. 1962. Induction of kidney tumours in the rat with dimethylnitrosamine. J. Path. & Bact. **84:** 19.
47. MAGEE, P. N. & J. M. BARNES. 1967. Carcinogenic nitroso-compounds. Advances Cancer Res. **10:** 164–246.
48. MCMAHON, R. E. 1966. Microsomal dealkylation of drugs. J. Pharm. Sci. **55:** 457.
49. MARQUARDT, H., F. K. ZIMMERMANN & R. SCHWAIER. 1964. Die Wirkung krebsauslösender Nitrosamine und Nitrosamide auf das Adenin-6-45 Rückmutationssystem von Saccharomyc.cer. Z. Vererbungsl. **95:** 82–96.
50. PASTERNAK, L. 1963. Untersuchungen über die mutagene Wirkung von Nitrosaminen und Nitrosomethylharnstoff. Acta Biol. Med. Germ. **10:** 436–438.
51. PIELSTICKER, K., O. WIESER, U. MOHR & H. WRBA. 1967. Diaplacentar induzierte Nierentumoren bei der Ratte. Z. Krebsforsch. **69:** 345–350.
52. PREUSSMANN, R., H. DRUCKREY & J. BÜCHELER. 1968. Carcinogene Wirkung von Phenyl-nitroso-harnstoff. Z. Krebsforsch. **71:** 63–65.
53. SCHMÄHL, D., R. PREUSSMANN & H. HAMPERL. 1960. Leberkrebs erzeugende Wirkung von Diaethylnitrosamin nach oraler Aabe bei Ratten. Naturwissenschaften **47:** 89.
54. SCHOENTAL, R. 1963. Induction of tumours of the stomach in rats and mice by N-nitroso-N-alkylurethanes. Nature (London) **199:** 190.
55. SCHOENTAL, R. & P. N. MAGEE. 1962. Induction of squamous carcinoma of the lung and of stomach and oesophagus by diazomethane and N-methyl-N-nitroso-urethane respectively. Brit. J. Cancer **16:** 92–100.
56. SPATZ, M. & G. L. LAQUEUR. 1967. Transplacental induction of tumors in Sprague

Dawley rats with crude cycad material. J. Nat. Cancer Inst. **38:** 233–239.

57. STROOBANDT, G. & J. M. BRUCHER. 1968. Etude de tumeurs nerveuses obtenues par l'administration de méthylnitrosourée au rat. Neurochirurgie **14:** 515–535.
58. THOMAS, C. & G. KERSTING. 1964. Zur Morphologie der durch Methyl-nitrosoharnstoff erzeugten Hirntumoren. Naturwissenschaften **51:** 144–145.
59. THOMAS, C., J. L. SIERRA & G. KERSTING. 1967. Hirntumoren bei Ratten nach oraler Gabe von N-nitroso-N-methyl-harnstoff. Naturwissenschaft **54:** 228.
60. VESSELINOVITCH, S. D., N. MIHAILOVIC & G. PIETRA. 1967. The prenatal exposure of mice to urethan and the consequent development of tumors in various tissues. Cancer Res. **27:** 2333–2337.
61. WECHSLER, W., P. KLEIHUES, S. MATSUMOTO, K. J. ZULCH, S. IVANKOVIC, R. PREUSSMANN & H. DRUCKREY. 1969. Pathology of experimental neurogenic tumors chemically induced during prenatal and postnatal life. Ann. New York Acad. Sci. (In press).
62. WEISBURGER, J. H., E. K. WEISBURGER, N. MANTEL, Z. HADIDIAN & T. FREDRICKSON. 1966. New carcinogenic nitrosamines in rats. Naturwissenschaften **53:** 508.
63. WRBA, H., K. PIELSTICKER & U. MOHR. 1967. Die diaplacentarcarcinogene Wirkung von Diaethylnitrosamin bei Ratten. Naturwissenschaften **54:** 47.

DISCUSSION OF THE PAPER

J. A. DIPAOLO (*National Cancer Institute, NIH, Bethesda, Md.*): You are probably aware that ethylnitrosourea has two teratogenic responses: brain malformation, reaching a maximum at nine days, and malformation of extremities around 13 days. I wonder if you could tell us something about the embryotoxicity as a result of treating animals at the period prior to the time we see manifestation of cancer, postnatally. In other words, during the 12 days of treatment, is the litter size decreased, or do you lose newborn animals, the ones that might have been at risk?

DR. DRUCKREY: I hope that I have understood you correctly. You are referring to embryotoxic and teratogenic effects. Surprisingly enough, we did not find a close relationship between teratogenicity and carcinogenicity. There are compounds that are very potent carcinogens in transplacental experiments and not teratogenic at all, and there are others that are teratogenic and not carcinogenic. Secondly, as you know, the teratogenic effects depend very much on the period of prenatal development. We tested all the compounds we have at comparable periods, and we found great differences, and again also in organotropic effects. The teratogenic effect in contrast to the carcinogenic effects is absolutely dependent upon the dosage given; the carcinogenic effect is not. This means that in order to get the teratogenic effect, you should give the highest possible concentration in one dose and not scatter this over many individual doses. In carcinogenesis, it does not matter whether you give a certain dose as a single treatment or a number of treatments. To give you an example: ethylnitrosourea, at the level of 60 mg per kg body weight, given to pregnant rats between the 12th and, approximately, 15th day of pregnancy, will produce malformations in 65% to 70% of the descendants. But when you divide this in repeated doses of 2.0 mg per kg each, given in intervals of 12 hr during the sensitive period, you will get no teratogenic effects at all.

DR. DIPAOLO: I was really asking what happens to the animals that were injected with ethylnitrosourea on the 12th day, when you say there would be a visible teratogenic effect. I am trying to determine how many of these groups would be left to be born prior to the time that you would see a carcinogenic effect?

DR. DRUCKREY: This depends, of course, upon the dose. With low doses, you get a 100% survival rate. You have practically normal survival time, and the malignant tumors of the nervous system develop mostly at the age between 150 and 250 days.

DR. DIPAOLO: In reference to transplacental carcinogenesis, would you comment on two things that may be relevant? Is there any evidence for the postnatal fetus' developing tumors if, instead of dosing the female, one doses the male before mating? Secondly, is there evidence for development of these tumors in the offspring if the embryos are removed from the mother and wombed by another mother?

DR. DRUCKREY: We did not do this, since the ethylnitrosourea is a very short-lived substance, persisting *in vivo,* at most, several hours. On the 15th day of pregnancy, we can be absolutely sure that the effect happens at that time, and it would not matter whether you get foster mothers to deliver the fetus.

CHEMICAL STRUCTURE AND CARCINOGENICITY OF ALIPHATIC HYDRAZO, AZO, AND AZOXY COMPOUNDS AND OF TRIAZENES, POTENTIAL *IN VIVO* ALKYLATING AGENTS*

R. Preussmann, H. Druckrey,
S. Ivankovic, and A. v. Hodenberg

Forschergruppe Praeventivmedizin
Freiburg, Germany

After having come to a certain end in our extensive studies on the carcinogenicity of organic N-nitroso compounds,[1] of which H. Druckrey gives an account in this monograph, we decided to continue and extend this work by the investigation of related groups of compounds. The search for new types of chemical carcinogens is important, since the successful prevention of cancer necessitates that all possible causes be known. The rationale was to look for compounds that are not active *per se,* but that might be activated *in vivo* by metabolic processes to form an alkylating agent as the proximate and ultimate carcinogen.

A similar biochemical reaction mechanism is very probable for carcinogenic nitrosamines, as has been shown mainly by the outstanding work of P. N. Magee and his colleagues,[2] of which he will give an account. I shall report here on our work on the carcinogenicity to experimental animals of two new classes of compounds: Aliphatic hydrazo, azo, and azoxy compounds, and aryl dialkyltriazenes, their structure-activity relationships and their possible mode of action.

Hydrazo, Azo, and Azoxyalkanes

Azoxyalkanes are structural isomers of nitrosamines, as shown in the following example:

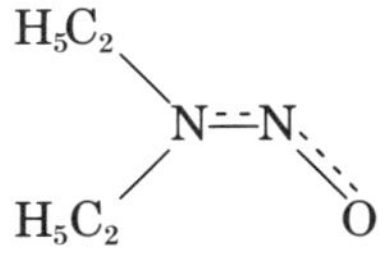

Diethylnitrosamine
$C_4H_{10}N_2O$

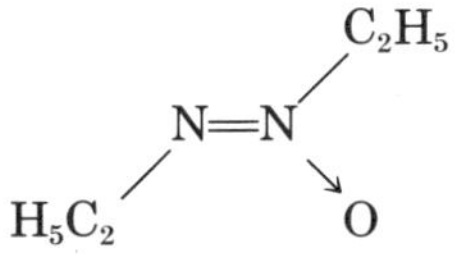

Azoxyethane
$C_4H_{10}N_2O$

However, not only azoxyalkanes seemed to be of interest as potential carcinogens, but also the corresponding azoalkanes, alkyl-N=N-alkyl, and hydrazoalkanes, alkyl-NH-NH-alkyl; hydrazoalkanes (1,2-dialkylhydrazines) are easily oxidizable to form the corresponding azo compounds. This oxidation is catalyzed by traces of heavy metals that also occur in the organism. Azoalkanes are quite reactive and are known to go easily into radical reactions. They also might be

* Supported by the Deutsche Forschungsgemeinschaft.

oxidized *in vivo* by microsomal N-oxidase, for example, to form azoxy compounds.

Some naturally occurring azoxyalkanes are known. The most important is cycasine, i.e., methylazoxymethanol-glucoside. It is the toxic component of several cycad plants widely distributed in the tropics and subtropics. It has been found to be carcinogenic in experimental animals.[3,4] Since Dr. Spatz will write on this subject, I shall say only that these results confirmed to us the importance of basic research in this group of compounds. 1,2-Disubstituted hydrazines have been tested as drugs; the most prominent example is procarbazine, N-isopropyl-(2-methyl-hydrazino)-p-toluamide, a recent cancer chemotherapeutic agent, which has recently been shown to have mutagenic[5] and carcinogenic[6] activity. Therefore, examination for carcinogenic activity in this group of compounds has not only scientific interest, but also practical importance for preventive medicine.

Structure-Carcinogenicity Relationship

Carcinogenicity experiments were performed with inbred strains of BD rats.[7] For chronic oral administration, compounds were either given daily in the drinking water or once a week by stomach tube. Subcutaneous (s.c.) injections of aqueous or oily solutions of the test compound were given once a week under the dorsal skin.

The methyl derivatives, 1, 2-dimethylhydrazine and azoxymethane (the gaseous azomethane has not been investigated), on repeated oral as well as s.c. application, produced selectively and in high yield malignant adenocarcinoma of the colon and rectum[8] (FIGURES 1 & 2). The specificity of action is absolutely identical for both compounds and for both methods of administration. In addition to the highly specific induction of intestinal carcinoma, we have seen some hemangioendothelioma of the liver and cystic degeneration of that organ after oral application. No local tumors at the site of administration have been observed after s.c. dosage, showing that both compounds are typical "indirect," resorptive carcino-

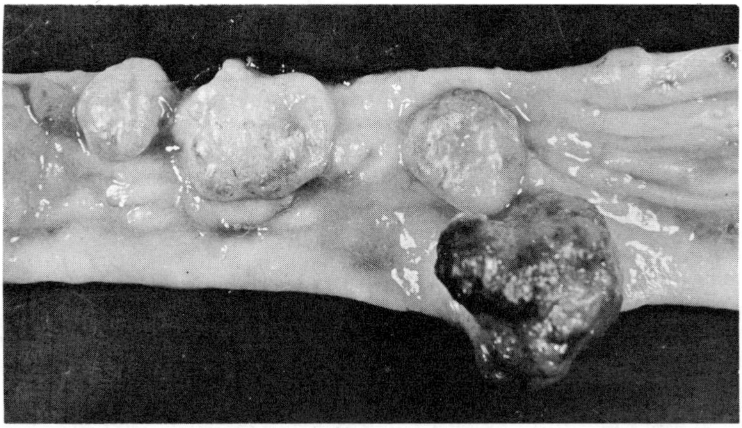

FIGURE 1. Adenocarcinoma of the colon after subcutaneous administration of 1,2-dimethylhydrazine.

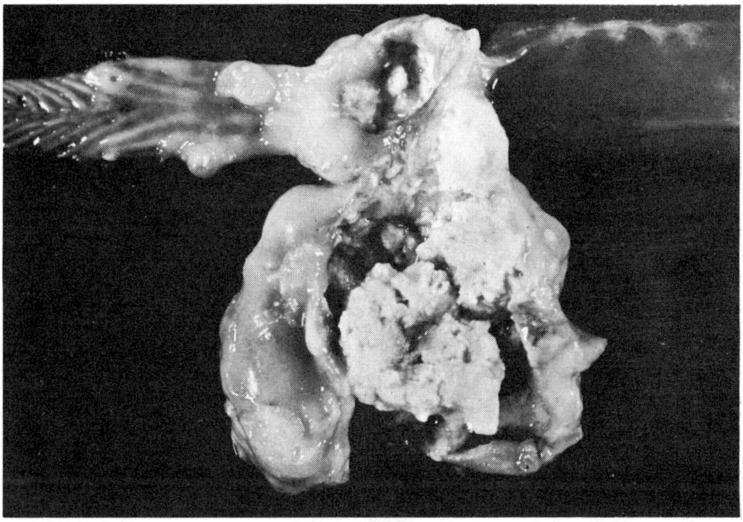

FIGURE 2. Adenocarcinoma of the rectum after oral administration of azoxymethane.

gens. The potent carcinogenic activity is further demonstrated by the induction of malignant carcinoma in single-dose experiments. Cycasine, also an azoxymethane derivative, has been shown to possess the same organ-specific activity,[4] which therefore is characteristic of methyl derivatives of hydrazo and azoxy compounds. The simple and regular induction of malignant intestinal tumors, at least in the rat, has become possible, according to these results.

On the other hand, the ınree ethyl compounds hydrazo-, azo-, and azoxyethane showed a totally different organ-specific multipotential carcinogenic activity.[9,10] With these three compounds we have never observed intestinal tumors, but regularly have seen neuroestesioepithelioma of the olfactory bulb, malignant brain tumors, mammary carcinoma, liver tumors, and leukemias on repeated s.c. as well as oral administration, as shown in FIGURE 3. Azoethane, a very volatile compound, is also carcinogenic after inhalation. Again, the tumor spectrum was identical with all three compounds, and again, no local tumors at the site of s.c. injection have been found. Again, single dose experiments were positive, demonstrating the potent carcinogenic activity of this class of compounds.

Certain isopropyl and n-butyl derivatives in this class were practically negative or only very weakly positive as carcinogens, but some of the experiments are not yet completed.

On the other hand, two hydrazoalkanes with different alkyl groups on the two hydrazine nitrogens, 1-methyl-2-n-butylhydrazine and 1-methyl-2-benzylhydrazine, could be shown to be potent carcinogens producing, interestingly enough, intestinal tumors as well as neurogenic carcinoma (FIGURES 4 & 5). Here, evidently the organotropic activities of the methyl derivatives (intestinal tumors), as well as those of the ethyl compounds (mainly neurogenic tumors), are combined in one molecule.

The astonishing difference in organ-specific activity between methyl and

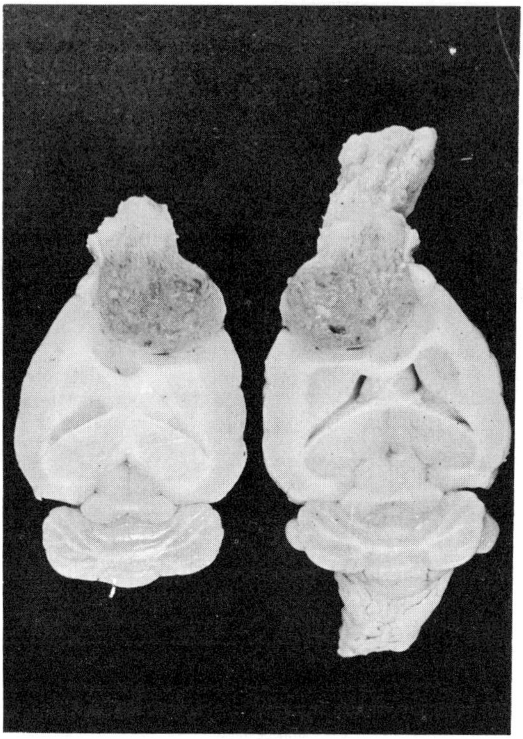

FIGURE 3. Neuroestesioepithelioma of the olfactory bulb after azoethane inhalation.

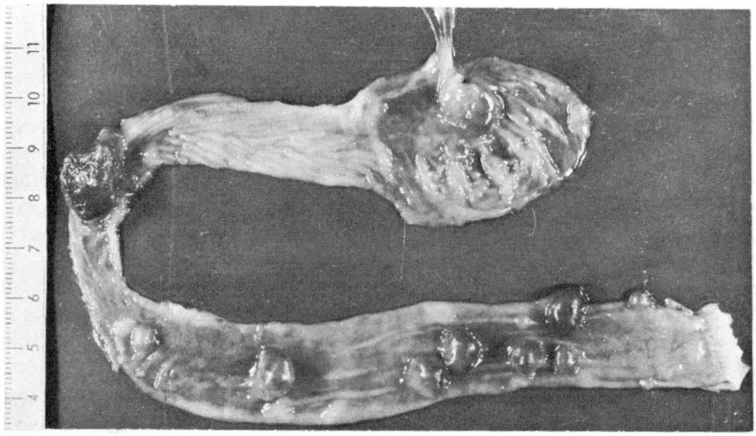

FIGURE 4. Intestinal tumors after oral administration of 1-methyl-2-n-butylhydrazine.

ethyl derivatives in this class of compounds can be further demonstrated very strikingly in transplacental carcinogenesis. Given to pregnant rats on the 15th day of gestation or later, in one single, low dose, the ethyl compounds produced malignant tumors of the brain, spinal cord and nervous system in practically all offspring (FIGURE 6). The methyl compounds, on the contrary, were absolutely noncarcinogenic for the offspring.[11]

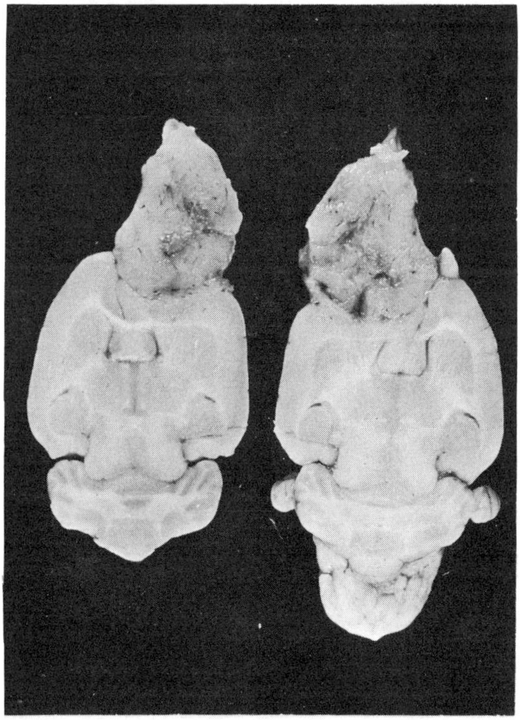

FIGURE 5. Olfactory bulb tumors after oral administration of 1-methyl-2-benzylhydrazine.

Several related compounds were found to have no carcinogenic properties and therefore gave an indication of the structural requirements for active compounds. Phenyl-alkyl derivatives of hydrazo, azo, and azoxy compounds were negative, showing that both organic residues must be alkyl groups for carcinogenic activity. 1,1-Dialkylhydrazines are practically noncarcinogenic,[1] showing that the hydrazo structure is necessary for activity. Azoisobutyronitrile, a well known initiator of radical reactions, was negative. Aliphatic azo compounds are easily rearranged to form the tautomeric alkylhydrazones: acetaldehyde-ethylhydrazone was therefore examined and found to be noncarcinogenic. The corresponding azine, acetaldehyde azine, and the respective hydrazide, 1-acetyl-1-2-ethyl-hydrazine, were also negative.

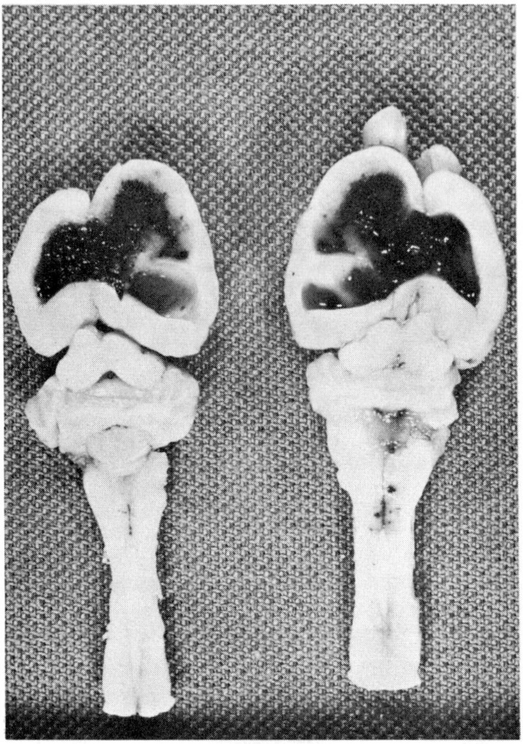

FIGURE 6. Transplacental induction of malignant brain tumor in the offspring. The mother was treated with a single i.v. dose of azoxyethane.

Mechanism of Action

Our structure-activity investigations have shown that aliphatic hydrazones, azines, and hydrazides, compounds that might be formed from hydrazo- or azo-alkanes, cannot be proximate carcinogens. The point has already been stressed that organ-specific effects can be obtained mainly by indirect, resorptive carcinogens. This fact indicates enzymatic activation *in vivo*. The investigated hydrazo-, azo-, and azoxyalkanes of one group with one given alkyl residue each show the same organotropic effects for all three compounds. This strongly suggests a common reactive intermediate.

We therefore want to discuss the following reaction mechanism postulating the formation of alkylating agents as proximate carcinogens by metabolic activation: hydrazoalkanes are easily oxidized to form the corresponding azoalkane as a first step of activation. This rapid oxidation is catalyzed by traces of heavy metals, as can easily be shown in experiments in the Warburg apparatus. Enzymatic monodealkylation of azo- as well as of azoxyalkanes by microsomes of liver and other organs should result in highly reactive intermediates with alkylating activity; namely, alkyldiimines, alkyldiimine oxides, or diazohydroxides.

To test this hypothesis we have incubated several azo- and azoxyalkanes with the microsomal fraction of rat liver and other organs. In the presence of a TPNH-generating system and molecular oxygen, the oxidative dealkylation of one alkyl group of the substrate could be demonstrated, since the oxidized alkyl group is removed and determined as aldehyde. Results with azoxymethane and azoxyethane are shown in TABLE 1 in comparison with the corresponding dealkylation of a typical nitrosamine, diethylnitrosamine.

TABLE 1

In Vitro DEALKYLATION OF AZOXYALKANES COMPARED WITH DIETHYLNITROSAMINE. INCUBATION AT 37° C WITH LIVER MICROSOMAL FRACTION AND NADPH.

Compound	μm Aldehyde after Incubation of 1 μm Substrate	% Yield
Azoxymethane	0.1	10
Azoxyethane	0.1	10
Diethylnitrosamine	0.07	7

There is growing evidence that the first step of microsomal N- or O-dealkylation is an enzymatic hydroxylation of the α-carbon-atom[12] and subsequent hydrolysis of this hydroxyalkyl derivative to form the corresponding aldehyde. The first reaction product for the enzymatic activation of azoxymethane, for example, is therefore supposed to be methylazoxymethanol, as shown in formula scheme 1. Methylazoxymethanol is the well-known proximate carcinogen of cycasine. It is easily hydrolyzed to formaldehyde and an alkylating agent, probably methyldiimine oxide, which is tautomeric with methyldiazohydroxide. Alkylations of phenols with methylazoxymethanol or cycasine have been demonstrated by Riggs,[13] of RNA and DNA *in vitro* by Matsumoto and Higa,[14] and *in vivo* by Shank and Magee.[15] The methylation products of nucleic acid bases are mainly 7-methylguanine. The alkylation hypothesis with carcinogenic azoxyalkanes therefore seems to be well founded and parallels the mechanism of action for nitrosamines.[1,2] Azoalkanes could be oxidized *in vivo* to form azoxyalkanes, although at present we have no direct chemical evidence for this. Dealkylation of azoalkanes could form alkyl-diimines, which have been shown[16] to have a certain alkylating activity, possibly by a radical mechanism. Further confirmation for an alkylating reactivity in this group of compounds comes from the work of W. Kreis[17] with Procarbazine, the previously mentioned 1-methyl-2-benzylhydrazine derivative. Working with a ^{14}C-methyl labeled compound, he also demonstrated the formation of 7-methylguanine *in vivo* as the most important alkylation product of nucleic acids.

Carcinogenic hydrazo-, azo- and azoxyalkanes therefore very probably are activated *in vivo* to form alkylating agents as proximate carcinogens, and alkylation of genetic material is very likely to be the cause of carcinogenesis with this type of compound.

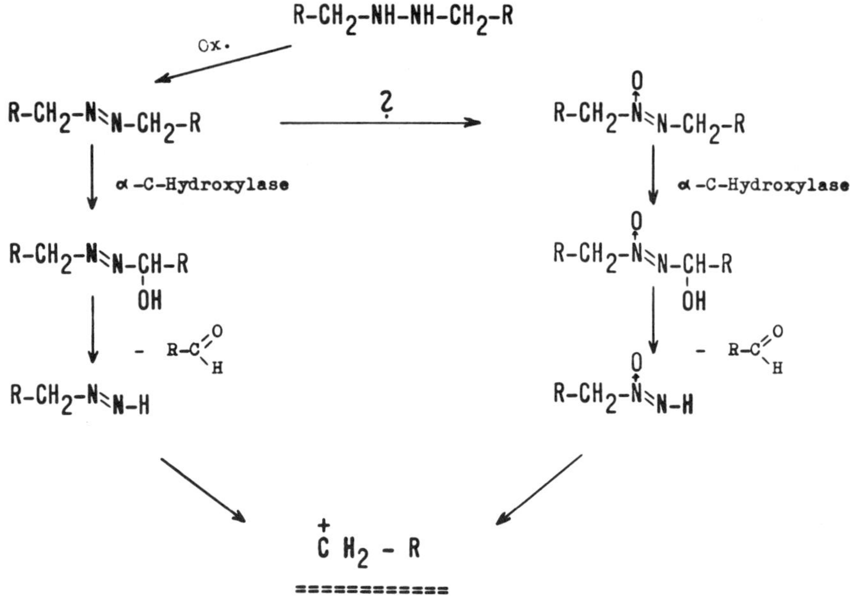

SCHEME 1. Proposed reaction mechanism of hydrazo-, azo-, and azoxyalkanes.

Of course, much further work, especially with labeled compounds, which cannot at present be done in our laboratory, will be necessary in order to elucidate a detailed mechanism of action. The proposed general mechanism, for example, does not explain highly organ-specific effects in carcinogenesis, and much additional work will be needed to obtain more information on the specifity of activating enzymes in different organs and on the chemical structure or metabolites in order to get a more detailed picture.

TRIAZENES

Our interest in triazenes also resulted from our earlier work with nitrosamines. We had found[18] that nitrosomethylaniline has carcinogenic activity in rats. We explained this action with the metabolic conversion of the compound to a benzenediazonium ion as the proximate carcinogen after enzymatic demethylation. Further confirmation came from the carcinogenicity of nitrosophenylurea,[19] which is easily hydrolyzed to a benzenediazonium ion. Carcinogenic effects of aromatic diazo compounds seemed possible, since several reactions with constituents of biological macromolecules are known that could account for the biological activity. For example, it has been shown to react with guanine to form 8-phenylazoguanine.[20] Reaction with the amino group of guanine also occurs with the formation of a guanosyl-phenyl-triazene.[21] Hoffman and Müller[22] have recently shown that benzene diazonium compounds can also act as arylating agents to form 8-arylguanosine. Furthermore, reaction of aromatic diazo compounds with protein has long been known as the Pauli reaction: diazotation of tyrosine and histidine occur as well as pentazadiene formation with free amino groups. Should such reactions occur in the organism, they could explain a carcinogenic effect of compounds of this type.

Clearly, further examination of the problem was indicated. We therefore followed a suggestion of R. Huisgen of Munich, and tested 1-phenyl-3, 3-dimethyltriazene for carcinogenic activity. Triazenes of this type are stabilized aromatic diazo compounds that are easily split, especially in acid medium, to form secondary amines and the corresponding diazo compounds.

The carcinogenic activity of 1-phenyl-3, 3-dimethyltriazene[23] prompted us to examine many other aryldialkytriazenes of the general formula

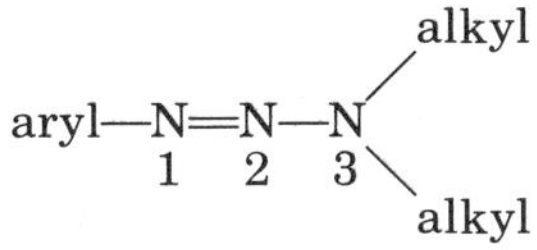

for structure-carcinogenicity relationships in this new group of biologically active compounds.

Certain triazenes have technical importance as intermediates in the so-called "Rapidogen" dyeing process. Other triazenes have been evaluated as carcinostatic agents on transplanted animal tumors.[24] Aryldialkyltriazenes in patents have been claimed as rodent repellents and herbicides.[25]

Carcinogenic Action

1-Phenyl-3,3-dimethyltriazene, C_6H_5—N=N—N$(CH_3)_2$, the most simple aryldialkyltriazene, was examined on oral as well as on s.c. administration to BD rats. Since no differences between the two groups were observed, results for both experiments will be discussed together.

At the time of the appearance of the first tumor, 41 animals were living. Of this number 34 (83%) died with malignant tumors. The great majority were located in the brain, the peripheral nervous system, and the spinal cord (FIGURE 7).

Therefore, a pronounced organotropic effect for the nervous tissue is evident. Some other malignant tumors have been found in the kidneys, the heart, and a few other organs. Only two local sarcomas at the site of s.c. injection have been observed. The median time for tumor induction was about 330 days; the median carcinogenic total dose amounted to 1.5 g triazene/kg body weight.

The potent carcinogenicity of phenyldimethyltriazene is further demonstrated by single-dose experiments. Several rats surviving a single dose of the LD_{50} subsequently died with malignant tumors of the brain and kidney.

Phenyldimethyltriazene is practically insoluble in water. A water-soluble analogue, 1-(pyridyl-3)-3, 3-dimethyl-triazene, therefore seemed to be interesting. On s.c. injection, 15 rats out of 20 died with malignant tumors, again predominantly in the brain and nervous system (FIGURE 8). In addition, carcinoma have been found in mammary tissue; they were also seen with the corresponding phenyl compound. No local tumors were formed.

The mammotropic activity is strongly enhanced without loss of the neurogenic action in the corresponding N-oxide, 3-(dimethyltriazeno)-pyridine-N-oxide.

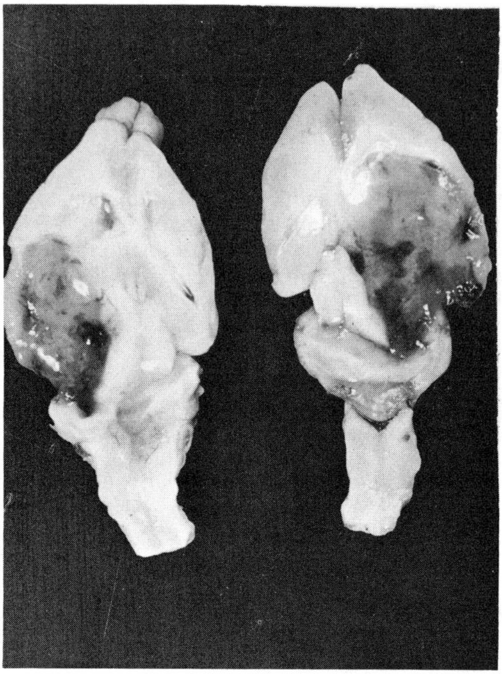

FIGURE 7. Malignant brain tumor after oral administration of 1-phenyl-3,3-dimethyl triazene.

Given intravenously, this compound produced malignancies in 12 out of 14 experimental animals. Seven of them had neurogenic tumors similar to those produced with the other triazenes, but eight showed multiple mammary carcinoma, often up to five mammary tumors in one animal (FIGURES 9 & 10). Carcinoma of the mammae often were associated with thymomas, which were not seen in the other triazene groups.

Several other triazenes with variations in the alkyl groups as well as with substituents in the aromatic group are presently being examined in chronic experiments, but the experimental time is too short for evaluation.

However, the most interesting results have been obtained in transplacental carcinogenesis, comparing phenyl- and pyridyl-dimethyl-triazenes and the corresponding ethyl compounds. Given on the 15th day of pregnancy, only the ethyl compounds produced neurogenic tumors in the offspring, while the methyl compounds were negative. However, given shortly before the end of pregnancy (23rd day of gestation), the methyl compounds also are carcinogenic for the offspring.

Hence, with triazenes also we have that most striking effect that has already been observed in the class of hydrazo-, azo-, and azoxyalkanes: On the 15th day of gestation, only the ethyl compounds of both classes of compounds are carcinogenic for the progeny, while the methyl derivatives are absolutely negative.

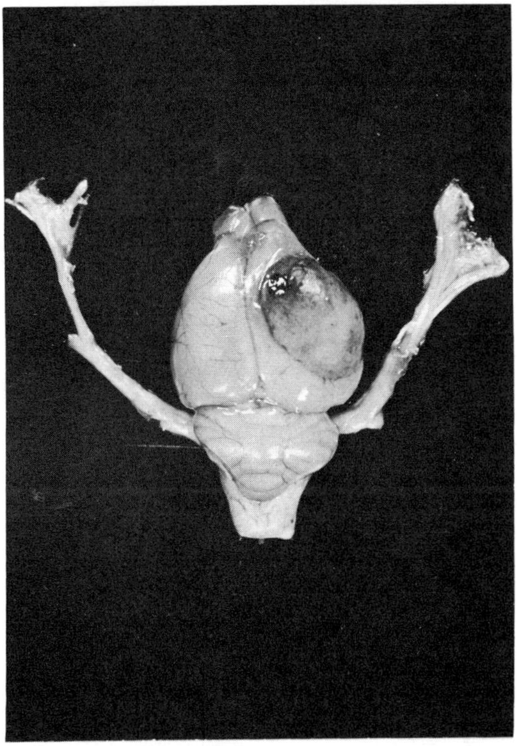

FIGURE 8. Malignant brain tumor after s.c. injection of 1-(pyridyl-3)-3,3-dimethyltriazene.

Mechanism of Action

The evaluated aryldialkyltriazenes in rats are potent carcinogens with pronounced organotropic action, especially toward nervous tissue. On oral administration, we saw no tumors in the stomach where the compounds should easily be decomposed at the acid pH to form aromatic diazonium compounds, the anticipated proximate carcinogen. On s.c. injection, we saw only very few local sarcomas. The examined triazenes are typical resorptive, "indirect" carcinogens, and activation to form the proximate carcinogen is therefore very probably not a simple hydrolytic scission of the triazene, but very likely an enzymatic process.

To investigate this possibility, a number of triazenes were incubated *in vitro* with isolated microsome fractions of rat liver and other organs in the presence of a NADPH-generating system and oxygen at 37° centigrade.[27]

Some of the results are shown in TABLE 2. Phenyldimethyltriazene on incubation with the complete system of rat liver is dealkylated in a yield of 50%, and formaldehyde can be shown to be the reaction product. There is dealkylation

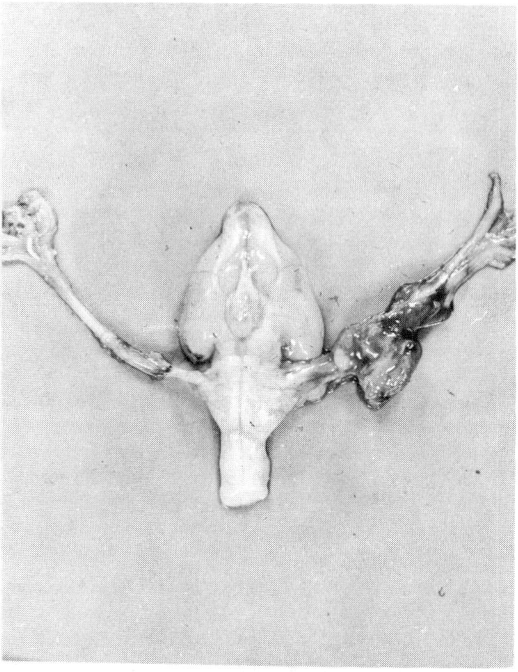

FIGURE 9. Tumor of the nervus trigeminus, induced by s.c. injection of 3-(dimethyltriazeno-)-pyridine-N-oxide.

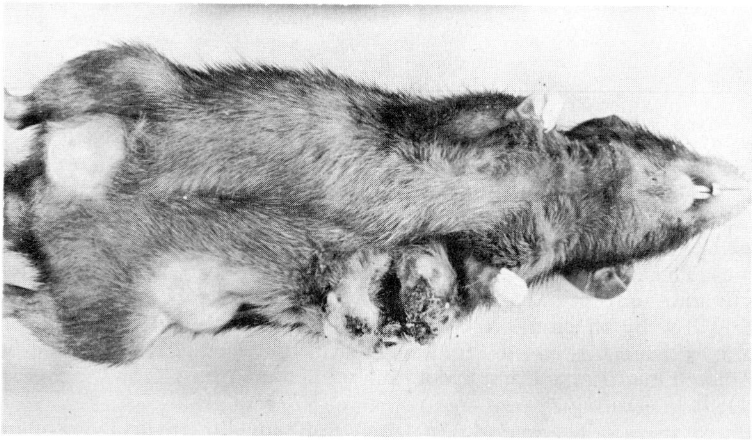

FIGURE 10. Multiple mammary carcinoma after treatment with 3-(dimethyltriazeno-) pyridine-N-oxide.

neither in the absence of the NADPH-generating system nor without microsomal fraction. No formaldehyde formation is observed in the absence of oxygen. All these results show that dealkylation is typical, as usually effected by microsomal preparations. Other organ preparations have been used showing that microsomes from lung have a very weak dealkylating activity, while microsomes from brain and kidney are not active in dealkylation.

Dealkylation of pyridyldialkyltriazenes is less than with the phenyl compounds, but still distinctly positive. For further details with other triazenes see reference 27.

Working with phenyldimethyltriazene and microsomal fractions *in vitro*, the formation of aromatic amine, probably aniline, has been demonstrated by us.[27] There is also evidence for the formation of aromatic amine *in vivo:* In acute toxicity experiments with several triazenes, methemoglobin formation could be demonstrated *in vivo*. This can best be explained by the formation of aromatic amines in the organism, known methemoglobin-forming compounds.

TABLE 2

In Vitro DEALKYLATION OF 1-PHENYL-3,3-DIMETHYLTRIAZENE WITH LIVER MICROSOMAL FRACTION AND NADPH.

Compound	μm Substrate Incubated	Incubation System	Organ	μm H_2—C=O	% Yield
1-Phenyl-3,3-dimethyltriazene	0.2	complete	liver	0.1	50
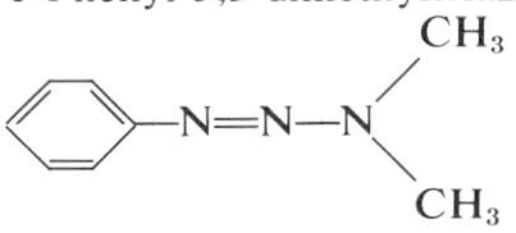	0.2	without NADPH	liver	—	—
	0.2	without oxygen	liver	—	—
	0.2	without microsomes	—	—	—
	0.2	complete	brain	—	—
	0.2	complete	lungs	0.01	5
	0.2	complete	kidney	—	—

We are well aware of the difficulties of extrapolating from *in vitro* results with isolated microsomal fractions to the intact organ or even to the whole organism. Nevertheless, on the basis of the results presented, we feel it is possible to propose a mechanism of action for carcinogenesis with phenyldimethyltriazene and other carcinogenic triazenes.

As shown in scheme 2, enzymatic hydroxylation of the triazene should form 1-phenyl-3-methyl-3-hydroxymethyltriazene as the first intermediate, which easily loses formaldehyde by hydrolysis to form phenylmonomethyltriazene as an intermediate.

Phenylmonomethyltriazene is a known compound and can be synthesized. Chemically, it reacts like a typical alkylating agent. The compound in aqueous solution is rather unstable, and is easily hydrolyzed to form the alkylating carbonium ion, nitrogen and aniline. As has been shown above, aniline is also a product of the *in vitro* and *in vivo* metabolism of the triazene.

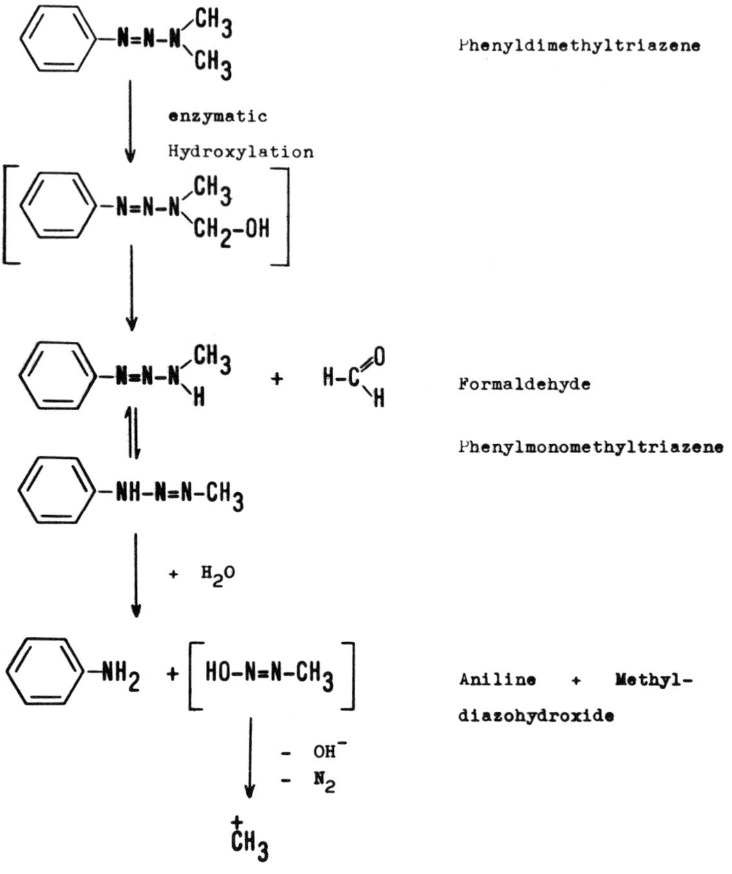

SCHEME 2. Proposed reaction mechanism for 1-phenyl-3,3-dimethyl-triazene.

The alkylating activity of phenylmonomethyltriazene can easily be demonstrated. Dimroth, as early as 1903, described this property and stated that it reacts like a "stabilized diazomethane."[28] Accordingly, it methylates carbonic acids and phenols in high yields.[28] Succinimide is N-methylated,[29] alcohols are methylated to form ethers in the presence of an $Al(OCH_3)_3$catalyst.[29] Acid decomposition of a monoalkyltriazene, 1-(4-nitrophenyl)-3-carbethoxymethyltriazene, has recently been shown to be a preparative method for diazoacetic ester, showing that diazoalkane is formed in fact on the decomposition of the monoalkyltriazene.[30]

In our laboratory, we have recently investigated the reaction of phenylmonomethyl- and monoethyltriazene with guanosine and DNA, using water/tetramethylurea as solvent and working at neutral or slightly acid pH. Reaction with guanosine under these conditions clearly forms the expected 7-alkylguanosine, which is isolated after acid hydrolysis by column chromatography on sephadex

G-10,[31] as shown in FIGURE 11, and identification by UV spectroscopy at acid, neutral, and alkaline pH. The reaction products are identical with authentic 7-methyl- or 7-ethylguanine.

In reactions with commercial, low molecular weight deoxyribonucleic acid from herring sperm *(Serva)* and high molecular weight DNA from salmon sperm, under similar conditions as for the reaction with guanosine, the formation of 7-alkylguanine could be demonstrated. Hydrolysis of DNA was effected either by total acid hydrolysis or by heating with water.[32] It has been found that ethylation is much less effective than methylation under the conditions used in the experiments.

Carcinogenic Activity of Phenylmonomethyltriazene

These results pointed to arylmonoalkyltriazene as the reactive intermediate of aryldialkyltriazene carcinogenesis. Therefore, phenylmonomethyltriazene has been tested for carcinogenic activity in BD rats. It is a powerful carcinogen. On oral administration, all animals died with "local" carcinoma in the esophagus and

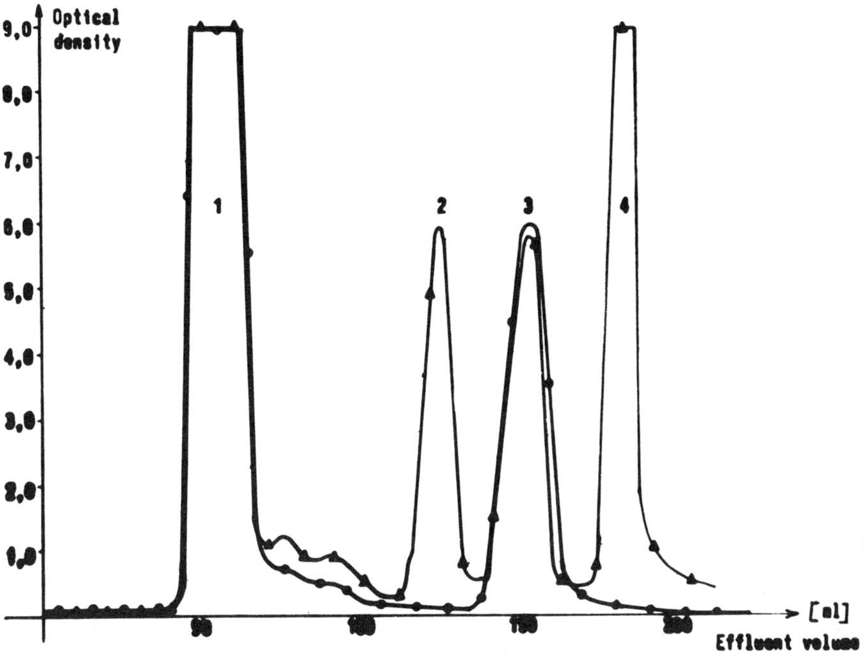

FIGURE 11. Reaction of guanosine with 1-phenyl-3-methyltriazene *in vitro*. Elution chromatogram (Sephadex G-10, elution with phosphate buffer, pH 7.0). Peak 1, solvent (tetramethylurea); peak 2, 7-methylguanine; peak 3, guanine; peak 4, aniline. ●—● = control; △—△ = experiment.

forestomach (FIGURE 12). Subcutaneous injection produced predominantly the expected local carcinoma at the site of injection, but also some neurogenic malignant tumors. This demonstrates that the compound is sufficiently stable *in vivo* to have "distant" effects, in addition. Compared with the corresponding phenyldimethyltriazene, the monomethyl compound fulfills conditions for a proximate carcinogen: It is more effective than the parent compound and produces predominantly local tumors.

Based on the results presented here, we feel justified in postulating that carcinogenic aryldialkyltriazenes are dealkylated *in vivo* to form arylmonoalkyltriazenes as proximate carcinogens, and that the carcinogenic activity of triazenes is caused by *in vivo* alkylation of biopolymers, probably nucleic acids. This places triazenes in one line with other groups of carcinogens, which are metabolized *in vivo* to form alkylating agents: the hydrazo-, azo-, and azoxyalkanes, as shown in this paper, and organic N-nitroso compounds.

The proposed reaction mechanism does not exclude the possibility that certain triazenes may act by a purely chemical heterolysis to form aryldiazonium ions as reactive intermediates. Experiments in this direction are under way.

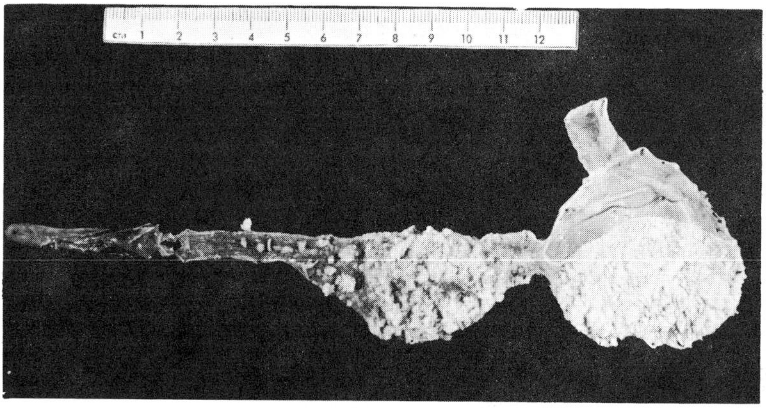

FIGURE 12. Carcinoma of esophagus and forestomach after oral administration of 1-phenyl-3-monomethyltriazene.

SUMMARY

Hydrazo-, azo-, and azoxyalkanes as a new group of potent chemical carcinogens have been investigated. 1,2-Dimethylhydrazine (hydrazomethane) and azoxymethane on repeated s.c. or oral administration produced selectively and in high yield carcinoma of the colon and rectum in rats. The corresponding ethyl compounds, 1,2-diethylhydrazine, azo- and azoxyethane, produced malignant tumors of the brain, the bulbus olfactorius, the mamma, and the liver, and leukemias, but never intestinal carcinoma. The structure/carcinogenicity relationship of this class of compounds and related substances is discussed.

The active compounds are typical resorptive carcinogens. Therefore an enzymatic activation *in vivo* to form the proximate and ultimate carcinogen is probable. Hydrazoalkanes are easily oxidized to form the corresponding azoalkanes. Azo- and azoxyalkanes are dealkylated by microsomal fraction of rat liver *in vitro*. Similar to nitrosamines, these compounds after dealkylation probably form unstable and reactive intermediates (alkyldiimides, alkyldiimide oxides and/or alkyldiazohydroxides), which decompose to form alkylating agents as ultimate carcinogens.

Another group of typical resorptive carcinogens are certain aryldialkyltriazenes. 1-Phenyl-3,3-dimethyltriazene (I), C_6H_5—N=N—$N(CH_3)_2$, after oral as well as s.c. injection, induced selectively malignant tumors in brain and nervous system in BD rats.

The potent carcinogenicity of certain triazenes was further demonstrated by the induction of malignant kidney tumors in single-dose experiments.

1-Phenyl-3,3-dimethyltriazene (I) produced practically no local tumors at the site of application. Therefore, reaction with isolated microsomal fraction of several rat organs was again investigated. It could be shown that (I) and other triazenes are enzymatically dealkylated. One alkyl group is split off as aldehyde. In the case of (I), aniline is also formed as metabolite.

Phenylmonomethyltriazene (II), C_6H_5—NH—N=N—CH_3, probably formed after dealkylation, is a powerful alkylating agent, which reacts to form carbonium ions, nitrogen, and aniline. Compound (II) methylates guanosine and nucleic acids to form 7-methylguanine. In rats, (II) is a more potent carcinogen than (I) with local activity: carcinoma of the esophagus and forestomach after oral, and sarcoma at the site of injection after s.c. administration have been observed.

These results suggest that carcinogenic aryldialkyltriazenes are dealkylated enzymatically to form arylmonoalkyltriazenes as proximate carcinogens, and that the carcinogenicity of triazenes is caused by *in vivo* alkylation of biopolymers.

References

1. Druckrey, H., R. Preussmann, S. Ivankovic, & D. Schmähl. 1967. Z. Krebsforsch. **69:** 103.
2. Magee, P. N. & J. M. Barnes. 1967. Advances Cancer Res. **10:** 163.
3. Laqueur, G. L., O. Michelsen, M. G. Whiting & L. T. Kurland. 1963. J. Nat. Canc. Inst. **31:** 919.
4. Laqueur, G. L. 1964. Fed. Proc. **23:** 1386.
5. Smith, D. W. E. 1966. Science **152:** 1273.
6. Kelley, M. G., R. W. O'Gara, K. Gadekar, S. T. Yancey & V. T. Oliverio. 1964. Cancer Chemother. Rep. **39:** 77.
7. Druckrey, H., P. Danneberg, W. Dischler & D. Steinhoff. 1962. Arzneimittelforschung **12:** 911.
8. Druckrey, H., R. Preussmann, F. Matzkies & S. Ivankovic. 1967. Naturwissenschaften **54:** 285.
9. Druckrey, H., R. Preussmann, S. Ivankovic, C. H. Schmidt, B. T. So & C. Thomas. 1965. Z. Krebsforsch. **67:** 31.
10. Druckrey, H., R. Preussmann, F. Matzkies & S. Ivankovic. 1966. Naturwissenschaften **53:** 557.
11. Druckrey, H., S. Ivankovic, R. Preussmann, C. Landschütz, J. Stekar, U. Brunner & B. Schagen. 1968. Experientia **24:** 561.
12. McMahon, R. E. 1966. J. Pharm. Sci. **55:** 457.

13. RIGGS, N. V. 1965. Nature (London) **207:** 632.
14. MATSUMOTO, H. & H. H. HIGA. 1966. Biochem. J. **98:** 20e.
15. SHANK, R. C. & P. N. MAGEE, 1966. Biochem. J. **100:** 35 P.
16. AKERMARK, B. 1967. Acta Chem. scand. **21:** 2909.
17. KREIS, W., J. H. BURCHENAL & D. J. HUTCHINSON. 1968. Proc. Amer. Ass. Cancer Res. **9:** 38.
KREIS, W., S. B. PIEPHO & H. V. BERNHARD. 1966. Experientia **22:** 431.
18. DRUCKREY, H., R. PREUSSMANN, D. SCHMÄHL & G. BLUM. 1961. Naturwissenschaften **48:** 722.
19. PREUSSMANN, R., H. DRUCKREY & J. BÜCHELER. 1968. Z. Krebsforsch. **71:** 63.
20. FISCHER, H. 1903. Hoppe-Seyler Z. Physiol. Chem. **60:** 69.
21. KÖSEL, H. 1965. Z. Physiol. Chem. 340: 210.
22. HOFFMANN, H. D. & W. MÜLLER. 1966. Biochem. Biophys. acta **123:** 421.
23. DRUCKREY, H., S. IVANKOVIC & R. PREUSSMANN. 1967. Naturwissenschaften **54:** 171.
24. PAPANASTASSIOU, Z. B., R. J. BRUNI, E. WHITE & P. L. LEVINS. 1966. J. Med. Chem. **9:** 725.
SHEALEY, Y. P., C. A. KRAUTH, L. B. HOLUM & W. E. FITZGIBBON. 1968. J. Pharm. Sci. **57:** 83.
25. CHEM. ABSTR. **60:** P 6788a; **61:** 6312d; **62:** 14568f.
26. DRUCKREY, H., S. IVANKOVIC & R. PREUSSMANN. 1967. Experientia **23:** 1042.
27. PREUSSMANN, R., A. v. HODENBERG & H. HENGY. 1968. Biochem. Pharmacol. **18:** 1.
28. DIMROTH, O. 1903. Ber. Dtsch. Chem. Ges. **36:** 909; 1905. ibid. **38:** 670.
29. POCHINOK, V. Y. & L. P. LIMARENKO. 1955. Ukr. Khim. Zh. **21:** 496 (Chem. Abstr. **50:** 5549i).
30. BAUMGARTEN, R. J. 1967. J. Org. Chem. **32:** 484.
31. SWEETMAN, L. & W. L. NYHAN. 1968. J. Chromatog. **32:** 662.
32. LAWLEY, P. D. 1968. Nature (London) **218:** 580.

DISCUSSION OF THE PAPER

DR. P. MAGEE (*Courtauld Institute of Biochemistry, London, England*): I wanted to ask you two questions. One is that I think I heard you say that one of the dialkyltriazene compounds was teratogenic, and yet you have spoken of this compound as a resultant carcinogen and not an approximate one. Now this would seem to be in contrast with the results of Alexanderoff and Nabolkov, who, as you know, found, for example, that dimethylnitroso amine was not tetratogenic at all. Could you comment on that?

DR. PREUSSMANN: Phenyldimethyl-triazene was given subcutaneously to the pregnant mother, and it certainly is teratogenic. We also have in our laboratory results showing that dialkylnitrosamines are not teratogenic. At present, I have no explanation for this. I think the mechanism for teratogenicity is different from that for carcinogenicity.

DR. MAGEE: Do you think it is possible that the triazene can be activated enzymatically in the fetus, perhaps?

DR. PREUSSMANN: It might be possible. After all, certain triazenes are carcinogenic for the embryo.

DR. MAGEE: That's exactly the point. Could I ask one other question? You spoke of a stabilized diazomethane a little while ago. Now in the earlier work—in this whole field—we have often spoken of the diazoalkane as being the likely intermediate. Now, I am sure you have seen the recent paper of Lijinsky and his colleagues, who used fully deuterated dimethylnitrosoamine and then extracted

7-methylguanine from the livers of rats treated with this compound. They found, very much to my surprise and theirs, too, that the molecular weight of this compound corresponded to CD_3 and not to CD_2H, which, it seems to me, makes it unlikely that the diazoalkane was the intermediate. Could you please comment on that?

DR. PREUSSMANN: May I have the last slide again. You will note that I did not put diazomethane on it, but methyldiazohydroxide, which might form the carbonium ion without intermediate formation of diazomethane. I only cited Dimroth* (1905). He stated that phenylmonomethyltriazene reacts "like a stabilized diazomethane." It can easily be shown that it methylates, say, benzoic acid in a yield of more than 95 percent. It also methylates phenols in very high yield. Chemically, it reacts really like diazomethane. Whether diazomethane or the diazonium ion is an intermediate *in vivo,* I cannot say.

UNIDENTIFIED SPEAKER: Certainly in this case, if the intermediate you postulate would be the diazonium ion, this would be an intermediate that would be formed from the diazomethane only by acquiring a proton from somewhere, but it would already have its proton in the mechanism you postulated. So this indeed should give you trideutero material. It would not have to pick up a proton it already had. The alkyl group, here, already has its proton. But in the diazomethane, the methyl group must pick up a proton; it starts out as CH_2. I think they both go through the same intermediate, but not really through diazomethane.

DR. PREUSSMANN: Yes, that would be my impression, also.

UNIDENTIFIED SPEAKER: As you pointed out before, procarbazine has both carcinogenic and carcinostatic properties. I was interested in knowing whether any of the hydrazines you have studied with respect to their carcinogenicity also have coexisting antitumor properties, which, as we know, exist with procarbazine.

DR. PREUSSMANN: We have not tested them for carcinostatic activity, but I think it is known from the work of the Swiss investigators who introduced it that quite specific requirements are necessary for cytostatic activity. I don't think that the simple 1,2-dialkylhydrazines are very effective as carcinostatic agents, but we haven't tested them in our laboratory.

DR. J. DI PAOLO (*National Institutes of Health, Washington, D.C.*): I should like to make two further observations on the dialkynitrosoamines. We have found them to be nonteratogenic in the hamster. Drunosky has reported that they are nonteratogenic to chick embryos, which seems to imply that some sort of conversion is required.

UNIDENTIFIED SPEAKER: For me as a biologist, I am concerned about the contradiction between the statements of Dr. Preussman and Dr. Price. Mainly, Dr. Price mentioned that diazomethane attacked most readily, whereas guanine is the most reactive base. I should like some comment on that.

DR. PREUSSMANN: I think that it is known that diazomethane reacts with guanine to form 7-methylguanine. We incubated commercial DNA *in vitro* with phenylmonomethyl-triazene and found 7-methylguanine. There can be no doubt about that. There are several other small peaks that we haven't identified yet. They may be other alkylated bases. Generally, in biological experiments, the main product of alkylation is 7-alkyl guanine. The only comment I might make is that the presumed reason why thymine is more readily alkylated by diazomethane is that it is a stronger acid. It can protonate diazomethane and add that extra

* Ber. 1903 **36:** 909; 1905 **38:** 670.

proton, which is essential to activate diazomethane. In your case, you do not need to add the proton to generate the carbonium ion to be an alkylating agent. It may be that the carbonium ion could be generated independently in the activation via the base and would prefer the 7-N of guanine, but there is no activation proton on the 7-N of guanine. In the case of diazomethane, you are only generating the carbonium ion by a strong acid, and one of the characteristics of the carbonium ion is that it exists for a relatively short time and may react only with the immediate site, which, as Dr. Shapiro pointed out, will be the anion formed by the loss of the proton. Thus, the thymidine anion would be reactive. So there is no real contradiction; one can rationalize those results.

DR. MAGEE: I must add a comment to what you just said. One paper, written two or three year ago by Emmelot and Kriek of Amsterdam, says that the action of diazomethane on nucleic acid was quite different, depending upon whether water is present. Of course, in biological systems, water is present.

IN VIVO REACTIONS OF NITROSO COMPOUNDS

P. N. Magee

Courtauld Institute of Biochemistry
Middlesex Hospital Medical School
London, England

A number of N-alkylnitroso compounds have very potent biological actions, including acute cellular injury in the liver and other organs, carcinogenesis, mutagenesis, and teratogenesis. Aspects of these biological actions have been discussed in several recent reviews.[1-3] The mechanism of toxic liver injury by nitrosamines has been discussed by Magee and Lee.[4]

The biological actions of the N-alkylnitroso compounds are determined to some extent by their chemical properties. The dialkylnitrosamines, of which dimethylnitrosamine is the simplest example (FIGURE 1), are relatively stable chemically, while some N-nitrosamides, for example, N-nitrosomethylurea (FIGURE 1), are relatively unstable in aqueous solution, the rate of decomposition being dependent on pH. According to Druckrey and co-workers[2] the half-life of N-nitrosomethylurea is 125 hours at pH 4.0, 24 hours at pH 6.5, 1.2 hours at pH 7, and 0.1 hours at pH 8.

BIOLOGICAL STUDIES

The biological actions of the N-alkylnitroso compounds that will be considered include acute cellular injury to the liver and other organs, carcinogenesis, mutagenesis, and teratogenesis.

Acute Cellular Injury

The sites of acute tissue injury induced by the nitrosamines and the nitrosamides vary and may be dependent on the chemical stability of the compounds, as mentioned above. The dialkylnitrosamines, with some exceptions, cause severe liver injury, with relatively little damage to other organs. The lesions produced are centrilobular haemorrhagic necrosis, the required dose increasing with increasing chain length of the alkyl groups. Notable exceptions are diphenylnitrosamine and tert-butylmethylnitrosamine. The latter compound does affect the liver, but causes periportal fatty change, which is quite distinct from the typical centrilobular lesions of the other nitrosamines. The chemically unstable nitrosamides such as N-nitrosomethylurethane and N-nitrosomethylurea cause local tissue injury of varying severity at the site of administration, and varying degrees of damage to distant organs. Nitrosomethylurethane causes very severe stomach lesions after oral intubation in the rat and marked lung damage as well as local tissue injury after subcutaneous (s.c.) injection. N-nitrosomethylurea, after oral or parenteral administration, damages organs with rapid cell division, including

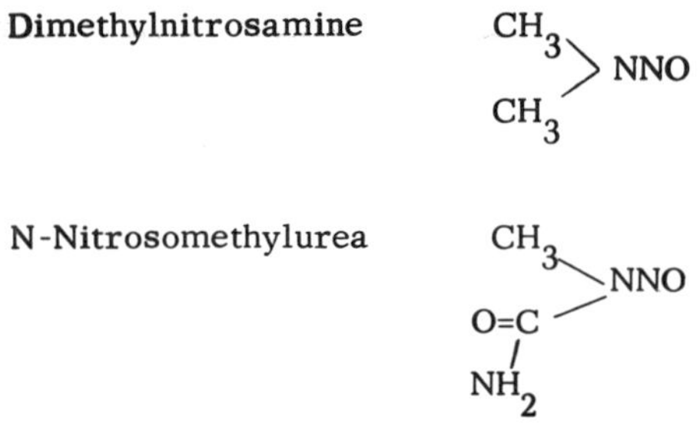

FIGURE 1. Chemical structures of dimethylnitrosamine and N-nitrosomethylurea.

bone marrow, lymphoid tissues, and intestinal tract.[6,7] The most probable explanation of the different patterns of acute cellular injury induced by the nitroso compounds is that the compounds themselves are not responsible for the lesions, but that they must first decompose to give the active form. The distribution of lesions would then depend on the distribution of the administered compound and the rate and site of its decomposition. This hypothesis will be further discussed below.

Carcinogenesis

The carcinogenic potency of the N-nitroso compounds is extraordinary, and they have several properties that make them particularly suitable for experimental studies on the mechanism of carcinogenesis. The range of animal species known to be susceptible to the induction of tumors by these compounds is remarkably wide,[8] and includes the monkey.[9] It therefore seems highly probable that man is also susceptible. As with acute tissue injury, the nitroso compounds show remarkable organ specificity in their carcinogenic action.[2] In general, the dialkylnitrosamines induce tumors of the liver. This appears to be true for all the species tested, including the rat. In the latter species, which has been the most frequently used, the carcinogenic action is not confined to the liver, and tumors of the esophagus have been induced, particularly by the unsymmetrical compounds.[2] The capacity of dibutylnitrosamine to induce bladder cancer in the rat is a notable example of organ specificity.[10] The hamster has proved especially susceptible to induction of tumors of the respiratory tract by diethylnitrosamine administered by a variety of routes.[11,12] The nitrosamines do not induce local tumors after topical application to the skin or s.c. injection,[6] but the nitrosamides may be locally active at either site. N-nitrosomethylurea is a potent topical carcinogen on the skin of mouse, rat, and hamster,[13] and also induced highly malignant tumors at the site of s.c. injection in the rat.[6] N′-nitro-N-nitrosoguanidine is also carcinogenic in rat s.c. tissue.[2] Another remarkable property of the nitroso carcinogens is their capacity to induce cancer after only one dose.[14,15,7] This property is the more remarkable since the compounds may not persist in the body for more than a few hours.[1-3] N-nitrosomethylurea has been shown to induce tumors of the squamous stomach, large and small intestine, kidney, skin, and dental tissues following a single oral dose.[7] As mentioned above, the half-life of this compound is only 1.2 hours at pH 7,[2] and studies of its fate after injection into rats have suggested a comparably brief half-life *in vivo*. The observation of Sanders and Burford[17] that exposure of hamster cells in culture to N-nitrosomethylurea for only one hour was sufficient to induce morphological conversion is of great interest in this connection. These authors also reported that dimethylnitrosamine was inactive in their system.

The balance of the available biological evidence suggests that the induction of cancer by the nitroso compounds is mediated by a decomposition product or activated form, rather than by the compounds themselves, but there are observations that are difficult to reconcile with this hypothesis (see below).

Mutagenesis

The mutagenic action of a number of N-alkylnitroso compounds is well known, and N′-nitro-N-nitrosomethylguanidine and N-nitrosomethylurea are among the most potent known chemical mutagens (see reference 3). The nitrosamides are mutagenic in all the usual microbial systems, in several plants, and in *Drosophila*.[18,3] By contrast, dimethylnitrosamine, until very recently, was reported to be active only in *Drosophila*,[18] suggesting that activation may be dependent on a metabolic system present in the insect that is absent in the microorganisms. This hypothesis receives striking support from the work of Malling,[19] who confirmed that dimethylnitrosamine was not mutagenic in *Neurospora* but became active in the presence of the reagent of Udenfriend, which is known to decompose dimethylnitrosamine in the presence of oxygen.[20] Very recently, however, Veleminsky and Gichner[21] have shown that some nitrosamines, including the dimethyl, ethylmethyl, and butylmethyl compounds, are mutagenic in the plant *Arabidopsis thaliana*. These observations indicate either that the plant is able to decompose the nitrosamines or that, in this case, the unchanged molecule is active.

Teratogenesis

N-nitrosomethylurea[22] and N-nitrosoethylurea[23] are potent teratogens, and both can induce tumors in the progeny of rats treated during pregnancy. The high incidence of tumors of the central and peripheral nervous system induced by N-nitrosoethylurea is remarkable. By contrast, dimethylnitrosamine is reported not to have teratogenic action in the rat but to induce renal and other tumors in the progeny of pregnant females treated during the third week of pregnancy.[24] A possible explanation of these results is that the developing embryo, at the stage when it is most susceptible to teratogenesis, lacks the metabolic capacity to decompose the nitrosamine, but at a later stage metabolism of the nitrosamine may occur to yield sufficient carcinogenic products to induce tumors. The newborn rat is capable of metabolism of dimethylnitrosamine during the first 24 hours after birth.[25,26]

The above brief summary of some of the biological actions of the N-alkylnitroso compounds suggests, but does not prove, that their action is wholly or partially dependent on their conversion to an active intermediate that then reacts with critical intracellular targets, resulting in the biological response.

If this hypothesis is correct, it is obviously important to determine the nature of the biologically active intermediate. An early suggestion was that this intermediate is the corresponding diazoalkane[1-3] derived by decomposition of the very unstable monoalkylnitrosamine formed metabolically from the dialkylnitrosamine and perhaps from the nitrosamide without requiring enzyme activity. Much of the biological data is consistent with such a hypothesis, e.g. lack of typical activity by diphenyl, tert-butylmethyl, and tert-butylethylnitrosamine,[2,3] none of which would be expected to yield a diazoalkane on decomposition. Other biological evidence, however, does not support such an alkylation hypothesis of the mechanism of action of the nitroso compounds. For example, phenylmethylnitrosamine, which, on dealkylation, could not yield a diazoalkane, is a potent esophageal carcinogen in the rat,[27] like other unsymmetrical nitrosamines.[2] Additionally, several cyclic nitrosamines, including N-nitrosomorpholine, N-nitrosopiperidine and N-nitrosopyrrolidine,[2] are carcinogenic in the rat, but it has been suggested that the metabolic opening of the rings required for the production of the diazoalkane is unlikely to occur.[28] Recent biochemical evidence, however, which will be discussed below, suggests that metabolism of heterocyclic nitrosamines does, in fact, occur, with ring opening and the formation of an alkylating intermediate *in vivo*.[29]

Biochemical Studies

The biochemical investigations to be discussed throw some light on some of the problems arising from the biological actions of the nitroso compounds. These problems include the specificity of action of the compounds, the nature of the biologically active molecular species, and the nature of the critical intracellular sites of action.

Specificity of Action

The selective hepatotoxic action of the nitrosamines, their organotropic carcinogenic action,[2] their failure to induce mutation in microorganisms, and their lack of teratogenic action can all possibly be explained by a requirement for metabolic conversion in target organs or cells. As mentioned above, metabolism of the nitrosamides may not be required, but they may decompose more rapidly in the presence of some cellular constituents such as sulphydryl compounds.[30] An explanation of the selective hepatotoxic action of dimethylnitrosamine was offered some years ago by Dutton and Heath[31] and by Magee,[32] who studied the metabolism of dimethylnitrosamine in rats and mice and suggested that the active toxic molecule was probably a metabolite of the nitrosamine. Since the liver is the organ mainly responsible for the metabolism of foreign compounds, it was suggested that the toxic metabolite would be formed in greatest concentration in this organ and thus account for the hepatotoxicity. On the basis of detailed studies of the rates of metabolism of several nitrosamines, Heath[33] concluded that the active molecular species involved in acute liver injury must be either the unstable monoalkylnitrosamine formed by dealkylation of the dialkyl compound or an alkylating agent derived from it. He drew no conclusions with regard to the carcinogenic action of the nitrosamines. Dimethylnitrosamine was found to be decomposed on incubation with rat liver slices *in vitro* in the presence of oxygen, but slices of other organs, with the possible exception of kidney,[34] were metabolically inactive. The capacity of rat kidney to metabolize dimethylnitrosamine is of great interest, since tumors have been induced in this organ by single doses of the compound.[14] The earlier metabolic studies[34] were based on measurement of disappearance of dimethylnitrosamine from the incubation medium, and the significance of small differences was difficult to assess. The problem has been recently studied again with use of a more sensitive method for the detection of metabolism of the nitrosamine. [^{14}C]Dimethylnitrosamine was incubated aerobically with slices of rat liver, kidney, or small intestine in a conventional Warburg apparatus. Oxygen uptake was measured, and CO_2 was trapped in alkali in the center well. The radioactive CO_2 was then precipitated as barium carbonate by conventional procedures and was washed before assay of radioactivity by scintillation counting. The results (TABLE 1) confirm the earlier observation of metabolism of dimethylnitrosamine by rat liver slices and clearly show that rat kidney slices, although considerably less active than liver, are definitely capable of metabolism of dimethylnitrosamine. It is interesting that no metabolic activity by the small intestine could be detected, although oxygen uptake was about the same as with liver, indicating that the tissue was viable. No evidence of cellular injury or carcinogenesis of the small intestine by dimethylnitrosamine or any other nitrosamine appears to have been reported, although several nitrosamides are active in this organ.[7,35]

Further information with implications for the organotropic action of the nitroso carcinogens has been obtained by injection of the intact animal with the compounds isotopically labeled in the alkyl groups. Earlier studies showed that nucleic acids and proteins of liver and some other organs become alkylated in animals treated with labeled dimethyl- and other nitrosamines.[36–41] The predominant site of alkylation of the nucleic acids is on the 7-position of guanine. Adenine and cytosine have recently been shown also to be methylated in nucleic acids from livers of rats treated with [^{14}C]dimethylnitrosamine, but to a considerably smaller extent than guanine. Adenine is methylated on the 1- and 3-positions, and cytosine on the 1-position.[42] Comparison of the degrees of methylation of RNA in different organs of rats treated with labeled dimethylnitrosamine showed that liver RNA was the most highly methylated (1–2% of guanine converted to 7-methylguanine) and that kidney and lung RNA were also methylated, but to a smaller extent.[40] These studies have now been extended to include DNA, and [^{14}C]dimethylnitrosamine of higher specific activity was used.[43] Rats were injected with [^{14}C]dimethylnitrosamine and killed 5 hours later, a time when

TABLE 1

PRODUCTION OF $^{14}CO_2$ FROM TISSUE SLICES INCUBATED AEROBICALLY WITH [^{14}C]DIMETHYLNITROSAMINE

Organ	Oxygen Uptake μl O_2/g/hour	Radioactivity of Evolved CO_2 cpm/g/hour
Liver	862	4,717
Kidney	2,547	807
Small intestine	955	0

previous work had shown methylation of nucleic acids to be near maximal. RNA and DNA were extracted from various organs by conventional phenol methods, and 7-methylguanine was isolated from acid hydrolysates of these radioactive nucleic acids by ion-exchange chromatography, as previously described.[37] The specific activity of the 7-methylguanine was measured and found to be virtually identical with that of the injected [^{14}C]dimethylnitrosamine, indicating direct transfer of the methyl group from the nitrosamine to the nucleic acid without appreciable dilution in metabolic pools. This observation allowed calculation of the degree of methylation of the nucleic acids, which is expressed as a percentage of the guanine methylated (i.e., converted to 7-methylguanine). The results of this experiment are shown in FIGURE 2. Clearly, liver has the highest level of methylation, as expected, and kidney and lung nucleic acids are appreciably methylated. Small-intestine nucleic acids are methylated to a small, but quite definite, degree, and even testis shows a minute level of methylation. Since kidney slices are capable of metabolism of dimethylnitrosamine, it seems probable that the methylation found in this organ is due to metabolism therein, and not to methylation by a circulating alkylating agent formed elsewhere or to incorporation of 7-methylguanine derived from the liver. This conclusion probably also applies to the smaller degrees of methylation observed in the other organs. Recent studies on the metabolism of 7-methylguanine,[44] using the compound labeled with ^{14}C in the methyl group, showed that almost all of the injected dose was excreted in

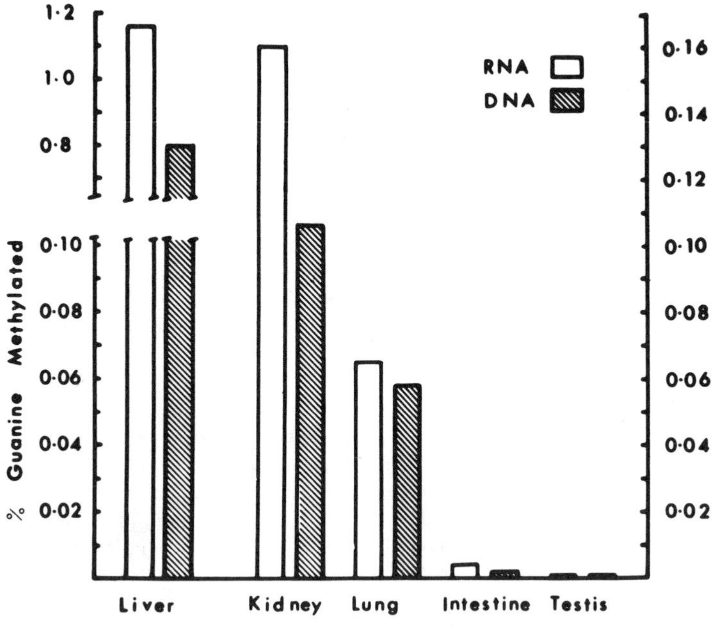

FIGURE 2. Degree of methylation of RNA and DNA of organs of rat 5 hours after intraperitoneal injection of dimethylnitrosamine (30 mg/kg body weight). Ordinate, percentage of guanine converted to 7-methylguanine.

the urine during the first 24 hours. There was no detectable incorporation of the administered 7-methylguanine into DNA or RNA, even in organs of rapid cell turnover or in the developing fetus.[44] The biochemical studies discussed in this section are consistent with the hypothesis that the selectively hepatotoxic and organotropic carcinogenic actions of the dialkylnitrosamines are probably dependent on their metabolic conversion in the target organs to form a biologically active intermediate. The problems raised by the biological behavior of the heterocyclic nitrosamines have already been mentioned. These compounds can induce typical acute liver injury in the rat and can certainly induce tumors, since N-nitrosomorpholine is a very potent liver carcinogen.[2] Lee and Lijinsky,[29] using these compounds labeled with tritium in the rings, have shown that metabolism does occur and have detected very low levels of alkylation of RNA in the livers of the treated animals. It is difficult to draw conclusions from this work on the rate and extent of metabolism of the heterocyclic nitrosamines and to make comparisons with the dialkyl compounds. Further investigation will be required before it can be concluded that the heterocyclic nitrosamines owe their hepatotoxic and carcinogenic activities to the formation of biologically active metabolites.

The postulated active products of the nitroso compounds are not necessarily alkylating agents (see below), but since tumors can be induced in rats given single doses of dimethylnitrosamine or N-nitrosomethylurea, it is of interest to know how long the methyl groups derived from the carcinogens remain combined with the nucleic acids in animals receiving such single doses. This has been studied in the DNA and RNA of liver and kidney of rats treated with [^{14}C]dimethylnitrosamine.[45] Previous work had shown that methylation of both nucleic acids in liver and kidney reached a peak about 5 hours after intraperitoneal injection, and started to fall about 12 hours after the injection.[38] These studies have now been extended to 12 days and 61 days after injection of a single dose of dimethylnitrosamine (30 mg/kg body weight, adequate to induce severe liver necrosis and kidney tumors in some of the survivors). At 12 days, labeled 7-methylguanine could still be detected in DNA and RNA of both organs, but it was not found at 61 days.[45] Such an experiment is clearly dependent on the specific radioactivity of the injected nitrosamine. Since it is extremely difficult to assess the exact point in time at which the renal tumors induced by dimethylnitrosamine actually arise, it is not possible to say whether the abnormally methylated base is still present in the nucleic acids at this time. The rapid removal of the methyl groups from DNA and RNA of liver and kidney of the nitrosamine-treated rats raises the question of the mechanism of their removal and of their fate. Injection of [^{14}C]dimethylnitrosamine into rats is rapidly followed by the excretion of radioactive 7-methylguanine in the urine.[46] This methylated base is, of course, a normal constituent of mammalian urine,[47] and the amount excreted in the first 24 hours after a dose of 30 mg/kg body weight of dimethylnitrosamine is about three times the normal amount. The available evidence suggests that some, at least, of the increased urinary excretion of 7-methylguanine must be derived from splitting out of this base from nucleic acids.[46]

Nature of the Biologically Active Intermediate

Although there is good evidence that alkylation of nucleic acids and proteins does occur in animals treated with carcinogenic nitrosamines[36–43] and of nucleic acids in rats treated with nitrosamides,[43,48,49] it does not necessarily follow that these alkylation reactions are causally related to the induction of cancer and the other biological actions of these compounds. Krüger and his colleagues[49] recently demonstrated methylation of RNA of several organs from rats treated with N-nitroso-[^{14}C]methylurea but did not find evidence of ethylation of RNA in animals receiving N-nitroso-[^{14}C]ethylurea. They concluded that alkylation of RNA is not related to carcinogenesis, since N-nitrosoethylurea is a very powerful carcinogen.

The chemical nature of the alkylating agent that must be formed from the nitroso compounds *in vivo* is not clear. The earlier suggestions involving the intermediate formation of the diazoalkane[1–3] now appear less likely in view of the recent work of Lijinsky and his colleagues.[50] These workers treated rats with fully deuterated dimethylnitrosamine and extracted nucleic acids from their livers. The 7-methylguanine isolated from these nucleic acids had a molecular weight corresponding to methylation by —CD_3 rather than —CD_2H, as would be expected if diazomethane had been an intermediate.

Several other powerfully biologically active molecules might be formed from nitroso compounds *in vivo,* including nitrous acid, derivatives of hydroxylamine and hydrazine, and the corresponding aldehyde formed by oxidative dealkylation. There is evidence for the formation of aldehydes from dimethyl and diethylnitrosamine after aerobic incubation with rat liver preparations *in vitro.*[51] Süss has reported the formation of the hydrazine derivative after anaerobic incubation of N-nitrosomorpholine with rat liver preparations.[52] The formation of nitrous acid might lead to deamination of nucleic acids, but no evidence of this was found in the DNA and RNA of livers from rats treated with dimethylnitrosamine, although very small degrees of deamination could not be excluded.[53]

The evidence for the formation of biologically active intermediates other than alkylating agents from the nitroso compounds is clearly not extensive, and further investigation is needed. The question obviously arises whether the various biological actions of the nitroso compounds can be reasonably explained on the basis of their capacity to alkylate cellular constituents. The cytotoxic action of the biological alkylating agents, particularly the bifunctional compounds, is well known,[54] and it seems possible that the acute cell-damaging action of the nitroso compounds may be attributable to alkylation. This suggestion, as it relates to the acute hepatotoxic action of the nitrosamines, receives considerable support from the work of Heath[33] mentioned above. Alkylation may also explain the mutagenic and teratogenic actions of the nitroso compounds, since several biological alkylating agents are potent in both these actions.[55,56] The position with regard to mutagenesis, however, is far from clear, and some evidence has been interpreted as indicating that the nitroso compounds are mutagenic by mechanisms other than alkylation (see reference 3).

A reasonable objection to alkylation as the necessary and sufficient mechanism of carcinogenesis by the nitroso compounds is that many of the well-known biological alkylating agents cannot be regarded as powerful carcinogens.[57] However, β-propiolactone is carcinogenic on s.c. injection in the rat and by topical application to the skin of mouse,[59] rat,[60] guinea pig,[61] and hamster.[62] This lactone is also a potent initiator of carcinogenesis in mouse skin[63,64] and alkylates nucleic acids *in vitro*[65] and *in vivo,*[64,66] reacting with guanine to form 7-2-carboxyethylguanine. Furthermore, the ethylating agent ethyl methanesulphonate was reported carcinogenic in mouse kidney by Alexander and Connell.[67] Similar results have recently been obtained in the rat with ethyl methanesulphonate.[68] With use of an experimental procedure rather similar to that of Alexander and Connell, rats were given three doses of ethyl methanesulphonate intravenously (i.v.) and then kept without further treatment. This work is still in progress, and several animals have developed large kidney tumors about nine months after the last injection. In a similar experiment using methyl methanesulphonate,[68] the survivors of a single large i.v. dose were also kept. There have been no kidney tumors among these animals, but several tumors of the brain have appeared (FIGURE 3). It seems, therefore, that simple ethylating and methylating agents may be effective carcinogens when administered under similar conditions to those used when inducing tumors with the nitroso compounds with single[7] or few repeated doses,[14] i.e., conditions in which lethal or almost lethal quantities are given and the survivors kept throughout their life spans.

Critical Intracellular Sites of Reaction

From the foregoing discussion it will be apparent that alkylation is far from being established as the critical intracellular reaction responsible for the biological activity of the nitroso compounds. Nevertheless, there seems sufficient evidence from a variety of sources to justify the retention of alkylation as a working hypothesis to explain the activity of these compounds. Satisfying explanations of the mechanisms of acute cellular injury by chemical agents are extremely

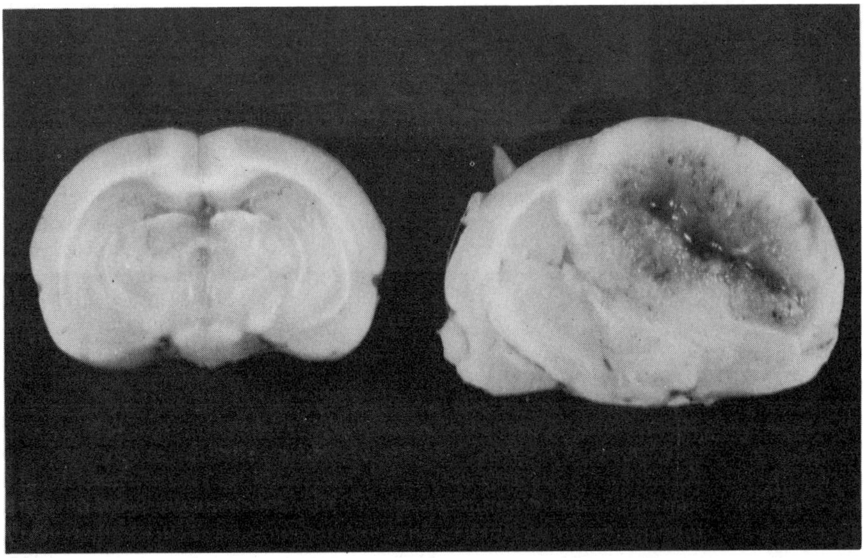

FIGURE 3. Brain of rat treated with methyl methanesulphonate sectioned to show large tumor (right). On left, brain of control rat sectioned at about the same level. The treated rat received 96 mg/kg body weight of methyl methanesulphonate intravenously 20 months before death.

difficult to formulate. This problem has been discussed in relation to mechanisms of acute liver necrosis induced by a variety of agents including the dialkylnitrosamines.[3,69] The marked cytotoxicity of bifunctional alkylating agents in dividing cells has been attributed to cross-linking of the strands of DNA by reaction with guanines on the 7-position by both arms of the agent,[54] e.g. sulphur mustard. Diguanyl derivatives were not detected, however, in hydrolysates of DNA from livers of rats treated with necrogenic doses of dimethylnitrosamine, although the predominant methylated base was 7-methylguanine.[42] It seems unlikely, therefore, that cross-linking of DNA plays a significant part in the acute hepatic necrosis induced by dimethylnitrosamine, which involves a large proportion of the parenchymal cells, while cell division in the liver is extremely rare. An early biochemical change in livers of rats treated with necrotizing doses of dimethylnitrosamine is inhibition of hepatic protein synthesis.[70,3] Whether this inhibition is directly related to the induction of liver necrosis is not clear, and there is evidence suggesting that it may not be. The mechanism of inhibition of hepatic protein synthesis by dimethylnitrosamine has been fairly extensively studied, and this work has provided suggestions which may be relevant to other biological actions of the nitroso compounds. Villa-Treviño[71] confirmed the earlier observations of Magee[70] and showed that the time course of inhibition of incorporation of amino acids into proteins of rat liver by dimethylnitrosamine runs closely parallel with disaggregation of the hepatic polyribosomes involving reduction in the polysomes and corresponding increase in monomers and dimers. These observations suggested the possibility of some defect either in synthesis or function of messenger RNA. The inhibition of protein synthesis preceded inhibition of nuclear RNA synthesis, suggesting that any relevant defect in messenger RNA must be in its function rather than in its biosynthesis. Villa-Treviño suggested that methylation of the messenger RNA might have occurred, with consequent failure of its function in maintaining the integrity of the polysomes.[71] Shank[72] showed that dimethylnitrosamine inhibits the induction of hepatic tryptophan pyrrolase in the rat in doses lower than are required for inhibition of amino acid incorporation. He concluded that his results were compatible with a primary action of dimethylnitrosamine on protein synthesis by methylation of messenger RNA. Regardless of its relevance to inhibition of hepatic protein synthesis, alkylation of messenger RNA and other species of RNA may be significant in carcinogenesis by the nitroso compounds. Recent studies of nucleic acids in the livers of rats treated with ethionine have shown that t-RNA is ethylated to a considerably greater extent than other RNA species[73] and that DNA is only ethylated to a very small extent, if at all.[74,75] There is evidence that 7-ethylguanine is among the ethylated bases present,[75] as is the case in RNA from the livers of rats treated with diethylnitrosamine.[41] Since ethionine is carcinogenic in rat liver, these observations focus attention on t-RNA as a possibly important intracellular site of alkylation and away from DNA. In mutagenesis, DNA is obviously a likely site of primary action by chemical mutagens, and theories have been put forward to explain the production of mutations as the result of alkylation of guanine bases on the 7-position with subsequent anomalous base-pairing or by deletion resulting from splitting out of the alkylated base from the DNA chain.[57] A similar mechanism may be operative in carcinogenesis, but there is no direct evidence for this. Much has been written on the possible significance of interaction of chemical carcinogens with proteins, and an interesting scheme has been put forward by Pitot and Heidelberger,[76] based on the well-known work of Jacob and Monod[77] with microorganisms. This scheme suggests an initial interaction of the carcinogen with an extranuclear entity, possibly proteins or RNA, which might lead to the necessary heritable change in the cell that must occur in carcinogenesis. As with theories postulating a primary reaction with DNA, there is no direct evidence in support of this scheme. There appear to have been no attempts, as yet, to explain the teratogenic action of the nitroso compounds in molecular terms.

Occurrence of Nitroso Compounds in the Environment

There is recent evidence that some biologically active nitroso compounds may occur in the environment either naturally or as the result of unsuspected chemical reactions.[78,2,3] The diabetogenic antibiotic streptozotocin, derived from *Streptomyces achromogenes,* is a nitrosamide,[79] chemically related to N-nitrosomethylurea, and it induces tumors of the kidney in rat.[80] A most remarkable example of unsuspected formation of a nitrosamine occurred in Norway, where a number of sheep became fatally ill with severe liver injury after consumption of fish meal preserved with nitrite.[81] Toxic levels of dimethylnitrosamine were found in this diet, presumably formed by reaction of the secondary amines present in the fish with the nitrite preservative. Reports have appeared of trace amounts of nitrosamines in human food and tobacco smoke (see references 3 and 78), but their significance is very difficult to assess.

Conclusions

The alkylnitroso compounds have very interesting biological actions. Among the large number of these compounds that have been investigated are included some of the most powerful known chemical carcinogens and mutagens. Some nitroso compounds are teratogenic, and several can induce severe acute cellular injury. These compounds are carcinogenic in a wide range of animal species and can induce tumors after only one dose, even though they are rapidly decomposed in the animal body and may not persist as the unchanged molecule for more than a few hours. There is evidence suggesting that the nitroso compounds derive their biological activity from conversion to more active molecular species in the affected cells. The compounds behave as alkylating agents in biological systems and react with the genetic material and other constituents of the cell. It is possible that the nitroso compounds owe their biological activity to these alkylation reactions, but this is not established, and other cellular interactions may be involved. Recent reports indicate that some nitroso compounds may occur in the environment and thus constitute a hazard to man and animals.

References

1. Magee, P. N. & R. Schoental. 1964. Brit. Med. Bull. **20:** 102.
2. Druckrey, H., R. Preussmann, S. Ivankovic & D. Schmähl. 1967. Z. Krebsforsch. **69:** 103.
3. Magee, P. N. & J. M. Barnes. 1967. Advances Cancer Res. **10:** 163.
4. Magee, P. N. & K. Y. Lee. 1963. Ann. N. Y. Acad. Sci. **104:** 916.
5. Schoental, R. & P. N. Magee. 1962. Brit. J. Cancer **16:** 92.
6. Herrold, K. M. 1966. J. Path. Bact. **92:** 35.

7. Leaver, D. D., P. F. Swann & P. N. Magee. (In preparation.)
8. Schmähl, D. & H. Osswald. 1967. Experientia **23:** 497.
9. Kelly, M. G., R. W. O'Gara, R. H. Adamson, K. Gadekar, C. C. Botkin, W. H. Reese & W. T. Kerber. 1966. J. Nat. Cancer Inst. **36:** 323.
10. Druckrey, H., R. Preussmann, S. Ivankovic, C. H. Schmidt, H. D. Mennel & K. W. Stahl. 1964. Z. Krebsforsch. **66:** 280.
11. Dontenwill, W. & U. Mohr. 1961. Z. Krebsforsch. **64:** 305.
12. Herrold, K. M. 1964. Brit. J. Cancer. **18:** 763.
13. Graffi, A., F. Hoffmann & M. Schütt. 1967. Nature (London) **214:** 611.
14. Magee, P. N. & J. M. Barnes. 1962. J. Path. Bact. **84:** 19.
15. Druckrey, H., D. Steinhoff, R. Preussmann & S. Ivankovic. 1963. Naturwissenschaften **50:** 735.
16. Swann, P. F. 1968. Biochem. J. **110:** 49.
17. Sanders, F. K. & B. O. Burford. 1967. Nature (London) **213:** 1171.
18. Pasternak, L. 1964. Arzneimittelforsch. **14:** 802.
19. Malling, H. V. 1966. Mutat. Res. **3:** 537.
20. Preussmann, R. 1964. Arzneimittelforsch. **14:** 769.
21. Veleminsky, J. & T. Gichner. 1968. Mutation Res. **5:** 429.
22. Kreybig, T. von. 1965. Z. Krebsforsch. **67:** 46.
23. Druckrey, H., S. Ivankovic & R. Preussmann. 1966. Nature (London) **210:** 1378.
24. Alexandrov, V. A. 1968. Nature (London) **218:** 280.
25. Lee, K. Y. & K. Spencer. 1964. J. Nat. Cancer Inst. **33:** 957.
26. Terracini, B. & P. N. Magee. 1964. Nature (London) **202:** 502.
27. Druckrey, H., R. Preussmann, D. Schmähl & G. Blum. 1961. Naturwissenschaften **48:** 722.
28. Arcos, J. C. & M. Arcos. 1962. Fortschr. Arzneimittelforsch. **4:** 407.
29. Lee, K. Y. & W. Lijinsky. 1966. J. Nat. Cancer Inst. **37:** 401.
30. Schoental, R. & D. J. Rive. 1963. Biochem. J. **87:** 22P.
31. Dutton, A. H. & D. F. Heath. 1956. Nature (London) **178:** 644.
32. Magee, P. N. 1956. Biochem. J. **64:** 676.
33. Heath, D. F. 1962. Biochem. J. **85:** 72.
34. Magee, P. N. & M. Vandekar. 1958. Biochem. J. **70:** 600.
35. Schoental, R. & J. P. M. Benstead. 1968. Brit. J. Cancer. **22:** 316.
36. Magee, P. N. & T. Hultin. 1962. Biochem. J. **83:** 106.
37. Magee, P. N. & E. Farber. 1962. Biochem. J. **83:** 114.
38. Craddock, V. M. & P. N. Magee. 1963. Biochem. J. **89:** 32.
39. Craddock, V. M. 1965. Biochem. J. **94:** 323.
40. Lee, K. Y., W. Lijinsky & P. N. Magee. 1964. J. Nat. Cancer Inst. **32:** 65.
41. Magee, P. N. & K. Y. Lee. 1964. Biochem. J. **91:** 35.
42. Lawley, P. D., P. Brookes, P. N. Magee, V. M. Craddock & P. F. Swann. 1968. Biochim. Biophys. Acta **157:** 646.
43. Swann, P. F. & P. N. Magee. 1968. Biochem. J. **110:** 39.
44. Craddock, V. M., A. R. Mattocks & P. N. Magee. 1968. Biochem. J. **109:** 75.
45. Frei, J. V. & P. N. Magee. (In preparation.)
46. Craddock, V. M. & P. N. Magee. 1967. Biochem. J. **104:** 435.
47. Krüger, M. & G. Salomon. 1898. Hoppe Seyler Z. Physiol. Chem. **26:** 350.
48. Schoental, R. 1967. Biochem. J. **102:** 5C.
49. Krüger, F. W., H. Ballweg & W. Maier-Borst. 1968. Experientia **24:** 592.
50. Lijinsky, W., J. Loo & A. E. Ross. 1968. Nature (London) **218:** 1174.
51. Mizrahi, I. J. & P. Emmelot. 1962. Cancer Res. **22:** 339.
52. Süss, R. 1965. Z. Naturforsch. **20b:** 714.
53. Craddock, V. M. & P. N. Magee. 1966. Biochem. J. **100:** 724.
54. Lawley, P. D. & P. Brookes. 1965. Nature (London) **206:** 480.
55. Loveless, A. 1966. *In* Genetic and Allied Effects of Alkylating Agents : 270. Butterworths. London, England.

56. FAVE, A. 1964. Thérapie. **19:** 43.
57. BROOKES, P. & P. D. LAWLEY. 1964. Brit. Med. Bull. **20:** 91.
58. DICKENS, F. & H. E. H. JONES. 1961. Brit. J. Cancer. **15:** 85.
59. ROE, F. J. C. & O. M. Glendenning. 1956. Brit. J. Cancer. **10:** 357.
60. SEARLE, C. E. 1961. Brit. J. Cancer. **15:** 804.
61. PARISH, D. J. & C. E. SEARLE. 1966. Brit. J. Cancer. **20:** 200.
62. PARISH, D. J. & C. E. SEARLE. 1966. Brit. J. Cancer. **20:** 206.
63. ROE, F. J. C. & M. H. SALAMAN. 1955. Brit. J. Cancer. **9:** 177.
64. COLBURN, N. H. & R. K. BOUTWELL. 1966. Cancer Res. **26:** 1701.
65. ROBERTS, J. J. & G. P. WARWICK. 1963. Biochem. Pharmacol. **12:** 1441.
66. COLBURN, N. H. & R. K. BOUTWELL. 1968. Cancer Res. **28:** 642.
67. ALEXANDER, P. & D. I. CONNELL. 1962. *In* Symposium on the Cellular Basis and Late Somatic Effects of Ionizing Radiation : 259. London, England.
68. SWANN, P. F. & P. N. MAGEE. (Unpublished results.)
69. MAGEE, P. N. 1966. Lab. Invest. **15:** 111.
70. MAGEE, P. N. 1958. Biochem. J. **70:** 606.
71. VILLA-TREVIÑO, S. 1967. Biochem. J. **105:** 625.
72. SHANK, R. C. 1968. Biochem. J. **108:** 625.
73. FARBER, E., J. MCCONOMY, B. FRANZEN, F. MARROQUIN, G. A. STEWART & P. N. MAGEE. 1967. Cancer Res. **27:** 1761.
74. FARBER, E., J. MCCONOMY & B. FRUMANSKI. 1967. Proc. Amer. Ass. Cancer Res. **8:** 16.
75. ORTWERTH, B. J., U. DELMONTE, ' ROSEN & G. D. NOVELLI. 1968. Fed. Proc. **27:** 803.
76. PITOT, H. C. & C. HEIDELBERGER. 1963. Cancer Res. **23:** 1694.
77. JACOB, F. & J. MONOD. 1961. J. Molec. Biol. **3:** 318.
78. MAGEE, P. N. 1968. Lancet **I:** 1071.
79. HERR, R. R., H. K. JAHNKE & A. D. ARGAUDELIS. 1967. J. Amer. Chem. Soc. **89:** 18.
80. ARISON, R. N. & E. L. FEUDALE. 1967. Nature (London) **214:** 1254.
81. SAKSHAUG, J., E. SÖGNEN, M. A. HANSEN & N. KOPPANG. 1965. Nature (London) **206:** 1261.

DISCUSSION OF THE PAPER

E. C. MILLER (*University of Wisconsin Medical School, Madison, Wis.*): There is a difference in the radioactivity in DNA and in 7-methylguanine. Is this difference due to the sensitivity of the method?

DR. MAGEE: When you measure total radioactivity of DNA, you measure activity in all the alkylated bases and that which has become incorporated into the purine and pyrimidine rings from the 1-carbon pool. The total radio-activity in the DNA, therefore, is higher than that in 7-methylguanine, and activity persists in the rings where the DNA does not turn over. The 7-methylguanine is split out from the nucleic acids *in vivo* at a rate greater than the normal turnover.

J. WEISBURGER: What happens with nitrosomethylurethane when it decomposes? Is this a spontaneous reaction without the intervention of an enzyme?

DR. MAGEE: The rate of breakdown of nitrosomethylurethane is increased by sulphydryl compounds.* I do not know whether there is any enzymic activity involved in the breakdown of nitrosomethylurethane or of nitrosomethylurea in

*Schoental, R. & D. J. Rive. 1956. Biochem. J. **97:** 466.

the animal. Nitrosomethylurea gives a fairly uniform level of methylation in all organs studied, and this level is very close to that seen in the kidney with dimethylnitrosamine. There is no organ that we measured that has as high a level as the liver does with dimethylnitrosamine, but virtually every organ has about the same degree of methylation – about 0.1–0.2%.

B. L. VAN DUUREN (*Institute of Environmental Medicine, New York University Medical Center, New York. N. Y.*): If I understood you correctly, you do get lung tumors with nitrosamines.

DR. MAGEE: We have observed very few lung tumors with dimethylnitrosamine until recently. I am talking about experiments with rats. What we have found is that when the metabolism of nitrosamines is slowed down by dietary means, we do start getting a few lung tumors.

DR. VAN DUUREN: In that case, I would like to add a comment. You mentioned in the beginning environmental factors, and I would just like to mention that there is at present a great deal of activity going on in search for nitrosamines in cigarette smoke, which would be very important in terms of lung-tumor induction.

DR. MAGEE: Yes, I think I would like to add a comment to that. If one wants to study lung-tumor induction, I suppose the hamster is the best animal. It is remarkably susceptible to lung-tumor induction by diethylnitrosamine. As far as we can see, it is not easy to get lung tumors with dimethylnitrosamine.

P. ALEXANDER (*Chester Beatty Research Institute, Belmont, Surrey, England*): It is possible that the carcinogenic intermediate is not alkylation at all, but that tumors arise as a result of the extensive tissue damage due to the immediate cytotoxic action of the agent. Extreme tissue damage and the resulting regeneration that takes place may be a real carcinogenic stimulus.

DR. MAGEE: Yes, that is a very important point, and we have thought about it. I think that there are certain observations that do not fit. One is, for example, in the treatment of the animal with dimethylnitrosamine or nitrosomethylurea, one is very hard put to see histologically any damage in the kidney at all after the single dose. It is the liver that kills the animal, and not the kidney. There may be damage visible with electron microscopy. Nevertheless, I think it is correct to say that there is no gross kidney damage, and yet you get kidney tumors.

UNIDENTIFIED SPEAKER: Is man included in the list of species that are susceptible to nitrosamines? Do you have some information on the fate of people exposed in industry to nitroso compounds?

DR. MAGEE: We have very little information on that, and we would like to have much more.

STUDIES ON THE MECHANISM OF ACTIVATION OF AROMATIC AMINE AND AMIDE CARCINOGENS TO ULTIMATE CARCINOGENIC ELECTROPHILIC REACTANTS*

Elizabeth C. Miller and James A. Miller

McArdle Laboratory for Cancer Research, University of Wisconsin Medical Center, Madison, Wis.

It is now generally recognized that the carcinogenicity and *in vivo* reactivity of aromatic amine and amide carcinogens must depend upon metabolic activation. N-Hydroxylation is generally regarded as the first step in the metabolic activation sequence because of the findings that aromatic amine and amide carcinogens are N-hydroxylated by the species in which they induce tumors and that these N-hydroxy amines and amides are more carcinogenic than the parent compounds, especially at sites of application.[1] While N-hydroxylation may be a sufficient activation step in some instances, an increasing body of evidence suggests to us that a second step, N-hydroxy esterification, is also necessary.[1] The evidence implicating N-hydroxy esterification in the carcinogenicity and *in vivo* reactivity of aromatic amine and amide carcinogens forms the body of this report. The data on the activation of N-hydroxy-2-acetylaminofluorene (N-hydroxy-AAF) (FIGURE 1) are the most complete, but supporting data will also be presented for a number of related carcinogens.

2-Acetylaminofluorene (AAF) is a versatile carcinogen for the rat and a number of other species, including the dog, hamster, mouse, rabbit, cat, and fowl.[2] The guinea pig has been notably resistant to tumor induction by AAF, even when large doses are administered for prolonged periods. Tumor induction in all species has most often been accomplished by long-term oral administration, although tumors can also be induced in rats and mice, at least, with repeated topical applications to the skin or with repeated injections. Regardless of the route of administration, the tumors generally develop in tissues distant from the site of application of AAF. In the rat, the most frequent sites of tumor formation are the liver, mammary glands, and ear duct glands, but low incidences of tumors are seen at a variety of other sites.

Metabolism of AAF proceeds along a number of pathways.[2–4] Quantitatively, ring-hydroxylation is a major pathway in the rat and the other species studied, but this appears to be only a detoxification mechanism. Deacetylation is also a major metabolic route. In most species deacetylation is accompanied by reacetylation of the product 2-aminofluorene (AF); where it has been studied the carcinogenicity of AF has not been markedly different from that of AAF.[2] On the other hand, N-hydroxylation, first demonstrated in our laboratory in 1960,[5,6] converts

*The research from the authors' laboratory has been supported by Program-Project Grant CA-07175 of the National Cancer Institute, USPHS, and by a grant from the Jane Coffin Childs Memorial Fund for Medical Research.

AAF into a more carcinogenic derivative.[7-10] The probable importance of N-hydroxy-AAF to the carcinogenic process is particularly evident from (a) its formation in all species susceptible to the carcinogenic activity of AAF,[9,11-13] (b) its greater carcinogenicity than that of AAF in a variety of species, especially at sites of application,[7-10] and (c) its carcinogenicity in the guinea pig, which appears to have a limited ability to synthesize N-hydroxy-AAF and is highly resistant to carcinogenesis by AAF.[9,14-16]

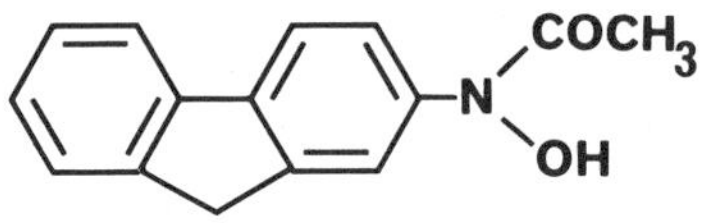

FIGURE 1. The structure of N-hydroxy-2-acetylaminofluorene (N-hydroxy-AAF).

Furthermore, administration of N-hydroxy-AAF results in the formation of higher levels of protein- and nucleic-acid-bound fluorene derivatives in the tissues than does administration of AAF.[17,18] While the functional significance of these protein- and nucleic-acid-bound derivatives is not known, they serve, as a minimum, as indicators of the extent to which metabolites of the carcinogen react with tissue macromolecules *in vivo*. This is important, since it appears inescapable that chemical carcinogens must act through some type of reaction with specific tissue macromolecules to effect, via either genetic or epigenetic mechanisms, or both, a permanent alteration of the control of cell multiplication. That the tissue-bound forms in animals administered N-hydroxy-AAF may reflect the formation *in vivo* of a reactive form important in the induction of neoplasia is indicated by the correlations observed between the levels of hepatic protein- and RNA-bound derivatives of AAF and susceptibility to carcinogenesis. Thus, the greater susceptibility of the livers of male rats as compared to those of female rats or of the livers of male hamsters, rabbits, or guinea pigs to carcinogenesis by N-hydroxy-AAF is reflected in the lower levels of hepatic protein- and RNA-bound fluorene derivatives in these animals as compared to the male rat.[17,19]

Reactivity of Esters of N-Hydroxy Amides and Amines

N-Hydroxylation does not appear to convert the aromatic amine and amide carcinogens into derivatives that react readily at neutral pH with tissue components. Thus, N-hydroxy-AAF and N-hydroxy-AF both have very low reactivity with nucleophiles at neutrality.[20-23] N-Hydroxy-AF, as first shown by Kriek,[20] is quite reactive at acid pH's with guanine in nucleic acids, and we have found acid-catalyzed reactions of N-hydroxy-AF with methionine and guanine-containing nucleosides and nucleotides.[23,24] In contrast, esterification of N-hydroxy-AAF converts it into derivatives that are very reactive at neutrality with a number of tissue nucleophiles.[1,21-23] Furthermore, the identity of some of the products formed by nonenzymatic reactions of esters of N-hydroxy-AAF with tissue nucleophiles at neutrality with some of those released from the proteins and RNA of rats administered AAF or N-hydroxy-AAF provided the first evidence for the biological formation of esters of N-hydroxy-AAF.[1,25,26]

The reactivity of esters of N-hydroxy-AAF can be depicted, at least formally, as resulting from the loss of an anion to yield positively charged amidonium and carbonium ions (FIGURE 2). Nonenzymatic reaction of the esters with methionine, free or in peptide linkage, yields 1- and 3-methion-S-yl derivatives, which are unstable and decompose gradually to 1- and 3-methylmercapto-AAF and homoserine or its lactone.[1,21] At least in the case of simple peptides such as methionylglycine this decomposition also results in cleavage of the peptide bond.[21] The presence of protein-bound 1- and 3-methion-S-yl-AAF in the livers of rats administered AAF or N-hydroxy-AAF has been demonstrated by the release with cold alkali of 1- and 3-methylmercapto-AAF from the solvent-extracted liver protein.[1,25] These methylmercapto derivatives contained ^{35}S if the rats were administered methionine-^{35}S in addition to N-hydroxy-AAF. Whether or not the decomposition of the sulfonium derivative *in vivo* involves an intramolecular attack of the methionyl carbonyl on the γ-carbon to result in peptide-bond cleavage has not been determined. Also the extent to which the sulfonium derivative may be S-demethylated *in vivo* has not been explored. In the former case, homoserine residues would replace methionine residues in the proteins, and possibly, cleavage

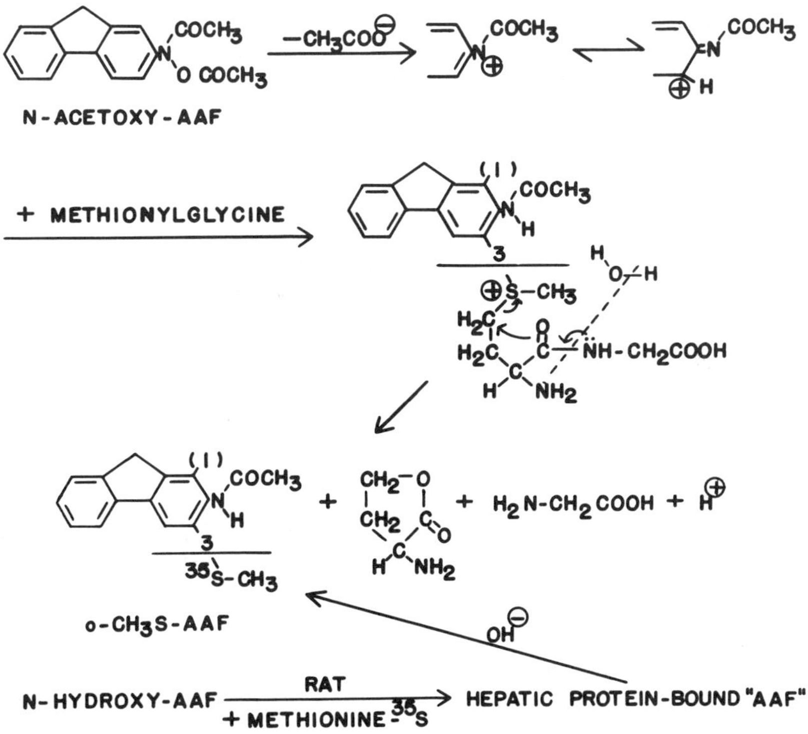

FIGURE 2. The nonenzymatic reaction of N-acetoxy-AAF with methionylglycine at neutrality to yield 1- and 3-methylmercapto-AAF and the liberation of 1- and 3-methylmercapto-AAF from the livers of rats administered N-hydroxy-AAF.[1,21,25]

of the peptide chain would occur. In the latter case the protein would be altered by the introduction of a large hydrophobic group. Either of these modifications could lead to important changes in secondary and tertiary structure of proteins with resultant alterations in biological activity.

In addition to methionine, the esters of N-hydroxy-AAF also react readily with tyrosine, tryptophan, and cysteine. In each case, two or more products are formed.[1] Except for one of the tryptophan derivatives (N-(tryptophan-2-yl)-AAF), these products have not been characterized, and it is not known whether or not they are formed in the tissues of N-hydroxy-AAF-treated animals.

Complementary information is available, however, with respect to the hepatocarcinogen N-methyl-4-aminoazobenzene (MAB), which also appears to be subject to N-hydroxylation and N-hydroxy esterification *in vivo*. Thus, in a manner analogous to the observations cited above for esters of N-hydroxy-AAF, N-benzoyloxy-MAB reacts nonenzymatically with methionine, tyrosine, tryptophan, and cysteine.[21,27] The sulfonium derivative that results from the reaction with methionine decomposes gradually to yield 3-methylmercapto-MAB and homoserine lactone (FIGURE 3).[21,27] 3-Methylmercapto-MAB is also liberated by cold alkali from the liver protein of rats administered MAB and contains ^{35}S if the rat is given methionine-^{35}S.[24,28] A second methionine derivative, 3-(homocystein-S-yl)-MAB, is the major component of the polar dye fraction released by enzymatic and alkaline hydrolysis of the liver proteins of rats administered MAB.[29] This is the product that would be expected if some of the protein-bound 3-(methion-S-yl)-MAB were S-demethylated *in vivo*. Two other polar dyes isolated from the digested liver protein are identical to the two dyes formed by reaction of tyrosine with N-benzoyloxy-MAB.[30] As shown in FIGURE 3, the probable structures of these dyes are N- and 3-(tyrosin-3-yl)-MAB. No tryptophanyl-MAB derivative has been detected among the polar dyes liberated by hydrolysis of the liver protein, but low levels might be missed since the derivative formed by reaction of tryptophan and N-benzoyloxy-MAB at neutrality is somewhat labile to alkali. Likewise, our inability to detect a cysteinyl-MAB polar dye has no meaning in view of the great alkali-lability of the derivative formed by reaction of cysteine and N-benzoyloxy-MAB.[30]

Among the purine and pyrimidine bases, esters of N-hydroxy-AAF show a marked preference for reaction with guanine, either in nucleosides or nucleotides or in nucleic acids (FIGURE 4 and TABLE 1).[1,22,31] The products of this nonenzymatic reaction are N-(guanin-8-yl)-AAF derivatives,[32] and as in the case of methionine, the same reaction occurs *in vivo*. Thus, as demonstrated both in our laboratory[1,25] and that of Kriek,[26] the hepatic RNA from rats treated with AAF or N-hydroxy-AAF can be degraded to yield products chromatographically identical with N-(guanosin-8-yl)-AAF or the corresponding nucleotide. Irving and associates[19] had previously inferred that the RNA-bound fluorene derivative of N-hydroxy-AAF retained the N-acetyl group on the basis of equal retention of label whether N-hydroxy-AAF-9-^{14}C or N-hydroxy-AAF-acetyl-^{14}C was administered. While esters of N-hydroxy-AAF react only to a very limited extent with adenosine, sufficient reaction to facilitate study of the product can be obtained by use of very large excesses of the sulfuric acid ester of N-hydroxy-AAF.[24]

A similar great preference for reaction with guanine as compared to adenine or the pyrimidine bases has also been observed for N-benzoyloxy-MAB[27] and esters of N-hydroxy-4-acetylaminobiphenyl.[24] However, the 0-acetyl derivatives of the potent subcutaneous carcinogens N-hydroxy-4-acetylaminostilbene and

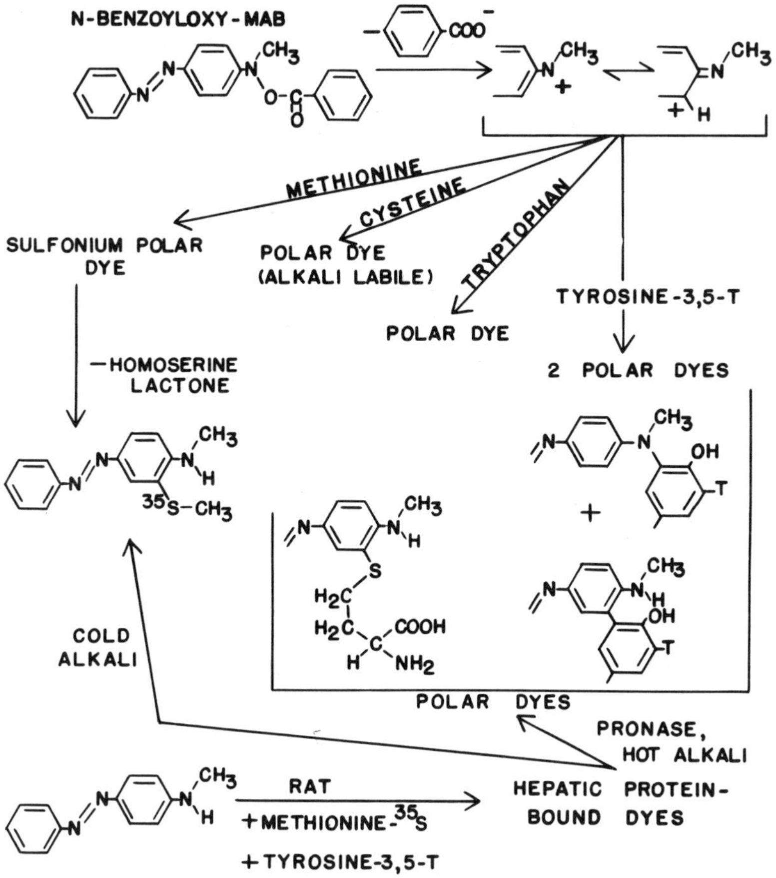

FIGURE 3. The nonenzymatic reaction at neutrality of N-benzoyloxy-N-methyl-4-aminoazobenzene (N-benzoyloxy-MAB) with methionine, cysteine, tryptophan, and tyrosine to yield polar dyes and the identity of the methionine and tyrosine derivatives with those liberated from the livers of rats administered MAB.[21,28-30]

4-hydroxyaminoquinoline-N-oxide show a different pattern. In each of these cases, guanine is the base that is preferentially substituted, but reactions one-fifth to one-half as great as those with guanine also occur with adenine and cytosine (TABLE 2).[24,33]

Enzymatic Formation of the Sulfuric Acid Ester of N-Hydroxy-AAF

Studies on the nonenzymatic reactivity of the benzoic acid, acetic acid, and sulfuric acid esters and with the glucuronide of N-hydroxy-AAF showed that they all reacted with the nucleophiles discussed above to yield similar products. With respect to the nature of the products, the only difference observed among

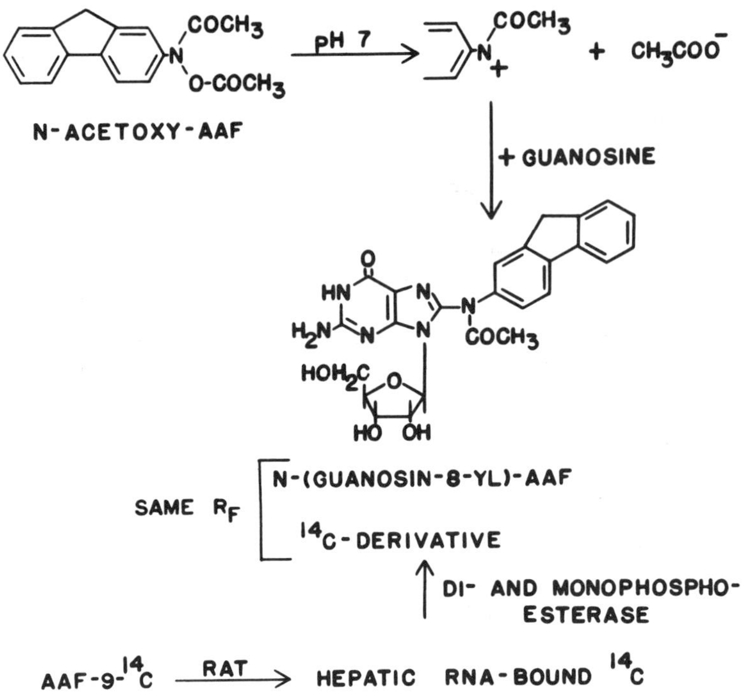

FIGURE 4. The nonenzymatic reaction at neutrality of N-acetoxy-AAF with guanosine to yield N-(guanosin-8-yl)-AAF and its chromatographic identity with a product released from the hepatic RNA of rats administered N-hydroxy-2-acetylaminofluorene.[25,32]

TABLE 1

THE REACTION OF N-ACETOXY-AAF WITH NUCLEOSIDES*

Nucleoside	Percent Reaction
Guanosine-8-^{14}C	50
Adenosine-8-^{14}C	0.5
Uridine-2-^{14}C	< 0.05
Cytidine-2-^{14}C	< 0.05
Thymidine-2-^{14}C	< 0.05

*The percent reaction is based on the nucleoside, the limiting reactant. The incubation mixture contained 1.8 μmoles of nucleoside and 7 μmoles of N-acetoxy-AAF in 1.25 ml of pH 7,0.005 M citrate buffer. After incubation for 3 hr at 37° C, the products were separated from the substrates by thin-layer chromatography on cellulose in acidic solvents. Other experiments in which the nonradioactive nucleosides were incubated with N-acetoxy-AAF-9-^{14}C confirmed that the products were fluorene derivatives.

TABLE 2
THE RELATIVE REACTIONS OF ESTERS OF N-HYDROXY DERIVATIVES WITH NUCLEIC ACID BASES*

		Relative Reaction			
	Guanine	Adenine	Cytosine	Uracil	Thymine
N-Acetoxy-AAF	(100)	1	n.d†	n.d.	n.d.
N-Acetoxy-4-acetyl-aminostilbene	(100)	15	30	n.d.	n.d.
Diacetyl derivative of 4-hydroxyaminoquinoline-1-oxide	(100)	50	25	n.d.	–

*The reactions of N-acetoxy-AAF and N-acetoxy-4-acetylaminostilbene were determined by incubation of the esters with ^{14}C-labeled nucleosides under the conditions described in the footnote to TABLE 1. The diacetyl derivative of 4-hydroxyaminoquinoline-1-oxide (presumably the 0,0′-diacetyl derivative) was reacted with polyriboguanylic acid, polyriboadenylic acid, polyribocytidylic acid, and polyribouridylic acid, and the extents of reaction were determined from the absorption at 354 mμ of each of the reisolated, purified polynucleotides.[33]

†The abbreviation "n.d." indicates that a reaction could not be detected.

the reactive conjugates of N-hydroxy-AAF was that considerable labilization of the N-acetyl group occurred on reaction of the glucuronide with guanosine. Thus, while essentially the only product from the reaction of esters of N-hydroxy-AAF with guanosine was N-(guanosin-8-yl)-AAF, approximately two-thirds of the product obtained by reaction with the glucuronide was N-(guanosin-8-yl)-AF.[23] There is, however, a major difference in the rates of reaction and half-lives of these conjugates. The glucuronide of N-hydroxy-AAF has a half-life of at least several days and reacts only slowly with nucleophiles. The acetic acid and benzoic acid esters have half-lives of one to one and one-half hours, and the half-life of the sulfuric acid ester is less than one minute.† Thus, while the glucuronide is sufficiently stable that Hill and Irving[34,35] could isolate it from the urine and bile of rabbits administered N-hydroxy-AAF, the isolation of the short-lived esters from animal tissues did not appear feasible.

Accordingly, we[36] and King and Phillips[37] independently developed *in vitro* systems in which esters of N-hydroxy-AAF were generated by soluble liver proteins and reacted with nucleic acids or methionine to give stable recognizable products. The formation of the sulfuric acid ester has been demonstrated unequivocally in both laboratories. The formation of appreciable amounts of reactive ester in the presence of ATP and Mg^{++} and in the absence of added $SO_4^=$ suggests that the phosphoric acid ester may also be formed by liver proteins,[36,37] but this has not been demonstrated rigorously. The formation of acyl derivatives

†The half-lives of N-acetoxy-AAF and N-benzoyloxy-AAF were obtained in 32% ethanol; the half-lives decrease with decreasing ethanol concentration and extrapolate to about 7 minutes for solutions in water.

by tissue preparations *in vivo* and *in vitro* also seems likely, but it has not been demonstrated.

Our assay for the sulfotransferase system depends on the enzymatic transfer of sulfate from 3′-phosphoadenosine-5′-phosphosulfate (PAPS) to N-hydroxy-AAF and the nonenzymatic reaction of the AAF-N-sulfate thus formed with methionine (FIGURE 5). The sulfonium product is unstable and decomposes‡ to 1- and 3-methylmercapto-AAF, which can be assayed by gas chromatography. This reaction is completely dependent on PAPS, either added or generated *in situ,* and is stimulated by Mg^{++} (TABLE 3).

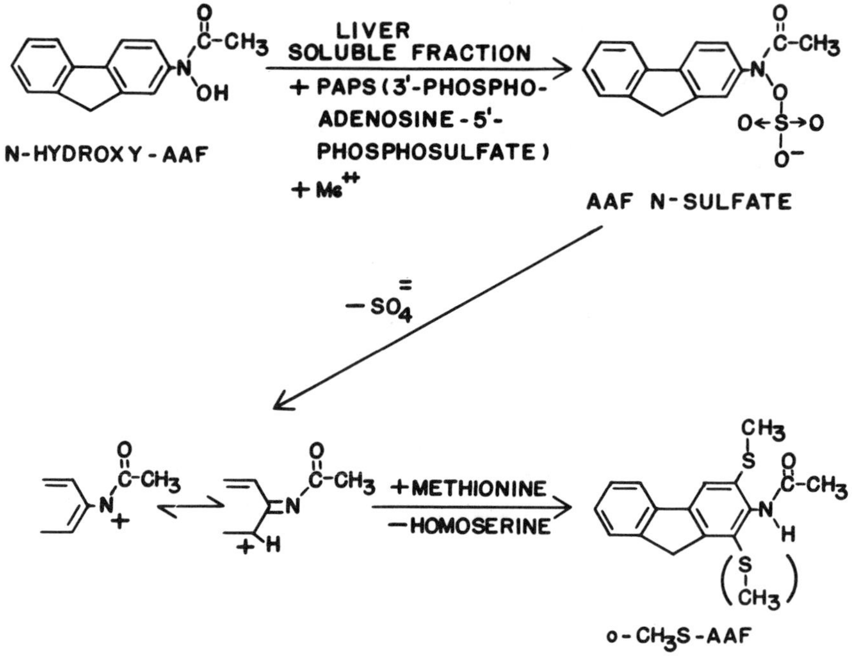

FIGURE 5. Assay for the enzymatic transfer of sulfate from 3′-phosphoadenosine-5′-phosphosulfate to N-hydroxy-AAF, as determined by the formation of o-methylmercapto-AAF.[36]

A survey of the capacities of livers from various animals to make the sulfuric acid ester of N-hydroxy-AAF indicates that the ability to transfer sulfate from PAPS to N-hydroxy-AAF could be a limiting factor in liver tumor induction (TABLE 3). Thus, male rat livers, which are much more susceptible to hepatic tumor induction by N-hydroxy-AAF than are female rat livers,[7] have a several-fold higher level of the sulfotransferase system for N-hydroxy-AAF. Similarly,

‡Complete decomposition of the sulfonium derivative is ensured by heating the reaction mixture at neutrality at 90° C for one hour.

TABLE 3

COFACTOR REQUIREMENTS FOR THE FORMATION OF THE SULFURIC ACID ESTER OF N-HYDROXY-AAF BY A SOLUBLE LIVER SYSTEM*

Additions	Sulfotransferase Activity (μg o-CH_3S-AAF)
PAPS (0.0006 M) + Mg^{++} (0.005 M)	60
PAPS + Mg^{++} + EDTA (0.004M)	32
PAPS	37
Mg^{++}	< 1.5
PAPS + Mg^{++} (but no enzyme)	< 1.5

*Each tube contained in a final volume of 1.0 ml 0.2 mg of N-hydroxy-AAF, 5 mg of L-methionine, 0.1 ml of liver supernatant (20% homogenate centrifuged at 105,000 × g for 1 hr, approximately 2.5 mg of protein), and 25 μmoles of tris (hydroxymethyl)-aminomethane·HCl buffer, pH 7.

the hepatic levels of sulfotransferase for N-hydroxy-AAF are very low in mice, guinea pigs, and hamsters. Mice and hamsters develop low incidences of liver tumors slowly when N-hydroxy-AAF is administered, while guinea pigs are very resistant.[9] The exception to this correlation is the rabbit. Rabbit liver has a level of hepatic sulfotransferase activity for N-hydroxy-AAF that is compatible with susceptibility to tumor induction,§ but liver tumors have not been found in rabbits treated with this carcinogen.[10] Resistance of rabbit liver to carcinogenesis may be a function of the high capacity of these livers to reduce administered N-hydroxy-AAF.[38] That the rabbit liver does not develop an appreciable level of esters of N-hydroxy-AAF after intraperitoneal injection of the carcinogen is indicated by our inability to liberate detectable amounts of o-methylmercapto-AAF from the liver protein (TABLE 4). The liver protein of other animals resistant to hepatocarcinogenesis also failed to yield more than small amounts of o-methylmercapto-AAF after administration of the hydroxamic acid, so that by this criterion, there is a good correlation between the apparent levels of esters of N-hydroxy-AAF formed in the liver and the susceptibility to hepatic carcinogenicity.

Although N-hydroxy-4-acetylaminobiphenyl is converted to the sulfuric acid ester by the soluble proteins of male rat liver about one-half as efficiently as is N-hydroxy-AAF, only very low amounts of 3-methylmercapto-4-acetylaminobiphenyl can be released from the liver protein after intraperitoneal injection of N-hydroxy-4-acetylaminobiphenyl into male rats.[39] This *in vivo* result is consistent with the very poor hepatocarcinogenic activity of 4-acetylaminobiphenyl and its N-hydroxy derivative.[40] The greater stability of the esters of N-hydroxy-4-acetylaminobiphenyl, as compared to those of N-hydroxy-AAF, may permit them

§Recent studies have shown that the sulfotransferase assay used to obtain the data in TABLE 3 was not fully limiting with respect to the amount of enzyme. With a system in which the sulfotransferase is limiting, rabbit liver has only 10% as much activity as rat liver.

to be cleared from the liver before significant reaction with tissue macromolecules occurs.

Much further work is necessary to determine what esters, other than the sulfate, can be formed by tissues susceptible to carcinogenesis by N-hydroxy-AAF and related compounds and to determine the relative importance of each of these esters, of other conjugates (e.g., the glucuronide), and of other possible metabolites to the carcinogenic process. The recent data of Kriek[26] on the isolation of N-(deoxyguanosin-8-yl)-AF-5′-phosphate after degradation of the hepatic DNA of rats administered AAF, while N-(guanosin-8-yl)-AAF[1,25] and N-(guanosin-8-yl)-AAF-5′-phosphate[26] have been obtained by hydrolysis of the hepatic RNA, raise new questions. Thus, is there a direct (enzymatic?) reaction of N-hydroxy-AF with DNA in the nucleus? Or, is the isolation of the DNA derivative evidence for the formation of esters of N-hydroxy-AF? Alternatively, is the isolation of this derivative evidence that the form that reacts with DNA is the glucuronide of N-hydroxy-AAF? Reaction of the glucuronide of N-hydroxy-AAF with guanosine results in labilization of the N-acetyl group and the formation of N-guanosin-8-yl-AF as the major product.[23] It is also pertinent to question whether there is a specificity among the metabolites of N-hydroxy-AAF for reaction with certain macromolecules or within certain morphological sites of the cell. Thus, it would not be surprising if the short half-life and negative charge of the sulfuric acid ester of N-hydroxy-AAF formed in the cytoplasm restricted the ability of this ester to penetrate to some parts of the cell, such as the nucleus.

Table 4

Comparison of the N-Hydroxy-AAF Sulfotransferase Activities, Amounts of Protein-Bound o-(Methion-S-yl)-AAF Formed *in Vivo* From N-Hydroxy-AAF, and Susceptibilities of Rodent Livers to Carcinogenesis by N-Hydroxy-AAF

Species and Sex	μg o-CH_3S-AAF		Liver Tumors from N-HO-AAF‡
	Liver Sulfotransferase* *(in vitro)*	Liver Protein† *(in vivo)*	
Rat (M)	31–39	31–41	++++
(F)	5–6	4–5	+
Hamster (M)	1–2	<2	+
Mouse (M)	1–2	<2	+
Guinea pig (M)	0–1	<2	—
Rabbit (M)	12–14§	<2	—

* Data from DeBaun *et al.*, 1968.[36]

† The amount of o-methylmercapto-AAF (μg/5 g of liver) released by alkali at room temperature from cold solvent-extracted liver protein. The animals were killed 20 hr after intraperitoneal injection of 5 mg of N-hydroxy-AAF per 100 g body weight.

‡ Data from Miller *et al.*, 1961,[7] Miller *et al.*, 1964,[9] and Irving *et al.*, 1967.[10]

§ o-Methylmercapto-AF plus o-methylmercapto-AAF.

Carcinogenicity of Esters of N-Hydroxy-AAF and Related Compounds

The high carcinogenicity of the neutral lipid-soluble acetic acid and benzoic acid esters of N-hydroxy-AAF at the site of subcutaneous injection in the rat is consistent with the premise that esters of the hydroxamic acids may be ultimate carcinogenic forms (TABLE 5). Under the conditions of our experiments, these esters were more carcinogenic at the subcutaneous site than any of the other metabolites tested, including N-hydroxy-AAF and N-hydroxy-AF. Similarly, the acetic acid esters of N-hydroxy-2-acetylaminophenanthrene, N-hydroxy-4-acetylaminostilbene, and N-hydroxy-4-acetylaminobiphenyl were each more carcinogenic for the subcutaneous tissue of the rat than the parent hydroxamic acid (TABLE 6). In contrast to these results with lipid-soluble neutral esters, the sulfuric acid esters of N-hydroxy-AAF and N-hydroxy-4-acetylaminobiphenyl have proved to have only low carcinogenic activity when injected subcutaneously into rats under the same conditions as the acetoxy derivatives. It appears likely that the negative charge and high reactivity of these compounds cause most of the reactivity to be expended on extracellular components and that very little of either sulfuric acid ester penetrates the cell membrane to be available for intracellular reactions.

N-Benzoyloxy-MAB, an ester of a hydroxylamine and presumably structurally related to the reactive metabolite(s) formed in the rat liver (see above), likewise induced a high incidence of sarcomas at the subcutaneous injection site,[27] while MAB was inactive at this site. The carcinogenic activity of N-benzoyloxy-MAB at the injection site and the finding of an AF derivative as a major DNA-bound form of AAF in the rat liver[26] emphasize the importance of studies on the carcinogenicity and reactivity of esters of N-hydroxy-AF and of other carcinogenic hydroxylamines. Syntheses for these compounds have not yet been devised.

TABLE 5

THE INDUCTION OF SARCOMAS AT THE SITE OF SUBCUTANEOUS INJECTION OF FLUORENE DERIVATIVES*

Compound Injected	No. of Injections	No. of Rats with Sarcomas		
		6 mo	9 mo	14 mo
N-Acetoxy-AAF	6	5	10	11†
N-Benzoyloxy-AAF	6	2	10	17
N-Hydroxy-AAF	6	0	3	12
N-Hydroxy-AF	6	0	2	5
2-Nitrosofluorene	6	0	2	10
AAF	10	0	0	0
AF	10	0	0	0
(Vehicle only)	10	0	0	0

*Trioctanoin (0.2 ml) containing 12.6 μmoles of fluorene derivative was injected subcutaneously once (groups receiving 6 injections) or twice (groups receiving 10 injections) per week. There were 17 male rats per group; initial weights were 110–130 g/rat.

†Five rats died tumor-free within the first 7 months from toxicity.

TABLE 6

THE RELATIVE INCIDENCES OF SARCOMAS INDUCED AT THE SITE OF SUBCUTANEOUS INJECTION OF VARIOUS N-ACETOXY AND N-HYDROXY AROMATIC AMIDES*

Compound	No. of Injections	No. of Rats with Sarcomas at Injection Site				
		5 mo	6 mo	8 mo	11 mo	16 mo
N-Acetoxy-2-acetyl-aminophenanthrene	3	7	11	13	15	15
N-Hydroxy-2-acetyl-aminophenanthrene	3	0	2	4	9	10
N-Acetoxy-4-acetyl-aminostilbene	5	4	8	10	11	–†
N-Hydroxy-4-acetyl-aminostilbene	5	1	4	7	11	–†
N-Acetoxy-4-acetyl-aminobiphenyl	15	0	0	0	1	5
N-Hydroxy-4-acetyl-aminobiphenyl	15	0	0	0	0	0
(Vehicle only)	15	0	0	0	0	0

*Each dose of 5 μmoles was injected in 0.2 ml of trioctanoin; injections were made at weekly intervals. Sixteen male rats with initial weights of 130–160 g comprised each group.

†All rats were dead by the 12th month.

Mutagenic Effects of N-Benzoyloxy-MAB and Esters of N-Hydroxy-AAF

The nature of the interaction(s) between the ultimately reactive carcinogenic form and some tissue constituent(s) to induce neoplasia is not known for any chemical carcinogen, but it seems clear that the perpetuable change in carcinogenesis must involve one or more of the macromolecules that can store or alter the use of genetic information, i.e., DNA, RNA, or protein. DNA is an attractive theoretical target, since alterations in the information coded in DNA are an obvious mechanism for development of a race of cells with a metabolic balance altered from that of the cells of origin. Hence it was important to determine whether the chemical alteration of DNA by esters of N-hydroxy-AAF and by N-benzoyloxy-MAB caused mutagenic effects.

Our studies, carried out in collaboration with Drs. Maher and Szybalski,[41] utilized the *Bacillus subtilis* transforming DNA system of Freese and Strack.[42] In this system the transforming DNA is treated with the test chemical in a non-metabolizing system, reisolated free of the test compound, and then assayed for its transforming and mutagenic effects. This system, since it avoids possible metabolic alteration of the test compound to more reactive or less reactive derivatives, permits assay of the mutagenic potentiality of the compound as such. Further, since the chemicals are tested on free native DNA, the assay is not influenced by differing rates of transfer of the test compounds across cellular and intracellular membranes.

In this assay, transformation depends on the incorporation of wild type DNA, which carries the gene for the enzyme that condenses indole or indole-3-glycerolphosphate with serine, into tryptophanless mutants of *B. subtilis*.[43] These transformants are the only cells that give rise to colonies on the test medium devoid of tryptophan. Mutation, by the test compound, of any one of three linked genes causes the accumulation in the progeny of the transformed cells of the fluorescent intermediates anthranilic acid or 1-(o-carboxyphenylamino)-1-deoxyribulose-5-phosphate. The accumulation of these intermediates causes such colonies of transformed cells to be fluorescent and thus easily scorable.

Treatment of the transforming DNA with N-benzoyloxy-MAB or with esters of N-hydroxy-AAF caused marked inactivation of transforming activity (FIGURE 6) and marked increases in the incidence of colonies of mutant fluorescing cells (FIGURES 7 and 8). Treatment of the DNA with MAB or with AF, AAF, 2-nitrosofluorene, N-hydroxy-AF, or N-hydroxy-AAF caused little loss of transforming activity or increase in the incidence of mutant colonies. It is tempting to speculate that these inactivating and mutagenic effects of N-benzoyloxy-MAB and the esters of N-hydroxy-AAF on transforming DNA may be analogous, at least in part, to two effects of these carcinogens on the target tissues *in vivo*, i.e.,

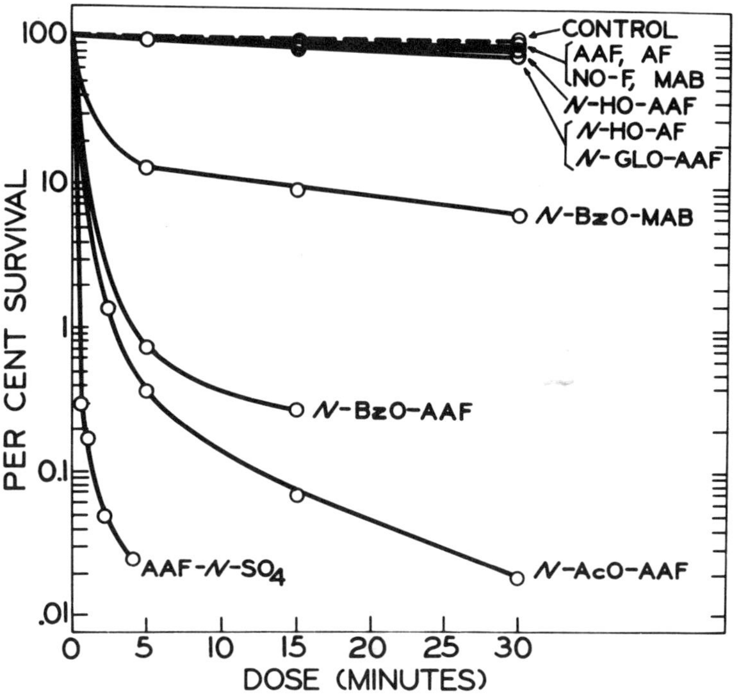

FIGURE 6. The reduction in transforming activity as a consequence of the *in vitro* reaction of DNA from *Bacillus subtilis* with esters of N-hydroxy-AAF or with N-benzoyloxy-MAB. Treatment of the DNA with the parent amines or amide (AAF, AF, or MAB) or with the metabolites N-hydroxy-AAF, N-hydroxy-AF, or 2-nitrosofluorene caused little or no loss of transforming activity.[41] (Reproduced by permission of the authors and Molec. Pharmacol. 1968. 4: 411–426.)

killing of cells and the occasional conversion of a normal cell to a neoplastic cell.

The nature of the chemical reaction that causes the mutational effects is not clear. It seems likely that the bulky AAF group (or the AF group) in the 8 position of guanine in DNA may inhibit DNA polymerase, and Troll and associates[44] have shown that DNA that has been reacted with N-acetoxy-AAF is a poor substrate for DNA polymerase. If substitution of AF or AAF in the 8 position of guanine residues in DNA does halt the progress of DNA polymerase, this substitution might be expected to yield deletion mutants. Deletion mutants are the type most frequently seen by Fahmy and Fahmy[41,45] on treatment of *Drosophila* males with N-acetoxy-AAF. However, most of the mutants obtained by treatment of transforming DNA with esters of N-hydroxy-AAF were spontaneously revertible, and thus they are presumed to be due to single base-pair changes.[41] As shown by Corbett and colleagues,[46] T4 phage is also mutated by N-acetoxy-AAF; their studies indicate that the revertible mutants were the consequence of A:T to G:C changes in the DNA. The latter observations suggest that the quantitatively minor reaction of adenine with esters of N-hydroxy-AAF may be of considerable importance in mutagenesis and, possibly, in carcinogenesis. Accordingly, the reactions of esters of N-hydroxyamides and N-hydroxyamines with adenine residues in nucleotides and polynucleotides are under further investigation.

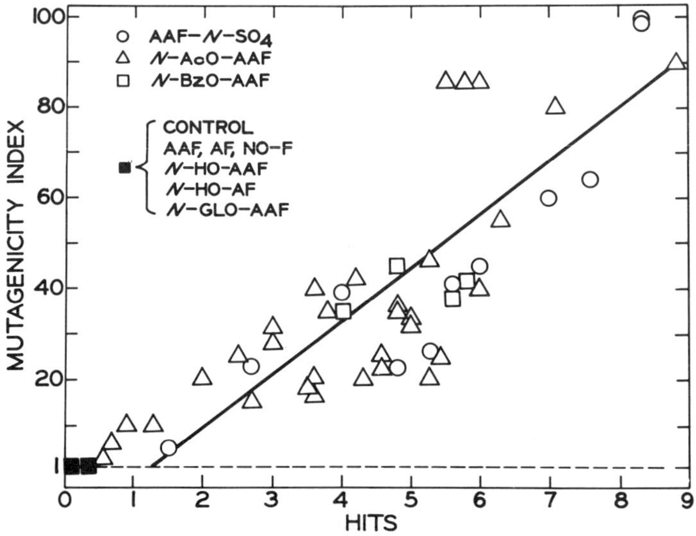

FIGURE 7. The mutagenic action of various esters of N-hydroxy-AAF on transforming DNA for *Bacillus subtilis*. AF, AAF, N-hydroxy-AAF, N-hydroxy-AF, and 2-nitrosofluorene had little or no effect on the incidence of mutant colonies. The mutation index is the ratio of the mutation rate for the colonies derived from cells treated with the reacted DNA to the control rate. The mutation rate parallels the extent of reaction of the DNA with the ester of N-hydroxy-AAF and the degree of inactivation (hits) of the DNA.[41] (Reproduced by permission of the authors and Molec. Pharmacol. 1968. **4:** 411–426.)

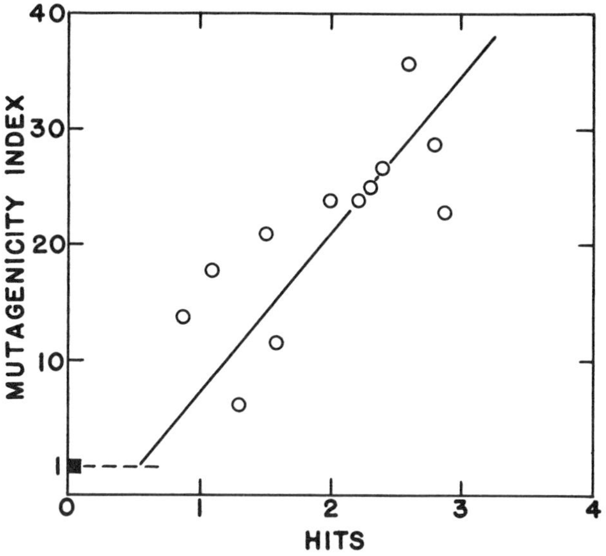

FIGURE 8. The mutagenic action of N-benzoyloxy-MAB (○) on transforming DNA for *Bacillus subtilis*.[41] Activity of control and MAB given by (■). (Reproduced by permission of the authors and Molec. Pharmacol. 1968. **4:** 411–426.)

An Overview of Chemical Carcinogenesis

The preceding discussion has emphasized the view that the aromatic amines and amides are really "precarcinogens" that are metabolically activated to ultimate carcinogenic forms and that these carcinogenic forms are electrophilic reactants. It now appears that this point of view can be broadened to include most, if not all, chemical carcinogens (FIGURE 9). Thus, as discussed by Price and coworkers[47] and by Shapiro[48] in this monograph, the alkylating agents are electrophilic reactants essentially in the form administered. Several classes of chemical carcinogens are now known to be converted, enzymatically or nonenzymatically, in animal tissues to alkylating agents. Evidence for this conversion of the nitrosamines and nitrosamides to electrophilic reactants has been discussed in this monograph by Preussman,[49] Druckrey,[50] and Magee.[51] Also, Preussman[49] and Druckrey[50] have discussed the conversion of 1,2-dialkyl hydrazines and the corresponding azo and azoxy compounds and of aryldialkyl triazenes to electrophilic reactants. Ethionine[52] and cycasin[53,54] undergo similar metabolic conversion. The carcinogenic pyrrolizidine alkaloids can be viewed as electrophilic reactants as administered, as originally shown by Culvenor and associates.[55] Furthermore, as first reported by Mattocks[56] and as emphasized in this monograph by Culvenor and colleagues,[57] the pyrrolizidine alkaloids are metabolized to pyrrole derivatives that are more reactive electrophiles. 4-Nitroquinoline-1-oxide is reduced *in vivo* to the more carcinogenic 4-hydroxyaminoquinoline-1-oxide,[58] and its diacetyl derivative reacts with nucleic acids *in vitro* to yield fluorescent conjugates with properties similar to those of the nucleic acid-bound derivatives formed on administration of 4-hydroxyamino-quinoline-1-oxide to rats.[33] The reactive and carcinogenic forms of the polycyclic aromatic hydrocarbons are still subjects of speculation. Fried and Schumm[59] and Wilk and Schwab[60] have pointed to the possible importance of radical cations formed by the action of one-electron transfer oxidants on the hydrocarbons *in vivo*. The withdrawal of a single electron to give a radical cation that could react with a tissue nucleophile is shown in FIGURE 10. Rearomatization could occur with the loss of a hydrogen ion and a second electron. The model experiments of Brookes and Dipple[61] further suggest that methyl substituents of the polycyclic aromatic hydrocarbons may also be subject to similar reactions.

The most critical cellular nucleophilic targets of the carcinogenic electrophilic reactants appear to be the bases of the nucleic acids and certain protein-bound amino acids. The covalently bound derivatives of carcinogens with proteins and nucleic acids appear to arise in this manner. However, some of the electrophilic reactant-macromolecule reactions may be transient and constitute "hit-and-run" reactions yielding macromolecules free of the carcinogen derivative. Similarly, other cellular targets may be involved and secondarily influence the properties of certain nucleic acids and proteins. The resultant altered DNA, RNA's, and proteins would thus initiate the carcinogenic process. The subsequent events that lead to the neoplastic state remain essentially uncharacterized. Carcinogenesis clearly involves heritable changes in growth control that appear to be irreversible under most circumstances. However, no carcinogenic mechanism, be it incited by a radiation, a virus, or a chemical, is understood today in molecular terms. At present, the four general mechanisms, two direct and two indirect, listed in FIGURE 9, appear to be the principal hypotheses that are under experi-

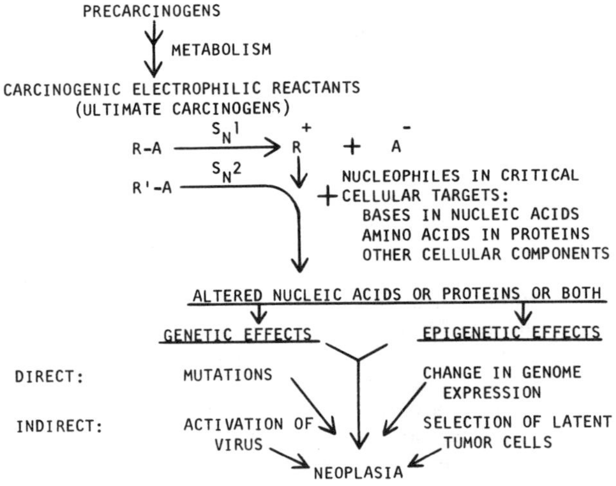

FIGURE 9. A unifying concept of chemical carcinogenesis that suggests that all or most chemical carcinogens are electrophilic reactants (i.e., the alkylating agents) or are activated by conversion to electrophilic derivatives that react with tissue nucleophiles to initiate the neoplastic transformation.

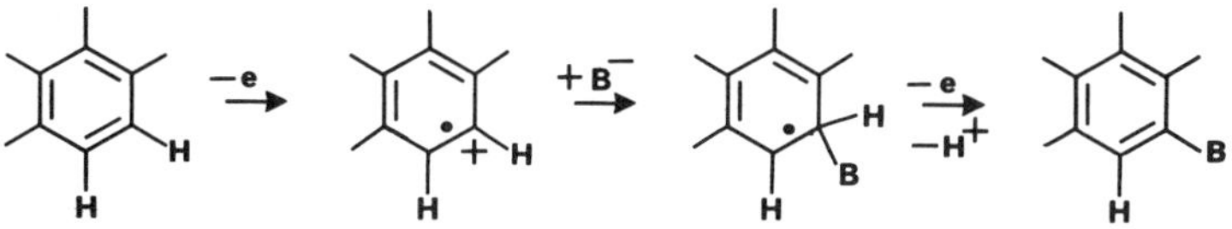

FIGURE 10. Scheme for the conversion of a polycyclic aromatic hydrocarbon to a radical cation[59,60] and the mechanism by which this derivative might react with tissue nucleophiles.

mental test. Any of these mechanisms or combinations thereof may account for the way in which a given carcinogenic agent operates.

The characterization of the ultimate carcinogenic forms of many if not all of the varied chemical carcinogens or precarcinogens as electrophilic reactants brings considerable unity to this aspect of chemical carcinogenesis. The stage now seems set for exciting new advances in concept and method.

ACKNOWLEDGMENTS

The collaboration of Dr. Jen-Kun Lin, Mr. Jack R. DeBaun, Mrs. Barbara W. Butler, Mrs. Cornelia Whelan, Mrs. Gudrun Rognerud, and Mrs. Huey-Jen Wei in some of the unpublished work is acknowledged with thanks.

REFERENCES

1. MILLER, J. A. & E. C. MILLER. 1969. The metabolic activation of carcinogenic aromatic amines and amides. Progr. Exp. Tumor Res. **11:** 273–301.
2. WEISBURGER, E. K. & J. H. WEISBURGER. 1958. Chemistry, carcinogenicity, and metabolism of N-2-fluorenamine and related compounds. Advances Cancer Res. **5:** 331–441.
3. MILLER, E. C. & J. A. MILLER. 1966. Mechanisms of chemical carcinogenesis: Nature of proximate carcinogens and interactions with macromolecules. Pharmacol. Rev. **18:** 805–838.
4. MILLER, J. A. & E. C. MILLER. 1966. A survey of molecular aspects of chemical carcinogenesis. Lab. Invest. **15:** 217–239.
5. CRAMER, J. W., J. A. MILLER & E. C. MILLER. 1960. N-Hydroxylation: A new metabolic reaction observed in the rat with the carcinogen 2-acetylaminofluorene. J. Biol. Chem. **235:** 885–888.
6. MILLER, J. A., J. W. CRAMER & E. C. MILLER. 1960. The N- and ring-hydroxylation of 2-acetylaminofluorene during carcinogenesis in the rat. Cancer Res. **20:** 950–962.
7. MILLER, E. C., J. A. MILLER & H. A. HARTMANN. 1961. N-Hydroxy-2-acetylaminofluorene: A metabolite of 2-acetylaminofluorene with increased carcinogenic activity in the rat. Cancer Res. **21:** 815–824.
8. MILLER, J. A., M. ENOMOTO & E. C. MILLER. 1962. The carcinogenicity of small amounts of N-hydroxy-2-acetylaminofluorene and its cupric chelate in the rat. Cancer Res. **22:** 1381–1388.
9. MILLER, E. C., J. A. MILLER & M. ENOMOTO. 1964. The comparative carcinogenicities of 2-acetylaminofluorene and its N-hydroxy metabolite in mice, hamsters, and guinea pigs. Cancer Res. **24:** 2018–2032.
10. IRVING, C. C., R. WISEMAN, JR. & J. M. YOUNG. 1967. Carcinogenicity of 2-acetylaminofluorene and N-hydroxy-2-acetylaminofluorene in the rabbit. Cancer Res. **27:** 838–848.

11. Irving, C. C. 1962. N-Hydroxylation of 2-acetylaminofluorene in the rabbit. Cancer Res. **22:** 867–873.
12. Poirier, L. A., J. A. Miller & E. C. Miller. 1963. The N- and ring-hydroxylation of 2-aminofluorene and the failure to detect N-acetylation of 2-aminofluorene in the dog. Cancer Res. **23:** 229–239.
13. Weisburger, J. H., P. H. Grantham & E. K. Weisburger. 1964. Metabolism of N-2-fluorenylacetamide in the hamster. Toxic. Appl. Pharmacol. **6:** 427–433.
14. Irving, C. C. 1964. Enzymatic N-hydroxylation of the carcinogen 2-acetylaminofluorene and the metabolism of N-hydroxy-2-acetylaminofluorene-9-^{14}C *in vitro.* J. Biol. Chem. **239:** 1589–1596.
15. Lotlikar, P. D., M. Enomoto, J. A. Miller & E. C. Miller. 1967. Species variations in the N- and ring-hydroxylation of 2-acetylaminofluorene and effects of 3-methylcholanthrene pretreatment. Proc. Soc. Exp. Biol. Med. **125:** 341–346.
16. Kiese, M. & I. Wiedemann. 1966. Excretion of N-hydroxy-2-aminofluorene by guinea pigs injected with 2-acetylaminofluorene. Biochem. Pharmacol. **15:** 1882–1885.
17. Marroquin, F. & E. Farber. 1965. The binding of 2-acetylaminofluorene to rat liver ribonucleic acid *in vivo.* Cancer Res. **25:** 1262–1269.
18. Miller, E. C., C. W. Cooke, P. D. Lotlikar & J. A. Miller. 1964. The metabolism and carcinogenicity of N-hydroxy-2-acetylaminofluorene and some of its possible metabolites. Proc. Amer. Ass. Cancer Res. **5:** 45.
19. Irving, C. C., R. A. Veazey & R. F. Williard. 1967. On the significance and mechanism of the binding of 2-acetylaminofluorene and N-hydroxy-2-acetylaminofluorene to rat-liver ribonucleic acid *in vivo.* Cancer Res. **27:** 720–725.
20. Kriek, E. 1965. On the interaction of N-2-fluorenylhydroxylamine with nucleic acids *in vitro.* Biochem. Biophys. Res. Commun. **20:** 793–799.
21. Lotlikar, P. D., J. D. Scribner, J. A. Miller & E. C. Miller. 1966. Reaction of esters of aromatic N-hydroxy amines and amides with methionine *in vitro:* A model for *in vivo* binding of amine carcinogens to protein. Life Sci. **5:** 1263–1269.
22. Miller, E. C., U. Juhl & J. A. Miller. 1966. Nucleic acid guanine: Reaction with the carcinogen N-acetoxy-2-acetylaminofluorene. Science **153:** 1125–1127.
23. Miller, E. C., P. D. Lotlikar, J. A. Miller, B. W. Butler, C. C. Irving & J. T. Hill. 1968. Reactions *in vitro* of some tissue nucleophiles with the glucuronide of the carcinogen N-hydroxy-2-acetylaminofluorene. Molec. Pharmacol. **4:** 147–154.
24. Miller, E. C. & J. A. Miller. Unpublished data.
25. DeBaun, J. R., E. C. Miller & J. A. Miller. 1967. Structures of protein- and RNA-bound forms of 2-acetylaminofluorene in the rat. Proc. Amer. Ass. Cancer Res. **8:** 12.
26. Kriek, E. 1968. Difference in binding of 2-acetylaminofluorene to rat liver deoxyribonucleic acid and ribosomal ribonucleic acid *in vivo.* Biochim. Biophys. Acta **161:** 273–275.
27. Poirier, L. A., J. A. Miller, E. C. Miller & K. Sato. 1967. N- Benzoyloxy-N-methyl-4-aminoazobenzene: Its carcinogenic activity in the rat and its reactions with proteins and nucleic acids and their constituents *in vitro.* Cancer Res. **27:** 1600–1613.
28. Scribner, J. D., J. A. Miller & E. C. Miller. 1965. 3-Methylmercapto-N-methyl-4-aminoazobenzene: An alkaline degradation product of a labile protein-bound dye in the livers of rats fed N,N-dimethyl-4-aminozobenzene. Biochem. Biophys. Res. Commun. **20:** 560–565.
29. Lin, J.-K., J. A. Miller & E. C. Miller. 1968. Studies on structures of polar dyes derived from the liver proteins of rats fed N-methyl-4-aminoazobenzene. II. Identity of synthetic 3-(homocystein-S-yl)-N-methyl-4-aminoazobenzene with the major polar dye P2b. Biochemistry **7:** 1889–1895.
30. Lin, J. -K., J. A. Miller & E. C. Miller. 1969. Studies on structures of polar dyes derived from the liver proteins of rats fed N-methyl-4-aminoazobenzene. III. Tyrosine and homocysteine sulfoxide polar dyes. Biochemistry. In press.
31. Miller, J. A. & E. C. Miller. 1967. Activation of carcinogenic aromatic amines and

amides by N-hydroxylation *in vivo*. *In* Carcinogenesis: A Broad Critique. : 397–420. The Williams and Wilkins Co. Baltimore, Md.
32. KRIEK, E., J. A. MILLER, U. JUHL & E. C. MILLER. 1967. 8-(N-2-Fluorenylacetamido) guanosine, an arylamidation reaction product of guanosine and the carcinogen N-acetoxy-N-2-fluorenylacetamide in neutral solution. Biochemistry **6:** 177–182.
33. ENOMOTO, M., K. SATO, E. C. MILLER & J. A. MILLER. 1968. Reactivity of the diacetyl derivative of the carcinogen 4-hydroxyaminoquinoline-N-oxide with DNA, RNA, and other nucleophiles. Life Sci. **7:** 1025–1033.
34. HILL, J. T. & C. C. IRVING. 1967. Biosynthesis and studies of the alkaline sensitivity of the NO-Glucuronide of the carcinogen N-2-fluorenylacethydroxamic acid. Biochemistry **6:** 3816–3821.
35. IRVING, C. C. 1965. On the structure of the glucuronide of N-hydroxy-2-acetylaminofluorene. J. Biol. Chem. **240:** 1011–1013.
36. DEBAUN, J. D., J. Y. ROWLEY, E. C. MILLER & J. A. MILLER. 1968. Sulfotransferase activation of N-hydroxy-2-acetylaminofluorene in rodent livers susceptible and resistant to this carcinogen. Proc. Soc. Exp. Biol. Med. **129:** 268–273.
37. KING, C. M. & B. PHILLIPS. 1968. Enzyme-catalyzed reactions of the carcinogen N-hydroxy-2-fluorenylacetamide with nucleic acid. Science **159:** 1351–1353.
38. LOTLIKAR, P. D., E. C. MILLER, J. A. MILLER & A. MARGRETH. 1965. The enzymatic reduction of the N-hydroxy derivatives of 2-acetylaminofluorene and related carcinogens by tissue preparations. Cancer Res. **25:** 1743–1752.
39. DEBAUN, J. R., E. C. MILLER & J. A. MILLER. Unpublished data.
40. MILLER, J. A., C. S. WYATT, E. C. MILLER & H. A. HARTMANN. 1961. The N-hydroxylation of 4-acetylaminobiphenyl by the rat and dog and the strong carcinogenicity of N-hydroxy-4-acetylaminobiphenyl in the rat. Cancer Res. **21:** 1465–1473.
41. MAHER, V. M., E. C. MILLER, J. A. MILLER & W. SZYBALSKI. 1968. Mutations and decreases in density of transforming DNA produced by derivatives of the carcinogens 2-acetylaminofluorene and N-methyl-4-aminoazobenzene. Molec. Pharmacol. **4:** 411–426.
42. FREESE, E. & H. B. STRACK. 1962. Induction of mutations in transforming DNA by hydroxylamine. Proc. Nat. Acad. Sci. USA **48:** 1796–1803.
43. CARLTON, B. C. 1967. Transformation mapping of the genes controlling tryptophan biosynthesis in *Bacillus subtilis*. J. Bact. **94:** 660–665.
44. TROLL, W., S. BELMAN, E. BERKOWITZ, Z. F. CHMIELEWICZ, J. L. AMBRUS & T. J. BARDOS. 1968. Differential responses of DNA and RNA polymerase to modifications of the template rat liver DNA caused by action of the carcinogen acetylaminofluorene *in vivo* and *in vitro*. Biochim. Biophys. Acta **157:** 16–24.
45. FAHMY, O. G. & M. J. FAHMY. 1967. Mutagenicity of aromatic amines and their metabolites. Brit. Empire Cancer Campaign. 45th Annual Report. : 81.
46. CORBETT, T., C. HEIDELBERGER & W. F. DOVE. Personal communication.
47. PRICE, C. C., G. M. GAUCHER, P. KONERU, R. SHIBAKAWA, J. R. SOWA & M. YAMAGUCHI. 1969. Mechanism of action of alkylating agents. Ann. N. Y. Acad. Sci. This monograph.
48. SHAPIRO, R. 1969. Reactions with purines and pyrimidines. Ann. N. Y. Acad. Sci. This monograph.
49. PREUSSMANN, R. 1969. Chemical structure and carcinogenicity of aliphatic hydrazo-, and azoxycompounds and of triazenes: potential *in vivo* alkylating agents. Ann. N. Y. Acad. Sci. This monograph.
50. DRUCKREY, H. 1969. N-Nitroso-compounds in organotropic and transplacental carcinogenesis. Ann. N. Y. Acad. Sci. This monograph.
51. MAGEE, P. N. 1969. *In vivo* reactions of nitroso compounds. Ann. N. Y. Acad. Sci. This monograph.
52. FARBER, E. 1963. Ethionine carcinogenesis. Advances Cancer Res. **7:** 383–474.
53. KOBAYASHI, A. & H. MATSUMOTO. 1965. Studies on methylazoxymethanol, the aglycone of cycasin. Isolation, biological, and chemical properties. Arch. Biochem. **110:** 373–380.

54. Matsumoto, H. & H. H. Higa. 1966. Studies on methylazoxymethanol, the aglycone of cycasin: Methylation of nucleic acids *in vitro*. Biochem. J. **98:** 20c–22c.
55. Culvenor, C. C. J., A. T. Dann & A. T. Dick. 1962. Alkylation as the mechanism by which the hepatotoxic pyrrolizidine alkaloids act on cell nuclei. Nature **195:** 570–573.
56. Mattocks, A. R. 1968. Toxicity of pyrrolizidine alkaloids. Nature **217:** 723–728.
57. Culvenor, C. C. J., D. T. Downing, J. A. Edgar & M. V. Jago. 1969. Pyrrolizidine alkaloids as alkylating and antimitotic agents. Ann. N. Y. Acad. Sci. This monograph.
58. Matsushima, T., I. Kobuna, F. Fukuoka & T. Sugimura. 1968. Metabolism of 4-nitroquinoline 1-oxide. IV. Quantitative determination of *in vivo* conversion of 4-nitroquinoline 1-oxide in subcutaneous tissue of rat. Gann **59:** 247–250.
59. Fried, J. & D. E. Schumm. 1967. One electron transfer oxidation of 7,12-dimethylbenz(a)anthracene, a model for the metabolic activation of carcinogenic hydrocarbons. J. Amer. Chem. Soc. **89:** 5508–5509.
60. Wilk, M. & H. Schwab. 1968. Zum Transportphanomen und Wirkungsmechanismus des 3,4-Benzpyrens in der Zelle. Z. Naturforsch. [B] **23b:** 431–438.
61. Brookes, P. & A. Dipple. 1967. Mechanism of hydrocarbon carcinogenesis. Brit. Empire Cancer Campaign. 45th Annual Report. : 20.

DISCUSSION OF THE PAPER

Unidentified Speaker: N-Acetoxy-AAF reacts with guanosine and guanylic acid. What happens if the ester is reacted with DNA?

Dr. Miller: Reaction of N-acetoxy-AAF with DNA results in substitution of the guanine bases at C-8 in the same manner as for the reaction of N-acetoxy-AAF with guanosine, as seen in Figure 4. With a sufficient excess of N-acetoxy-AAF, most of the guanine in denatured DNA will react. Extensive reaction also occurred when we started with native DNA. No reaction of the other bases in DNA has been detected, but the methods that have been used to search for these products have not been very sensitive (for example, base analyses after formic acid hydrolysis).

Unidentified Speaker: The reaction you have discussed between esters of N-hydroxy-AAF and DNA is a chemical one. Have you examined possible physical interactions that might disrupt the tertiary structure of the DNA within the cells?

Dr. Miller: We have not investigated this problem.

IN VIVO REACTIONS OF β-PROPIOLACTONE

R. K. Boutwell, Nancy H. Colburn, and Carolyn C. Muckerman

McArdle Laboratory, University of Wisconsin, Madison, Wis.

Introduction

The fundamental mechanisms of *in vitro* alkylation were reviewed before a conference of the New York Academy of Sciences in 1957.[11,15] It was pointed out that alkylation may be regarded as the conversion of a target molecule, H-X, a nucleophile, to RX by the alkylating agent R-Y. The alkylating agent is capable of reacting with agents possessing nucleophilic character, that is agents with electron-rich centers, to form the alkylated derivative, RX.

Our interest in this reaction is that it appears to be a reaction with cellular constituents that is common to all carcinogens. However, in the case of many classes of carcinogens, R^+ is the end product of metabolic activation, whereas R^+ forms spontaneously in the case of the carcinogenic alkylating agents. The question remains, is this the determining reaction of carcinogenesis and what is (or are) the critical cellular nucleophilic center(s)?

In this research, we have studied the reaction of β-propiolactone with the DNA, RNA, and protein of the skin of intact mice. This choice was predicated on the following facts. First, β-propiolactone has been found to be both a carcinogen[13] and an initiator[4,14] for mouse skin. Second, the lability of β-propiolactone to nucleophilic attack is well known, and the reaction with DNA and RNA *in vitro* to form the 7-alkylated guanine, 7-(2-carboxyethyl)guanine, has been studied.[12] Also well studied is the *in vitro* reaction of β-propiolactone with albumin,[17] cysteine,[7] and 18 amino acids.[10,19] Finally, some information is available on the consequences of alkylation of proteins and nucleic acids with β-propiolactone and on the possibility of functional significance for this reaction in carcinogenesis.[1]

The reaction of nucleophilic centers with β-propiolactone is a second-order nucleophilic displacement reaction, as illustrated in Figure 1. The nucleophile is represented by XNH, and nitrogen is shown as the electron-rich, nucleophilic center. The final product is the carboxyethyl derivative of the nucleophile. A number of nucleophilic centers exist in both nucleic acids[1] and proteins[16] and most commonly involve nitrogen, sulfur, or oxygen atoms.

β-propiolactone is a highly reactive molecule; it has a half-life of about three hours in water at 25° C, and at body temperature in the presence of nucleophiles in aqueous solution, the half-life is much less. Furthermore, much of the β-propiolactone administered to an animal reacts with the extracellular water and nucleophiles, and it is likely that only a small part of the administered dose reaches the intracellular macromolecules, particularly the nuclear components.

Experiments and Results

The work to be reported was concerned with investigating the molecular mechanism of mouse skin carcinogenesis by β-propiolactone. It will be presented

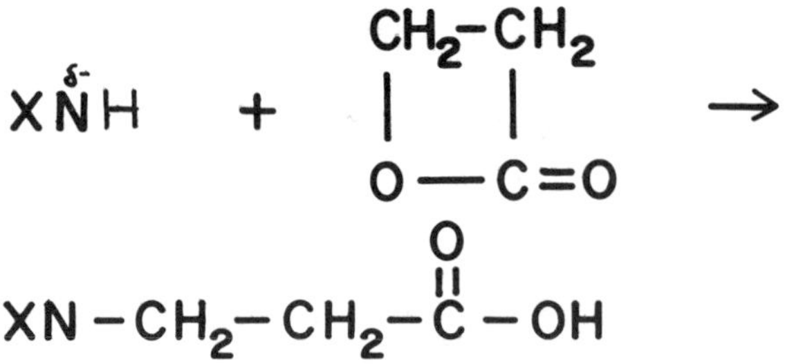

FIGURE 1. The interaction of β-propiolactone with a nucleophilic nitrogen-containing compound.

under the following headings: (1) the binding of β-propiolactone to DNA, RNA, and protein *in vivo* and the quantitation and kinetics of this binding, (2) the nature of the binding products of β-propiolactone to DNA, RNA, and protein, (3) studies of the significance to carcinogenesis of DNA, RNA, and protein binding, and (4) studies on the functional consequences of the formation of 7-(2-carboxyethyl)guanine in DNA.

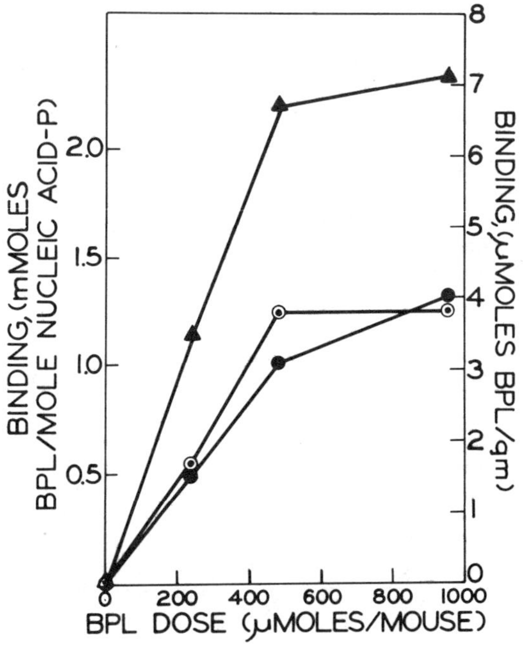

FIGURE 2. The binding of β-propiolactone-^{3}H to mouse skin DNA, RNA, and protein as a function of dose. Tritiated β-propiolactone was applied once to the skin of skin-tumor-susceptible (STS) mice in 0.3 ml of acetone solution per mouse. Mice were killed and the skins taken at four hours after application of β-propiolactone. ●, DNA; ⊙, RNA; ▲, protein; nucleic acid-P, nucleic acid phosphate.

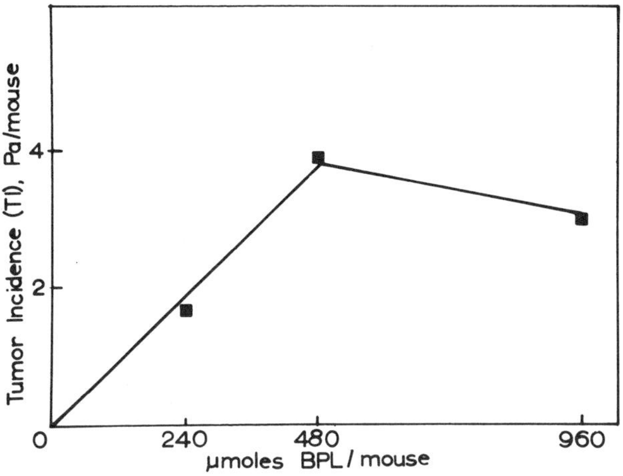

FIGURE 3. Variation in tumor incidence with dose. An initiating dose of β-propiolactone was applied to STS mice once in 0.3 ml of acetone per mouse. A solution of oil was applied repeatedly beginning one month later. Each point represents the average number of papillomas per mouse in groups of 10 mice. Tumor incidence is plotted at the 19th week after initiation. Skin carcinomas began to appear at the 18th week.

The Binding of β-Propiolactone to DNA, RNA, and Protein[4,5]

Tritiated β-propiolactone (specific activity varied from about 20 to 288 mc/mmole) was applied to the shaved backs of mice as a freshly prepared solution in 0.3 ml of acetone. The DNA, RNA, and protein were extracted according to a modification of the procedure of Kirby.[8] Skins from five mice were pooled for analysis, and, typically, we recovered 1 mg each of DNA and RNA and 200 mg of protein. Both DNA and RNA samples had protein contents of 3% or less. DNA samples contained less than 2% RNA.

Groups of mice given doses increasing from 0 to 960 μmoles of tritiated β-propiolactone in acetone were killed four hours after treatment, and the specific activities of the extracted DNA, RNA, and protein were determined. The results are shown in FIGURE 2. The extent of binding of β-propiolactone to all three macromolecules was linear up to a dose of 480 μmoles per mouse. The binding of β-propiolactone to both DNA and RNA at the 480-μmole dose corresponds to about 1 mmole β-propiolactone per mole of nucleic acid phosphate. On a per-gram-weight basis, binding to protein was about twice as high as binding to either nucleic acid.

The effect of increasing doses of β-propiolactone applied once to the skin of the backs of groups of mice on the tumor incidence elicited by multiple applications of croton oil is shown in FIGURE 3. A maximum tumor incidence of about four papillomas per mouse resulted from the 480-μmole dose of β-propiolactone, the same dose that gave maximum binding to each macromolecule.

The time course of binding of tritiated β-propiolactone to skin DNA, RNA, and protein is interesting (FIGURE 4). Mice that received 480 μmoles of tritiated β-propiolactone were killed at various times afterwards, and the specific activity of the DNA, RNA, and protein extracted by the Kirby procedure was determined. (There was one exception: The solid circles represent the specific activity

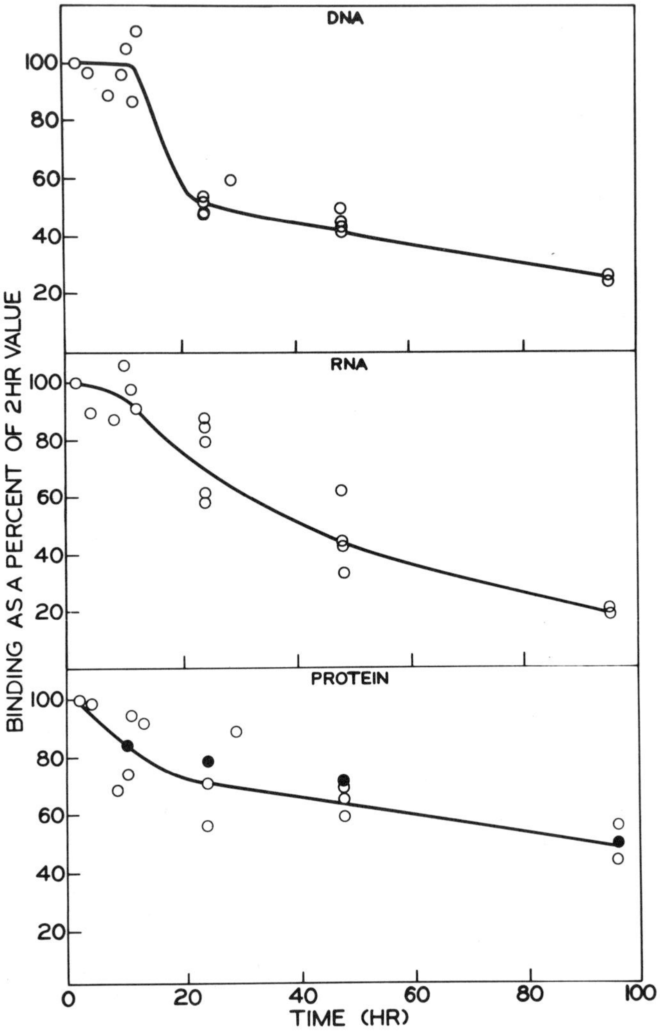

FIGURE 4. The time course of binding of β-propiolactone-^{3}H to skin DNA, RNA, and protein. A single application of 480 μmoles of tritiated β-propiolactone in 0.3 ml acetone was made to the back of each mouse. Mice were killed and skins taken for analysis from 2 to 96 hr after the treatment. Each symbol represents the data from one experiment. (The solid circles represent data for insoluble protein[18] rather than protein isolated by the modified Kirby procedure.)

of insoluble protein.)[18] The graph shows the binding as percent of the two-hour value plotted against the time of determination.

The DNA binding appears to remain constant from 2 to 12 hr, drops sharply to 50% of the 2-hr value at 24 hr, and then decreases at a slower but constant rate through 96 hr. The sharp fall in specific activity corresponds to the period of rapid synthesis of DNA that follows treatment of mouse skin with β-propiolactone, while the slow, constant fall in specific activity is accounted for by the normal rate of turnover of DNA plus the specific loss of labeled carboxyethylguanine from DNA due to the fact that alkylation of guanine in the 7 position labilizes the deoxyribose bond to the 9 position.[9] We found this deguanylation reaction to have a half-life of 150 hr in the case of DNA containing 7-(2-carboxyethyl)guanine.

The RNA binding decreases slowly through the first 12 hr, then faster at a constant rate to about 20% of the 2-hr value at 96 hr. This *in vivo* decrease of RNA specific activity after alkylation might be occurring by RNA turnover in the skin and by enzymatic excision, since the 39-hr half-life for the alkylated RNA exceeded the half-life of 100 hr for RNA of normal mouse skin. Chemical depurination has been shown not to occur in polyribonucleotides at neutral pH.[2]

Finally, the protein binding appears to decrease faster during the first 24 hr than subsequently, reaching about 50% of the 2-hr value at 96 hr.

Warwick and Roberts[20] have reported a persistent binding of azo dye derivative to liver DNA in contrast to a complete loss of bound dye from RNA and protein within a few weeks. We attribute their observation to the fact that DNA turnover in liver is very much slower than in skin and to the possibility that azo dye bound to DNA may not labilize the purine-deoxyribose bond. Therefore the altered base could remain persistently bound to the DNA.

The Nature of the Binding Products of β-Propiolactone to DNA, RNA, and Protein[4,5]

To identify the products formed when β-propiolactone reacts with skin macromolecules *in vivo,* DNA, RNA, and protein were isolated by the Kirby procedure from the skins of mice treated four hours earlier with from 120 to 480 μmoles per mouse of the tritiated propiolactone.

The RNA was hydrolyzed in 1N HCl for one hour at 100° C, and the hydrolysate was subjected to two-dimensional paper chromatography with carrier 7-(2-carboxyethyl)guanine. The UV-absorbing spots were traced (FIGURE 5).

FIGURE 5 shows the positions of the origin, guanine (G), 7-(2-carboxyethyl)-guanine (CEG), pyrimidine nucleotides (PyNT), and adenine (A) as well as the solvent fronts for the first and second dimensions (SF_1 and SF_2). The chromatogram of the RNA hydrolysate as a function of position along the chromatogram is shown in FIGURE 6. Some radioactivity appeared to be incorporated into the normal bases, but the major peak of radioactivity cochromatographed with authentic 7-(2-carboxyethyl)guanine and appeared to be identical to it. No unidentified radioactivity was found on the paper.

Similar results were obtained when DNA was hydrolyzed and chromatographed and the radioactivity was determined. FIGURE 7 shows a radioactive profile of a paper chromatogram made from the hydrolysate of radioactive mouse skin DNA.

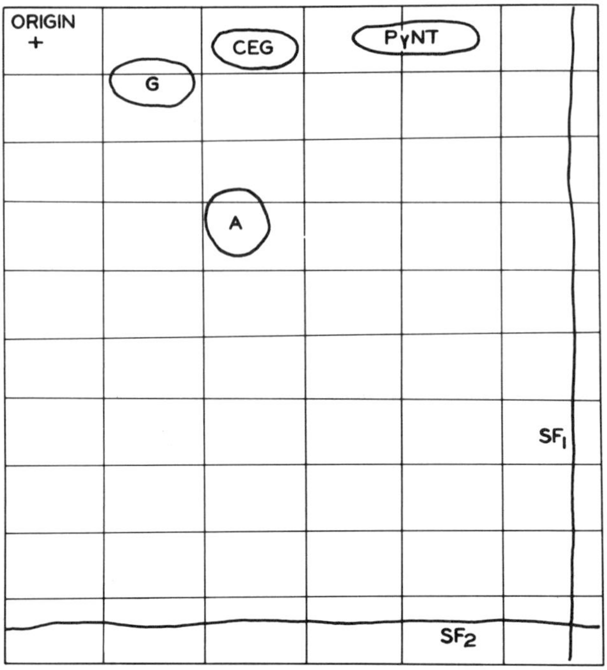

FIGURE 5. Chromatogram of the hydrolysate of RNA extracted from β-propiolactone-^3H-treated mouse skin. Mice were treated with 120 μmoles (2,070 μc) of tritiated propiolactone per mouse, and skins were taken four hours later. The extracted RNA was hydrolyzed in 1N HCl (125 μg of RNA in 50 ml) at 100° C for one hour. The hydrolysate was chromatographed in two dimensions with unlabeled carrier 7-(2-carboxyethyl)guanine (20 μg). Shown are the positions of the origin, 7-(2-carboxyethyl)guanine, pyrimidine nucleotides, adenine, and the two solvent fronts.

On the basis of these experiments, we conclude that 7-(2-carboxyethyl)-guanine, shown in FIGURE 8 in the enol form, is the major binding product of β-propiolactone with both DNA and RNA *in vivo*.

To determine the nature of the binding products of β-propiolactone with protein,[10] we first determined the reaction products of the lactone with individual amino acids *in vitro*, utilizing high-voltage paper electrophoresis and the Beckman amino acid analyzer to locate the reaction products.

Protein, isolated by the Kirby procedure from the skin of mice treated with radioactive β-propiolactone, was subjected to HCl hydrolysis in a sealed tube for 22 hr at 110° C. The hydrolysate was subjected to electrophoresis at pH 2 or pH 5 at 5,000 v for 20–30 min and to analysis on the amino acid analyzer.

The lower portion of FIGURE 9 shows the electrophoretic pattern at pH 2 of a skin protein hydrolysate to which was added carboxyethylcysteine, noted as CEC. The other spots are identified with standard abbreviations. The chromatogram was cut into rectangles as shown, the paper pieces eluted with 50% ethanol, the ninhydrin color destroyed with hydrogen peroxide, and the radioactivity

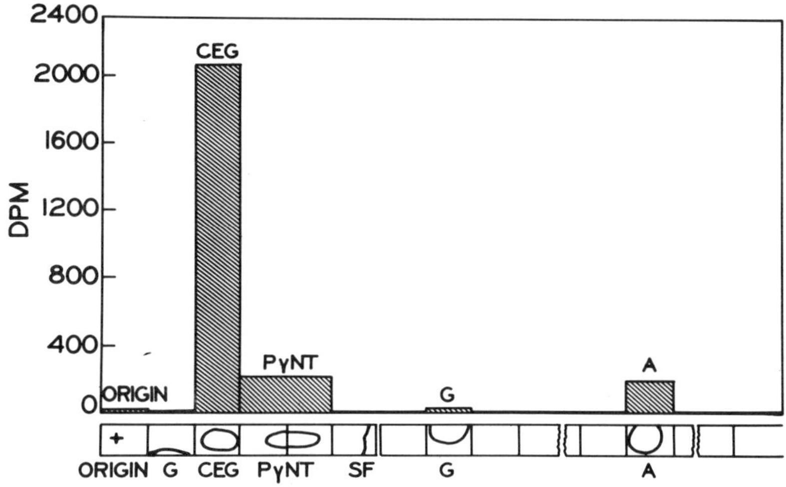

FIGURE 6. Radioactive profile of a paper chromatogram of the hydrolysate of radioactive mouse skin RNA (125 μg) isolated four hours after treatment with β-propiolactone. The chromatogram shown in FIGURE 5 was cut into rectangles as shown in that figure, eluted, and the radioactivity of the eluates determined. The radioactivity eluted, expressed as disintegrations per minute (DPM) per rectangle, is plotted as a function of position along the chromatogram. There was no radioactivity in any of the rectangles not shown in this profile.

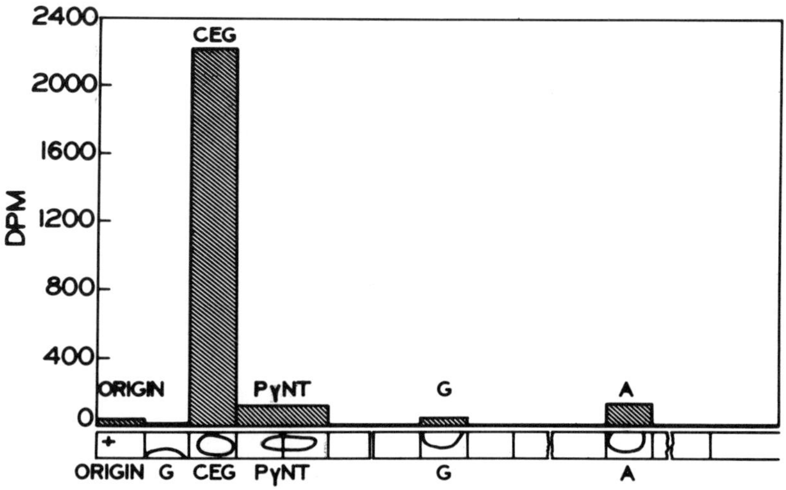

FIGURE 7. Radioactive profile of a paper chromatogram prepared from the hydrolysate of radioactive mouse skin DNA (150 μg). The procedure was similar to that described under FIGURE 6. No radioactivity was found in any of the rectangles not shown in this profile.

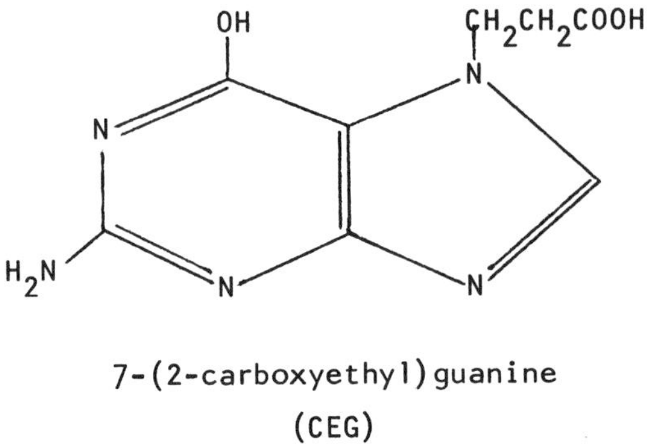

FIGURE 8. The enol form of 7-(2-carboxyethyl)guanine.

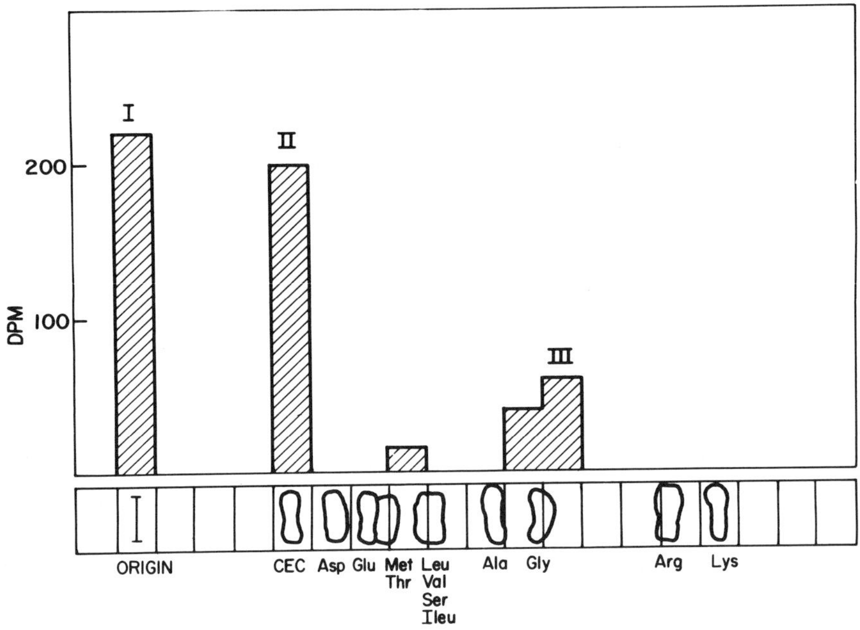

FIGURE 9. The radioactive profile of an electropherogram prepared from the hydrolysate of radioactive mouse skin protein (approx. 200 μg). A group of five mice was treated with 480 μmoles (approx. 100 μc) each of β-propiolactone-^{3}H and skin samples removed four hours later. The extracted protein was hydrolyzed in constant boiling HCl for 22 hr at 110° C in a sealed tube. The hydrolysate was subjected to electrophoresis at 5,000 v for 20 min with unlabeled carrier S-2-carboxyethyl-L-cysteine. The electropherogram was cut into rectangles as shown, eluted, and the radioactivity determined. Peak II was identified as carboxyethylcysteine and Peak I as 3-hydroxypropanoic acid, while the nature of the other peaks remains unknown.

determined by scintillation counting. The radioactivity from each rectangle is shown in the bar graph. Peak I was identified as 3-hydroxypropanoic acid resulting from the breakdown of acid labile products during hydrolysis of the protein. Peak II was identified as S-2-carboxyethyl-L-cysteine, the major acid stable product. The nature of the other peaks remains unknown.

The results of chromatography of the skin protein hydrolysate on the long column of the amino acid analyzer are shown in FIGURE 10. The amino acid

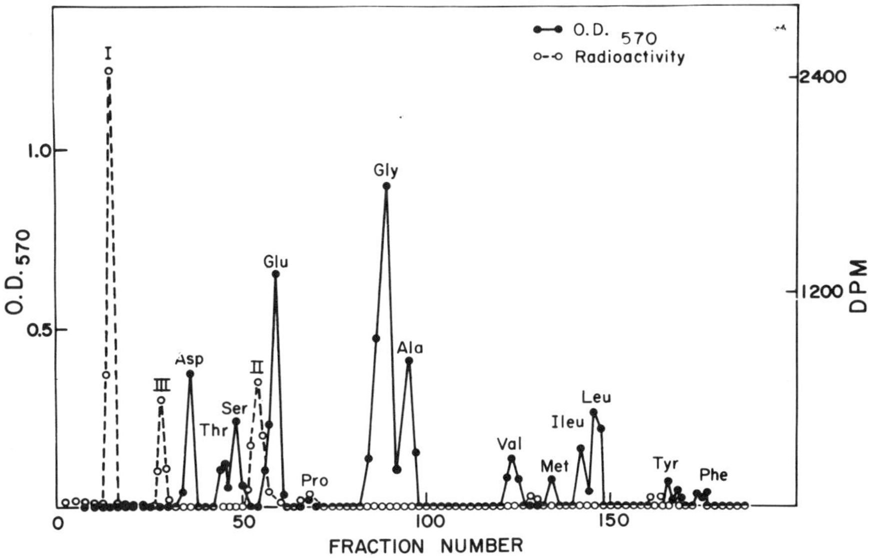

FIGURE 10. The results of chromatography of an hydrolysate of radioactive protein on the amino acid analyzer. The mice were treated and the hydrolysate prepared as described in the legend for FIGURE 9. A sample containing 5 μmoles total material was dissolved in 10 ml of pH 2.2 citrate buffer. Analysis of 1-ml aliquots was made on the Beckman model 120 C amino acid analyzer at 56° C and a buffer flow rate of 40 ml per hour. Radioactive peak II was identified as carboxyethylcysteine, peak I was identified as 3-hydroxypropanoic acid, and peak III was not identified.

peaks are identified with standard abbreviations, and the radioactive peaks are designated by numerals. As in the case of the high-voltage electrophoresis, peak I was identified as 3-hydroxypropanoic acid. Peak II was identified as S-2-carboxyethyl-L-cysteine, and as before, peak III could not be identified with any of the reaction products of β-propiolactone with individual amino acids *in vitro*. It is possible that peak III was also an artifact of the hydrolysis reaction, as was peak I. We have not been successful in achieving adequate hydrolysis by enzymatic methods, thereby obviating the artifacts introduced by acid hydrolysis.

Studies on the Significance to Carcinogenesis of DNA, RNA, and Protein Binding[6]

It was shown earlier in this report that the binding of β-propiolactone to DNA, RNA, and protein reached a maximum at a dose level of about 480 μmoles of propiolactone per mouse; higher levels did not increase the binding. Similarly, the maximum initiating response was reached at 480 μmoles of the lactone. These data provide no clue on the significance to carcinogenesis of the binding to a particular macromolecular species.

An attempt was made to distinguish the significance of the different types of binding by comparing the binding properties of β-propiolactone and some related alkylating agents differing in their initiating ability. The agents chosen for study were β-propiolactone, 3-iodopropanoic acid, 3-chloropropanoic acid, and iodoacetic acid.

Tumors were induced in groups of STS mice as follows. Mice were treated twice weekly for three weeks with 0.3 ml of an acetone solution containing 120 μmoles of β-propiolactone, 3-iodopropanoic acid, and 3-chloropropanoic acid; or 10 μmoles of iodoacetic acid. The choice of these levels was based on the corrosive nature of some of these chemicals for mouse skin as well as on prior experience in tumor response. After these six applications were completed, twice-weekly applications of croton oil were begun and continued until the end of the experiment. Control groups were treated with the six applications of the appropriate alkylating agent without subsequent croton oil treatment. The tumor

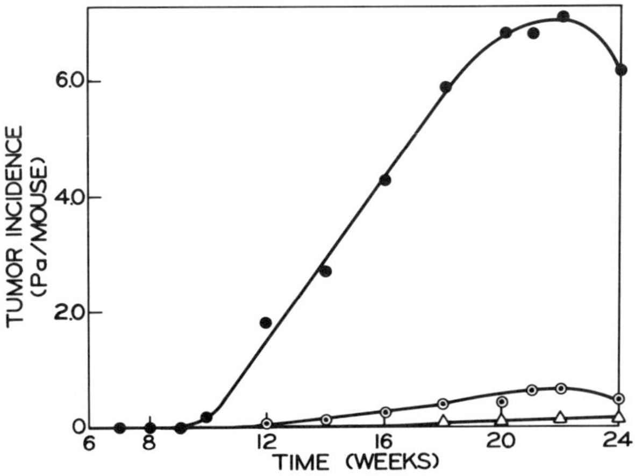

FIGURE 11. Tumor incidence in average number of papillomas per mouse (Pa/mouse) as a function of time after the beginning of initiation. The skin of the back of mice was treated twice weekly for three weeks with 120 μmoles/mouse of β-propiolactone, 3-iodopropanoic acid, or 3-chloropropanoic acid, or with 10 μmoles/mouse of iodoacetic acid followed either by repeated applications of croton oil or no further treatment. ●, β-propiolactone followed by croton oil; ⊙, 3-iodopropanoic acid followed by croton oil; △, β-propiolactone alone without further treatment. No tumors were obtained in 30 weeks in the groups treated with 3-chloropropanoic acid or iodoacetic acid with or without subsequent treatment with croton oil or in the group treated with 3-iodopropanoic acid without subsequent treatment. Each group consisted of 30–35 STS mice.

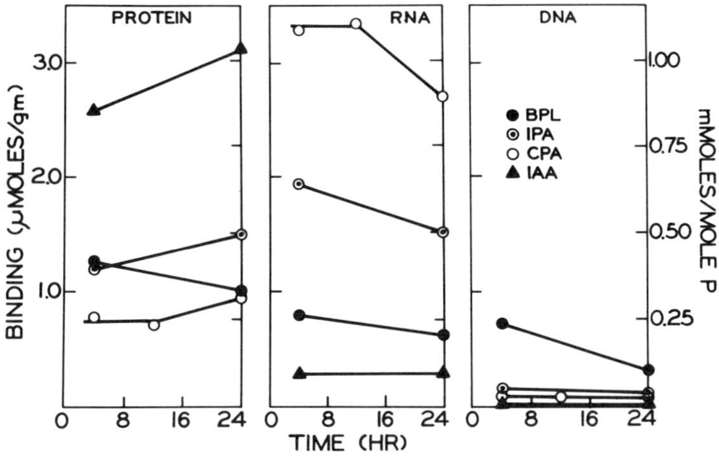

FIGURE 12. The time-course of binding of β-propiolactone-^{3}H, 3-iodopropanoic acid-^{3}H, 3-chloropropanoic acid-^{3}H, or iodoacetic acid-^{3}H to mouse skin DNA, RNA, and protein. Mice were killed and the skins taken for analysis at times from 4 to 24 hr after treatment. Data from one experiment is shown for each compound. BPL, β-propiolactone; IPA, 3-iodopropanoic acid; CPA, 3-chloropropanoic acid; IAA, iodoacetic acid; P, phosphate.

incidence resulting from this experiment is shown in FIGURE 11. The tumor incidence in average number of papillomas per mouse is plotted as a function of time after the beginning of initiation. At 22 weeks, there was an average of 7.1 papillomas per mouse in the group initiated with β-propiolactone and promoted with croton oil. There was an average of 0.7 papillomas per mouse in the group initiated by iodopropanoic acid followed by croton oil. There was a barely detectable response in the group treated with β-propiolactone without subsequent applications of croton oil. No tumors resulted from any of the other treatments. β-propiolactone was clearly much more effective than iodopropanoic acid as an initiator; iodoacetic acid and chloropropanoic acids were ineffective.

The binding of each of the four alkylating agents to the DNA, RNA, and protein of mouse skin was determined. Animals were killed for analysis 4, 12, and 24 hr after a single application of 120 μmoles of tritiated β-propiolactone, 3-iodopropanoic acid, and 3-chloropropanoic acid or of 10 μmoles of tritiated iodoacetic acid.

The results are shown in FIGURE 12. The binding of β-propiolactone to protein and RNA did not distinguish itself from the other alkylating agents; certainly binding bore no relation to the initiating property of these agents as shown in the previous figure. In contrast, the binding of β-propiolactone to DNA was several times greater than that of the other three agents. That there is indeed a strong correlation of DNA binding with tumor-initiating activity is shown in FIGURE 13. The binding of each agent to DNA of mouse skin four hours after application is expressed in terms of μmoles bound per mole of DNA phosphorus. This is plotted against tumor incidence in terms of papillomas per mouse at 22 weeks. β-propiolactone shows the highest degree of binding and the highest tumor incidence, iodopropanoic acid initiated only a few tumors and was bound pro-

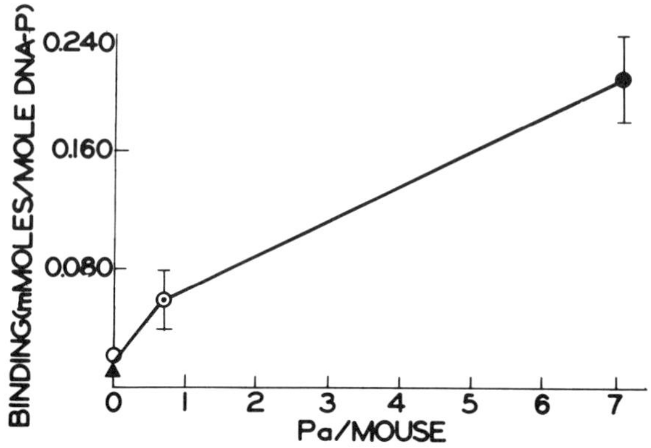

FIGURE 13. Binding of tritium-labeled alkylating agents to DNA of mouse skin four hours after application, in relation to the initiating potency as represented by the tumor incidence at 22 weeks in papillomas (Pa) per mouse. The symbols are the same as those shown in FIGURE 12.

portionately less to DNA, while chloropropanoic acid and iodoacetic acid did not initiate and were bound to DNA at a very low level.

The strong correlation of tumor-initiating ability and DNA binding supports the view that DNA is the significant cellular receptor of carcinogenic alkylating agents, in accordance with the somatic mutation theory of carcinogenesis.

Studies on the Functional Consequences of the Formation of 7-(2-Carboxyethyl)guanine in DNA

The template properties of β-propiolactone-alkylated DNA in an *in vitro* RNA polymerase system was found to decrease the template activity of DNA for the synthesis of RNA product when the incorporation of ^{14}C-labeled precursors, namely AMP (adenosine monophosphate), CMP (cytidine monophosphate), or UMP (uridine monophosphate) was measured. There was a further decrease in template activity when the alkylated DNA was allowed to undergo depurination.

The possible mechanisms by which DNA alkylation at the N-7 position of guanine might be important in carcinogenesis include anomalous base-pairing of the alkylated guanine with thymine, as suggested by Brookes and Lawley.[3] However, no evidence could be obtained for the anomalous base pairing of the N-7-alkylated guanine in DNA with uracil in an RNA polymerase system.

SUMMARY

β-propiolactone, an initiator of mouse skin tumors, was found to bind *in vivo* to mouse skin DNA, RNA, and protein. The major binding product formed with both DNA and RNA was 7-(2-carboxyethyl)guanine. Carboxyethylcysteine was found in the acid hydrolysate of protein isolated from the skin of propiolactone-treated mice.

Utilizing four structurally-related alkylating agents, it was found that the extent of binding to DNA correlated with initiating activity; no such correlation with tumor-initiating activity was found for binding to RNA or protein.

Finally, it was shown that the template activity of alkylated DNA in an RNA polymerase system is defective. However, no difference could be detected in the level of transcription error of normal or of alkylated DNA.

References

1. Brookes, P. 1966. Cancer Res. **26:** 1994.
2. Brookes, P. & P. D. Lawley. 1960. Biochem. J. **77:** 478.
3. Brookes, P. & P. D. Lawley. 1964. Brit. Med. Bull. **20:** 91.
4. Colburn, N. H. & R. K. Boutwell. 1966. Cancer Res. **26:** 1701.
5. Colburn, N. H. & R. K. Boutwell. 1968. Cancer Res. **28:** 642.
6. Colburn, N. H. & R. K. Boutwell. 1968. Cancer Res. **28:** 653.
7. Dickens, F. 1964. Brit. Med. Bull. **20:** 96.
8. Kirby, K. S. 1962. Biochim. Biophys. Acta **55:** 89.
9. Lawley, P. D. & P. Brookes. 1963. Biochem. J. **89:** 127.
10. Muckerman, Carolyn C. 1968. M.S. Thesis. University of Wisconsin. Madison, Wis.
11. Price, C. C. 1958. Ann. N. Y. Acad. Sci. **68**(3): 663.
12. Roberts, J. J. & G. P. Warwick. 1963. Biochem. Pharmacol. **12:** 1441.
13. Roe, F. J. C. & O. M. Glendenning. 1956. Brit. J. Cancer **10:** 357.
14. Roe, F. J. C. & M. H. Salaman. 1955. Brit. J. Cancer **9:** 177.
15. Ross, W. C. J. 1958. Ann. N. Y. Acad. Sci. **68**(3): 669.
16. Ross, W. C. J. 1962. *In* Biological Alkylating Agents. Butterworths. London, England.
17. Searle, C. E. 1961. Brit. J. Cancer **15:** 804.
18. Somerville, A. R. & C. Heidelberger. 1961. Cancer Res. **21:** 581.
19. Taubman, M. A. & M. Z. Atassi. 1968. Biochem. J. **106:** 829.
20. Warwick, G. P. & J. J. Roberts. 1967. Nature **213:** 1206.

DISCUSSION OF THE PAPER

Dr. P. Alexander (*Chester Beatty Research Institute, London, England*): You say without any qualification that your data show that the principal reaction product of β-propiolactone with DNA was 7-carboxyethylguanine. You may be perfectly right, but I think one must stress the point that the technique that you used to study this problem does not, in my view, allow you to make such a statement without any qualifications. If you hydrolyze at 100° C for six hours in acid, many reactions can occur.

Dr. Boutwell: Protein was hydrolyzed with constant boiling HCl in a sealed tube for 22 hrs at 110° C. In contrast, both DNA and RNA were hydrolyzed in 1 N HCl at 100° for one hour (about 250 μg of nucleic acid in 0.1 ml). The conditions used for nucleic acid hydrolysis open the phosphate ester linkages, but are not sufficiently drastic to degrade nucleic acids completely to the constituent bases, sugars, and phosphoric acid.

Dr. Alexander: It could possibly rupture other bonds, also. One must not be too dogmatic, because in the protein you fail to find any reaction with the mutagen. The carboxy group of proteins is the principal site of alkylation in proteins in addition to SH groups.

DR. BOUTWELL: In the case of protein isolated from the skins of β-propiolactone-H^3-treated mouse skin, S-2-carboxyethylcysteine was demonstrated to be the principal acid stable product; it typically accounted for about a third of the recovered radioactivity. The presence of 3-hydroxypropanoic acid, resulting from the breakdown of acid-labile products, was established, and accounted for about half the recovered radioactivity. Because the presence of 3-hydroxypropanoic acid is readily detected, its presence in the hydrolysis mixture has proved to be a useful indicator of alkylations that have been cleaved during the work-up for the detection of reaction products of β-propiolactone with cellular constituents.

DR. ALEXANDER: I should like to add a word of caution, that I do not think it is right to state, without qualification, that N-7 of guanine in DNA is the principal site of reaction.

DR. BOUTWELL: Nearly all of the radioactivity in the hydrolysate of both DNA and RNA was recovered as 7-(2-carboxyethyl)guanine; only minor peaks of radioactivity were found in the region of pyrimidine nucleotides, adenine, and guanine. However, if the products of alkylation of either DNA or RNA were labile to the acid hydrolysis (e.g. alkylation in the sugar-phosphate chain), one would expect to find radioactive hydroxypropanoic acid among the hydrolysis products. None was found.*

DR. P. MAGEE: We thought for some time that in the case of animals treated with dimethylnitrosamine, the primary reaction is at the N-7 of guanine. We examined liver RNA and DNA. It turns out that there are other alkylated bases present. Could it be so in your case? This is a very important point.

DR. BOUTWELL: This could be true. We saw this morning the great contrast in reactivity of the various positions of the nucleotides, and it strengthens your point that, with higher specific activity and better methods, other alkylated bases might be detected. The amount of radioactivity found in the carboxyethylguanine was at least 2,000 dpm. No unaccounted radioactivity was detected, so if β-propiolactone alkylates bases other than guanine in DNA or RNA to form acid-stabile derivates, the extent of reaction is considerably less than for the N-7 of guanine.

UNIDENTIFIED SPEAKER: Have you examined, by any chance, the γ-lactones, which, I believe, are very weak carcinogens? I think they would be of interest here.

DR. BOUTWELL: No, we have not included the γ-lactones in this series. Have you, Dr. Van Duuren?

B. L. VAN DUUREN, *New York University Medical Center, New York, N.Y.:* We have not, but there is no reason to believe that they should be alkylating agents.

* Colburn and Boutwell (1968a).

CONSEQUENCES OF ALKYLATION FOR THE BEHAVIOR OF DNA*

B. Strauss,† M. Coyle, and M. Robbins

Department of Microbiology
The University of Chicago
Chicago, Ill.

Bifunctional alkylating agents form cross-links binding the two strands of DNA together (Lawley & Brookes, 1967; Kohn, *et al.*, 1966; Kohn & Spears, 1967).‡ Such bifunctional compounds are toxic, but are relatively not as mutagenic as their monofunctional analogs, presumably because interstrand cross-linking prevents replication. The monofunctional alkylating agents can be extremely efficient mutagens. Ethyl methanesulfonate is widely used as a mutagen for plants (Amano & Smith, 1965) and animals (Carlson & Oster, 1962) and N-methyl-N′-nitro-N-nitroso-guanidine (NTG), one of the most efficient of mutagens (Adelberg *et al.*, 1965), does methylate DNA to form the same sort of products as does methyl methanesulfonate (MMS) (Lawley, 1968). The alkylated bases serve as sites at which replication errors can be made, resulting in transitions (Krieg, 1963). However, MMS is a relatively toxic substance producing an unfavorable ratio of mutations per lethal hit as compared to NTG (Cerdá-Olmedo & Hanawalt, 1967), which is remarkable among mutagens for its mutagenic efficiency at low lethality. Some factor other than the methylation of bases must determine the ratio between mutagenic effect and the toxicity of monofunctional alkylating agents.

In this paper we would like to discuss the probable events that occur when DNA is alkylated *in vitro* or *in vivo* with monofunctional methylating agents. We should like to establish the following points: 1) Three results of *in vitro* reaction of DNA with alkylating agents can be demonstrated; the production of DNA with alkylated (methylated) sites, with apurinic sites, and with single-strand breaks. 2) The methylated bases serve as recognition sites for an endonuclease that produces breaks at or near the site of some of the methylated bases. 3) Damage produced by reaction with methylating agents can be repaired, and it is likely that the repair is of single-strand breaks produced either spontaneously or as a result of endonuclease action. 4) Those methyl groups not recognized by the endonuclease or spontaneously lost by depurination may escape the repair systems and serve as sites at which mutagenic change can occur.

* Supported by grants from the National Science Foundation (GB 5419) and the National Institute of Health (GM 07816).

† Recipient of a Research Career Development Award (GM-K3-823) from the National Institutes of Health.

‡ Recently Lawley *et al.* (1969. J. Mol. Biol. **39:** 181–198) have demonstrated the formation of intrastrand crosslinks as a result of bifunctional alkylation.

In Vitro *Effects of Alkylation*

Treatment of DNA with MMS results in the formation of 7-methyl guanine and 3-methyl adenine (Lawley & Brookes, 1963). These bases are eventually lost, leaving apurinic residues that are susceptible to hydrolysis. The sequence of events can be demonstrated at low doses of MMS with use of a physically homogeneous virus DNA. Coliphage T7 DNA was alkylated with 0.0125 M MMS for 10 minutes to give about 16 added methyl groups/2.5 × 10^7 daltons (Strauss & Robbins, 1968). Methyl groups added by 1 hr reaction were labile on heating (FIGURE 1), as required by the experiments of Lawley and Brookes (1963). The alkylated DNA was stable to alkali, as determined by sucrose gradient centrifugation (FIGURE 2). Heating at 100° C for 2.5 minutes or at 50° for longer periods converted the alkylated DNA into a product that showed a diminished

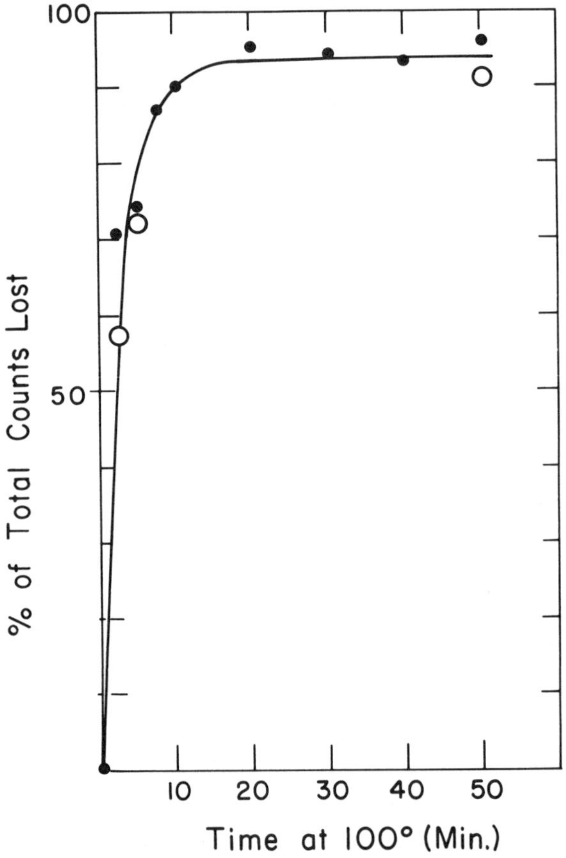

FIGURE 1. Acid solubilization of the radioactivity fixed to T7 DNA by reaction with 0.0125 M MMS for 120 minutes at 37° C. DNA was treated, dialyzed, and then heated in a boiling water bath. Open and closed circles give the results of different experiments.

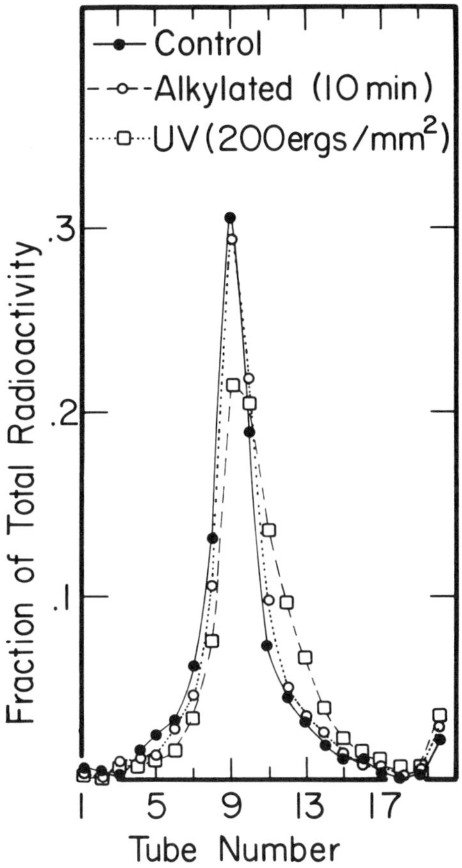

FIGURE 2. Sedimentation of methylated (0.0125 M MMS), UV-treated, and control T7 DNA through an alkaline sucrose gradient. Centrifugation was for three hours at 20° C at 35,000 rpm in the SW 39 rotor of the Spinco L-2 ultracentrifuge.

sedimentation rate in alkali (FIGURE 3) but not in neutral sucrose after formamide denaturation, as compared with the controls (Strauss *et al.*, in press). Heating presumably produced alkali-labile apurinic sites that did not hydrolyze readily in neutral solution, a conclusion in accordance with the findings of Laurence (1963).

At higher doses of MMS, breaks are produced immediately in the DNA, and these breaks are responsible for the inactivation of transforming activity when *B. subtilis* DNA is treated with MMS. DNA can be methylated with little loss of transforming activity (Strauss & Wahl, 1964), but heating such alkylated DNA reduces its activity without affecting the control (FIGURE 4). Extensive methylation does inactivate. Wahl-Synek (1967) showed that the transforming activity of DNA treated with MMS was correlated with its single strand molecular weight as estimated from sedimentation coefficients of formamide-denatured and

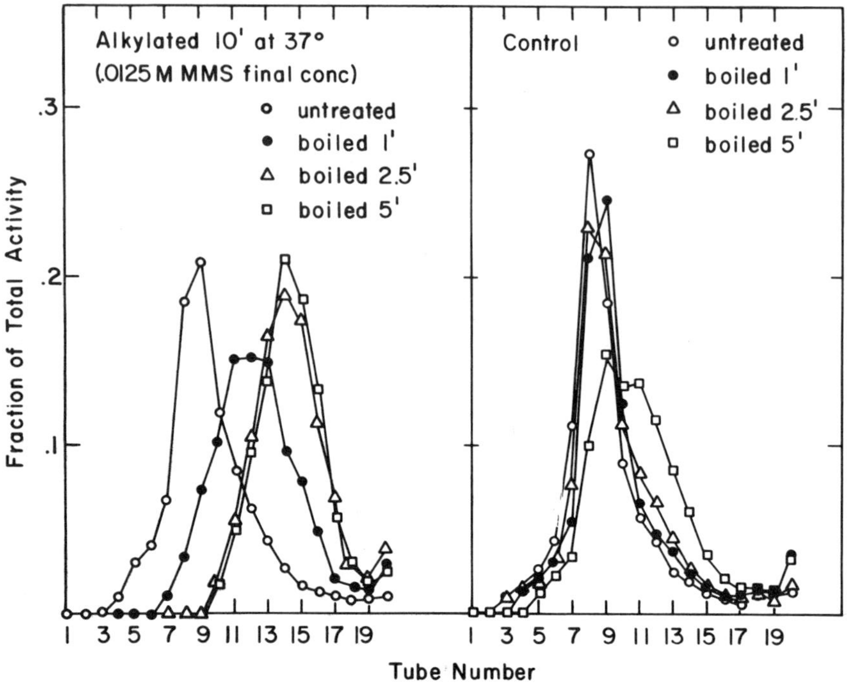

FIGURE 3. Effect of immersion in a boiling water bath on the sedimentation of methylated and control T7 DNA through an alkaline sucrose gradient. The DNA was placed in a screw-cap tube, which was immersed in a boiling water bath for the time indicated and then quenched in an ice bath.

formaldehyde-fixed DNA, a procedure that does not introduce breaks into apurinic DNA (FIGURE 5). Methylated and methylated and heated samples gave results falling on a curve which coincided exactly with the curve obtained on treating DNA with pancreatic deoxyribonuclease. These data, coupled with observations on the relative stability of alkylated and apurinic sites (Laurence, 1963; Lawley & Brookes, 1963; Strauss *et al.*, 1968), make it probable that in the presence of MMS, breaks appear more rapidly than might be supposed on the basis of the sequential mechanism:

alkylated bases → apurinic sites → single strand breaks.

Regardless of mechanism, it is clear that a) methylated DNA is biologically active, at least as far as its ability to participate in bacterial transformation is concerned, b) DNA with single-strand breaks is biologically inactive as measured by the same criterion, a result supported by the work of Bodmer (1966), c) single-strand breaks are produced in DNA as a result of MMS treatment, and d) it is nonetheless possible to obtain a methylated DNA free of breaks and apurinic sites as judged by the coincidence of the sedimentation of alkylated and untreated DNA through alkaline sucrose gradients.

Enzymatic Recognition of Methylated Sites

Although *B. subtilis* DNA methylated *in vitro* has a specific transforming activity about 60% that of control DNA, DNA from *B. subtilis* methylated *in vivo* has a specific transforming activity only about 3% of the control (TABLE 1). The difference in the results of *in vivo* and *in vitro* MMS treatment is due to the action of an endonuclease with specificity for methylated sites. *B. subtilis* and *M. lysodeikticus* extracts decrease the sedimentation of alkylated phage T7 DNA in alkaline, but not in neutral sucrose (FIGURE 6). The sedimentation of enzyme-treated, alkylated DNA is also reduced in neutral sucrose after formamide denaturation. Magnesium ion is not required. These experiments indicate that enzyme action produces single-strand breaks rather than apurinic sites. The sedimentation of alkylated DNA in alkaline sucrose can be reduced either by heating the DNA or by enzyme treatment. Treatment with enzyme before heating in a

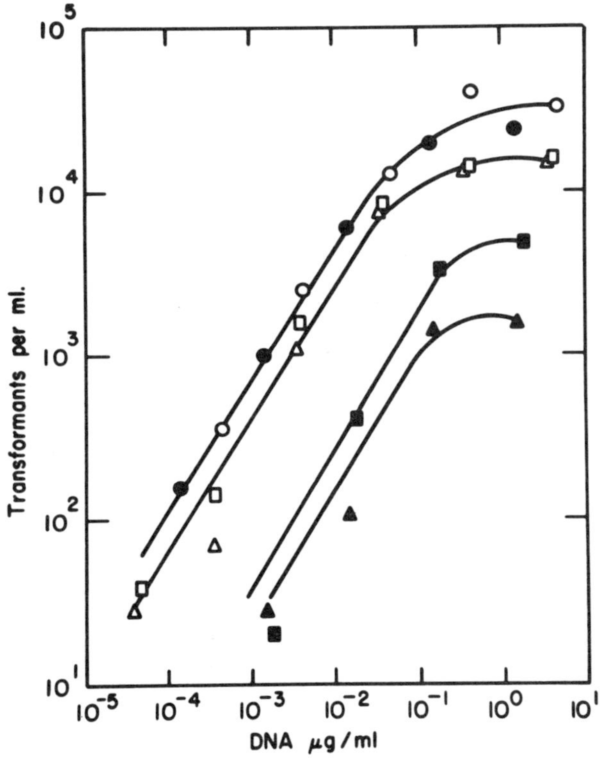

FIGURE 4. Transforming activity for the *ind*$^+$ marker of *B. subtilis* DNA after reaction with MMS. Open circles: control DNA. Closed circles: control DNA heated six hours at 50° C. Open squares: DNA-treated for 30 minutes with 0.025 M MMS at 37° C. Closed squares: MMS-treated DNA heated six hours at 50° C after removal of the MMS. Open triangles: DNA-treated for 60 minutes with MMS. Closed triangles: 60 minutes' reaction with MMS followed by six-hour heating at 50° C.

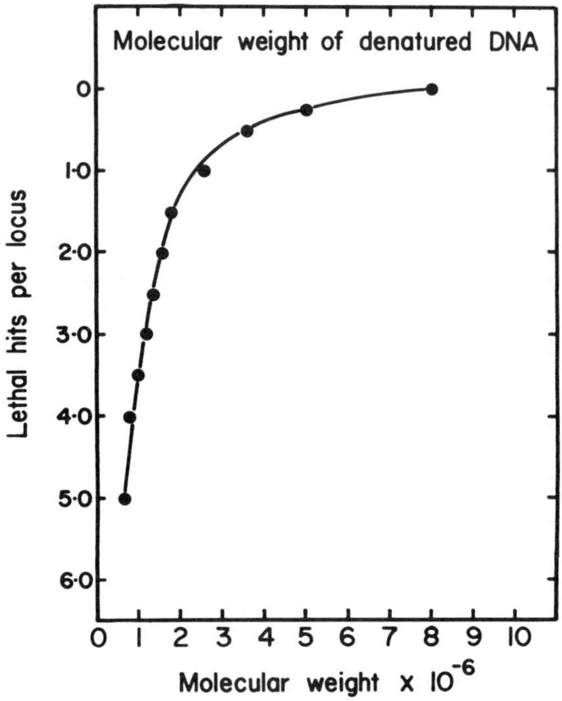

FIGURE 5. Transforming activity of MMS-treated *B. subtilis* DNA as a function of single-strand molecular weight determined by sedimentation after formamide denaturation and formaldehyde fixation. Transforming activity as lethal hits/locus for the *ind*$^+$ marker. Individual points represent different MMS doses. (Data of R. Wahl-Synek, 1967).

TABLE 1

PROPERTIES OF *B. subtilis* DNA AFTER ALKYLATION *in Vitro* AND *in Vivo**

		Survival of Transforming Activity (relative to activity at t_0) after	
Treatment	Relative Transforming Activity	6 hr at 50°	15 min with *M. lysodeikticus* extract
None	1.0	1.0	0.40
in vitro	0.59	0.17	0.008
in vivo	0.03	0.16	0.14

* MMS treatment: 60 min. at 37° C with 0.025 M MMS (data from Strauss & Wahl, 1964).

boiling water bath did not increase the amount of degradation (FIGURE 7). This experiment indicates that it is the heat-sensitive sites that are attacked, and that breaks occur on the same strand as the alkylated bases and close to them. If the enzyme caused a single-strand break opposite a strand carrying a methylated base, heat-labile sites would still be present, and these would become alkali-labile on heating. The effect of such additional degradation would be to reduce the molecular weight by an additional factor of about two, since heat-induced apurinic sites would be formed across from the site of enzyme attack as well as

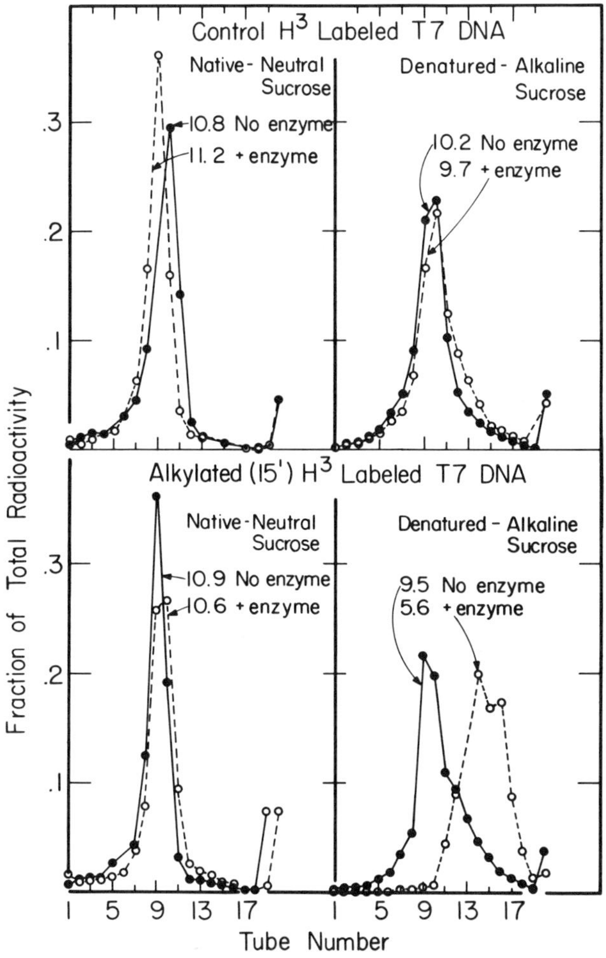

FIGURE 6. Effect of the *M. lysodeikticus* extract on methylated and control T7 DNA. All samples were centrifuged three hours. The numbers indicate the average number of tubes traversed.

at the position of methylated bases whose complements might not have been attacked by the enzyme. An effect of this magnitude would have been detected.

Enzymatic and heat-induced degradation occur at the sites of the same population of alkylated bases, but not all heat-labile sites are sites for enzyme action, since enzyme treatment did not result in as much degradation as heating. The amount of reaction obtained was not limited by the *M. lysodeikticus* enzyme preparation, since increasing the amount of alkylation increased the amount of degradation obtained without changing the proportion of enzyme-labile to heat-labile sites (TABLE 2). All methyl groups added by MMS are heat-labile (FIGURE 1), but only a proportion are sites for enzyme attack. This accounts for the finding (TABLE 1) that DNA can be extracted from alkylated cells with heat-labile sites still remaining. The difference between sensitive and nonsensitive alkylated sites is not known. Both 7-methylguanine and 3-methyladenine are produced by *in vitro* methylation (Lawley, 1968) in a molar ratio of about eight to one. Since

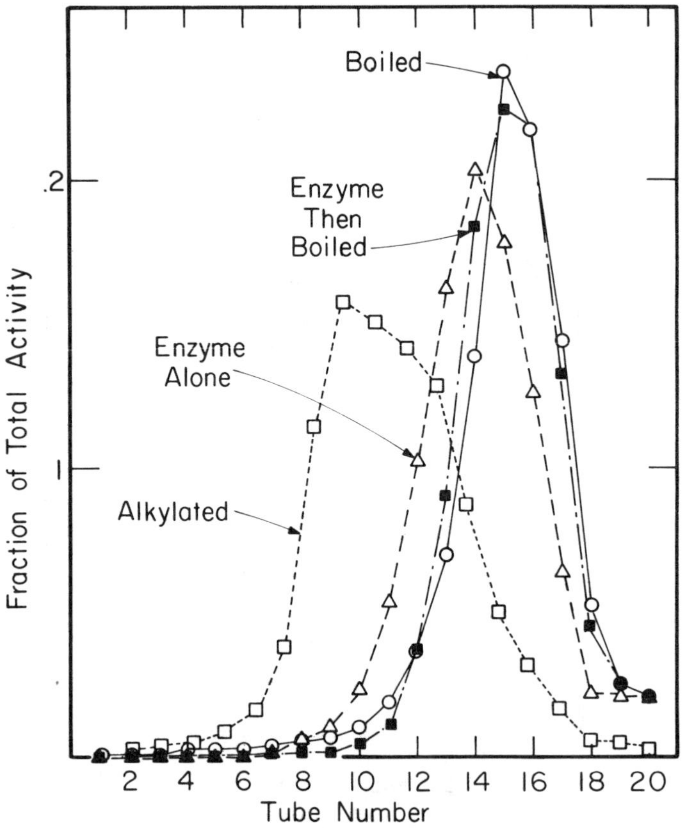

FIGURE 7. Effect of enzyme treatment followed by boiling on the sedimentation of methylated T7 DNA. The T7 DNA was alkylated 15 minutes with 0.0125 M MMS. Centrifugation was through an alkaline sucrose gradient.

TABLE 2

SEDIMENTATION OF ALKYLATED DNA

Treatment	Time of Alkylation with 0.0125 M MMS					
	None		10 minutes		20 minutes	
	Sed. (cm)	Relative MW	Sed. (cm)	Relative MW	Sed. (cm)	Relative MW
None	2.03	1	1.88	1.2	1.78	1.5
Boiled	1.88*	1.2	1.09	4.7	0.71	14.
Heated 5 hours at 50° C	1.84	1.3	1.09	4.7	0.71	14.
M. lysodeikticus extract 7.5 minutes	—	—	1.47	2.2	0.99	6.0
M. lysodeikticus extract 15 minutes	2.09	0.93	1.37	2.7	1.07	4.8
M. lysodeikticus extract 22.5 minutes	—	—	1.41	2.5	0.95	6.7

*The control sample was immersed 3 minutes in a boiling water bath, alkylated samples were immersed 2.5 minutes. Sedimentation is the average distance moved through an alkaline sucrose gradient after 3 hours at 35,000 rpm in the SW 39 rotor of the Spinco L-2 centrifuge. Average distance moved (converted to cm) and relative molecular weight (control/treated) were calculated as described by Strauss and Robbins (1968). Treatment with *M. lysodeikticus* extract was as described by Strauss and Robbins (*loc. cit.*).

about 50% of all available sites seem to be split by enzyme, it is unlikely that the type of methylated base is the only distinction.

Transforming activity is lost when alkylated *B. subtilis* DNA is treated with enzyme. This loss may be used as an assay that (probably) measures endonucleolytic breaks, since such breaks inactivate transforming activity. Methylated transforming DNA is more susceptible to enzyme when alkylated *in vitro* than when extracted from alkylated *B. subtilis* cells (TABLE 1) since DNA extracted from cells is necessarily exposed to enzyme during the course of extraction. This difference between *in vitro* and *in vivo* inactivation of DNA by methylation was not obtained by Terawaki and Greenberg (1965) on treatment with NTG. At a level of treatment in which there was a surviving fraction of *B. subtilis* transformants of 0.6 after *in vitro* treatment of DNA, 0.5 survived when DNA was extracted from cells treated with the same dose. If methylation is the major mechanism of NTG action (Lawley, 1968), one possible interpretation is that different methylating agents place methyl groups in positions of varying enzyme sensitivity.

The transformation assay has been used to demonstrate enzyme activity against alkylated DNA in extracts of lymphocytes obtained from calf thymus and peripheral human blood (TABLE 3). This demonstration is supported by the finding that in the presence of magnesium ion, ^{32}P from uniformly labeled, alkylated *E. coli* DNA is made acid-soluble (TABLE 4). The transformation results are more convincing than the solubilization data, since the ^{32}P-labeled substrate had been extensively alkylated. This means that numerous single strand breaks were probably present along with the required methyl groups. It is therefore not certain that this assay measured endonuclease activity, since some exonuclease that attacks at the site of those breaks formed during alkylation could have been

TABLE 3
EFFECT OF LYMPHOCYTE EXTRACTS ON THE TRANSFORMING ACTIVITY OF *B. subtilis* DNA*

	DNA Treatment			
	none	MMS		UV
Extract		30 min	60 min	
None	2,510	1,030	300	1,060
Blood lymphocytes (1.2 × 10^6 cells)	1,530	175	80	485
Calf thymus lymphocytes (6 × 10^6 cells)	1,710	215	40	695

*MMS treatment was with 0.025 M MMS for the time indicated. The UV dose was 720 ergs/mm². Reaction mixtures contained 0.2 ml DNA (A_{260} = 1.0) in SSC plus 0.05 ml of the supernatant of a suspension of frozen and thawed cells. Sodium lauryl sulfate (0.03 ml of a 2½% solution) was added after 15 min at 37° C and the mixture was diluted 10^{-2} before transformation assay for the *ind*$^+$ marker of *B. subtilis.*

TABLE 4
EFFECT OF LYMPHOCYTE EXTRACTS ON ^{32}P-LABELED *E. coli* DNA*

	DNA Treatment			
Extract	None	MMS	UV	Boiled
A. Peripheral blood lymphocytes				
None	213	258	–	176
Blood lymphocytes (2.2 × 10^6 cells)	209	804	201	902
B. Calf thymus lymphocytes				
None	540	233	157	–
Calf thymus lymphocytes (9 × 10^6 cells)	571	3,350	514	–
Diluted 1:4	277	1,160	275	–

*Extracts are the supernatant after freezing and thawing. Reaction mixture: 3.6 μM $MgSO_4$, 11.6 μM tris, pH 8; DNA, 0.1 ml, alkaline phosphatase 10 μg in a total of 0.4 ml. Total counts/min added: MMS DNA, 1.87 × 10^5 (calf), 1.62 × 10^5 (blood); control & UV, 1.55 × 10^5 (calf), 1.34 × 10^5 (blood). Recorded acid soluble cpm after 30 min at 37° C + 15 min at 65° C with alkaline phosphatase. MMS treatment: 3 hrs at 37° C with 0.1 M MMS. UV treatment: 4.4 × 10^3 ergs/mm². Boiled: 5 minutes in a boiling water bath.

present. This criticism does not apply to the transformation assay. Erythrocyte preparations from which leukocytes had been removed had no enzyme activity.

The *M. lysodeikticus* extracts have activity against DNA treated with either MMS or with ultraviolet light (UV), but there is evidence that at least two enzymes are involved. *B. subtilis* extracts have activity against alkylated but not UV-treated DNA (Reiter & Strauss, 1965), which accounts for the finding that

DNA can be extracted from UV-treated cells so that it still contains the UV-induced lesion. A mutant of *M. lysodeikticus* that has diminished enzyme activity against UV-treated DNA has been isolated (Okubo *et al.*, 1967) and this mutant still retains enzyme activity against alkylated DNA (Okubo, personal communication). Different enzymes with the ability to recognize DNA damaged in various ways can be found in cells.

Repair of Alkylated DNA

Damage induced in cells by both UV and by ionizing radiation can be repaired (see Strauss, 1968, for review). The enzymatic details of the process are still being investigated and there may be more than one pathway, but a major portion of the UV repair goes by the following steps: a) The damaged bases (pyrimidine dimers in the case of UV repair) are recognized by a nucleolytic system and are removed, taking with them a presently undetermined number of nucleotides. b) The gap in the DNA molecule is then filled by "repair synthesis," in which the remaining, undamaged strand of DNA serves as template. c) At the conclusion of repair synthesis an enzyme similar or identical with the recently described polynucleotide ligase (Weiss & Richardson, 1967; Gefter *et al.*, 1967) reforms the phosphodiester bond to complete the repair.

Damage induced by alkylating agents can be repaired, although it is not absolutely clear just what damage is repaired, whether all alkylated sites are repaired, or whether different alkyl groups are repaired with different efficiency. The evidence that repair does occur comes first from the isolation of bacterial mutants peculiarly sensitive to MMS (Searashi & Strauss, 1965). Not only are the bacteria themselves sensitive, but phage treated with alkylating agent are more sensitive when assayed on this MMS-sensitive host than when assayed on the wild type (FIGURE 8). This implies that some metabolic event occurs subsequent to MMS treatment that determines whether the treated organisms survive. The demonstration that a class of UV-sensitive mutants was unable to remove pyrimidine dimers from their DNA was one of the major steps in the elucidation of the pathways of UV repair. No similar finding has been made with the MMS-sensitive strains. The strain of *B. subtilis* isolated by Searashi degrades its DNA after MMS treatment (Searashi & Strauss, 1967), but the mechanism is not known. Numerous other MMS-sensitive strains have been isolated (Mahler, 1966; Howard-Flanders & Boyce, 1966), but in no case is the nature of the metabolic defect known.

Transforming activity increases when cultures of *B. subtilis* are treated with MMS and then incubated prior to lysis and assay (TABLE 5). The increase in transforming activity takes place in the absence of net DNA synthesis, but is accompanied by the incorporation of thymine (Strauss, 1963). We suppose that inactivated transforming DNA contains single-strand breaks produced by purely chemical reaction and by specific nuclease action during extraction. Removal of enzyme-sensitive alkyl groups during incubation and sealing of the single-strand breaks would be observed as an increase in extractable transforming activity in the absence of net DNA synthesis, i.e., as repair.

If single-strand breaks are produced either directly or as a result of enzyme action, repair should be detectable as an increase in the average size of DNA molecules extracted after incubation from MMS-treated organisms. Such an increase has been observed with MMS-treated *B. subtilis* (Reiter *et al.*, 1967).

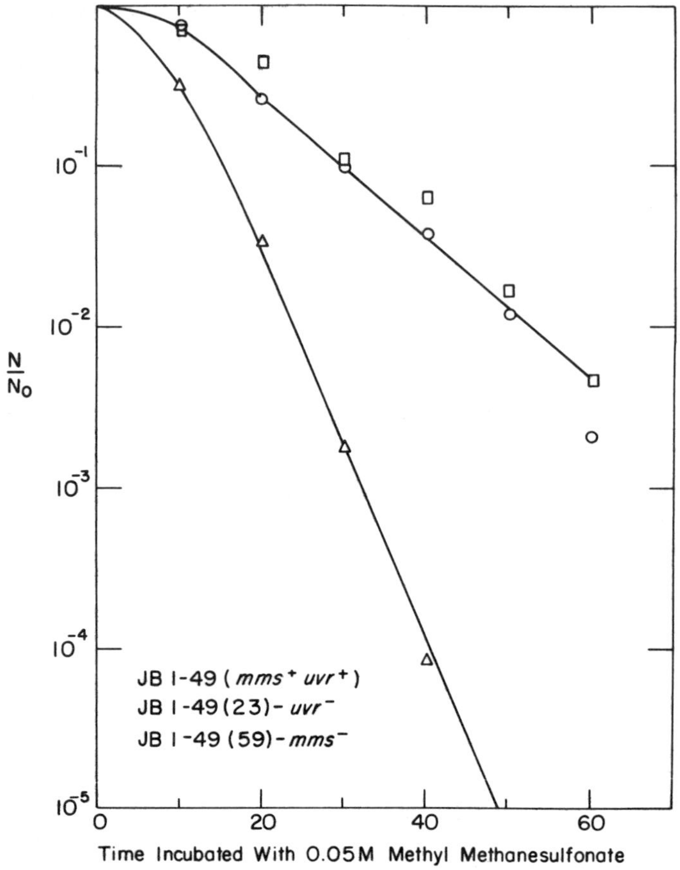

FIGURE 8. Lethal effect of MMS on the *B. subtilis* phage SPO1 when assayed on a UV-sensitive (uvr$^-$) and MMS sensitive (mms$^-$) host. Data from Searashi and Strauss (1965).

TABLE 5
EFFECT OF INCUBATION ON TRANSFORMING ACTIVITY*

Treatment	Time Incubated after Treatment (min)	DNA (% of amount at start of incubation)	ind$^+$ Transformants per μg DNA $\times 10^{-3}$
MMS	0	100	0.53
(0.025 M, 30 min)	120	100	1.31
None	0	100	6.15
	80	152	7.10

* *B. subtilis* cells were treated in salt solution and then incubated in growth medium for the time indicated before lysis. Data from Strauss (1963).

Transforming activity is found in molecules of different sizes. After incubation of alkylated cells, the extractable transforming activity both increases and is recovered in faster sedimenting material (FIGURE 9). A much more elegant method for the demonstration of the repair of single-strand breaks following x-ray or MMS treatment has recently been published (Boyce & Tepper, 1968; Boyce & Farley, 1968). This method employs homogeneous, circular viral DNA. The results are perfectly clear. A decrease in the number of breaks in DNA is observed on incubation of MMS-treated organisms.

If MMS repair follows the same pathways taken by the UV-repair scheme, repair synthesis should be demonstrable. Such synthesis has been reported (Reiter & Strauss, 1965) and has also been reported in the DNA of cells treated with NTG (Cerda-Olmedo and Hanawalt, 1967). There are differences between the UV and MMS repair pathways since cells unable to repair UV damage can

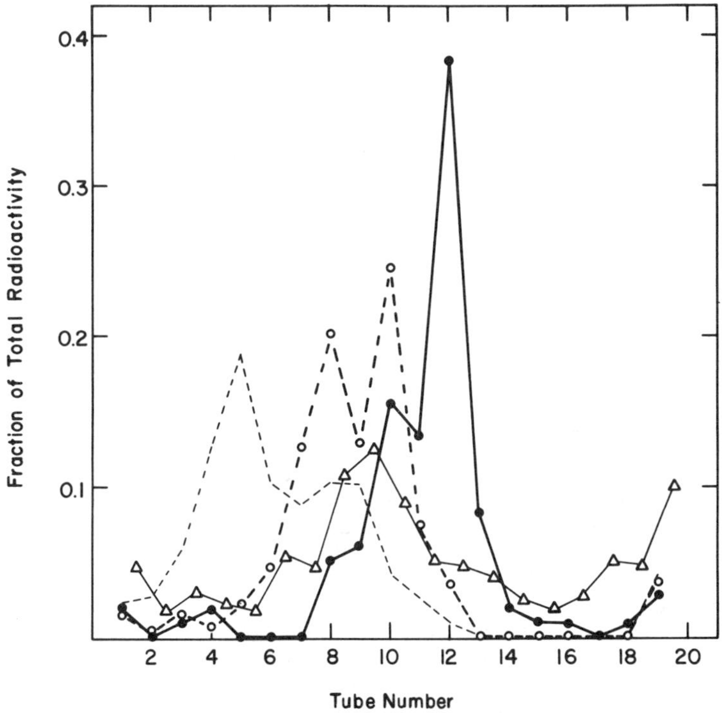

FIGURE 9. Sedimentation of transforming activity in lysates of MMS treated cells before and after recovery. *Ind*$^+$*thy*$^-$ cells were treated with 0.16 M MMS for 10 minutes to give a surviving fraction of 5.2×10^{-2}. Lysates were prepared immediately or after 40 minutes' recovery in a medium containing radioactive thymidine; total transforming activity increased by a factor of 2.1 during the recovery. The lysates were diluted and centrifuged through a neutral sucrose gradient. Alternate fractions were used to assay transforming activity and acid insoluble radioactivity. Closed circles: transforming activity from MMS treated cells. Open circles: transforming activity of recovered cells. Dotted lines: transforming activity of control. Triangles: radioactivity. Data from Reiter and co-workers. (1967).

repair MMS-induced damage, but this might reflect a difference in only the first step; i.e., if breaks are spontaneously produced by MMS treatment, a deficiency in the excision enzyme would not be noticed. If different "excision" enzymes were involved, the initial stages would be under the control of different genes. The exact number of nucleotides removed is not known in any case of repair synthesis.

We were interested in the report of Crathorn and Roberts (1966) that tissue culture cells were able to remove alkyl groups from their DNA, since this indicated that mammalian cells carry out repair reactions. Since that time there have been numerous reports that mammalian cells repair UV- (Cleaver, 1968) and x-ray-induced damage, although the repair after x rays is observable at doses so high that its physiological significance is not apparent (Painter & Cleaver, 1967; Lett *et al.,* 1967). Roberts and co-workers (1968) have shown repair synthesis after treatment of Hela cells with sulfur mustard, and they report that they have also observed repair synthesis after physiologically significant doses of MMS.

We have attempted to obtain evidence for repair in HEP-2 tissue culture cells and in peripheral blood lymphocytes after doses of methylating agent low enough to inhibit DNA synthesis only slightly. We have attempted to detect repair by looking for a gradual increase in the sedimentation rate of DNA extracted from HEP-2 cells treated with MMS and then incubated for increasing times prior to extraction. Since it was not possible to obtain and centrifuge intact mammalian DNA, a rigorously standardized protocol for DNA preparation was devised. The method involves pronase digestion of isolated and lysed nuclei, phenol extraction, dialysis, and standing at low temperature for one to two weeks to ensure complete solution (Strauss *et al.,* 1968).

When cells treated with MMS were incubated, there was first a slight decrease in the average sedimentation rate and then a gradual increase in the size of the extracted fragments (FIGURE 10). The DNA was labeled with tritiated thymidine for six hours, one day before the start of the experiment. The medium (Eagles Minimal Medium) was replaced, and incubation in large petri dishes continued until the start of the experiment. Degradation of the labeled DNA and utilization of the fragments for the resynthesis of larger molecules after MMS treatment could account for our data, especially considering the long period required for the rejoining, but we have not observed breakdown of the DNA of treated cultures. Furthermore, if breakdown and resynthesis accounted for our results, the addition of unlabeled thymidine would be expected to inhibit the observed "repair," since the unlabeled thymidine should compete with degradation products for incorporation into the DNA. Addition of 300 μg/ml of thymidine to the medium, a 250-fold greater amount than the radioactive thymidine added, had no inhibitory effect on the recovery observed (FIGURE 11), even though it did inhibit DNA synthesis by both control and MMS-treated cultures (TABLE 6). We may therefore have observed a rejoining of DNA fragments after treatment of cells with doses of MMS that only slightly inhibit DNA synthesis by the culture. In these experiments DNA synthesis proceeded at a normal rate after a six-hour lag, even though the DNA extracted from the cells still appeared to contain alkali-labile bonds.

Peripheral blood lymphocytes do not synthesize DNA until stimulated either by antigen or by plant mitogens such as phytohemagglutinin (PHA) (Robbins, 1964). If the repair mechanisms are connected with replication, as seems likely, it should be possible to demonstrate that lymphocytes are more sensitive to alkylation before PHA stimulation, when they cannot make DNA. Such a differential

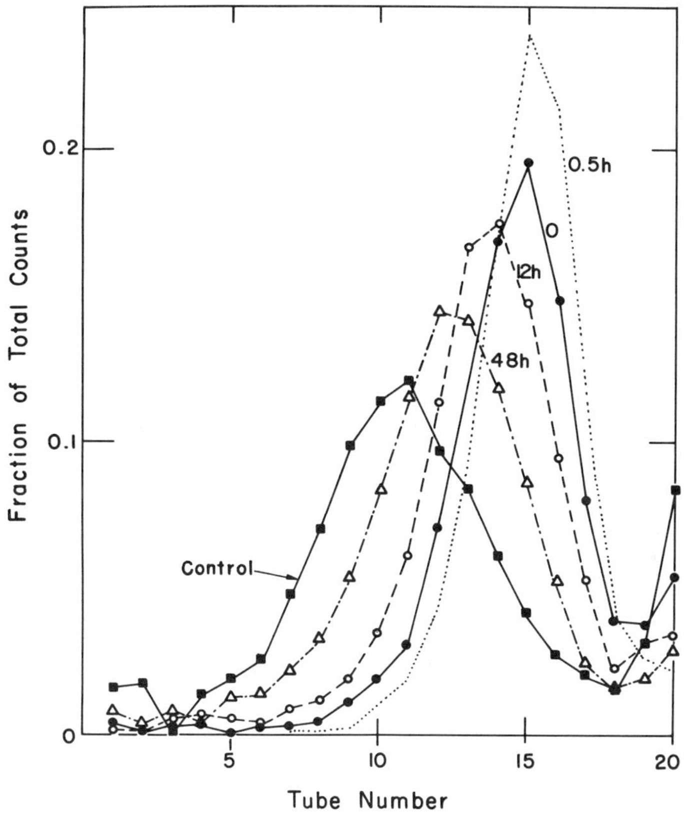

FIGURE 10. Recovery of DNA from MMS-treated HEP-2 cells. Alkaline sucrose gradients (5–20% w/w sucrose in 0.9 M NaCl + 0.1 M NaOH) centrifuged three hours at 25,000 rpm in the SW 39 rotor of a Spinco L-2 ultracentrifuge at 20° C.

effect has been reported for lymphocytes treated with x rays (Schrek & Stefani, 1964) or with nitrogen mustard (Stefani & Schrek, 1964). Stefani and Schrek used a vital stain to determine the viability of cultures seven days after treatment. We decided to determine whether a direct effect on DNA synthesis could be observed.

The ability of cells to synthesize DNA was determined by the amount of tritiated thymidine fixed in acid insoluble form. Peripheral blood lymphocytes were prepared from freshly drawn human blood by sedimentation in the presence of gelatin (Coulson & Chalmers, 1964) followed by passage through a washed column of glass wool and nylon fiber (Greenwalt *et al.*, 1962). The cells were adjusted to about 10^6/ml by suspension in Eagles minimal medium plus nonessential amino acids containing streptomycin and penicillin and supplemented with 20% heat inactivated calf serum. PHA (Difco Phytohemagglutinin P) was added to give a concentration of 50 μg/ml. Cultures of 4 ml in screw-cap tubes were

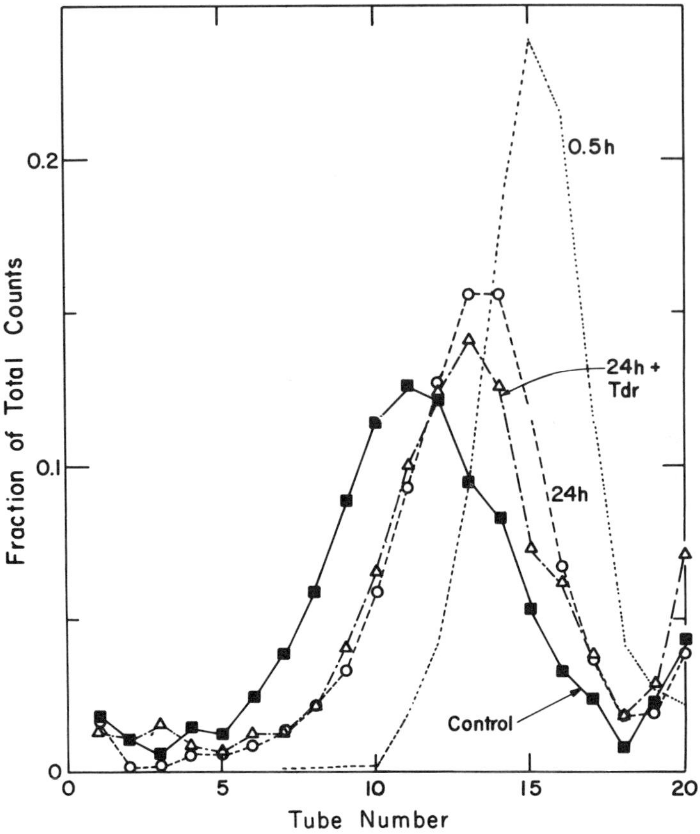

FIGURE 11. Effect of nonradioactive thymidine on the recovery of DNA from MMS-treated HEP-2 cells. Thymidine 300 μg/ml. Incubation time 24 hours (recovered). MMS-treated not recovered; incubated 30 minutes. Alkaline sucrose gradients as in the legend to FIGURE 10.

gassed with a mixture of 5% CO_2: 95% O_2 before incubation at 37° C. A net increase in DNA could be demonstrated colorimetrically after four days. Cultures treated with MMS were incubated one hour with MMS made up in the culture medium and then washed with medium and resuspended in fresh medium. Washing and resuspension were eliminated when cultures were treated with dimethyl sulfate (DMS), since the half-life of this compound in solution of 37° is less than 20 minutes. Labeled thymidine was present for 24 hours before the cultures were harvested. Acid insoluble radioactivity was determined by scintillation counting.

Lymphocytes were treated with MMS either immediately after harvest or one or two days after incubation with PHA. Cells incubated with PHA prior to MMS treatment were more resistant to the alkylating agent (TABLE 7). In some of the experiments with DMS, a concentration of reagent that completely inhibited the capacity to make DNA when added before PHA stimulation had almost no effect when added two days after stimulation at the time rapid DNA synthesis begins in these cultures. Those cells able to synthesize DNA after MMS treatment of PHA-stimulated cells appeared to do so at the same rate as untreated cells (FIGURE 12). Cells after one day's incubation with PHA had swelled and oc-

TABLE 6

EFFECT OF THYMIDINE ON SYNTHESIS OF DNA BY ^{3}H-LABELED HEP-2 CELLS*

Set	Time Incubated (hours)	Total DNA μg	cpm/μg	Total cpm $\times 10^{-5}$	Inhibition %
Control	0	107.	1064	1.14	
	24	237.	639	1.52	
	48	432.	325	1.40	
Control & TdR (300 μg/ml)	24	160.	869	1.36	68
	48	231.	575	1.33	55
MMS treated (10^{-3} M, 60 minutes)	0	97.6	1141	1.11	
	0.5	108.	1290	1.39	
	12	179.	852	1.53	
	24	218.	662	1.44	
	48	411.	330	1.36	
MMS & TdR (300 μg/ml)	24	152.	930	1.41	70
	48	213.	638	1.36	52

*Cultures were incubated in plastic petri dishes. The values represent the total content of single cultures.

TABLE 7

INCORPORATION OF THYMIDINE BY LYMPHOCYTES AFTER TREATMENT WITH MMS*

Time of Treatment: Days after PHA	MMS Concentration (M) 0	5×10^{-4} cpm	10^{-3}
0	648	79	13
	(1.0)	(0.12)	(0.02)
1	1438	2132	133
	(1.0)	(1.4)	(0.09)
2	1707	2148	262
	(1.0)	(1.3)	(0.15)

*Isotope present from day 2–3. Values in parentheses are ratios of activity. Cpm are averages of triplicate cultures each with 3.9×10^6 lymphocytes. Medium was changed after MMS treatment and at day two.

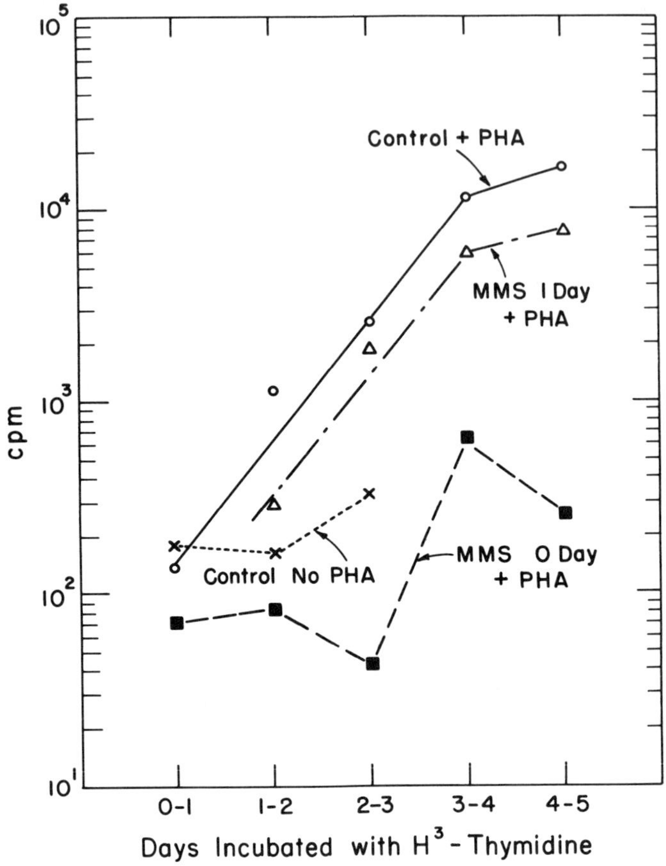

FIGURE 12. DNA synthesis by lymphocytes. Lymphocytes were treated as described in the text. MMS-0 refers to cells treated with MMS (5×10^{-4} M, 60 minutes) before PHA addition; MMS-1 day cells were treated one day after the start of incubation with PHA.

curred in small clumps, but differentiation into transformed cultures did not occur until three days' incubation.

If we assume that DNA is the primary target for methylating agents, then either the DNA is protected from the action of the alkylating agent in stimulated cells or the cells are able to cope with methylation damage in a manner not available before stimulation; i.e., by some repair or recovery mechanism. It is unlikely that unstimulated cells are completely deficient in such mechanisms, since Evans and Norman (1968) have reported that both UV and x irradiation stimulate the incorporation of thymidine into the DNA of freshly prepared human lymphocytes incubated with hydroxyurea to prevent normal replication. Our data permit the assumption that the repair mechanisms are more active in transformed cells.

Conclusion

Repair of alkylation damage has been reported in viruses, in bacteria, and in mammalian cells. The loss of the alkylation lesion has been demonstrated after bifunctional alkylation of bacteria (Lawley & Brookes, 1965; Papirmeister & Davison, 1964) and HeLa cells (Crathorn & Roberts, 1966), and can be inferred from the partial loss of heat sensitivity seen in the DNA of bacteria recovering from MMS-induced damage (Strauss, 1963). Repair synthesis has been shown to accompany the repair process. Nucleolytic enzymes that recognize alkylation damage have been demonstrated, and these have a different specificity from those recognizing UV damage. An enzymatic basis for the differences observed in UV- and MMS-repair is available.

The studies from this laboratory and from others indicate the following possibilities for DNA treated with alkylating agents: 1) Production of single-strand breaks during the alkylation. 2) Production of alkylated sites that are converted to single-strand breaks enzymatically. 3) Production of alkylated sites that are resistant to enzyme attack. Single-strand breaks produced by either mechanism are repaired. It is likely that repaired DNA no longer contains alkyl groups at the repaired sites.

What is not known is the fate of the alkylated sites that are resistant to enzyme attack. Some of these must be stable during replication. Alkylation *per se* is not inactivating, as shown by the efficiency of alkylated DNA for transformation and by the production of mutations in phage treated with ethyl methanesulfonate both in the first and later rounds of DNA replication (Green & Krieg, 1961). This implies that enzyme-resistant sites of alkylation can participate in replication. Cerdá-Olmedo and Hanawalt (1967) conclude that the mutagenic action of NTG "must depend on another hypothesized alteration of DNA by nitrosoguanidine that will not be recognized by the repair mechanism." We would suggest that mutation occurs at those sites resistant to nucleolytic action.

Alkylated DNA on storage does accumulate lethal damage, presumably via spontaneous depurination (Loveless & Stock, 1959). Why should there be both enzymatic and spontaneous mechanisms to accomplish the same thing? One may suppose that the enzyme is designed to recognize naturally occurring damage other than that produced by alkylating agents. Secondly, the spontaneous processes take a long time. DNA with a few alkyl groups is relatively stable. It may be that the enzyme is designed to prevent altered DNA from replicating with a consequent increased chance of mutation.

Summary

In vitro methylation with a monofunctional alkylating agent produces DNA with methylated bases and with single-strand breaks. Methylated DNA is active for transformation; DNA with single-strand breaks is inactive. Methylated DNA with no single-strand breaks or apurinic sites is attacked by an endonuclease present in bacterial and mammalian cell extracts. The enzyme splits DNA at or near the site of the methylated bases. Not all methylated bases are attacked; a proportion appears immune. Methylated DNA is repaired by systems found in bacteria and in animal cells. During this repair, single-strand breaks produced from alkylated DNA, either spontaneously or enzymatically, are converted to phosphodiester bonds. It is not clear whether methylated bases that have not been removed either spontaneously or enzymatically are repaired.

ACKNOWLEDGMENTS

The work on lymphocytes was performed at CSIRO Division of Animal Genetics, Australia, and we should like to thank Dr. James Rendel of that organization and Dr. Gordon Archer of the Sydney Blood Bank for their hospitality and their help. The technical assistance of Mrs. J. Smith at CSIRO is gratefully acknowledged.

REFERENCES

1. ADELBERG, E., M. MANDEL & G. CHEIN-CHING-CHIN. 1965. Optimal conditions for mutagenesis by N-methyl-N′-nitro-N-nitrosoguanidine in *Escherichia coli* K12. Biochem. Biophys. Res. Commun. **18:** 788–795.
2. AMANO, E. & H. SMITH. 1965. Mutations induced by ethyl methane sulfonate in maize. Mutat. Res. **2:** 344–351.
3. BODMER, W. 1966. Integration of deoxyribonuclease treated DNA in *Bacillus subtilis* transformation. J. Gen. Physiol. **49(2):** 233–258.
4. BOYCE, R. & J. FARLEY. 1968. Production of single-strand breaks in covalent circular λ phage DNA in superinfected lysogens by monoalkylating agents and the joining of broken DNA strands. Virology **35:** 601–609.
5. BOYCE, R. & M. TEPPER. 1968. X-ray induced single strand breaks and joining of broken strands in superinfecting λ DNA in *Escherichia coli* lysogenic for λ. Virology **34:** 344–351.
6. CARLSON, E. & I. OSTER. 1962. Comparative mutagenesis of the dumpy locus in *Drosophila melanogaster*. II. Mutational mosaicism without apparent breakage by a monofunctional alkylating agent. Genetics **47:** 561–576.
7. CERDÁ-OLMEDO, E. & P. HANAWALT. 1967. Macromolecular action of nitrosoguanidine in *Escherichia coli*. Biochim. Biophys. Acta **142:** 450–464.
8. CLEAVER, J. 1968. Defective repair replication of DNA in *Xeroderma pigmentosum*. Nature **218:** 652–656.
9. COULSON, A. & D. CHALMERS. 1964. Separation of viable lymphocytes from human blood. Lancet **i:** 468–469.
10. CRATHORN, A. & J. ROBERTS. 1966. Mechanisms of the cytotoxic action of alkylating agents in mammalian cells and evidence for the removal of alkylated groups from deoxyribonucleic acid. Nature **211:** 150–153.
11. EVANS, R. & A. NORMAN. 1968. Radiation stimulated incorporation of thymidine into the DNA of human lymphocytes. Nature **217:** 455–456.
12. GEFTER, M., A. BECKER & J. HURWITZ. 1967. The enzymatic repair of DNA. I. Formation of circular λ DNA. Proc. Nat. Acad. Sci. USA **58:** 240–247.
13. GREEN, D. & D. KRIEG. 1961. The delayed origin of mutants induced by exposure of extracellular phage T4 to ethyl methanesulfonate. Proc. Nat. Acad. Sci. USA **47:** 64–72.
14. GREENWALT, T., M. GAJEWSKI & J. MCKENNA. 1962. A new method for preparing buffy coat-poor blood. Transfusion **2:** 221–229.
15. HOWARD-FLANDERS, P. & R. BOYCE. 1966. DNA repair and genetic recombination studies on mutants of *Escherichia coli* defective in these processes. Radiat. Res. (Suppl.) **6:** 156–184.
16. KOHN, K. W., C. L. SPEARS, & P. DOTY. 1966. Inter-strand crosslinking of DNA by nitrogen mustard. J. Molec. Biol. **19:** 266–288.
17. KOHN, K. & C. SPEARS. 1967. Stabilization of nitrogen mustard alkylations and inter-strand crosslinks in DNA by alkali. Biochim. Biophys. Acta **145:** 734–741.
18. KRIEG, D. 1963. Ethyl methanesulfonate-induced reversion of bacteriophage T4rII mutants. Genetics **48:** 561–580.
19. LAURENCE, D. 1963. Chain breakage of deoxyribonucleic acid following treatment with low doses of sulphur mustard. Proc. Roy. Soc. Sect. A **271:** 520–530.

20. Lawley, P. 1968. Methylation of DNA by N-methyl-N-nitrosourethane and N-methyl-N-nitroso-N′-nitroguanidine. Nature **218:** 580–581.
21. Lawley, P. & P. Brookes. 1963. Further studies on the alkylation of nucleic acids and their constituent nucleotides. Biochem. J. **89:** 127–138.
22. Lawley, P. & P. Brookes. 1965. Molecular mechanism of the cytotoxic action of difunctional alkylating agents and of resistance to this action. Nature **206:** 480–483.
23. Lawley, P. & P. Brookes. 1967. Interstrand crosslinking of DNA by difunctional alkylating agents. J. Molec. Biol. **25:** 143–160.
24. Lett, J., I. Caldwell, C. Dean & P. Alexander. 1967. Rejoining of X-ray induced breaks in the DNA of leukaemia cells. Nature **214:** 790–792.
25. Loveless, A. & J. Stock. 1959. The influence of radiomimetic substances on deoxyribonucleic acid synthesis and function studied in *Escherichia coli* phage systems. I. The nature of the inactivation of T2 phage *in vitro* by certain alkylating agents. Proc. Roy. Soc. Sect. B **150:** 423–445.
26. Mahler, I. 1966. Effect of Mitomycin C on five excision-repair mutants of *Bacillus subtilis*. Biochem. Biophys. Res. Commun. **25:** 73–79.
27. Okubo, S., H. Nakayama, M. Sekiguchi & Y. Takagi. 1967. A mutant of *Micrococcus lysodeikticus* defective in a deoxyribonuclease activity specific for ultraviolet-irradiated DNA. Biochem. Biophys. Res. Commun. **27:** 224–229.
28. Painter, R. & J. Cleaver. 1967. Repair replication in HaLa cells after large doses of X-irradiation. Nature **217:** 369–370.
29. Papirmeister, B. & C. Davison. 1964. Elimination of sulfur mustard-induced products from DNA of *Escherichia coli*. Biochem. Biophys. Res. Commun. **17:** 608–617.
30. Reiter, H. & B. Strauss. 1965. Repair of damage induced by a monofunctional alkylating agent in a transformable, ultraviolet-sensitive strain of *Bacillus subtilis*. J. Molec. Biol. **14:** 179–194.
31. Reiter, H., B. Strauss, M. Robbins, & R. Marone. 1967. Nature of the repair of methyl methanesulfonate induced damage in *Bacillus subtilis*. J. Bact. **93:** 1056–1062.
32. Robbins, J. 1964. Tissue culture studies of the human lymphocyte. Science **146:** 1648–1654.
33. Roberts, J., A. Crathorn & T. Brent. 1968. Repair of alkylated DNA in mammalian cells. Nature **218:** 970–972.
34. Schrek, R. & S. Stefani. 1964. Radioresistance of phytohemagglutinin-treated normal and leukemic lymphocytes. J. Nat. Cancer Inst. **32:** 507–517.
35. Searashi, T. & B. Strauss. 1965. Relation of the repair of damage induced by a monofunctional alkylating agent to the repair of damage induced by ultraviolet light in *Bacillus subtilis*. Biochem. Biophys. Res. Commun. **20:** 680–687.
36. Searashi, T. & B. Strauss. 1967. Glucose requirement for DNA breakdown resulting from treatment of *Bacillus subtilis* with ultraviolet radiation or methyl methane sulfonate. Mutat. Res. **4:** 372–375.
37. Stefani, S. & R. Schrek. 1964. *In vitro* effect of phytohemagglutinin on the sensitivity of human lymphocytes to nitrogen mustard (HN_2). J. Lab. Clin. Med. **63:** 1027–1032.
38. Strauss, B. 1963. Recovery of deoxyribonucleic acid from the effects of alkylation. J. Gen. Microbiol. **30:** 89–103.
39. Strauss, B. 1968. DNA repair mechanisms and their relation to mutation and recombination. Current Topics in Microbiology and Immunology **44:** 1–85.
40. Strauss, B., M. Coyle & M. Robbins. 1968. Alkylation damage and its repair. Cold Spring Harbor Symposium of Quantitative Biology. **33:** 277–287.
41. Strauss, B. & M. Robbins. 1968. DNA methylated *in vitro* by a monofunctional alkylating agent as a substrate for a specific nuclease from *Micrococcus lysodeikticus*. Biochim. Biophys. Acta **161:** 68–75.
42. Strauss, B. & R. Wahl. 1964. The presence of breaks in the deoxyribonucleic acid of *Bacillus subtilis* treated *in vivo* with the alkylating agent, methyl methanesulfonate. Biochim. Biophys. Acta **80:** 116–126.

43. TERAWAKI, A. & J. GREENBERG. 1965. Effect of some radiomimetic agents on deoxyribonucleic acid synthesis in *Escherichia coli* and transformation in *Bacillus subtilis*. Biochim. Biophys. Acta **95:** 170–173.
44. WAHL-SYNEK, R. 1967. Production of single strand breaks as an inactivating effect of the chemical mutagen methyl methanesulfonate on *Bacillus subtilis* DNA. Ph.D. Thesis. University of Chicago, Chicago, Ill.
45. WEISS, B. & C. RICHARDSON. 1967. Enzymatic breakage and joining of deoxyribonucleic acid. I. Repair of single-strand breaks in DNA by an enzyme system from *Escherichia coli* infected with T4 bacteriophage. Proc. Nat. Acad. Sci. USA **57:** 1021–1028.

DISCUSSION OF THE PAPER

UNIDENTIFIED SPEAKER: Do you find a possible difference between methylmethane sulfonate and methyl nitrosoguanine? Did you try any nitrogen mustards, and if so, were they like these compounds?

DR. STRAUSS: I have just one experiment in which nitrogen mustaıd was used. However, most of the nitrogen mustard lesions are still monofunctional alkylations, and so the susceptibility of DNA treated with this compound to the enzyme cannot be interpreted.

UNIDENTIFIED SPEAKER: Chemical data suggest that single-stranded breaks are induced via triester formation. Would the methyl esters formed after rupture of the triester be susceptible to your enzyme, in cleaving it first and then repairing it?

DR. STRAUSS: We have no evidence that would permit an answer, since a pure enzyme is not available. We do know that DNA with no breaks is a good substrate for the enzyme. We do not know whether the initial product of enzyme action still has the methylated base or the methylated site attached to it. There is no *a priori* reason that I can think of why methylated, i.e., the triester phosphate, might not serve as a substrate. However, since DNA with no breaks is a substrate, methyl esters cannot be the sole substrate.

P. ALEXANDER *(Chester Beatty Research Institute, Belmont, Surrey, England)*: I would like to make an appeal to Dr. Strauss, when he talks of alkylation in these areas of experimentation, to refer to it specifically as methylation, because of the differences in physicochemical changes that monofunctional alkylating agents produce at different targets.

DR. STRAUSS: I think that you are correct in distinguishing between methylation, ethylation, and treatment with bifunctional agents. It may also be important to know the particular patterns of methylation, because as I pointed out, it is possible that not all methyl groups behave in the same way.

P. N. MAGEE *(Courtauld Institute of Biochemistry, Middlesex Hospital Medical School, London, England)*: I really have a question quite closely related to what you just said, because we heard yesterday of the differences between ethylating and methylating, carcinogens, which often are quite striking. Is there any reason to believe that ethylated DNA is more resistant to the enzyme than methylated DNA, since you said that it is a substrate for the enzyme?

DR. STRAUSS: I have not yet made the same careful studies with ethylated DNA that were done with methylated DNA, but suppose that about 50% of the alkyl groups—ethyl or methyl—that are still on the DNA are in positions sensitive to enzyme. After ethylation, there might be no chain breakage in contrast to the results after methylation. Chain breakage, if I am correct, is a signal for the repair processes to start. Therefore, one would expect that ethylated DNA would retain its ethyl groups to a greater proportion, than would methylated DNA, since ethylated DNA might yield breaks only by the enzymatic mechanism. That would mean that ethylated DNA would replicate with a greater proportion of the ethyl groups still attached, which would in turn mean that one would expect more replication errors to occur. Such a mechanism could account for the greater mutagenic efficiency of ethylating agents.

UNIDENTIFIED SPEAKER: Have you tested any of the methylated RNA species or any methylated synthetic polynucleotides for their ability to act as substrates for your ribonuclease?

DR. STRAUSS: Briefly, the answer is no. The reason is that our enzyme is highly impure. We are fortunate that the lack of the standard type of nucleases in the *M. lysodeikticus* preparation permits us to do some work with these preparations. We hope to do such studies. I should also point out that there are known methylating enzymes, but DNA methylated by such enzymes does not appear to be a substrate for our nuclease.

MUTAGENICITY OF ALKYLATING CARCINOGENS*

H. V. Malling and F. J. de Serres

Biology Division, Oak Ridge National Laboratory, Oak Ridge, Tenn.

In many ways, the initiation and growth of a tumor parallels the development of a cell culture in which a change has occurred because of a somatic mutation. In the past, the similarity of these two events led to the hypothesis that the occurrence of somatic mutations was the important event in the origin of a tumor. It was soon apparent, however, that the cancer by somatic mutation hypothesis was inadequate, because it could not account for the following observations: (1) viruses seem to induce certain kinds of tumors; (2) compounds exist that are highly carcinogenic but not mutagenic; and (3) Compounds exist that are highly mutagenic but that have no, or only a weak, carcinogenic activity.

The study of the relationship between the carcinogenic activity and mutagenic activity of different compounds has been complicated by the fact that these two activities are rarely tested in the same organism. This is particularly important because it may not be the compound itself but some metabolic breakdown product that functions either as a proximate or ultimate carcinogen.[1–3] Previous experiments with *Neurospora*[4] strongly suggest that an activation of two potent carcinogens, diethylnitrosamine (DEN) and dimethylnitrosamine (DMN) (TABLE 1), similar to that which occurs during their metabolism in the liver, was required before they showed mutagenic activity. Analogously, the potent carcinogen cycasin, a glycone, seems to require a deglucosylation to achieve both its mutagenic[5] and carcinogenic activity.[6]

Another difficulty with the cancer by somatic mutation hypothesis was the existence of potent mutagens that differed drastically in their carcinogenic activity. We know now that gene mutations result from a wide variety of genetic alterations and that the spectrum of genetic alterations is mutagen-specific. Thus, it is possible that potent mutagens differ in the type of mutations they can induce. A characterization at the molecular level of the genetic alterations in the mutations produced by different carcinogens could provide some understanding as to whether carcinogenic activity is correlated with the production of a particular type of genetic alteration.

Methyl methanesulfonate (MMS) and N-methyl-N′-nitro-N-nitrosoguanidine (MNNG) (see TABLE 1) are examples of compounds that give the same reaction products with DNA, and that are potent mutagens but differ in their carcinogenic activity. Both these compounds are methylating, and it is likely that the main methylation products in DNA in both cases are 7-methylguanine and 3-methyladenine.[7,8] MMS and MNNG are both strong mutagens in microorganisms.[9–12] MNNG is a potent carcinogen,[13,14] whereas MMS has very weak carcinogenic activity.[15] We have used these two compounds to try to determine whether there is any correlation between carcinogenic and mutagenic activity. Clearly both

* The research for this study was jointly sponsored by the National Cancer Institute and by the U. S. Atomic Energy Commission under contract with the Union Carbide Corporation.

TABLE 1
MUTAGENS AND CARCINOGENS

Name	Formula	Abbreviation
Diethylnitrosamine	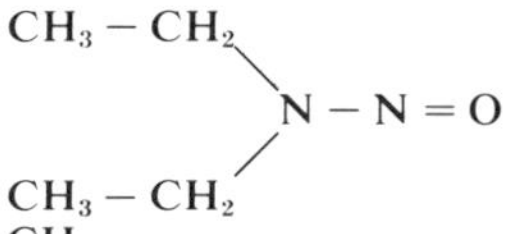	DEN
Dimethylnitrosamine	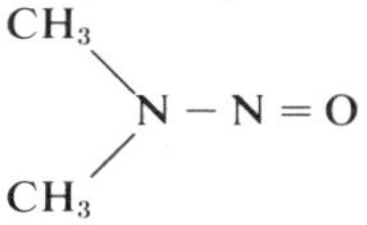	DMN
N-methyl-N′-nitro-N-nitrosoguanidine	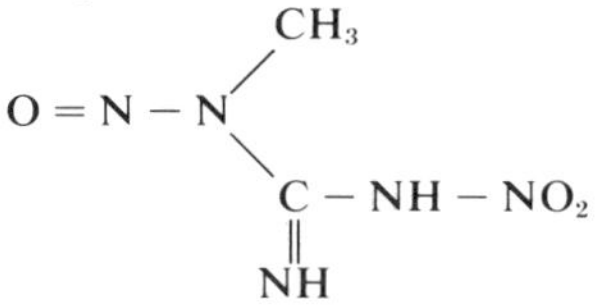	MNNG
Methyl methanesulfonate	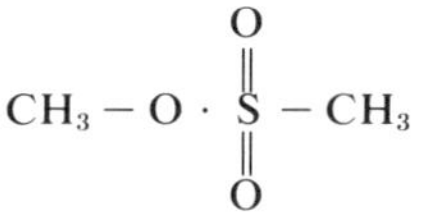	MMS

compounds are mutagenic; therefore, our investigation has been designed expressly to determine whether there is any difference between the spectrum of genetic alterations produced by each and whether carcinogenic activity is correlated with the production of a particular type of mutational event.

THE ad-3 TEST SYSTEM

Characterization of the mutagenic activity of MMS and MNNG was made with the ad-3 test system of *Neurospora*.[16] This system consists of a heterokaryon between two different, biochemically marked haploid strains. Since the heterokaryotic condition effectively mimics a diploid, it is possible to study a spectrum of genetic effects similar to that found with higher diploid organisms.[17] This spectrum includes dose-effect curves for cellular inactivation and induction of recessive lethal mutation both over the entire genome as well as at two specific loci in the ad-3 region. The specific locus mutations are characterized by a series of genetic tests to distinguish point mutations from chromosome deletion mutations and to obtain a presumptive identification of the genetic alterations at the molecular level by means of tests for allelic complementation.

MEASURABLE BIOLOGICAL PARAMETERS IN THE DIKARYON SYSTEM (FIGURE 1)

Inactivation of the Nuclei. Conidia from a dikaryon can either contain different nuclei (heterokaryotic) or be homokaryotic for one or the other type of

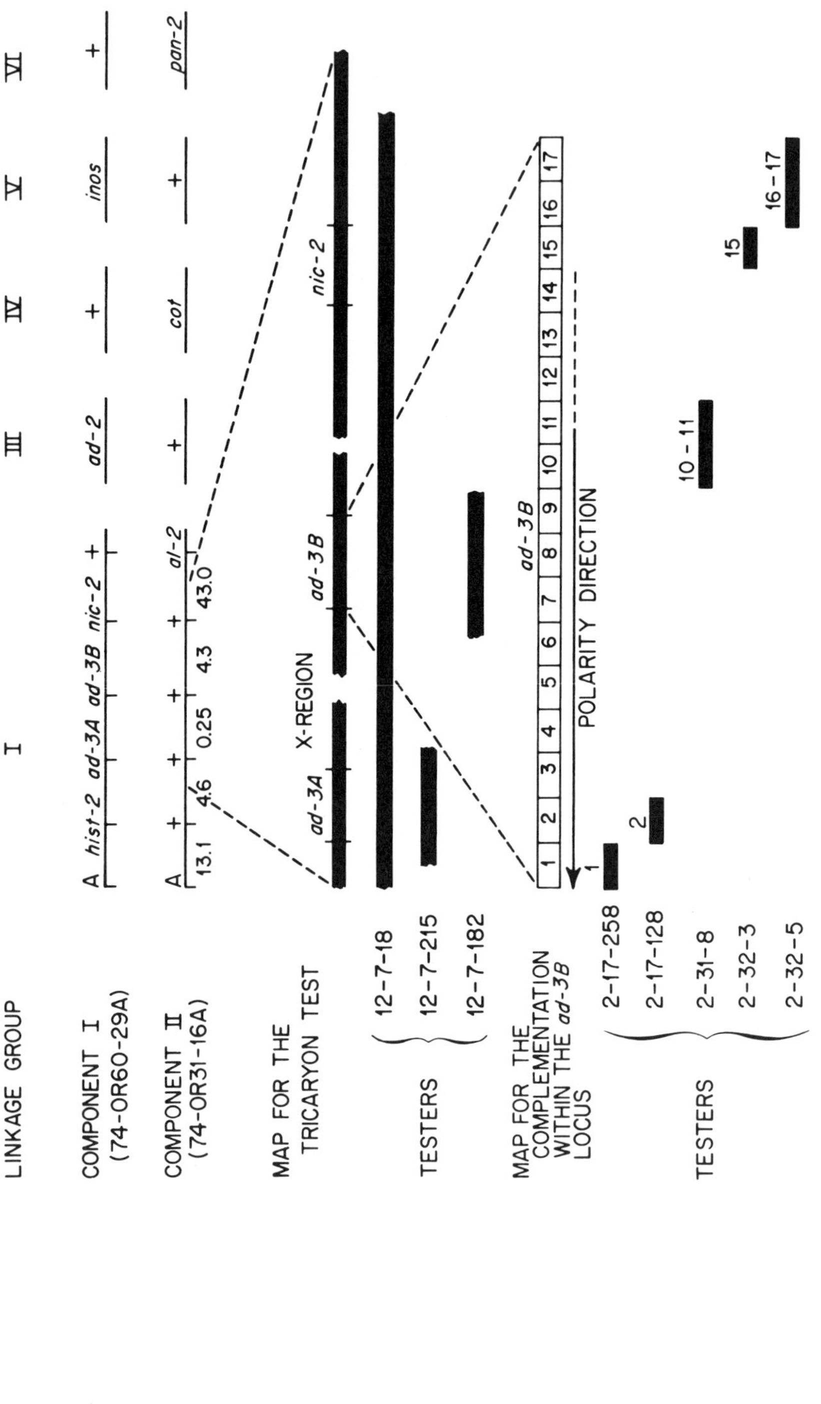

FIGURE 1. Genetic composition of the mutants used in the dikaryon system and the series of tester mutants used to characterize the mutants obtained in the dikaryon.

nuclei. The conidia from the heterokaryon are plated on (a) minimal medium, (b) minimal medium supplemented with the compounds required by the biochemical markers in component I, (c) minimal medium supplemented with the compounds required by the biochemical markers in component II, and (d) completely supplemented medium. From the colony counts on these four different media, the surviving fractions of heterokaryotic and homokaryotic conidia can be determined. For a conidium to survive on minimal medium, it must contain at least one functional nucleus from each of the two components, but to survive on any of the supplemented media, it needs only one functional nucleus. These results can be used to calculate the inactivation of the nuclei in the heterokaryotic conidia during the treatment, and hence to determine the kinetics of nuclear inactivation.

Forward-Mutations in the ad-3 Region. In heterokaryotic conidia, component I nuclei carry both an ad-3A and ad-3B mutation. A point mutation or deletion of either one or both of the wild-type alleles in component II nuclei will make the heterokaryotic conidia respectively homozygotic or hemizygotic for an ad-3 mutation.

Recessive Lethal Mutations in the Whole Genome. Component II of the heterokaryon has a genetic marker the temperature-sensitive mutant cot. Conidia homokaryotic for this mutation will form very dense colonies at 35° C, whereas conidia heterokaryotic or homokaryotic for the wild-type allele will form more sparse colonies.

Dikaryons in which component II nuclei contain a recessive lethal mutation will not give rise to the dense cot colonies at 35° Centigrade. By plating conidia from the dikaryon and scoring for the presence of the cot marker, we can determine the frequency of spontaneous and induced recessive lethal mutations in the entire genome of the nucleus of component II.

Mapping of Deletions in the ad-3 Region. By a genetic test called the "trikaryon test,"[18] (FIGURE 1) we can distinguish between the following classes of genetic alterations: (1) multilocus deletions covering either the ad-3A or ad-3B locus or both, and (2) point mutations at the ad-3A or ad-3B locus, with a separate site of recessive lethal damage located elsewhere in the genome. In the trikaryon test, heterokaryons are formed between (a) the dikaryon containing the ad-3 mutant with the unknown genetic damage and (b) a series of adenine-requiring tester dikaryons containing small deletions covering either or both of the ad-3 and adjacent loci.

Complementation. Point mutations in the ad-3A locus do not show allelic complementation. Point mutations in the ad-3B locus can be noncomplementing or can show allelic complementations, with either polarized or nonpolarized complementation patterns.[19] Brockman and co-workers[20] have selected a series of tests by which the genotype and complementation type of the ad-3 mutant can be determined (FIGURE 1). A correlation has been found between complementation pattern and genetic alteration;[21] essentially all mutants with nonpolarized complementation patterns result from base-pair substitution, whereas mutants with polarized patterns or noncomplementing mutants result from base-pair substitution, base-pair addition and deletion, and other genetic alterations. Thus the relatively simple heterokaryon test for allelic complementation provides a presumptive identification at the molecular level of the genetic alterations in reparable ad-3B mutations (ad-3B^{R}). A reparable ad-3B mutant can grow as a homokaryon on minimal medium supplemented with adenine.

Comparison of the Mutagenicity of MNNG and MMS

A comparison of the mutagenic actions of MNNG and MMS was made by studying the genetic effects of individual treatments on each of the biological parameters that can be measured in the dikaryon system.

Forward-Mutation Frequency. The treatment of *Neurospora* conidia with MMS and MNNG was performed under identical conditions (in a 0.067 M phosphate buffer adjusted to pH 7.0, at 25° C, and incubated on a rotary shaker). The kinetics of the induction of ad-3 mutants by these two compounds are illustrated in Figures 2 and 3. The mutation frequency increases as the square of the concentration of MMS (Figure 2). For MNNG at short treatment times and low concentrations, the mutation frequency increases as the square of the treatment time. However, at higher concentrations of MNNG and longer treatment times, the power of the function declines toward one (Figure 3).

A direct comparison of the efficiency of the two compounds as mutagens (Table 2) showed that, in *Neurospora,* MNNG is approximately 3,000–4,000 times more mutagenic than MMS. It is also noteworthy that MMS is less mutagenic than MNNG, but much more toxic. However, the quantitative difference in mutagenicity of the two compounds might not necessarily be related to carcinogenic activity. Factors such as the penetration of the compounds into the cell and into the nucleus might influence the mutation rate as much as 3,000–4,000 times.

Recessive Lethal Mutations. Another striking and unexpected difference between the mutagenic activities of MNNG and MMS was found in the relative

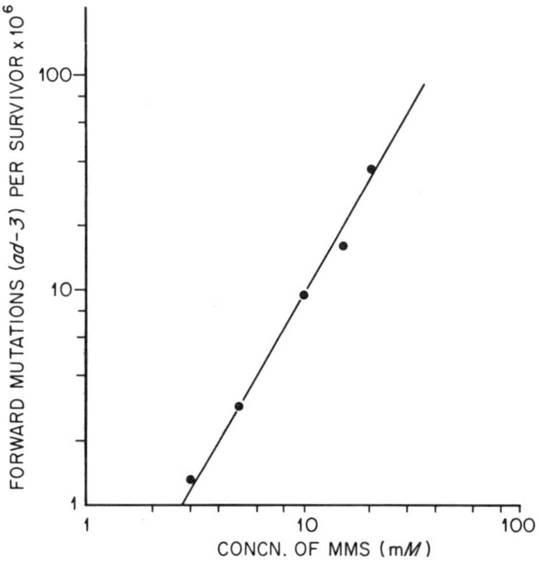

Figure 2. Frequency of purple mutations (ad-3) obtained after treatment of *Neurospora* conidia with various concentrations of MMS for 300 minutes.

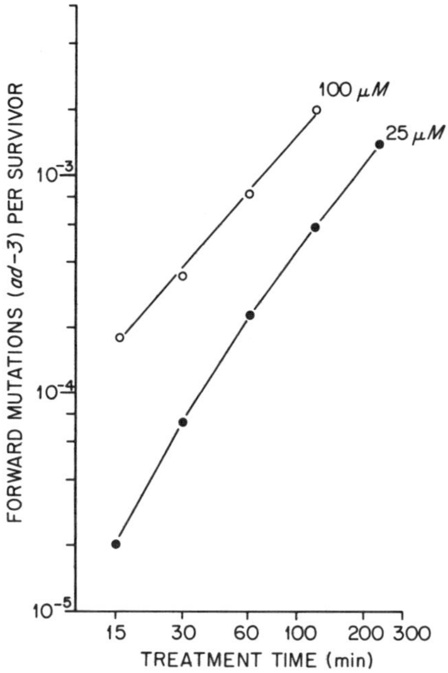

FIGURE 3. Frequency of purple mutations (ad-3) obtained after treatment of dikaryotic conidia of *Neurospora* with 25 μM or 100 μM MNNG for various lengths of time.

frequencies of ad-3 mutations and recessive lethal mutations elsewhere in the entire genome. We can see that at equivalent ad-3 frequencies MNNG is approximately 10 times more efficient than MMS in inducing recessive lethal mutations elsewhere in the genome (FIGURE 4).

The high frequency of recessive lethal mutations per ad-3 mutation among the MNNG-induced mutants as compared with MMS-induced mutants may be explained by the observation of Cerdo-Olmedo and colleagues,[10] who found that in *Escherichia coli* the area of the DNA closest to the replication point is more susceptible to mutagenic attack by MNNG than any other part of the DNA in the

TABLE 2

COMPARISON OF THE FORWARD MUTATION FREQUENCY OBTAINED AFTER TREATMENT OF NEUROSPORA CONIDIA WITH MMS AND MNNG*

Compound	Concentration	Hours of Treatment	Percent Survival	ad-3 Mutations per Survivors
MMS	20×10^3 μM	5	26	3.5×10^{-4}
MNNG	25 μM	4	65	1.5×10^{-3}

* The conidia were treated at 25° C, suspended in a phosphate buffer 0.067 M at pH 7.0, and incubated in a waterbath on a rotary shaker.

cell. The conidia used for the mutagenic treatment were derived from a growing culture, so it is possible that a small fraction of the conidia contained nuclei that had not completed their division cycles. Nuclei in this stage may be more sensitive to the mutagenic action of MNNG than nuclei in other stages, which would result in a high probability of simultaneous induction of recessive lethals and ad-3 mutations. Zimmerman and Schwaier[22] found two different classes of cells in the same yeast culture, one very sensitive to the mutagenicity of carcinogenic nitrosoamides and the other more resistant. For single-cell systems such as mammalian cells, this would mean that MNNG will induce many mutations in the same cell simultaneously.

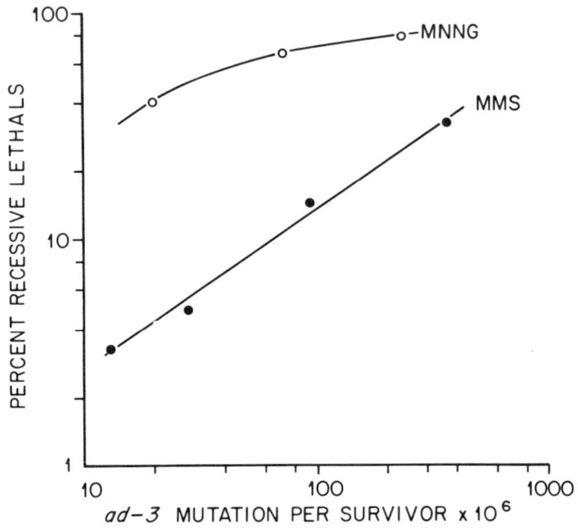

FIGURE 4. Correlation between frequencies of the recessive lethal mutations occurring in the entire genome and the frequencies of ad-3 mutations. Both frequencies are obtained after treatment of *Neurospora* conidia with MMS and MNNG. The conidia were treated with various concentrations of MMS for 300 minutes and with 25 μM MNNG for various lengths of time.

Chromosome Deletions in the ad-3 Region. By means of the trikaryon test, the frequency of the chromosome deletions in the ad-3 region were determined. Among the MNNG-induced mutants the frequency of multilocus deletions is extremely low; with increasing concentration of MMS an increasing proportion of the ad-3 mutants are multilocus deletions (TABLE 3). We can therefore conclude that MMS, compared with MNNG, induces relatively more chromosome aberrations than point mutations.

Complementation Pattern. One striking difference between the mutagenicity of MNNG and MMS at the molecular level was found by comparing the allelic complementation spectra among MMS- and MNNG-induced ad-3B mutants (TABLE 4). Among the MNNG-induced ad-3B mutants, 81% had nonpolarized

TABLE 3

FREQUENCY OF IRREPARABLE ad-3 MUTANTS (ad-3^{IR}), ad-3 MUTANTS WITH ADDITIONAL RECESSIVE LETHAL DAMAGE SOMEWHERE ELSE IN THE GENOME (ad-3^{R} + RL), AND REPARABLE ad-3 MUTANTS (ad-3^{R}) AMONG MMS-INDUCED ad-3 MUTANTS

Treatment with MNNG 25 μM (min)	Total No. of Mutants Analyzed	Frequency of ad-3 Mutations per 10^6 Survivors	Frequency in Percent		
			ad-3^{IR}	ad-3^{R}+RL	ad-3^{R}
0	4	1.3	(25)*	(25)*	(50)*
15	57	20	2.1	39.2	58.7
30	177	72	0.6	66.3	33.1
60	201	238	0.5	77.6	21.9
120	309	592	1.0	75.2	23.8
240	217	1451	0.9	87.7	11.4
Treatment with MMS for 300 min (mM)					
0	4	0.6	0	0	100
3	160	13	1.3	3.1	96.4
5	132	29	2.3	4.9	92.8
10	125	160	4.0	13.6	82.4
20	115	367	15.7	27.8	56.5

*Only a total of four mutants were found in the control; the frequency estimated from such a low total number is extremely inaccurate.

TABLE 4

PERCENTAGE OF DIFFERENT TYPES OF COMPLEMENTATION PATTERNS AMONG ad-3B MUTANTS INDUCED BY FIVE DIFFERENT MUTAGENS*

Mutagen	Complementation Patterns		
	NP	P	NC
MNNG	81	1	18
NA†	75	7	18
HA	52	12	36
OMHA	45	12	43
MMS	37	13	50

*Abbreviations not defined in TABLE 1: NP = ad-3B mutants with nonpolarized complementation pattern; P = ad-3B mutants with polarized complementation pattern; NC = noncomplementing ad-3B mutants; NA = Nitrous acid; HA = Hydroxylamine; OMHA = O-methylhydroxylamine.

†Complementation pattern among the NA-induced mutants, with a base-pair transition at the mutant site.

complementation patterns, 1% had polarized complementation patterns, and 18% were noncomplementing. Among the MMS-induced ad-3B mutants, 37% had nonpolarized complementation patterns, 13% had polarized complementation patterns, and 50% were noncomplementing.

Identification of the Genetic Alteration at the Molecular Level

When the spectra of complementation patterns induced by MNNG and MMS in *Neurospora* are compared with similar spectra induced by such specific mutagens as nitrous acid (NA), hydroxylamine (HA), and 0-methylhydroxylamine (OMHA) (Table 4), tentative conclusions can be reached about the mutation mechanism of MMS and MNNG. The genetic alterations in the NA-induced and HA-induced mutants have been identified by tests for revertibility after treatment with specific mutagens. We found that the predominant portion of the nitrous-acid-induced base-pair transitions have GC at the mutant site,[23] whereas most of the HA-induced mutants have AT at the mutant site (H. V. Malling, unpublished data). HA is an extremely specific reagent for cytosine in the DNA[24] and induces predominantly base-pair transitions from GC to AT.

It is easy to see that the spectra of the complementation patterns among mutants induced by these two mutagens reflects the genetic alteration identified at the mutant site. From what is known about the genetic code, we know that mutants induced by a GC → AT transition can be nonsense mutations, whereas mutants by an AT → GC transition will never give rise to a nonsense codon.

Mutants with a nonsense codon will code either for a fraction of the polypeptide chain or for no polypeptide at all. Therefore, these mutants will have a polarized complementation pattern or be noncomplementing. Mutants induced by an AT → GC transition should be predominantly missense mutations, and therefore code for a complete polypeptide with only a single erroneous amino acid. The great majority of these mutants will have a nonpolarized complementation pattern, like the mutants induced by NA.

As we can see in Table 4, the spectrum of complementation patterns for a certain mutagen seems to have a diagnostic value for the determination of the genetic alteration induced by this mutagen at the molecular level. If we compare the spectrum of complementation patterns among MNNG-induced ad-3B mutants with the spectrum among mutants induced by NA, HA, or OMHA, which is more specific in its mutagenic action than HA, we can arrive at the tentative conclusion that mutants induced by MNNG preferentially have GC at the mutant site. The predominant mechanism of mutation induction by MNNG appears to be base-pair transition from AT → GC (this point is currently being investigated by studying the revertibility of MNNG-induced mutants after treatment with specific mutagens).

This conclusion is in contrast to chemical data indicating that, among the bases in the DNA, guanine is the major point of attack for methyl nitrosoamides and -amines.[8,25] Some investigators, however, have found that diazomethane reacts readily with thymine,[26] a result that could be rationalized to explain our data.

Noncomplementing mutants and mutants with polarized complementation patterns can arise from a broad spectrum of genetic alterations[23] that result in the production of polypeptide fragments or nonfunctional gene products. When the complementation spectrum of MMS-induced mutants is compared with the spectra of HA-induced and NA-induced mutants (TABLE 2), it resembles that of HA-induced mutants. By analogy, this suggests that most MMS-induced mutants may have AT at the mutant site, a result in good agreement with the observation that MMS reacts predominantly with guanine in the DNA. It is likely, however, that the MMS-induced mutants are composed of a wide variety of genetic alterations, similar to the EMS-induced mutants in *Neurospora*.[27]

Chromosome Breaks Contra Point Mutations

MNNG can break chromosomes in higher plants[28,29] and in mammalian cells in tissue culture (M. S. Legator, personal communication; E. H. Y. Chu, personal communication). In *Neurospora*, MNNG can introduce approximately 0.1% mutation in the ad-3A and ad-3B loci at treatments that gave very little cellular inactivation (68% survival) (FIGURE 4). Genetic analysis of MNNG-induced mutants has shown that 99% were point mutations at either the ad-3A or ad-3B locus. If we compare these data with results obtained after treatment with x rays, we can see that at a mutation frequency approximately 10 times lower than the highest frequency obtained for MNNG, more than half of the ad-3 mutations are chromosome deletions in the ad-3 region.[17]

It is difficult to predict the extent to which one can extrapolate data from *Neurospora* to mammalian cells in tissue culture or *in vivo*. To elucidate this problem, one must have a biological system in which point mutations, chromosome aberrations, and carcinogenic activities can be scored quantitatively. Mammalian cells in culture appear to meet these requirements, especially in view of the recent finding[30,31] that point mutations can be induced in these cells by chemical mutagens. Chu and Malling[31] found that MNNG was at least 100 times more effective than MMS in the induction of point mutations. These results are in good agreement with the *Neurospora* data.

Relationship Between Carcinogenicity and Type of Genetic Alteration at the Molecular Level

A comparison of the spectra of genetic alterations induced by compounds with different carcinogenic activity, such as MNNG and MMS, may indicate whether the induction of a particular type of genetic alterations is correlated with carcinogenic activity. The spectra of genetic alterations induced by MNNG and MMS showed great differences between the ratio of point mutations to chromosome deletions and between the genetic alterations among the point mutations.

Relative Efficiency for the Induction of Multilocus Deletions and Point Mutations. The frequency of multilocus deletions (i.e., irreparable ad-3 mutations (ad-3^{IR})) among the MMS-induced mutants increased with increasing concentration (TABLE 3). Thus, the spectrum of genetic alterations induced by MMS is dose-dependent. Therefore, a determination of the relative efficiency of MNNG and MMS for the induction of point mutations and multilocus deletions has to be made at similar forward-mutation frequencies. Treatment with 25 μM MNNG for 60 and 120 minutes induced respectively 238×10^{-6} and 592×10^{-6} ad-3 mutations per survivor, and 0.5 and 1.0% chromosome deletions, respectively, were found among the induced mutants. Treatment with 20 mM MMS for 300 minutes induced 367 $\times 10^{-6}$ ad-3 mutations per survivor; 15.7% of these were chromosome deletions. We can conclude, therefore, that MMS is more efficient than MNNG in the production of multilocus deletions. Furthermore, the production of multilocus deletions may be correlated with weak carcinogenic activity, or, conversely, the production of point mutations may be correlated with potent carcinogenic activity. But is carcinogenic activity independent of the type of point mutation induced?

Significance of the Differences in the Spectra of Point Mutations. A significant difference between the spectra of point mutations induced by these two mutagens is indicated by the fact that the frequency of mutants with nonpolarized complementation patterns is much higher among the MNNG-induced mutants (81%) than among the MMS-induced mutants (37%). Mutants with nonpolarized complementation patterns are believed to produce a complete polypeptide chain. Many of these mutants have a residual enzyme activity[21] and can grow to varying extent on minimal medium (leaky mutants). Noncomplementing mutants or mutants with polarized complementation patterns are believed to produce a polypeptide fragment or no polypeptide at all. In general, such mutants do not possess enzyme activity, and they are never leaky. On the basis of the spectra of complementation patterns among MNNG- and MMS-induced mutants, we can conclude that most MMS-induced mutants specify a gene product with a complete loss of function, whereas MNNG-induced mutants mainly specify a gene product with an altered function. It would appear, then, that potent carcinogenic activity is associated with the production of enzymes with altered function, rather than enzymes with no function.

Summary

When we compared the mutagenic actions of two methylating compounds, methyl methanesulfonate (MMS) and N-methyl-N′-nitro-N-nitrosoguanidine (MNNG), we found that MMS induced chromosome abnormalities but that MNNG did not. A high proportion of the intragenic genetic alterations induced by MMS led to metabolically inactive gene products, whereas a high proportion of the MNNG-induced mutants gave rise to gene products with altered function. These have led us to formulate the following working hypothesis: Compounds that induce a high percentage of mutants in which the specific gene product has an altered function are strong carcinogens, whereas compounds that induce a high percentage of mutants in which the specific gene product is nonfunctional have only a limited carcinogenic activity.

References

1. Schoental, R. 1958. Carcinogenic activity and O-alkylation. Nature **182:** 719–720.
2. Magee, P. N. & E. Farber. 1962. Toxic liver injury and carcinogenesis. Methylation of rat-liver nucleic acids by dimethylnitrosamine *in vivo*. Biochem. J. **83:** 114–124.
3. Miller, E. C. & J. Miller. 1966. Mechanisms of chemical carcinogenesis: Nature of proximate carcinogens and interactions with macromolecules. Pharmacol. Rev. **18:** 803–838.
4. Malling, H. V. 1966. Mutagenicity of two potent carcinogens, dimethylnitrosamine and diethylnitrosamine, in *Neurospora crassa*. Mutat. Res. **3:** 537–540.

5. SMITH, D. W. E. 1966. Mutagenicity of cycasin aglycone (methyl azoxymethanol), a naturally occurring carcinogen. Science **152:** 1273–1274.
6. LAQYER, G. L. 1964. Carcinogenic effects of cycad meal and cycasin, methylazoxymethanol glycoside, in rats and effects of cycasin in germfree rats. Fed. Proc. **23:** 1386–1387.
7. LAWLEY, P. D. & P. BROOKES. 1963. Further studies on the alkylation of nucleic acids and their constitutent nucleotides. Biochem. J. **89:** 127.
8. LAWLEY, P. D. 1968. Methylation of DNA by N-methyl-N-nitrosourethane and N-methyl-N-nitroso-N′-nitroguanidine. Nature **218:** 580–581.
9. MANDELL, J. & J. GREENBERG. 1960. A new chemical mutagen for bacteria, 1-m ethyl-3-nitro-1-nitrosoguanidine. Biochem. Biophys. Res. Commun. **3:** 575–584.
10. CERDÁ-OLMEDO, E., P. C. HANAWALT & N. GUEROLA. 1968. Mutagenesis of the replication point by nitrosoguanidine: Map and pattern of replication of *Escherichia coli* chromosome. J. Molec. Biol. **33:** 705–719.
11. MALLING, H. V. & F. J. DE SERRES. 1967. N-methyl-N′-nitro-N-nitrosoguanidine (MNNG) as a mutagenic agent for *Neurospora crassa.* (abst.) Genetics **56:** 575.
12. LOPRIENO, N. 1966. Differential response of *Schizosaccharomyces pombe* to ethyl methanesulfonate and methyl methaesulfonate. Mutat. Res. **3:** 486–493.
13. DRUCKREY, H., R. PREUSSMANN, S. IVANKOVIC, B. T. SO, C. H. SCHMIDT & J. BÜCHELER. 1966. Zur Erzeugung subcutaner Sarkome an Ratten. Carcinogene Wirkung von Hydradicarbonsäuve-bis-(methylnitrosamid), N-Nitroso-N-n-butyl-harnstoff, N-Methyl-N-nitroso-nitroguanidine und N-Nitro-so-imidazolidon. Z. Krebsforsch. **68:** 87–102.
14. SUGIMURA, T., M. NAGAO & Y. OKADA. 1966. Carcinogenic action of N-methyl-N′-nitro-N-nitrosoguanidine. Nature **210:** 962–963.
15. CLAPP, N. K. & A. W. CRAIG. 1968. Ongogenicity by methyl methanesulfonate in male RF mice. Science **161:** 913–914.
16. DE SERRES, F. J. & R. S. OSTERBIND. 1962. Estimation of the relative frequencies of X-ray-induced viable and recessive lethal mutations in the *ad-3* region of *Neurospora crassa.* Genetics **47:** 793–796.
17. WEBBER, B. B. & F. J. DE SERRES. 1965. Induction kinetics and genetic analysis of X-ray-induced mutations in the ad-3 region of *Neurospora crassa.* Proc. Nat. Acad. Sci. USA **53:** 430–437.
18. DE SERRES, F. J. 1968. Genetic analysis of the extent and type of functional inactivation in irreparable recessive lethal mutations in the *ad-3* region of *Neurospora crassa.* Genetics **58:** 69–77.
19. DE SERRES, F. J. 1964. Mutagenesis and chromosome structure. J. Cell. Comp. Physiol. **64** (Suppl. 1): 33–42.
20. BROCKMAN, H. E., F. J. DE SERRES & W. E. BARNETT. 1968. Analysis of *ad-3* mutants induced by nitrous acid in a heterokaryon of *Neurospora crassa.* Mutat. Res. (In press.)
21. MALLING, H. V. & F. J. DE SERRES. 1967. Relation between complementation patterns and genetic alterations in nitrous acid-induced *ad-3B* mutants of *Neurospora crassa.* Mutat. Res. **4:** 425–440.
22. ZIMMERMANN, F. K. & R. SCHWAIER. 1963. Eine ungewöhnliche Dosiswirkungs—Beziehung der N-nitroso-N-methylacetamid induzierten Mutationsraten bei *Saccharomyces cerevisiae.* Z. Verebungsl. **94:** 261–268.
23. MALLING, H. V. & F. J. DE SERRES. 1968. Correlation between base-pair transition and complementation pattern in nitrous acid-induced *ad-3B* mutants of *Neurospora crassa.* Mutation Res. **5:** 359–371.
24. FREESE, E., E. BAUTZ & E. B. FREESE. 1961. The chemical and mutagenic specificity of hydroxylamine. Proc. Nat. Acad. Sci. USA **47:** 845–855.
25. LEE, K. Y., W. LIKINSKY & P. N. MAGEE. 1964. Methylation of ribonucleic acids of liver and other organs in different species treated with C^{14}- and H^3-dimethylnitrosamines *in vivo.* J. Nat. Cancer Inst. **32:** 65–76.

26. FRIEDMAN, O. M., G. N. MAHAPATRA & R. STEVENSON. 1963. The methylation of deoxyribonucleosides by diazomethane. Biochim. Biophys. Acta **68:** 144–146.
27. MALLING, H. V. & F. J. DE SERRES. 1968. Identification of genetic alterations induced by ethyl methanesulfonate in *Neurospora crassa*. Mutat. Res. **6:** 181–193.
28. MÜLLER, A. J. & T. GICHNER. 1964. Mutagenic activity of 1-methyl-3-nitro-1-nitrosoguanidine on *Arabidopsis*. Nature **201:** 1149–1150.
29. SAX, K. & H. J. SAX. 1966. Radiomimetric beverages, drugs and mutagens. Proc. Nat. Acad. Sci. USA **55:** 1431–1435.
30. KAO, F. T. & T. T. PUCK. 1968. Genetics of somatic mammalian cells, VII. Induction and isolation of nutritional mutants in Chinese hamster cells. Proc. Nat. Acad. Sci. USA **60:** 1275–1281.
31. CHU, E. H. Y. & H. V. MALLING. Mammalian cell genetics. II. Chemical induction of specific locus mutations in Chinese hamster cells *in vitro*. Proc. Nat. Acad. Sci. USA. (In press.)

DISCUSSION OF THE PAPER

UNIDENTIFIED SPEAKER: Although methylhydroxylamine becomes incorporated in RNA, these compounds are completely innocuous, that is, noncarcinogenic. Would you care to comment on this?

DR. MALLING: At low concentration, hydroxylamine and its derivatives are readily oxidized, a process that leads to formation of highly reactive compounds. I would assume that at concentrations used in mammals, oxidation of hydroxylamines is a likely process, and one is therefore studying the effect of many different compounds. In order to get the high specificity of hydroxylamine, Freese has shown that it is necessary to treat with high concentrations of hydroxylamine under anaerobic conditions or in the presence of catalase.‡

UNIDENTIFIED SPEAKER: At low concentrations, hydroxylamine behaves like hydrogen peroxide in that it forms hydroxyl radicals, and these do not induce any mutations, but they do lead to backbone cleavage, and a mechanism for this has been proposed. Therefore, the data for hydroxylamine at low concentrations should not be considered in relation to mutagenesis or carcinogenesis.

DR. MALLING: I agree, but I have included hydroxylamine to show the diagnostic value of the spectrum of complementation patterns and how we arrived at the conclusion that MNNG has GC as the mutant site.

P. N. MAGEE (*Courtauld Institute of Biochemistry, Middlesex Hospital Medical School, London, England*): Did you say that MMS could be a mutagen?

DR. MALLING: Yes, and MMS seems to produce predominantly base-pair transitions from GC to AT.

‡Freese, E. and E. B. Freese. 1965. Biochemistry **4:** 2419–2433.

TERATOGENIC AGENTS: MAMMALIAN TEST SYSTEMS AND CHEMICALS

Joseph A. DiPaolo

Biology Branch, Etiology
National Cancer Institute
Bethesda, Md.

Teratology must be considered a complex subject that has evolved from a purely morphological or descriptive phase to a discipline that encompasses pharmacology, embryology, genetics, and oncology. A series of useful definitions is given by Dorland's Medical Dictionary: "Teratogenesis is the production of physical defects in offspring *in utero;* of teratology, that division of embryology and pathology which deals with abnormal development and congenital malformations; and abnormality, a malformation." [1] A current concept of teratology should include the realization that the fetus also is susceptible to the development of abnormalities, some of which may be enzymopathic or produce their effects at different stages of postnatal life, perhaps in the form of cancer. For a variety of reasons, including the fact that its liver detoxifying enzymes are absent or poorly developed, the fetus may react to a drug's pharmacological action more severely than the mother does.

The embryo may be particularly susceptible to developmental anomalies during the critical phases of differentiation and to other conditions, such as cancer and drug addiction, during completion of organogenesis and fetal life. It has been concluded that experimental teratogenesis depends upon administration of a specific treatment, of a particular dose, to a genetically susceptible animal, when embryos are in a susceptible stage of development.[2] These four conditions summarize the requirements for production of young with congenital malformations.

One problem lies in determining what constitutes congenital malformations. The relationship between teratogenicity and embryotoxicity requires investigation. Some gross anomalies not visible on the body surface may be recognized only when they interfere with functions. Failure to recognize anomalies of the heart or potentially lethal malformations of the urinary tract make it difficult to determine whether or not embryotoxicity should be considered an abnormality.

In some instances a close parallelism between the results obtained in animal experiments and phenomena observed in human experience has led to analogous reasoning. This is best exemplified by irradiation of the gravid uterus. In other areas the response of experimental animals differs widely from that of man.

Although the search for environmental teratogenic factors recently has been intensive, only a few environmental agents have so far been clearly implicated as causes of congenital malformation in human beings. Probably the first of these to be identified was radiation, either therapeutic or atomic.[3,4] From the experimental point of view, radiation has been an ideal tool because the time of insult coincides accurately with the stage of development under examination.[5] Subsequently, another environmental teratogen was discovered—maternal infection with rubella, which led to a characteristic syndrome of defects in some children.[6] The risk of malformation is estimated as being between 5 and 30% even when the infection with rubella has occurred in the first trimester of pregnancy,[7] a point to which I shall refer again subsequently. A potent folic acid antagonist, aminopterin, was also found to be teratogenic. Aminopterin, which is used in cancer chemotherapy, has been given to women to induce therapeutic abortions, but in cases where treatment was unsuccessful, the embryos were malformed.[8] About 1958 it was determined that progestin used in treatment of threatened or habitual abortions occasionally produced abnormalities in female babies.[9] Then in 1962 occurred that horrendous tragedy with thalidomide[10] and the resultant attempts to explain the mechanism of action of thalidomide on the human fetus. How thalidomide acts on the human fetus is not yet understood.

The difficulties in attempting to extrapolate experimental results to humans or in estimating the danger of chemicals to humans are astronomical. One can make lists of compounds that are suspect because they are teratogenic and others that indicate observable relationships between maternal medication and fetal or neonatal changes.[11] Much attention is being directed to the evaluation of the safety of drugs in animals and the subsequent extrapolation of animal data to man. The early investigations carried out on laboratory animals were concerned with the demonstration of teratological response, not with a pharmacological drug effect. Proper evaluation must include consideration of therapeutic dose and body weight, or better yet, relative blood values. Materials may pass through the cells forming the placenta by diffusion, facilitated diffusion, or active transport, since placentas are composed of several types of cells and have thick and thin spots rather than uniform thickness. If one is concerned with immediate deleterious effects to the human embryo or fetus during "critical" periods one can assume that any drug given to a mother will pass through the placenta; however, one must then determine whether the drug or its necessary metabolite crosses rapidly enough, in effective concentration in blood and tissues at a time in development when the embryo or fetus might be affected by it. Another difficulty in extrapolation from experimental data is in the possible interference by the insult with the normal pattern of multifactorial inheritance so that the drug influences a developmental threshold in an individual with a hereditary predisposition to produce a malformation. A renewed interest that is part of the discussion of this conference has dealt with the relationship between oncogenesis and teratogenesis. The lists of agents capable of inducing cancer as well as malformations is growing.[12] In some childhood situations there is a significant concurrence of cancer with other malformations.[13] The final outcome—be it cancer, a congenital malformation, or normal development—will also depend upon the particular individual developmental threshold to a given drug or other teratogen.

Polyfunctional Alkylating Agents

Alkylating agents are part of the clinical armament against cancer. They are of extreme practical interest since they are usually given in the range of maximum tolerated dose and thus become potential teratogens for man. Alkylating agents have been reported to produce a wide spectrum of teratogenic responses in pregnant animals. On the basis of published case reports, however, the alkylating agents have been much less toxic for the human fetus than might have been expected from extrapolation from animal experiments. It appears that alkylating agents as a group do not entail the risk that folic acid antagonists do.

Probably the first alkylating agent to be reported as having deleterious effects on pregnant animals was the simple mustard, methyl-bis(β-chloroethyl)-amine (HN_2). A number of malformations have been reported for both the mouse and the rat; the type of malformation produced varied with the dose and the exact time during gestation in which the compound was given. A subcutaneous injection of 0.5 or 1 mg HN_2/kg body weight to rats of a hybrid strain resulted in total resorption of fetuses from treatment on day 12; malformations resulted from treatment on day 13 or 14; normal offspring were produced by animals treated on day 15. The abnormalities consisted of reduction in size, exencephaly restricted to the occipital region, cleft palate, and a variety of skeletal deformities involving limbs, absence and fusion of digits, short tails, and unusual body proportions.[14] More recently, a series of papers has extended the observation of HN_2 on Wistar rats.[15] Single injections from the 9th to 16th day of gestation have resulted in abnormalities similar to those described previously. In addition, encephalocele as well as marked angulations of the ribs and fusions and bifurcations of sternebrae were found by clearing the bones with potassium hydroxide and staining with alizarin red. In the mouse, intraperitoneal injection of HN_2 during the 10th to 12th day of pregnancy produced a number of malformations; the kind of anomaly produced depended upon the exact time of treatment.[16] The most common anomalies involved the feet and the digits, although other malformations were associated with the head, eyes, ears, and tail.

The administration of triethylene thiophosphoramide (thiotepa) to pregnant rodents resulted in malformed fetuses. In addition there was decreased weight in both rat and mouse fetuses that had been treated with thiotepa, as compared to control animals. Rats treated on the 12th day of pregnancy had gross and skeletal abnormalities similar to those that were produced by treatment with other alkylating agents at this time in gestation; however, thiotepa did not produce cleft palate in the rat.[17] The known teratogenicity of thiotepa in mice is generally limited to the skeletal system.[18] Gold thioglucose that induced obesity decreased the frequency of fetuses with malformations caused by thiotepa but did not have an effect on fetal mortality.[19] It did produce a slight growth retardation relative to nonobese mice. When pregnant mice were given daily amphetamine orally and in addition thiotepa intraperitonally on day 10 in gestation, there was no modification of the teratogenicity of thiotepa.[20] Nor was amphetamine alone found to be teratogenic. Although the combination caused reduction in the average body weight of fetuses, no significant interaction between the two agents was observed. However, potentiation of teratogenicity was achieved in the mouse offspring of alloxan-induced diabetic mothers that were treated with thiotepa.[21] In one report the offspring of thiotepa-treated mice were permitted to survive. The only malformation noted was polydactylism; the fertility of these surviving mice was not impaired, and no malformations were seen in their offspring.[22]

Triethylene melamine (TEM) has been shown to produce a variety of malformations in both mice and rats. In mice, intraperitoneal injections of aqueous solution in the first half of gestation caused lethal effects on embryos.[23] A relatively high frequency of abnormalities resulted from treatment during day 10 to day 12, and a relatively low frequency of abnormalities after this period.[24] Growth suppression was noted particularly with treatment on the 11th to 13th day of gestation. Most malformations occurred in the skeletal system; others such as hernias, hydrocephalic protrusion, and skin vesicles were also noted. Cleft palate was found; it occurred from treatment at different periods of susceptibility in two strains of mice.[25] The toxic effect of TEM for mice embryos,[26] which resulted in prenatal mortality, is a marked characteristic of the drug, especially when injected into pregnant females 3–5 days after implantation. With earlier injections, 1–3 days after implantation, when embryos are in the late primitive streak stage, drug toxicity is less. Abnormal development of the eyeball, which appeared to be fairly frequent after administration of teratological dose of TEM, may be considered a phenocopy described as microphthalmia, which has been reported as a mutant for a strain of mice.[27] Such a condition has also resulted from the x-irradiation of pregnant females.[28] Abnormalities characteristic of exposure to alkylating agents were produced in rats by TEM, although, as in the case with thiotepa, the cleft palate, a common result with other alkylating agents, was absent in fetuses treated with TEM on the 12th day.[17]

Chlorambucil, an aromatic nitrogen mustard less toxic than nitrogen mustard, has a teratogenic effect on fetal mice and rats. Injection of chlorambucil into rats on the 10th day of pregnancy resulted in multiple malformations among 95% of the young; abnormalities of the urogenital system were most numerous.[29] Injections into pregnant rats on the 12th day in relation to the litter LD_{50} produced a teratogenic action greater than that which was produced by other alkylating agents injected at comparable doses at identical times.[17] A woman with Hodgkin's disease who had been treated with a variety of agents became pregnant while being treated with chlorambucil.[30] A hysterectomy was performed at four and one-half months, and a normal-appearing male fetus was obtained. A complete dissection revealed that although the right kidney and ureter were normally located, the left side lacked both the kidney and ureter. In some other instances in which alkylating agents were used in cases of pregnancy with Hodgkin's disease, no evidence of harm to infants was noted or the pregnancies ended in spontaneous abortion or were terminated artificially.[31]

Another polyfunctional alkylating compound, busulfan, has been shown to be teratogenic in rats. Of the alkylating agents that were injected into rats on day 12, busulfan was the least active.[17] It was thought that the placental level was of insufficient concentration to produce the required effect, possibly due to the low solubility of busulfan. Nevertheless, there was a significant incidence of severe stunting of fetus, cleft palate, and digital deformity. These lesions were also seen as a result of treatment with a variety of alkylating agents, but encephaloceles common with other agents were not produced with busulfan. When busulfan was fed to pregnant rats, testicular necrosis and possibly tail necrosis were noted in male offspring.[32] Other studies have shown that litters born to female rats receiving busulfan in early pregnancy show a diminished weight gain and a persistent absence of the germinal elements of the gonads.[33,34] Busulfan has been considered a potential human teratogen, but in a number of cases investigated, it has been found that all the pregnancies resulted in grossly normal infants.[35] However, in one case, busulfan was indicted in the causation of cytomegaly in the human female infant whose mother had been treated during pregnancy with busulfan and 6-mercaptopurine.[36] Since in a previous pregnancy the mother had been receiving 6-mercaptopurine alone and had delivered a normal infant, it was postulated that busulfan was a teratogenic agent. The infant was born with several congenital anomalies, including microphthalmia and cleft palate as well as an absence of the germinal elements of the ovaries, as has been reported in animal experiments.

Cyclophosphamide is teratogenic for mice and rats and has been implicated in the production of congenital anomalies in the human infant. Fetal anomalies occur at doses that produce no toxic manifestations in the adult. In rats there is a single *in utero* mortality peak at day 12.[37] The variety of teratogenic effects are consistent with those that resulted from other alkylating agents or x-irradiation.[37,38] In mice, fetal mortality followed a biophasic response, with a peak resulting from administrations on day 9 and 10 as well as on days 13 and 14.[39] The abnormalities include cleft palate, exencephaly, digital defects, fusion of the long bones, curvature of the long bones, and missing ribs as well as soft tissue malformations including cleft palate, open eye, aphakia, or microaphakia. To a lesser degree, both hydrocephalus and hydronephrosis were also seen. The time of induction of cleft palate by cyclophosphamide treatment coincided in mice,[39] rabbits,[40] and rats.[38] This is particularly interesting since in the mouse cortisone affects the palate later, at the time of palatine closure,[41] and not prior to the closure. Therefore the action of cyclophosphamide on this target is probably different from cortisone. A woman with Hodgkin's disease received a course of x-irradiation prior to pregnancy.[42] During the first trimester cyclophosphamide was given intravenously and orally. Therapy was maintained after the patient volunteered the information that she was pregnant since it was probably too late to prevent possible abnormal development. A premature male infant was born with hand and foot defects, a groove extending to the uvula on each side of the midline arc palate, bilateral inguinal hernia sac, flattened naval ridge, and a small skin tag from the abdomen. One year postnatally, no further evidence of additional congenital malformation was observed, and chromosomal analysis of the peripheral blood leukocyte cultures appeared normal. The possibility of mongolism was thus disposed of, and since cyclophosphoramide therapy was begun at approximately the postulated date of conception and continued throughout the duration of pregnancy, it is concluded that cyclophosphamide played a significant teratogenic role.

Another class of alkylating agents, the nitroso compounds, have members that can produce teratogenic and/or carcinogenic effects. The details concerning transplacental carcinogenic properties are reported elsewhere in this conference.[43,44] Dimethylnitrosamine (DMNA), although nonteratogenic, has proven embryotoxic when given intraperitonally or orally to rats at a time of maximum sensitivity.[45] The same is true for the Syrian hamster[46] and chick embryos.[47] The latter is interesting since it demonstrates that direct exposure to the compound at a sensitive stage of development is toxic but does not result in malformations contributable to the compound. The arylalkylnitrosoamines tested did not induce malformations; these were diethylnitrosoaniline and dibutylnitrosoaniline.[45] Experiments with methyl- and ethyl- nitrosoaniline showed that these compounds also had marked embryotoxic effects; in fact, the toxicity encountered with MNA was similar to that with DMNA. Both of these compounds were slightly teratogenic at doses approaching the LD_{50} in pregnant female rats. Malformations of the eyes, toes, and brains did occur among those fetuses that survived. The alkylnitrosourea group contains a number of compounds that have been demonstrated to be transplacental carcinogens and teratogens. After the demonstration of teratogenicity of methylnitrosourea (MNU) by Von Kreybig,[48] the toxicity and teratogenicity responses as the result of injection at specific stages in development were reported.[45] MNU was toxic on the third day of embryogenesis, a period prior to implantation, as well as on the ninth day of embryonic growth. Of the fetuses surviving the ninth day injection, 80% were malformed. Malformations involved the brain, spinal cord, maxilla, and eye. When pregnant animals were injected on the 13th day of pregnancy, an even higher incidence of malformations was reported. The majority of these appeared to involve the skeletal system and retardation of growth. Ectrodactylia was the most common type of abnormality of the forelimbs, while polydactylia and syndactyly were found to affect the hind feet. Some progeny that were allowed to be born died at about two months with brain anomalies. Such an observation has also been reported in rats after treatment with ethylnitrosourea,[49] The rat showed biphasic teratogenic response as a result of treatment on the ninth and 13th days with dimethyl-, ethyl- and propylnitrosourea.[45] Brain defects were predominant as a result of an injection on the ninth day, while abnormalities of the extremities were the most common when treatment occurred on the 13th day of embryogenesis. At this time dimethylnitrosourea produced phocomelia, which was a stigma of thalidomide in humans and was seen in mice after treatment with thalidomide.[50]

N-ethyl-N-nitrosourea (ENU) is a potent teratogen in the hamster with a specific effect on the eye as well as a broad spectrum of other malformations.[51] Injection of 0.5 mmole/kg of ENU on day 6 or 7 resulted in 100% resorptions and deaths. Injection on days 11 to 13 had no adverse effect on the fetuses, while injection on days 8, 9, or 10 resulted in malformations as well as in deaths and resorptions. The numbers of malformations and resorptions in the control groups are combined, as there were so few.

The most consistent series of malformations found on days 11 to 15 after injection on day 8 were in the eye. Except for day 11, when only 90% of malformed animals had eye defects, nearly 100% of the malformed fetuses had some combination of anophthalmia or microphthalmia.

Of those hamsters killed on day 15, 97.3% of the fetuses from animals injected on day 8 were either dead, resorbed, or malformed. The comparable figures for day 9 and 10 are 87.0% and 52.2%, respectively. The types and severity of malformation differ markedly according to day of treatment. Injection on day 10 resulted in malformations limited to the digits, including syndactyly, polydactyly, and macrodactyly. Malformations from fetuses injected on day 9 were all microphthalmia. By contrast, the malformed fetuses from mothers treated on day 8 and killed on day 15 have a 67% incidence of total or hemianophthalmia in addition to central nervous system and limb defects.

FIGURE 1 represents graphically the percentage of live, dead, resorbed, and malformed fetuses present on days 11 to 15. For the first three days (days 11, 12, 13), the percentage of live fetuses is approximately constant around 70% (controls average about 92%). The percentage of malformed fetuses drops slightly, and the percentage of adverse effects oscillates between 75 and 82%. The number of dead fetuses declines to 9.5%, and the number of resorption sites shows a corresponding rise. Between day 13 and day 14, the percentage of live fetuses declines markedly; the percentage of resorptions and total adverse effects rises.

In the experiment in which the pups were permitted to be born, transplacental carcinogenic effect was not demonstrated. This is in contrast to the transplacental carcinogenic effects of ENU[49] or cycad[52] material demonstrated in rats. Also, treatment of pregnant hamsters from days 11 to 15 with diethylnitrosamine and the subsequent nursing of the young by untreated mothers resulted at 25 weeks in tracheal papilloma or squamous metaplasia of the trachea,[53] while in mice lung adenomas were noted.[54] The time of the single injection in our work is probably critical; treatment at day 8 produced maximum teratologic effects resulting in animals that were too severely malformed to survive. The type of malformations found by treating pregnant animals on day 10 would be less severe and would probably be compatible with life as well as consistent with the type of malformations and time of treatment associated with transplacental carcinogenesis and teratogenesis.

Aflatoxins, toxic products of the mold *Aspergillus flavus,* have in recent years

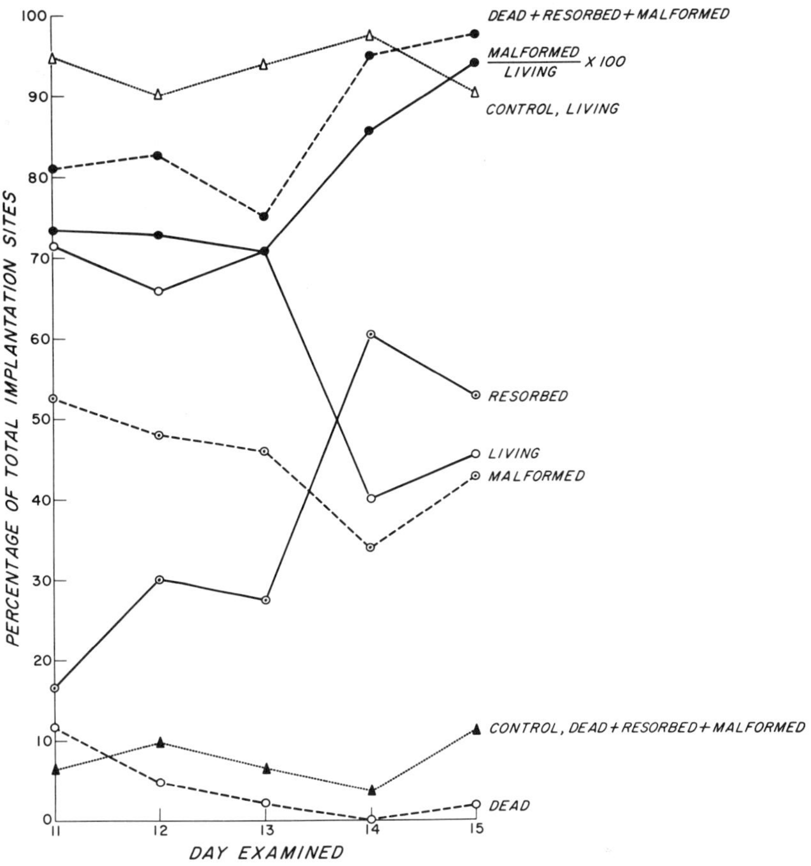

FIGURE 1. Results obtained with an intraperitoneal injection of 0.5 mmole/kg N-ethyl-N-nitrosourea on day 8.

been isolated and studied. The most toxic component of the aflatoxin group has been designated Aflatoxin B_1, a lactone, and its chemical structure has been determined.[55] Aflatoxin is carcinogenic to rat liver,[56] produces congenital malformations in hamsters,[57] and is embryotoxic to rats[58] and mice.[59] Aflatoxin B_1 binds to DNA and results in rapid and drastic alteration of nuclear RNA metabolism *in vivo*.[60,6]

Aflatoxin was dissolved in purified triethyleneglycol (1 mg/ml). Hamsters were injected intraperitonally once on day 8 or 13 of pregnancy. Mice received an intraperitoneal injection for several days, commencing on day 6 or 7. Control animals were injected with the same amounts of solvent alone. Hamsters were killed by intraperitoneal injections of pentobarbital sodium on day 9, 11, or 15; all mice were killed on day 18. The uterus was removed and transferred to a petri dish containing warm saline; implantations were counted, and each sac was opened and the contents examined under a dissecting microscope.

TABLE 1 summarizes the influence of single intraperitoneal injections of 4 mg/kg of aflatoxin B_1 on the development of malformations in fetuses whose mothers were killed on days 9, 11, 13, or 15. The number of malformed fetuses and the severity of malformations decreased as the stage of development at time of treatment increased. The incidence of normal fetuses after aflatoxin treatment was constant for all groups, approximately 50%. The number of malformed embryos on day 9 is approximately five times higher than that of day 15. An opposite situation exists for the number of dead, which on day 15 is 2.5 times higher than on day 9. In early stages of development, severe damage such as anencephaly, disorganization of cranial end of neural tube, severe growth retardation, and ectopia cordis were observed. Usually the malformations were incompatible with life. On day 11 head malformations were also severe and probably not compatible with postuterine life. In 13-day-old fetuses, the most common malformations were microcephaly and umbilical hernia. Malformations in 15-day-old fetuses were few and minor, consisting of soft tumorous formations on the head, harelip, and umbilical hernia.

TABLE 1

RESULTS OF INTRAPERITONEAL INJECTION OF 4 MG AFLATOXIN B_1/KG INTO PREGNANT HAMSTERS ON DAY 8 OF GESTATION

Day of Examination	Number of Implantations	Percent of Normal Fetuses	Percent of Malformed Fetuses	Percent of Resorbed Fetuses
9	51	52.9	29.4	17.6
11	36	47.2	22.2	30.5
13	52	51.9	9.6	38.3
15	48	50.0	6.2	43.7
Control	210	88.8	–	11.1

The number of malformed fetuses following injection of aflatoxin B_1 on day 8 decreased with gestation time, while the number of fetuses resorbed or in the process of resorption increased. The aflatoxin probably damaged most of the fetuses—some of them so severely that development could not proceed, and they died and were resorbed. Thus, incidence of malformations found was decreased when fetal examination occurred several days after the teratogenic insult.

Animals examined in earlier stages of gestation had malformations more severe than the malformations in more advanced stages of development. Possibly in the earlier stages of development only the most severe malformations are noted because the minor ones are usually so minute on a small fetus that they are overlooked. Because the severe malformations are incompatible with life, these fetuses die and are resorbed, and only healthy fetuses and fetuses with slight malformations survive. As fetal development progresses, these malformations become more prominent, and therefore malformations compatible with intrauterine life such as hernia umbilicalis and harelip are found in older fetuses. The compatibility of some malformations with life after delivery is questionable.

Since aflatoxin B_1 binds to DNA, the effect of aflatoxin B_1-DNA mixture was tested. A viscous DNA solution was made by mixing 10 mg DNA/ml of saline for 24 hr in a cold room. For some injections, the DNA solution and the aflatoxin

B_1 solutions in a 100-to-1 ratio were mixed for 24 hours. The injection of DNA aflatoxin B_1 mixture was much less teratogenic to the fetuses than the aflatoxin B_1 alone in the same doses. The incidence of malformed fetuses after the injection of 4 mg/kg of aflatoxin B_1 mixed with 400 mg DNA/kg is almost one-ninth the incidence obtained with aflatoxin B_1 alone.

When aflatoxin B_1 and DNA were injected separately into different areas of the abdominal cavity, the incidence of malformed fetuses appeared reduced with a dose of 4 mg of aflatoxin B_1/kg, but the number of examined fetuses was too small to be significant. The decreased incidence of malformations following injection of DNA-bound aflatoxin may be due to the inability of the complex to cross the placenta, or possibly its release by deoxyribonucleases was below the threshold required to produce malformations. The latter possibility is validated, since the fetal livers showed preservation of cytoplasmic integrity lacking in the maternal livers.

The lack of protection by repeated fractionated injections of DNA following injection of aflatoxin B_1 may reflect a rapid absorption of aflatoxin B_1, or it may indicate that the hamster can preferentially eliminate a foreign DNA, such as calf thymus DNA. Although relatively large amounts of DNA were nontoxic, its administration in fractionated doses subsequent to aflatoxin B_1 demonstrated enhanced toxicity.

The C3H mouse response was extremely limited.[59] Repeated injections of aflatoxin commencing at half the LD_{50} dose for mice and decreasing to one-eighth the LD_{50} dose (1 mg of aflatoxin/kg) resulted in no malformations, but there was a varying incidence of dead or resorbed embryos. The differences in size and weight of fetuses of treated and control groups were not statistically significant at the 0.05 level of confidence.

Histological examination of the placenta of the mouse and hamster failed to reveal any obvious differences. Nor did the placentas of treated mothers show any macroscopic or histological signs of abnormality.

These contrasting results in the mouse and hamsters may also be compared to those reported for the rat. A dose of less than 200 μg of aflatoxin B_1 per animal was found to cause retardation of growth, and a dose of 300 μg caused fetal death with hemorrhages at the uteroplacental junction.[58] In another study using Wistar rats and aflatoxin B_1 at a dose equivalent to one-fourth of LD_{50} dose for nonpregnant female rats, no evidence of toxic effects on the fetus or placenta, other than a slight reduction of placental weight at term, was found.[62] This was considered a secondary effect due to toxicity for the mothers and perhaps due to maternal liver damage. Thus the toxic effect of aflatoxin B_1 may vary in different species.

Summary

Basically, experimental teratology depends upon administration of a specific substance, in a particular dose, to a genetically susceptible animal, when embryos are in a susceptible stage of development. The final outcome—be it cancer, a congenital malformation, or normal development—will also be influenced by the developmental threshold of the particular embryo or fetus to a given drug or other teratogen. Polyfunctional alkylating agents have had a deleterious effect on mice, rats, rabbits, and hamsters. The alkylating agents similar to radiation have caused a variety of malformations involving skeletal and soft tissue. In some cases they have mimicked mutations. Although many alkylating agents are used in man for cancer chemotherapy at maximum tolerated dose, they have not had the serious deleterious effects that might be expected from extrapolation of data from animal experimentation.

References

1. Arey, L. B., W. Burrows, J. P. Greenhill & R. M. Hewitt, Eds. 1957. *In* Dorland's Medical Dictionary. : 1370. W. B. Saunders Company. Philadelphia, Pa. and London, England.
2. The Federation of American Societies for Experimental Biology. 1964. Report of the Commission on Drug Safety. Washington, D. C.
3. Murphy, D. P. 1929. Ovarian irradiation and the health of the subsequent child. Surg. Gynec. Obstet. **48:** 766–779.
4. Plummer, G. 1952. Anomalies occurring in children exposed in utero to the atomic bomb in Hiroshima. Pediatrics **10:** 687–693.
5. Russell, L. B. 1960. X ray. Induced developmental abnormalities in the mouse and their use in the analysis of embryological patterns. J. Exp. Zool. **114:** 545–601.
6. Gregg, N. M. 1942. Congenital cataract following German measles in mother. Trans. Ophthal. Soc. Aust. **3:** 35–46.
7. Hill, A. B., R. Doll, T. Galloway & J. P. W. Hughes. 1958. Virus diseases in pregnancy and congenital defects. Amer. J. Hum. Genet. **9:** 98–116.
8. Thiersch, J. B. 1952. Therapeutic abortions with folic acid antagonist, 4-aminopteroyl glutomine acid administered by oral route. Amer. J. Obstet. Gynec. **63:** 1298–1325.
9. Wilkins, L., H. W. Jones, G. H. Holman & R. S. Stempfel. 1958. Masculinization of the female fetus associated with administration of oral and intramuscular progestins during gestation. J. Clin. Endocr. **18:** 559–585.
10. Lenz, W. 1964. Chemicals and malformations in man. Proc. Second Int. Conf. Congenital Malformations: 263–276.
11. Apgar, V. 1964. Drugs in pregnancy. JAMA **190:** 840–841.
12. DiPaolo, J. A. & P. Kotin. 1966. Teratogenesis-oncogenesis: A study of possible relationships. Arch. Path. **81:** 3–23.
13. Miller, R. W. 1965. Environmental carcinogenesis. Yale J. Biol. Med. **37:** 487–507.
14. Haskin, D. 1948. Some effects of nitrogen mustard on the development of external body form in the fetal rat. Anat. Rec. **102:** 493–511.
15. Murphy, M. L. & D. A. Karnofsky. 1959. Effect of azaserine and other growth-inhibiting agents on fetal development of the rat. Cancer **9:** 955–962.
16. Danforth, C. H. & E. Center. 1954. Nitrogen mustard as a teratogenic agent in the mouse. Proc. Soc. Exp. Biol. Med. **86:** 705–707.
17. Murphy, M. L., A. D. Moro & C. Lacon. 1958. The comparative effects of five polyfunctional alkalating agents on the rat fetus with additional notes on the chick embryo. Ann. N. Y. Acad. Sci. **68:** 762–781.
18. Tanimura, T. & H. Nishimura. 1962. Teratogenic effect of thio-TEPA, a potent amineoplastic compound, upon the offspring of pregnant mice. Acta Anat. Nippon. **37:** 66–67.
19. Nashimura, H., M. Terada & N. Yasuda. 1967. Mitigated teratogenicity of thio-TEPA in goldthioglucose obese mice. Proc. Soc. Exp. Biol. Med. **124:** 1190–1193.
20. Yasuda, M., F. Ariyuki & H. Nishimura. 1967. Effect of successive administration of amphetamine to pregnant mice upon the susceptibility of the offspring to the teratogenicity of thio-tepa. Cong. Anom. **7:** 66–73.
21. Takana, K., T. Tanimura & H. Nishimura. 1965. The susceptibility of the offspring of alloxan-diabetic mice to a teratogen. J. Embryol. Exp. Morph. **14:** 63–73.

22. Tanaka, T. 1967. The postnatal fate of mouse young treated with thio-TEPA during the embryonic stage. Acta Anat. Nippon. (Kaibogaku Zasshi) **42:** 94–98.
23. Kaguyama, M. 1961. Multiple developmental anomalies in offspring of albino mice injected with triethylene melamine during pregnancy. Acta Anat. Nippon. **36:** 10–23.
24. Kaguyama, M. & H. Nishimura. 1961. Developmental anomalies in mouse embryos induced by triethylene melamine. Acta Sch. Med. Univ. Kioto **37:** 318–327.
25. Kaguyama, M. 1961. Disturbances in the skeletal development of mouse embryos induced by injection of triethylene melamine during pregnancy. Acta Anat. Nippon. **36:** 246–255.
26. Jurand, A. 1959. Action of triethanomelamine (TEM) on early and later stages of mouse embryos. J. Embryol. Exp. Morph. **7:** 526–538.
27. Chase, H. B. & E. B. Chase. 1911. Studies on an anophthalmic strain of mice. I. Embryology of the eye region. J. Morph. **68:** 279–295.
28. Russell, L. B. 1950. The effect of radiation on the preimplantation stages of the mouse embryo. Anat. Rec. **108:** 521.
29. Monie, I. W. 1961. Chlorambucil-induced abnormalities of the urogenital system of rat fetuses. Anat. Rec. **139:** 145–153.
30. Shotton, D. & I. W. Monie. 1963. Possible teratogenic effects of chlorambucil on a human fetus. JAMA (Oct.): 74–75.
31. Smith, R. B. W., T. W. Sheehy & H. Rothberg. 1958. Hodgkin's disease and pregnancy: Case reports and discussion of treatment of Hodgkin's disease and leukemia. Arch. Intern. Med. **102:** 777.
32. Light, A. E. 1967. Additional observations on the effects of busulfan on cataract formation, duration of anesthesia, and reproduction in rats. Toxic. Appl. Pharmacol. **10:** 459–466.
33. Hemsworth, B. N. & H. Jackson. 1962. Effect of busulfan on the foetal gonad. Nature **195:** 816.
34. Heller, R. H. & H. W. Jones. 1964. Production of ovarian dysgenesis in the rat and human by busulfan. Amer. J. Obstet. Gynec. **89:** 414.
35. Williams, D. W. 1966. Busulfan in early pregnancy. Obstet. Gynec. **27:** 738–740.
36. Diamond, I., M. M. Anderson & S. R. McCreadie. 1960. Transplacental transmission of busulfan (Myleran) in a mother with leukemia: Production of fetal malformation and cytomegaly. Pediatrics **25:** 85–90.
37. Von Kreybig, T. 1965. Die teratogene Wirkung von Cyclophosphamide wahrend der Embryonales Entwicklung phase bie der ratte. Naunyn Schmiedeberg Arch. Exp. Path. **252:** 173–195.
38. Chaube, S., G. Kury & M. L. Murphy. 1967. Teratogenic effects of cyclophosphamide in the rat. Cancer Chemother. Rep. **51:** 363–379.
39. Gibson, J. E. & B. A. Becker. 1968. The teratogenicity of cyclophosphamide in mice. Cancer Res. **28:** 475–480.
40. Gerlinger, P. & J. Clavert. 1965. Anomalies observees chez des lapins issus de méres traitées au cyclophosphamide. Compt. Rend. Soc. Biol. **159:** 1462–1466.
41. Kalter, H. 1965. Interplay of intrinsic and extrinsic factors. *In* Teratology Principles and Techniques. J. C. Wilson & J. Warkany, Eds. : 57–80. The Univ. of Chicago Press. Chicago, Ill.
42. Greenberg, L. H. & K. R. Tanaka. 1964. Congenital anomalies probably induced by cyclophosphamide. JAMA **188:** 423–426.
43. Druckrey, H., R. Preussmann & S. Ivankovic. 1969. N-nitroso-compounds in organotropic and transplacental carcinogenesis. This monograph.
44. Rice, J. M. 1969. Transplacental carcinogenesis in mice by 1-ethyl-1-nitrosourea. This monograph.
45. Napalkov, N. P. & V. A. Alexandrov. 1967. On the effects of blastomogenic substances on the organism during embryogenesis. Krebsforsch. **71:** 32–50.
46. DiPaolo, J. A. & H. Givelber. Unpublished results.
47. Karnofsky, D. A. 1955. Investigation of diverse systems for cancer chemotherapy

screening assay of chemotherapeutic agents on developing chick embryo. Cancer Res. (Suppl.) **3:** 83–85.

48. Von Kreybig, T. 1965. Die Wirkung einer carcinogen Methylnitroso-Harnstoff-Dosis auf die Embryonalentwicklung der Ratte. Z. Krebsforsch. **67:** 46–50.
49. Druckrey, H., S. Ivankovic & R. Preussmann. 1966. Teratogenic and carcinogenic effects in the offspring after single injection of ethylnitrosourea to pregnant rats. Nature **210:** 1378–1379.
50. DiPaolo, J. A. 1963. Congenital malformations in strain A mice: Its experimental production by thalidomide. JAMA **183:** 139–141.
51. Givelber, H. & J. A. DiPaolo. Teratogenic effects of N-ethyl-N-nitrosourea in the Syrian hamster. Cancer Res. In press.
52. Spatz, M. & G. Laquer. 1967. Transplacental induction of tumors in Sprague-Dawley rats with crude cycad material. J. Nat. Cancer Inst. **38:** 233–245.
53. Mohr, U. & A. Authaler. 1966. Diaplacental effect of the carcinogen diethylnitrosamine in the golden hamster. Cancer Res. **26:** 2349–2352.
54. Mohr, U. & J. Althoff. 1965. Die diaplacentare Wirkung des Cancerogens Diathylnitrosamin bie der Maus. Z. Krebsforsch. **67:** 152–155.
55. Asao, T. *et al.* 1964. The structures of aflatoxin B_1 and G_1. *In* Mycotoxins in Foodstuffs. G. N. Wogan, Ed. : 265–273. MIT Press. Cambridge, Mass.
56. Barnes, J. M. & W. H. Butler. 1964. Carcinogenic activity of aflatoxin to rats. Nature **202:** 1016.
57. Elis, J. & J. A. DiPaolo. 1967. Aflatoxin B_1. Arch. Path. **83:** 53–57.
58. LeBreton, E., C. Frayssinet, C. Lafarge & A. M. DeRecondo. 1964. Aflatoxine – mechanisme de l'action. Food Cosmet. Toxic. **2:** 675.
59. DiPaolo, J. A., J. Elis & H. Erwin. 1967. Teratogenic response by hamsters, rats and mice to aflatoxin B_1. Nature **215:** 638–639.
60. Clifford, J. I. & K. R. Rees. 1966. Aflatoxin: A site of action in the rat liver cell. Nature **209:** 312–313.
61. Sporn, M. *et al.* 1966. Aflatoxin B_1: Binding to DNA in vitro and alteration of RNA metabolism in vivo. Science **151:** 1539–1541.
62. Butler, W. H. & J. S. Wigglesworth. 1966. The effects of aflatoxin B_1 on the pregnant rat. Brit. J. Exp. Path. **47:** 242.

TRANSPLACENTAL CARCINOGENESIS IN MICE BY 1-ETHYL-1-NITROSOUREA

Jerry M. Rice*

Biology Branch, Etiology
National Cancer Institute
Bethesda, Md.

Transplacental carcinogenesis refers to the development of neoplastic disease as a result of prenatal exposure to a causative agent circulating in the mother's blood. In this discussion we shall consider only chemical agents experimentally introduced into the circulation of a pregnant laboratory animal. Carcinogenesis can also be effected during prenatal life by direct injection or implantation of suitable chemicals into the amnionic sac, thus circumventing the placental barrier, but such experiments will not be dealt with here.

Attempts to produce tumors in mice by transplacental exposure to a chemical carcinogen first appeared in the literature in the late 1940's, shortly after the discovery of the carcinogenic properties of ethyl carbamate (urethan).[1] Several investigators administered single or repeated doses of this anesthetic to pregnant mice at different times during the final week of gestation, and observed the subsequent development of pulmonary tumors in the offspring of treated animals.[2–4] The results were less than striking, however, for multiple adenomas were observed only in mice exposed to the carcinogen less than 24 hours prior to birth, and in these the average number of tumors was lower than in the mother animals. Our interest in the subject was stimulated by the recent announcement of Druckrey and co-workers[5] that neurogenic tumors developed in the offspring of BD rats given a single dose of 1-ethyl-1-nitrosourea (ENU) on the 14th day of gestation, approximately seven days before parturition. In contrast with urethan, this substance obviously was active relatively early in gestation, and we decided to use it to reinvestigate the susceptibility of mouse tissues to neoplastic transformation during fetal life.

Gestation in the mouse continues for a period of 18–21 days, depending on the genetic history of the animals and, to a lesser extent, on the size of a given litter and the treatment to which pregnant mice may be subjected. In many inbred lines, including A, C57B1, and the Carworth Farms CFI-S strain,† the duration of normal pregnancy is approximately 19 days; the NIH General Purpose (GP) mouse, from a Swiss-derived closed colony maintained by random mating, generally delivers on the 21st day of gestation. A partial synopsis of events during a 19–day pregnancy is presented in TABLE 1.

It is convenient to subdivide this time into three sequential intervals: a period of embryogenesis, comprising the first seven days of gestation, from fertilization

*Present address: Building 37, Room 2B-08, National Institutes of Health, Bethesda, Md. 20014.

†The CFI-S strain has been used as the model for an excellently illustrated text on murine embryology: The Mouse: Its Reproduction and Development, by Roberts Rugh, 1968, the Burgess Publishing Co., Minneapolis, Minn., 430 pages.

TABLE 1

SEQUENCE OF EVENTS DURING A 19-DAY PERIOD OF GESTATION IN THE MOUSE

Stage of Development (Vulnerability)	Day of Gestation	Major Events
Embryogenesis (lethal damage)	1	fertilization
	2	
	3	
	4	implantation
	5	
	6	
	7	mesoderm
		neural plate
Early organogenesis (teratogenesis)	8	
		placenta
	9	liver
	10	lung
	11	
	12	thymus (epithelial)
Tissue differentiation (carcinogenesis)	13	
	14	thymus (lymphoid)
	15	
	16	
Fetus (carcinogenesis)	17	
	18	
	19	
		birth

to the appearance of the third germ layer (the mesoderm); a period of early organogenesis, from the seventh to approximately the 12th day, during which the major organ systems form; and, finally, between the 12th day and birth, a period during which differentiation of most tissues is largely completed. Most differentiation is in fact complete by the 16th day, except in certain organs (such as the cerebellum) that do not mature until after birth; the final three days or so of gestation comprise a true fetal stage of development, characterized more by growth than by differentiation. It is during the second of these periods that gross malformations are most easily induced by teratogens, and during the third and part of the second that chemical carcinogenesis is most readily demonstrable.

By exposing embryos to appropriate compounds at various stages of development, one can attempt to explore a number of problems in carcinogenesis, among them the following:

1. Adult mice are characterized by strain- and sex-specific differences in susceptibility to induction of certain types of tumors. How far into prenatal life can these differences be demonstrated, and what can be inferred from this about the biochemical basis for these genetically determined differences?

2. Multiple primary tumors can be induced in certain organs of adult mice, among them the liver and the lungs, by a single exposure to an appropriate

carcinogen. Will the demonstrable tumor incidence in these organs resulting from transplacental carcinogenesis simply parallel the increasing volume of target tissue as development proceeds, or will this response be modified at some point by other factors?

3. Will the histological features, or even the tissue of origin, of tumors characteristic of a given organ change as differentiation proceeds? For example, the liver functions largely as a hematopoietic organ prior to birth; will one see an increased incidence of leukemias or reticulum-cell sarcomas and related conditions in strains of mice prone to hepatoma induction in adult life? Or will one see embryonic mixed-cell tumors, analogous to the hepatomas containing an osteogenic component that are sometimes found in human infants?[6]

4. Finally, the synthesis of many enzymes involved in drug metabolism is repressed in fetal tissues, and is not inducible until differentiation has reached an advanced stage. What effect will this have on carcinogenesis, especially by compounds that require metabolic modification to generate proximate carcinogens?

In our experiments, pregnant mice were given a single intraperitoneal injection of ENU in trioctanoin, in doses ranging from 0.25–1.0 mmoles/kg of body weight. Groups of animals were treated at daily intervals from the 12th through the 19th days of gestation. The size of the dose was adjusted according to the mother's total weight; no account was taken of the increasingly larger proportion of that weight consisting of fetal tissue as pregnancy approaches term. Care was taken to avoid intrauterine or intraamniotic injections. Experiments have been performed with inbred strains A/J, A/He, C3Hf/He, C57B1/6, and certain of their F_1 hybrids, and with the random-bred GP mouse, but comprehensive data are not yet available for all of these. Most of our work to date has been done with GP mice, which are the easiest of these strains to breed and raise; adults of this line are highly responsive to chemical induction of both pulmonary adenomas and lymphocytic leukemias. We have observed pulmonary adenomas and occasional lymphocytic leukemias in the offspring of all strains tested, and hepatomas in strains A and C3Hf. Latent periods for tumors induced transplacentally are generally the same or slightly shorter than those observed for tumors of the same organs in animals treated as adults, ranging from a few weeks for pulmonary tumors to 40 weeks or more for hepatomas. Pulmonary tumors have the shortest latent period, and their multiplicity in treated animals varies with the dose of carcinogen administered, providing a parameter for statistical analysis. We have accordingly directed most of our attention to the effects of this treatment on the lungs.

Within a few weeks after birth, some pulmonary tumors are visible in mice prenatally exposed to ENU. In GP mice, the number of tumors seen as a result of any given set of treatment conditions does not increase significantly after the age of 12 weeks, at which time most experiments were terminated. These included investigations of dose-response relationships and of the variation in tumor yield resulting from exposure to the carcinogen at different times during gestation. There is no difference in pulmonary tumor response attributable to sex; male and female animals are not distinguished in tabulations. In the mouse, the typical pulmonary neoplasm is alveologenic, and early tumors have the histological appearance of adenoma; their border is well-defined and they grow by expansion, compressing the surrounding tissues (FIGURES 1 & 2). We routinely count pulmonary tumors after fixing the lungs in formalin, and reserve only questionable or atypical lesions for histological processing.

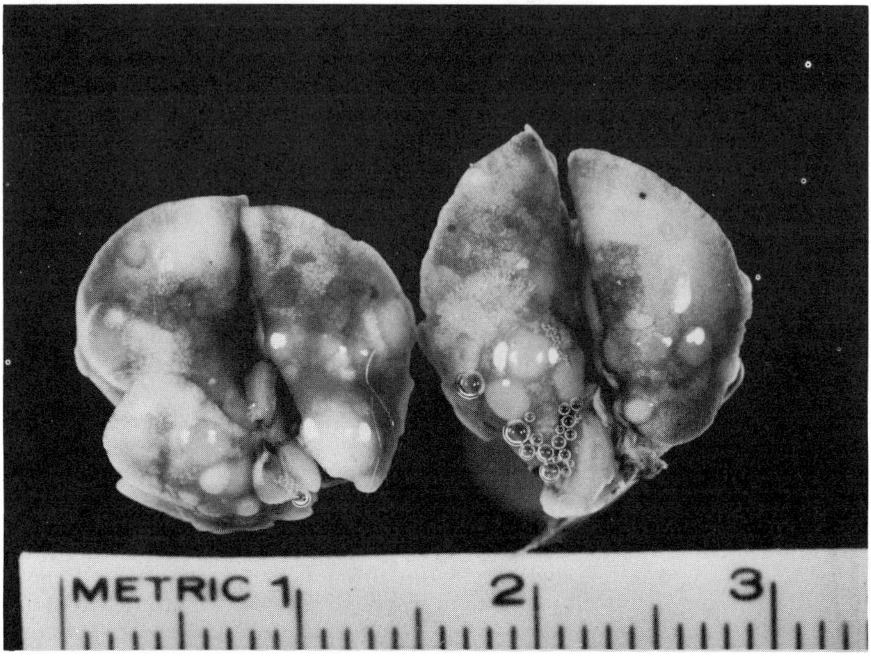

FIGURE 1. Pulmonary tumors in the lungs of A/J mice at age 40 weeks, prior to fixation; 0.5 mmole/kg ENU transplacentally, day 14.

The pulmonary tumor incidence at 12 weeks of age in the offspring of GP mice treated once during pregnancy with ENU is summarized in TABLE 2. The major conclusions from this data are the following:

1. Tumors can be induced in the lungs of animals treated as early as the 12th day of intrauterine life. Lung buds first appear on the tenth day of the 19-day gestational period of CFI-S mice, and probably form a day or so later in embryos of the GP strain. Tumor indiction in the lungs is possible, therefore, from the time that these organs begin to differentiate. The tumors that result from such early treatment are not demonstrably different in histological appearance from those induced in adult animals.

2. The tumor incidence in mice treated with ENU at any given stage of gestation is linearly dose-dependent, at least at dosage levels of 0.5 mmole/kg and below (FIGURE 3). Doses of 1.0 mmole/kg are embryocidal prior to the 14th day of gestation, and mice exposed on the 14th day fail to breed or gain weight normally and often exhibit neurological abnormalities in adult life.

3. The slope of the dose-response curve is greatest on the 16th day of gestation. When the average tumor yield for a given dose of ENU is plotted against the time of administration of the carcinogen, the curve therefore exhibits a maximum at day 16 (FIGURE 4).

4. The standard deviations in pulmonary tumor incidence among animals of a given litter are generally rather large, often on the order of one-fourth to one-

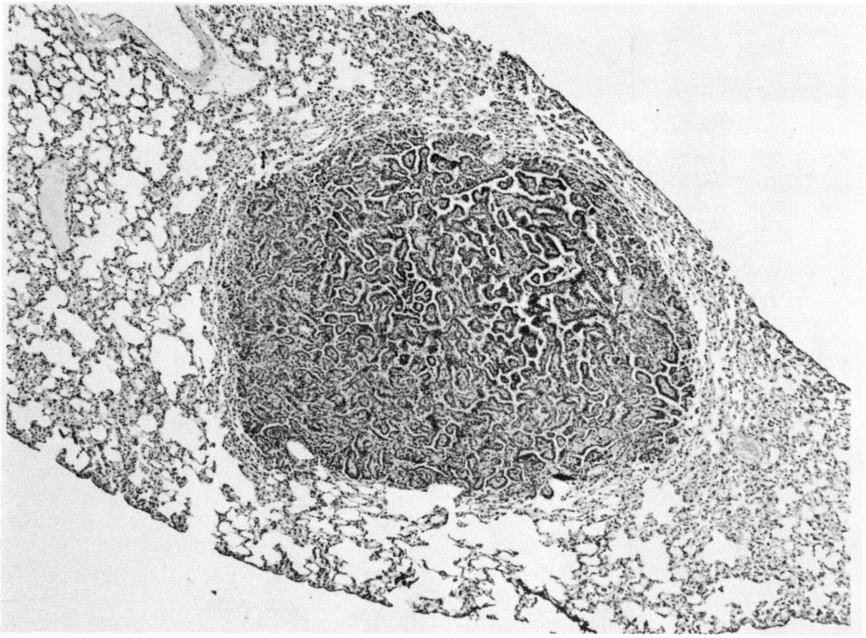

FIGURE 2. Typical alveologenic pulmonary tumor induced transplacentally by ENU. Strain GP, age 21 weeks; 1.0 mmole/kg ENU, day 14. H & E, × 50.

TABLE 2

PULMONARY TUMORS IN GP MICE AT 12 WEEKS OF AGE, RESULTING FROM A SINGLE PRENATAL TREATMENT WITH ENU*

Injected on Day of Gestation:	Tumors per Mouse: Mean ± Standard Deviation			
		ENU, mmoles/kg maternal body weight		
	control	0.25	0.5	1.0
12	0	0.5 ± 1.0	0.3 ± 0.5	embryocidal
14	0	–	5.5 ± 2.1	9.6 ± 2.9
15	–	–	9.5 ± 3.8	–
16	0	14.0 ± 4.4	26.5 ± 7.0	33.9 ± 9.0
17	–	–	21.3 ± 8.0	–
18	–	7.5 ± 3.4	11.8 ± 4.6	26.6 ± 9.0
....				
...				
21 (birth)				
Mothers	0	0	1.8 ± 3.0	12.3 ± 12.9

*Mice from at least two litters were averaged for each point.

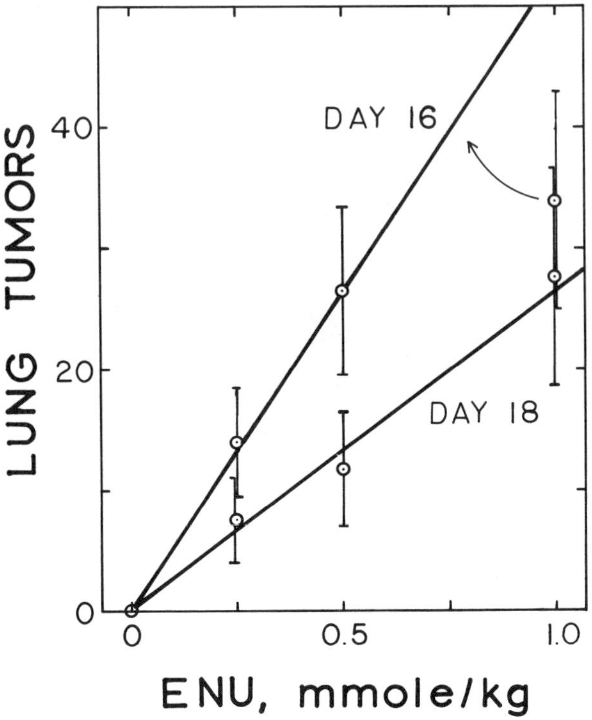

FIGURE 3. Dose-response curves for transplacental pulmonary carcinogenesis in GP mice by ENU, administered on day 16 or on day 18 of gestation. Data is taken from TABLE 2; error bars indicate one standard deviation from the mean tumor incidence in mice treated *in utero* and necropsied at 12 weeks of age. The slopes and intercepts of the lines were calculated by the method of least squares, using data from all four dosage levels for day 18, and dosage levels of 0.5 mmole/kg and below for day 16.

half the mean. So far, there does not seem to be any significant difference in the magnitude of the standard deviation among littermates in random-bred versus inbred strains. Whether the pulmonary tumor response of mice given ENU as adults generally tends to be less uniform than that seen in animals exposed by the transplacental route remains to be seen. It is apparent, however, that no figures for tumor incidence resulting from a given set of treatment conditions can be considered reliable unless they are derived from averages over a number of individuals. The answer to the question "How many are enough?" is, of course, "However many will provide reproducible results." By this criterion, given the magnitude of the standard deviation encountered in this work, we have generally found data derived from ten or more animals from two or more litters to be satisfactory.

5. Doses marginally or negligibly carcinogenic to pregnant mice can be extremely effective in their unborn young if the latter are exposed during the period of maximal sensitivity. We have not yet seen a pulmonary tumor in adult

GP mice given 0.25 mmole/kg ENU, but the offspring of females given this dose on the 16th day of pregnancy develop an average of 14 pulmonary tumors per mouse.

Although our data from other strains of mice are less extensive, we can say at this point that similar maxima appear in the curves of pulmonary tumor response versus time of carcinogen administration for all strains examined, and that they seem always to occur at least four to five days prior to parturition. In TABLE 3, some preliminary data for strains A/J and C57B1/6N are compared with an older study involving urethan. Adult A/J mice are among the most sensitive to pulmonary tumor induction, while C57B1/6N are extremely resistant. When exposed transplacentally to ENU five days prior to birth, mice of both strains suffer a much higher tumor incidence than treated adults; as gestation approaches term, the tumor incidence in the offspring approaches that observed in the mother. C57B1/6N mice are as resistant as adults at least two days prior to birth, but earlier in gestation their sensitivity relative to A/J is markedly increased. A large fraction of the resistance of C57B1/6N mice to pulmonary tumor induction therefore seems to develop late in gestation, sometime after the 15th day. Urethan, as stated earlier, generates a markedly different response; the number of tumors seen in strain A offspring is much lower than that seen in adults when treatment

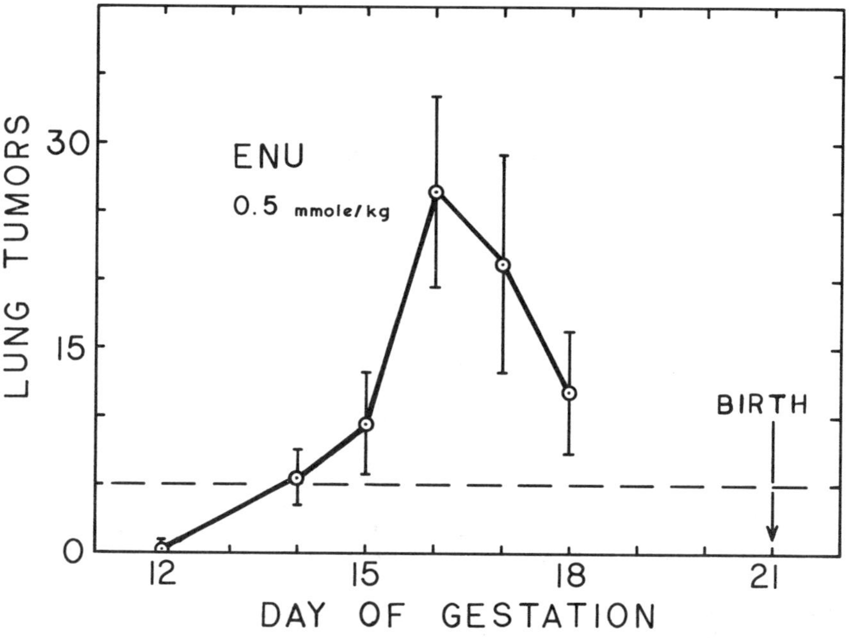

FIGURE 4. Pulmonary tumor induction in GP mice exposed *in utero* to a single dose of 0.5 mmole/kg ENU at various times during gestation. Necropsies at 12 weeks of age; data from TABLE 2. The dashed horizontal line refers to the pulmonary tumor incidence in the mothers, and is drawn one standard deviation above the mean.

TABLE 3

PULMONARY CARCINOGENESIS IN INBRED MICE FOLLOWING SINGLE TRANSPLACENTAL EXPOSURES TO CHEMICAL CARCINOGENS*

Days Between Injection and Birth (Estimated Day of Gestation)	Tumors per Mouse: Mean ± Standard Deviation			
	25 mg (0.28 mmole) urethan (pooled litters, strain A) Data from Larsen, 1947[2]	0.5 mmole/kg ENU (single litters) A/J	C57B1/6N	Ratio A/J : C57B1/6N
6 (13)	–	14.7 ± 2.1 (b)	–	–
5 (14)	1.6 (c)	33.6 ± 8.3 (b)	14.3 ± 5.1 (b)	2.4
		35.5 ± 7.0 (d)		
4 (15)	1.3 (c)	34.4 ± 10.5 (b)	11.1 ± 4.5 (a)	3.1
3 (16)	1.2 (c)	–	–	–
2 (17)	1.8 (c)	12.2 ± 4.2 (b)	1.3 ± 2.3 (a)	9.4
1 (18)	8.9 (c)	–	–	–
Mothers	18.2	9.0 ± 4.8	1.4 ± 1.4	6.4

* Age at autopsy: (a) 14 weeks; (b) 20 weeks; (c) 20 weeks or more; (d) 40 weeks.

is given earlier than 24 hours prepartum, and approaches the adult level *from below* as the time of treatment approaches to within hours of parturition.

Our results with ENU thus indicate that the lungs of mice are extraordinarily sensitive to this substance during a period of less than 48 hours, centered on the fifth day prior to birth. During this period, either a higher proportion of cells at risk become transformed or, of the cells that undergo whatever carcinogen-induced process is necessary for neoplastic transformation, a much larger than usual fraction subsequently gives rise to tumors. A number of possible explanations can be formulated for the manner in which the pulmonary tumor response varies during gestation, and some of these are subject to test. Among the more interesting possibilities are the following:

1. There may exist a period of exceptional sensitivity to neoplastic transformation that is inherent in rapidly proliferating pulmonary tissue in certain stages of development. Such time-dependent vulnerability is observed, for example, in the developing skeleton and in other structures subject to teratogenic insult.

2. What we observe as a maximum may result from the intervention of a corrective process that is increasingly effective after the fifth day prior to birth, and that reduces the number of tumors that would otherwise result from exposure to a given dose of ENU. This might consist of an intracellular repair mechanism; such a process has been shown to account for the differential sensitivity of different sublines of tissue-cultured cells exposed to sulfur mustard.[7] This might operate with varying efficiency in different strains of mice, and thereby contribute to the strain-specific differences in susceptibility to pulmonary tumor induction. Or, since lymphoid differentiation begins in the thymus approximately five days prior to birth, an immunological response may inhibit the growth of an increasing fraction of latent neoplastic cells transformed after this time. This response might also operate with varying degrees of efficiency in different strains of mice.

3. The maximum may result from an enhancement of the carcinogenic effect of ENU through its simultaneous effects on both pulmonary and differentiating lymphoid tissues. It is well known that alkylating agents constitute a group of powerful immunosuppressive drugs,[8] and we have found that a single dose of ENU is extremely effective in preventing tumor allograft rejections in adult mice. It is possible that immature lymphoid tissues are especially susceptible to damage by ENU. There is evidence that damage to the lymphoid system can enhance chemical carcinogenesis: neonatal thymectomy has been shown in at least one laboratory to increase the pulmonary tumor incidence in Swiss mice subsequently treated with urethan.[9]

This last alternative is the most easily tested of the three; it is receiving initial attention in our current search for experimental data to support or eliminate one or another of these hypotheses.

We should also like an explanation of why urethan is ineffective as a transplacental carcinogen during all but the last 24 hours of gestation. It has been suggested[10] that passage of urethan through the placenta is facilitated just prior to birth, but this hypothesis seems insufficient to account for the difference in effectiveness between this compound and ENU earlier in gestation. Although the factors controlling passage of drugs across the placenta are not known in great detail, to a first approximation the placental membranes act as simple lipoid barriers to diffusion, allowing nonionized, highly fat-soluble organic molecules to pass readily from maternal to fetal circulation or vice versa, depending on the direction of the concentration gradient.[11] The transplacental passage of substances such as urethan or ENU is therefore a passive process, probably controlled primarily by factors such as their oil-water partition coefficients, and should not vary greatly with the stage of gestation. What probably does change during gestation is the ability of fetal tissues to synthesize the enzymes required for drug "detoxification." It is known that fetal tissues lack many of these enzymes,[12] and it seems most likely that urethan is ineffective early in gestation because an actively carcinogenic metabolite cannot be formed. The role of N-hydroxyurethan in urethan carcinogenesis is controversial,[13] but this substance is an obvious candidate for such a metabolite, and it should be possible to demonstrate whether or not it can be formed from urethan by fetal tissues. The problem could best be approached, of course, by studying the transplacental carcinogenic activity, at different times during gestation, of a compound known to require metabolic activation. Such a substance is diethylnitrosamine (DENA), which produces lung tumors in the offspring of mice given daily subcutaneous injections during the final week of pregnancy.[14] Metabolic activation of this compound involves hydroxylation of an alpha-carbon atom,[15] followed by spontaneous dissociation into acetaldehyde and ethyldiazotic acid, an unstable species that spontaneously decomposes, generating a nascent ethyl carbonium ion. We hope to correlate transplacental carcinogenesis by this compound with the development in fetal lung tissue of enzymes capable of metabolizing it. The homologous compound, dimethylnitrosamine (DMNA), was found to be a weaker carcinogen for the kidneys of fetal rats than for the mothers when pregnant animals were treated daily during the final week of gestation.[16] It has been shown that demethylation of DMNA in the rat kidney is very inefficient prior to birth.[17] The present state of knowledge concerning metabolism and transplacental carcinogenic activity of ENU, DENA, and urethan is summarized in TABLE 4.

This question of the role of fetal enzymes poses a very practical question; namely, when during gestation should one test for transplacental carcinogenesis?

TABLE 4

METABOLIC ACTIVATION OF TRANSPLACENTAL CARCINOGENS

	Transplacental Pulmonary Carcinogen in Mice		
Compound	Effective Period	Metabolism	Formation of Reactive Species
ENU	day 12 and after	none required	$H_2NCO{-}N(N{=}O){-}CH_2CH_3 \xrightarrow{OH^-}$ $CH_3CH_2{-}N{=}N{-}OH + H_2NCOO^-$
DENA	sometime during final week	enzymic hydroxylation of alpha carbon	$CH_3CH_2{-}N(N{=}O){-}CH_2CH_3 \xrightarrow[(Enz.)]{O_2}$ $CH_3CH_2{-}N(N{=}O){-}CH(OH)CH_3 \longrightarrow$ $CH_3CH_2{-}N{=}N{-}OH + CH_3CHO$
Urethan	day 18–19	possibily N-hydroxylation	$CH_3CH_2OCO{-}NH_2 \xrightarrow[(Enz.)]{O_2\ (?)}$ $CH_3CH_2OCO{-}NH(OH)$

If metabolic activation is prerequisite for carcinogenic activity by a compound, then it may not be effective until just prior to parturition. If it does not require metabolic alteration, a compound should be maximally effective earlier in gestation, as is ENU. However, for compounds that are effective only late in gestation, and for which no active metabolite has been identified, studies of fetal metabolism of the substances may assist in identification of such a metabolite. It should be emphasized, however, that not all substances requiring metabolic change for the acquisition of carcinogenic activity are necessarily inactive as transplacental carcinogens early in pregnancy. Druckrey, Preussmann and their co-workers have shown that 1,2-diethylhydrazine, azoethane, and azoxyethane, which presumably require metabolic activation, are effective transplacental carcinogens for the nervous system of the rat on the 15th day of gestation.[18] The demonstration of transplacental carcinogenicity early in gestation therefore cannot be considered evidence against a hypothetical requirement for metabolic activation.

By contrast with pulmonary tumors, the development of hepatomas in the adult mouse (and in the rat as well) is known to be strongly dependent on the presence of circulating sex hormones; this applies both to spontaneous and to induced tumors. In the strains of mice most prone to hepatomas – C3H, CBA, and their F_1 hybrids with other strains – males develop far more urethan-induced hepatomas than females, but the same intermediate response is observed in castrated animals of both sexes.[19] It thus seems that circulating male hormones promote, and female hormones repress, the development of hepatomas. In rats,

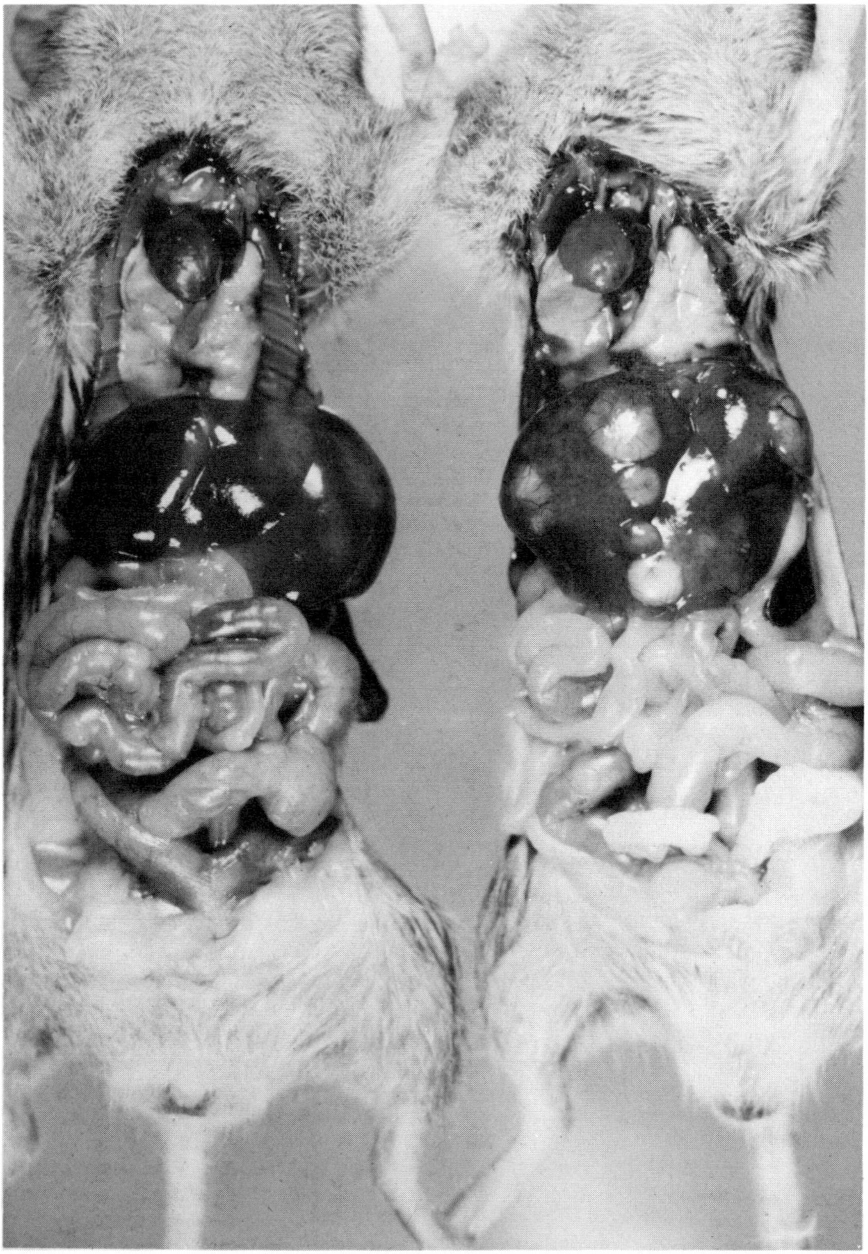

FIGURE 5. Female (left) and male (right) C3Hf littermates at age 40 weeks. Note hepatomas in the male; none were found in the female, or in male or female controls. Treatment: 0.66 mmole/kg ENU transplacentally, day 16.

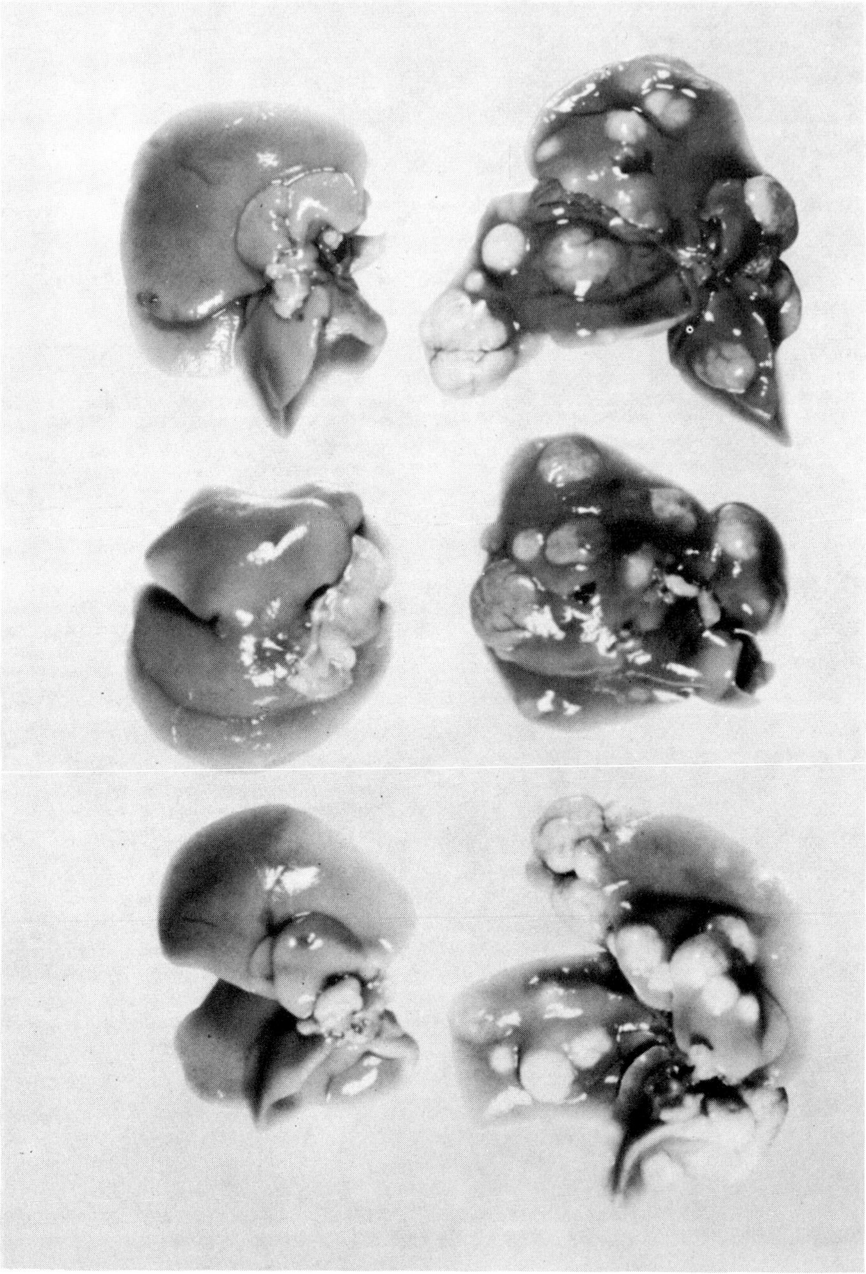

FIGURE 6. Livers from the three female (left) and three male (right) C3Hf siblings comprising the litter described in the legend to FIGURE 5.

part of the sex effect on hepatic carcinogenesis by compounds known to require metabolic activation occurs at the microsomal level. There are demonstrable differences in the rate of metabolism of various drugs by microsomes from rats of different sexes.[20] Part of the sex effect on hepatoma development in rats thus may involve different levels of exposure to endogenously generated proximate carcinogens.

We were interested in determining, first, whether ENU would effect transplacental hepatocarcinogenesis in the mouse; second, whether the carcinogenic response would be limited to strains of mice known to be sensitive to hepatocarcinogenesis as adults; and finally, whether sex would affect the dose response in mice exposed transplacentally to a hepatic carcinogen that does not require metabolic activation. The answers to all three of these questions are affirmative. We find that multiple hepatomas appear in the livers of male C3Hf mice at 40 weeks of age, following transplacental exposure to ENU on the 14th day of gestation or thereafter. The hepatoma incidence in their female siblings is far lower (FIGURES 5 & 6). A few hepatomas are also seen in similarly treated strain A mice at 40 weeks of age, but none are observed in GP mice at this time. We have no data for mice of any strain older than 40 weeks. The tumors are first apparent as hyperplastic nodules of parenchymal cells, which grow progressively and assume an increasingly neoplastic appearance in histological sections; those so far examined, like the pulmonary tumors, are identical histologically with those induced in adults. The relatively long latent period and pronounced sex dependence of these transplacentally induced hepatomas are consistent with the hypothesis that it is the development of tumors from latent neoplastic liver cells, rather than some aspect of the transformation process itself, that is affected by the levels of circulating sex hormones in these animals.

We have not yet seen any embryonal mixed tumors, nor any significant incidence of unusual neoplasms in the offspring of mice treated with ENU during gestation. Probably we have not kept our animals long enough to observe the entire range of neoplastic responses engendered by transplacental exposure to ENU. It is also quite possible that the unusual neoplasms we have so far failed to observe might conceivably be generated by exposure of less differentiated tissues at times earlier in gestation than the 12th day. The difficulty, of course, is that serious malformations result from treatment with ENU during the period of early ogranogenesis, between the seventh and twelfth days of gestation,[21] and that fetuses so afflicted will not live long enough to develop tumors.

We are presently extending our studies in an effort to cast some light on certain questions raised by the results presented here, especially the variation in pulmonary tumor response with time of administration of ENU, and the role of fetal metabolism in transplacental carcinogenesis by various classes of alkylating agents.

ACKNOWLEDGMENT

I wish to take this opportunity to thank Miss Jacqueline Davidson for excellent technical assistance, Miss Johanna Zuefle and her staff for histological preparations, and Dr. Richard Bates for advice on matters of pathology and for many helpful discussions.

References

1. Nettleship, A. & P. S. Henshaw. 1943. Induction of pulmonary tumors in mice with ethyl carbamate (urethane). J. Nat. Cancer Inst. **4:** 309.
2. Larsen, C. D. 1947. Pulmonary-tumor induction by transplacental exposure to urethan. J. Nat. Cancer Inst. **8:** 63.
3. Smith, W. E. & P. Rous. 1948. The neoplastic potentialities of mouse embryo tissues. IV. Lung adenomas in baby mice as a result of prenatal exposure to urethan. J. Exp. Med. **88:** 529.
4. Klein, M. 1952. The transplacental effect of urethan on lung tumorigenesis in mice. J. Nat. Cancer Inst. **12:** 1003.
5. Druckrey, H., S. Ivankovic & R. Preussmann. 1966. Teratogenic and carcinogenic effects in the offspring after single injection of ethylnitrosourea to pregnant rats. Nature **210:** 1378.
6. Allison, R. M. & R. A. Willis. 1956. An ossifying embryonic mixed tumor of an infant's liver. J. Path. Bact. **72:** 155.
7. Crathorn, A. R. & J. J. Roberts. 1966. Mechanism of the cytotoxic action of alkylating agents in mammalian cells and evidence for the removal of alkylated groups from deoxyribonucleic acid. Nature **211:** 150.
8. Santos, G. W. 1967. Immunosuppressive drugs. Fed. Proc. **26:** 907.
9. Trainin, N., M. Linker-Israeli, M. Small & L. Boiato-Chen. 1967. Enhancement of lung adenoma formation by neonatal thymectomy in mice treated with 7,12-dimethylbenz(*a*)anthracene or urethan. Inter. J. Cancer **2:** 326.
10. DiPaolo, J. A. 1962. Effects of oxygen concentration on carcinogenesis induced by transplacental exposure to urethan. Cancer Res. **22:** 299.
11. Fingl, E. & D. M. Woodbury. 1965. *In* The Pharmacological Basis of Therapeutics. L. S. Goodman and A. Gilman, Eds. : 11. Macmillan Company, New York, N. Y.
12. Fouts, J. R. 1965. The metabolism of drugs by the fetus. *In* Embryopathic Activity of Drugs – A Symposium. J. M. Robson, F. M. Sullivan & R. L. Smith, Eds. : 43–55. Little, Brown and Company. Boston, Mass.
13. Mirvish, S. S. 1966. The metabolism of N-hydroxyurethan in relation to its carcinogenic action; conversion into urethan and an N-hydroxy-urethan glucuronide. Biochim. Biophys. Acta **117:** 1.
14. Mohr, U. & J. Althoff. 1965. Die diaplacentare Wirkung des Cancerogens Diäthylnitrosamin bei der Maus. Z. Krebsforsch. **67:** 152.
15. Mizrahi, I. J. & P. Emmelot. 1962. The effect of cysteine on the metabolic changes produced by two carcinogenic N-nitrosodialkylamines in rat liver. Cancer Res. **22:** 339.
16. Alexandrov, V. A. 1968. Blastomogenic effect of dimethylnitrosamine on pregnant rats and their offspring. Nature **218:** 280.
17. Lee, K. Y. & K. Spencer. 1964. Methylation of liver and kidney ribonucleic acids in newborn rats treated with H^3-dimethylnitrosamine. J. Nat. Cancer Inst. **33:** 957.
18. Druckrey, H., S. Ivankovic, R. Preussmann, C. Landschutz, J. Stekar, U. Brunner & B. Schagen. 1968. Transplacentar induction of neurogenic malignomas by 1,2-diethylhydrazine, azo-, and azoxyethane in rats. Experientia **24:** 561.
19. Vesselinovitch, S. D. & N. Mihailovich. 1967. The effect of gonadectomy on the development of hepatomas induced by urethan. Cancer Res. **27:** 1788.
20. Schenkman, J. B., I. Frey, H. Remmer & R. W. Estabrook. 1967. Sex differences in drug metabolism by rat liver microsomes. Molec. Pharmacol. **3:** 516.
21. Napalkov, N. P. & V. A. Alexandrov. 1967. On the effects of blastomogenic substances on the organism during embryogenesis. Z. Krebsforsch. **71:** 32.

DISCUSSION OF THE PAPER

H. DRUCKREY (*Forschergruppe Praeventivmedizin, Freiburg, Germany*): What is the distinction between the benign lung adenomas you observed and malignant lung tumors? Did you observe any tumors of the nervous system?

DR. RICE: The lung tumors initially have a very benign appearance; later on many of them do develop invasive properties, and eventually many of them can be transplanted. The transplanted tumors will metastasize and kill the host. Histologically, primary lung tumors capable of progressive growth after transplantation are invariably alveologenic adenocarcinomas. Bronchogenic carcinomas of the sort most frequently seen in man have rarely been demonstrated in the mouse.

We have not seen any neurogenic tumors in any of our strains of mice. We have seen neurological abnormalities of various sorts, indicating some damage to the central nervous system, but none of these has so far been traced to neoplastic disease.

THE MUTAGENICITY AND INITIATING ACTIVITY OF SOME AROMATIC AMINE METABOLITES*

Frank Mukai and Walter Troll

New York University Medical Center
New York, N.Y.

The nature of the biological target remains one of the fundamental unanswered questions regarding the mechanism of carcinogenesis. Most chemical carcinogens have been found to react with three of the biologically important macromolecules: deoxyribonucleic acid (DNA), ribonucleic acid (RNA), and protein.[1] Therefore, it is not surprising that no general agreement exists concerning the primary cellular site of action of a carcinogen and that, depending upon the carcinogen used, various authors favor the importance of one of these macromolecules over the others.[2–6]

In the case of aromatic amines and amides, attempts to delineate the biological target are further complicated by the fact that these carcinogens have been shown to be metabolically converted in susceptible species to a number of active derivatives that are generally more carcinogenic at sites of application than the parent compounds are.[1] Thus, the identification of the active metabolites becomes an additional problem.

Several papers have recently appeared concerning the interaction of aromatic amines and their carcinogenic metabolites with nucleic acid constituents. In the case of 2-acetylaminofluorene (2-AAF), the parent compound did not react *in vitro* with nucleic acids,[1] whereas a possible *in vivo* metabolite, N-hydroxy-2-aminofluorene (N-OH-2AF), reacted with the guanine moiety of DNA and RNA at low pH.[7] The related carcinogenic derivative, N-acetoxy-2-acetylaminofluorene (N-acetoxy-2AAF), also reacted with guanine of the nucleic acids and with guanosine *in vitro* at neutral pH.[8] The reaction product of guanosine and N-acetoxy-2AAF has been identified as 8-(N-2-fluorenylacetamido) guanosine.[9]

The effects of another aromatic amine, the bladder carcinogen 2-aminonaphthalene (2AN), and its carcinogenic metabolites on the thermal stability of DNA and synthetic polynucleotides[10] and on the RNA polymerase priming activity of DNA[11] have revealed a general correlation between reactivity and carcinogenicity.

It seems reasonable to expect that these interactions with nucleic acids, particularly DNA, would result in mutation. In the present report, we have utilized the bacterial back-mutation system to determine whether any relationship exists between the reported carcinogenicity of aromatic amine metabolites and their mutagenicity. Further, to check the relevance of mutagenic activity to carcinogenic activity, selected metabolites have been used as initiators and promoters in mouse skin tumorigenesis. The results indicate that the parent compounds are

* This investigation was supported by Project Grants from the NIH (USPHS) Research Grants nos. CA-09568 and CA-08491 and by a grant from Allied Chemical Corporation, and it is part of a Core Program supported by the USPHS, Bureau of State Services Grant ES-00014, and the National Cancer Institute Grant CA-06989.

neither mutagenic nor initiators in mouse skin, while several carcinogenic N-hydroxy metabolites are mutagens and initiators.

Materials and Methods

Strains of Organisms Used

Most of the experiments were done with 44 nutritional mutants derived from *Escherichia coli* strain 15. Three tryptophan-requiring mutants of *E. coli* K-12—A23, A46, and A58—kindly supplied by Dr. C. Yanofsky, Stanford University, were used to check for base-pair specificity. All three mutants are considered to have AT (adenine-thymine) at the mutant site.[12]

Compounds Tested for Mutagenicity

The aromatic amines and derivatives selected for study are listed in Table 1 together with data on their effects on thermal stability of DNA and on the RNA polymerase priming activity. Preparation of the derivatives of 1AN, 2AN, and 2AAF has been described previously.[13,14] β-Propiolactone (BPL), hydroxylamine HCl (HA), and 2-aminopurine (2AP) were obtained commercially.

Mutagenic Treatments

All platings for scoring revertant colonies were made by spreading treated cultures on the surface of Petri plates containing M-9 agar medium[15] enriched

Table 1

Compounds Tested and Their Effects on Thermal Stability and on RNA Polymerase Priming Activity of Treated DNA

Compound (Abbreviation)	Property Affected: Thermal Stability	Property Affected: Priming Activity
2-aminonaphthalene (2AN)	−	−
N-hydroxy-2-aminonaphthalene (N-OH-2AN)	+ (pH 5)	+
N-acetoxy-2-acetylaminonaphthalene (N-acetoxy-2AAN)	−	(+)*
1-hydroxy-2-aminonaphthalene (1-OH-2AN)	+	+
1-aminonaphthalene (1AN)	−	−
N-hydroxy-1-aminonaphthalene (N-OH-1AN)	+ (pH 5)	+
N-acetoxy-1-acetylaminonaphthalene (N-acetoxy-1AAN)	−	(+)
2-acetylaminofluorene (2AAF)	−	−
N-hydroxy-2-acetylaminofluorene (N-OH-2AAF)	−	(+)
N-acetoxy-2-acetylaminofluorene (N-acetoxy-2AAF)	+	+
N-hydroxy-2-aminofluorene (N-OH-2AF)	+ (pH 5)	+

*(+) denotes moderate effect.

with 1.25% nutrient broth. Revertant colonies were counted after two to four days incubation at 37° C.

The experiments with BPL and the initial tests with the aromatic amine compounds were performed according to the spot test method.[16] For experiments involving treatment in liquid medium, a glycerol-acetone solvent system was used[13] at a final concentration of 100 gammas of each compound/ml.

For 2AP mutagenesis, logarithmic growth phase cultures at a cell concentration of approximately 10^8 bacteria/ml were treated for 60 min in M-9 medium containing the appropriate nutritional factor and 250 μg 2AP/ml. 2AP was removed by centrifugation before the cells were plated.

For HA mutagenesis, stationary growth phase cultures were used. Five milliliters of an overnight broth culture were centrifuged and washed once with saline. The washed pellet was then resuspended in 2.5 ml of the HA reaction mixture,[17] which was 1.0 M for HA and 0.05 M for sodium pyrophosphate at a pH of 7.0. For control cultures, 0.5 ml of this suspension was immediately added to L-broth to stop the action of HA.[18] The remainder of the suspension was incubated without aeration at 37° C for 45 min and the reaction stopped by a similar dilution into L-broth. HA was removed by centrifugation before plating.

Mouse Skin Tumorigenesis

Initiating activity was tested by applying a single l-mg dose, in acetone, of the compounds on test to the backs of female Swiss-Millerton mice, followed 18 days later by three-times-weekly application of 25 μg croton resin.[19] Promoting activity was tested by first initiating with a single subcarcinogenic[20] dose (480 μmoles) of BPL, followed by three-times-weekly application of 100 μg of the compounds on test.

Results and Discussion

Mutagenicity Studies

Perez and Radomski[21] first reported that the parent amine 2AN was not mutagenic, whereas the N-hydroxy metabolite N-OH-2AN, as well as N-OH-1AN, was mutagenic for *E. coli.* Since the N-hydroxy compounds reverted only a purine-dependent mutant, and not a methionine- and histidine-dependent mutant, they suggested that this locus specificity implied a nucleotide pair specificity.

Our studies were extended to 44 nutritional mutants originating from 2AP treatment to determine the mutagenicity of the aromatic amine compounds and to see whether such a specificity did indeed exist. This base analogue was selected to induce the forward mutations since 2AP is considered capable of producing both guanine-cytosine-to-adenine-thymine (GC-AT) base pair transitions as well as AT-GC transitions.[22,23] Based on the following criteria, 30 of the mutants were classified as transitional mutants: (1) They were back-mutated by the base analogue 2AP, (2) they were back-mutated by BPL and/or HA, and (3) they were able to back-mutate spontaneously. The remaining 14 mutants were considered to be of the deletion or the transversion types of mutants, since they did not meet any of the criteria mentioned.

The number of mutants responding to the mutagens used for their characterization and to the parent amines, 1AN and 2AN, and their N-hydroxy metabolites, N-OH-1AN and N-OH-2AN respectively, as tested by the spot test method, is presented in TABLE 2. Seven of the 44 mutants responded to N-OH-1AN, two of these seven also gave back-mutants with N-OH-2AN, and all seven mutants belonged to the group of 30 transitional mutants.

Although these results appear to be compatible with the previous findings of Perez and Radomski that N-OH-1AN is a better mutagen than N-OH-2AN,[21] mutagenicity tests using the glycerol-actone solvent system indicate that both N-hydroxy compounds are active on the same transitional mutants. This is shown in TABLE 3, which summarizes the results of the two methods of testing. Among the remaining 23 transitional mutants which were negative by the spot test method, 15 additional mutants were also back-mutated when treated with the N-hydroxy compounds, but not by the parent amines.

The revertant frequencies produced by all of the aromatic amine compounds

TABLE 2

NUMBER OF MUTANTS RESPONDING TO VARIOUS MUTAGENS

Compound	Type of Response	
	Revertible	Nonrevertible
Control (spontaneous)	30	14
2-Aminopurine	30	14
Beta-propiolactone	25	19
Hydroxylamine	28	16
1-Aminonaphthalene	0	44
2-Aminonaphtalene	0	44
N-hydroxy-1-aminonaphthalene	7	37
N-hydroxy-2-aminonaphthalene	2	42

TABLE 3

COMPARISON OF TWO METHODS OF BACK-MUTATION INDUCTION*

Mutant	Spot Test		Liquid Medium	
	N-OH-1AN	N-OH-2AN	N-OH-1AN	N-OH-2AN
A11	++	+	++	++
A12	+	−	++++	++
A23	+	−	+	+
A38	+	−	++++	++++
B14	+	−	++	+
B36	++	+	+	++
H2	+	−	+++	++

* A minus sign denotes no increase in reversion frequency over controls; + = 2- to 5-fold increase; ++ = 5- to 10-fold increase; +++ = 10- to 20-fold increase; ++++ = greater than 20-fold increase.

using the more reliable liquid medium system are shown in TABLE 4 and TABLE 5. The mutants used for the experiments were all capable of being back-mutated by treatment with HA, BPL, and 2AP. The compounds found to be mutagenically active were N-OH-1AN, N-OH-2AN, N-acetoxy-2AAF, and N-OH-2AF. None of these metabolites or HA were able to increase the frequency of revertants when tested on the three tryptophan mutants of *E. coli* K12 (A23, A46, A58) known to have AT at their mutant sites.[12] On the basis of the results presented thus far, it could be postulated that all of the mutagenically active metabolites are specifically causing GC-AT transitions. Verification of this apparent nucleotide pair specificity is dependent upon the validity of the hypothesis that the mutagenic effect of HA is due solely to its reaction with cytosine.[22,23] One method of proof would be to show that HA-induced forward mutations could not be back-mutated by either HA or any of the active metabolites. When we did this,

TABLE 4
MUTATION INDUCTION BY AROMATIC AMINE COMPOUNDS AS TESTED BY LIQUID MEDIUM METHOD (NONMUTAGENIC COMPOUNDS)

	Frequency of Revertants/10^8 Cells*							
Mutant	Control	2AN	N-acetoxy-2AAN	1-OH-2AN	1AN	N-acetoxy-1AAN	2AAF	N-OH-2AAF
A11	14.6	20.1	12.6	23.6	19.2	10.1	6.8	13.6
A12	1.8	2.8	—	2.5	4.8	—	1.7	4.3
A23	4.5	4.4	—	3.2	6.3	—	4.2	4.9
A38	2.1	5.9	1.5	10.1	4.2	1.5	4.7	2.9

* A dash denotes not tested.

however, we found that five of 11 HA-induced forward mutants were back-mutated by treatment with HA, N-OH-1AN, and N-OH-2AN. This indicates that HA is also capable of producing AT-GC transitions and is in agreement with the recent findings of Osborn and associates,[24] who found that about 58% of HA-induced revertants in an amber mutant of *E. coli* WWU were the result of

TABLE 5
MUTATION INDUCTION BY AROMATIC AMINE COMPOUNDS AS TESTED BY LIQUID MEDIUM METHOD (MUTAGENIC COMPOUNDS)

	Frequency of Revertants/10^8 Cells				
Mutant	Control	N-OH-2AN	N-OH-1AN	N-acetoxy-2AAF	N-OH-2AF
A11	14.6	92.6	76.2	64.0	380.0
A12	1.8	11.2	59.6	7.3	461.0
A23	4.5	10.9	10.0	24.0	501.0
A38	2.1	277.0	114.0	12.8	320.0

AT-CG transitions. Thus, it would be premature to assign a particular base-pair specificity to the mutagenically active aromatic amine metabolites. Nonetheless, the bacterial back-mutation tests have enabled us to show that the parent amines are not mutagenic, while several carcinogenic derivatives are mutagens.

Mouse Skin Tumorigenesis

The four mutagenically active metabolities—N-OH-1AN, N-OH-2AN, N-OH-2AF, and N-acetoxy-2AAF—have all been found to be carcinogenic *in situ*.[23,25,26] In order to clarify the relation of our mutagenic findings to carcinogenesis, skin-painting experiments were performed with the purpose of identifying these compounds as initiators, or promoters, of carcinogenesis, according to the two-stage scheme of cancer induction proposed by Berenblum.[27]

The results of the skin tumor induction experiments with N-OH-1AN and N-OH-2AN are shown in TABLE 6. The single 1-mg application of both metabolites, followed by croton resin promotion, resulted in 6/20 and 5/20 animals with papillomas as compared with 7/14 in the BPL-initiated, croton-resin-promoted, positive-control group of animals. First tumors appeared 49 days after beginning of promotion as compared to 41 days in the control group, and the average number of papillomas was 2.4 as compared to 4.0. It does not appear that either of the metabolites has any promoting activity, although the data presented may indicate that N-OH-1AN is a weak whole carcinogen, since 2/15 animals had papillomas appearing after 349 days. Thus, both N-OH-1AN and N-OH-2AN are initiators of mouse skin tumors when promoted by croton resin.

TABLE 6

MOUSE SKIN TUMORIGENESIS*

Treatment: Initiator	Treatment: Promoter	Tumor Bearers / No. Surviving	Days to First Appearance†	Average No. Papillomas per Tumor Bearer
N-OH-1AN	Croton resin	6/20	49	2.4
N-OH-2AN	Croton resin	5/20	49	2.4
BPL	Croton resin	7/14	41	4.0
N-OH-1AN	Acetone	0/18	—	—
N-OH-2AN	Acetone	0/19	—	—
BPL	Acetone	0/16	—	—
BPL	N-OH-1AN	2/15	178, 303	2.0
BPL	N-OH-2AN	0/14	—	—
None	N-OH-1AN	2/15	349	2.0
None	N-OH-2AN	0/15	—	—
None	Croton resin	0/14	—	—

* A preliminary report of this work was presented at the meeting of the American Association for Cancer Research in April, 1968.[31]

† From start of promotion.

In experiments now in progress, preliminary observations indicate that the mutagenic derivative of 2AAF, N-acetoxy-2AAF, is an initiator, while the nonmutagenic metabolite, N-OH-2AAF, is not. Both N-acetoxy esters of 1- and 1AN, N-acetoxy-1AN and N-acetoxy-2AN respectively, which we found were not mutagenic, appear to have initiating activity. All three parent compounds are devoid of initiating activity.

Summarizing the results of the mutagenicity and tumor induction data of the compounds tested thus far: (1) Three derivatives possessing the properties of being carcinogenic, mutagenic, and initiating are N-OH-1AN, N-OH-2AN, and N-acetoxy-2AAF, (2) two metabolities reportedly carcinogenic, but neither mutagenic nor able to initiate, are 1-OH-2AN and N-OH-2AAF, and (3) two compounds not yet tested for carcinogenicity, but found not mutagenic, yet having initiating activity are N-acetoxy-1AAN and N-acetoxy-2AAN.

In these experiments, we have attempted to ascertain whether carcinogens are mutagens and whether mutagenic carcinogens are initiators. The results indicate that such relationships are not complete for aromatic amine compounds. To determine whether a better correlation would be found for epoxides and lactones, which may be considered direct carcinogens, we have examined the mutagenicity of 10 of these alkylating agents. The results are shown in TABLE 7.

TABLE 7

THE MUTAGENICITY OF SOME EPOXIDES AND LACTONES

Compound	Carcinogenicity*	Mutagenicity†
Beta-propiolactone	+	+
Beta-butyrolactone	+	+
Glycidaldehyde	+	+
Ethylglycidyl ether	−	−
1,2-Epoxybutane	−	−
1,2,3,4-Diepoxybutane	+	+
1,2,4,5-Diepoxypentane	+	+
1,2,5,6-Diepoxyhexane	+	+
1,2,7,8-Diepoxyoctane	+	+
Vinylcyclohexene-3-diepoxide	+	+

* Van Duuren and associates.[32]
† Present study.

In the case of these compounds, it can be seen that there is an excellent correlation between carcinogenicity and mutagenicity. Further, Van Duuren and colleagues[28] have shown that BPL, beta-butyrolactone, glycidaldehyde, and 1,2,3,4-diepoxybutane are initiators of mouse skin tumors when promoted by croton resin. Therefore, our failure to obtain a better correlation with N-acetoxy-1-AAN and N-acetoxy-2-AAN may lie in the fact that these compounds are further converted into the active derivatives. For example, these compounds may be deacetylated in the mouse skin to yield N-OH-1AN and N-OH-2AN respectively, compounds which possess the three properties of carcinogenicity, mutagenicity, and initiation. The possibility of deacetylation has been raised recently by the report[29] that the N-acetyl group of 2AAF is not retained in the case of *in vivo* binding to liver DNA, which suggested that the reaction of the hydroxylamine N-OH-2AF was favored in the nucleus.

Neoplasia certainly is a complex phenomenon. Two steps have clearly been delineated in mouse skin carcinogenesis—initiation and promotion. Our results support the suggestion that DNA is the cellular target in the process of initiation.[30] The promoting agent croton resin is not mutagenic in our system, which may indicate that promoting agents have different cellular targets, i.e., RNA or proteins.

Acknowledgments

We gratefully acknowledge the significant contributions of Dr. Sidney Belman and Mrs. Irene Hawryluk.

References

1. Miller, E. C. & J. A. Miller. 1966. Mechanisms of chemical carcinogenesis: Nature of proximal carcinogens and interactions with macromolecules. Pharmacol. Rev. **18:** 805–838.
2. Brooks, P. 1966. Quantitative aspects of the reaction of some carcinogens with nucleic acids and the possible significance of such reactions in the process of carcinogenesis. Cancer Res. **26:** 1994–2003.
3. Brooks, P. & P. D. Lawley. 1964. Evidence for the binding of polynuclear aromatic amines to nucleic acids of mouse skin. Relation between carcinogenic power of hydrocarbons and their binding to deoxyribonucleic acid. Nature **202:** 781–784.
4. Heidelberger, C. 1959. The relation of protein binding to hydrocarbon carcinogenesis. *In* Carcinogenesis: Mechanism of Action. Ciba Found. Symp. G. E. W. Wolstenholme & M. O'Conner, Eds. : 179–192. Churchill Ltd. London, England.
5. Marroquin, F. & E. Farber. 1965. The binding of 2-acetylaminofluorene to rat liver ribonucleic acid *in vivo*. Cancer Res. **25:** 1262–1269.
6. Roberts, J. J. & G. P. Warwick. 1966. The covalent binding of metabolites of dimethylaminobenzene, β-naphthylamine and aniline to nucleic acids in vivo. Int. J. Cancer **1:** 179–196.
7. Kriek, E. 1965. On the interaction of N-2-fluorenylhydroxylamine with nucleic acids *in vitro*. Biochem. Biophys. Res. Commun. **20:** 793–799.
8. Miller, E. C., V. Juhl & J. A. Miller. 1966. Nucleic acid guanine: Reaction with the carcinogen N-acetoxy-2-acetylaminofluorene. Science **153:** 1125–1127.
9. Kriek, E., J. A. Miller, J. Juhl & E. C. Miller. 1967. 8-(N-2-fluorenylacetamido) guanosine, an arylamidation reaction product of guanosine and the carcinogen N-acetoxy-N-2-fluorenylacetamide in neutral solution. Biochemistry **6:** 177–182.
10. Troll, W., S. Belman & E. Levine. 1963. The effect of metabolites of 2-naphthylamine and the mutagen hydroxylamine on the thermal stability of DNA and polyribonucleotides. Cancer Res. **23:** 841–847.
11. Belman, S., T. Huang, E. Levine & W. Troll. 1964. The effect of chemical modification of DNA on its priming activity with RNA polymerase. Biochem. Biophys. Res. Commun. **14:** 463–467.
12. Yanofsky, C., E. C. Cox & V. Horn. 1966. The unusual mutagenic specificity of an *E. coli* mutator gene. Proc. Nat. Acad. Sci. USA **55:** 274–281.
13. Belman, S., W. Troll, G. Teebor & F. Mukai. 1968. The carcinogenic and mutagenic properties of N-hydroxy-aminonaphthalenes. Cancer Res. **28:** 535–542.
14. Troll, W., E. Rinde & P. Day. 1968. A comparison of C-8 and N-7 substitution of guanine in calf thymus DNA. Biochim. Biophys. Acta. Accepted for publication.
15. Adams, M. H. 1959. *In* Bacteriophages. Interscience Publishers, Inc. New York, N. Y.
16. Iyer, V. N. & W. Szybalski. 1958. Two simple methods for the detection of chemical mutagens. Appl. Microbiol. **6:** 23–29.

17. FREESE, E. & E. BAUTZ FREESE. 1965. The oxygen effect of deoxyribonucleic acid inactivation by hydroxylamines. Biochemistry **4:** 2419–2433.
18. WEINBERG, R. & H. W. BOYER. 1965. Base analogue induced arabinose-negative mutants of *Escherichia coli.* Genetics **51:** 545–553.
19. VAN DUUREN, B. L. & L. ORRIS. 1965. The tumor-enhancing principles of *Croton tiglium L.* Cancer Res. **25:** 1871–1875.
20. COLBURN, N. H. & R. K. BOUTWELL. 1966. The binding of β-propiolactone to mouse skin DNA *in vivo.* Its correlation with tumor-initiating activity. Cancer Res. **26:** 1701–1706.
21. PEREZ, G. & J. L. RADOMSKI. 1965. The mutagenicity of the N-hydroxy naphthylamines in relation to their carcinogenicity. Ind. Med. and Surg. **34:** 714–716.
22. FREESE, E. 1963. Molecular mechanism of mutations. *In* Molecular Genetics. J. H. Taylor, Ed. : 207–269. Academic Press, Inc. New York, N. Y.
23. PHILLIPS, J. H. & D. M. BROWN. 1967. The mutagenic action of hydroxylamine. *In* Progress in Nucleic Acid Research and Molecular Biology. J. N. Davidson & W. E. Cohn, Eds. : 349–368. Academic Press, Inc. New York, N. Y.
24. OSBORN, M., S. PERSON, S. PHILLIPS & F. FUNK. 1967. A determination of mutagen specificity in bacteria using nonsense mutants of bacteriophage T4. J. Molec. Biol. **26:** 437–447.
25. BOYLAND, E., E. R. BUSBY, C. E. DUKES, P. L. GLOVER & D. MANSON. 1964. Further experiments on implantation of materials into the urinary bladder of mice. Brit. J. Cancer **18:** 575–581.
26. MILLER, E. C., C. W. COOKE, P. D. LOTLIKAR & J. A. MILLER. 1964. The metabolism and carcinogenicity of N-hydroxy-2-acetylaminofluorene (N-HO-AAF) and some of its possible metabolites. Proc. Amer. Assoc. Cancer Res. **5:** 45.
27. BERENBLUM, I. 1954. Carcinogenesis and tumor pathogenesis. *In* Advances in Cancer Research. J. P. Greenstein & A. Haddow, Eds. : 129–175. Academic Press, Inc. New York, N. Y.
28. VAN DUUREN, B. L., L. ORRIS & N. NELSON. 1965. Carcinogenicity of epoxides, lactones, and peroxy compounds. J. Nat. Cancer Inst. **35:** 707–717.
29. KRIEK, E. 1968. Difference in binding of 2-acetylaminofluorene to rat liver deoxyribonucleic acid and ribosomal ribonucleic acid *in vivo.* Biochim. Biophys. Acta **161:** 273–275.
30. COLBURN, N. H. & R. K. BOUTWELL. 1968. The binding of β-propiolactone and some related alkylating agents to DNA, RNA, and protein of mouse skin; relation between tumor-initiating power of alkylating agents and their binding to DNA. Cancer Res. **28:** 653–660.
31. MUKAI, F., S. BELMAN, I. HAWRYLUK & W. TROLL. 1968. The initiating activity of arylhydroxylamines. Proc. Amer. Assoc. Cancer Res. **9:** 52.
32. VAN DUUREN, B. L., L. LANGSETH, B. M. GOLDSCHMIDT & L. ORRIS. 1967. Carcinogenicity of epoxides, lactones, and peroxy compounds. VI. Structure and carcinogenic activity. J. Nat. Cancer Inst. **39:** 1217–1228.

PART IV. ENVIRONMENTAL ALKYLATING AGENTS

PYRROLIZIDINE ALKALOIDS AS ALKYLATING AND ANTIMITOTIC AGENTS*

C. C. J. Culvenor, D. T. Downing† and J. A. Edgar

Division of Applied Chemistry, CSIRO, Melbourne, Australia

and

M. V. Jago

Division of Animal Health, CSIRO, Melbourne, Australia

Introduction

The pyrrolizidine alkaloids occur most frequently in the plant families Compositae (tribe Senecioneae), Boraginaceae (subfamilies Heliotropioideae and Boraginoideae), and Leguminosae (genus *Crotalaria*), but in recent years they have been found also in the families Celastraceae, Gramineae, Orchidaceae, Rhizophoraceae, Santalaceae, and Sapotaceae, as well as in the genus *Eupatorium,* which belongs to a different section of the Compositae.[1] Depending on the dose level, the hepatotoxic alkaloids produce peracute, acute, or chronic toxic effects in animals, the chronic syndrome being the one usually encountered in natural occurrences of pyrrolizidine poisoning. The characteristic feature of the chronic syndrome is a megalocytosis of the liver in which the liver becomes composed of a small number of giant cells. This lesion appears to result from a long-lasting antimitotic effect combined with an increased rate of cell death, which gives a stimulus to liver growth.

Structure-Activity and Alkylating Properties

The three alkaloids that have been most studied biologically, heliotrine (I), lasiocarpine (II), and monocrotaline (III), have structures typical of the hepatotoxic alkaloids. With one exception, the minimum structural requirements for hepatotoxicity can be expressed as in (IV) (R = branched chain alkyl, R′ = H,OH or O-acyl), which has a 1,2-double bond in the pyrrolizidine ring and the primary hydroxyl esterified with a branched-chain acid.[2] This conclusion is now based on 28 alkaloids known to be hepatotoxic in the chronic sense and nine alkaloids that are not hepatotoxic.[1] The exception, 7-angelylheliotridine (V), which has the aminoalcohol esterified on the secondary rather than the primary hydroxyl and produces a mild degree of megalocytosis, will be discussed later. Some pyrrolizidine alkaloids have mutagenic and tumor-inhibitory properties or cause chromosome breakage, and these also conform to the structure (IV). Partial correlations can be made between hepatotoxicity and physical properties. In particular, in-

* Presented by Dr. Downing.

† Present Address: Department of Dermatology, Boston University Medical Center, Boston, Mass.

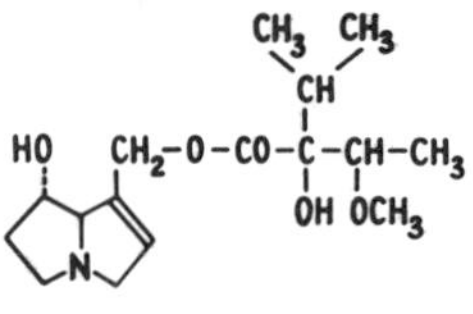

(I)

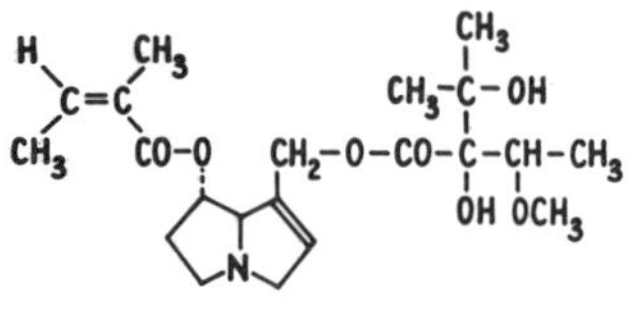

(II)

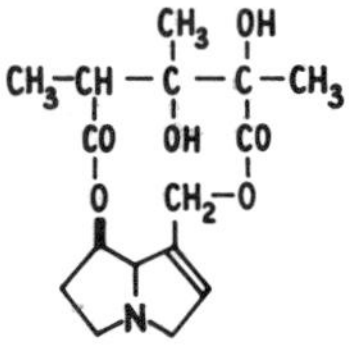

(III)

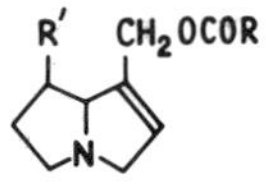

(IV)

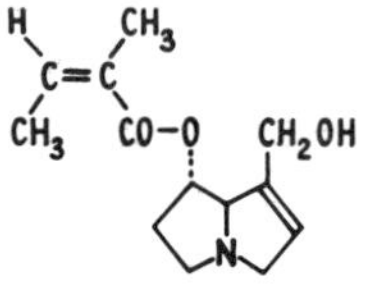

(V)

verse relationships are apparent between acute hepatotoxicity and both base strength and water solubility (TABLE 1),[1] and there is reason to believe that acute hepatotoxicity parallels chronic hepatotoxicity and thus antimitotic activity. The hepatotoxic alkaloids have weak alkylating reactivity associated with the possi-

TABLE 1

INVERSE RELATIONSHIPS BETWEEN ACUTE TOXICITY OF ALKALOIDS AND (A) WATER SOLUBILITY, AND (B) BASE STRENGTH[1]

Alkaloid	LD_{50} in Male Rats (mg/kg)	Solubility in Water (g/100 ml)	pK_a (in Water)
Heliosupine	60	medium	ca 7.6
Lasiocarpine	72	low (0.68)	7.6
Seneciphylline	77	low	ca 7.6
Senecionine	85	low (0.030)	ca 7.7
Latifoline	125	low	ca 7.6
Heleurine	140	low	9.6
Monocrotaline	175	medium (1.21)	ca 7.9
Echimidine	200	medium	
Spectabiline	220	low	ca 7.9
Cynaustine	260	medium	ca 9.6
7-Angelylheliotridine	260	medium	ca 9.7
Heliotrine	300	medium (2.64)	8.5
Echinatine	350	high (87.5)	8.4
Supinine	450	low (0.29)	9.6
Rinderine	550	high	ca 8.5
Europine	>1000	high	ca 8.5
Intermedine + lycopsamine	>1000	high	ca 8.5
Heliotridine	1200	high	9.0
Heliotrine N-oxide	5000	high	very weak

bility of alkyl-oxygen cleavage of the allylic ester grouping, as is evident in the following reactions:[2]

(1) Hydrogenolysis of the ester anion occurs during catalytic hydrogenation and also as a metabolic reaction in sheep's rumen. In the *in vivo* reaction, rearrangement occurs to form 1-methylene pyrrolizidine derivatives. This metabolic reaction appears to be of general application.

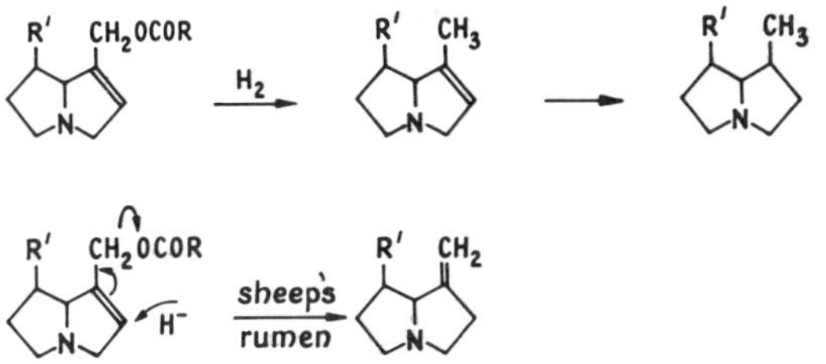

(2) Heliotrine reacts with benzyl mercaptan under alkaline conditions to give an allylic sulphide. The reaction apparently proceeds only slowly, if at all, at neutral pH.

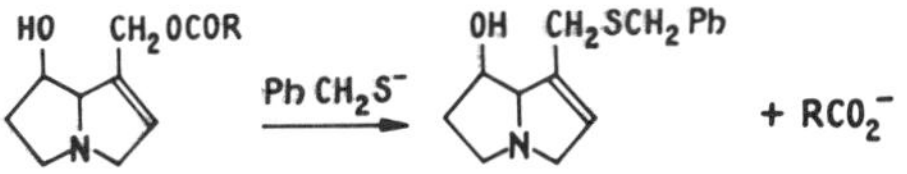

Thus the alkylating ability of pyrrolizidine alkaloids is weak but definite, and might be expected to become effective if the alkaloids should become held by hydrogen-bonding in close contact with the nucleophilic centers of cell constituents. A causal relationship between alkylating ability and nucleotoxic properties, including chronic hepatotoxicity, has been postulated.[2]

Antimitotic Effect

The antimitotic effect of the alkaloids has been measured quantitatively by a technique that also illustrates its long duration.[3] Rats were given one dose of alkaloid, left for four weeks, and subjected to partial hepatectomy. The frequency of mitosis was then determined. With heliotrine and lasiocarpine, the cumulative mitotic index (eight-hour period) varies with dose of alkaloid, according to the curves in FIGURE 1. A dose as low as 0.05 LD_{50} led to 50% inhibition of mitosis, while 0.4 LD_{50} produces almost complete inhibition. The degree of inhibition was the same if the interval between dosing and hepatectomy was increased to eight weeks. Lasiocarpine N-oxide gives a similar degree of mitotic block at equivalent molar doses, although its acute hepatotoxicity is much less than that of lasiocarpine. The nonhepatotoxic platyphylline and heliotridine had no significant effect. The tedious counting required has prevented measurements from being made on a wider range of alkaloids.

Binding to Liver Nucleic Acid and Protein

An attempt has been made to demonstrate *in vivo* alkylation of nucleic acid or protein in rat liver with use of lasiocarpine randomly labeled with ^{14}C. The lasiocarpine was prepared by growing *Heliotropium europaeum* in an atmosphere of $^{14}CO_2$ and was of specific activity 0.12 millicuries/millimole. Of this activity, 44% was present in the aminoalcohol. A dose of 5 mg lasiocarpine containing 1.5 μc ^{14}C was administered to a rat by intraperitoneal (i.p.) injection and the distribution of activity in body tissues determined after four hours, when expiration of $^{14}CO_2$ in the breath had ceased. The results in TABLE 2 show that the liver nucleic acids were very lightly labeled and the liver protein labeled to a somewhat greater extent, the activity per milligram being 2.5 and 14 DPM, respectively. In case labeled aminoalcohol was removed from the nucleic acid fairly rapidly by a repair mechanism or by hydrolysis, a second experiment was performed in which the rat was killed after 10 minutes and the activity distribution was measured as before. The degree of labeling of liver nucleic acid was only slightly higher (3.2 DPM/mg) than in the first experiment. The low specific activity of the labeled nucleic acid precluded an attempt to determine whether the labeling was specific or nonspecific. The distribution of activity within the protein has also not been investigated.

The level of labeling of the DNA is equivalent to one aminoalcohol unit/160,000 nucleotides, probably somewhat less than one aminoalcohol unit/molecule of DNA. Although this level seems too low to be significant, it may be noted that mustard gas is said to inactivate phage T4 DNA at the level of one alkyl group/30,000 nucleotides,[4] and a similar level is attained in the DNA of Ehrlich ascites cells in mice dosed with 0.1 mg mustard gas/mouse, a dose of similar magnitude to that which inhibits the growth of certain mouse tumors.[5]

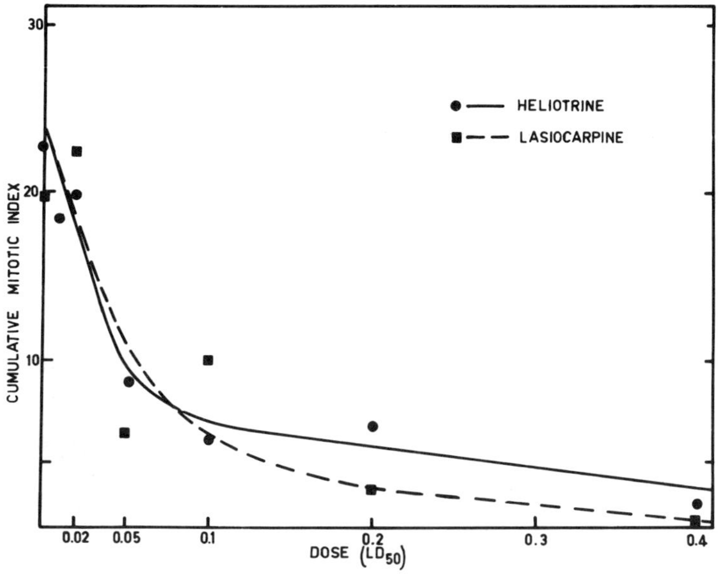

FIGURE 1. Persistent antimitotic activity of heliotrine and lasiocarpine in rat liver; dose response. (Adapted from Downing & Peterson.[3])

TABLE 2

DISTRIBUTION OF ^{14}C, 260 MINUTES AFTER ADMINISTRATION OF ^{14}C-LASIOCARPINE TO A RAT[1]

Tissue, Fraction	Weight (g)	Dpm	% ^{14}C given
Carcase	120	202,000	6.4
Intestines	22	270,000	8.6
Testes	1.15	3,000	0.1
Lung	1.3	1,400	0.05
Kidney	1.45	8,200	0.26
Heart	1.0	1,400	0.05
Spleen	0.3	330	0.01
Brain	0.9	930	0.03
Urine	(100 μl)*	860,000	27.2
Liver-TCA ext.		54,000	1.73
Liver lipids		14,800	0.48
Liver protein	1.36	19,100	0.61
Liver nucleic acids	0.064	160	0.005
Expired CO_2		294,000	9.3

* Part of the urine was lost.

The Possibility of an Antimitotic Metabolite

The distribution of the megalocytic lesions, very largely confined to the liver but occasionally in the kidney and lung, suggests that the antimitotic action may be due not to the alkaloids themselves, but to a metabolite produced in liver cells and so reactive that it does not normally escape from the cell in which it is formed. If it actually existed, we expected the metabolite to have the following features: (1) The possibility of formation from all hepatotoxic alkaloids, (2) strong alkylating reactivity or similar binding properties, and (3) strong antimitotic action. Three types of derivatives of the alkaloids seemed likely to fit this description: the pyrrole analogues (VI), the 1,2-epoxides (VII) and the sulphonium salts (VIII). The first two have now been prepared and a preliminary examination has been made of their biological properties.

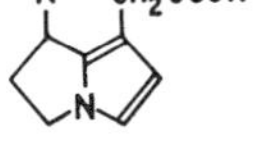

(VI)

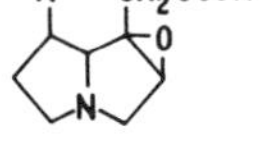

(VII)

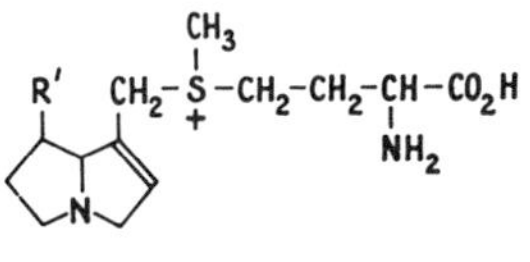

(VIII)

The α- and β-epoxides of monocrotaline were prepared by methods similar to those used for the epoxidation of supinidine.[6] The β-epoxide is chemically reactive, as is the naturally occurring supinidine β-epoxide, but, so far, neither the β- nor the α-form has shown any relevant biological activity. They are not hepatotoxic and have no inhibitory action against the KB cell culture system. The pyrrolic esters (VI), on the other hand, have proved to be of great interest. As recently reported also by Mattocks,[7] the formation of pyrrolic metabolites from the alkaloids *in vivo* is also readily demonstrable, and it seems probable that the metabolites of this type are involved in pyrrolizidine toxicity.

Preparation and Properties of Pyrroles

The pyrrole analogues of the hepatotoxic alkaloids may be prepared in high yield by the action of acetic anhydride on the alkaloid N-oxides;[8] for example, heliotrine N-oxide (IX) gives dehydroheliotrine (X). Mattocks has utilized this reaction for the quantitative estimation of the alkaloids,[9] but obtained only mixed methyl ethers and acetyl derivatives when he applied it in a preparative manner to retrorsine N-oxide.[7]

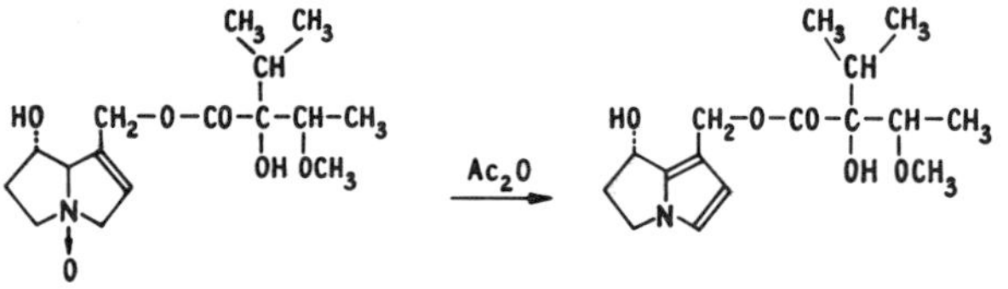

(IX) (X)

Related pyrrole derivatives have been prepared also by catalytic dehydrogenation of 1,2-dehydropyrrolizidines or by oxidation of the bases with mild oxidants such as manganese dioxide and permanganate in acetone.[8] These procedures give reasonable yields only with the aminoalcohols of the alkaloids and related compounds. In this way the pyrrole analogues of the aminoalcohols (XI) and (XII) and the oxidation products (XIII)-(XV) have been obtained.

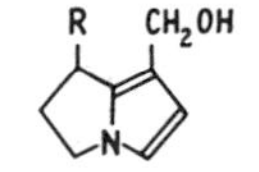

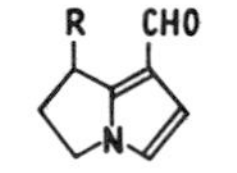

(XI) R = OH
(XII) R = H

(XIII) R = OH
(XIV) R = H
(XV) R = =O

The pyrrole analogues of heliotrine and lasiocarpine, known as dehydroheliotrine (X) and dehydrolasiocarpine, are highly unstable compounds, particularly in the presence of acid, which converts them into red or red-black insoluble solids. Dehydromonocrotaline and dehydrosenecionine are crystalline and somewhat more stable. Their chemical properties are not yet fully explored, but high alkylating reactivity is evident. Thus dehydrosenecionine (XVI) is completely converted into the dimethyl ether (XVII) when left in methanol solution for 30 minutes at room temperature. Nucleophilic attack may occur at both C7 and C9 in the diesters and also in the diol (XI), which is the analogue of heliotridine. Thus, these compounds are bifunctional alkylating agents with potential for cross-linking nucleic acid strands. The diol (XI) is less reactive than the ester pyrroles and forms a monoether, probably (XVIII), when refluxed in methanol for 30 minutes. If the pyrroles mediate chronic liver damage, their bifunctional character would explain the hepatotoxicity of 7-angelylheliotridine (V) (c.f. above).

The attempted preparation of (XIX) from desoxyretronecine and manganese

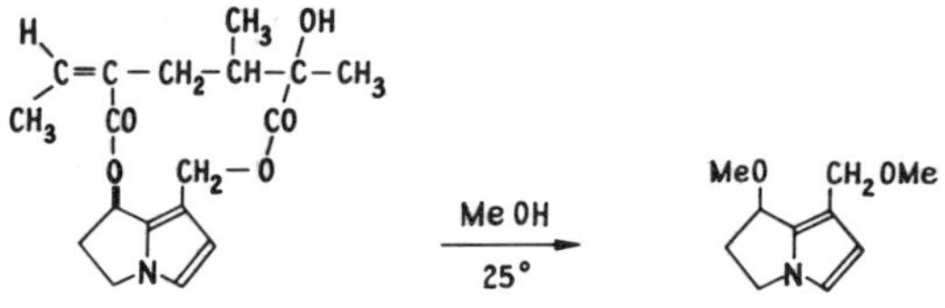

(XVI) (XVII)

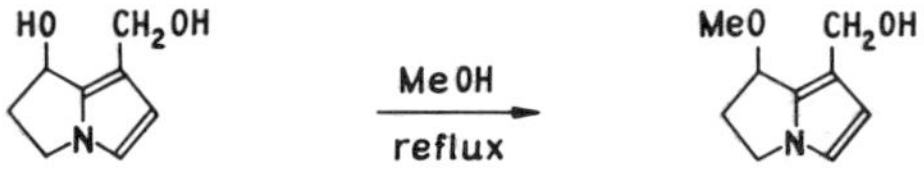

(XI) (XVIII)

dioxide leads to an unstable aldehyde (XX) as a major product. Aldehydes of this type are also potentially strong alkylating agents, particularly for amines, which should react to form a Mannich intermediate (XXI) of favorable structure for ring closure to (XXII).

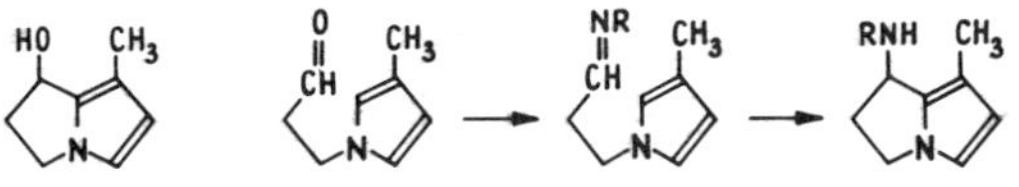

(XIX) (XX) (XXI) (XXII)

Metabolic Formation of Pyrroles

Utilizing the Ehrlich color reaction of pyrroles, Mattocks[7] has shown that pyrrole derivatives are formed in rats from a number of hepatotoxic pyrrolizidine alkaloids. Pyrroles were detected in bound form in the liver, particularly in the solid debris and microsomes, and in soluble form in the urine. The proportion of alkaloid excreted as pyrrole derivatives was estimated as 0.2–12% for several alkaloids. In a study of the metabolism of heliotrine and lasiocarpine in liver homogenates and microsomal preparations, we have also observed the formation of pyrrolic metabolites. We have isolated the main soluble metabolite from heliotrine and lasiocarpine and identified it by mass and nuclear magnetic resonance spectra as 7-hydroxy-1-hydroxymethyl-dihydro-5H-pyrrolizine (XI). The diol (XI) is also one of the main urinary metabolites.

Different pyrrolic metabolites are formed from the supinidine esters, supinine and heleurine, and from the nonhepatotoxic alkaloid, platyphylline. The pyrroles retaining the original ester groupings of the alkaloids have not been detected and, if formed, might be too unstable to be isolated. Although it seemed likely that the pyrroles are formed metabolically via the N-oxides, which are already known to be formed metabolically,[1] we find that only trace amounts of pyrroles are produced by liver microsomes *in vitro* from lasiocarpine N-oxide. The facility of the dehydropyrrolizidine → dihydropyrrolizine transformation is so great that other mechanisms are readily envisaged and other N-dealkylation pathways are especially indicated.

Biological Properties of the Pyrroles

In an attempt to determine whether the pyrrole analogues of the alkaloids (VI), the known metabolite (XI), or other pyrroles that might be derived from these unstable substances act as the hypothetical "antimitotic metabolite," we have examined them initially for hepatotoxic, cytotoxic, and nucleotoxic properties. In assessing the results, the instability of the pyrroles and the difficulty of ensuring that they become effective at the appropriate site of action should be borne in mind. So far, there has been no indication that any of the pyrroles can induce a megalocytic condition of the liver. The pyrrole analogues of heliotrine, lasiocarpine, monocrotaline, and senecionine, administered i.p. to young rats as aqueous alcoholic solutions, were found to be much less toxic than the parent alkaloids, apparently because of decomposition. When dehydromonocrotaline and dehydrosenecionine were injected as solutions in dimethylsulphoxide, all rats receiving doses as low as 1–5 mg/kg died within a week. Severe hemorrhagic effects and adhesions were observed in the peritoneum and on the outer surface of some organs, but there was no liver necrosis. Detailed studies of subacute and chronic toxicity have yet to be made.

TABLE 3

INHIBITION OF KB CELL CULTURE BY DIHYDROPYRROLIZINE DERIVATIVES*

Compound	ED_{50} ($\mu g/ml$)
Dehydroheliotrine	>100
Dehydrolasiocarpine	>100
Dehydromonocrotaline	17
Dehydrosenecionine	14
Dihydro-5H-pyrrolizine-1-carboxaldehyde	>100
7-Hydroxy-dihydro-5H-pyrrolizine	22
7-Hydroxy-1-hydroxymethyl-dihydro-5H-pyrrolizine	19
1-Hydroxymethyl-dihydro-5H-pyrrolizine	1.9
c.f. Alkaloids: Heliotrine	15
Lasiocarpine	25
Monocrotaline	>100

*These results were obtained under the auspices of the Cancer Chemotherapy National Service Center, Washington, D.C.

Further evidence of cytotoxicity was sought by measuring the activity of the pyrroles against bacteria, the KB cell culture, and Ehrlich ascites tumor systems. Dehydroheliotrine, dehydrolasiocarpine, and several derivatives inhibit *Trichophyton* at high concentrations (ca 10^{-4} M) but were inactive against *Staphylococcus, Salmonella, Pseudomonas,* and *Candida* species.[10] Heliotrine and lasiocarpine are themselves active against *Pseudomonas pyocyanea* and *Candida albicans* at approximately 10^{-5} molar. Under the conditions of the

National Institutes of Health protocol,[11] the pyrroles are only weakly inhibitory to KB cell culture, their activity being of the same order for heliotrine and lasiocarpine (TABLE 3). The apparent lack of inhibitory action of dehydroheliotrine and dehydrolasiocarpine is thought to be due to decomposition under the test conditions. Dehydromonocrotaline and dehydrosenecionine are more active than the parent alkaloids. The multiplication of Ehrlich ascites cells in mice is completely inhibited by the metabolite (XI) but not by dehydroheliotrine if the compound is added to the cell suspension before i.p. injection.

More indicative of specific nucleotoxic effects has been the observation of mutagenic and antiviral activity. Preliminary experiments[12] disclose a weak mutagenic activity of dehydroheliotrine and dehydrolasiocarpine in *Drosophila*, more definite activity of the metabolite (XI) in both *Drosophila* and *Aspergillus*, and activity of several related compounds in *Aspergillus*. A number of the available pyrroles were tested for inhibition of the reproduction of a DNA virus, infectious bovine rhinotracheitis (IBR) and an RNA virus, parainfluenza virus (PI3), in a culture of bovine kidney cells.[13] The metabolite (XI) inhibits IBR virus at a concentration of 8×10^{-5} molar and heliotrine-pyrrole and its 7-keto-derivative inhibit the same virus at approximately 3×10^{-4} molar. PI3 Virus was not inhibited at these concentrations.

Thus it seems that the pyrrole analogues (VI) of the hepatotoxic pyrrolizidine alkaloids are highly reactive alkylating agents of high acute toxicity, exhibiting local cytotoxicity in animals, weak cytotoxicity against KB cell culture, mutagenic activity in *Drosophila*, and weak inhibition of reproduction of IBR virus. Their metabolic formation has not been detected, possibly because of their great instability. The pyrrole analogue of heliotridine (XI) has been identified as the main soluble pyrrolic metabolite of heliotrine and lasiocarpine, has mild alkylating reactivity and a medium acute toxicity in rats, is weakly cytotoxic to KB cell culture, is mutagenic in *Drosophila* and in *Aspergillus*, and inhibits reproduction of IBR virus. The other related pyrroles discussed above have similar properties but are not especially distinguished. It is therefore probable that some of these compounds are involved in the expression of pyrrolizidine toxicity, but whether one compound or type of compound can be identified with the "antimitotic metabolite" will be known only after more detailed studies.

Comparison with Mitomycin C

Attention has previously been drawn to the similarity in structure between the pyrrolizidine alkaloids and the mitomycin group of antibiotics.[14] The comparison is even more striking between the pyrrole analogues of the alkaloids, e.g. dehydrolasiocarpine (XXIII) from lasiocarpine (II), and the reduced (activated) form (XXIV) of, for example, mitomycin C (XXV). Dehydrolasiocarpine and reduced mitomycin C are both strong, bifunctional alkylating agents with the same linkage points in the dihydropyrrolizine moiety. The ability of reduced mitomycin C to cross-link the strands of the DNA helix suggests a similar property for the alkaloid-derived pyrroles. There is evidence that lasiocarpine brings about inhibition of DNA-dependent RNA-polymerase in rat liver.[15]

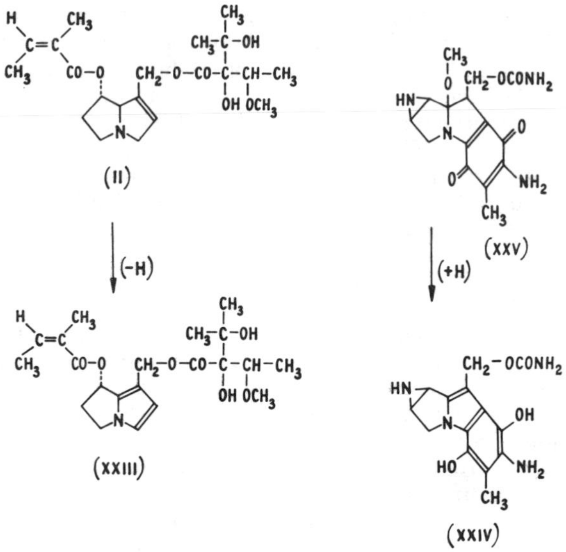

Summary and Conclusion

The chronic liver lesion produced by pyrrolizidine alkaloids, megalocytosis, owes its development to a long-lasting antimitotic effect on liver cells, together with an acceleration of cell death that provides a stimulus to liver growth. A single dose of heliotrine or lasiocarpine of 0.4 LD_{50} completely prevents mitosis in liver cells when a partial hepatectomy is performed one month after administration of the alkaloid. The alkaloids have weak alkylating reactivity, which makes them capable of selective attack on cell constituents. Administration of ^{14}C-labeled alkaloid to a rat resulted in low levels of incorporation into liver protein and nucleic acid. The alkaloids are readily converted *in vitro* and to some extent *in vivo* into pyrrole derivatives that are highly reactive and exert cytotoxic and other biological actions suggestive of attack on nucleic acids. The main soluble pyrrolic metabolite from heliotrine and lasiocarpine is 7-hydroxy-1-hydroxymethyldihydro-5H-pyrrolizine.

The significance, if any, of alkylation in the antimitotic and nucleotoxic effects of pyrrolizidine alkaloids remains obscure, but a new stage in the understanding of these effects has been foreshadowed with the demonstration that pyrrolic metabolites are formed *in vivo* and become firmly bound in liver cells. The pyrrole analogues of the alkaloids, a known pyrrole metabolite, and several likely breakdown products are now undergoing chemical and biological study, and clarification of the role of the pyrrole metabolites should be forthcoming in the near future.

References

1. Bull, L. B., C. C. J. Culvenor & A. T. Dick. 1968. The Pyrrolizidine Alkaloids. North Holland Publishing Co. Amsterdam, The Netherlands.

2. CULVENOR, C. C. J., A. T. DANN & A. T. DICK. 1962. Nature (London) **195:** 570.
3. DOWNING, D. T. & J. E. PETERSON. 1968. Aust. J. Exp. Biol. Med. Sci. **46:** 493.
4. LAWLEY, P. D. & P. BROOKES. 1965. Nature (London) **206:** 480.
5. BROOKES, P. & P. D. LAWLEY. 1960. Biochem. J. **77:** 478.
6. CULVENOR, C. C. J., G. M. O'DONOVAN & L. W. SMITH. 1967. Aust. J. Chem. **20:** 757.
7. MATTOCKS, A. R. 1968. Nature (London) **217:** 723.
8. CULVENOR, C. C. J., J. A. EDGAR, L. W. SMITH & H. J. TWEEDDALE. (In preparation.)
9. MATTOCKS, A. R. 1967. Anal. Chem. **39:** 443.
10. CULVENOR, C. C. J., and D. S. ROBERTS. (Unpublished data.)
11. Cancer Chemotherapy Reports. 1962. No. 25. Cancer Chemotherapy National Service Center.
12. CLARK, A. M. & C. C. J. CULVENOR. (Unpublished data.)
13. FRENCH, E. L. (Unpublished data.)
14. IYER, V. N. & W. SZYBALSKI. 1964. Science **145:** 55.
15. REDDY, J., C. HARRIS & D. SVOBODA. 1968. Nature (London) **217:** 659.

DISCUSSION OF THE PAPER

DR. VAN DUUREN: Have you been able to introduce hepatomas with any of these compounds? Several of the compounds would be of great interest in view of Schoental's reports.

DR. DOWNING: It is the general impression that these compounds are not carcinogenic.

UNIDENTIFIED SPEAKER: In Schoental's experiments, a single large dose was needed. The survivors developed hepatomas after a latent period of a year or more. Did you have any animals on test as long as Dr. Schoental?

DR. DOWNING: Some animals were kept for extended periods and were subjected to repeated small doses of alkaloids but gave no hepatomas. Dr. Schoental suggests that a large single dose is required for the production of hepatomas. This might indicate that the induction of these tumors is a secondary effect that requires severe liver damage. The pyrrolizidine alkaloids in a large single dose, four tenths of the LD_{50}, can give complete inhibition of cell division. There are also reports that, on the contrary, there is induction of cell division. The two situations seem to be paradoxical.

TOXIC AND CARCINOGENIC ALKYLATING AGENTS FROM CYCADS

Maria Spatz

Section on Histochemistry, Laboratory of Experimental Pathology
National Institute of Arthritis and Metabolic Diseases
National Institutes of Health, Bethesda, Md.

Several studies have been published during the last five years dealing with the biologic effects of a naturally occurring glucoside cycasin, β-D glucosyloxyazoxymethane, and of its aglycone, methylazoxymethanol (MAM). There is no need, therefore, to repeat all the details contained in these reports. This presentation will essentially be limited to the mechanism of action of cycasin and MAM, emphasizing certain effects on the prenatal and postnatal life of the animals.

Both compounds, cycasin and MAM, are extractable from seeds, roots and leaves of *Cycas circinalis* (Guam) and *Cycas revoluta* (Japan). These palmlike plants belong to the family Cycadaceae, which are found in the tropical and subtropical regions of the world. They are survivors of ancient plants whose ancestors were common during the Mesozoic Era. The seeds of cycad plants were and still are used as a source of food in some parts of the world.

Toxic properties of cycad seeds were well known to the consumers long before their chemical identification was established. According to Dr. Whiting's survey, the method for detoxication of the seeds has been similar on different continents without apparent intercommunications. The dehusked, sliced, or halved fruits were repeatedly washed and dried in the sun before being ground into a flour. Consumption of insufficiently washed seeds has led to sickness and death of people.[1] At present, a study by Hirono is in progress in which the long-term effects of eating meals prepared from cycads during a period of natural disaster following a series of typhoons are being examined in the population of the island of Mijakoshima.[2]

Postnatal Effects

Chemistry

Cycasin and its aglycone MAM are aliphatic azoxy compounds that were not considered to exist in nature until 1951. At that time Langley isolated and identified macrozamin as β-D primeverosyloxyazoxymethane from the Australian cycad *(Macrozamia spiralis)*.[3] In 1955 Nishida isolated cycasin, β-D glucosyloxyazoxymethane, from *Cycas revoluta*,[4] and in 1956 Riggs found cycasin in *Cycas circinalis*.[5] Pure methylazoxymethanol (MAM) can be obtained by enzymic hydrolysis of cycasin *in vitro* with use of almond emulsion as the source for β-D glucosidase.[6] MAM was synthesized by Matsumoto as MAM acetate, which is stable and biologically as effective as the natural MAM.[7] Paper and thin-layer chromatography are used in the identification of cycasin, MAM, and MAM acetate in biological materials.

Biological Effects and Mechanism of Action

Cycasin and MAM are hepatotoxic, carcinogenic, teratogenic, and neurotoxic. The LD50 in rats for cycasin is 562 mg/kg body weight and for MAM acetate, 90 mg/kg body weight.[8,9] Acute toxicity is best observed in two target organs, the liver and the developing brain. The severity of the lesion is dose-dependent. With use of low concentrations of cycasin, the early changes in the liver consist of loss of centrilobular basophilia and glycogen preceded by a decrease in glucose-6-phosphatase.[10,11] With large doses, hemorrhagic centrilobular liver cell necrosis is accompanied by loss in RNA and phospholipids.[12] Inhibition of protein synthesis was suggested by the diminished rate in catalase synthesis in the liver.[13] Recently, Shank and Magee reported an inhibition of (^{14}C) leucine incorporation into hepatic proteins with sublethal doses of cycasin.[14] The early and acute toxic effects on the developing brain will be discussed below.

The tumorogenic and late effect is a rather general one, and frequent sites for tumor formation have been liver, kidney, large and small intestine, lung, and brain. Tumors often develop multiply, but dose, route of administration, and age of animals determine, to some extent, sites of predilection. Tumors have been induced by single and repeated doses of cycasin or MAM in rats,[15,16] guinea pigs,[17] mice,[18] hamsters,[19] and fish.[20] A detailed description of these studies is beyond the scope of this paper. I should like to mention two important aspects, however, which bear on the following discussion of cycasin metabolism: 1. In weanling and adult animals, cycasin is toxic and carcinogenic only when given orally, whereas MAM is active irrespective of the route of administration. 2. The tumor incidence with cycasin is variable, whereas MAM produces neoplasms in 100% of the rats.

Cycasin Metabolism in Vivo

Weanling and Adult Animals

The Japanese investigators Yoshimura (1922) and Nishida (1935 & 1936) thought that the formaldehyde liberated in the breakdown of *Cycas revoluta* accounted for the toxic symptoms seen following cycad poisoning.[21] Both Cooper, who had originally isolated macrozamin, and Nishida, who had identified cycasin, mentioned that oral administration of these substances was a prerequisite for toxicity to become apparent in guinea pigs and mice.[22,23] These results led Nishida and his co-workers to implicate digestive juices or enzymes as being responsible for the hydrolysis of both glucosides to their common aglycone part, and he suggested further that the toxicity was due to the aglycone itself. This theory received support from the studies of Kobayashi and Matsumoto (1964), who recovered all of the intraperitoneally (i.p.) injected cycasin in the urine of rats.[24] At the same time, Laqueur observed an absence of ill effects from ingested cycasin in germfree rats, when compared with conventional animals. Thus, cycasin given in high concentration to germfree rats was well tolerated without affecting body-weight gain during an experimental period of 20 days, whereas the same dose led to hepatic centrilobular necrosis and demise of the conventional animals within a few days.[25] In subsequent experiments, the quantitative recovery of injected cycasin from urine and feces of germfree rats and the varied but low urinary excretion of orally given cycasin in conventional rats strongly suggested that bacterial enzymes in the intestinal tract might be responsible for cycasin deglucosylation.[26] Supportive evidence for this hypothesis was obtained from studies in which the excretion of ingested cycasin and the presence of hepatic injury were compared between germfree rats and germfree rats monocontaminated with bacteria containing varying activities of β-D glucosidase. Indeed, it could be shown that the most severe hepatic necrosis was found in those animals that showed the lowest excretion of cycasin and that had been monocontaminated with bacteria of high β-D glucosidase activity. Conversely, monocontamination with microorganisms lacking glucosidase activity resulted in high urinary excretion of cycasin and in structurally normal livers. A role of the intestinal microflora in significantly determining cycasin toxicity was thus demonstrated.[27]

Newborn

The successful induction of kidney tumors in rats following a single subcutaneous (s.c.) injection of cycasin in newborns, communicated to us by Magee in 1965, which was subsequently confirmed in our laboratory, required a new approach in explaining the deglucosylation of cycasin.[8] Acute cycasin toxicity and the age-limiting effectiveness of cycasin by s.c. route during the neonatal period was examined, and it was shown by Hirono in our laboratory that cycasin in concentration of 2 mg/g body weight resulted within 48–72 hours in death of all babies and of three uninjected mothers when cycasin was given s.c. between the first and seventeenth days of life. Cause of death was severe, hepatic, centrilobular necrosis in babies and mothers. Saline-injected control rats survived unharmed. At this stage it was thought that the mother had licked the urine containing cycasin while cleaning her young, swallowed the cycasin, which was subsequently hydrolyzed in the mother's intestinal tract, and, after absorption, excreted the MAM through the mammary gland. This possibility appeared logical, because it had been shown that MAM can be excreted in the milk.

Objections to this theory as the sole mechanism for the noted effect came from the observations by Hirono in which he showed that s.c. injected germfree rats and artificially fed baby rats were not protected from hepatic death.[28] There was the additional observation that eight-day-old rats receiving i.p. injections of cycasin showed less liver injury than those that received the same amount s.c., as judged from their survival rates at two weeks. The possibility of a direct cycasin effect in the postnatal life was then considered, but was ruled out by finding MAM in homogenates of cycasin-injected germfree and conventional baby rats.[29]

These studies led us to search for β-D glucosidase activity in the subcutis. Indeed, a β-D glucosidase was found in the crude skin homogenate from both germfree and conventional rats, using as substrates the synthetic β glucosides p- and o-nitrophenyl-β-D-glucoside and the cycasin. The activity of this skin enzyme was related to the age of the rats, being highest during the prenatal and early postnatal days. Thus, the deglucosylation of cycasin by crude skin β-D glucosidase *in vitro* corresponded well to the observations made *in vivo*, in which the toxicity of s.c. injected cycasin had been found to be age-dependent. The broader physiologic significance of a skin β-D glucosidase is unknown at present. It seems likely that this "short-term activity" enzyme is only one of several enzymes present during tissue maturation.[30]

The transient nature of β-D glucosidase activity in the skin may well be responsible for cycasin deglucosylation in newborn mice that show neurotoxic and hepatotoxic effects after s.c. injection of cycasin, according to Hirono, who described ataxia and paralysis of the hind legs in mice so treated.[31] Since the mice showed signs of cerebellar injury, the observed effect may be related to the most sensitive period of cerebellar development as judged from the observations of radiation-induced injury.[32]

It may be recalled that the question whether cycasin exerted neurotoxic effects was raised by Whiting years ago. Indeed, the investigations into the possible neurotoxicity of cycads were originally undertaken as a search for an environmental toxin to explain the high incidence of amyotrophic lateral sclerosis observed on the island of Guam. In addition, a paralysis of cattle grazing on land where cycads grow, which was later pathologically confirmed as being due to demyelination of the fasciculus gracilis and dorsal spinocerebellar tracts, seemed to strengthen the need for searching for a neurotoxic factor in cycad material.[33,34]

Biological Effects of MAM on Fetal Tissues

Following our observation that MAM was demonstrable in fetuses when the mothers were given cycasin enterically, it was not surprising that this very reactive compound of low molecular weight and soluble in aqueous solutions would interact with fetal tissues.[35] In the following paragraphs, our experiences of short- and long-term effects of MAM on the fetuses will be reviewed.

Teratogenesis

Whereas malformations at first were not observed in rats exposed *in utero* to MAM, the golden hamster proved to be useful in our studies in teratogenesis. The method we used was that described by Ferm. MAM given in a concentration of 20 mg/kg body weight intraveneously (i.v.) on the eighth day of gestation produced a variety of malformations in the fetuses. The most common were hydrocephalus, microcephalus, cranioschisis, rachischisis, anophtalmia, and microphtalia.[36]

In later studies, a microencephaly was produced in rats with surprising regularity, and I should like to review some of our observations to date.

Originally, the microencephaly was found in four 13-month-old litters, which had been exposed to MAM on the 14th, 15th, and 16th day of intrauterine life. These rats were parts of an experiment designed to establish whether site and frequency of transplacentally induced tumors had a relationship to the stage of fetal development at the time of exposure to MAM.

The experiment was successfully repeated in 10 pregnant rats, and their offspring had uniformly smaller brains at 28 days, when they were killed and compared with saline-injected controls. More recent data showed that microencephaly could be produced most effectively by a single injection of MAM, 20 mg/kg body weight, on the 14th or 15th day of gestation. (Figure 1). The MAM-induced microencephaly was unaccompanied by other malformations and was consistent with long survival. Brain tumors have developed thus far in 10% of the long-term survivors. The microencephalic rats, when tested by the Webb-

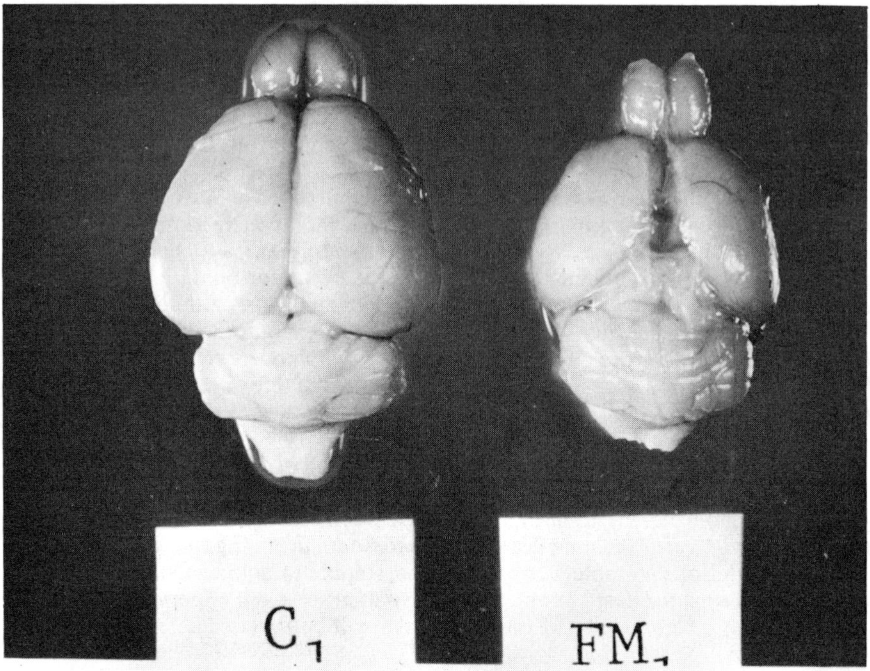

FIGURE 1. Brains from 28-day-old rats. Control, left; MAM-treated on day 14 of fetal life, right.

Williams maze method at four months of age, had a significantly poorer scoring than the controls indicating some intellectual deficit.[37] These studies are now being extensively explored by our collaborators Dr. Haddad and Dr. Rabe. Limited observations on other physiologic parameters indicate that reproduction in these rats was not significantly altered unless associated with very severe microencephaly, in which case successful mating did not occur. Otherwise, sister-brother matings of microencephalic rats resulted in normal offspring.

Grossly, the affected brains showed a marked diminution of the cerebral hemispheres, resulting in exposure of the corpora guadrigemia. The midbrain, pons, medulla, and cerebellum appeared normal. A narrowing of the parietal bone was noted in rats having microencephaly. The suture lines were soft and open at birth when the malformation was already recognizable, although the maturation of the brain is still incomplete at that time.

Extensive focal cellular necrosis was seen microscopically in the subependymal neuroblastic cell layer between the ventricular space and the outer cortical zone of the brain as early as 24 hours after exposure to MAM.[38] Detailed morphological investigations are under way to reconstruct the sequential events leading to the development of microencephaly. The damage appears to be similar to the one induced by x-ray radiation.[32]

Postnatal followup studies of MAM-treated and control rats revealed an abrupt cessation of growth on the 14th day of life in the experimental rats. The observed difference in growth occurred at the time when the rate of cerebral lipid deposition is greatest.[39–41] Thus, the amount of total cortical lipids in microencephalic rats was significantly diminished when compared with that of controls on dry-weight basis. No such change was seen in the rest of the brain (TABLE 1). As illustrated in FIGURE 2, no difference was found in cortical water content at any time, but a significant decrease in total proteins on wet-weight basis at 28 days was noted in experimental rats when compared with that in control animals (total protein: control, 9.79 mg ± .881; experimental, 7.98 ± .708; P = <.001).

It remains to be seen whether cortical lipids and proteins remain low in later life of microencephalic rats. If this occurs, then these findings would suggest permanent impairment in lipid and protein metabolism. If not, the diminution of these solids in early life would suggest an altered rate of lipid and protein metabolism as a reflection of inhibited synthesis. A fractionation of the lipids is now necessary to determine whether MAM affects myelin or both myelin and cerebroside formation, since cerebrosides are deposited later than myelin. Protein and carbohydrate, as well as mineral metabolisms, should also be examined for a better understanding of the basic relationship of the brain composition and its function in microencephalic rats.

The transplacentally MAM-induced effect on the developing brain cortex is not unique, and x-ray radiation,[32] high temperature,[42] and methylnitrosourea[43] have produced microencephaly. As seen in TABLE 2 methylnitrosourea is one of four nitroso compounds tested in our laboratory that induced microencephaly. We have thus been able to confirm the observations of Von Kreybig[44] and of Napalkow and Alexandrov.[43]

TABLE 1

COMPARISON OF TOTAL LIPIDS IN BRAINS FROM CONTROL AND MICROENCEPHALIC RATS.

	Control				Experimental				
Age	Rats	Assays	% Lipids* in mg	S.E.	Rats	Assays	% Lipids* in mg	S.E.	Significance Between Means P†
Cortex									
7	11	1	25.6		10	1	23.00		
14	23	3	44.18	±1.70	32	2	31.80	±.90	S
28	25	7	44.44	±1.48	43	6	32.22	±1.21	S
Rest of Brain									
7	11	1	24.30		10	1	22.50		
14	23	3	35.54	±2.90	32	2	34.85	±5.35	N.S.
28	25	7	47.91	±3.24	43	6	42.33	±3.04	N.S.

* Based on dry weight.

† P = <.001.

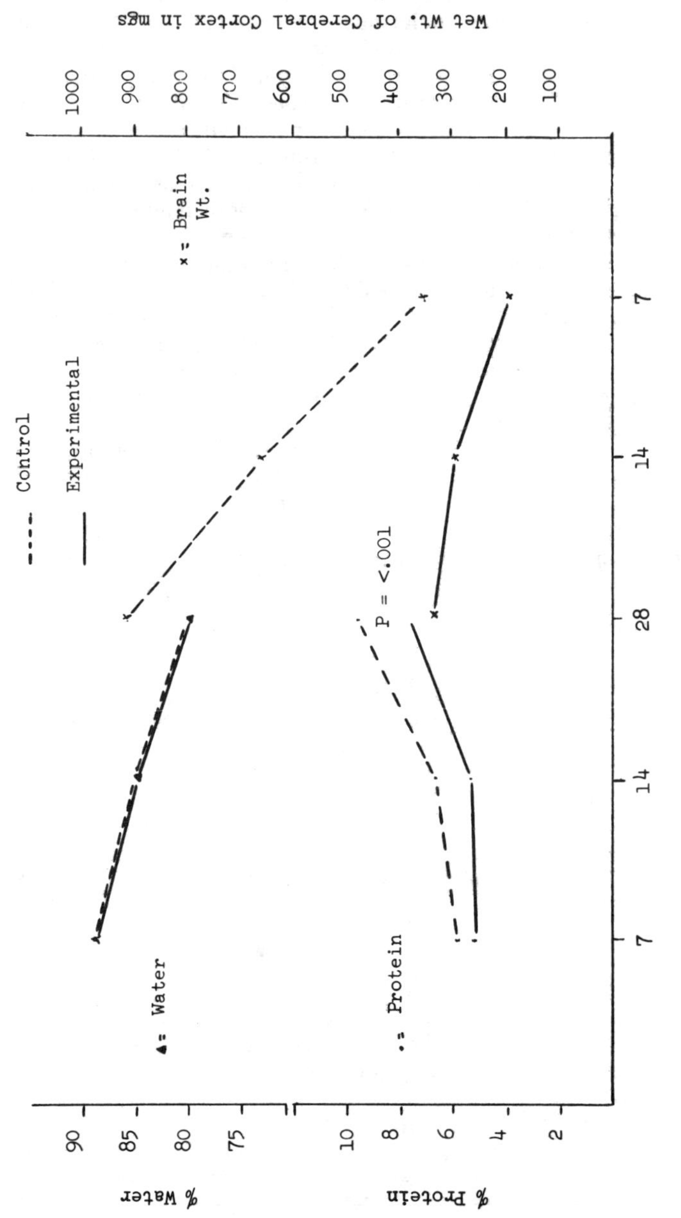

FIGURE 2. Changes in Composition of Cerebral Cortex in Control and Microencephalic Rats.

TABLE 2
OCCURRENCE OF MICROENCEPHALY IN FISHER RATS
TREATED WITH NITROSO COMPOUNDS

Substance	Route	Dose in mg/kg Body Weight	Result
Diethylnitrosamine	i.p.	15	negative
	i.p.	30	negative
Dimethylnitrosamine	i.p.	7.5–50	lethal to fetuses and mother
Ethylnitrosourea	i.v.	80	negative
Methylnitrosourea	i.p.	80	positive
	i.p.	100	positive

Neoplasia

Among the long-term effects of cycad materials on fetal tissues, neoplastic growths were the only important findings, and tumors were produced by feeding, at various periods during gestation, crude cycad meal containing 3% cycasin. The minimal induction time for tumor development was about six months, and thus the same as in older animals. Although the overall incidence of neoplasia was only 18.5%, several facts came to light. They were: (1) a high mortality of 42% in the offsprings before weaning time due to hypoplasia of the maternal mammary glands and to a decreased suckling stimulus of the baby rat; (2) the most frequent sites of neoplasia were jejunum and brain, sites rarely involved when cycad meal, cycasin, or MAM are given enterically, but not uncommon in rats receiving injections of MAM; (3) the occurence of similar tumors in several litter mates; (4) the presence of neoplasia in the cycad meal-fed mothers as well as in their offsprings, and (5) the absence of malformation in such rats.[45]

MECHANISM OF ACTION

The similarities between the chemical structure and the biological effects of the synthetic dimethylnitrosamine and the naturally occurring cycasin was noted by Laqueur and co-workers.[15] It was suggested by Miller that both substances may have a common metabolic pathway forming diazomethane, a compound known to possess alkylating properties and to be a strong carcinogen. In the case of cycasin, this involves as the first step the deglucosylation of cycasin to MAM, which is well documented. This compound is highly unstable and releases formaldehyde and forms azoxymethane, which in turn loses water producing diazomethane.[46]

Thus far the metabolites of MAM have not been identified, but it would seem significant from the studies of Druckrey that azoxymethane may be an important possible metabolite of MAM, since this compound is highly carcinogenic for colon and rectum, sites showing a predilection for carcinomas after feeding cycasin or injecting MAM.[16,17]

In the metabolic breakdown of cycasin and MAM, methylation of nucleic acids occurs *in vitro*[48] and *in vivo*.[14] Thus, Matsumoto and Higa have shown that incubation of MAM acetate with liver RNA and DNA at pH 7.4 *in vitro* resulted in methylation of the bases and in the appearance of 7-methyl guanine. In a comparative biochemical investigation, Shank and Magee demonstrated *in vivo* that cycasin and MAM had the same ability to methylate nucleic acids as did dimethylnitrosamine. The amount of detectable 7-methyl guanine in liver was greater in DNA (approximately 0.24%) than RNA base (approximately 0.1%) with cycasin. However, the RNA base in the liver was more susceptible to methylation of cycasin than that in the kidney and small intestine. Furthermore, about 2% of liver RNA was methylated in the 7 position of guanine, when animals were tested with MAM. The greater methylating effect of MAM than that of cycasin was not unexpected, since deglucosylation is necessary for cycasin activity. Recently, Matsumoto found 7-methyl guanine in fetal rat brain after i.p. administration of MAM acetate to the mother on the 15th day of pregnancy (personal communication).[49]

This observation is of particular interest, considering the possibility that alkylation of nucleic acids may be one of the important mechanisms in carcinogenesis. Our observation that about 10% of the microencephalic rats developed brain tumors later in life therefore assumes some importance in the context. It is unknown whether the cytotoxic effect of MAM on the neuroblast resulting in microencephaly is also due to this mechanism.

In addition to the alkylating effects of cycasin and MAM, these compounds have been shown to have mutagenic and radiomimetic effects. For example, Smith has demonstrated in our laboratory that treatment of histidine requiring mutants of Salmonella typhimurium with MAM resulted in high reversion to the histidine independent mutants. No such effect was seen with cycasin since the Salmonella strain lacks the β-D glucosidase.[50] And Teas and co-workers demonstrated that MAM and MAM acetate induced a high incidence of sex-linked recessive lethal mutation in *Drosophila melanogaster*. Cycasin failed to produce this effect because of the absence of β-D glucosidase activity in these flies.[51]

Addition of cycasin to the onion seeds, *Allium cepa,* containing β-D glucosidase, induced as many chromosomal aberrations as were produced by about 200-roentgen of gamma radiation.[52] It is of interest, therefore, that it has been possible to protect rats from a lethal dose of cycasin by simultaneous administration of radioprotective agents, though without altering the ultimate development of neoplasms.[8] The mechanisms involved appear to be multiple, and they are being investigated.

Conclusion

The aglycone of cycasin, methylazoxymethanol, is the active component of the naturally occurring glucoside cycasin. It is a small molecule, water miscible, but an unstable azoxy compound possessing hepatotoxic, neurotoxic, teratogenic, carcinogenic, mutagenic, alkylating, and radiomimetric properties. Whether one, some, or all of the biological effects can be attributed to alkylation of nucleic acids cannot be answered at the present time. The broad spectrum of effects in experimental animals that is produced by this natural compound, used as a source of food by man in certain parts of the world, requires an open mind in searching for possible relationships between diseases in general and the availability and consumption of such food resources.

REFERENCES

1. WHITING, M. G. 1963. Toxicity of cycads. Economic Botany **17:** 271.
2. HIRONO, I. 1968. (Personal communication.)
3. LANGLEY, B. W., LYTHGOE, B. & N. V. RIGGS. 1949. Macrozamin. Part II. The Aliphatic Azoxy Structure of the Aglycone Part. J. Chem. Soc. **4:** 2309.
4. NISHIDA, K., A. KOBAYASHI & T. NAGAHAMA. 1955. Studies on cycasin, a new toxic glycoside, of Cycas revoluta Thunb. Bull. Agr. Chem. Soc. **19:** 77.
5. RIGGS, N. V. 1956. Glucosylazoxymethane, a constituent of the seeds of *Cycas circinalis* L. Chem. Ind. **35:** 926.
6. KOBAYASHI, A. 1962. Biochemical studies on cycasin. Part I. Purification and properties of cycad β-glucosidase. Agr. Biol. Chem. **26:** 203.
7. MATSUMOTO, H., T. NAGAHAMA & H. O. LARSON. 1965. Studies on methylazoxymethanol, the aglycone of cycasin: a synthesis of methylazoxymethyl acetate. Biochem. J. **95:** 13c.
8. HIRONO, I., G. L. LAQUEUR & M. SPATZ. 1968. Tumor induction in Fischer and Osborne-Mendel rats by a single administration of cycasin. J. Nat. Cancer Inst. **40:** 1003.
9. GANOTE, C. E. & A. S. ROSENTHAL. 1968. Characteristic lesions of methylazoxymethanol induced liver damage. A comparative ultrastructural study with dimethylnitrosamine, hydrazine sulfate and carbon tetrachloride. Lab. Invest. **19:** 382.
10. LAQUEUR, G. L. 1964. Acute and long-term effects from ingestion of cycad plant material. Introductory remarks. Fed. Proc. **23:** 1373.
11. SPATZ, M. 1964. Effects of cycad meal and cycasin on histochemically demonstrable liver phosphatases and nonspecific esterases. Fed. Proc. **23:** 1381.
12. WILLIAMS, J. N. & G. L. LAQUEUR. 1965. Response of liver nucleic acids and lipids in rats fed *Cycas circinalis* L. endosperm or cycasin. Proc. Soc. Exp. Biol. Med. **118:** 1.
13. RECHCIGHL, JR., M. & G. L. LAQUEUR. 1968. Carcinogen-mediated alteration of the rates of enzymes synthesis and degradation. Enzym. Biol. Clin. (Basel) **9:** 209.
14. SHANK, R. C. & P. N. MAGEE. 1967. Similarities between the biochemical actions of cycasin and dimethylnitrosamine. Biochem. J. **105:** 521.
15. LAQUEUR, G. L., O. MICKELSEN, M. G. WHITING & L. T. KURLAND. 1963. Carcinogenic properties of nuts from *Cycas circinalis* L. indigenous to Guam. J. Nat. Cancer Inst. **31:** 919.
16. LAQUEUR, G. L., E. G. MCDANIEL & H. MATSUMOTO. 1967. Tumor induction in germfree rats with methylazoxymethanol (MAM) and synthetic MAM acetate. J. Nat. Cancer Inst. **39:** 355.
17. SPATZ, M. 1964. Carcinogenic effect of cycad meal in guinea pigs. Fed. Proc. **23:** 1384.
18. O'GARA, R. W., J. M. BROWN & M. G. WHITING. 1964. Induction of hepatic and renal tumors by the topical application of aqueous extract of cycad nut to artificial skin ulcers in mice. Fed. Proc. **23:** 1383.
19. SPATZ, M. (Unpublished data.)
20. STANTON, M. E. 1966. Hepatic neoplasms of aquarium fish to *Cycas circinalis*. Fed. Proc. **25:** 661.
21. NISHIDA, K. & A. YAMADA. 1935. Biochemistry of Japanese sago plant. III. Enzyme chemistry of the formaldehyde containing constituent. I. J. Agr. Chem. Soc. Japan **11:** 357.
22. COOPER, J. N. 1941. Isolation of a toxic principle from the seed of *Macrozamia spiralis*. J. Proc. Roy. Soc. N.S. Wales **74:** 450.

23. NISHIDA, K., A. KABAYASHI, T. NAGAHAMA, K. KOJIMA & M. JAMANE. 1956. Cycasin, a new toxic glucoside of *Cycas revoluta*. IV. Pharmacology of cycasin. Seikagakis **28:** 218.
24. KOBAYASHI, A. & H. MATSUMOTO. 1965. Studies on methylazoxymethanol, the aglycone of cycasin isolation, biological, and chemical properties. Arch. Biochem. Biophys. **110:** 373.
25. LAQUEUR, G. L. 1964. Carcinogenic effects of cycad meal and cycasin (methylazoxymethanol glycoside) in rats and effects on cycasin in germfree rats. Fed. Proc. **23:** 1386.
26. SPATZ, M., E. G. MCDANIEL & G. L. LAQUEUR. 1966. Cycasin excretion in conventional and germfree rats. Proc. Soc. Exp. Biol. Med. **121:** 417.
27. SPATZ, M., D. W. E. SMITH, E. G. MCDANIEL & G. L. LAQUEUR. 1967. Role of intestinal microorganisms in determining cycasin toxicity. Proc. Soc. Exp. Biol. Med. **124:** 691.
28. HIRONO, I. (Unpublished data.)
29. SPATZ, M. (Unpublished data.)
30. SPATZ, M. 1968. Hydrolysis of cycasin by *β-D* glucosidase in skin of newborn rats. Proc. Soc. Exp. Biol. Med. **128:** 1005.
31. HIRONO, I. & C. SHIBUYA. 1967. Induction of a neurological disorder by cycasin in mice. Nature (London) **216:** 1311.
32. HICKS, S. P., C. J. D'AMATO & M. J. LOWE. 1959. The development of the mammalian nervous system. J. Comp. Neurol. **113:** 435.
33. HALL, W. T. & M. D. MCGAVIN. 1968. Clinical and neuropathological changes in cattle eating the leaves of *Macrozamia lucida* and *Bowenia serulata* (family Zamiaceae) Path. Vet. (Basel) **5:** 26.
34. MASON, M. M. & M. G. WHITING. 1966. Demyelination in the bovine spinal cord caused by Zamia neurotoxicity. Fed. Proc. **25:** 533.
35. SPATZ, M. & G. L. LAQUEUR. 1968. Evidence for transplacental passage of the natural carcinogen cycasin and its aglycone. Proc. Soc. Exp. Biol. Med. **127:** 281.
36. SPATZ, M., W. DOUGHERTY & D. W. E. SMITH. 1967. Teratogenic effects of methylazoxymethanol. Proc. Exp. Biol. Med. **124:** 476.
37. HADDAD, R. K., A. RABE, G. L. LAQUEUR, M. SPATZ & M. P. VALSAMIS. 1969. Intellectual deficit associated with transplacentally induced microcephaly in rat. Science **163:** 88.
38. SPATZ, M. & G. L. LAQUEUR. 1968. Chemical induction of microencephaly in two strains of rats. Part I. Proc. Soc. Exp. Biol. Med. **129:** 705.
39. WATSON, J. B. 1903. Animal education. An experimental study on the physical development of the white rat, correlated with growth of its nervous system. Ph.D. Thesis. University of Chicago. Chicago, Ill.
40. KOCH, W. & M. L. KOCH. 1913. Contributions to the chemical differentiation of the central nervous system. III. The chemical differentiation of the brain of the albino rat during growth. J. Biol. Chem. **15:** 423.
41. FOLCH, J., J. CASALS, A. POPE, J. A. MEATH, F. N. LEBARON & M. LEES. 1959. Chemistry of myelin development. Progr. Neurobiol. **4:** 122.
42. EDWARDS, M. J. 1967. Congenital defects in guinea pigs following induced hyperthermia during gestation. Arch. Path. **84:** 42.
43. NAPALKOV, N. P. & V. A. ALEXANDROV. 1967. On the effects of blastomogenic substances on the organism during embryogenesis. Z. Krebsforsch. **71:** 32.
44. VON KREYBIG, T. 1965. Die Wirkung einer carcinogenen Methylnitroso-Harnstoff-Dosis auf die Embryonalentwicklung der Ratte. Z. Krebsforsch. **67:** 46.
45. SPATZ, M. & G. L. LAQUEUR. 1967. Transplacental induction of tumors in Sprague-Dawley rats with crude cycad material. J. Nat. Cancer Inst. **38:** 233.
46. MILLER, J. A. 1964. Comments on chemistry of cycads. Fed. Proc. **23:** 1361.
47. DRUCKREY, H. (Personal communications to Dr. Laqueur.)
48. MATSUMOTO, H. & H. H. HIGA. 1966. Studies on methylazoxymethanol, the aglycone of cycasin: methylation of nucleic acids *in vitro*. Biochem. J. **98:** 20c.

49. MATSUMOTO, H. (Personal communication.)
50. SMITH, D. W. E. 1966. Mutagenicity of cycasin aglycone (methylazoxymethanol), a naturally occurring carcinogen. Science **152:** 1273.
51. TEAS, H. W. & J. G. DYSON. 1967. Mutation in *Drosophila* by methylazoxymethanol, the aglycone of cycasin. Proc. Soc. Exp. Biol. Med. **125:** 988.
52. TEAS, H. J., H. J. SAX & K. SAX. 1965. Cycasin; radiomimetic effect. Science **149:** 541.

DISCUSSION OF THE PAPER

H. DRUCKREY (*Vorschergruppe Praeventivmedizin, Freiburg, Germany*): Neither 1,2-dimethylhydrazine nor azoxymethane is carcinogenic to offspring when administered to pregnant rats, even on the fifteenth day of gestation. But, as you have shown, methylazoxymethane is active, and I think this proves convincingly that the decisive process in activating dimethylhydrazine as well as azoxymethane is, in fact, the hydroxylation on an opposite carbon atom. Did you ever observe cancer of the skin in the progeny?

DR. SPATZ: No, we have never observed skin cancer in the progeny. As a matter of fact, we also have never seen neoplasms in the mother rat at the site of injection.

P. N. MAGEE (*Courtauld Institute of Biochemistry, London, England*): Would you care to speculate at all on the possible relationship of the brain lesions or nerve lesions you saw to what I think was the original purpose of your investigation?

DR. SPATZ: Our study did not show any relationship; namely, we have not found central nervous system lesions in rats resembling the one seen in amyotrophic lateral sclerosis in man. However, we ought to keep in mind the prospects of species difference. In this conjunction, if a compound is neurotoxic in one species producing one effect, it might be neurotoxic in another species but producing a different effect.

UNIDENTIFIED SPEAKER: You mentioned that you saw early changes in the liver such as necrosis after giving the animal cycasin. How early?

DR. SPATZ: Within 24 hours.

ALKYLATING AGENTS AS INSECT CHEMOSTERILANTS

Alexej B. Bořkovec

Entomology Research Division, Agricultural Research Service
U.S. Department of Agriculture, Beltsville, Md.

Introduction

Birth control pills are becoming widely accepted as one of the means for regulating human populations. However, the concept of decreasing populations of rapidly reproducing organisms by reducing their birth rates rather than by increasing their death rates found its most striking application in the realm of insect pests (Knipling, 1960). Obviously, the reason was not an effort for a humanitarian treatment of some of our most destructive enemies, but an attempt to strike at the very base of the pest problem: the high reproductive capacity. The principle of population control by sterility is simple. If the ratio of the sterile to fertile organisms is made sufficiently large, matings between fertile males and females will become scarce, and the population will gradually diminish. The most important factor for success of this method is not the actual size of the population, but the ratio of the sterile to fertile individuals. Thus, some of the members of the population can be sterilized directly in their habitats or artificially reared and sterilized organisms can be released in sufficient numbers to establish the desired sterile:fertile ratio.

Sexual sterilization of insects can be accomplished in many ways, but only two methods appear to be practical now—irradiation with gamma rays and treatment with chemicals. In distinction to birth control pills, sterilizing chemicals or chemosterilants should have a permanent and irreversible effect, but, like birth control pills, they must not interfere with mating and should have a minimum of side effects. One of the first guidelines in the search for effective chemosterilants was the analogy between carcinostatic and sterilizing effects. There is a certain similarity between tumor cells and germ cells, and it appeared logical that the same compounds might interfere with the propagation of either system. Indeed, the first successful insect chemosterilants were antimetabolites and biological alkylating agents that had been used previously with some success in cancer chemotherapy. The alkylating agents were of particular interest because they usually sterilized both sexes, and an extensive program of synthesis and testing was initiated in 1961 by chemists and entomologists of the U.S. Department of Agriculture. Following the discovery of nonalkylating male-insect sterilants (Chang *et al.*, 1964), the emphasis has shifted toward these less toxic compounds, but the high activity and versatility of alkylating chemosterilants has not yet been surpassed.

Physiological Effects of Alkylating Chemosterilants in Insects

The effects of sexual sterility are easy to detect, but its causes are variable and difficult to trace because the chain of events between the cause and effect may be very long. A simple diagram (FIGURE 1) outlines the pathway leading from the male and female gamete to the formation of a zygote. In insects, the interaction of the sterilant with the gonocyte or with any of its more advanced stages may lead to sterility, but because the developing sperm cells and ova are under nutritional and regulatory control of the organism, any interference with these control processes may produce the same final effect. When adult males are sterilized, a direct action of the chemical on mature spermatozoa is highly probable, because in most economically important species of insects a full complement of mature sperm is available at the time of eclosion. Spermicidal action, which would also result in sterility, is not a common effect of alkylating chemosterilants, but it has been observed at high doses of the agent (Mendoza & Peters, 1968). In most tests in which the sperm of treated males was examined, motility appeared to be normal and no pathological changes could be seen even with an ultramicroscope (Chang *et al.*, 1966). *In vitro* sterilization of bee (*Apis mellifera* L.) sperm with the alkylating sterilant tepa was achieved recently (Taber &

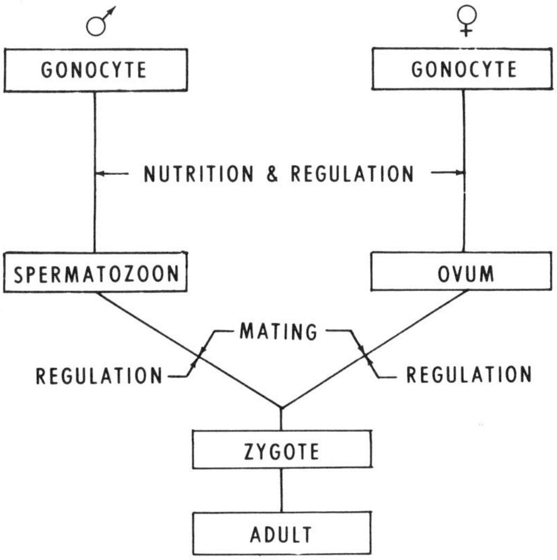

FIGURE 1. Diagram of the reproductive processes in sexually reproducing insects.

Bořkovec, unpublished results), and thus the assumption of a primary interaction between a sperm cell and the alkylating agent is well justified. Nevertheless, degeneration and necrosis of the testicular tissues after treatment with alkylating agents have also been observed (for references, see Bořkovec, 1966), and such effects undoubtedly contributed to sterility of males that mated more than once.

In distinction to these infrequent pathological findings in males, the reproductive organs of treated females were almost always visibly affected, and the distinction between primary and secondary effect of alkylating agents was usually obscure. A sterilized female lays either no eggs or the seemingly normal eggs fail to hatch when fertilized with sperm of fertile males (for references, see Bořkovec, 1966), but the type of physiological and morphological changes in the ovaries depends on the structure and dose of the sterilant as well as on the age of the treated female. Successful sterilization of fertilized females (Henneberry *et al.*, 1967) and of females containing mature eggs suggests that a direct interaction between the sterilant and the ovum can also be the main mechanism of sterility.

Mutagenic Effects of Alkylating Chemosterilants in Insects

Since in two recent monographs on genetic effects of alkylating agents (Kihlman, 1966; Loveless, 1966) chemosterilants were not even mentioned, it may seem that the sterility induced by these compounds in insects was nongenetic in nature. Much of the early experimental work on chemical mutagenesis was done on *Drosophila* (Auerbach, 1967; Fahmy & Fahmy, 1964) and unhatchability of insect eggs (i.e., sterility) was frequently used as a measure of the induction of dominant lethal mutations. There are some limitations to this method of assessing dominant lethality, but there is little doubt that mutagenic effects are largely responsible for the activity of alkylating chemosterilants in insects. Because this subject has been discussed in detail in two recent reviews (Bořkovec, 1966; LaChance *et al.*, 1968), it may be sufficient to note that besides dominant lethal mutations, alkylating chemosterilants induce other nonlethal genetic changes that are of considerable importance in sterilization of insects. House flies subjected for 30 generations to substerilizing doses of an alkylating agent became gradually more susceptible to the sterilizing effects of the compound (Morgan *et al.*, 1967). Testicular chromosomes of flies released from the pressure of the chemosterilant showed typical abnormalities that could be transmitted to following generations. However, the increased sensitivity to sterilization was not permanent, because it became almost normal after the treated colony was kept for an additional 50 generations (LaBrecque, 1968). Similar sensitizing effects of a different alkylating agent were reported by Saccà and co-workers (1964). Another type of genetic effects apparently caused by selection was described by Hazard and associates (1964) in the yellow-fever mosquito (*Aedes aegypti* L.) and by Saccà and co-workers (1966) in the house fly. The development of resistance to insecticides is well known, and a similar development with respect to chemosterilants was not unexpected. Resistance to alkylating agents appears to be of a relatively low level, and no reliable data regarding cross-resistance to related compounds is available.

Conventional testing of chemosterilants (Bořkovec, 1966; LaBrecque, 1968) does not yield any information on recessive or nonlethal mutations, and the structure-activity relationships in alkylating sterilants that may be valid for dominant lethality are not necessarily valid for other genetic effects.

Aziridinyl Chemosterilants

In the many classes of biological alkylating agents (Ross, 1962), the derivatives of aziridine (ethylenimine) are the most effective insect chemosterilants with a broad spectrum of activity. Most of the work on structure-activity relationship and metabolism in insects has been done with aziridinyl compounds (Bořkovec, 1962, 1964, 1966) and the conclusions will be briefly reviewed here.

The basicity of aziridines is determined by the characteristics of substituents on the ring nitrogen. Electron-withdrawing groups reduce the availability of the pair of electrons on nitrogen and the basicity of the compound. All highly active aziridinyl sterilants contain a polar π-electron system attached to the ring nitrogen

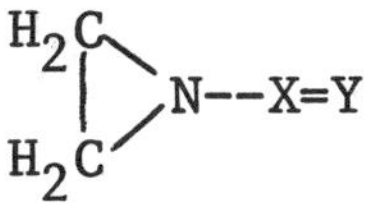

X = C, P, S   Y = O, S, N

FIGURE 2. Generalized structure of aziridinyl chemosterilants.

(FIGURE 2), and thus are only weakly basic. Insertion of a methylene group between the ring and the XY system reduces substantially the sterilizing activity of the compound. In general, basic aziridines in which the ring is easily protonated are inactive or only poorly active as insect chemosterilants. The effects of polarity of the XY system on sterilizing activity are difficult to assess. Although in aziridinyl compounds of a general structure shown in FIGURE 2 the XY group determines the basicity of the nitrogen and the alkylating activity of the ring, the biological properties of aziridinyl compounds depend to a large extent on transport characteristics, i.e., physical properties of the whole molecule, and on the ability of the compound to interact with systems that are not directly related to reproduction. A quantitative study of the effects of bis(1-aziridinyl)alkylaminophosphine oxides in male house flies (Chang & Bořkovec, 1966b) demonstrated not only the profound influence of different alkyl groups on the sterilizing activity of these closely related compounds, but also their seemingly unrelated toxic effects. TABLE 1 shows the median sterilizing doses (SD_{50}) and median lethal doses (LD_{50}) of compounds arranged by increasing alkyl substitution. With the exception of the isopropyl derivative, the sterilizing activity decreases with the size of the alkyl group, but the toxicity varies without any apparent regularity. The compounds were soluble in polar and nonpolar solvents, but with increasing chain length the nonpolar characteristics predominated. The high toxicity of the octyl compound that may be related to its lipophilic character could have also influenced the results of sterility tests, because only few individuals survived any

TABLE 1

MEDIAN STERILIZING AND TOXIC DOSES OF BIS(1-AZIRIDINYL)(ALKYLAMINO)PHOSPHINE OXIDES INJECTED INTO MALE HOUSE FLIES*

$(\triangleright N)_2PO$—R R	SD_{50} (nanomoles)	LD_{50} (nanomoles)
NH CH_3	0.348	153
$N(CH_3)_2$	1.49	432
NH C_2H_5	1.40	325
NH $(CH_2)_2CH_3$	3.18	11.3
NH CH $(CH_3)_2$	1.21	450
NH $(CH_2)_3CH_3$	4.59	94.3
NH $(CH_2)_7CH_3$	19.1	38.1

*Calculated from Chang and Bořkovec (1966b).

fertility-affecting treatment. Although the question of structure-activity with regard to the polarity and other properties of the XY group is far from being answered, semiquantitative testing data on several hundred aziridinyl derivatives in house flies (Bořkovec *et al.*, 1968) indicate that high sterilizing activity is more likely to be associated with more polar, rather than with less polar, compounds. In many respects, substituted bis(1-aziridinyl)phosphine oxides or sulfides are well suited for studying effects of substituents, because the configuration of the two aziridinyl rings remains constant. In other difunctional or polyfunctional aziridines and similar alkylating agents, the mean distance between the functional groups changes, and thus a new variable is introduced. For example, compounds of the general structure ▷N—CO—R—CO—N◁ reach a peak of activity at a certain chain-length that is related to the nature of R and the test species. With R = $NH(CH_2)_nNH$, the optimal activity was reached at n = 5–8 in house flies (Borkovec *et al.*, 1968), and at n = 4–7 in screw-worm flies, *Cochliomyia hominivorax* (Coq.), (Crystal, 1967). With R = $(CH_2)_n$, the optimal activity was at n = 4 in house flies, but the compounds were only slightly active in the screw-worm fly. As I have mentioned earlier, the insertion of a methylene group between the carbonyl and the aziridinyl groups (e.g. ▷N—CH_2—CO—NH—$(CH_2)_n$—NH—CO—CH_2—N◁) reduces greatly the sterilizing activity; nevertheless, Skinner *et al.* (1966) reported that even these weakly active compounds show an optimum at chain length of n = 8–9.

Any substitution on the carbon of the aziridine ring decreases the sterilizing activity of the candidate compounds. The effects of methyl substituents have been studied most extensively (for references see Bořkovec, 1966), and in all instances in which the differences between substituted and unsubstituted compounds were determined quantitatively, the activity of the unsubstituted compound was higher than that of its substituted homologue. This simple relationship appears to be valid without regard to the electronic characteristics or to the size of the substituent, although bulky substituents decrease the sterilizing activity of the parent compounds more drastically than do the small substituents. Multiple substitution of the four hydrogens attached to the two aziridinyl carbons also reduces sharply the activity of the parent compound.

Polyfunctionality is not required for activity of alkylating chemosterilants. Monoaziridinyl compounds can be effective if they fulfill two basic conditions: no substitution on the aziridinyl carbon and a suitable XY substitution on the aziridinyl nitrogen. Because even the best monoaziridinyl chemosterilants were never as active as some of the polyaziridinyl compounds, most of the research on the effects of chemosterilants in insects was done with trifunctional and hexafunctional aziridines shown in FIGURE 3.

Nevertheless, there is no evidence that the physiological or genetic effects of monofunctional aziridines would be qualitatively different from those of polyfunctional compounds.

Other Alkylating Chemosterilants

Nitrogen mustards and alkanesulfonates are two groups of alkylating agents that received considerable attention as candidate chemosterilants. Historically, nitrogen mustards were among the first compounds that induced mutations in insects, but in comparison with aziridines their sterilizing activity was disappointing. High toxicity to insects is a standard feature of the more promising mustards,

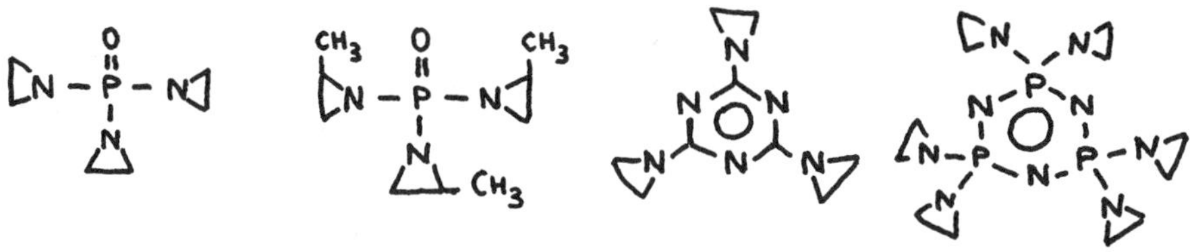

Tepa Metepa Tretamine Apholate

FIGURE 3. Structures of aziridinyl chemosterilants tested extensively in insects.

but as always in the realm of insects, the differences among various species were large. A recent report (Klassen *et al.*, 1968) on the activity of certain alkyl alkanesulfonates, R—SO_2—O—R′—O—SO_2R, illustrates the point. Apholate, a moderately effective sterilant of the boll weevil, *Anthonomus grandis* Boheman, (Lindquist *et al.*, 1964) decreases the longevity and mating ability of this insect by damaging the vitally important intestinal tissues. Busulfan (R = CH_3, R′ = $(CH_2)_4$), a drug still considered of merit in cancer therapy, does not cause extensive damage to the intestine of the boll weevil, although its sterilizing effects are similar to those of apholate. Other alkanesulfonates were also found to be effective in the boll weevil and screw-worm fly (Crystal, 1968). Detailed structure-activity relationship of nonaziridinyl alkylating chemosterilants are not available, but if a mustard or sulfonate highly active in some economically important species were discovered, additional studies would be forthcoming.

Mode of Action of Alkylating Agents in Insects

Adult insects are organisms with few actively reproducing tissues. Because testes in the male and ovaries in the female are the most conspicuous systems of dividing cells, it is not surprising that alkylating agents often sterilize without affecting longevity or other characteristics of the insect. However, in spite of the localization of effects and the long history of insect-alkylating-agent interaction, the mode of action of these compounds remains unknown. Cytological and cytogenetic investigations of organisms treated with alkylating agents indicate no basic differences between affected insect cells and the cells of other organisms. Attempts for detecting a possible alkylation of guanine in nucleic acid from eggs of treated house flies (Painter & Kilgore, 1967) were negative, but similar experiments with sperm of sterilized insects have not been performed. Thus, the fundamental question of whether and how the alkylating agent interacts with the gamete remains unanswered. The indirect sterilization process in which the alkylating agent is thought to affect some of the nutritional or regulatory processes of reproduction are even more complicated because of the multitude of biochemical steps that are involved. It cannot be excluded, however, that the direct (usually dominant lethal mutations) and indirect effects of the sterilant have a common mechanism. If nucleic acid in ovarian nurse cells or similar follicular tissues were the target of alkylation, abnormal eggs could result that either would not be laid or, if laid, would be infertile. Similarly, if nucleic acid in oocytes or even mature eggs were attacked, no oviposition or infertile eggs could be expected. As yet, the research on insect chemosterilants has brought about little of new insight into the mechanism of action of alkylating agents. Nevertheless, the versatility of insects as experimental organisms and their sensitivity to the sterilizing effects of alkylating agents offer much promise in future work.

Practical Application of Alkylating Chemosterilants

In any application of toxic chemicals in nature, the problem of contamination and residues must be seriously considered. Chemosterilants can be used in two ways: for treatment of existing pest populations in their natural habitat, or for treatment of artificially reared insects in a strictly controlled environment. The first method does not differ greatly from the application of insecticides, and it would have to be governed by the same precautions with regard to residues and general safety. The second method may be compared to the use of antibiotics, food additives, and similar materials in the management of certain economically important animals. Again, there is ample precedent for the acceptable and safe use of these chemicals. Generalizations about the toxicity of alkylating agents are of questionable value. The tremendous variations between activities of related compounds in a given insect, the differences in susceptibility of even closely related species to the same compound, the specificity of sex, developmental stage, and mode of application all point to the probability of similar differences in other organisms. Nevertheless, toxicological characteristics of some of the better-known alkylating chemosterilants have been described (Hayes, 1968) and in absence of such specific information, each alkylating chemosterilant should be handled with utmost care. Many, but not all, alkylating agents are reactive compounds, and their persistence in the environment is usually limited. Even so, a highly toxic and possibly mutagenic or carcinogenic chemosterilant could not be used safely for the treatment of natural insect populations. Whether other less toxic alkylating agents could be used in this manner remains to be seen, but it appears that the greatest potential of alkylating chemosterilants lies in their use for sterilization of artificially reared insects. That a chemosterilant applied to insects dissipates rapidly from the body has been shown by Chang and Bořkovec (1966a), Collier and Tardif (1967), Maitlen and McDonough (1967), and Morgan and colleagues (1968). In general, the longer the period between treatment and release, the smaller the amount of contamination that the insects can impart to the environment. Sterilization of immature stages of insects appears to be especially favorable from the standpoint of residues and safety.

In the rapidly approaching age of integrated pest control operations, chemosterilants will probably fill only one of the slots in the arsenal of weapons of increasing complexity. Whether alkylating agents will be among the practical compounds cannot be predicted. Tepa, a well-known alkylating agent, was the first chemosterilant used in the field (Shaw *et al.,* 1966) for controlling the Mexican fruit fly, *Anastrepha ludens* Loew. Similar application of other alkylating agents may follow in the future.

Summary

Certain alkylating agents induce sexual sterility in insects, but their activity varies greatly with the sex, age, developmental stage, and species of the insects, as well as with the physical and chemical characteristics of the compounds. Structure-activity relationship has been extensively investigated in the derivatives of aziridine. The most effective aziridines were unsubstituted on the ring carbons but had polar substituents on the ring nitrogen. Among the other types of alkylating agents, only nitrogen mustards and alkanesulfonates had some effects on the reproduction of insects. Although the sterility induced by alkylating agents is in some instances of clearly genetic origin, nongenetic effects of the same compounds may also affect fertility by interfering with the regulatory processes in reproductive organs. From a practical standpoint, the sterilizing effects of alkylating agents can be utilized for controlling populations of pest insects provided that such applications would not contaminate the environment.

References

1. Auerbach, C. 1967. The chemical production of mutations. Science **158:** 1141–7.
2. Bořkovec, A. B. 1962. Sexual sterilization of insects by chemicals. Science **137:** 1034–7.
3. Bořkovec, A. B. 1964. Insect chemosterilants: Their chemistry and application. Residue Rev. **6:** 87–103.
4. Bořkovec, A. B. 1966. Insect Chemosterilants. Interscience Publishers. New York, N. Y.
5. Bořkovec, A. B., R. L. Fye & G. C. LaBrecque. 1968. Aziridinyl chemosterilants for house flies. ARS **33–129,** U.S. Dept. Agric., Washington, D.C. 60 pp.
6. Chang, S. C. & A. B. Bořkovec. 1966a. Determination of tepa residues on chemosterilized Mexican fruit flies. J. Econ. Entom. **59:** 102–4.
7. Chang, S. C. & A. B. Bořkovec. 1966b. Structure-activity relationship in analogs of tepa and hempa. J. Econ. Entom. **59:** 1359–62.
8. Chang, S. C., P. H. Terry & A. B. Bořkovec. 1964. Insect chemosterilants with low toxicity for mammals. Science **144:** 57–8.
9. Chang, S. C., A. B. Bořkovec & C. W. Woods. 1966. Fate of tepa uniformly labeled with C^{14} in male house flies. J. Econ. Entom. **59:** 937–44.
10. Collier, C. W. & R. Tardif. 1967. Analysis of male gypsy moths for microgram quantities of tepa. J. Econ. Entom. **60:** 28–30.
11. Crystal, M. M. 1967. Chemical structure and sterilizing activity of N,N′-alkylenebis (1-aziridine carboxamides) in screw-worm flies. J. Econ. Entom. **60:** 1005–7.
12. Crystal, M. M. 1968. Sulfonic acid esters as chemosterilants of screw-worm flies with particular reference to methanediol dimethanesulfonate. J. Econ. Entom. **61:** 446–9.
13. Fahmy, O. G. & M. J. Fahmy. 1964. The chemistry and genetics of the alkylating chemosterilants. Trans. Roy. Soc. Trop. Med. Hyg. **58:** 318–26.
14. Hayes, W. J., Jr. 1968. Toxicological aspects of chemosterilants. *In* Principles of Insect Chemosterilization. G. C. LaBrecque & C. N. Smith, Eds. Appleton-Century-Crofts, Inc. New York, N. Y.
15. Hazard, E. I., C. S. Lofgren, D. B. Woodard, H. R. Ford & B. M. Glancey. 1964. Resistance to the chemical sterilant apholate in *Aedes aegypti.* Science **145:** 500-1.
16. Hennéberry, T. J., H. C. Mason & W. L. McGovern. 1967. Some effects of gamma radiation and apholate on the fertility of *Drosophila melanogaster.* J. Econ. Entom. **60:** 853-7.
17. Kihlman, B. A. 1966. Actions of Chemicals on Dividing Cells. Prentice-Hall, Englewood Cliffs, N.J.
18. Klassen, W. & F. Matsumura. 1966. Resistance to a chemosterilant metepa in *Aedes aegypti* mosquitoes. Nature **209:** 1155-6.

19. KNIPLING, E. F. 1960. Use of insects for their own destruction. J. Econ. Entom. **53:** 415–20.
20. LABRECQUE, G. C. 1968. Laboratory procedures. *In* Principles of Insect Chemosterilization. G. C. LaBrecque and C. N. Smith, Eds. Appleton-Century-Crofts, Inc. New York, N.Y.
21. LACHANCE, L. E., D. T. NORTH, AND W. KLASSEN. 1968. Cytogenic and cellular basis of chemically induced sterility. *In* Principles of Insect Chemosterilization. G. C. LaBrecque and C. N. Smith, Eds. Appleton-Century-Crofts, Inc. New York, N.Y.
22. LINDQUIST, D. A., L. J. GORZYCKI, M. S. MAYER, A. L. SCALES & T. B. DAVICH. 1964. Laboratory studies on sterilization of the boll weevil with apholate. J. Econ. Entom. **57:** 745–50.
23. LOVELESS, A. 1966. Genetic and Allied Effects of Alkylating Agents. The Pennsylvania State University Press. University Park, Pa., and London, England.
24. MAITLEN, J. C. & L. M. MCDONOUGH. 1967. Residues of tepa on chemosterilized codling moths. J. Econ. Entom. **60:** 1391–3.
25. MENDOZA, C. E. & D. C. PETERS. 1968. Histochemical effects of apholate on the reproductive organs of southern corn rootworms. J. Econ. Entom. **61:** 416–20.
26. MORGAN, P. B., M. C. BOWMAN & G. C. LABRECQUE. 1968. Uptake and persistence of metepa and hempa in the house fly. J. Econ. Entom. **61:** 805–8.
27. MORGAN, P. B., G. C. LABRECQUE, C. N. SMITH, D. W. MEIFERT & C. M. MURVOSH. 1967. Cumulative effects of substerilizing dosages of apholate and metepa on laboratory populations of the house fly. J. Econ. Entom. **60:** 1064–7.
28. PAINTER, R. R. & W. W. KILGORE. 1967. The effect of apholate and thiotepa on nucleic acid synthesis and nucleotide ratios in house fly eggs. J. Insect Physiol. **13:** 1105–18.
29. ROSS, W. C. J. 1962. Biological Alkylating Agents. Butterworths. London, England.
30. SACCÀ, G., A. SCIROCCHI, E. STELLA, M. L. MASTRILLI & G. M. DEMEO. 1966. A strain of *Musca domestica* selected with the chemosterilant metepa. Atti. Soc. Pelorit. Sci. Fis. Mat. Nat. **12:** 447–56.
31. SACCÀ, G., E. STELLA & R. MAGRONE. 1964. Ricerche preliminari sull'azione dell' afoxide (ossido di tris (1-aziridinyl)fosfato) su *Musca domestica* L. Parasitology **6:** 229–34.
32. SHAW, J. G., W. P. PATTON, R. M. SANCHEZ, L. M. SPISHAKOFF & B. C. REED. 1966. Mexican fruit fly control. Calif. Citrograph **51:** 200–3.
33. SKINNER, W. A., M. CORY, T. E. SHELLENBERGER & J. I. DEGRAW. 1966. Effects of organic compounds on reproductive processes. III. Alkylating agents derived from various diamines. J. Med. Chem. **9:** 520–2.

DISCUSSION OF THE PAPER

B. L. VAN DUUREN (*New York University Medical Center, New York, N. Y.*): Has any of the isosters of aziridines been tested as chemosterilants, particularly epoxides and episulfides?

DR. BOŘKOVEC: Quite a number of them has been tested, but none of them appeared to be particularly effective.

DEGRADATION AND RESIDUES OF ALKYLATING AGENTS

Lawrence Fishbein

National Institute of Environmental Health Sciences
Research Triangle Park, N. C.

Introduction

The main objective of this presentation is to bring into focus from an environmental health standpoint the degradation products and residues of a number of alkylating agents that have both current and potential industrial, food-processing, sterilization, and insecticidal application, e.g. epoxides, lactones, and aziridines. Also of paramount interest is the question of nitrosamines that have been reported to be formed *in situ* in foods and tobacco smoke.

The mechanisms of action,[1–6] as well as the toxicity and carcinogenicity[7–12] and in the latter case of the aziridines, the clinical utility of these agents[13] have been well documented.

Epoxides: Ethylene and Propylene Oxide

Ethylene oxide is available in unrestricted quantities and is used largely for the production of ethylene glycol and its derivatives e.g. polyethylene glycols, mixed polyglycols, and glycol ethers and esters. Substantial amounts are also used in the preparation of such chemicals as monoethanolamine, acrylonitrile, and surface-active agents.

Propylene oxide is also available in unrestricted amounts and is mainly used for the production of propylene glycol and its derivatives e.g. polypropylene glycols, mixed polyglycols, and various propylene glycol ethers and esters.

Significant quantities are also used for the preparation of hydroxy propyl celluloses and sugars, surface active agents, isopropanol amine, and a host of other chemicals.

Ethylene and propylene oxides are extensively used for the sterilization of a broad spectrum of materials ranging from medical instruments to foodstuffs such as spices, cocoa, flour, dried egg powder, desiccated coconut, dried fruits, and vegetables.

These epoxides are capable of elimination or of greatly diminishing the numbers of viable organisms present without imparting any after-odor of flavor tint to foods by direct action or by leaving chemical residues, if properly used.

Residues are produced mainly by two reactions of epoxides e.g. (a) their slow chemical combination with water to form the corresponding glycols or (b) their combination with hydrochloric acid to form the corresponding chlorohydrins. Since even dry materials contain moisture, it is apparent that glycol formation is unavoidable. Moreover, without the presence of some moisture, sterilization cannot be effected. However, residues of glycols are generally regarded as harmless and permissible.

Wesley and co-workers[14] described the formation of persistent toxic chlorohydrins in foodstuffs by fumigation with ethylene oxide and with propylene oxide. Under conditions for effective fumigation (e.g. 750 ml/m^3 for five hours) with either oxide, these reagents were found to combine not only with moisture, but also with chlorine from the natural inorganic chloride content of foodstuffs, forming the corresponding chlorohydrin. Concentrations of ethylene chlorohydrin up to about 1,000 ppm were found in whole spices after commercial fumigation with ethylene oxide. These chlorohydrins are not volatile and are unreactive chemically to persist under food-processing conditions, but they are highly toxic substances by all accounts.

TABLE 1 depicts the chlorohydrin residues obtained from a variety of materials following commercial fumigation with ethylene oxide for five hours at a concentration of 750 ml/cubic meter. Attempts were made to determine the requirements for eliminating chlorohydrin residues from foodstuffs by decomposition at elevated temperatures under food-processing conditions and also by volatilization during cooking. It was found, for example, that canned soup with 6.8 ppm ethylene chlorohydrin initially present still contained 5.1 ppm chlorohydrin after 70 minutes of autoclaving at 246° F. Similar results were obtained with soup in which a mixture of the two propylene chlorohydrins were present initially at approximately the same total concentration.

TABLE 1

RESIDUES OF CHLOROHYDRIN FOLLOWING FUMIGATION WITH ETHYLENE OXIDE*

Sample	Chlorohydrin Found (ppm)	Initial Cl in Sample (% NaCl)
Flour	260	0.24
Desiccated coconut	42	0.52
Currants	4	0.57
Spray-dried albumin	310	2.10
Sliced freeze-dried French beans	8	0.39
Whole air-dried green peas	1	0.14
Ground air-dried green peas	36	0.14

* Fumigation for five hours at a concentration of 750 ml/cubic meter.

Hence, under conditions precluding volatilization, little or no loss of chlorohydrins was found to occur, despite prolonged heat treatment.

However, there remains the possibility of volatilization of chlorohydrins when foodstuffs are cooked under special conditions.

Under existing food and drug regulations, seven different foodstuffs (cocoa, glazed fruits, gums, processed nut meats, dried prunes, processed spices, and starches) may be commercially treated with propylene oxide and three products (whole spices, black walnut meats, and cocoa) with ethylene oxide. It has been demonstrated that such fumigation can result in the formation of toxic chlorohydrins.[14,15]

The isolation and determination of chlorohydrins in foods fumigated with ethylene oxide or with propylene oxide has been further investigated.[15] The levels of 2-chloroethanol found in five foods commercially fumigated with ethylene oxide ranged from 45 ppm for paprika to 110 ppm for pepper. Levels of 1-chloro-2-propanol found in six food products commercially treated with propyl-

TABLE 2
ANALYSIS OF 2-CHLOROETHANOL IN FOOD FUMIGATED WITH ETHYLENE OXIDE

Sample	2-Chloroethanol Found, ppm Methods of Analysis	
	Sweep Codistribution	Ether Extension
Celery seed	83	66
Paprika	45	–
Turmeric	53	–
Pepper	–	110
Gum tragacanth	–	<5

ene oxide ranged from 4 ppm for cocoa to 47 ppm for glazed citron. TABLES 2 and 3 illustrate the analysis of 2-chloroethanol and 1-chloro-2-propanol in foods fumigated with ethylene oxide and propylene oxide, respectively. Gas chromatography and infrared spectroscopy were used to determine and identify the chlorohydrin present.

Gordon and co-workers[16] explored the effect of fumigating dried prunes with ethylene oxide under controlled conditions in order to provide data on the quantity and identity of these relatively unknown food constituents. Dried prunes fumigated with ethylene oxide-^{14}C reacted with the fumigant to yield nonvolatile and relatively nontoxic alkylation products. More than 50% of the total radioactivity was combined as insoluble hydroxyethyl cellulose in the prune skin, 30% as hydroxy ethylated sugars in the pulp and 3% as glycols (mostly diethylene glycol). The remainder was tentatively identified as hydroxy ethylated amino acids and proteins.

The major fraction of the ethylene oxide is bound to prune cellulose. The hydroxyethylated sugars in prune pulp are present in fairly large amounts (0.5–1% of the dry weight). Little is known of the toxicity of alkylated sugars, although 3-methyl glucose has been shown to be completely nontoxic to the rat.[17]

TABLE 4 illustrates the distribution of hydroxy ethyl derivatives in ethylene oxide-fumigated prunes, and TABLE 5 depicts the radioactivity in fractions of ^{14}C-ethylene oxide-treated prune.

TABLE 3
ANALYSIS OF 1-CHLORO-2-PROPANOL IN FOODS FUMIGATED WITH PROPYLENE OXIDE

Sample	1-Chloro-2-propanol Found, ppm		
	Sweep Codistribution	Ether Extension	Steam Distribution
Walnut meats	33	–	9
Tapioca starch	–	–	–
Flour	–	10	–
Cocoa	–	4	–
Glazed cherries	–	–	5
Glazed citron	–	–	47

TABLE 4

DISTRIBUTION OF HYDROXYETHYL DERIVATIVES IN ETHYLENE OXIDE-FUMIGATED PRUNES

Solubility of Derivative	Prune Constituent Labeled*	Location in Prune	Total Radioactivity (Percentage)	Major 2-Hydroxyethyl H Derivatives	Reactive Groups Labeled, %
Insoluble	. . .	pit	1 (64 with skin; 68 total)		
	cellulose	skin	63	6-H- and 6-HH-cellulose	~13
	cellulose	pulp	(1)	6-H-cellulose	~ 1
	(protein)	pulp	(3)	(H-histidine and H-methionine)	~15
Water-soluble	(protein)	pulp	(4) (7 with next; 32 total)	(H-histidine and H-methionine)	
	(amino acids)	pulp	(3)	(H-amino acids)	~ 5–15
	sugars	pulp	24	6-H-glucose and 1-H-glucose	0.7
Ether-soluble	water	pulp	0.4	diethylene glycol, ethylene glycol	0.0003

* Names in parentheses indicate tentative or speculative identification only.

TABLE 5
RADIOACTIVITY IN FRACTIONS OF ^{14}C-ETHYLENE OXIDE-TREATED PRUNE

Prune Tissue	Total Weight, mg	Observed, Counts/ Min/ mg	Estimated* mμ/mg	Approximate Total μc	Total Activity Percentage
Skin	1,290	3,370	35	45	63
Pulp, whole†	3,750	1,160	7	25	
Ether-extractable	8	40,500	48	0.4	0.5
Water-extractable	2,550	1,510	9	22	31
Insoluble residue	190	3,020	18	3	4
Pit (less kernel)	650	119	1.4	0.8	1
Kernel	162	54	0.6	0.1	0.1

* Empirically determined factors ranging from 0.0012 (for samples with negligible self-absorption) to 0.014 (for samples with very high self-absorption) were used to convert counts/minute to millimicrocuries. Activity of original C^{14}-ethylene oxide is 4,200 mμc/mg, and would be 3,000 mμc/mg if converted to ethylene glycol.

†Whole pulp weight includes 26% water, not included in weights of three subfractions below.

There is a growing awareness of the need for methods to monitor all types of pesticide residues in foods. Most attention has been given to the problem of the highly persistent insecticide. However, a substantial proportion of the national consumption of a commodity may be treated with a less persistent pesticide, methyl bromide or ethylene oxide as fumigants for grain; it is of importance that minute amount of such toxic agents be detectable and its significance assessed.

The extent of ethylene chlorohydrin formation by ethylene oxide in flour under normal fumigation conditions is being studied at present.[18]

These reactions and the volatility of the fumigants suggest that most of any residual methyl bromide or ethylene oxide will quickly disappear after treatment and subsequent processing. However, more efficient and more sensitive methods than have been hitherto available are required, in order to indicate whether this disappearance is complete.

Heuser and Scudamore[18,19] described cold solvent extraction and gas chromatographic methods for the analysis of free methyl bromide and ethylene oxide as well as fumigant residues (ethylene chlorohydrin) in wheat and flour.

Initial exposure of flour to ethylene oxide for periods of one to six hours as well as with periods of preliminary aerations from three-quarters to two hours and main aeration from three to four hours, resulted in recoveries of free ethylene oxide of 95.0–95.8% with a lower detection limit of about 0.3 ppm, hence, suggesting *in situ* residues of ethylene oxide reaction products of approximately four to five percent resulting from the partial aeration of flour with ethylene oxide.

Wiseblatt[20] described the reduction of the microbial populations in flours incorporated into refrigerated foods following the utilization of propylene oxide vapor. The flours were inoculated with several microorganisms representing sources of food spoilage and food poisoning, e.g. *B. subtilis*, *S. aureus*, *A. flavus*, and *E. coli*.

TABLE 6 illustrates the recovery of epoxide after treatment of two flours e.g. pastry and patent flour with 1,000 ppm of propylene oxide.

TABLE 6

RECOVERY OF RESIDUAL PROPYLENE OXIDE FROM FLOUR*

Days after Exposure	Residual Propylene Oxide Pastry Flour ppm	Patent Flour ppm
2	208	228
16	111	114
30	57	60

* Flours exposed to 1,000 ppm propylene oxide. L. Wiseblatt. 1967. Cereal Chem. **44:** 269–280.

Whether the decreases shown were due to volatilization or to slow reaction with the flour was not determined, although the latter was thought to prevail, since the flours were stored in air-tight containers.

Ethylene oxide has been used in the tobacco industry both to shorten the aging process[21] and to reduce the nicotine content in tobacco leaves.[22,23] The reaction products of nicotine with gaseous ethylene oxide and the aspects of their pyrolysis has been reported.[24] It was found that N-hydroxyethyl nicotine was the main reaction product when tobacco leaves were treated with ethylene oxide. In the reaction with nicotine monoacetate, two products were formed: N′-hydroxyethyl nicotine and N-hydroxyethyl nicotine in the weight ratio of 1 : 3.5.

TABLE 7 depicts the relative quantity of pyrolyzed compounds of nicotine, hydroxyethyl nicotine, and their hydrochlorides on pyrolysis at 600 and 800° C (the ratio of relative amount of pyrolysis products to 3-cyano pyridine).

The substantial pyrolysis of nicotine and N-hydroxyethyl nicotine on smoking could be expected in considering the pyrolysis pattern of the hydrochloride, because these compounds are believed to be present as salts of organic and/or inorganic acids in tobacco leaves. It was also found that a considerable amount of nicotine and pyridine derivatives was regenerated by pyrolysis of N-hydroxyethyl nicotine, and N-hydroxyethyl nicotine dihydrochloride′ and N′-hydroxyethyl nicotine dihydrochloride.

In recent years ethylene oxide sterilization has become an important tool, primarily where sterilization by autoclaving is either impractical or, as in the case of many plastic devices, destructive to the product.

The use of ethylene oxide for sterilization has thus raised a number of significant questions regarding (a) the possible entrapment of ethylene oxide in a plastic that may then exert a toxic effect when placed in contact with living tissue, and (b) the effect of (sorbed) ethylene oxide on the possible changes in the physical and chemical properties of the medical plastics, *per se*. It had been earlier shown that plastic tubings that have been ethylene oxide-sterilized can cause significant hemolysis when placed in contact with human blood.[25–27] For example, Bain and Lowenstein[27] reported that when mixed leukocyte cultures were incubated in disposable plastic tubes sterilized with ethylene oxide, the cell survival was severely affected by a toxic residue left on the plastics. The residue was dissipated only after four or five months' storage at room temperature, and the cell survival returned to values obtained with ultraviolet-sterilized control tubes.

TABLE 7

RELATIVE QUANTITY OF PYROLYZED COMPOUNDS OF NICOTINE, HYDROXYETHYLNICOTINE AND THEIR HYDROCHLORIDES (3-CYANOPYRIDINE = 1)*

Products	Free Nicotine		Free N-hydroxyethyl-Nicotine		Nicotine Dihydrochloride	N-hydroxyethyl-Nicotine Dihydrochloride	N′-hydroxyethyl-Nicotine Dihydrochloride
Pyrolysis temp. (° C)	600	800	600	800	600	600	600
Low boiling compounds	5	5	2	5	3	15	3
Pyridine	1.5	4	0.5	3	1	1	1
3-Picoline	4	1.5	0.3	1	4	5	5
3-Ethylpyridine	1.5	0.2	0.5	0.2	0.8	1	1
3-Vinylpyridine	10	5	5	2	4	5	5
3-Cyanopyridine	1	1	1	1	1	1	1
Nicotine	8	4	10	5	5	3	4
Quinoline	0.2	1	1	1.5	1.5	1.5	0.5
Isoquinoline	0.1	0.3	0.5	0.8	0.3	0.8	0.2
Myosmine	0.5	0.5	0.5	1.5	1.5	1	1

* Y. Obi, Y. Shimada, K. Takahashi, K. Nishida & T. Kisaki. 1968. Tobacco **166:** 26–30.

O'Leary and Guess,[28] in their study of the toxicologic potential of medical plastics sterilized with ethylene oxide vapors, presented data demonstrating the ability of ethylene oxide to remain entrapped in a nonclosed system such as surgical tubing, gas washing bottles, plastic syringe, or plastic bottles at various temperatures above its boiling point. In this same study, the hemolyzing ability of known amounts of ethylene oxide to that of freshly gas-sterilized plastic pharmaceutical products was shown. Additionally, the effects of plasticizers of the ester type upon the sorption of ethylene oxide into polyvinyl chloride products was described.

One of the interesting observations on the solubility of ethylene oxide in phthalic acid esters was that this gaseous vapor could remain in a nonclosed system in high equilibrium concentrations at relatively high temperature.

TABLE 8 illustrates the effect of temperature on residual ethylene oxide in glass bottles. At 71.5° C, seven times the boiling temperature of ethylene oxide (b.p. 10.7° C), there was still almost half a gram of residual sterilant.

This residual ethylene oxide could present a hazard in the sterilization of such devices as syringes. The residual gas, for example, might produce toxicity due to some of the oxidation products as indicated: epoxide → glycol → glyoxalic acid → glycolic acid → oxalic acid.

In addition, the effect of residual ethylene oxide (or its oxidation products) upon the contents of the sterilized syringe adds still another dimension to the potential hazard and novel toxicities that could result. This is especially true of the rubber components of many devices. It has also been shown that ethylene oxide (a relatively polar ether) possesses significant ability to solvate nonpolar hydrocarbon esters such as dinonyl phthalate and dioctyl phthalate. Since polyvinyl chloride tubing can contain approximately 35% of phthalate esters (such as dioctyl phthalate), the possibility was suggested that a flexible tubing weighing 1 g can absorb as much as 40 mg of ethylene oxide (an amount sufficient to cause significant hemolysis in human blood). However, at the present time it is not known whether or not the plasticizer in the polymer will attain the same solubility limits for ethylene oxide as it does in the pure state.

TABLE 9 illustrates the toxicity to cell cultures for 18 pharmaceutical plastics with ethylene oxide. It should be noted that the more plasticized formulations caused cell death, reflecting a higher degree of ethylene oxide solubility in the plasticizer and/or a more rapid release of the gas from this material. The cell

TABLE 8

THE EFFECT OF TEMPERATURE ON RESIDUAL ETHYLENE OXIDE IN GLASS BOTTLE

Experiment Number	Weight in mg of residual Ethylene Oxide at Various Temperatures		
	45.5° C	57.0° C	71.5° C
1	459	399	382
2	473	456	391
3	481	452	371
4	482	413	399
5	466	399	439
Mean values	472	424	396
Std. error	3.0	8.5	7.8

TABLE 9

CELL CULTURE TOXICITY RESULTS FOR 18 PHARMACEUTICAL PLASTICS STERILIZED WITH ETHYLENE OXIDE*

Plastics (10 mil film)	"L" Cell Culture	Chick Cell Culture
Cellulose acetate	cell death	complete cell lysis
Polycarbonate	no effect evident	no effect evident
Polyethylene	cell death	no effect evident
Teflon® 7	no effect evident	no effect evident
Polyvinyl chloride with 35% dioctyl phthalate	cell death	not tested
Nylon 6,6	no effect evident	no effect evident
Polyphenylene oxide	cell death	complete cell lysis
Polypropylene	no effect evident	no effect evident
Polyvinyl chloride with 15% dioctyl phthalate	cell death	complete cell lysis
Rigid polyvinyl chloride	no effect evident	no effect evident
Cellulose triacetate	cell death	complete cell lysis
Rigid polyurethane	cell death	no effect evident
Flexible polyurethane	not tested	no effect evident
Cellulose acetate-butyrate	cell death	no effect evident
Polymonochlorotrifluoroethylene	no effect evident	no effect evident
Polybutylene	no effect evident	no effect evident
Acrylonitrile-Butadiene-Styrene	cell death	no effect evident
Polyvinyl acetate	cell death	complete cell lysis

* Plastics were placed on the culture plates within 15 minutes after the sterilization procedure was completed. Toxicity observations were made with the unaided eye, after 24 hours' exposure to the culture plates.

deaths noted with the nonplasticized plastics were related to the complex desorption relationships resulting from various degrees of crystallinity, branching, and molecular weights of the polymers. The tests indicated that the polypropylene devices would perhaps have to be classified as the best potential candidates for making a medical product that would undergo ethylene oxide sterilization. The above studies of O'Leary and Guess also disclosed that hemolysis may result from the sterilization of medical plastics of many diverse types (See TABLE 10).

The determination of residual ethylene oxide in catheters has been carried out utilizing gas-liquid chromatography.[29]

According to standard hospital practice, catheters (long cardiac type made of plastic and short urinary type [rubber]) were sterilized in an autoclave at 22 inches of vacuum; then the mixture of 12% ethylene oxide and 88% Freon was let in to obtain a pressure 5–7 psi at 135° F for four hours. Vacuum was applied to remove the gases and the chamber was flushed with filtered room air to remove the residual ethylene oxide.

FIGURE 1 illustrates the retention of ethylene oxide in catheters following various aeration times. The decrease in ethylene oxide was especially large after the 48-hour aeration, after which the decrease leveled off to a constant value of 0.4 mg ethylene oxide/gm catheter for plastic catheters and 0.1 mg/gm for the rubber catheters. The levels of retention of ethylene oxide by plastic and rubber catheters appeared to remain essentially constant from 48–168 hours of standing in room air, wrapped in cellophane covers. This retention of ethylene oxide for a period of one week indicated that aeration as used in this work was not effective

TABLE 10

THE HEMOLYSIS LIABILITY OF SELECTED PHARMACEUTICAL PLASTICS STERILIZED WITH ETHYLENE OXIDE

Name of Device	Polymer Type	Time Blood Exposed to Plastics	% Absorption @ 540 mμ
Disposable venoclysis set	flexible polyvinyl chloride	60 minutes	68
		100	87
Blood administration set	flexible polyvinyl chloride	60	22
Disposable syringe I	polypropylene	40	18
		140	18
Disposable syringe II	polypropylene	45	2
		135	8
Disposable syringe III	polystyrene	85	15
		195	18
Blood collection unit	polyethylene	95	18
		190	24
Whole blood container	high density polyethylene	75	33
		135	33
Nylon bottle	polyamide	80	3
		150	14
Teflon® bottle	fluoroethylene propylene	30	0
		143	30
Polyolefin bottle	blend of polypropylene and linear polyethylene	100	8

in removing all the ethylene oxide from the catheters. It was pointed out that ethylene oxide, if not removed, might be released later under use and might cause hemolysis, erythema, and edema of the tissues.[26–30]

Other cogent studies relating to the general problem of interaction of ethylene oxide with rubber and plastic constituents have been reported.

Downey[31] demonstrated that the mercaptobenzothiazole vulcanization accelerators found in rubber reacted rapidly with ethylene oxide to produce (hydroxyethyl-mercapto)-thioazole despite the fact that residual ethylene oxide concentration in rubber tubing had been reported dissipated after five hours' aeration.

Little is known about the parenteral toxicity of these compounds or of the other possible reaction products in ethylene oxide sterilized rubber.

Cunliffe and Wesley[32] have shown that ethylene chlorohydrin was given off from PVC tubing six days after ethylene oxide sterilization.

It has also been demonstrated by Gunther[33] that high concentrations of ethylene oxide can be taken up by polyethylene, gum rubber, and plasticized polyvinyl chloride. This reemphasizes the general problem of gas entrapment occurring in plastics.

Lactones: Beta Propiolactone

Beta propiolactone (BPL) has a broad spectrum of current and suggested industrial utility e.g. in wood processing, protective coatings, and impregnation of textiles, modification of flax cellulose, urethane foam manufacture, intermediate in the preparation of insecticides, plasticizers, medicinals, and additive for leaded gasolines, and in the modification of tobacco flavors.

The chemical properties and reactions of BPL have been delineated by Machell.[34] BPL is produced commercially from formaldehyde and ketene in the presence of a catalyst such as zinc chloride, hydrated aluminum silicate, or zinc trifluroacetate, viz:

$$CH_2=CO + HCHO \rightarrow \begin{array}{ccc} CH_2 & - & CH_2 \\ | & & | \\ O & \text{———} & CO \end{array}$$

It is a colorless liquid at room temperature, boiling at 162.3° C. The 97% grade BPL (which can contain trace quantities of the reactants) is stable for several years when stored at 4° C, and the half-life of aqeuous solutions is approximately three to one-half hours at 25°C.

The common commercial product contains about 18% impurities e.g. acrylic acid, acetic anhydride, and polymers.

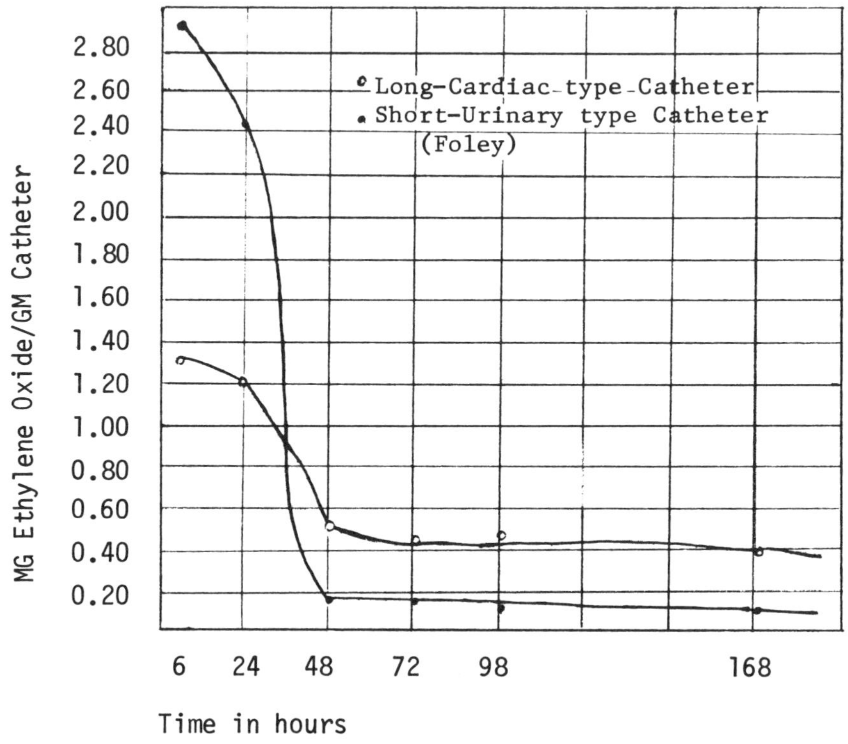

FIGURE 1. Ethylene oxide (mg) catheter (g) vs time (hr). (By permission of the authors and the publishers of the Journal of Biomedical Material Research.[29])

Beta propiolactone is hydrolyzed at the alkyl and acyl bonds with the formation of substituted beta propionic acids and hydracrylic acid as shown:

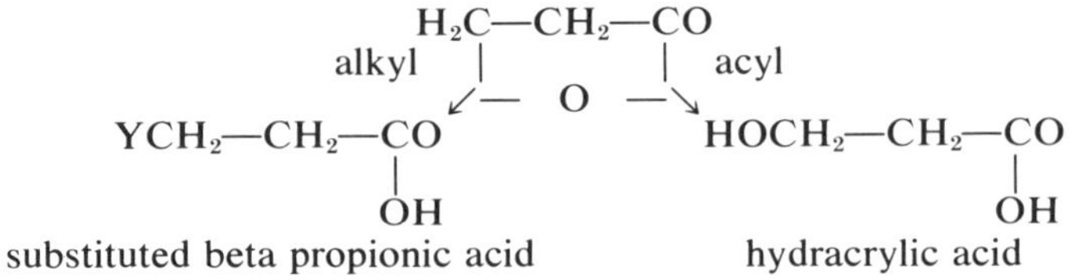

Chemically, β-propiolactone is highly reactive, due to the strained four-membered ring. It is an alkylating carcinogen,[35] undergoing rapid electrophilic reactions e.g. with thiols (-SH) forming thio-ethers. In the case of cysteine, the compound formed is S-2-carboxyethyl-cysteine.[36]

β-Propiolactone has been used fairly extensively as a sterilizing agent, particularly as an aerosol for sterilizing rooms, plasma, arterial or homografts, or as a toxoiding agent in place of formalin. Roe and Salaman[37] have drawn attention to the possible carcinogenic hazard involved in such uses.

Beta-propiolactone (BPL) has been shown to be an effective vaporphase decontaminant for the treatment of enclosed areas (it is effective against bacterial spores and vegetative cells as well as viruses).

Because liquid BPL is a good organic solvent, problems are often encountered when it is used as a decontaminent, e.g. the dissolution of paints, lacquers, and waxes on surfaces in the enclosure treated. The problem of BPL vapor decontamination has been reviewed by Hoffman and colleagues.[38] It has been shown that BPL vapor does adsorb on surfaces and may require a relatively long time to desorb.

The virucidal, toxicological, and biological effects of beta propiolactone as well as its degradation products hydracrylic- and beta-chloropropionic acids have been described by Kelly and Hartman.[39–41] Beta-propiolactone itself is hepatotoxic and nephrotoxic to the rabbit and guinea pig, but not to mice. Hydracrylic and beta-chloropropionic acids produce peripheral vasodilation in the mouse and rabbit. (Acrylic acid itself also elicits this response.) Both degradation products in large repeated doses depress the platelet count in the peripheral blood of animals.

Aziridines: Tepa, Metepa, and Thiotepa

Tepa {tris(1-aziridinyl)-phosphine oxide} has been the most extensively employed of all the aziridinyl phosphine oxides. Its industrial applications include the flame-proofing of textiles, its use with water-repellent, wash-and-wear, and crease-resistant fabrics, and treatment of paper and wood.

The above utility of tepa (as well as other aziridines) is illustrative of the ability of these compounds to act as cross-linking agents for polymers containing active hydrogen groups such as carboxyl, phenol, sulfhydryl, amide, and hydroxyl. This can be represented schematically as follows, with ZH representing the active hydrogen group in the polymer chain:

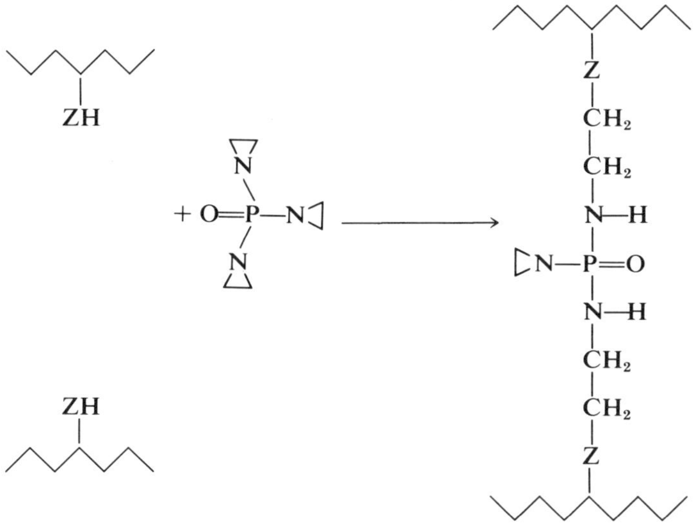

The availability of aziridine compounds, notably tepa, thiotepa, and metepa, as well as the development of new methods of administration, has strongly suggested the potential use of chemosterilants for large scale control or eradication programs. Inherent in such programs, however, is the dispersion of large numbers of treated insects into the environment. Hence, it is of paramount importance to elucidate chemosterilant stability, residues, and degradation products on and in the insect, as well as its persistence.

The effects of temperatures and pH on the stability of tepa and a number of other aziridinyl chemosterilants have been investigated by Beroza and Bořkovec.[42]

FIGURE 2 shows the effect of pH on the rate of degradation of tepa in D_2O buffers. Tepa in acidic or neutral solutions gave a stable degradation product that, with the aid of nuclear magnetic resonance spectrum (NMR) was identified as ethyleneimine. Other products involving C—N bond cleavage were postulated, based on NMR data, and it was suggested that the decomposition of tepa in D_2O could be represented as shown in FIGURE 3.

In aqueous solutions, tepa degradation is accompanied by liberation of inorganic phosphate.[42,43]

Recognition of the effect of pH on decomposition of azridine chemosterilants led to modification of insect diets used in screening tests.

A number of investigations have dealt with the identification of reaction products and their persistence following chemosterilization with tepa.

Chang and co-workers[44] reported that 50% of ^{14}C-tepa injected into male houseflies was retained in the fly after five hours of normal activity. Radioactivity was present in treated flies as tepa or aziridinyl metabolites; the radioactive metabolites in the excreta did not contain aziridinyl groups. Further radiometric and colorimetric determinations indicated that treated flies retained about nine percent of the radioactivity and five percent of the azridinyl content over prolonged periods (72 hours).

Hedin and associates[45] investigated the fate of ^{14}C-tepa in weevils. Depending on the diet, the radioactivity was reduced to 50% in 6–48 hours. For example,

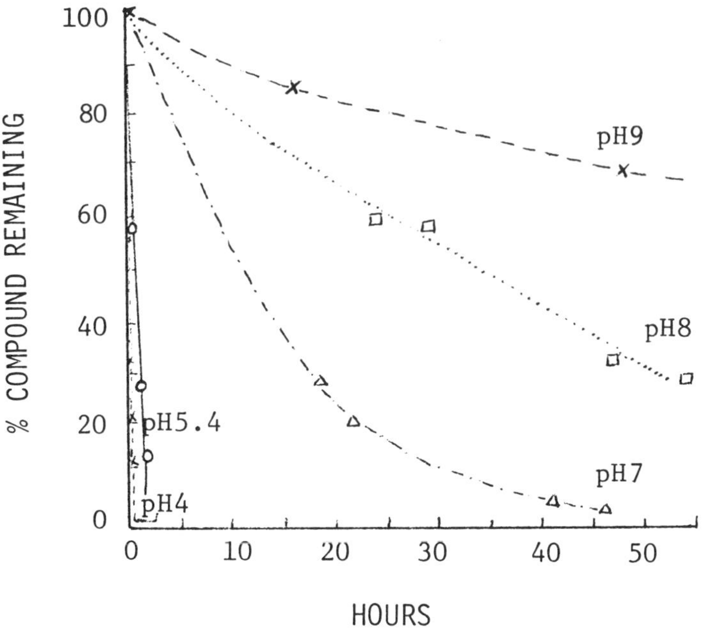

FIGURE 2. Stability of 2.5% tepa in D_2O buffered at different pH values as determined from NMR spectra.

weevils fed cotton buds were able to excrete the radioactivity more rapidly than those fed an artificial diet. However, between 10 and 20 percent of the radioactivity was retained for at least 10 days.

Collier and Tardiff[46] described the analysis of male gypsy moths, *Portetria dispar* L for microgram quantities of tepa following eight-hour exposure to residual films of 1 mg/dm^2 of tepa. It was found that a combination of washing and an eight-hour post treatment holding period reduced the level to the order of 1–5 mg and that low levels were attained only after prolonged periods.

Ladd and co-workers[47] reported on the mass sterilization of Japanese beetles, *Popillia Japonica* Nervman, with tepa and the determination of residues. TABLE 11 illustrates the mean residues of tepa in and on male Japanese bettles at different times after dipping in a 0.0625% concentration of tepa. Residues in and on treated beetles were 2.0 μg/beetle 1.5 hours after treatment, and 0.3 μg/beetle after 48 hours. Washing with water one day after treatment did not measurably reduce the residues. The above analyses for tepa residues was carried out with use of the colorimetric technique of Chang and Bořkovec.[48] The results are indicative of the total alkylating function of the eluates: they include tepa and any degradation product such as ethyleneimine still possessing alkylating activity. Hence, the indicated tepa values are maximum values.

The persistence of tepa in male and female fall armyworm moths, *Spodoptera frugiperda*, was determined by radiometric and gas chromatographic (GLC) procedures.[49] The radiometric analyses showed considerably more tepa on and

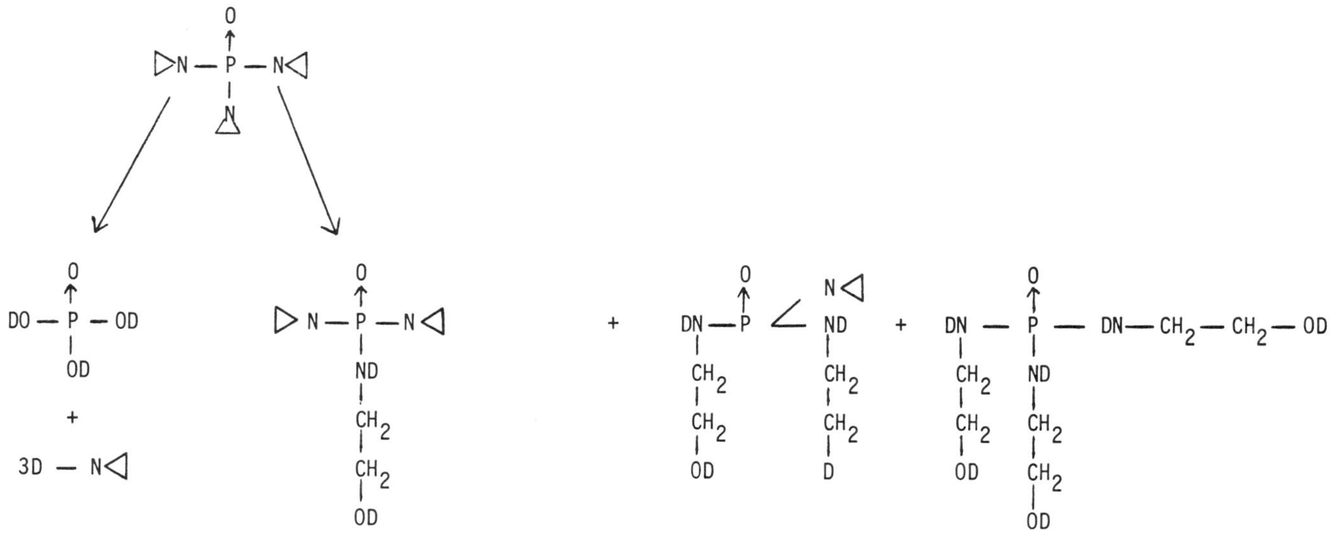

FIGURE 3. Decomposition of tepa in D_2O. (Adapted from M. Beroza and A. B. Borkovec.[42])

TABLE 11

MEAN RESIDUES OF TEPA IN AND ON MALE JAPANESE BEETLES AT DIFFERENT TIMES AFTER DIPPING IN A 0.0625% CONCENTRATION OF TEPA*

Time After Treatment (hr)	No. Insects in Test	Mean Tepa Residue (μg/male)
1.5	30	2.0
22.5	20	0.6
22.5 (washed)	20	.6
48.0	10	.3

*T. L. Ladd, C. W. Collier & E. L. Plasket. 1968. J. Econ. Entom. **61:** 9421.

in the insects than did the specific GLC analyses, an indication that ^{14}C-labeled fragments of the tepa molecule were being analyzed as tepa. Within 24 hours, >90% of the tepa disappeared from moths that ingested as much as 100 μg per moth. More than 95% disappeared within 48 hours.

The residues of tepa on chemosterilized codling moths, *Carpocapsa pomonella* L., has been studied by Maitlen and McDonough,[50] following initial levels of 4.5 and 22.8 μg/moth. The results are summarized in TABLE 12 and illustrate tepa residues found on codling moths at various intervals after two different levels of aerosol treatment. FIGURE 4 depicts the logarithm of the concentration (μg/moth) versus time and illustrates the linear decrease of tepa with time. The slope and correlation coefficients were 0.012 log units/hour and 0.994 for the high-level treatment and 0.022 log units/hour and 0.997 for the low-level treatment. Although the linear relationships suggest that the degradation reaction is first order, the variation of the slope with initial concentration reveals that it is more complicated. The loss of tepa after 72 hours was 88 and 97% for the high and low-level treatment, respectively. These values are roughly similar to the 93% loss in 72

TABLE 12

TEPA RESIDUES FOUND ON CODLING MOTHS AT VARIOUS INTERVALS AFTER TWO DIFFERENT LEVELS OF AEROSOL TREATMENT

Interval After Application (hr)	Residues of Tepa (av. of 3 replicates)			
	Low-level Treatment μg/moth	Low-level Treatment ppm	High-level Treatment μg/moth	High-level Treatment ppm
0	4.5	140.3	22.8	926.5
3	4.2	123.3	23.0	1045.2
6	3.7	119.6	21.1	880.5
12	2.3	76.1	16.0	732.7
24	1.3	45.1	12.0	568.6
36	0.64	22.2		
48	.46	16.2	5.1	242.2
72	.13	5.3	2.6	145.1
144			0.56	31.8

hours on Mexican fruit flies, *Anastrepha Ludens* Loew.[48] The initial residue on the fruit flies of 1.68 μg/fly corresponds to 1500 ppm.

Puparia of Mexican fruit flies, *Anastrepha Ludens* Loew, that had been dipped in a 5% solution of tepa were analyzed by Chang and Bořkovec[48] to determine the amount of residue on the surface of each puparium.

Adult flies that emerged from treated pupae became sterile after contacting the chemosterilant deposited on the pupal cases. The quantity of tepa incorporated in an adult fly decreased by more than 90% within the first three days of its life and constituted only a small fraction of the sterilant deposited.

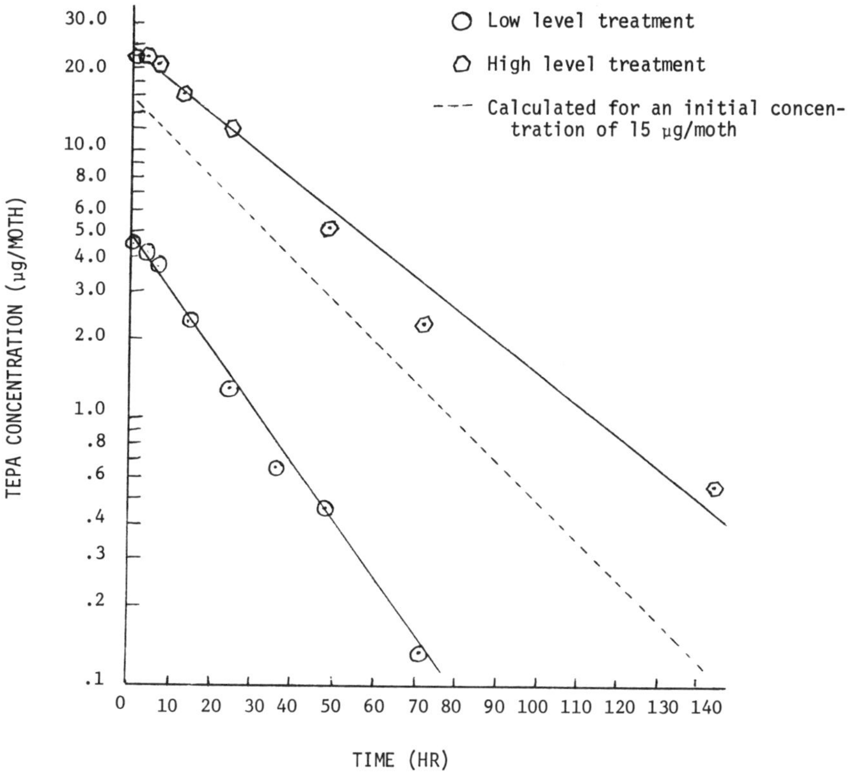

FIGURE 4. Logarithm of tepa concentration (μg/moth) vs time. Low-level treatment was 4.5 μg/moth; high-level, 22.8 μg/moth.

The determination of tepa was accomplished with γ-(4-nitrobenzyl)-pyridine, using the colorimetric procedure of Epstein and co-workers,[51] which is based on the quantitative determination of the aziridinyl fraction and not on the content of the intact tepa molecule.

TABLE 13 depicts the analysis of tepa residues on Mexican fruit flies treated by dipping in five-percent solutions of tepa. The data suggest that since two-to-

TABLE 13

COLORIMETRIC ANALYSIS OF TEPA RESIDUES ON MEXICAN FRUIT FLIES TREATED BY DIPPING IN 5% SOLUTIONS OF TEPA

	Age of Flies After Treatment or Emergence	μg Tepa/Individual Puparium	
		Lot 1 (washed)	Lot 2 (unwashed)
Intact pupae	4 days	44.8	50.8
Pupal cases	6 days	38.9	35.5
Adult flies	1–24 hours	1.68	1.35
	24–48 hours	0.30	0.19
	52–72 hours	0.14	0.09

three-day-old flies contain approximately .30 and 0.14 μg tepa/individual puparium, eight-to-nine-day-old flies (the average age at which they are being released in infested areas in Mexico) would not contain any detectable residues of tepa. Caution, however, was advised by the authors in the interpretation of the data in TABLE 13, since pickup and retention of chemosterilant may vary with environmental conditions as well as with thickness of the layer of pupae in emergence cages, relative size of cage, or length of time adults are in contact with treated puparia and empty pupal cases.

Metepa (tris-(2-methyl-1-aziridinyl)-phosphine oxide was found to be as sensitive to acidic conditions as the other chemosterilants; for example, degradation in acidic media was complete within two hours.[52]

Plapp and associates[53] studied the distribution and fate of ^{32}P-metepa in chloroform extracts of house flies, mosquitoes, and mice. Following topical administration to house flies, ^{32}P-metepa was found to be rapidly absorbed (50% in 1.5 hours), and rapidly detoxified following absorption, as 50% in two hours.

Fifty percent degradation occurred in slightly more than one hour following injection of the material, with more than 95% being degraded in 24 hours. Since the rate of degradation in two strains of house flies resistant to organophosphorus insecticides was the same as that observed in the susceptible strain, it was concluded that degradation of the sterilant proceeded via a pathway different from that responsible for organophosphate detoxification.

In mosquito larvae, degradation was rapid and virtually complete within 48 hours after termination of treatment. Although an amount of ^{32}P remained through pupal and adult stages, very little of the radioactivity was associated with metepa.

Adult mosquitoes fed sugar solutions of metepa degraded metepa even more rapidly, with degradation being complete within 24 hours after the sterilant solution was removed.

Chamberlain and Hamilton[54] studied the absorption, excretion, and metabolism of ^{32}P-labeled metepa by the screw-worm fly, *Cochliomyia hominivorax* Coquerel and the stable fly, *Stomoxys Calcitrans* L.

The excreta of screwworm flies fed ^{32}P-labeled metepa contained 62–67% phosphoric acid and only 11–15% of radioactivity as metepa (or closely related compounds) 24 hours after treatment. However, five unknown metabolites accounted for 17–20% of the radioactivity in the feces.

Dame and Schmidt[55] studied the uptake of ^{32}P-metepa and its effect on two species of mosquitoes (*Anopheles quadrimaculatus, Aedes aegypti*) and house flies (*Musca domestica*). ^{32}P-labeled metepa was found to be quite volatile on glass surfaces and highly sorptive on masonite. The distribution of metepa in the insects was rapid and apparently nonselective. Excretion was found to be rapid in insects exposed to residual deposits of 10 mg/foot^2. Insects exposed to treated larval medium and food retained a high percentage of their original radioactivity over prolonged periods. This activity was believed to represent detoxified metepa.

TABLE 14 indicates the percent loss of total radioactivity in excreta of mosquitoes exposed to ^{32}P-labeled metepa residues of 100 mg/foot^2 on masonite.

In other studies based on the decrease of radioactivity of mosquitoes and house flies treated on glass surfaces, it was found that after 24 hours, the residual activity approximated only 11% in house flies, and after 8–11 days, only 1–3% in house flies and mosquitoes.

In these studies it was shown that the distribution of metepa was both rapid and general. Metepa was distributed in proportion to the weights of the various body sections. In mosquitoes, however, radioactivity was predominantly located in the legs.

The nonselective nature of metepa suggests that only a minor portion of the total uptake was involved in the mechanism of sterilization. The rapid uptake and basically unchanged distribution pattern further suggests that the compound reacted very rapidly within the insect. Plapp and co-workers[53] also found that metepa was rapidly metabolized, with only a minor amount of unmetabolized metepa remaining in the insects after six to eight hours.

Metepa and its metabolites were shown to be excreted rapidly in large quantities. For example, house flies exposed to residual deposits on glass lost 89% of their radioactivity within 24 hours. However, a greater percentage of the original radioactivity remained in the adults that had obtained the material during the larval stage or during the three-day adult feeding period than in those adults subjected to residual deposits.

It was suggested that the residual radioactivity in these insects did not represent unmetabolized metepa, because of the high degree of chemical activity of this compound. This hypothesis receives support from the findings of Plapp and co-workers.[53]

The uptake and persistence of metepa in the house fly has been studied by Morgan and colleagues.[56]

The amounts of metepa on and in house flies and in their environment (determined by gas chromatography) at 0–72 hours after one-hour exposure to a sugar but containing 0.8% of metepa revealed that metepa was excreted by the insects

TABLE 14

PERCENT LOSS OF TOTAL RADIOACTIVITY IN EXCRETA OF MOSQUITOES EXPOSED TO ^{32}P-LABELED METEPA RESIDUES OF 100 MG/FT^2 ON MASONITE

Hours after Treatment	*quadrimaculatus*	*aegypti*
0	—	—
6	9	12
12	23	8
24	30	33
48	35	27

during the entire test period. However, about 9.3% of the total was still present in the females and 0.94 in the male after 72 hours.

It was suggested from this study that the low persistence of the chemosterilants and the minute quantities of residues present indicated that they could not contribute sufficient amounts of metepa and hempa to adversely affect the environment.

Thiotepa (tris(1-aziridinyl)-phosphine sulfide tends to polymerize in aqueous solutions (like most of the aziridine chemosterilants), or in the presence of moisture, especially at acidic pH.

Benckhuijsen[57] studied the behavior of thiotepa in acid medium and presented evidence of an intramolecular alkylation of the sulfur on protonation of the molecule. The resultant five-membered ring was hydrolyzed slowly in neutral solution at room temperature, liberating an SH group. In the SH derivative, two ethyleneimine rings were retained and were shown to be more reactive toward water and sulfhydryl than were those of thiotepa.

FIGURE 5 illustrates the above sequence of reactions.

It has been previously reported[58] that thiotepa was highly unstable at pH 4.2 and 37° C; 95% of the alkylating groups was destroyed within 30 minutes. However, Benckhuijsen[57] found a decrease in alkylating activity of only 1.2% in 30 minutes under these conditions. Hence, it was interesting to find a remarkable stability against hydrolysis at low pH for two-thirds of the alkylating groups of thiotepa.

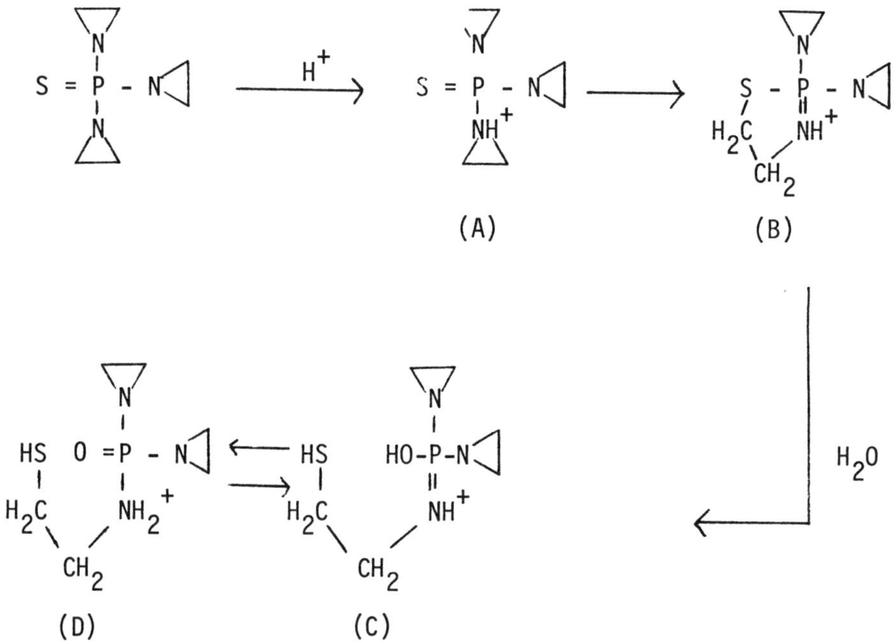

FIGURE 5. Intramolecular alkylation of thiotepa. (By permission of the author and the publishers of Biochemical Pharmacology.[57]

The metabolism of ^{32}P-labeled thiotepa following topical application to the German cockroach (*Blatella germanica*), house fly (*Musca domestica*), stable fly (*Stomoxys calcitrans*), and boll weevil (*Anthonomus grandis*) was studied by Parish and Arthur.[59]

TABLE 15 indicates the percentage of ^{32}P-thiotepa absorbed and the fractionation of the internal extracts recovered from the insects treated topically at 100 mg/kg.

TABLE 15

PERCENTAGE OF ^{32}P-THIOTEPA ABSORBED AND THE FRACTIONATION BY SILICA GEL CHROMATOGRAPHY OF THE INTERNAL EXTRACTS RECOVERED FROM INSECTS TREATED TOPICALLY AT 100 mg/kg*

Insect	Time after Treatment (hr.)	Absorbed	% Internal Extracts Present Thiotepa	Tepa
German cockroach	0	18.8	–	–
	1	43.6	65.1	34.9
	4	85.0	49.3	50.7
	24	69.1	17.9	82.1
House fly	0	15.2	–	–
	1	81.6	50.2	49.8
	4	87.8	24.3	75.7
	24	75.7	18.0	82.0
Stable fly	0	86.0	–	–
	1	75.6	64.2	35.8
	4	81.2	66.5	33.5
	24	40.7	52.9	47.1
Boll weevil	0	1.5	–	–
	1	41.2	37.2	62.8
	4	60.7	37.7	62.3
	24	73.5	62.8	37.2

*J. C. Parish & B. W. Arthur. 1965. J. Econ. Entom. **58:** 976–979.

It was found that a period of less than one hour to 24 hours was required for the treated insects to oxidize one-half of the thiotepa to tepa. German cockroaches, house flies, and stable flies metabolized thiotepa at a regular rate after treatment. Boll weevils, however, exhibited a buildup of thiotepa that did not exist in the other species. It was speculated that a mechanism is present in boll weevils that initially degrades thiotepa but then is inactivated by the thiotepa or inhibited.

Nitrosamines

N-Nitrosamines have recently attracted much attention because of their carcinogenic and mutagenic action,[60] and because their presence has been suggested in tobacco smoke,[61] in tobacco,[62] in fish meals,[63,64] and in wheat kernels.[65]

In fish meal, the occurrence of dimethyl-N-nitrosamine may, in the majority of cases, be explained by the occurrence of dimethylamine and the use of sodium nitrite as a preservative. However, the demonstration of dimethyl-N-nitrosamine in meal from fish where no nitrite has been added raises the problem of the nature of the nitrite precursor, whether it is nitrate or some other compound.

Samples of sodium nitrite preserved herring meal that had caused hepatic toxicity in sheep similar to that produced by dimethylnitrosamine were shown to contain 30–100 ppm of dimethylnitrosamine after prolonged storage at 2 to 4° C.[63] Although diethylnitrosamine was not found in any of the samples, other unidentified nitroso compounds were detected. Sakshaug and co-workers concluded from these studies that a relationship existed between dimethylnitrosamine and the toxic effects of some batches of herring meal. This possibility suggests the general need for investigations as to whether dialkylnitrosamines are formed in other foods or feeds where sodium nitrite is used for preservation.

Devik[66] has studied the possibility that the necessary precursors for N-nitrosamines in fish meals might be formed by side reactions occurring during the condensation of amino acids and of aldoses (the Maillard reaction). This condensation is assumed to be an initial step for the subsequent formation of pigments responsible for the browning of various food products.

In the case of the diethyl-N-nitrosamine in wheat, nitrite has been shown to be present, but here the problem is to identify the source of the diethylamine.

In the case of tobacco, the occurrence of N-nitrosamines is more readily explained by the presence in tobacco of various secondary amines and of nitrate.

Druckrey and Preussmann[67] first suggested that during the burning of tobacco conditions exist that could produce nitrosamines. Tobacco is known to contain nitrates plus a number of amines that, when burned in tobacco in an atmosphere of limited oxygen, favor the production of nitrosamines. However, the establishment of the presence of nitrosamines in cigarettes *per se* has been difficult because of the paucity of procedures for their measurement in a very complex mixture. For example, Serfontein and Hurter[68] indicated the probable presence in cigaratte smoke condensate of at least three nitrosamines. It was estimated that 1–5 μg of N-nitrosopiperidine could be formed per cigarette under the given conditions.

Neurath and co-workers[69,70] have shown (in model experiments) that the conditions for the formation of nitrosamines in tobacco smoke require an equimolar mixture of NO and NO_2 plus a secondary amine to yield two moles of the corresponding nitrosamine. The reaction was found to be time-dependent and temperature-sensitive and required the exclusion of oxygen. Under normal smoking conditions, very little of the nitrosamines could be detected. However, when smoke condensate was collected in a cold trap, some nitrosamines were found. In the latter instance, more time for interaction could prevail. However, Neurath suggested that the nitrosamines formed under these conditions were probably artifacts produced primarily by oxidation of NO to NO_2 in the cold trap, generating a required intermediate for the production of nitrosamines. It had been earlier reported by Norman and Keith[71] that only NO is found in tobacco smoke under normal smoking conditions (very little, if any, NO_2 could be found).

Evidence for the occurrence of nitrosamines in unburned tobacco has been reported by Serfontein and Smit.[62]

Unburned Burley tobacco yielded, on chromatographic analysis, a zone of compounds that appeared to be nitrosamines. The possibility was suggested that nitrosamines in tobacco smoke condensate could originate in part from material in the tobacco plant *per se*.

Neurath and colleagues[69] identified N-nitrosdibutyl amine in cigarette smoke condensate in a 10–15% yield following its addition to a cigarette. Much of the loss was attributed to side-stream smoke or to combustion processes. It was also found that the recovery of N-nitrosodimethylamine was considerably poorer than for the corresponding dibutyl compound.

The presence of N-nitrosamines in tobacco smoke has been most recently studied by Johnson and associates.[72]

Examination of neutral smoke condensates, utilizing a highly selective gas chromatographic system[73] (a detector selective for amine compounds, including nitrosamines, and eliminating many classes of nitrogen compound in addition to standard hydrocarbons, chlorine, and phosphorus containing compounds), revealed no detectable nitrosamine peaks.

From the available literature, it appears that if nitrosamines are present in tobacco smoke under conditions similar to those prevailing in cigarettes smoked by humans, they are present in concentrations not exceeding 0.01 μg/cigarette (for cigarettes not enriched with nitrates). This quantity would be increased somewhat for nitrate-enriched cigarettes.

Because of the importance of nitrosamines and the known high incidence of lung cancer in smokers, the unequivocal establishment of their presence in smoke is of importance. Hence, additional studies are required to improve methods of collection and cleanup of samples as well as to enhance detection procedures greatly both in regard to selectivity and sensitivity. However, the unequivocal identification of nitrosamines in cigarette smoke at a certain level still requires the further establishment as to whether they contribute to the total carcinogenicity of the tobacco smoke.

Summary

Man is subjected to a whole galaxy of environmental agents such as pesticides, food additives, water, and air pollutants, and perhaps various synergistic combinations of these. Attention has been focused on only a very small number from one category: the alkylating agents. Their degradation, alkylation-reaction products, and residues were described with a view toward both drawing attention to possible areas of concern and the need for more intensive development of analytical methodology and toxicologic investigations.

References

1. Brooks, P. & P. D. Lawley. 1964. Alkylating agents. Brit. Med. Bull. **20:** 91–95.
2. Dickens, F. 1964. Carcinogenic lactones and related substances. Brit. Med. Bull. **20:** 96–101.
3. Wheeler, G. P. 1962. Studies related to the mechanisms of action of cytotoxic alkylating agents." Cancer Res. **22:** 651–688.
4. Hochester, R. M. & J. H. Quastel. 1963. Metabolic Inhibitors. Academic Press. New York, N. Y.
5. Stacey, K. A., M. Cobb, S. F. Cousens & P. Alexander. 1958. The reactions of the radiomimetic alkylation agents with macromolecules in vitro. Ann. N. Y. Acad. Sci. **68:** 682–701.
6. Magee, P. N. 1966. Alkylation of nucleic acids and carcinogenesis. Colloquium der Gesellschaft für Physiologische Chemie. April 21–23. Mosbach/Baden: 80–95.

7. PATTY, F. A. 1967. Industrial Hygiene and Toxicology. 2nd edit. Interscience. New York, N. Y. 1623–1634, 1642–1648, 2171–2178.
8. HAYES, W. J., JR. 1964. The toxicology of chemosterilants. Bull. WHO **31:** 721–736.
9. HEATH, D. F. 1961. Mechanism of the hepatotoxic action of dialkylnitrosamines. Nature (London) **192:** 170.
10. TORKELSON, T. R., R. A. HOYLE & V. K. ROWE. 1968. Toxicological hazards and properties of fumigants. Pest Control. July: 1–8.
11. MILLER, J. A. & E. C. MILLER. 1965. Metabolism of drugs in relation to carcinogenicity. Ann. N. Y. Acad. Sci. **123:** 125–140.
12. VAN DUUREN, B. L., N. NELSON, L. ORRIS, E. D. PALME & F. L. SCHMITT. 1963. Carcinogenicity of epoxides, lactones and peroxy compounds. J. Nat. Cancer Inst. **31:** 41–55.
13. GOODMAN, L. S. & A. GILMAN. 1967. The Pharmacological Basis of Therapeutics. 3rd edit. Macmillan Co. New York, N. Y. 1357–1358.
14. WESLEY, F., B. ROURKE & O. DARBISHIRE. 1965. The formation of persistent toxic chlorohydrins in foodstuffs by fumigation with ethylene oxide and propylene oxide. J. Food Sci. **30:** 1037–1042.
15. RAGELIS, E. P., B. S. FISHER & B. A. KLIMECK. 1968. Isolation and determination of chlorohydrin in foods fumigated with ethylene oxide or with propylene oxide. J. Ass. Offic. Anal. Chemists **51:** 709–715.
16. GORDON, H. T., W. W. THORNBURG & L. N. WERUM. 1959. Hydroxyethyl derivatives in prunes fumigated with C^{14}-ethylene oxide. J. Ag. Food Chem. **7:** 196–200.
17. CAMPBELL, P. N. & F. G. YOUNG. 1952. Metabolic studies with 3-methyl glucose. Biochem. J. **52:** 439–444.
18. HEUSER, S. G. & K. A. SCUDAMORE. 1968. Fumigant residue in wheat and flour: solvent extraction and gas chromatographic determination of free methyl bromide and ethylene oxide. Analyst **93:** 252–258.
19. HEUSER, S. G. & K. A. SCUDAMORE. 1967. Determination of ethylene chlorohydrin, ethylene dibromide and other volatile fumigant residues in flour and whole wheat. Chem. Industr.: 1557.
20. WISEBLATT, L. 1967. Reduction of microbial populations in flours incorporated into refrigerated foods. Cereal Chem. **44:** 269–280.
21. BOBIER, M. A. & A. L. LEPIGRE. 1957. Fermentation of Tobacco and Other Plant Products. Ger. Patent 1,020,554. Dec. 5 Chem. Abstr. **54:** 2318 (1960).
22. GROSS, P. M. & L. F. DIXON. 1934. Method of Reducing the Nicotine Content of Tobacco. U. S. Patent 1,962,145. June 28. Chem. Abstr. **28:** 4842.
23. SAMFIELD, M. M., E. E. LOCKLAN AND B. A. BROCK. 1957. Decreasing the Nicotine Content of Tobacco Smoke. U. S. Patent 2,760,495. August 28. Chem. Abstr. **51:** 677A.
24. OBI, Y., Y. SHIMADA, K. TAKAHASHI, K. NISHIDA & T. KISAKI. 1968. Reaction products of nicotine with ethylene oxide and their pyrolysis. Tobacco **166:** 26–30.
25. ROSE, T. H., R. GOLDSTEIN & C. BAILEY. 1953. Hemolysis of blood due to exposure to different types of plastic tubing and the influence of ethylene oxide sterilization. J. Thoracic. Cardiov. Surg. **45:** 245–251.
26. CLARKE, C., W. DAVIDSON & J. B. JOHNSTON. 1966. Haemolysis of blood following exposure to an Australian manufactured plastic tubing sterilized by means of ethylene oxide gas. Aust. So. New Zeal. J. Surg. **36:** 53–55.
27. BAIN, B. & L. LOWENSTEIN. 1967. Effect of type of culture tubes to the mixed leucocyte reaction. Rept. to Med. Res. Council of Canada (Grant MBT 1664).
28. O'LEARY, R. K. & W. L. GUESS. 1968. Toxicological studies on certain medical grade plastics sterilized by ethylene oxide. J. Pharm. Sci. **57:** 12–17.
29. KULKARNI, R. K., D. BARTAK, D. K. OUSTERHOUT & F. LEONARD. 1968. Determination of residual ethylene oxide in catheters by gas liquid chromatography. J. Biomed. Mater. Res. **2:** 165–171.
30. SYKES, G. 1964. Disinfection and Sterilization. J. P. Lippincott Co. Philadelphia, Pa. 202–227.

31. Downey, P. M. 1950. 2-(2-Hydroxyethyl-Mercapto)-Thiazole. U. S. Patent 2,513,922. July 4. Chem. Abstr. **44:** 9484C.
32. Cunliffe, A. C. & F. Wesley. 1967. Hazards from plastics sterilized by ethylene oxide. Brit. Med. J. : 575–576.
33. Gunther, D. 1965. Determination of adsorbed ethylene and propylene oxides. Anal. Chem. **37:** 1172–1174.
34. Machell, G. 1960. Properties and reactions of Beta propiolactone. Indust. Chem. **36:** 13–20.
35. Dickens, F. & H. E. H. Jones. 1961. Carcinogenic activity of a series of reactive lactones and related substances. Brit. J. Cancer **15:** 85–100.
36. Dickens, F. 1967. Drugs with lactone groups as potential carcinogens. UICC Monograph. R. Truhaut, Ed. **7:** 144–151. Springer-Verlag. Berlin, Germany.
37. Roe, F. J. C. & M. H. Salaman. 1958. Sterilization of arterial grafts. Brit. Med. J. **1:** 942–943.
38. Hoffman, L. M. Buchanan & D. R. Spiner. 1966. Beta propiolactone vapor decontamination. Appl. Microbiol. **14:** 989–992.
39. Kelly, A. R. & F. W. Hartman. 1951. Beta propiolactone: its toxicity, degradation products and comparison with nitrogen mustard. Fed. Proc. **10:** 361.
40. Kelly, A. R. & F. W. Hartman. 1952. Biological effects of Beta propiolactone. Fed. Proc. **11:** 419.
41. Kelly, A. R. 1952. Effects of virucide Beta propiolactone and its degradation products on blood platelets. Fed. Proc. **11:** 419.
42. Beroza, M. & A. B. Bořkovec. 1964. The stability of tepa and other aziridine chemosterilants. J. Med. Chem. **7:** 44–49.
43. Craig, A. W. & H. Jackson. 1955. The metabolism of P^{32}-labelled triethylene phosphoramide in relation to its antitumor activity. Brit. J. Pharmacol. **10:** 321–325.
44. Chang, S. C., A. B. Bořkovec & C. W. Woods. 1966. Fate of tepa uniformly labeled with C^{14}- in male house flies. J. Econ. Entom. **59:** 937–944.
45. Hedin, P. A., G. Wiygul, D. A. Vickers, A. C. Bartlett & N. Mitlin. 1966. Sterilizing effect of the chemosterilant tepa on the male boll weevil with respect to dosage, permanency of sterility, gonadal changes and its biological turnover. J. Econ. Entom. **60:** 209–214.
46. Collier, C. W. & R. Tardif. 1967. Analysis of male gypsy moths for microgram quantities of tepa. J. Econ. Entom. **60:** 28–30.
47. Ladd, T. L., C. W. Collier & E. L. Plasket. 1968. Mass sterilization of Japanese beetles with tepa and the determination of residue. J. Econ. Entom. **61:** 942–946.
48. Chang, S. C. & A. B. Bořkovec. 1966. Determination of Tepa Residues on Chemosterilized Mexican Fruit Flies. J. Econ. Entom. **59:** 102–104.
49. Cox, H. C., J. R. Young & M. C. Bowman. 1967. Persistence of tepa in fall armyworm moths. J. Econ. Entom. **60:** 1111–1115.
50. Maitlen, J. & L. M. McDonough. 1967. Residues of tepa on chemosterilized codling moths. J. Econ. Entom. **60:** 1391–1393.
51. Epstein, J., R. W. Rosenthal & R. J. Ess. 1955. Use of γ-(4-nitrobenzyl)-pyridine as analytical reagent for ethyleneimines and alkylating agents. Anal. Chem. **27:** 1435–1439.
52. Bořkovec, A. B., S. C. Chang & A. M. Limburg. 1964. Effect of pH on sterilizing activity of tepa and metepa in male house flies. J. Econ. Entom. **57:** 815–817.
53. Plapp, F. W., Jr., W. S. Bigley, G. A. Chapman & G. W. Eddy. 1962. Metabolism of metaphoxide in mosquitoes, house flies and mice. J. Econ. Entom. **55:** 607–613.
54. Chamberlain, W. F. & E. W. Hamilton. 1964. Absorption, excretion and metabolism of P^{32}-metepa by screw-worm and stable flies. J. Econ. Entom. **57:** 800–803.
55. Dame, D. A. & C. H. Schmidt. 1964. Uptake of metepa and its effect on two species of mosquitoes (*Anopheles quadrimaculatus,* Aedes *aegypti*) and house flies (*Musca domestica*). J. Econ. Entom. **57:** 77–81.
56. Morgan, P. B., M. C. Bowman & G. C. LaBrecque. 1968. Uptake and persistence of metepa in the house fly. J. Econ. Entom. **61:** 805–808.

57. Benckhuijsen, C. 1968. Acid catalyzed conversion of triethylene amine thiophosphoramide (thio-tepa). Biochem. Pharmacol. **17:** 55–64.
58. Mellett, L. B. & L. A. Woods. 1960. Comparative physiological disposition of thiotepa and tepa in the dog. Cancer Res. **20:** 524–532.
59. Parish, J. C. & B. W. Arthur. 1965. Mammalian and Insect Metabolism of the Chemosterilant Thiotepa. J. Econ. Entom. **58:** 976–979.
60. Druckrey, H., R. Preussmann, S. Ivankovic & D. Schmähl. 1967. Organotropic carcinogenic effects of 65 different N-nitroso compounds on BD Rats. Z. Krebsforsch. **69:** 103–201.
61. Neurath, G., B. Pirmann, W. Luttich & H. Wichern. 1965. Zur Frage der N-Nitrosoverbindungen im Tabakrauch. II. Beitr. Tabaksforsch **3:** 251–262.
62. Serfontein, W. J. & H. Smit. 1967. Evidence for the occurrence of nitrosamines in tobacco. Nature (London) **214:** 169–170.
63. Sakshaug, J., E. Sognen, M. A. Hansen & N. Koppang. 1965. Dimethylnitrosamine—its hepatoxic effect in sheep and its occurrence in toxic batches of herring meal. Nature (London) **206:** 1261–1262.
64. Ender, G., G. Havre, A. Helgebosted, N. Koppang, R. Madsden & L. Ceh. 1964. Isolation and identification of a hepatoxic factor in herring meal produced from sodium nitrate preserved herring. Naturwissenschaften **51:** 637–638.
65. Marquardt, P. & L. Hedler. 1966. Über das Vorkommen von Nitrosaminen. Arzneimittelforschung **16:** 778–779.
66. Devik, O. G. 1967. Formation of N-Nitrosamines by the Maillard Reaction. Acta Chem. Scand. **21:** 2302–2303.
67. Druckrey, H. & R. Preussmann. 1962. Production of lung cancer in rats by means of subcutaneous injection of N,N-diamylnitrosamine. Naturwissenschaften **49:** 498–499.
68. Serfontein, W. J. & P. Hurter. 1966. Nitrosamines as environmental carcinogens. II. Evidence for the presence of nitrosamines in tobacco smoke condensate. Cancer Res. **26:** 575–579.
69. Neurath, G., B. Pirmann & H. Wichern. 1964. Zur Frage der N-Nitrosoverbindungen in Tabakrauch. Beitr. Tabakrauch. Beitr. Tabaksforsch. **2:** 311–319.
70. Neurath, G. 1967. Zur Grage des Vorkummens von N-Nitroso-Verbindungen in Tobakrauch. Experientia **23:** 400–404.
71. Norman, V. and C. H. Keith. 1965. Nitrogen oxides in tobacco smoke. Nature (London) **205:** 915–916.
72. Johnson, D. E., J. D. Millan & J. W. Rhoades. 1968. Nitrosamines in tobacco smoke. *In* Toward a Less Harmful Cigarette. Nat. Cancer Inst. Monograph **28:** 181–189.
73. Johnson, D. E., J. W. Rhoades & R. J. Wheeler. 1967. A comparison of selective detectors for nitrogen-containing compounds. 154th National ACS Meeting. Sept. 14. Chicago, Ill.

ANALYSIS OF ALKYLATING AGENTS: APPLICATIONS TO AIR POLLUTION

E. Sawicki and C. R. Sawicki

U. S. Department of Health, Education, and Welfare
Consumer Protection and Environmental Health Service
National Air Pollution Control Administration
Chemical and Physical Research and Development Program
Cincinnati, Ohio

Since a large number of alkylating agents and analogous compounds are known that can cause discomfort, injury, or death to human beings (TABLE 1), their presence in the human environment must be kept at some minimum level through judicious use of controls, with the help of analytical techniques.

A variety of methods has been developed to determine trace amounts of alkylating agents of known structure that have been added to the human internal and external environments. The development of analytical procedures for these molecules and their products is then based on knowledge concerning the physical properties of these molecules and the test mixtures in which they are present. To determine whether trace amounts of unknown alkylating agents are present in some particular human environment, it is necessary to develop general analytical methods to detect these compounds. Once alkylating agents are known to be present in the unknown mixture, then general methods of colorimetric and/or fluorimetric analysis can be developed to study the variation in concentration of this family of alkylating agents in the environment. The next step is the characterization of the unknowns. With this knowledge, specific analytical procedures can then be developed for the assay of these compounds.

EXPERIMENTAL*

Chemicals. All alkylating agents were obtained from Aldrich Chemical Company or from Consolidated Midland Corporation, Katonah, N. Y. 4-p-Nitrobenzylpyridine, 1,3-propanediamine and tetraethylenepentamine were obtained from Matheson, Coleman and Bell. 4-Pyridinealdehyde 4-nitrophenylhydrazone, 4-pyridinealdehyde 2-benzothiazolylhydrazone, 4-acetylpyridine 4-nitrophenylhydrazone and 4-acetylpyridine 2-benzothiazolylhydrazone were synthesized by literature procedures.[23]

Equipment. Absorption spectral measurements were obtained with a Cary Model 11 spectrophotometer.

Silica gel plates were obtained from the Brinkmann Company.

Location reagents. R_1 = 0.1% 4-pyridinealdehyde p-nitrophenylhydrazone in acetone.

* Mention of commercial products does not constitute endorsement by the Public Health Service.

TABLE 1

ALKYLATING AGENTS: THEIR BIOLOGICAL EFFECTS, USAGE AND ASSAY

Alkylating Agent	Biological Effects	Usage*	Assay Method
Epoxides	carcinogens,[1–4] mutagens[5–7]	CT[8]	colorimetry[9]
Episulfides	–	CT[8]	–
Aziridines	antimitotagens,[5] mutagens[5–7]	CT,[10] insect chemosterilant[11]	colorimetry[12]
Diazoalkanes	alkylation of RNA[13] and DNA[14]	–	colorimetry[15]
N. Mustards	vesicants, antimitotagens,[5] mutagens,[5] carcinogens,[16]† obesifier[17]‡	CT[18]	colorimetry[12]
S. Mustards	vesicants,[19] Carcinogens[16]	CT[20]	colorimetry[21]
α-Haloacyl derivatives	lachrymators[19]	–	colorimetry[22,23]
Phosphates, thiophosphates	–	pesticides[24]	colorimetry[25]
Fluoro- and cyanophosphates	–	nerve gases[26]	fluorimetry[27]
Alkyl halides	toxic	–	colorimetry[12,23]
Benzyl halides	lachrymators,[19] vesicants[19]§	–	colorimetry[12,23,30]
Pyrrolizidine alkaloids	carcinogens[29]	–	colorimetry[30]
Alkane sulfonates	antimitotagens,[5] mutagens,[5] carcinogens[31]	CT[32]	colorimetry[12,23,30]
Benzene sulfonates	–	–	colorimetry[23,30]
Sulfates	–	–	colorimetry[12,23]
α-Halo ethers	vesicants,[19] carcinogens[33]	–	colorimetry,¶ fluorimetry¶
1-Nitroso-1-halo alkanes	vesicant,[19] orticant[36]		colorimetry[36]
Nitrosamines	carcinogens[16,37,38]	CT[5]	colorimetry¶
Triazine halides		Herbicides[39]	colorimetry[23,39]
Lactones	carcinogens,[1–3,40,41]		
Polyhaloalkanes	toxic		colorimetry[42,43]
Iodoform			colorimetry[23,30]
Aryl halides	vesicants		colorimetry[23]
Acylating agents	vesicants		colorimetry[12,44]
Sulfenyl halides			colorimetry[45]
Chloroarsines	vesicants[19]		colorimetry[12]
Chlorosilanes			colorimetry[12]

* CT = Tried in cancer treatment.

† Uracil mustard is carcinogenic.[16]

‡ Bipiperidyl mustard.[17]

§ Example is the skin irritation by 9-bromofluorene.[28]

¶ This paper. Modifications of previously published colorimetric[34] and fluorimetric[35] procedures.

R_2 = 0.25% 4-pyridinealdehyde 2-benzothiazolylhydrazone in acetone. This is approximately the maximum amount that will dissolve in hot acetone.
R_3 = 2% 4-p-nitrobenzylpyridine in acetone;
R_4 = 0.05% 4-acetylpyridine 2-benzothiazolylhydrazone in acetophenone;
R_5 = 0.1% 4-acetylpyridine 4-nitrophenylhydrazone in acetophenone;
5% aqueous ammonium acetate;
10% 1,3-propanediamine in acetone;
10% triethylamine in acetophenone;
10% tetraethylenepentamine in acetone.

Location Procedures. Silica Gel Spraying Method. Spray silica gel plate with R_1, R_2 or R_3 until slightly wet. Spray with 5% aqueous ammonium acetate. Let acetone evaporate. Heat plate at 110° C for 10 minutes. Spray with 10% 1,3-propanediamine in acetone. From the appropriate color (TABLE 2), the presence of alkylating agents can be ascertained.

DETECTION PROCEDURE ON A SPOT PLATE. To a drop of R_1 or R_2 in acetophenone or R_3 or R_4 add a drop of the test solution in acetophenone. Read color. Add a drop of 10% triethylamine in acetophenone and read color again.

Detection Procedure on Paper. The paper is impregnated with an acetone solution containing p-nitrobenzylpyridine or one of the hydrazones in the given percentages. A drop of the test solution is placed on the dry paper. Heat at 110° C for 10 minutes. Read color. Dip in 10% 1,3-propanediamine in acetone. This last step intensifies the color.

Location of Aziridines on Silica Gel Plates.[11] Spray with 0.1 M aqueous potassium hydrogen phthalate and then with a 5% acetone solution of 4-(p-nitrobenzyl)pyridine. Heat at 110° C for 30 minutes, cool and spray with M aqueous potassium carbonate. Spots containing aziridines turned blue.

Location of Chloro-1,3,5-triazines and Dialkyl Thiophosphates on Silica Gel Plates.[48] Spray with 2% 4-(p-nitrobenzyl)pyridine in acetone. Let air dry. Heat in an oven at 110° C for 15 minutes. Once the plate is cool, spray with 10% tetraethylenepentamine in acetone. For most compounds of these types, red spots are obtained; for zinophos, a blue spot.

Determination of α-Chloroalkyl Ethers. Following separation or distillation, the ether is collected in warm water. To 1 ml of this aqueous test solution add 1 ml of aqueous 0.8% 3-methyl-2-benzothiazolinone hydrazone hydrochloride, followed by 2 ml of 0.5% aqueous ferric chloride. Read the absorbance at λ max 625 mμ at 14–40 minutes after the addition of the last solution. Results are given in TABLE 3.

DISCUSSION

A fairly large number of alkylating agents is known (TABLE 1). Most of these compounds are volatile. The greater knowledge about the physiological activity of these chemicals most probably stems from the fact that they are more readily available than analogous high-boiling compounds and are more readily usable as antipersonnel weapons because of this volatility. The alkylating agents comprise the most numerous group of chemical mutagens.[70] Quite a few of them have definite carcinogenic activity. They appear to be active as such, or through the formation of transient intermediates. In each case the carbon atom adjacent to the hetero atom in these agents combines with electron-rich centers e.g. N, O, S, or an activated C atom. This type of reactivity is also useful in analytical work.

TABLE 2
REAGENTS FOR LOCATION OR DETECTION OF ALKYLATING AGENTS AND ANALOGOUS COMPOUNDS

Analyzed Compound	Reagent	Media	Color[a]	Determination Limit μg	Reference
Epoxides	Pyridine	–	–	–	46
1,2,3,4-Diepoxybutane	4-pyridineald. 2-benzothiazolylhydrazone, PBH	silica gel plate, SGP	R	0.2[b]	[c]
1,2,3,4-Diepoxybutane	4-(4-nitrobenzyl)pyridine, NBP	SGP	P	0.4[b]	[c]
Epoxyethylbenzene	NBP	SGP	P	16[b]	[c]
Aziridine	PBH	SGP	R	0.2[b]	[c]
Aziridine	NBP	SGP	P	0.2[b]	[c]
Aziridine	4-pyridineald. 4-nitro phenylhydrazone, PAN	SGP	G	0.2[b]	[c]
Aziridines	I_2 vapor	paper chromatogram, PC	–	–	11
Aziridines	NBP	PC	B	–	11
N-Carbamoylaziridines[d]	DDQ[e]	silicic acid plate, SAP	Br,[f] BG,[g] O[g]	–	47
N-Carbamoylaziridines[d]	tetracyanoethylene	SAP	Y to YG	–	47
N-Carbamoylaziridines[d]	gibbs R[h]	SAP	B → Pk;[i] O[j]	–	47
N-Carbamoylaziridines[d]	NBP	SAP	BV,[k] p[l]	–	47
N-Carbamoylaziridines[d]	rhodamine B	SAP	PR[m]	–	47
Tris-1-aziridinyl phosphine oxide	NBP	SGP	P	1[b]	[c]
Tris-1-aziridinyl phosphine oxide	PBH	SGP	R	0.2[b]	[c]
Tris-1-aziridinyl phosphine oxide	PAN	SGP	P	1[b]	[c]
Diazoalkanes, diazoketones and diazoesters	NBP	solution	P	–	15
1,6-Bis-(2-chloroethylamino)-1,6-dideoxy-D-mannitol	NBP	SGP	P	18[b]	[c]
1,6-Bis-(2-chloroethylamino)-1,6-dideoxy-D-mannitol	PAN	SGP	G	7[b]	[c]
1,6-Bis-(2-chloroethylamino)-1,6-dideoxy-D-mannitol	PBH	SGP	R	4[b]	[c]

Bis-2-chloroethylsulfide	NBP	SGP	P	24^{b}	[c]
Bis-2-chloroethylsulfide	PAN	SGP	G	24^{b}	[c]
Bis-2-chloroethylsulfide	PBH	SGP	R	5^{b}	[c]
α-Haloketones	1,1-Diphenylhydrazine	solution	Y	–	22
α-Bromoacetophenone	PBH	solution on paper	P	3^{b}	[c]
α-Bromoacetophenone	4-Acetylpyridine 2-benzothiazolyl hydrazone, ABH	solution on paper	V	1^{b}	[c]
Diazinon[n]	potassium iodoplatinate	SGP	B	~5	48
Diazinon	NBP	SGP	R	~5	48
Zinophos[o]	NBP	SGP	B	~5	48
Phosphate and thiophosphate pesticides[p]	NBP	PC or SGP	B	5	49
Phosphoryl fluorides and cyanides	Luminol	solution	BG[q]	0.5	26
Phosphoryl fluorides and cyanides	indole, alk. peroxide	solution	BG fl.	0.03	27
1-Iodo-n-hexadecane	NBP	SGP	P	2	[c]
1-Iodo-n-hexadecane	PAN	SGP	G	13	[c]
p-Nitrobenzyl bromide	PBH	solution on paper	P	2	[c]
p-Nitrobenzyl bromide	ABH	solution on paper	V	2	[c]
1,4-Tetramethylene-bis-methanesulfonate	NBP	SGP	P	3^{b}	[c]
1,4-Tetramethylene-bis-methanesulfonate	PBH	SGP	R	4^{b}	[c]
1,4-Tetramethylene-bis-methanesulfonate	PAN	SGP	G	7^{b}	[c]
Ethyl p-toluenesulfonate	NBP	SGP	B	2^{b}	[c]
Ethyl p-toluenesulfonate	PAN	SGP	G	13^{b}	[c]
Alkyl bisulfates	2,3,5-triphenyltetrazolium halide	solution	R	–	50
α-Halo ethers	3-Methyl-2-benzothiazolinone hydrazone, MBTH	solution on paper	B	–	[c]
α-Halo ethers	3-Methyl-2-benzothiazolinone hydrazone, MBTH	gas on alumina	B	–	[c]

TABLE 2 (*continued*)

Analyzed Compound	Reagent	Media	Color[a]	Determination Limit	Reference
				μg	
Cyanogen bromide	PBH	SGP	P	0.4[b]	[c]
Cyanogen bromide	ABH	SGP	B	0.4[b]	[c]
Cyanuric chloride	PBH	SGP	BG	0.05[b]	[c]
Cyanuric chloride	ABH	SGP	B	0.05[b]	[c]
Simazine[r]	NBP	SGP	R	~5	48
Atrazine[s]	NBP	SGP	R	~5	48
Propazine[t]	NBP	SGP	R	~5	48
1-Methyl-2-iodoquinolinium methosulfate	PBH	SGP	P	2[b]	[c]
1-Methyl-2-iodoquinolinium methosulfate	ABH	SGP	V	1[b]	[c]
Acetyl chloride	PBH	solution on paper	V	0.2	23
Acetyl chloride	ABH	solution on paper	V	0.2	23
Nonanoyl chloride	PBH	solution on paper	V	0.06	23
Nonanoyl chloride	ABH	solution on paper	V	0.06	23
Benzoyl chloride	PBH	solution on paper	V	0.3	23
Benzoyl chloride	NBP	solution on plate	O	0.5	[c]
Benzoyl chloride	ABH	solution on plate	V	0.3	[c]
Benzoyl chloride	PAN	solution on paper	P	0.5	[c]
Benzoyl chloride	ANH	solution on paper	V	1	[c]
α-Furoyl chloride	PBH	SGP	V	0.1	23
α-Furoyl chloride	ABH	SGP	B	0.3	23
p-Toluenesulfonyl chloride	PBH	SGP	P	7	23
p-Toluenesulfonyl chloride	ABH	SGP	V	7	23
Methanesulfonyl chloride	PBH	SGP	P	7	23
Methanesulfonyl chloride	ABH	SGP	V	4	23
Acetic anhydride	PBH	SGP	P	50	23
Acetic anhydride	ABH	SGP	V	50	23
Acetic anhydride	nickel dimethylglyoximate	solution	R	12	51

Methanesulfonic anhydride	PBH	SGP	P	1	23
Methanesulfonic anhydride	ABH	SGP	V	2	23
Trifluoroacetic anhydride[u]	PBH	SGP	OY	1	23
Trifluoroacetic anhydride[u]	ABH	SGP	OY	3	23
Phosgene	NBP	paper	R	V	52
Carbon suboxide	o-dianisidine and sodium perborate	solution	YBr	3	53
Carbon suboxide	Di-isonitrosoacetone	solution	R	30	53
Carbon suboxide	Indole and sodium perborate	solution	fluorescence	0.1	53

[a] B = blue, Br = brown, G = green, O = orange, P = purple, Pk = pink, R = red, V = violet and Y = yellow.
[b] $\mu g/cm^2$.
[c] This paper.
[d] 24 N-alkyl and N-aryl derivatives tested.
[e] 2,3-Dichloro–5,6-dicyano-1,4-benzoquinoneimine.
[f] Alkyl derivatives, after NH_3 = BG.
[g] Aryl derivatives, after NH_3 = OR.
[h] 2,6-Dibromo-N-chloro-p-benzoquinoneimine.
[i] Alkyl derivatives, after NH_3 = YG.
[j] Aryl derivatives, after NH_3 = Y to Br.
[k] Alkyl derivatives, after NH_3 = B.
[l] Aryl derivatives, after NH_3 = B.
[m] Orange fluorescence; after NH_3, no fluorescence.
[n] 0,0-Diethyl-0-(2-isopropyl-4-methylpyrimidyl-6)-thiophosphate.
[o] 0,0-Diethyl-0-(pyrazinyl-2)thiophosphate.
[p] All 20 gave positive results at 5 μg. Dipterex, malathion, dimethoate, methyl parathion, parathion, and diazinon gave positive results at 1 μg or less.
[q] Chemiluminescence
[r] 2-Chloro-4,6-bis(ethylamino)-1,3,5-triazine.
[s] 2-Chloro-4-ethylamino-6-isopropylamino-1,3,5-triazine.
[t] 2-Chloro-4,6-bis-isopropylamino-1,3,5-triazine.
[u] Many other acid chlorides and anhydrides tested.
[v] 0.25 ppm detected in air.

TABLE 3

DETERMINATION OF ALKYLATING AND ANALOGOUS AGENTS

Alkylating Agent	Reagent	Test Mixture	λ Max, mε	Reference
Epoxides	picric acid	heated fats	480, 18.8[a]	9
1-Phenyloxirane	NBP	–	572, 4.0	9
1-Phenoxymethyloxirane	NBP	–	572, 4.4	23
Aziridine[b]	NBP	–	565, ~34	12
Diazoalkanes	NBP	–	545	15
Tris(B-chlorethyl)amine, HN-3	NBP	–	565, ~35	12
Bis(B-chlorethyl)amine, nor HN-2	NBP	tissue	565	54
Methyl bis(B-chlorethyl)amine, HN-2	NBP	tissue	565	54
HN-2	NBP	biological fluids	540[c]	55
Nitrogen mustards	NBP	biological fluids	565	56
Phenylalanine mustard[d]	NBP	blood	565, 21.6	57
Uracil mustard	NBP	blood plasma	600, 21.8	58
Dopan[e]	NBP	blood plasma	590, 24.6	58
Chlorambucil[f]	NBP	blood plasma	590, 30.2	58
HN-3	NBP	blood plasma	570, 24.4	58
HN-2	NBP	blood plasma	570, 11.2	58
Bis-(2-haloethyl)amines[g]	8-quinolinol	–	468[h]	21
HN-2	4-hydroxybiphenyl, HB	biological fluids	F 285/340[i]	59
Sesquimustard, $CH_3CH(SCH_2CH_2Cl)_2$	o-dianisidine, cupric acetate	–	540	60
4′-Phenyl-2-bromoacetophenone	NBP	–	561, 6.0	23
α-Haloketones	1,1-diphenylhydrazine	–	–	22
Phosphate pesticides	NBP	fruit and vegetables	520	25
0,0-Dimethyl-2,2,2-trichloro-1-hydroxyethyl phosphonate	NBP	–	572, 8.0	23
Diazinon	NBP	–	571, 12.0	23

Alkyl alkoxy phosphoryl fluorides	benzidine, sodium perborate	–	~440[j]	61
Alkyl alkoxy phosphoryl fluorides[k]	indole, sodium perborate	–	~F 365/475	27
Dialkylamino alkoxy phosphoryl cyanides[k]	indole, sodium perborate	–	~F 365/475[l]	27
Nerve gases	Luminol	–	chemiluminescence	26
n-Butyl iodide	NBP	–	565, 7.3	12
1-Iodo-n-octadecane[m]	NBP	–	556, 123	23
1-Iodo-n-octadecane	PAN	–	625, 62	23
1-Iodo-n-octadecane	PBH	–	560, 1480	23
1-Iodo-n-octadecane	ABH	–	567,161	23
1-Iodo-n-octadecane	4-acetylpyridine 4-nitrophenyl-hydrazone, ANH	–	642,190	23
1-Iodo-n-octadecane	4-picoline and o-dinitrobenzene	–	617, 32.2	30
1-Bromo-n-octadecane	ANH	–	640, 33	23
1-Bromo-n-octadecane	4-picoline and o-dinitrobenzene	–	620, 20.8	30
1-Chloro-n-octadecane	ANH	–	642, 0.7	23
Iodoacetic acid[n]	NBP	–	558, 112	23
Benzyl chloride	NBP	–	561, 7.9	23
Benzyl chloride	quinoline	–	o	62
9-Bromofluorene	NBP	–	560, 4.6	23
Benzyl thiocyanate	NBP	–	516, 13.0	23
Ethyl methanesulfonate	ANH	–	640, 35[p]	23
Ethyl p-toluenesulfonate	ANH	–	642, 38[p]	23
Diethyl sulfate	NBP	–	570, 11[q]	23
Chloromethyl methyl ether	MBTH	–	625, 58	[c]
Bis-chloromethyl ether	MBTH	–	625, 97	[c]
Cyanuric chloride	NBP	–	490, 40	23
Atrazine	Pyridine, ethyl cyanoacetate	–	550	39
Dimethyl tetrachloroterephthalate[r]	NBP	–	565, ~55	63
sym.-Dimethylhydrazine	Chromotropic acid, CA	–	578, 15.7 (64)	65
sym.-Diethylhydrazine	4-Hydroxybiphenyl	–	570	65
sym.-Di-n-propylhydrazine	MBTH	–	666	65
Phenylazomethane	CA	–	578	65
Azoethane	4-Hydroxybiphenyl	–	570	65
Azopropane	MBTH	–	666	65

TABLE 3 *(continued)*

Alkylating Agent	Reagent	Test Mixture	λ Max, mε	Reference
1,1-Dimethylhydrazine	CA	–	578	66, 67
Trimethylhydrazine	CA	–	578	67
Tetramethylhydrazine	CA	–	578	67
Tetramethyltetrazene	CA	–	578	67
1-Chloro-1-nitrosoacetone	NBP	–	500, 6.0	36
Dichloroformoxime	NBP	–	520, 7.0	36
Iodoform[p]	ANH	–	640, 112	23
2,4-Dinitrochlorobenzene	NBP	–	547, 12	23
Acetyl chloride	NBP	–	451, 24	44
Benzoyl chloride	NBP	–	450, 15	44
Ethyl chloroformate	NBP	–	452, 13	44
Phosgene	Aniline	–	257	68
Phosgene[s]	NBP	–	450, 15	44
Carbon suboxide	o-dianisidine and sodium perborate[t]	–	–	53
Carbon suboxide	di-isonitroso acetone[u]	–	Red	53
Carbon suboxide	indole and sodium perborate[v]	–	fluorescent	53
Acyl anhydrides	4-sulfo-1-naphthylamine, sodium nitrite	–	–	69
Trichloromethanesulfenyl chloride	resorcinol	–	415	45

Footnotes to this table are on the opposite page.

Footnotes to TABLE 3

[a] Value obtained with the pure picric ether of propylene oxide.
[b] Similar values for the 2-ethyl-, 2,2-dimethyl- and N-ethyl derivatives of aziridine.
[c] Method detects less than 0.1 μg of nitrogen mustard in 1 ml of plasma, lymph, urine, or tissue homogenate.
[d] p-Di-(2-chloroethyl)phenylalanine. Also investigated were methyl bis(β-chloroethyl)amine, HN-2, and uracil mustard or 5-(bis(2-chloroethyl)amino uracil. HN-2 gave a molar absorptivity of 30,600.
[e] 5-Bis-(2-chloroethyl)amino-6-methyluracil.
[f] 4′-Bis-(2-chloroethyl)amino-3-phenylbutyric acid.
[g] Reaction stated to be specific for bifunctional type of compound.
[h] Limit of determination for nitrogen mustard was approximately 0.2 μ mole per ml.
[i] As little as 0.02 μg of drug/ml can be estimated.
[j] To produce color at least 1 to 2 μg of sarin, tabun, DFP, TEPP, HETP, paraoxon, or benzoyl chloride necessary while 10 μg of parathion is necessary.
[k] Nerve gases.
[l] As little as 0.05 μg of sarin, Me(iPrO)(PO)F in 10 ml of solution can be determined.
[m] Approximately 50 haloalkanes tested by this autocatalytic procedure.
[n] Can also be determined by other reagents in references 23 and 30.
[o] Can determine 2 μg.
[p] Compound can also be determined by NBP, PAN, PBH, ABH[23] or by the 4-picoline-o-dinitrobenzene methods.[30]
[q] Higher molar absorptivity probably obtained by Epstein and co-workers.[12]
[r] Data given on six other analogous compounds.
[s] Results given for 34 acylating agents. See also reference 52 for the determination of phosgene.
[t] Detection limit 3 μg.
[u] Detection limit 30 μg.
[v] Detection limit 0.1 μg.

TABLE 4
ANALYSIS OF ALKYLATING AGENTS AS ALDEHYDE PRECURSORS

Alkylating agent	Aldehyde	Reagent[a]	Reference
$ClCH_2$-O-CH_3	CH_2O	MBTH	b
$ClCH_2O$-CH_2Cl	CH_2O	MBTH	b
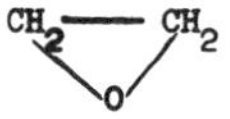	CH_2O	CA	71, 72
CH_2Cl_2	CH_2O	CA	73
Azoalkanes	RCHO, R'CHO	CA, HB, MBTH	65
Dialkylhydrazines	RCHO, R'CHO	CA, HB, MBTH	65, 67
Tri- and tetra-alkylhydrazines	RCHO, R'CHO	CA, HB, MBTH	67
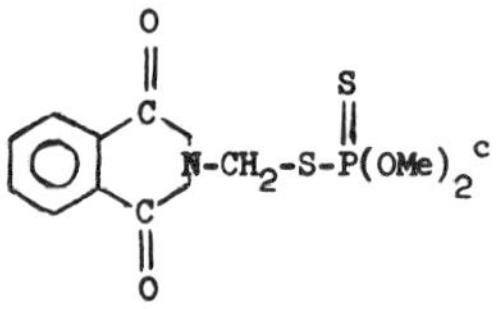 [c]	CH_2O	CA	74
p-$(Eto)_2P(=S)$-S-CH_2-S-C_6H_4-Cl[d]	CH_2O	CA	75
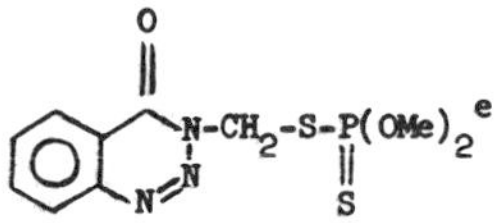 [e]	CH_2O	CA	75
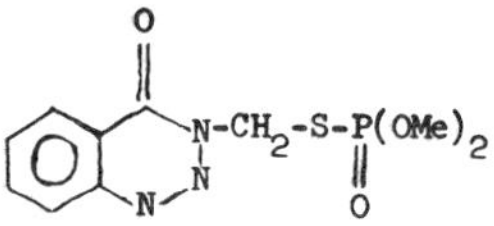	CH_2O	CA	75
p-$(Eto)_2P(=S)$-S-CH_2-S-C_6H_4-Cl[f]	CH_2O	CA	75
p-$(Eto)_2$-$P(=O)$-S-CH_2-S-C_6H_4-Cl	CH_2O	CA	75
$(Eto)_2$-$P(=S)$-S-CH_2-S-$P(=S)(OEt)_2$[g]	CH_2O	CA	75
$(Eto)_2$-$P(=O)$-S-CH_2-S-$P(=O)(OEt)_2$	CH_2O	CA	75

[a] MBTH is 3-methyl-2-benzothiazolinone hydrazone. Other terms are defined in previous tables; [b] This paper; [c] Imidan; [d] Phorate or thimet; [e] Guthion; [f] Trithion; [g] Ethion.

TABLE 5

ALDEHYDE REAGENTS THAT CAN BE USED IN THE ASSAY OF ALKYLATING AGENT ALDEHYDE PRECURSORS

Reagent	Aldehydes Analyzed	λ* max, mε or F† exc/em	Reference
Chromotropic acid	CH_2O	578, 15.7	64
J-Acid (dication endproduct)	CH_2O	468, 21.0	64
J-Acid (monocation endproduct)	CH_2O	612, 34.0	64
Phenyl J-Acid	CH_2O	660, 51.4	64
J-Acid (dication endproduct)	CH_2O	F 470/522	76
2,4-Pentanedione	CH_2O	F 410/510	35, 77
2,4-Pentanedione	CH_2O	412, 7.7	77, 78
1,1-Dimethoxy-3-butanone	CH_2O	F 400/480	‡
1,3-Cyclohexanedione, Procedure 1	aldehyde	F 395/460	35
1,3-Cyclohexanedione, Procedure 2	aldehyde	F 460/505	35
Dimedon, Procedure 1	aldehyde	F 395/460	35
Dimedon, Procedure 2	aldehyde	F 465/520	35
Phenylhydrazine	aliphatic aldehyde	520, 34.2	79
2-Hydrazinobenzothiazole	CH_2O +	582, 48.0	80
3-Methyl-2-benzothiazolinone hydrazone	aliphatic aldehyde	635, 670; 65.0, 65.0§	34, 81
4-Hydroxybiphenyl	CH_3CHO	570	65
1-Ethylquinaldinium iodide	CH_2O +	608, ~73	76
o-Aminobenzaldehyde	aliphatic aldehyde	440, 2.5	82
Oxaldihydrazide	aldehyde and ketones	610, 6.6§	83
Ninhydrin	C_2H_5CHO	595	84
Sodium nitroprusside, morpholine	CH_3CHO	575	85
Fructose, resorcinol, HCl	CH_3CHO	555	86

* Colorimetry
† Fluorimetry
‡ This paper
§ With formaldehyde

Determining the presence and quantity of an alkylating agent in material to which it has been knowingly added directly or indirectly simplifies the problem of detection and assay. Various nitrogen mustard derivatives have been assayed in this fashion in various biological fluids.[55–59]

Establishing the presence of alkylating agents of known structure in the human environment is difficult because of the lack of sensitive and selective procedures for measuring these compounds. Although little work has been done in the gas chromatographic analysis of volatile alkylating agents, this technique should eventually prove of value, not only in the establishment of the purity of a pure alkylating agent,[33] but also in its trace analysis.

Of interest to the investigator of our polluted environment are the alkylating agents of higher boiling point. Very little is known about the presence of these types of molecules in the environment, and very little is also known about the physiological activity of such molecules.

The same alkylating properties of use in assay are probably reflected in the biological effects and the usages of the alkylating agents (TABLE 1). Some of the more recently reported chemicals with carcinogenic, mutagenic, and teratogenic properties such as the aliphatic hydrazo, azo, and azoxy compounds[65,67] could be assayed through the aldehyde formed from them by the many methods available for aldehydes (TABLES 4 and 5). However, since they are alkylating agents *in vivo*,[87] it should be possible to assay them by forming the alkylating agent in the test tube.

Methods useful in the location or detection of alkylating agents on a thin-layer plate, on a paper chromatogram, or in solution are described in TABLE 2. Most of the methods involve the use of 4-p-nitrobenzylpyridine or a 4-pyridine-aldehyde or 4-acetylpyridine hydrazone as reagent. Heat is also necessary to insure formation of the chromogen. Much more selective and sensitive methods are needed in the field of trace analysis of complicated environmental mixtures.

The structures of many of the reagents that have been used in the determination of alkylating agents are shown in FIGURE 1. These include aza heterocyclic compounds to which the alkylating agent adds directly to form an azonium derivative. The azonium derivative can be measured directly or can be reacted with another reagent to form a chromogen (FIGURE 2) or, in the case of a pyridine as a reagent, the pyridinium ring can be split and measured as the glutaconaldehyde or as a glutaconaldehyde derivative (FIGURE 3).

The most common type of reagent containing an aza nitrogen consists of a pyridine ring attached through an insulating group in the 4-position to another conjugation system. Examples are 4-p-nitrobenzylpyridine and the 4-pyridine aldehyde and 4-acetylpyridine hydrazones. The type of reaction involved in the analysis is shown in FIGURE 4.[12] The chromogens formed in the determination of alkylating agents with 4-p-nitrobenzyl pyridine show a very strong solvent effect (FIGURE 5). There is a strong red shift in going from a carbonyl solvent to an aqueous solvent.

Another somewhat similar reaction is shown in FIGURE 6.[23] However, this reaction is autocatalytic when alkyl iodides are analyzed. The hydrogen iodide formed as a byproduct is oxidized by air to iodine; the iodine then reacts with the solvent acetophenone to form α-iodoacetophenone. This molecule then undergoes the reaction. A chromogen is formed that absorbs at about 557 millimicrons. In addition, hydrogen iodide is formed that is oxidized by air to iodine, which reacts with more solvent molecules, et cetera. Beer's law is not obeyed in the autocatalytic methods. However, in some cases, molar absorptivities of well

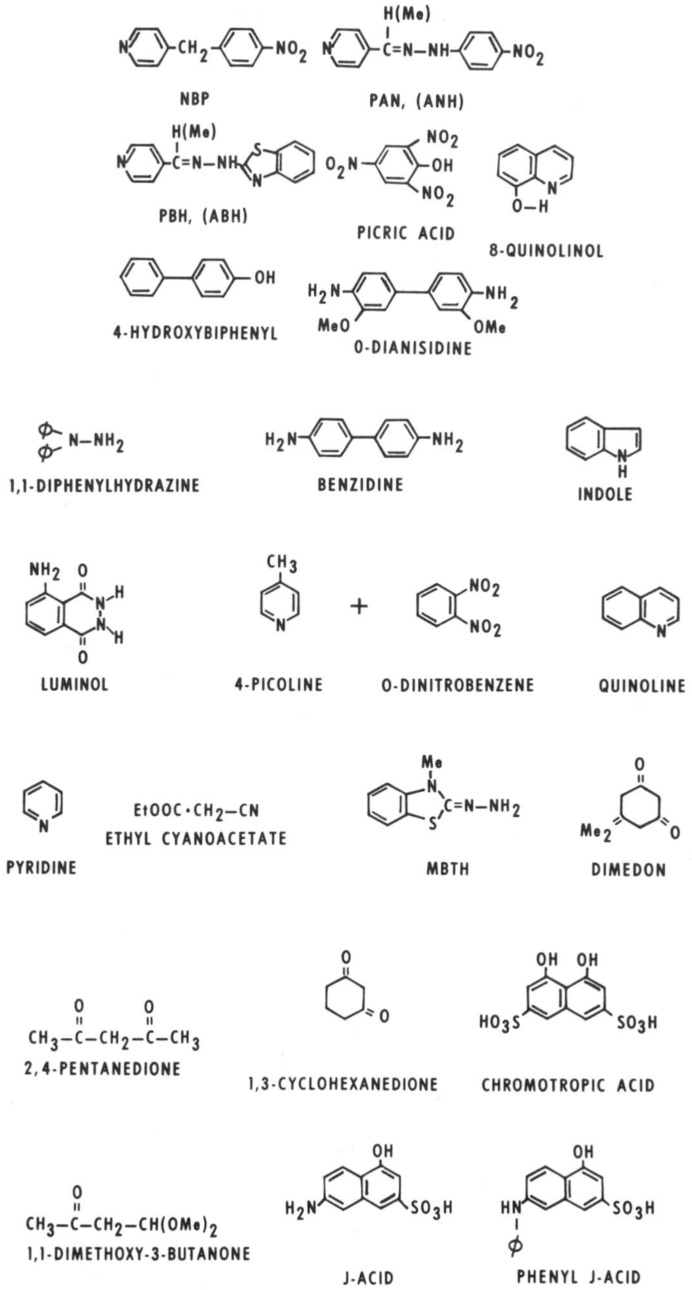

FIGURE 1. Reagents used in the assay for alkylating agents.

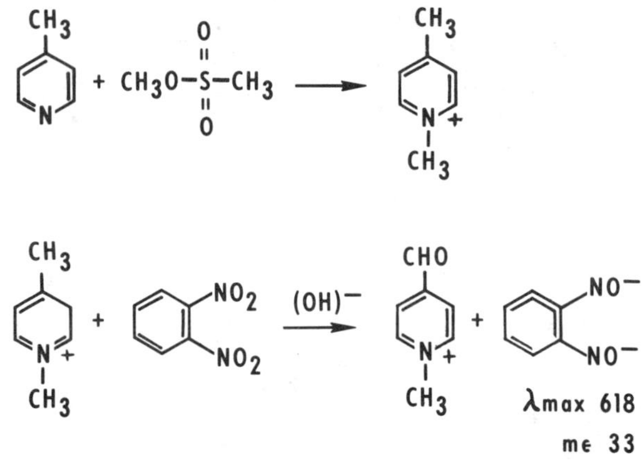

FIGURE 2. Determination of methyl mesylate with 4-picoline and o-dinitrobenzene.

over a million are obtained. The potentiality of these autocatalytic methods in the analysis of the various types of alkylating agents has not yet been explored. Extremely sensitive kinetic methods of analysis could be developed from the autocatalytic methods.

Another family of reactions involves the alkylation of phenols. Thus, epoxides can be measured through their alkylation of picric acid.[9] As can be seen in FIGURE 7, alkylated picric acid absorbs at much longer wavelength than does picric acid in alkaline solution. A second type of phenolic alkylation useful in the

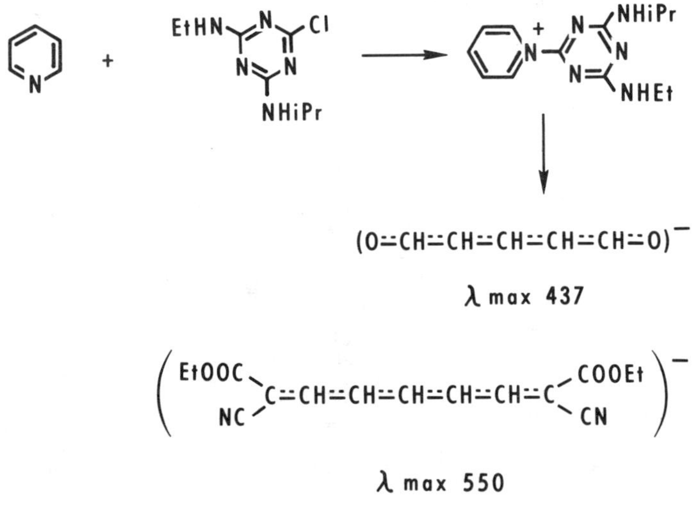

FIGURE 3. Determination of atrazine with pyridine and ethyl cyanoacetate.

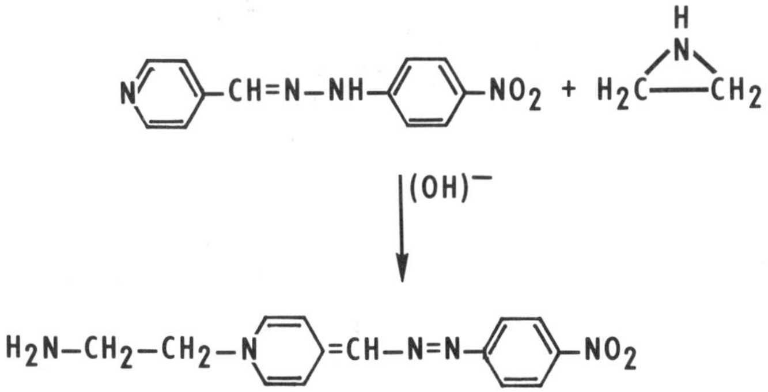

FIGURE 4. Determination of an alkylating agent with 4-pyridinealdehyde 4-nitrophenylhydrazone.

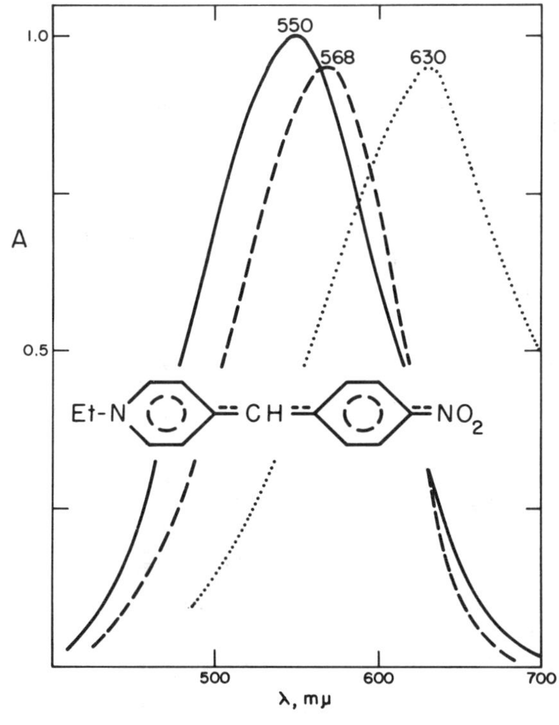

FIGURE 5. Visible absorption spectra of N-ethyl-4-(4-nitrobenzyl)-pyridinium p-toluenesulfonate (3×10^{-5}M). (——), in acetone containing 7.5% triethylamine. (- - - -), in acetophenone containing 0.25% cyclohexylamine. (· · · ·), in water-methanol (3:1) containing 7.5% of 10% aqueous tetraethylammonium hydroxide.[23]

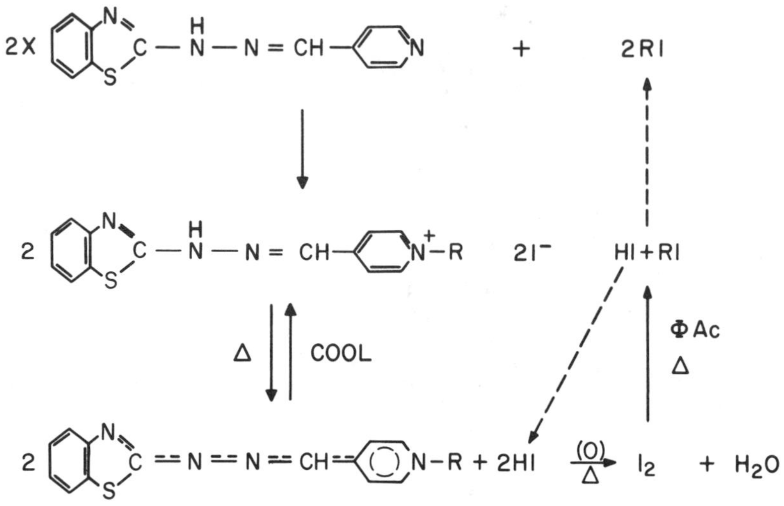

III

FIGURE 6. Autocatalytic reaction in the determination of an alkyl iodide with 4-pyridinealdehyde 2-benzothiazolylhydrazone.

analyses of these agents involves the liquid-liquid separation of the alkoxy derivative from a basic solution of the phenolic anion, followed by measurement of the fluorescence of the alkoxy derivative. This has been done with 4-hydroxybiphenyl as the reagent for the analysis of nitrogen mustard.[59]

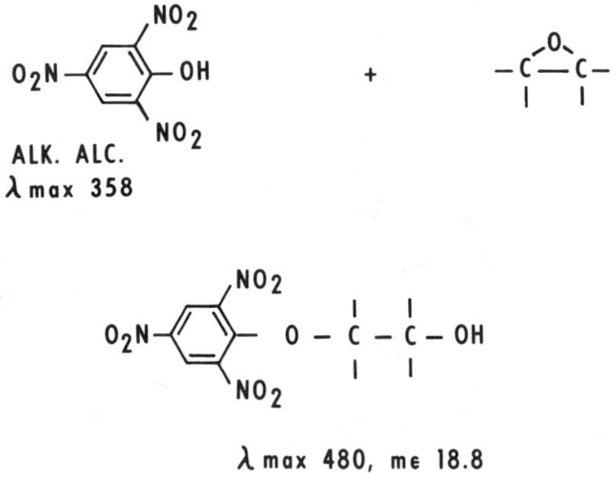

FIGURE 7. Determination of an epoxide with picric acid.

Oxidizing reactions have also been used in the analysis of alkylating and allied agents. Thus, sesquimustard is analyzed through the quinonic dye formed by oxidation of o-dianisidine with the help of cupric acetate.[60] Similarly, carbon suboxide is determined through the oxidation of o-dianisidine with the help of sodium perborate.[53] In the same way, nerve gas[27] and carbon suboxide[53] can be estimated through the oxidation of indole to highly fluorescent indoxyl or indigo white. Another assay of potential usefulness is the measurement of the chemiluminescence produced by the oxidation of luminol with the help of a nerve gas.[26]

An entirely different type of reagent useful in the analysis of alkylating agents is the type used for the analysis of aldehydes. With these reagents all alkylating agents that can be converted to aldehydes can be determined. A list of the various alkylating agents, the aldehydes derived from them and the reagent used to analyze the aldehyde is given in TABLE 4. A typical colorimetric reaction of this type is shown in FIGURE 8. A reaction ending in a fluorogen is shown in FIGURE 9.

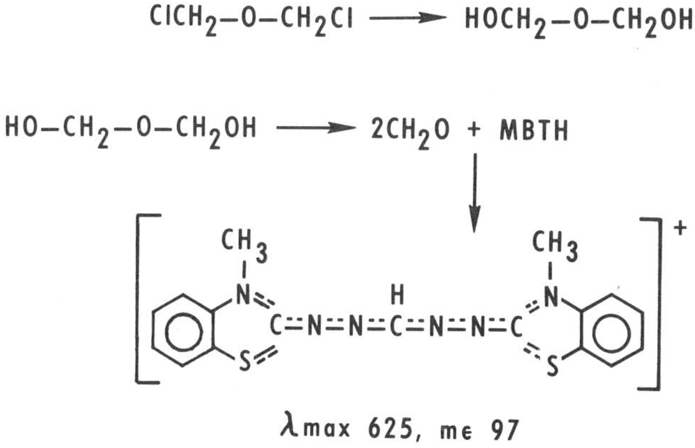

FIGURE 8. Colorimetric determination of bis(chloromethyl) ether.

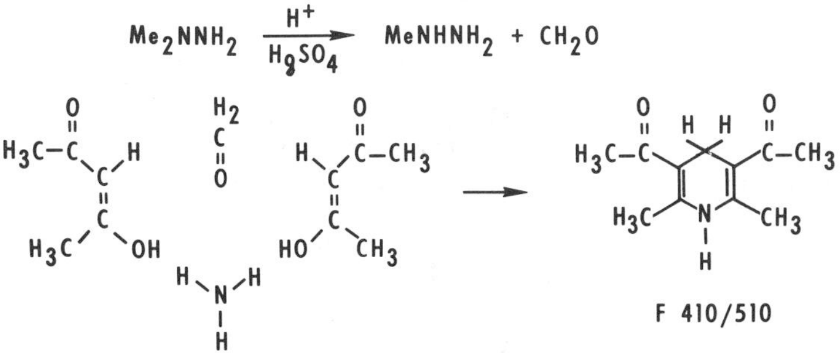

FIGURE 9. Fluorimetric determination of 1,1-dimethylhydrazine with 2,4-pentanedione.

A variety of reagents has been used in the determination of aldehydes. The results obtained with many of these is shown in TABLE 5. Only a few of these reagents have been applied to the analysis of alkylating agents. Their application would be advantageous from the viewpoint of increased sensitivity and selectivity.

The fluorimetric methods are more sensitive than the colorimetric ones. However, because of this sensitivity, the fluorimetric procedures have more of a blank problem. This is because air, distilled water, and many solvents are contaminated with low concentrations of aldehydes. Consequently, unless a clean laboratory and highly purified solvents and reagents are used, all blanks will show the presence of aldehydes when the highly sensitive fluorimetric methods are used.

Acyl halides are measured by reaction with the 4-p-nitrobenzylpyridine type of reagent. The presence of a carbonyl group on the aza N decreases the electron-donor strength of this resonance terminal and shifts the long wavelength maximum to shorter wavelengths. The further away the carbonyl group is from the aza N, the weaker is this effect as shown for I, II, and III:

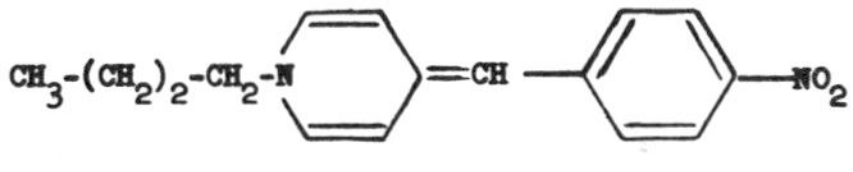

I. λ max 572

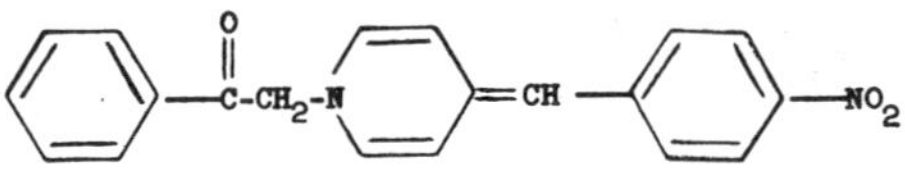

II. λ max 557

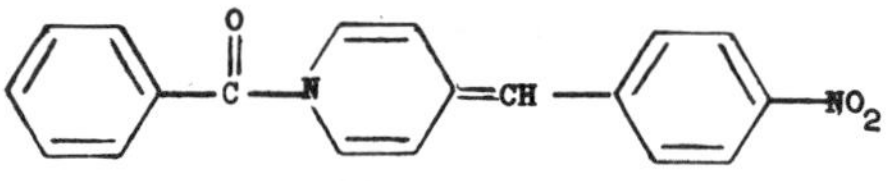

III. λ max 450

Acid anhydrides are analyzed by reaction with nitrite to form an acyl nitrite that is subsequently separated, hydrolyzed to nitrous acid, and then reacted with 4-sulfo-1-naphthylamine to form an azo dye.[69]

APPLICATION

Epoxides are found in environmental mixtures. Some PVC food-packaging film is plasticized with epoxidized glycerides. Traces of epoxides are generated in heated fats via the hydroperoxides.[9] A long chain inner epoxide was found to react with picric acid to the largest extent. Thus, the epoxide that most resembles those found in fats, reacts to the greatest extent. The physiological effect of these epoxides is not yet fully understood. The biological effects of such compounds known to be present[88,89] in autoxidized fats and oils is of importance because these materials are extensively used for human consumption.

Since fats and oils are present in many urban atmospheres, knowledge about the identity and physiological effects of their photooxidized products becomes of some concern, especially since the aliphatic and oxygenated fractions of some urban airborne particulates have been shown to be carcinogenic to mice.[88]

Large amounts of olefins are present in the atmosphere. For some communities the aliphatic fraction of the benzene-soluble extracts of urban airborne particulates is the largest fraction, much larger than the aromatic, acidic, neutral oxygenated, basic and water-soluble fractions.[89] Aliphatic fractions free of aromatic hydrocarbons have produced skin tumors in mice.[90] It was suggested that the activity of this material was due to the presence of epoxides that have been formed by the oxidation of olefins. In line with this is the report that ozonized gasoline is carcinogenic to animals.[91]

Because the aliphatic fraction is nonpolar and, on the basis of infrared spectral examination shows the absence of carbonyl compounds, it would appear that epoxides would probably be the carcinogenic component present in this fraction. Consequently, it was necessary to test for the presence of such alkylating agents in the aliphatic fraction. Tests were performed on 4–40 mg of sample. With the 4-(4-nitrobenzyl)pyridine procedure, aliphatic fractions of particulate samples obtained from submarine atmospheres, auto exhaust fumes, and urban atmospheres gave a positive test for alkylating agents.[23] A composite aliphatic fraction of urban airborne particulates obtained from approximately 200 American cities also gave a positive test in the procedure.

When tested for alkylating agents, aromatic, acidic, and neutral oxygenated fractions obtained from the benzene extract of urban airborne particulates also gave positive results. For samples that were colored a shade of yellow, the 4-acetylpyridine 4-nitrophenylhydrazone procedure was used. With this reagent, a neutral fraction from cigarette smoke tar gave a positive result. Many of the urban air fractions have been shown to have varying carcinogenic activity.[88] Whether some of this activity is due to the alkylating agents is still to be determined.

Data on tumor induction in mice following cutaneous administration of benzene or methylene chloride extracts of urban airborne particulates as reported in nine different publications by various groups have been summarized by Epstein and co-workers.[92] Local tumors were reported by all groups, while two groups reported pulmonary adenomas, and a third group, hepatomas, lymphomas, and pulmonary adenomas. Analytical and biological data indicate that a wide variety of carcinogens are present in polluted atmospheres. Some of these could be alkylating agents, especially since analytical data indicates that alkylating agents are present in air particulates.

Analysis of a composite benzene extract of the airborne particulates from about 200 American cities gave an average molecular formula of $C_{32.4}H_{48}O_{3.3}N_{0.16}S_{0.083}X_{0.065}(OR)_{0.12}$, where X represents chloride, bromide, and iodide reported in terms of chloride, and OR represents alkoxy groups reported in terms of the methoxy group. The average molecular weight of this material is about

460. A test for alkylating agents with the 4-acetylpyridine 4-nitrophenylhydrazone procedure gave positive results.

Due to the widespread use of pesticides in the control of insects and other pests, their presence in some river waters, foods, and atmospheres is to be expected. Of the pesticides that could be classified as alkylating agents, some polyhalides and the alkyl thiophosphates and phosphates are very prominent members. The alkylation properties of alkyl thiophosphates and phosphates have been reviewed.[93] Extensive spraying of DDT in various Florida communities has been used to control mosquitoes. At these times, therefore, extremely high concentrations of DDT are present in the atmosphere.

Many of the insecticidal dialkyl thiophosphates can be determined colorimetrically by their inhibiting effect on the enzyme cholinesterase. Thus, thiometon, disulfoton (di-syston) and carbophenothion (trithion) can be determined after collection from contaminated air.[94]

The paper, thin-layer, and gas chromatographic separation and the location, detection, and assay of these types of pesticides has been covered in many publications.[24,95,96]

Since N, N-dialkyl N-nitrosamines are carcinogenic alkylating agents, their presence in the human environment is of some concern. The probable presence of nitrosamines in cigarette smoke condensate has been shown by Serfontein and colleagues[97,98] and Neurath and co-workers[99,100] Nitrosamines can be converted to strong alkylating agents such as the diazoalkanes by microsomal enzyme systems, and these compounds can alkylate cellular constituents such as DNA and RNA. The evidence is equivocal for the presence of the nitrosamines in cigarette smoke, for under the conditions of cold or liquid trapping, they are produced by chemical reaction in the trapped liquid.[101] The identification of these nitroso compounds has usually been through gas chromatography[101] or through reduction to a 1,1-dialkylhydrazine followed by reaction with 4-(4-nitrophenyl)-azobenzoyl chloride[97] or 5-nitrosalicylaldehyde[96] and absorptiometric examination. Obviously, one of the aldehyde reagents could be used to analyze the dialkylhydrazine.

Nitrosamine compounds have been found in wheat flour, smoked fish, and a product known as "liquid smoke." [101] Since they are formed by the reaction between a secondary amine, NO and NO_2,[100] they could be present in atmospheres containing these three components.

With the presence of many types of carcinogens and cocarcinogens in polluted atmospheres throughout the civilized world,[102] the spread and probable increase of aerial allergens in wide areas of the world and the presence of alkylating agents in so many diverse fractions of urban particulates, continuous watch over and control of our aerial environment must be kept, in order to insure that our pollution problems of today do not become the superproblems of tomorrow.

References

1. Van Duuren, B. L., N. Nelson, L. Orris, E. D. Palmes & F. L. Schmitt. 1963. Carcinogenicity of epoxides, lactones and peroxy compounds. J. Nat. Cancer Inst. **31:** 41.
2. Van Duuren, B. L., L. Orris & N. Nelson. 1965. Carcinogenicity of epoxides, lactones and peroxy compounds. Part II. J. Nat. Cancer Inst. **35:** 707.

3. VAN DUUREN, B. L. & B. M. GOLDSCHMIDT. 1966. Carcinogenicity of epoxides, lactones and peroxy compounds. Part III. Biological activity and chemical reactivity. J. Med. Chem. **9:** 77.
4. KOTIN, P. & H. L. FALK. 1963. Organic peroxides, hydrogen peroxide, epoxides and neoplasia. Radiat. Res. (Suppl.) **3:** 193.
5. WHEELER, G. P. 1962. Studies related to the mechanism of action of cytotoxic alkylating agents: A review. Cancer Res. **22:** 651.
6. AUERBACH, C. 1958. Mutagenic effects of alkylating agents. Ann. N. Y. Acad. Sci. **68:** 731.
7. FAHMY, O. G. & M. J. FAHMY. 1958. Discussion of paper by C. Auerbach. Ann. N. Y. Acad. Sci. **68:** 736.
8. BRATZEL, R. P., T. H. GOODRIDGE & W. T. HUNTRESS. 1963. A survey of alkylating agents—Nitrogen mustards. Cancer Chemother. Rep. **26:** 1.
9. FIORITI, J. A., A. P. BENTZ & R. J. SIMS. 1966. Reaction of picric acid with epoxides. I. A colorimetric method. J. Amer. Oil Chem. Soc. **43:** 37.
10. GOODRIDGE, T. H., W. T. HUNTRESS & R. P. BRATZEL. 1963. A survey of alkylating agents—Aziridines. Cancer Chemother. Rep. **26:** 341.
11. BEROZA, M. & A. B. BOŘKOVEC. 1964. The stability of tepa and other aziridine chemosterilants. J. Med. Chem. **7:** 44.
12. EPSTEIN, J., R. W. ROSENTHAL & R. J. ESS. 1955. Use of γ-(4-nitrobenzyl)pyridine as analytical reagent for ethyleneimines and alkylating agents. Anal. Chem. **27:** 1435.
13. KRIEK, E. & P. EMMELOT. 1963. Methylation and breakdown of microsomal and soluble ribonucleic acid from rat liver by diazomethane. Biochemistry (Wash.) **2:** 733.
14. KRIEK, E. & P. EMMELOT. 1964. Methylation of deoxyribonucleic acid by diazomethane. Biochim. Biophys. Acta. **91:** 59.
15. PREUSSMAN, R., H. HENGY & H. DRUCKREY. 1965. Studies on the detection of alkylating agents. I. Spectrophotometric determination of diazoalkanes with 4-(4-nitrobenzyl)pyridinium perchlorate. Chem. Ann. **684:** 57.
16. HUEPER, W. C. & W. D. CONWAY. 1964. Chemical Carcinogenesis and Cancers. Charles C. Thomas. Springfield, Ill.
17. RUTMAN, R. J., F. S. LEWIS & W. D. BLOOMER. 1966. Bipiperidyl mustard, a new obesifying agent in the mouse. Science **153:** 1000.
18. BRATZEL, R. P., R. B. ROSS, T. H. GOODRIDGE, W. T. HUNTRESS, M. T. FLATHER & D. E. JOHNSON. 1963. A survey of alkylating agents—Nitrogen mustards. Cancer Chemother. Rep. **26:** 1.
19. SARTORI, M. 1939. The War Gases. D. Van Nostrand Co., Inc. New York, N. Y.
20. HUNTRESS, W. T., T. H. GOODRIDGE & R. P. BRATZEL. 1963. A survey of alkylating agents—Sulfur mustards. Cancer Chemother. Rep. **26:** 323.
21. TRAMS, E. G. 1958. Determination of bis-(beta-chloroethyl)amines and related compounds with 8-quinolinol. Anal. Chem. **30:** 256.
22. STACHLEWSKA-WROBLOWA, A. 1966. Application of 1,1-diphenylhydrazine to detection and determination of α-haloketones. Chemia Analit. **11:** 1099.
23. SAWICKI, E., D. F. BENDER, T. R. HAUSER, R. M. WILSON, JR. & J. E. MEEKER. 1963. Five new methods for the spectrophotometric determination of alkylating agents including some extremely sensitive autocatalytic methods. Application to air pollution. Anal. Chem. **35:** 1479.
24. ZWEIG, G., ED. 1963–1967. Analytical Methods for Pesticides, Plant Growth Regulators, and Food Additives. Vols. I–V. Academic Press. New York, N. Y.
25. GETZ, M. E. & R. R. WATTS. 1964. Application of 4-(p-nitrobenzyl)pyridine as a rapid quantitative reagent for organophosphate pesticides. J. Ass. Offic. Agr. Chem. **47:** 1094.
26. GOLDENSON, J. 1957. Detection of nerve gases by chemiluminescence. Anal. Chem. **29:** 877.
27. GEHAUF, B. & J. GOLDENSON. 1957. Detection and estimation of nerve gases by fluorescence reaction. Anal. Chem. **29:** 276.
28. POWELL, E. W. 1967. Skin irritation by 9-bromofluorene. Chem. Ind. 2080.

29. MILLER, J. A. & E. C. MILLER. 1966. A survey of molecular aspects of chemical carcinogenesis. Laboratory Investigation **15:** 217.
30. BENDER, D. F., E. SAWICKI & R. M. WILSON. 1965. Spectrophotometric determination of alkylating agents with 4-picoline and o-dinitrobenzene. Analyst **90:** 630.
31. HADDOW, A. 1958. Chemical carcinogens and their mode of action. Brit. Med. Bull. **14:** 79.
32. CCSNC. 1960. A survey of alkanesulfonic acid esters. Cancer Chemother. Rep. **9:** 78.
33. VAN DUUREN, B. L., B. M. GOLDSCHMIDT, C. KATZ, L. LANGSETH, G. MERCADO & A. SIVAK. 1968. Alpha-halo ethers: A new type of alkylating carcinogen. Arch. Environ. Health (Chicago) **16:** 472.
34. SAWICKI, E., R. SCHUMACHER & C. R. ENGEL. 1967. Comparison of the 3-methyl-2-benzothiazolinone hydrazone and other methods for the determination of sugars and other α-glycolic derivatives. Application to air pollution. Microchem. J. **12:** 377.
35. SAWICKI, E. & R. A. CARNES. 1968. Spectrophotofluorimetric determination of aldehydes with dimedone and other reagents. Mikrochim. Acta. 148–159.
36. MALATESTA, P. & A. LORENZINI. 1958. Colorimetric microdetermination of orticant substances. Ann. Chim. (Rome) **48:** 1336.
37. MAGEE, P. N. & J. M. BARNES. 1962. Carcinogenicity of nitrosamines. J. Path. Bact. **84:** 19.
38. MAGEE, P. N. & R. SCHOENTAL. 1964. Carcinogenesis by nitroso compounds. Brit. Med. Bull. **20:** 102.
39. RADKE, R. O., D. E. ARMSTRONG & G. CHESTERS. 1966. Evaluation of the pyridine-alkali colorimetric method for determination of atrazine. J. Agr. Food Chem. **14:** 70.
40. DICKENS, F. 1964. Carcinogenic lactones and related substances. Brit. Med. Bull. **20:** 96.
41. ROSS, W. C. J. 1962. Biological alkylating agents. Buttersworth. London, Eng.
42. LIEBMAN, K. C. & J. D. HINDMAN. 1964. Modification of the Fujiwara reaction for determination of polyhalogenated organic compounds. Anal. Chem. **36:** 348.
43. LUGG, G. A. 1966. Fujiwara reaction and determination of carbon tetrachloride, chloroform, tetrachloroethane, and trichloroethylene in air. Anal. Chem. **38:** 1532.
44. AGREE, A. M. & R. L. MEEKER. 1966. Determination of micro and semi-micro concentrations of acylating agents by using 4-(4-nitrobenzyl)pyridine as reagent. Talanta **13:** 1151.
45. NVOTOVA, V. & Z. VESELA. 1964. Colorimetric determination of trichloromethanesulfenyl chloride in the atmosphere. Pracovni Lekarstvi **16:** 372.
46. LEHMANN, H. 1939. A new identification reaction for ethylene oxides and pyridine derivatives. Angew. Chem. **52:** 407.
47. FISHBEIN, L. 1967. Detection and thin-layer chromatography of derivatives of ethyleneimine. I. N-Carbamoylaziridines. J. Chromatog. **26:** 522.
48. GUTH, J. A. & L. P. MANNER. 1967. 4-(p-Nitrobenzyl)pyridine as a reagent for the thin-layer chromatographic detection and estimation of some aza heterocyclics. J. Chromatog. **30:** 514.
49. WATTS, R. R. 1965. 4-(p-Nitrobenzyl)pyridine, a new chromogenic spray reagent for organophosphate pesticides. J. Ass. Off. Agr. Chem. **48:** 1161.
50. RENAULT, J. & L. BIGOT. 1963. Microcharacterization of sulfate and sulfonate surface-active agents by means of 2,3,5-triphenyltetrazolium halides. Ann. Pharm. Franc. **21:** 847.
51. SOSNOVSKY, G. 1963. New Approach to the detection of acylating agents. Chemist-Analyst **52:** 81.
52. DIXON, B. E. & G. C. HANDS. 1959. A field method for the determination of phosgene in air. Analyst **84:** 463.
53. HOLDOWAY, M. J., E. S. LANE & J. L. WILLANS. 1962. The detection and estimation of carbon suboxide. Chem. Ind. **603.**
54. FRIEDMAN, O. M. & E. BOGER. 1961. Colorimetric estimation of nitrogen mustards in aqueous media. Hydrolytic behavior of bis(beta-chloroethyl)amine, nor HN_2. Anal. Chem. **33:** 906.

55. TAN, Y. L. & D. R. COLE. 1965. New method for determination of alkylating agents in biological fluids. Clin. Chem. **11:** 58.
56. TRUHAUT, B., E. DELACOUX, G. BRULE & C. BOHUON. 1963. Assay of alkylating agents in biological fluids. Method involving the color reaction with 4-p-nitrobenzylpyridine in alkaline medium. Clin. Chim. Acta. **8:** 235.
57. KLATT, O., A. C. GRIFFIN & J. S. STEHLIN, JR. 1960. Method for determination of phenylalanine mustard and related alkylating agents in blood. Proc. Soc. Exp. Biol. Med. **104:** 629.
58. PETERING, H. G. & G. J. VAN GIESSEN. 1963. Colorimetric method for determination of uracil mustard and related alkylating agents. J. Pharm. Sci. **52:** 1159.
59. MELLETT, L. B. & L. A. WOODS. 1960. The fluorimetric estimation of mechlorethamine (mustargen) and its biological disposition in the dog. Cancer Res. **20:** 518.
60. KOBLIN, A. 1958. Colorimetric determination of sesquimustard. Anal. Chem. **30:** 256.
61. GEHAUF, B., J. EPSTEIN, G. B. WILSON, B. WITTEN, S. SASS, V. E. BAUER & W. H. C. RUEGGEBERG. 1957. Reaction for colorimetric estimation of some phosphorus compounds. Anal. Chem. **29:** 278.
62. BYKHOVSKAYA, M. S. & G. A. KONDAUROVA. 1964. Separate determination of benzyl chloride, α,α-dichlorotoluene and α,α,α-trichlorotoluene present together in air. Zhur. Anal. Khim. **19:** 504.
63. SCHULDT, P. H., H. P. BURCHFIELD, D. E. STALLARD, W. E. PRIDDLE & S. KLEIN. 1961. Colorimetric determination of micro amounts of dimethyl tetrachloroterephthalate. Contrib. Boyce Thompson Inst. **21:** 163.
64. SAWICKI, E., T. R. HAUSER & S. MCPHERSON. 1962. Spectrophotometric determination of formaldehyde and formaldehyde-releasing compounds with chromotropic acid, 6-amino-1-naphthol-3-sulfonic acid (J-Acid), and 6-anilino-1-naphthol-3-sulfonic acid (Phenyl J-Acid). Anal. Chem. **34:** 1460.
65. PREUSSMANN, R., H. HENGY, D. LUBBE & A. VON HODENBERG. Photometric determination of aliphatic azo and hydrazo compounds. Anal. Chim. Acta. **41:** 497.
66. SUTTON, N. V. 1964. Spectrophotometric determination of unsymmetrical dimethylhydrazine, employing chromotropic acid. Anal. Chem. **36:** 2120.
67. PREUSSMANN, R., H. HENGY & V. VON HODENBERG. 1968. A new photometric method for the determination of 1,1-dialkylhydrazines. Anal. Chim. Acta. **42:** 95.
68. CRUMMETT, W. B. & J. D. MCLEAN. 1965. Ultraviolet spectral determination of trace quantities of phosgene in gases. Anal. Chem. **37:** 424.
69. LIDDELL, H. F. & B. SAVILLE. 1957. Determination of acid anhydrides. Chem. Ind. **16:** 493.
70. BROOKES, P. & P. D. LAWLEY. 1964. Reaction of some mutagenic and carcinogenic compounds with nucleic acids. J. Cell. Comp. Physiol. 64 (Suppl. I): 111.
71. JAWORSKI, M., A. ZIELASKO & K. GASIOR. 1961. Colorimetric determination of epoxyethane. Chem. Anal. (Warsaw) **6:** 1005.
72. BOLTON, N. E. & N. H. KETCHAM. 1964. Determination of ethylene oxide in air. Arch. Env. Health **8:** 711.
73. GRONSBERG, E. S. 1964. Determination of methylene chloride in presence of chlorinated hydrocarbons. Tr. Khim. Khim. Technol. (Gorki) 131; Anal. Abstr. (1965) **12:** 4879.
74. BOWMAN, M. C. & M. BEROZA. 1965. Analysis for imidan colorimetrically and by electron-affinity gas chromatography. J. Ass. Off. Agr. Chem. **48:** 922.
75. GIANG, P. A. & M. S. SCHECHTER. 1960. Formaldehydogenic organophosphorus compounds. J. Agr. Food Chem. **8:** 51.
76. SAWICKI, E., T. W. STANLEY & J. PFAFF. 1963. Spectrophotofluorimetric determination of formaldehyde and acrolein with J-Acid. Comparison with other methods. Anal. Chim. Acta. **28:** 156.
77. BELMAN, S. 1963. Fluorimetric determination of formaldehyde. Anal Chem. **29:** 120.
78. NASH, T. 1953. The colorimetric estimation of formaldehyde by means of the Hantzsch Reaction. Biochem. J. **55:** 416.

79. TANENBAUM, M. & C. E. BRICKER. 1951. Microdetermination of free formaldehyde. Anal. Chem. **23:** 354.
80. SAWICKI, E. & T. R. HAUSER. 1960. Spot test detection and colorimetric determination of aliphatic aldehydes with 2-hydrazinobenzothiazole. Application to air pollution. Anal. Chem. **32:** 1434.
81. SAWICKI, E., T. R. HAUSER, T. W. STANLEY & W. ELBERT. 1961. The 3-methyl-2-benzothiazolinone test. Sensitive new methods for the detection, rapid estimation and determination of aliphatic aldehydes. Anal Chem. **33:** 93.
82. ALBRECHT, A. M., W. I. SCHER, JR. & H. J. VOGEL. 1962. Determination of aliphatic aldehydes by spectrophotometry. Anal. Chem. **34:** 398.
83. BARTOS, J. & J. F. BURTIN. 1961. Colorimetry of some aldehydes and ketones with the aid of oxalyldihydrazide. Ann. Pharm. Franc. **19:** 769.
84. JONES, L. R. & J. R. RIDDICK. 1954. Colorimetric determination of propionaldehyde. Anal. Chem. **26:** 1035.
85. CLANCY, D. J. & D. E. KRAMM. Determination of acetaldehyde by colorimetry. Anal. Chem. **35:** 1987.
86. ARSENAULT, G. P. & W. YAPHE. 1966. Fructose—resorcinol—hydrochloric acid for detection and determination of acetaldehyde. Anal. Chem. **38:** 503.
87. PREUSSMANN, R. 1968. Chemical structure and carcinogenicity of aliphatic hydrazo-, azo-, and azoxy compounds and triazenes: potential *in vivo* alkylating agents. This monograph.
88. HUEPER, W. C., P. KOTIN, E. C. TABOR, W. W. PAYNE, H. FALK & E. SAWICKI. 1962. Carcinogenic Bioassays on Air Pollutants. Arch. Pathol. **74:** 89.
89. TABOR, E. C., T. R. HAUSER, J. P. LODGE & R. H. BURTTSCHELL. 1958. Characteristics of the organic particulate matter in the atmosphere of certain American cities. A.M.A. Arch. Ind. Health **17:** 58.
90. KOTIN, P. & H. L. FALK. 1955. Production of tumors in C57BL mice with atmosphere-extracted aliphatic hydrocarbons. Proc. Amer. Ass. Cancer Res. **2:** (No. 1)30.
91. KOTIN, P., H. L. FALK & C. J. MCCAMMON. 1958. Carcinogenicity of ozonized gasoline. Cancer **11:** 473.
92. EPSTEIN, S. S., N. MANTEL & T. W. STANLEY. 1968. Photodynamic assay of neutral subfractions of organic extracts of particulate atmospheric pollutants. Env. Sci. Technol. **2:** 132.
93. HILGETAG, G. & H. TEICHMANN. 1965. About the alkylation properties of alkyl thiophosphates. Angew. Chem. **77:** 1001.
94. BATORA, V. & J. KOVAC. 1964. The determination of small amounts of some insecticidal dialkyl phosphorodithioates in factory air. Chem. Tech. (Berlin) **16:** 230.
95. BARRY, H. C., J. G. HUNDLEY & L. Y. JOHNSON. 1963. (Revised continually). Pesticide Analytical Manual. Vol. I. Methods which detect more than one pesticide residue. U.S. Department of Health, Education and Welfare. Food and Drug Administration. Washington, D.C.
96. DUGGAN, R. E., H. C. BARRY, L. Y. JOHNSON & S. WILLIAMS. 1964. (Revised continually). Pesticide Analytical Manual. Vol. II. Methods for individual pesticide residues. U.S. Department of Health, Education and Welfare. Food and Drug Administration. Washington, D.C.
97. SERFONTEIN, W. J. & J. H. SMIT. 1967. Evidence for the occurrence of N-nitrosamines in tobacco. Nature (London) **214:** 169.
98. SERFONTEIN, W. J. & P. HURTER. 1966. A method for identifying small amounts of nitrosamines in biological material. Nature (London) **209:** 1238.
99. NEURATH, G., B. PIRMANN & H. WICHERN. 1964. On the question of N-nitroso compounds in tobacco smoke. Beitr. Tabakforsch **2:** 311; **3:** 251.
100. NEURATH, G. 1967. On the question of N-nitroso compounds in tobacco smoke. Experentia **23:** 400.
101. JOHNSON, D. E., J. D. MILLAR & J. W. RHOADES. 1968. Nitrosamines in tobacco smoke. *In* Toward a Less Harmful Cigarette. Nat. Cancer Inst. Monograph **28:** 181.

Part V. Chemotherapy by Alkylating Agents

ALKYLATING AGENTS IN CLINICAL CANCER CHEMOTHERAPY*

Manuel Ochoa, Jr.

Division of Chemotherapy Research, Sloan-Kettering Institute for Cancer Research; Department of Medicine, Memorial Hospital for Cancer and Allied Diseases and James Ewing Hospital; Department of Medicine, Cornell University Medical College, New York, N. Y.

In the fall of 1942, the first dose of nitrogen mustard was administered to a terminal cancer patient in a deliberate and most instructive clinical experiment.[1,2] The decision to test the therapeutic usefulness of this class of chemical warfare agents, whose impressive local and systemic toxicity had been known since the turn of the twentieth century,[3,4] was based on numerous investigations during and between the two World Wars on the chemical properties and biological effects of the sulfur and nitrogen mustards.[2,5] In point of fact, the therapeutic utility of the alkylating agents had already been demonstrated in 1931 by Adair and Bagg[6] at the Memorial Hospital when they demonstrated that the intratumoral injection of sulfur mustard in a patient with recurrent neurogenic sarcoma caused measurable tumor regression. However, the fear surrounding mustard gas created technical difficulties that interfered with further work until the exigencies of national survival during World War II overcame them.

The striking carcinostatic activity of the first alkylating agents was accompanied by almost equally pronounced toxicity to the host. (Indeed, it was the vesicant toxicity that led Dr. James Ewing in 1927 to suggest to Bagg that mustard gas might influence the growth of tumors.) The narrow distance between the minimum effective and maximum tolerated doses of nitrogen mustard might well have discouraged extensive exploration, but the war years had witnessed such spectacular successes in the improvement of the therapeutic indices of other pharmacological agents by the systematic pursuit of structure-activity studies that the decision to apply an analogous approach to the development of more useful anticancer compounds could hardly have been avoided. In the next two and one-half decades, countless contributions from countless laboratories and clinics around the world recorded an incredible number of effects of practically all conceivable structural variations of the alkylating moieties. Many dozens of reviews have been written on the subject, and many dozens of times scientists and clinicians have assembled to discuss the formulae, properties, and clinical value of this group of drugs. Despite these labors, only a few alkylating agents have gained a lasting place in the armamentarium of the clinical oncologist. It is probable, on the basis of the acute pharmacologic effects, the types of neoplasms affected, and the therapeutic indices, that the alkylating agents thus far adjudged to warrant clinical status have, in general, a similar spectrum of therapeutic activity. The fact that a variety of alkylating agents with different physiochemical properties

*Supported in part by Public Health Service research grants CA-05826 and CA-08748 from the National Cancer Institute.

exert similar clinical effects suggests that the enhancement of their therapeutic specificity, measured in terms of cytotoxic potential, will be difficult. It seems important at this juncture to select the most promising and meaningful next steps with some care, rather than simply recommend the further pursuit of all conceivable investigative efforts with equal priority. This paper will, therefore, summarize the clinical utility of representative alkylating agents and use the summary as a point of departure for brief proposals for future clinical investigations.

Absorption

The six alkylating drugs commonly considered for nonexperimental clinical chemotherapy in the United States are: mechlorethamine (HN2) (Mustargen®); chlorambucil (Leukeran®); melphalan (Alkeran®); cyclophosphamide (Cytoxan®); busulfan (Myleran®); and triethylene thiophosphoramide (Thio-TEPA®). It is clear that a variety of routes of administration can be employed for these agents. They are absorbed, with the possible exception of nitrogen mustard, from the gastrointestinal tract. Mechlorethamine, administered orally, produces neither bone marrow depression nor therapeutic effects despite doses of 1.3 mg/kg.[7] Tris(2-chloroethyl)amine (HN3) is absorbed and its tumor-inhibitory effects are heightened by fasting,[8] suggesting that the interaction of gastrointestinal contents and the nitrogen mustards may account for the variability in absorption. The oral absorption of the other five agents is probably incomplete and erratic.[7] Comparison of the total amounts of drug and radiolabeled end products, excreted in the urine after oral or intravenous administration, does not reveal significant differences; 25–85% of the radiolabel may be recovered. Plasma levels and recovery of the radiolabel from the stools are correspondingly variable and indicate incomplete absorption, which may potentially result in sharp excursions in antitumor effect or toxicity.[7] In practice, however, these agents are administered in an individualized fashion, and these variations generally are minimized. When rapid administration is desirable, a parenteral preparation is used for initial treatment and the therapy is maintained with an oral preparation. It is reasonable to conclude that further comparison of the oral and parenteral effects of alkylating agents is unlikely to yield new data of significant clinical value.

Distribution and Metabolism

The mustards act directly on susceptible cells of animals to cause injury. There is no evidence that the cytotoxic effects are the indirect consequence of a systemic host effect. Extensive studies have revealed time-dependent differences in tissue distribution but have failed consistently to demonstrate selective concentration of alkylating agents in the tissues exhibiting the most severe injury; that is, the bone marrow, lymph nodes, intestinal epithelium, or tumor tissues.[9] Boursnell,[10] for example, in early pharmacologic studies, demonstrated the retention of the label after administration to rabbits of ^{35}S-labeled sulfur mustard, in the kidney, lung, and liver and suggested that concentration in these tissues might be related to their excretory function. Accumulation in bone marrow was low. Subsequent studies demonstrated that the distribution of nitrogen mustard depends in part on the route of administration; the more rapid the exposure of tissue to drug, the greater the uptake of isotope.[11] Fractionation into cellular components demonstrated the radioactivity from HN2 to be equally distributed in the nuclear, mitochondrial, microsomal, and supernatant portions as well as in the DNA of both sensitive and resistant tumors. A plethora of subsequent studies, conducted primarily on animals but in a few instances on humans, led us[9] to conclude that the quest for selective localization of these cytotoxic agents in tumor cells had, in essence, met with failure. Despite the diversity of the carrier molecules and of the alkylating functions, these compounds are distributed widely, if not ubiquitously, in the tissues of the host. The tumor implants, when present, may be among the tissues with lower, rather than higher, content of the alkylating agents. The fact that most of the compounds under discussion do, after all, have a therapeutic index greater than unity must, therefore, be based on factors other than the gross distribution patterns. This impression, valid as a generality, may require modification, because Bolt and co-workers[12] reported that cyclophosphamide, which may modestly prolong the survival of patients with lung cancer, may localize in bronchial carcinoma in human subjects.

The alkylating agents remain as the parent compounds in the fluids and the patient for short periods, usually minutes. Triethylene thiophosphoramide (thio-TEPA), however, persists for several hours. None of the parent compounds can be found in the urine after administration to man of busulfan, triethylene phosphoramide (TEPA), thio-TEPA, or triethylene melamine (TEM). When busulfan-^{14}C is given, 75% of the dose is recovered in the urine as unknown metabolites. With busulfan-^{35}S, 95% is recovered as methane sulfonic acid. About 90% of TEPA-^{32}P is recovered as inorganic phosphates. Ten percent of TEM-^{14}C is excreted as urea and creatinine with 90% of the label in 12 unidentified metabolites. Triethylene thiophosphoramide, as such, is not found in the urine, but there are small amounts of TEPA.[7] These and similar observations in man led Oliverio and Zubrod,[7] to postulate that there are two pharmacologic categories of alkylating agents. One group (nitrogen mustard, busulfan and TEM) remain as the parent compound in plasma for only a few minutes; the radiolabels appear in the urine in a variety of degradation products. A second group (cyclophosphamide, thio-TEPA, N(3-oxapentamethylene)-N′, N″-diethylene thiophosphoramide [OP-SPA]) have a much longer plasma half life; parent compounds can be found in the urine in small amounts, and the number of metabolites is relatively small. It remains to be seen whether the differences on which this classification is based can be exploited to achieve a significantly greater therapeutic index for alkylating agents of clinical interest. In view of the similarities in carcinostatic effectiveness in experimental tumor systems and the ubiquitous distribution *in vivo,* these expectations should probably not be raised too high.

The metabolic fate of drugs depends in part upon the route of administration and, in this regard, the effects of the structure of alkylating compounds on properties that may be of pharmacologic significance appear to warrant continued study. Linford[13] observed that the rates of hydrolysis and of chemical condensation with proteins of human serum were more rapid with chlorambucil than with cyclophosphamide, and he interpreted the hydrolytic and condensation reactions of chlorambucil as therapeutic wastes. Serum proteins adsorbed chlorambucil but not cyclophosphamide, presumably by van der Waals binding; this physical binding may limit the extent of diffusion at certain locations. Sanderson and associates[14] demonstrated that following the injection of phenylalanine mustard into rabbits, there was a sharp decrease in reactive chloroethyl groups but a thousandfold increase in cytotoxicity. The suggestion was made that phenylalanine mustard is hydrolyzed to a metabolite that alkylates protein; and that this compound may be more cytotoxic than the parent molecule. In this instance, then, the interaction of protein and drug would not be a therapeutic waste. These metabolic data further suggest that, whereas the basic mechanism(s) of action at the molecular level may be similar for the various classes of alkylating agents, the pharmacologic disposition may modulate their clinical utility. Further studies of the relation of structure to activity[15] may be useful in enhancing the therapeutic efficiency of the alkylating agents, but the expectation is for a limited increment. A further commentary in this regard is provided by the National Cancer Institute, which has reduced the input of new alkylating agents into their screening program from 12% of all new agents in 1965 to three percent in 1968.

Toxicity

In a general way, the toxicities of the alkylating agents resemble those of other anti-tumor drugs acting upon rapidly dividing cells, such as those of bone marrow, the gastrointestinal tract, and hair roots. The most frequent serious toxicity of the alkylating agents resides mainly in their effects upon the marrow granulocytes and platelets. This property is common to all six of the clinically useful agents. Cyclophosphamide may be an exception in that it is often stated that this agent demonstrates a relative sparing of the platelets.[7] Well-controlled studies that might serve to document this clinical impression are difficult to locate. However, it does produce chemical cystitis in approximately 20% of patients, usually the dehydrated patients. Another potential difference, to extrapolate from clinical impressions, is that mucosal ulceration rarely occurs with alkylating agents but may be seen with phenylalanine mustard and cyclophosphamide.[7] Karnofsky[16] has summarized the late toxic effects, in patients, attributed to the use of the various polyfunctional alkylating agents. They include bone marrow aplasia, the stimulation of amyloidosis, pulmonary fibrosis, cytologic abnormalities, teratogenic effects, possibly carcinogenesis, amenorrhea and inhibition of spermatogenesis, increased susceptibility to infection possibly due to the bone-marrow depression and immunosuppression, and a questionable decrease in survival time. As with the acute toxicities, certain alkylating agents may produce effects more closely related to their prosthetic groups: these include the syndrome of hyperpigmentation, weakness, anorexia, and weight loss associated with busulfan, bladder cancer with β-naphthyl-di(β-chloroethyl)amine, and alopecia with cyclophosphamide. Certain of these apparently selective toxicities could, in theory, be translated into therapeutically useful reactions. They have not been. The explanation is provided by the systematic appraisal of the toxicity of alkylating agents in rodents, dogs, and monkeys conducted by Schmidt and co-workers.[17] These investigators detailed gross variations in the quantitative aspects of the toxicity of these agents but concluded that "there were, in reality, few significant differences in the quality of reactions." Except for the quinolone and acridine mustards, almost every agent produced severe anorexia and depression, myelopenia, erythropenia, lymphopenia, gastrointestinal hemorrhage, and thrombocytopenia or disturbed platelet function. With regard to toxicity, then, the similarities among alkylating agents clearly overshadow the differences between them. That this conclusion applies equally to humans is attested to by reports in the literature suggesting that the aforementioned selective toxicities may be general if the alkylating agents are appropriately administered. Thus, the pulmonary fibrosis attributed to busulfan has also been noted after long-term cyclophosphamide therapy by Karnofsky.[17] A somewhat advantageous therapeutic index has generally been more the result of fortunate happenstance than of deliberate design.

This conclusion must stand even when one reviews the repeated attempts by several investigative groups to widen the distance between the minimum effective and the maximum tolerated doses of alkylating agents by the simultaneous addition of protective compounds. A brief account of some of these efforts will show that they met only partial success at the experimental level and have not reached the stage of clinical application. L-cysteine protects rabbits and humans against HN2-induced leukopenia when the protective agents are administered 15 minutes prior to the HN2.[18] There is apparently little effect on the mustard's carcinostatic potential in humans.[19] Other studies[9] have demonstrated quantitative differences in the degree of protection provided by substances possessing sulfhydryl groups. Only slight protection was obtained with cysteine against Eponate, and none against busulfan or thio-TEPA. Mercaptoalkylamines protect against the toxicity of HN2 and cyclophosphamide (but not of phenylalanine and chloroquine mustards.) The reduction of toxicity is not accompanied by loss of anti-tumor activity. Indeed, quantitative studies suggest preferential destruction of tumor cells after administration of 1-mercapto-2-aminobutane, and the suggestion was made by Rutman and colleagues[20] that the SH-binding sites differ in normal and tumor cells. Finally, the toxicity of a series of phosphoramides and thiophosphoramides, containing the mercaptoethylamino group of a radioprotective grouping and the ethyleneimino group as the radiomimetic component, was one-fourth to one-eighth that of thio-TEPA, but carcinostatic activity was equivalent. These agents nevertheless depressed the marrow elements, produced hyperglycemia, and increased the sensitivity of the peripheral cholinergic nervous system. More indirect attempts to lessen the toxicity of the alkylating agents include glucose pretreatment, administration of hormones, introduction of serotonin or histamine antagonists, and changes of pH. It may be reiterated that these and similar techniques have not surpassed the status of laboratory curiosities.

Therapeutic Effects

The foregoing rather sober enumeration of the pharmacology of the alkylating agents has been presented not to test the reader's fortitude and attention, but to provide documentation for the clinician's impression that the selection of particular alkylating agents for nonexperimental clinical chemotherapy is based, not upon the rational exploitation of the different physicochemical properties of these agents, but upon experience, convenience, convention, commercial promotion, or national derivation. A potentially significant exception, and an area for future clinical exploration, is the relation of the alkylating drugs and the immunological responses of the host.

Chemotherapy is the treatment of choice for trophoblastic tumors including choriocarcinomas, in females. Whereas methotrexate, actinomycin D, and vinblastine may be the preferred drugs,[21] nitrogen mustard, nitromin, and other alkylating agents have caused definite regressions and, in some cases, possible cure of the disease both alone and in combination with one of the preferred agents.[21,22] The favorable responses using the alkylating agents alone probably do not exceed 5–10%, compared with a complete regression rate approaching 70% when the preferred agents or combination therapy is employed.[21,22]

Following the demonstration that mouse leukemia can be transplanted by a single cell, the studies of Skipper and associates[23,24] have demonstrated that in the mouse, the eradication of all leukemic cells is possible in some instances, and that this may be set as a goal for clinical chemotherapy.[25] Studies of intensive chemotherapy such as the VAMP, BIKE, and POMP programs suggest that such a goal may be attainable in some acute leukemia patients.[25] Whereas vincristine, 6-mercaptopurine, methotrexate, and prednisone are the preferred agents, cyclophosphamide has also produced remissions and may be unique among the alkylating agents in its ability to produce remissions in childhood leukemia in a significant number of patients.[25–27]

The status of cyclophosphamide is advanced to that of preferred drug, along with another alkylating agent, orthomerphalan or 3-(0-[bis(2-chloroethyl)amino] phenyl)alanine, DL in the treatment of Burkitt's tumor in Africa. Approximately 15–20% of patients with Burkitt's tumor have survived in unmaintained remission from one to seven years after the original course of therapy.[28,29] It appears possible, on the basis of continued observation, that many of these cases will continue in remission. The implication is clear that the eradication of all Burkitt's tumor cells may be possible.[29] Additionally, if the patient relapses a few months after the first or even subsequent remissions, further treatment still may produce a long-term remission.

Synergism of an immune mechanism and drug therapy may contribute to the success of the long-term regression of choriocarcinoma in the female. Li[30] has unsuccessfully attempted to detect evidence for activation of immunological factors. His findings of a delayed homograft rejection by patients with uterine choriocarcinoma are compatible with the general phenomenon of tolerance of skin homografts in cancer subjects. It appears that in Burkitt's tumor in Africa, host resistance may have an important role in the response to therapy. Klein and co-workers[31] have shown that patients with Burkitt's tumor in complete remission have a higher level of antibody demonstrated by an indirect membrane immunofluorescence test against allogeneic and autochthonous Burkitt's target cells than do patients with Burkitt's tumor who have not responded well to chemotherapy. This suggests that the long-term remissions seen in this disease may be due, not to chemotherapy alone, but rather to the combination of chemotherapy and host defenses. It is of interest to note that the third disease category in which long-term remissions can be induced by chemotherapeutics, although not efficiently with the alkylating agents, is the leukemia of childhood. Histologically, this group of illnesses is characterized as lymphoid, again suggesting the obvious relation between the lymphoreticular tissues and immunologic responses. It may well be that the postulated synergism between alkylating agents and other chemotherapeutic drugs on the one hand and host immunity on the other represent the most promising approach to anti-cancer therapy in the immediate future. Old and Boyse[32] have recently summarized the many issues that the immunotherapy of cancer raises; suffice it to state that although the experiences related above engender optimism, there is reason for restraint at a time when there are so few positive experimental results to guide the clinician. Nevertheless, it is of additional interest to report that Klein[33] attributes the response of patients with intractable multiple epitheliomatoses to the topical application of Trenimon (2,3,5-tri-ethylene-imino(1,4)-benzoquinone), to the induction of a delayed hypersensitivity response.

The alkylating agents have been effective in controlling chronic myelocytic leukemia. At present, the most useful analogue appears to be busulfan, which can induce remissions for 12 months or more even without maintenance therapy.[34]

Rundles and co-workers[35] demonstrated, however, that the primacy of busulfan notwithstanding, chronic myelocytic leukemia will respond in lesser or greater degree to chlorambucil.

Karnofsky and associates[36] and Wolf and co-workers[37] failed to prolong survival significantly by treating patients with bronchogenic carcinoma with mechlorethamine. More recently, Wolf[38] has reported that the survival time in a cyclophosphamide-treated group of patients with this condition was statistically significantly greater when compared with a concurrent control group. However, the survival of the treated group was only approximately 10% greater than that of the control group at 90 and 120 days—hardly of great clinical import, especially since in some of his studies, 40% of the control group lived to 120 days. This study, which may be interpreted as possibly demonstrating a superior antitumor effect for cyclophosphamide, is best evaluated in the perspective of another study (Karrer, *et al.*[39]) These investigators demonstrated that those patients with bronchogenic carcinoma who developed leukopenia during cyclophosphamide treatment survived longer than nonleukopenic patients. Taken together, these two studies emphasize that the minimal statistical prolongation of survival is small, and apparent only when systemic toxicity is manifest.

The contrast between chronic myelocytic leukemia, relatively sensitive to alkylating agents, and bronchogenic carcinoma, relatively resistant to these agents, serves as the clinical counterpart to the pharmacological data previously presented. The conclusion is similar: with regard to therapeutic effectiveness, the similarities between the alkylating agents—considered alone and not in combination chemotherapy or as an adjunct to immunotherapy—clearly overshadow the differences between them. This conclusion applies to the treatment of other malignancies: chronic lymphatic leukemia, Hodgkin's disease, lymphosarcoma, reticulum cell sarcoma, mycosis fungoides, multiple myeloma, and carcinomas of the breast and of the ovary, all of which appear to exhibit lesser or greater sensitivity to the alkylating agents. Bergel[40] has evaluated various proposals for the potential improvement of alkylating agents and has concluded that none of them has so far come up to expectations. The attempts to utilize thiol neutralizers, such as the quinol-quinones, to exploit the increase in disulphide demonstrated by leukemia leukocytes, to apply short-lived, rapidly acting compounds for infusion therapy, to exploit the pH differences between normal and neoplastic cells by simultaneous administration of glucose and of alkylating agents with basic groups, or to utilize differences in oxidation potential between normal and malignant tissues by the application of alkylating compounds with quinone-quinol structures, have not yielded clinically significant techniques. The application of cell-generation time to combination therapy[23–25] has resulted in enhanced therapeutic efficiency, but the advance has been, as we have noted, limited to the lymphoreticular malignancies.

In a general review presented at the 1945 AAAS-Gibson Island Research Conference on Tumor Chemotherapy,[41] the following statement was accepted as an authoritative conclusion: "If we have no cure today, surely it is not from lack of trying . . . Those who have not been trained in chemistry or medicine . . . may not realize how difficult the problem of treatment really is. It is almost—not quite, but almost—as hard as finding some agent that will dissolve away the left ear, say, yet leave the right ear unharmed: so slight is the difference between the cancer cell and its normal ancestor." This conclusion remains authoritative. It has been shown here once again that the pharmacologic and therapeutic effects of the clinically utilized alkylating agents are, on the whole, quite reminiscent of each other. Furthermore, these agents have been known for over a decade, lending additional emphasis to the awareness that the numerous endeavors directed at enhancing the therapeutic indices of alkylating agents have not yielded major clinical advances. Haddow,[40] indeed, has always given the alkylating agents a higher place in basic research than in their medical application.

This formulation need not cause despair. A sound foundation upon which a scientific discipline can be erected is being established by the understanding of the principles of cellular biochemistry, by the pharmacologic analysis of drug action on cells, by an appreciation of the clinical behavior of various forms of cancer, and by the techniques of evaluating the clinical benefits from new forms of treatment. Future chemotherapists may be concerned with agents that alter the genetic expression of the tumor cell. The observations that some tumor cells can inappropriately secrete substances with hormonal activity[42] and that single-cell transplantations of embryonal cells result in the formation of organized tissues[43] lead to the conclusions (1) that some tumor cells retain genetic information for differentiating into normal cells, and (2) that some cancer cells are not irreversibly altered but can, under the appropriate conditions, become apparently benign. The hypothesis that the biological phenomenon termed "cancer" is, in some instances, a deviation from the normal in the expression of gene action, suggests the possibility that the alkylating agents, by virtue of their versatile reactivity, may be utilized to redirect some cancer cells rather than to kill them. This clearly speculative proposal, which diverts chemotherapy from the goal of cytotoxicity to "cyto-regulation," is offered to complement Karnofsky's formulation of the present position of the chemotherapy of cancer, to wit:[44] "The great visions have yet to be seen, and the great discoveries yet to be made before one can make a great prophesy of an imminent cure."

Acknowledgment

The author is grateful for the secretarial assistance of Miss Linda Neaus and Mrs. Edith Testa.

References

1. Gilman, A. 1963. The initial clinical trial of nitrogen mustard. Amer. J. Surg. **105:** 574–578.
2. Gilman, A. & F. S. Philips. 1946. The biological actions and therapeutic applications of the β-chloroethyl amines and sulfides. Science **103:** 409–415.
3. Ehrlich, P. 1898. Ueber die Beziehungen von chemischer Constitution, Vertheilung und pharmakologischer Wirkung. *In* "The Collected Papers of Paul Ehrlich." F. Himmelweit, Ed. **1:** 570–595. 1956. Pergamon Press. New York, N.Y.
4. Meyer, V. 1887. Medicinisch-chemische Notizen. II. Physiologische Wirkung der gechlorten Schwefelaethyle. Ber. **20:** 1729–1731.
5. Philips, F. S. 1950. Recent contributions to the pharmacology of bis(2-haloethyl)-amines and sulfides. J. Pharmacol. Exp. Ther. **99:** 281–323.
6. Adair, F. E. & H. J. Bagg. 1931. Experimental and clinical studies on the treatment of cancer by dichlorethylsulfide (mustard gas). Ann. Surg. **93:** 190–199.
7. Oliverio, V. T. & C. G. Zubrod. 1965. Clinical pharmacology of the effective anti-tumor drugs. Ann. Rev. Pharmacol. **5:** 335–356.
8. Peczenik, O. 1952. Inhibition of tumor-growth after oral and parenteral treatment with nitrogen mustards and triethylene melamine. Brit. J. Cancer **6:** 262–269.

9. Ochoa, M., Jr. & E. Hirschberg. 1967. Alkylating Agents. *In* "Experimental Chemotherapy." R. J. Schnitzer & F. Hawking, Eds. **5:** 1–132. Academic Press. New York, N.Y.
10. Bournsnell, J. C., J. A. Cohen, M. Dixon, G. E. Francis, G. D. Greville, D. Needham & A. Wormall. 1946. Studies on mustard gas ($\beta\beta'$-dichlorodiethyl sulphide) and some related compounds. 5. The fate of injected mustard gas (containing radioactive sulphur) in the animal body. Biochem. J. **40:** 756–764.
11. Boone, I. U., B. S. Rogers, J. R. Maxfield & J. B. Storer. 1957. Nitrogen mustard and triethylene melamine content in normal and tumor tissues after intra-arterial and intravenous injection in rats. Cancer Res. **17:** 1120–1126.
12. Bolt, W., F. Ritzl, R. Toussaint & H. Nahrmann. 1961. Verteilung und Ausscheidung eines cytostatisch wirkenden, mit Tritium markierten N-Lost-Derivates beim krebskranken Menschen. Arzneimittelforschung. **11:** 170–175.
13. Linford, J. H. 1961. Some interactions of nitrogen mustards with constituents of human blood serum. Biochem. Pharmacol. **8:** 343–357.
14. Sanderson, R. P., J. M. McKenna & W. S. Blakemore. 1965. Cytotoxic activity compared with photometric measurements of selected alkylating agents. Nature (London) **205:** 479–481.
15. Bardos, T. 1969. Structure-activity relationships of alkylating agents in cancer chemotherapy. This monograph.
16. Karnofsky, D. A. 1967. Late effects of immunosuppressive anti-cancer drugs. Fed. Proc. **26:** 925–932.
17. Schmidt, L. H., R. Fradkin, R. Sullivan & A. Flowers. 1965. Comparative pharmacology of alkylating agents. Cancer Chemotherapy Rep. (Suppl.) **2:** 1–1528.
18. Weisberger, A. S. & R. W. Henle. 1950. The protective effect of cysteine on leucopenia induced by nitrogen mustard. J. Lab. Clin. Med. **36:** 872–876.
19. Weisberger, A.S., R. W. Henle & B. Levine. 1952. The effect of L-cysteine on nitrogen mustard therapy. Amer. J. Med. Sci. **224:** 201–211.
20. Rutman, R. J., F. S. Lewis & C. C. Price. 1964. Experimental chemotherapy studies. IV. The protective action of mercapto alkylamines against alkylating agents. Cancer Res. **24:** 626–633.
21. Hertz, R. 1967. Eight years' experience with the chemotherapy of choriocarcinoma and related trophoblastic tumors in women. *In* Choriocarcinoma. J. F. Holland & M. M. Hreshchyshyn, Eds. **3:** 66–71. UICC Monographs. Springer-Verlag. Berlin, Germany.
22. Ishizuka, N. 1967. Chemotherapy of chorionic tumors. *In* Choriocarcinoma. J. F. Holland & M. M. Hreshchyshyn, Eds. **3:** 116–118. UICC Monographs. Springer-Verlag. Berlin, Germany.
23. Skipper, H. E., F. M. Schabel, Jr., M. Bell, J. R. Thomson & S. Johnson. 1957. On the curability of experimental neoplasms. I. A-metopterin and mouse leukemias. Cancer Res. **17:** 717–726.
24. Skipper, H. E., F. M. Schabel, Jr., M. W. Trader & J. R. Thomson. 1961. Experimental evaluation of potential anti-cancer agents. VI. Anatomical distribution of leukemic cells and failure of chemotherapy. Cancer Res. **21:** 1154–1165.
25. Frei, E., III, & E. J. Freireich. 1965. Progress and perspectives in the chemotherapy of acute leukemia. Advances Chemother. **2:** 269–298.
26. Tan, C. T. C., J. Phoa, M. Lyman, M. L. Murphy, H. W. Dargeon & J. H. Burchenal. 1961. Hematological remissions in acute leukemia with cyclophosphamide. Blood **18:** 808.
27. Greenwald, E. S. 1967. Alkylating Agents. *In* Cancer Chemotherapy. E. S. Greenwald, Ed.: 35–93. Medical Examination Publishing Co. New York, N. Y.
28. Burchenal, J. H. 1968. Long-term survivors in acute leukemia and Burkitt's tumor. Cancer **21:** 595–599.
29. Zubrod, C. G. 1968. Acute leukemias and Burkitt's Lymphoma. Present status of therapy. Cancer **21:** 553–557.
30. Li, M. C. 1967. Chemotherapeutic and immunological considerations on the response

of choriocarcinomas. *In* Choriocarcinoma. J. F. Holland & M. M. Hreshchyshyn, Eds. **3:** 138–145. UICC Monographs. Springer-Verlag. Berlin, Germany.

31. Klein, G., P. Clifford, E. Klein & J. Stjernswärd. 1967. Search for tumor-specific immune reactions in Burkitt lymphoma patients by the membrane immunofluorescence reaction. *In* Treatment of Burkitt's tumor. J. H. Burchenal & D. P. Burkitt, Eds.: 209–232. Springer-Verlag. Berlin, Germany.
32. Old, L. J. & E. A. Boyse. 1968. Prospects for immunotherapy of human cancer. Ann. Intern. Med. **69:** 393–397.
33. Klein, E. 1968. Tumors of the skin. X. Immunotherapy of cutaneous and muscosal neoplasms. N. Y. J. Med. **68:** 900–911.
34. Haut, A., W. S. Abbott, M. M. Wintrobe & G. E. Cartwright. 1961. Busulfan in the treatment of chronic myelocytic leukemia. The effect of long term intermittent therapy. Blood **17:** 1–19.
35. Rundles, R. W., J. Grizzle, W. N. Bell, C. C. Corley, W. B. Frommeyer, Jr., B. G. Greenberg, C. M. Huguley, Jr., G. W. James, R. Jones, Jr., W. E. Larsen, V. Loeb, L. A. Leone, J. G. Palmer, W. H. Riser, Jr., & S. J. Wilson. 1959. Comparison of chlorambucil and Myleran in chronic lymphocytic and granulocytic leukemia. Amer. J. Med. **27:** 424–432.
36. Karnofsky, D. A., W. H. Abelmann, L. F. Craver & J. H. Burchenal. 1948. The use of the nitrogen mustards in the palliative treatment of carcinoma. Cancer **1:** 634–656.
37. Wolf, J., P. Spear & R. Yesner. 1960. Nitrogen mustard and the steroid hormones in the treatment of inoperable bronchogenic carcinoma. Amer. J. Med. **29:** 1008–1016.
38. Wolf, J. 1966. Controlled therapeutic trials in lung cancer. Ninth International Cancer Congress. Tokyo, Japan. October 23–29, 1966. Abst. S0992. Also personal communication.
39. Karrer, K., S. R. Humphreys & A. Goldin. 1965. Relationship of drug toxicity to chemotherapeutic effectiveness. *In* Antimicrobial Agents and Chemotherapy. G. L. Hobby, Ed.: 539–543. American Society for Microbiology. Michigan.
40. Bergel, F. 1964. Development possibilities and prospects of alkylating agents. *In* Chemotherapy of Cancer. P. A. Plattner, Ed.: 21–31. Elsevier Publishing Co. Amsterdam, the Netherlands.
41. Woglom, W. H. 1947. General review of cancer therapy. *In* Approaches to Tumor Chemotherapy. F. R. Moulton, Ed.: 1–12. Amer. Assoc. Advance. Sci. Washington, D. C.
42. Myers, W. P. L., C. K. Tashima & E. O. Rothschild. 1966. Endocrine syndromes associated with nonendocrine neoplasms. Med. Clin. N. Amer. **50:** 763–778.
43. Kleinsmith, L. J. & G. B. Pierce, Jr. 1964. Multipotentiality of single embryonal carcinoma cells. Cancer Res. **24:** 1544–1552.
44. Karnofsky, D. A. 1964. Chemotherapy of cancer and its present position in the management of neoplastic diseases. *In* Chemotherapy of Cancer. P. A. Plattner, Ed.: 3–17. Elsevier Publishing Co. Amsterdam, the Netherlands.

SOME EFFECTS OF ALKYLATING AGENTS ON EPITHELIA IN MAN AND IN AN EXPERIMENTAL SYSTEM IN THE RAT*

Leopold G. Koss

The Memorial Hospital for Cancer and Allied Diseases and the Sloan-Kettering Institute for Cancer Research, New York, N. Y.

Alkylating agents used in the treatment of human cancer affect not only their intended target, the cancer cells, but also noncancerous cells and tissues. This is not surprising, since there are no known basic qualitative biochemical differences between the metabolic pathways of cancer cells and noncancerous cells.[10]

Three drugs have been observed to exercise marked effect on human epithelial cells and other tissues. These are: triethylenethio-phosphoramide (thio-tepa), busulfan, and cyclophosphamide. The information on thio-tepa is, at this time, very scanty. Abnormalities of epithelium of the uterine cervix have been observed.[10] Considerable information, however, is available on the effects of the other two agents.

Busulfan

Busulfan is a bivalent alkylating agent mainly used in relatively small doses over prolonged periods of time in the treatment of chronic myelogenous leukemia.[5,7] Known clinical complications regarding the use of this drug are: bone-marrow depression, amenorrhea, and a syndrome resembling adrenal cortical insufficiency, and pulmonary fibrosis.[3,5,8,14,15,17,19,20]

Cellular Abnormalities

Nuclear gigantism in various tissues was first described by Waller in autopsy material.[21] This was subsequently followed by observations on patients under treatment.[6,13,16,22] Personal observations[3,10,13] indicate that cellular abnormalities akin to those observed in spontaneously occurring human cancer and precancerous states may be observed in patients. Such cells may be observed in smears of the uterine cervix, in urinary sediment, and in sputum. In one such patient the abnormalities persisted for six months after discontinuation of treatment, and were confirmed in autopsy material.

Autopsy findings revealed major cellular abnormalities in a great many organs. A recent report from this laboratory[3] illustrates well the abnormalities attributable to busulfan. The patient was a 58-year-old woman who had been receiving busulfan almost continuously for a period of nearly 10 years for chronic myelogenous

*Supported in part by National Cancer Institute grant CA 08748.

leukemia. After six years of treatment, she developed a carcinoma of the vulva, successfully treated. At the time of autopsy, three years later, there were cellular abnormalities of the thyroid, adrenal cortex, and pancreas, and in the epithelia of pulmonary alveoli and terminal bronchioles, renal tubules, renal pelvis, bladder, exo- and endocervix, and mammary ducts. Giant fibroblasts were also observed in several organs. In addition, there were adenomas of the kidney and of the pancreas.

Pulmonary Changes

The first clinical observations that busulfan therapy may produce significant pulmonary disease were reported by Oliner and co-workers[17] and by Leake and colleagues.[15] The full significance of these changes has not become clear until recently. Patients receiving the drug may develop an alveolar-capillary block associated with significant respiratory difficulty after variable duration of therapy ranging from 16 months to eight years. The chest roentgenograms show diffuse bilateral nodular opacities that may occur rather suddenly in the course of the disease. Histologic findings disclose nodular fibrosis, irregularly distributed and occupying intra- and extraalveolar spaces. Significant nuclear abnormalities occur in the epithelium of the alveoli and of the terminal bronchioles.[3,10,16] Heard and Cooke[9] pointed out the presence of deposits of fibrin in the terminal bronchioles and in the alveoli and considered this the first step in the genesis of the "busulfan lung." This observation could not be confirmed on the patient material observed at the Memorial Hospital.

Busulfan and Neoplasia

Nelson and Andrews[16] were the first to record a case of mammary carcinoma observed in a patient receiving busulfan therapy for chronic myelogenous leukemia. A case of invasive carcinoma of the uterine cervix occurring after five years of busulfan therapy was subsequently encountered.[10] In the most recently reported case,[3] a carcinoma on the vulva was observed after six years of therapy, and, at autopsy three years later, there were adenomas of the pancreas and the kidney. It is thus entirely possible that the cellular abnormalities simulating cancer are more than just a morphologic curiosity.

Cyclophosphamide

Cyclophosphamide, also a bivalent alkylating agent, has been shown to produce ulcerations of the urinary bladder epithelium in experimental animals by Philips and co-workers.[18] These authors demonstrated that cyclophosphamide was inactive *per se,* and that its metabolites, presumably formed in the liver, were excreted in the urine; adequate hydration of the experimental animals prevented to some extent the ulcerative effect of the drug on the epithelia of the lower urinary tract.

In man, significant cytologic abnormalities were observed in the urinary sediment of patients undergoing treatment with this drug.[4] Cytologic abnormalities included marked nuclear changes that in some instances simulated cancer cells. The effect was not dose-dependent and was observed in some patients who received only a small amount of the drug.

Biopsies of the bladder and postmortem material demonstrated epithelial abnormalities akin to those observed under the impact of busulfan.[10]

In a single instance, pulmonary abnormalities were also observed: these occurred in a 60-year-old man who was receiving large daily doses of cyclophosphamide for a period of three years. The findings were those of an organizing intraalveolar fibrinous exudate. There were no nuclear abnormalities within the alveoli.[10]

Experimental System Based on Cyclophosphamide

The observations of Philips and colleagues[18] led to further investigation of the effects of cyclophosphamide on the epithelium of the urinary bladder.[11] Single doses of the drug in the amounts of 200 or 400 mgm/kg administered intraperitoneally to the male rats resulted in the following sequence of events:

Epithelium. Within two hours after administration of the drug, epithelial necrosis set in. Within 24 hours, the epithelium was almost completely necrotic, except for small islets of cells. From these remnants of the epithelial structure, there originated a vigorous proliferation of cells, resulting in a marked rapid epithelial regeneration and hyperplasia that was quite obvious at 48 hours after administration of the drug. Two weeks after initiation of the experiments, a marked papillary hyperplasia persisted.

Long-term studies, presently still under way, indicate that with the passage of time the epithelium reverted to a morphologic appearance approaching normal; however, some degree of cellular abnormality persisted for as long as 16 months.

Electron microscopic studies during the initial phase of the experiments revealed evidence of epithelial necrosis. Two hours after injection, peculiar intranuclear granules were observed, resembling those hitherto described only in experiments involving multiplication of viruses (for summary, see reference 11).

Smooth Muscle. The drug also affected the smooth muscle of the bladder, causing necrosis of individual muscle fibres.

Discussion

It is evident that the alkylating agents busulfan and cyclophosphamide are capable of producing significant cellular abnormalities in noncancerous tissues of man. These effects are not unique and have been occasionally associated with other drugs as well (for summary, see reference 13). However, the significance of the changes attributable to busulfan is enhanced by the report of three patients who developed carcinoma of breast, uterine cervix, and vulva while under treatment.[16,10,3] In the last patient, two histologically benign adenomas were also observed. Boyland[1] stated: "It is probable that the biochemical lesions caused by nitrogen mustard, or other alkylating agents used either in controlling malignant disease or inducing cancer, are similar."

Ample biochemical evidence is presented in this monograph documenting the biochemical bases of carcinogenesis by alkylating compounds. Repeating this evidence here would be redundant.

The effects of cyclophosphamide on the epithelium of the urinary bladder in man has been the basis of an experimental system in the rat described above. Chaves[2] recently confirmed my original observations. To date, this system does not appear to be carcinogenic in the rat, but has served as a basis for a series of other experiments. Thus, problems of regeneration of the epithelium and of generation time of epithelial cells are presently being investigated. Carcinogenesis in the urinary bladder is also being studied.[12]

Summary

The alkylating agents busulfan and cyclophosphamide produce marked cellular changes in apparently healthy tissues of man. In the case of busulfan, the changes at the cellular level are akin to those observed in human cancer, affect primarily epithelial structures, and may involve virtually every organ. Severe pulmonary fibrosis that may be associated with the cellular changes may be fatal. Three cases of human cancer occurring during treatment of chronic myelogenous leukemia with this drug are recorded.

Cyclophosphamide affects primarily the human urinary bladder, wherein marked epithelial abnormalities may be observed. An experimental system utilizing this drug to produce marked hyperplasia in the epithelium of the urinary bladder in the rat is described, and its applications are briefly discussed.

[NOTE ADDED IN PROOF: A case of lung cancer in a patient receiving busulfan therapy was recently described by Min and Györkey in Cancer **22:** 1027, 1968. Wada *et al.* have also pointed out that mustard gas has been shown to produce lung cancer in workers exposed to this substance (Lancet, 1161, June 1, 1968).]

References

1. Boyland, E. 1964. The carcinogenic activity of drugs employed in the treatment of cancer and leukemia. Bull. Union internat. contre cancer, **2:** 6.
2. Chaves, E. 1968. Induction of bladder hyperplasia in rats after a single dose of cyclophosphamide. Rev. Franc. Etud. Clin. Biol., **13:** 56–61.
3. Feingold, M. L. & L. G. Koss. Effects of long term administration of busulfan. Report of a case with generalized nuclear abnormalities, carcinoma of vulva, and pulmonary fibrosis. A.M.A. Arch. Int. Med. (In press.)
4. Forni, A. M., L. G. Koss & W. Geller. 1964. Cytological study of the effect of cyclophosphamide on the epithelium of the urinary bladder in man. Cancer **17:** 1348–1355.
5. Galton, D. A. G., M. Till & E. Wiltshaw. 1958. Busulfan (1,4-dimethanesulfonyloxybutane, Myleran): Summary of clinical results. Ann. N. Y. Acad. Sci. **68:** 967–973.
6. Güreli, N., S. W. Denham & S. W. Root. 1963. Cytologic dysplasia related to busulfan (Myleran) therapy: Report of a case. Obstet. Gynec. **21:** 466–470.
7. Haddow, A. & G. M. Timmis. 1953. Myleran in chronic myeloid leukemia: Chemical constitution and biological action. Lancet **i:** 207–208.
8. Harrold, B. P. 1966. Syndrome resembling Addison's disease following prolonged treatment with busulfan. Brit. Med. J. **5485:** 463–464.
9. Heard, B. E. & R. A. Cooke. 1968. Busulfan lung. Thorax **23:** 187–193.

10. Koss, L. G. 1968. Diagnostic Cytology and Its Histopathologic Bases. 2nd edit. J. B. Lippincott Co. Philadelphia, Pa.
11. Koss, L. G. 1967. A light and electron microscopic study of the effects of a single dose of cyclophosphamide on various organs in the rat. I. The urinary bladder. Lab. Invest. **16:** 44–65.
12. Koss, L. G. (Unpublished data.)
13. Koss, L. G., M. R. Melamed & K. Mayer. 1965. The effect of busulfan on human epithelia. Amer. J. Clin. Path. **44:** 385–397.
14. Kyle, R. A., R. S. Schwartz, H. L. Oliner & W. Dameshek. 1961. A syndrome resembling adrenal cortical insufficiency associated with long term busulfan (Myleran) therapy. Blood **18:** 497–510.
15. Leake, E., Smith, W. G. & Woodliff, H. J. 1963. Diffuse interstitial pulmonary fibrosis after busulphan therapy. Lancet **ii:** 432–434.
16. Nelson, B. M. & G. A. Andrews. 1964. Breast cancer and cytologic dysplasia in many organs after busulfan (Myleran). Amer. J. Clin. Path., **42:** 37–44.
17. Oliner, H., R. Schwartz, F. Rubio & W. Dameshek. 1961. Interstitial pulmonary fibrosis following busulfan therapy. Amer. J. Med. **31:** 134–139.
18. Philips, F. S., S. S. Sternberg, A. P. Cronin & P. M. Vidal. 1961. Cyclophosphamide and urinary bladder toxicity. Cancer Res. **21:** 1577–1589.
19. Sprunt, J. G., & C. R. Rizza. 1966. Pigmentation and busulfan therapy. Brit. Med. J. **5489:** 736–737.
20. Vivacqua, R. J., I. Haurani & A. J. Ersley. 1967. "Selective" pituitary insufficiency secondary to busulfan. Ann. Int. Med. **67:** 380–387.
21. Waller, U. 1960. Riesenkerne nach Myleranthérapie und Milzbestrahlung bei chronischer myeloischer Leukaemie. Path. Microbiol. **23:** 283–290.
22. Ward, H. N., N. Konikov & E. H. Reinhard. 1965. Cytologic dysplasis occurring after busulfan (Myleran) therapy. A syndrome resembling adrenocortical insufficiency and atrophic bronchitis. Ann. Int. Med. **63:** 654–660.

PROPERTIES OF L5178Y LYMPHOBLASTS HIGHLY RESISTANT TO NITROGEN MUSTARD*

Gerald J. Goldenberg

Department of Internal Medicine
University of Manitoba, and
The Manitoba Cancer Foundation
Winnipeg, Canada

Introduction

The distinct possibility exists that there is no single mode of action for alkylating agents because of their capacity to react with several nucleophilic groups in the cell.[1-3] A technique that has proven useful in investigating mechanisms of action of other chemotherapeutic agents, particularly the antimetabolites, has been the comparison of physical and chemical properties of two closely related cell lines differing only with respect to sensitivity to a particular drug.[4-8] Therefore, the object of this study was to obtain a cell line markedly resistant to nitrogen mustard that might serve as a model for the investigation of the mechanism of action of that drug by comparing the properties of sensitive and resistant cells.

Materials and Methods

Induction of Resistance to Nitrogen Mustard

Murine leukemia L5178Y lymphoblasts were treated *in vitro* with nitrogen mustard (HN2)† as previously described.[9,10] Surviving cells were retreated with HN2 with the object of inducing resistance to that drug. A series of growth curves obtained by the sequential treatment of surviving cells is plotted semilogarithmically in Figure 1. The broken line in each pair of curves represents an untreated control; the open circle and solid line represent the growth curve of a treated culture. With each subsequent treatment, the growth curve of the treated flask more closely approximates that of the untreated control (i.e., the cells are becoming more resistant). The initial dose of HN2 was 0.06 μgm/ml, and this was subsequently increased.

An overall perspective of the sequential treatment program and the induction of resistance to HN2 is illustrated in Figure 2. Resistance to HN2, as measured by D_0 (the dose of drug required to reduce survival by 1/e along the exponential portion of the dose-survival curve) is plotted against time. D_0, which in this instance was an approximate value, was calculated from the equation: $D_0 = C_2 - C_1/\log_e S_1 - \log_e S_2$, where C_1 and $\log_e S_1 = 0$, C_2 = concentration of HN2 in μgm/ml and S_2 = surviving cell fraction derived from the growth curves

* Supported by a grant from the National Cancer Institute of Canada.

† Nitrogen mustard (Mustargen®) kindly supplied by Dr. W. Dorian, Merck Sharpe & Dohme of Canada Ltd., Montreal, Canada.

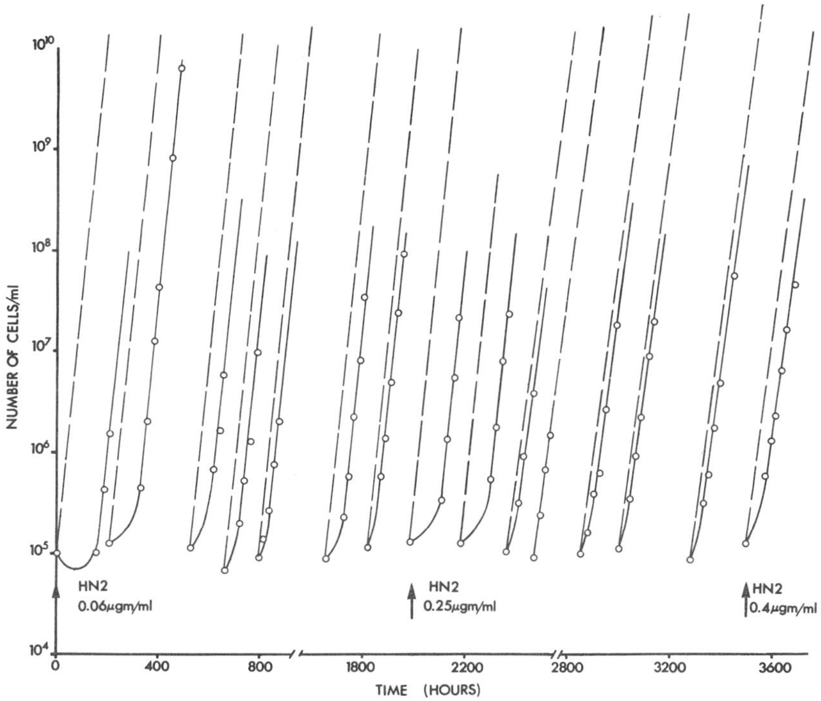

FIGURE 1. A series of growth curves of L5178Y lymphoblasts treated with progressively larger doses of nitrogen mustard (HN2). The broken line in each pair of curves represents an untreated control; the open circle and solid line represent the growth curve of a treated culture.

shown in FIGURE 1 with use of the extrapolation method of Alexander and Mikulski.[11]

The initial dose of HN2 was 0.06 μgm/ml, and the surviving cells were retreated at that dose for a total of seven treatments over a period of 77 days (FIGURE 2). Thereafter, the dose of HN2 was gradually increased sequentially to 0.25, 0.4, 0.5, and subsequently to 1.25 μgm/ml.

In order to assess stability of the induced resistance, cells were removed from the sequential treatment program at points A and B and were maintained *in vitro* without further exposure to HN2.

Cells were also removed from the sequential treatment scheme at seven and one-half months (line 1) and 18 months (line 2), and these were transplanted back into normal DBA/2 female mice and maintained *in vivo* as ascites tumors by serial intraperitoneal (i.p.) transplantation every five to seven days. These two cell lines will be referred to as resistant line 1 (L5178Y/HN2-1) and resistant line 2 (L5178Y/HN2-2), respectively. Periodically, cell cultures were established *in vitro* from these two resistant mouse ascites tumors and the original sensitive line for study of the various properties described in this report.

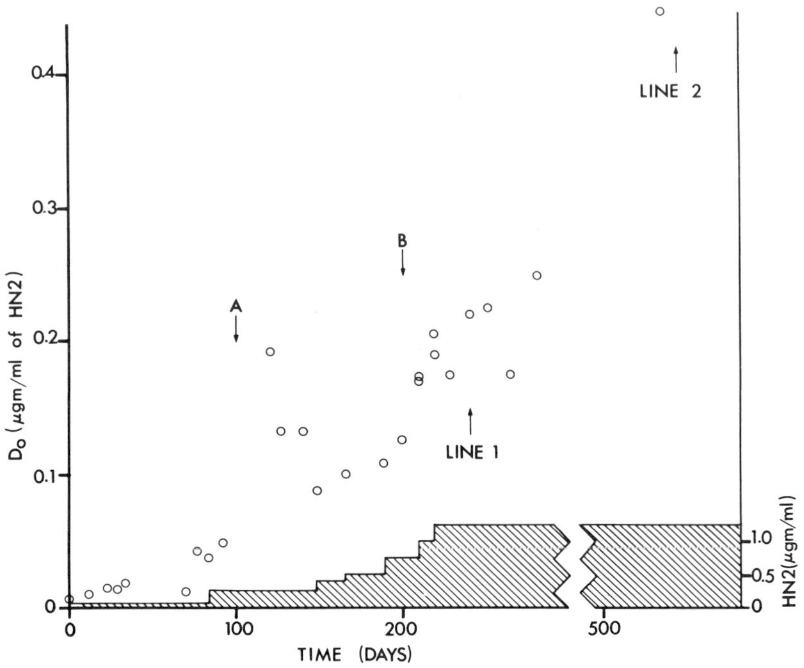

FIGURE 2. An overall perspective of the sequential treatment program and the induction of resistance to HN2 is illustrated. Resistance to HN2 is expressed as D_0 (see text for derivation of this value). The sequential increase in dosage of HN2 is depicted by the hatched area at the bottom. Cells removed at points A and B were kept *in vitro* without further exposure to HN2 in order to assess stability of the induced resistance (see below). Cells removed at the points marked line 1 and line 2 were transplanted back into normal DBA/2 female mice and maintained *in vivo* as HN2-resistant ascites tumors.

Method of Determination of Dose-Survival Curves

The extrapolation method of Alexander and Mikulski[11] was employed; the limitations and assumptions inherent in this method have been described in detail previously.[9,12] The extrapolation method tends to exaggerate cell kill if a significant fraction of surviving cells has a doubling time longer than that of untreated controls (slow-growing variants), or if the surviving cells are arrested for some time in interphase before undergoing cell division (division delay). Both these phenomena have been observed at higher drug concentrations than those used here, in which cell kill exceeds four logs. Slow-growing variants are recognized by prolongation of the doubling time and division delay by curvilinear deviation of the dose-survival curve.[12] At the drug concentrations used in this experiment, dose-survival curves were exponential throughout and surviving cells grew up promptly with a doubling time identical to that of untreated controls.

Chromosome preparations

L5178Y lymphoblasts at a concentration of 2–5 × 10^5 cells/ml were treated with 4 μg/ml colchicine (Colcemid®)‡ at 37° C for five hours. The cells were centrifuged at 750 rpm for three minutes, the supernate was decanted, and the cells were swollen by incubation in one percent sodium citrate at 37° C for 15 minutes. The cells were then fixed in ethanol:glacial acetic acid (3:1), mounted on slides, and stained with aceto-orcein.

Life-Cycle Analysis

Life-cycle analysis of HN2-sensitive and -resistant L5178Y lymphoblasts was performed following the method of Stanners and Till.[13] The cells were incubated in 0.25 μc/ml of ^{3}H-thymidine (Schwarz Bioresearch Inc., Orangeburg, N.Y.) at 37° C for 11 hours; aliquots were removed at 15-minute intervals for the first two hours and at hourly intervals thereafter. The fixed cells were mounted, stained with aceto-orcein, coated with Ilford Type K-2 nuclear research emulsion (Ilford Ltd., Ilford, Essex), and exposed for eight days before developing.

Biochemical Determinations

RNA was extracted from cells by the hot phenol-SDS method of Scherrer and Darnell[14] and measured by ultraviolet (UV) absorption at 260 millimicrons. The kinetics of RNA sythesis were studied in sensitive and resistant cells by following rate of incorporation of radioactive phosphorus (^{32}P) into RNA.

RNA and DNA were also extracted from the cells by a modification of the Schmidt and Thannhauser method,[15] as previously described.[16] RNA was determined colorimetrically by a modification of the orcinol reaction[17] with use of 8.3 N HCl, 0.08% $FeCl_3$, and 0.23% orcinol, and boiling for 15 minutes; DNA was determined by the diphenylamine reaction.[18]

Sulfhydryl levels were determined by the method of Ellman,[19] which detects all thiol groups, free or protein-bound, available to react with the reagent 5,5^1-dithiobis(2-nitrobenzoic acid).

Physical Determinations

Cell size was measured with use of a model A Coulter electronic particle counter. The instrument was calibrated with giant ragweed pollen (mean particle diameter 19.5 μ) in order to determine cell volume.

Cell mobility was determined with the whole cell electrophoresis apparatus and method described by Bangham.[20]

Osmotic fragility studies were performed by incubating 10^6 cells at room

‡Colchicine (Colcemid) kindly supplied by Dr. C. W. Murphy, Ciba Company Limited, Dorval, Quebec, Canada.

temperature for 30 minutes in a series of tubes ranging from 0–0.9% NaCl concentration. Cell viability was determined by exclusion of dye (0.2% trypan blue), and viable cells were counted in a hemocytometer.

Results

Induction of Resistance to Nitrogen Mustard

Induction of resistance to HN2 was a slow process (Figure 2). An increase in resistance was not detected until the seventh course of HN2 was given on day 77 of the sequential treatment program. Thereafter, a slow but steady induction of resistance was noted, and even after 18 months, resistance to HN2 was still increasing. This slow development of resistance explains our previous unsuccessful attempt to induce resistance to HN2, since in that study the effort was abandoned after only four courses of HN2 were administered.[9]

Dose-response curves obtained for three cell lines—the original sensitive line, resistant line 1, and resistant line 2—following treatment with nitrogen mustard are shown in Figure 3. A comparison of the D_0 reveals that the two resistant lines are approximately ten- and thirtyfold more resistant to HN2 than the original line. The magnitude of the resistance is such that a dose of HN2 that previously permitted only 1 in 10^6 sensitive cells to survive now allows approximately 50% of HN2-resistant cells to recover.

Reversibility of Resistance

The cells that were removed from the sequential-treatment scheme at points A and B (Figure 2) and kept *in vitro* without further exposure to HN2 were used to assess stability of the induced resistance. For cells removed at point A, resistance to HN2 was stable for up to 117 days *in vitro,* but resistance began to diminish sometime between 117 and 279 days (Figure 4, A). For cells removed at point B, resistance was stable for 80 days *in vitro,* declined between 80 and 158 days, and completely disappeared by 307 days, so that the sensitivity of the original cell line was restored (Figure 4, B). Thus resistance was stable for more than 80 days *in vitro,* but thereafter declined and completely disappeared at approximately 300 days.

Resistant line 1 (L5178Y/HN2-1) was transplanted back into normal six-to-ten-week-old DBA/2 female mice and carried *in vivo* by serial intraperitoneal (i.p.) transplantation every five to seven days. Dose-survival curves of resistant line 1 cells treated with HN2 before and after transplantation *in vivo* are shown in Figure 5. Sensitivity to HN2 decreased initially after transplantation *in vivo,* then stabilized between the first and ninth transplant, and has remained stable up to 39 transplantations *in vivo* (i.e., approximately 200 days). A similar pattern was observed on transplantation of resistant line 2 *in vivo.*

Biological Properties

Virulence. A comparison of the median survival time of mice inoculated i.p. with sensitive and resistant cells revealed no significant difference; mice receiving

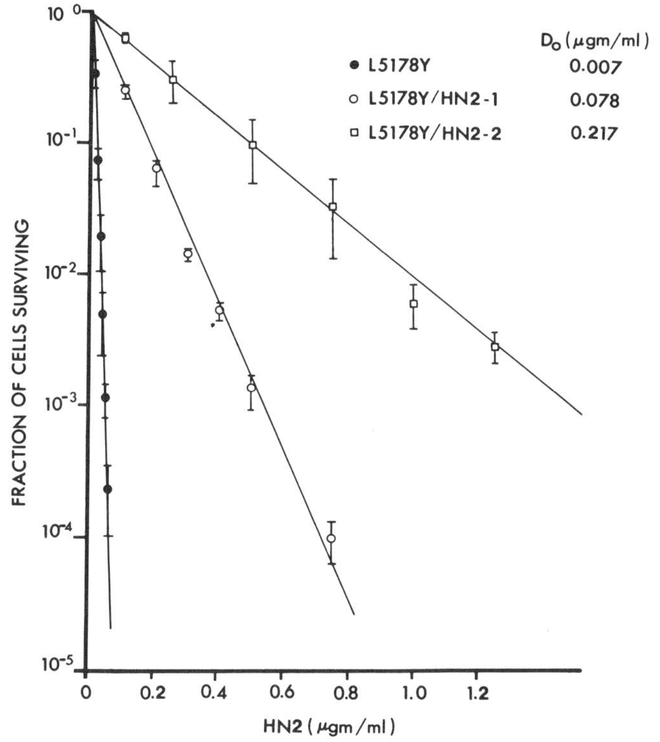

FIGURE 3. Dose-survival curves following treatment with HN2 of three L5178Y cell lines, the original sensitive line (L5178Y), resistant line 1 (L5178Y/HN2-1), and resistant line 2 (L5178Y/HN2-2).

sensitive L5178Y cells had a median survival time of 10.9 days compared with 11.1 and 11.2 days for mice inoculated with resistant lines 1 and 2, respectively.

The doubling time *in vitro* of resistant cells was slightly longer than that of sensitive cells, but only the difference between sensitive (10.9 ± 0.14 hours) and resistant line 2 cells (11.7 ± 0.33 hours) was statistically significant ($p < 0.05$). This finding is less striking but similar to the report of Reid and Walker,[21] in which the doubling times of strain L cells sensitive and resistant to sulfur mustard were 16 and 21 hours, respectively.

Chromosomes. During induction of resistance to HN2 *in vitro,* a linear relationship was observed between percent tetraploidy and resistance to HN2 as measured by D_0 (FIGURE 6); the correlation coefficient of the regression line was 0.90 and was statistically significant ($p < 0.05$). However, examination of resistant lines maintained *in vivo* for several generations revealed a poorer correlation, with considerable overlap between HN2-resistance and percent tetraploidy. Tetraploidy varied from 1–4% in the sensitive line, from 2.6–18% in resistant line 1, and from 35.5–56% in resistant line 2.

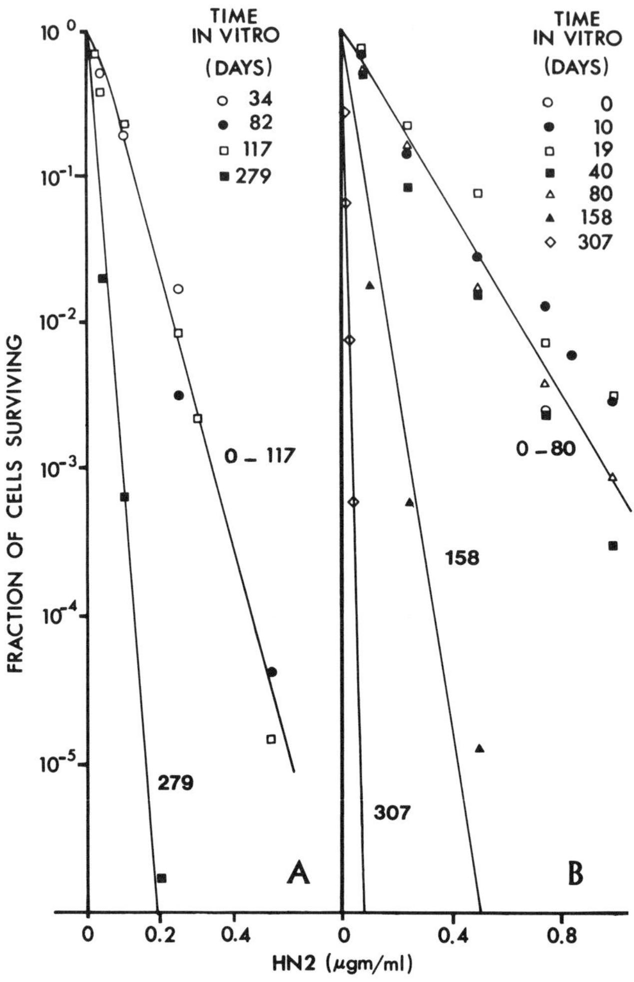

FIGURE 4. A: Dose-survival curves of HN2-resistant lymphoblasts removed from the sequential treatment program at point A, FIGURE 1, and treated with HN2 at various intervals following their last exposure to drug to assess stability of the induced resistance. B: Same as for A, except that it relates to cells removed at point B, FIGURE 1.

On serial transplantation of both resistant lines *in vivo*, an exponential decline in tetraploidy was observed over a period of time (FIGURE 7).

Chromosome analysis of diploid cells revealed that both sensitive (L5178Y) and resistant (L5178Y/HN2-1) lines contained a predominance of cells with 40 chromosomes, which is the normal chromosome number for the mouse. The karyotype of the resistant line appeared more homogenous with 73.8 ± 3.2% of cells containing 40 chromosomes, compared with 38.5 ± 3.6% of cells in the sensitive line.

Cross-Resistance. To determine whether cross-resistance existed between HN2 and ionizing radiation, sensitive and resistant cells (L5178Y/HN2-2) were treated with ionizing radiation from a Co^{60} source. No difference was observed in the dose-survival curves of the two cell lines, indicating a lack of cross-resistance between HN2 and ionizing radiation. This finding confirms that of Hirono,[22] who reported that a Yoshida ascites tumor resistant to alkylating agents was not cross-resistant to x rays.

Life-Cycle Analysis. The mitotic index of sensitive L5178Y cells was 2.15 ± 0.11%, that of resistant L5178Y/HN2-2 cells was 1.68 ± 0.15%, and the difference was statistically significant ($p < 0.01$). The mitotic index of both cell lines increased approximately eightfold on incubation with Colcemid; the mitotic index of the resistant line after Colcemid was 13.90 ± 1.26%, that of the sensitive line 18.91 ± 1.88%, and again the mitotic index of the resistant line was significantly lower than the sensitive line ($p < 0.05$). No apparent explanation of the

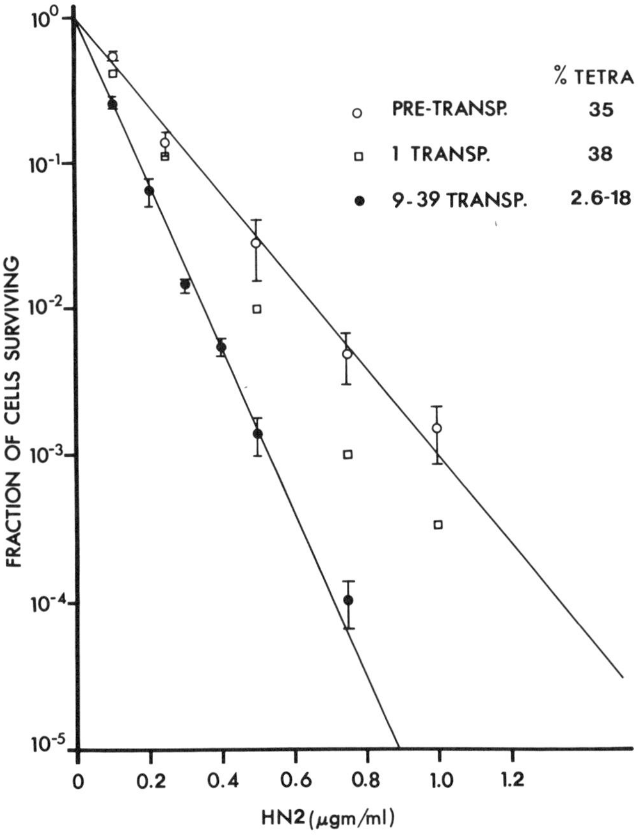

FIGURE 5. Dose-survival curves of resistant line 1 (L5178Y/HN2-1) before and after transplantation *in vivo*.

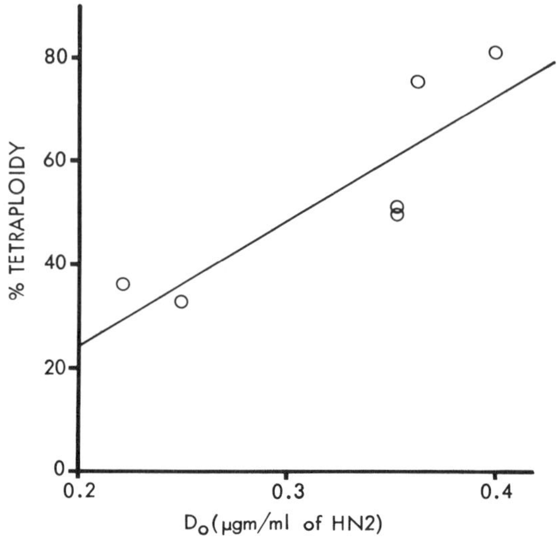

FIGURE 6. The relationship of resistance to HN2 (as measured by D_0) and the percentage of tetraploid cells in a culture, during induction of resistance to HN2.

lower mitotic index of resistant cells was found, but the observation prompted a study of the life cycle of sensitive and resistant cells.

Life-cycle analysis revealed a striking similarity between HN2-sensitive and resistant lymphoblasts (TABLE 1), and these data correspond closely with the results reported by Watanabe and Okada.[23,24] The percentage of labeled cells

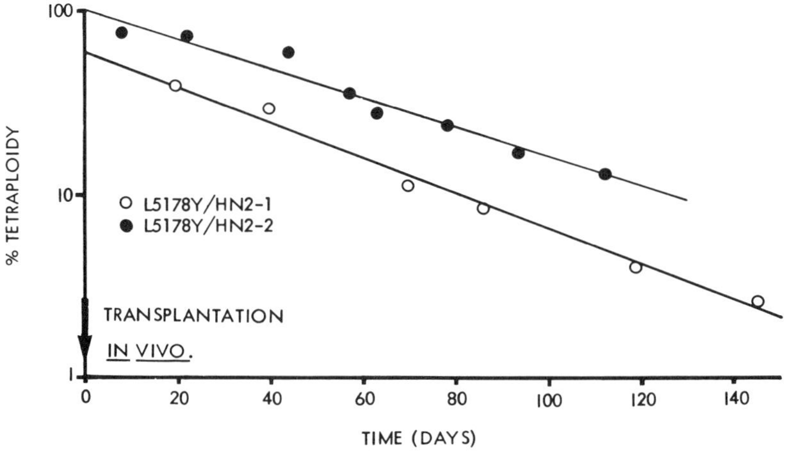

FIGURE 7. Semilogarithmic plot of rate of decline of percent tetraploidy in resistant lines 1 and 2 after transplantation *in vivo*.

TABLE 1
LIFE-CYCLE ANALYSIS OF HN2-SENSITIVE AND -RESISTANT L5178Y LYMPHOBLASTS

Cell Line	Generation Time (hours)	M hours	M %	G_1 hours	G_1 %	S hours	S %	G_2 hours	G_2 %
L5178Y	11.5	0.36	3.1	2.36	20.5	7.67	66.7	1.11	9.7
L5178Y/HN2-2	10.0	0.24	2.4	1.81	18.1	6.74	67.4	1.21	12.1

reached a maximum at 97.7% for the sensitive line and 97.8% for the resistant line, indicating that for each cell line, approximately two percent of cells are in the noncycling or G_0 phase.

Biochemical Properties

Nucleic Acid Content. Rate of synthesis of total cellular RNA was similar in HN2-sensitive and -resistant cell lines (FIGURE 8). The kinetics of ribosomal precursor RNA synthesis and degradation of precursor to ribosomal RNA were also similar in sensitive and resistant lines.[25] Total RNA content in resistant cells (L5178Y/HN2-2), as measured by O.D.$_{260}$ following hot phenol extraction, was 14% higher than that of sensitive cells (TABLE 2), and this difference was statistically significant ($p < 0.05$).

Nucleic acids were also extracted from sensitive and resistant lymphoblasts with use of a modification of the Schmidt and Thannhauser method.[16] RNA content of both cell lines was lower with this method than the values obtained by phenol extraction (TABLE 2). The RNA content of HN2-resistant cells was $8.37 \pm 0.50 \times 10^{-12}$ g/cell compared with $7.71 \pm 0.46 \times 10^{-12}$ g/cell for the sensitive line, but the difference was not statistically significant, although it was in the same direction obtained with the phenol method.

DNA content of resistant cells was $4.61 \pm 0.32 \times 10^{-12}$ g/cell, which was approximately 18% higher than the DNA content of sensitive cells, but the differ-

TABLE 2
NUCLEIC ACID CONTENT OF HN2-SENSITIVE AND -RESISTANT L5178Y LYMPHOBLASTS

Cell Line	RNA ($\times 10^{-12}$ g/cell) Phenol*	RNA ($\times 10^{-12}$ g/cell) S&T†	DNA ($\times 10^{-12}$ g/cell) S&T†	RNA/DNA S&T†
L5178Y	9.88 ± 0.40	7.71 ± 0.46	3.92 ± 0.21	1.97
L5178Y/HN2-2	11.26 ± 0.50	8.37 ± 0.50	4.61 ± 0.32	1.82

* Hot phenol extraction[14] and O.D.$_{260}$ determination of RNA.
† Modified Schmidt and Thannhauser extraction of nucleic acids; RNA determined by orcinol reaction (see text) and DNA by the diphenylamine reaction.[18]

ence fell short of statistical significance (TABLE 2). The ratio of RNA to DNA was 1.97 and 1.82 in sensitive and resistant cells, respectively.

Sulfhydryl Content. The thiol content in the sensitive line was $40.2 \pm 1.6 \times 10^{-16}$ moles/cell, that in resistant line 1 was $56.3 \pm 1.7 \times 10^{-16}$ moles/cell, and that in resistant line 2 was $81.6 \pm 3.9 \times 10^{-16}$ moles/cell. A t-test comparing the significance of the difference of mean thiol content between each of the three cell lines was highly significant ($p < 0.001$). A direct correlation was observed between HN2 resistance, as expressed by D_0, and cellular thiol content; the correlation coefficient of the regression line was 0.99, and was statistically significant ($p < 0.05$) (FIGURE 9).

Physical Properties

Cell Size. A size distribution plot of sensitive and resistant cells obtained in a Coulter particle counter revealed that resistant cells were smaller than sensitive

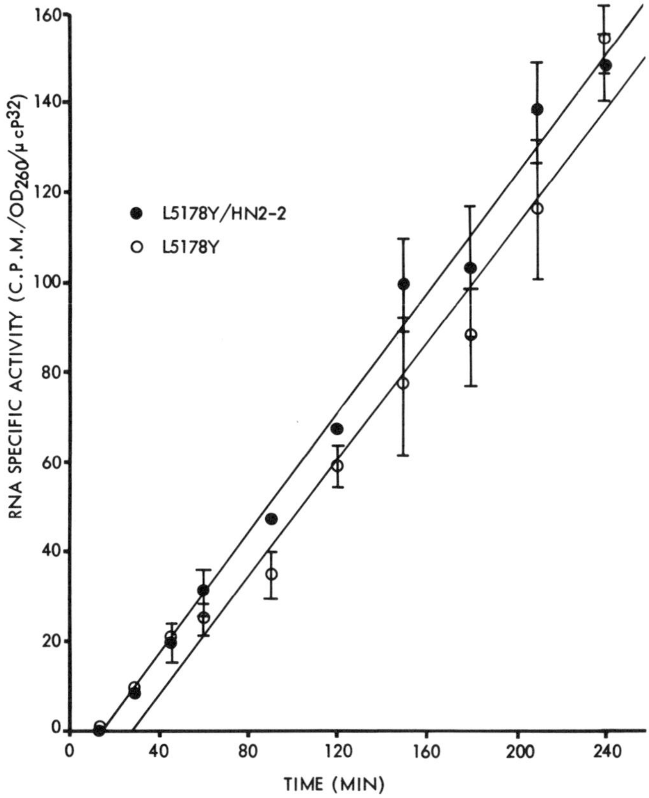

FIGURE 8. Rate of synthesis of total cellular RNA in HN2-sensitive and -resistant cells *in vitro* as measured by rate of incorporation of ^{32}P.

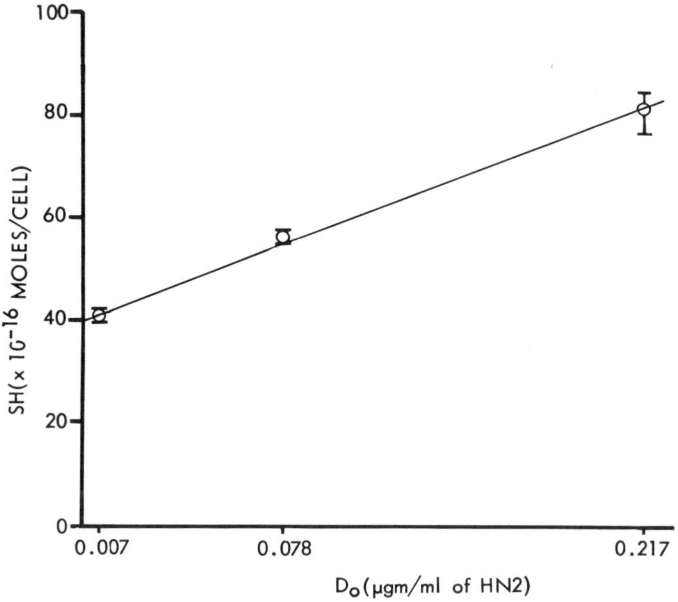

FIGURE 9. The relationship of resistance to HN2 (as measured by D_0) and cellular sulfhydryl content.

cells (FIGURE 10). A t-test comparing the difference of mean cell volumes was highly significant ($p < 0.001$). With use of giant ragweed pollen as a standard, the sensitive cell was calculated to have a mean cell volume of 633 μ^3 and a mean cell diameter of 10.56 μ; resistant cell line 1 was found to have a mean cell volume of 527 μ^3 and a mean cell diameter of 9.93 microns. No difference in cell size was noted between resistant cell lines 1 and 2.

Cell Mobility. Electrophoretic mobility of sensitive (L5178Y) and resistant (L5178Y/HN2-2) lymphoblasts revealed no significant difference. The mobility of sensitive cells was 0.83 ± 0.04 μ/sec/volt/cm, and that of resistant cells was 0.86 ± 0.05 μ/sec/volt/cm. An interesting observation was that after being *in vitro* for more than 30 weeks, cell mobility of both sensitive and resistant cells increased.

Osmotic Fragility. Osmotic fragility curves of sensitive and resistant cells were identical.

DISCUSSION

The degree of resistance induced to HN2 *in vitro* in this study greatly exceeds the level of resistance reported previously for alkylating agents.[21,26,27] Reid and Walker reported on a sulfur mustard-resistant subline of strain L cells in which the D_0 was 1.33-fold greater than the sensitive line.[21] Crathorn and Roberts described a sulfur mustard-resistant lymphoma line in which the dose-survival

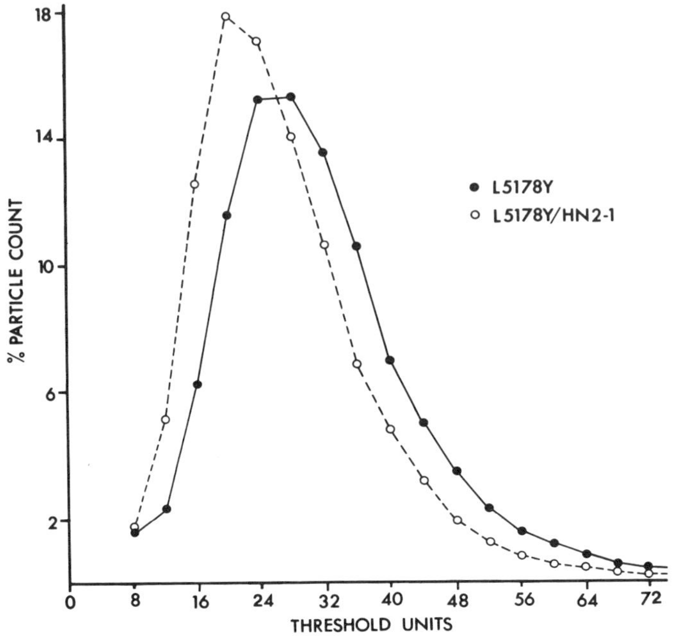

FIGURE 10. Size distribution plots of HN2-sensitive and -resistant cells obtained in a Coulter particle counter.

curve differed from that of the sensitive line in having a more prominent shoulder, but in which the D_0 was only fractionally greater.[27] Levis isolated an HN2-resistant subline of guinea pig cells cultured *in vitro* in which the D_0 of the resistant line was 1.5 times that of the sensitive line (estimated from his dose-survival curves).[26] In this study, the D_0 of HN2-resistant line 2 was some thirtyfold greater than the D_0 of the original Fischer line (FIGURE 3).

In addition to the magnitude of the resistance, certain biological features of the HN2-resistant L5178Y cell line make it an attractive model for studying mechanism of action of and/or resistance to HN2. The resistant line closely resembles the sensitive line in several respects: 1) virulence, as indicated by the median survival time of mice inoculated with the resistant lines (11.1 and 11.2 days) compared with the sensitive line (10.9 days); 2) doubling time *in vitro* of the sensitive line was 10.9 hours and that of the resistant lines was 11.3 and 11.7 hours; 3) life-cycle analysis was very similar in sensitive and resistant lines; 4) similar cell mobility and osmotic fragility studies; and 5) the same rate of RNA synthesis in sensitive and resistant cells.

Another attractive feature of this model is the relative stability of the resistant line for more than 80 days *in vitro* (FIGURE 4) and the retention of resistance on transplantation *in vivo* for approximately 200 days following an initial decline in resistance (FIGURE 5).

During the induction of resistance to HN2, a linear relationship was demonstrated between percent tetraploidy and HN2-resistance (FIGURE 6). Once resistance was established and the cells were no longer exposed to HN2, percent tetraploidy decreased in an exponential fashion (FIGURE 7); however, decline in HN2-resistance was not as predictable, and considerable overlap was noted between HN2-sensitivity and tetraploidy. This weaker correlation may merely reflect the inability of dose-survival curves of this type to detect differences of tetraploidy of 5–50% in mixed cell populations; alternatively, it may indicate that tetraploidy is not the only change that cells undergo in developing resistance to nitrogen mustard.

The finding of tetraploidy in association with resistance to HN2 is consistent with an earlier report of "radiosensitive" and "radioresistant mutants."[9] In that study it was found that a tetraploid mutant, which had been isolated on suboptimal culture media, was more resistant to nitrogen mustard but not to x-radiation. In this investigation, the induction of resistance to HN2 was associated with an increase in tetraploidy. Thus a correlation would appear to exist between HN2-resistance and tetraploidy.

The formation of tetraploid cells in this study provides biologic evidence supporting the hypothesis that one mechanism of cytocidal action of nitrogen mustard is the cross-linking of DNA. Wheeler has suggested that cross-linked DNA may remain intact, and if replication of each template molecule occurred, the resulting tetra-strand DNA could not cleave to yield two daughter double strands, and interference with mitosis would be likely.[1]

The doubling times of both resistant lines (one of which contains a large percentage of tetraploid cells) are approximately 11 hours. The rate of decline of tetraploidy, however, is slow; the $T\frac{1}{2}$ for tetraploidy in resistant lines 1 and 2 is 31 and 37 days, respectively (FIGURE 7). These data suggest that diploid and/or tetraploid cells are dividing and forming tetraploid daughter cells, since if diploid cells were dividing to form diploid daughter cells exclusively, the rate of dilution of tetraploid cells would be much more rapid.

The absence of cross-resistance between HN2 and Co^{60} radiation confirms similar reports by several other investigators.[22,26,28] This finding strongly suggests that the mechanism of action of HN2 differs from that of ionizing radiation.

The concentrations of RNA and DNA were higher in resistant than in sensitive cells (TABLE 2). This finding may be explained by the higher percentage of tetraploidy in resistant cells. Whisson reported a 30% increase in DNA content of a plasma-cell tumor resistant to alkylating agents, which was also characterized by a higher chromosome number than the sensitive tumor.[29]

Previously, it was noted that "radiosensitive" L5178Y cells were larger in size than "radioresistant" cells.[9] Reid and Walker, using a Coulter particle counter to measure cell size, found that the volume of strain L cells varied inversely with resistance to sulfur mustard; they postulated that the smaller target size accounted for the greater degree of drug-resistance of S-mustard-resistant cells (21). In this investigation, resistant cells were also found to be smaller than sensitive cells (FIGURE 10). However, no difference in cell volume was noted between the two resistant lines, although the D_0 of resistant line 2 was approximately threefold greater than that of resistant line 1. To explain the smaller cell size of resistant cells in conjunction with an increase of tetraploidy, one might postulate that the nuclear/cytoplasmic ratio of resistant cells was greatly increased. No attempt was made to determine the nuclear/cytoplasmic ratio of sensitive and resistant cells in this study, but such an investigation would be of interest.

The mechanism of induction of resistance to HN2 is unknown, but several possibilities might be considered, including: 1) selection of a resistant clone of cells; 2) alteration of membrane permeability to the drug; 3) induction of enzyme(s) either to circumvent a specific metabolic block or to enhance capacity for repair (the latter being more likely with alkylating agents); and 4) increased cellular concentration of protective agents (*viz,* thiol groups) that would "spare" the target sites from lethal injury by alkylation.

Firstly, the attempt to induce a resistant mutant was undertaken after it was noted that the dose-survival curve of sensitive L5178Y cells was becoming biphasic, with a sharp increase in D_0 at higher doses of HN2. This suggested the existence of two cell populations of differing sensitivity to HN2, and that by repeated treatment of surviving cells the sensitive population might be eliminated with selection of a resistant clone of cells. This observation lends support to the first mechanism, selection of a resistant clone of cells.

Secondly, alteration of membrane properties was not detected with respect to surface charge or cell shape as measured by cell mobility and osmotic fragility, respectively; however, these negative findings do not rule out a change in membrane permeability to HN2.

With respect to enzyme induction as a mechanism of resistance, there is suggestive evidence that HN2 may act at several biochemical sites,[1-3] so that induction of a single enzyme is not a plausible mechanism of resistance. However, differences in repair enzymes may well explain the superior ability of resistant cells to recover following treatment with HN2.

Finally, convincing evidence was obtained in this investigation indicating a strong correlation between cellular thiol content and HN2-resistance as measured by D_0 (FIGURE 9). This observation is consistent with the report of Calcutt and Connors,[30] who found that tumor sensitivity to the alkylating agent merophan varied directly with the ratio of protein-bound:free thiol content of the tumor and with the earlier experience of Hirono,[31] who found elevated nonprotein sulfhydryl levels in nitromin-resistant tumors. Furthermore, Ball and co-workers[32] reported a 50% increase in glutathione in an HN3-resistant Yoshida sarcoma. Thus, the protective effect of elevated cellular thiol content appears to be an important mechanism in the development of resistance to HN2. Whether the elevation of cellular sulfhydryl content represents a specific mechanism of resistance to HN2 or whether it is merely a nonspecific manifestation of tetraploidy has not been resolved by this study.

Induction of resistance to nitrogen mustard in L5178Y cells was found to be a slow process (FIGURE 2), in marked contrast with the rapid development of resistance reported for the antimetabolite methotrexate.[33,34] On reviewing mechanisms of drug resistance in microorganisms, Moyed indicated that single-step mutations may be expected to have a single biochemical alteration that is solely responsible for resistance.[35] However, in situations where resistant microorganisms are selected by repeated or prolonged exposure to a drug, several biochemical alterations might exist, each making an unspecified contribution to the total resistance.[35]

The same principle may apply to mammalian cells; a single-step mutation has been described during induction of resistance to methotrexate in association with a single biochemical alteration, induction of the enzyme dihydrofolate reductase.[34] By contrast, in this investigation induction of resistance to nitrogen mustard was found to be a slow process, which required repeated exposure to the drug, suggesting that resistance may consist of several biochemical alterations. One such biochemical alteration would appear to be elevation of cellular thiol content, and a biological alteration would appear to be the emergence of tetraploid cells.

Summary

A cell line thirtyfold more resistant to the cytocidal action of nitrogen mustard has been induced by sequential treatment of L5178Y lymphoblasts with HN2 *in vitro*. Resistance was stable for more than 80 days *in vitro*, but thereafter declined, and completely disappeared at approximately 300 days. On transplantation of resistant cell lines *in vivo*, there was an initial loss of resistance, followed by stabilization of drug responsiveness for up to 200 days. Median survival time of mice transplanted with resistant lines was identical to that of mice inoculated with the sensitive line. Doubling time, life-cycle analysis, cell mobility, and osmotic fragility were similar in HN2-sensitive and -resistant cells. Cells resistant to HN2 differed from sensitive cells in having a lower mitotic index, smaller cell volume, an increased percentage of tetraploid cells, and an increased concentration of RNA, DNA, and thiol groups. A direct correlation was observed between HN2-resistance and percent tetraploidy, and also between HN2-resistance and cellular thiol content. The slow development of resistance to nitrogen mustard suggested that resistance may consist of several biochemical alterations.

Acknowledgments

The author wishes to thank Mrs. Candice Vanstone, Miss Dorise Hamel, and Mrs. Marjorie Hutchison for their technical assistance, and Miss Isobel Steedman and Miss Nan Christie for typing the manuscript. The critical discussions and interest of Dr. P. Alexander, Dr. J. A. Hildes, and Dr. L. G. Israels are gratefully acknowledged.

References

1. Wheeler, G. P. 1967. Some biochemical effects of alkylating agents. Fed. Proc. **26:** 885–892.
2. Ross, W. C. J. 1962. Biological Alkylating Agents. Butterworths. London, England.
3. Stacey, K. A., M. Cobb, S. F. Cousens & P. Alexander. 1958. The reactions of radiomimetic alkylating agents with macromolecules *in vitro*. Ann. N.Y. Acad. Sci. **68:** 682–701.
4. Wheeler, G. P. 1963. Studies related to mechanisms of resistance to biological alkylating agents. Cancer Res. **23:** 1334–1349.
5. Warwick, G. P. 1963. The mechanism of action of alkylating agents. Cancer Res. **23:** 1315–1333.
6. Brockman, R. W. 1963. Mechanisms of resistance to anticancer agents. Advances Cancer Res. **7:** 129.
7. Hutchison, D. J. 1963. Cross resistance and collateral sensitivity studies in cancer chemotherapy. Advances Cancer Res. **7:** 235.
8. Hutchison, D. J. 1965. Studies on cross-resistance and collateral sensitivity (1962–1964). Cancer Res. **25:** 1518.
9. Goldenberg, G. J. & P. Alexander. 1965. The effects of nitrogen mustard and

dimethyl myleran on murine leukemia cell lines of different radiosensitivity *in vitro*. Cancer Res. **25:** 1401–1409.

10. GOLDENBERG, G. J. 1966. Comparison of direct and indirect effect of alkylating agents and radiation on murine leukemia cells *in vitro*. Nature (London) **211:** 427–428.
11. ALEXANDER, P. & Z. B. MIKULSKI. 1961. Differences in response of leukemic cells in tissue culture to nitrogen mustard and dimethyl myleran. Biochem. Pharmacol. **5:** 275–282.
12. GOLDENBERG, G. J. 1968. Repair of sub-lethal damage of L5178Y lymphoblasts *in vitro* treated with dimethyl myleran and nitrogen mustard. Biochem. Pharmacol. **17:** 820–824.
13. STANNERS, C. P. & J. E. TILL. 1960. DNA synthesis in individual L-strain mouse cells. Biochem. Biophys. Acta **37:** 406–419.
14. SCHERRER, K. & J. E. DARNELL. 1962. Sedimentation characteristics of rapidly labelled RNA from Hela cells. Biochem. Biophys. Res. Comm. **7:** 486–489.
15. SCHMIDT, G. & S. J. THANNHAUSER. 1945. A method for the determination of desoxyribonucleic acid, ribonucleic acid and phosphoproteins in animal tissues. J. Biol. Chem. **161:** 83–89.
16. GOLDENBERG, G. J. 1965. The metabolism of polyamines by normal and neoplastic mammalian cells. Ph.D. Thesis. Univ. of Minnesota, Minneapolis, Minn. (University Microfilms, Ann Arbor, Mich.)
17. HUTCHISON, W. C. & H. N. MUNRO, 1961. The determination of nucleic acids in biological materials. Analyst **86:** 768–813.
18. BURTON, K. 1956. A study of the conditions and mechanisms of the diphenylamine reaction for the colorimetric estimation of deoxyribonucleic acid. Biochem. J. **62:** 315.
19. ELLMAN, G. L. Tissue sulfhydryl groups. Arch. Biochem. Biophys. **82:** 70–77.
20. BANGHAM, A. D., R. FLEMANS, D. H. HEARD & G. V. F. SEAMAN. 1958. An apparatus for microelectrophoresis of small particles. Nature (London) **182:** 642–644.
21. REID, B. D. & I. G. WALKER. 1966. Resistance to sulfur mustard: a comparison of some properties of strain L cells and a resistant subline. Cancer Res. **26:** 1801–1805.
22. HIRONO, I. 1955 A comparative study of the mode of action of x rays and alkylating agents. Nature (London) **176:** 1168–1169.
23. WATANABE, I. & S. OKADA. 1966. Study of mechanisms of radiation-induced reproductive death of mammalian cells in culture. Estimation of stage at cell death and biological description of processes leading to cell death. Radiat. Res. **27:** 290–306.
24. WATANABE, I. & S. OKADA. 1967. Effects of temperature on growth rate of cultured mammalian cells (L5178Y). J. Cell Biol. **32:** 309–323.
25. GOLDENBERG, G. J. & C. L. VANSTONE. (Unpublished observations.)
26. LEVIS, A. G. 1963. X-irradiation sensitivity of nitrogen mustard-resistant mammalian cells *in vitro*. Nature (London) **198:** 498–499.
27. CRATHORN, A. R. & J. J. ROBERTS. 1965. Reactions of cultured mammalian cells of varying radiosensitivity with the radiomimetic alkylating agent, mustard gas. Prog. Biochem. Pharmacol. **1:** 320–326.
28. SKIPPER, H. E. & F. M. SCHABEL, JR. 1962. Experimental evaluation of potential anticancer agents. VII. Cross resistance of alkylating agent-resistant neoplasms. Cancer Chemother. Rep. **22:** 1–22.
29. WHISSON, M. E. 1966. Action of alkylating agents on plasma cell tumors. Brit. Emp. Cancer Camp. Rep. Part II: 10.
30. CALCUTT, G. & T. A. CONNORS. 1963. Tumor sulphydryl levels and sensitivity to the nitrogen mustard merophan. Biochem. Pharmacol. **12:** 839–845.
31. HIRONO, I. 1960. Non-protein sulphydryl group in the original strain and sub-line of the ascites tumor resistant to alkylating reagents. Nature (London) **186:** 1059–1060.
32. BALL, C. R., R. A. CONNORS, E. H. COOPER & M. E. WHISSON. 1966. Studies of acquired drug resistance in tumors. Brit. Emp. Cancer Camp. Reports: 12–13.
33. FISCHER, G. A. 1959. Nutritional and amethopterin-resistant characteristics of leukemic clones. Cancer Res. **19:** 372–376.

34. Fischer, G. A. 1961. Increased levels of folic acid reductase as a mechanism of resistance to amethopterin in leukemic cells. Biochem. Pharmacol. **7:** 75–80.
35. Moyed, H. S. 1964. Biochemical mechanisms of drug resistance. Ann. Rev. Microbiol. **18:** 347–366.

PRECLINICAL INVESTIGATION OF ALKYLATING AGENTS IN CANCER CHEMOTHERAPY

Abraham Goldin and Harry B. Wood, Jr.

Cancer Chemotherapy National Service Center
Chemotherapy, National Cancer Institute
Bethesda, Md.

A broad chemotherapy program has been in progress at the National Cancer Institute for more than 10 years, and notable contributions have been made in making available chemotherapeutic agents that are active against clinical neoplasia.[1,2] Also, in the chemotherapy program, a number of potentially useful chemotherapeutic agents are in various stages of development.[1] The program encompasses a progressive series of steps, initiating with the procurement and synthesis of new candidate agents and the screening of these agents in appropriate test systems. Compounds that emerge from the primary screen as positive are subjected to further evaluation and development designed to identify the most promising compounds. The activity of new compounds is compared with that of available congeners. Toxicologic and pharmacologic studies of candidate agents are conducted, and the most desirable compounds are formulated and subjected to clinical investigation.[3,4] In the testing program, compounds fall by the wayside when they cannot meet the progressively increasing demands for chemotherapeutic effectiveness. A "decision-point network" has been established in which the data are examined at designated levels of development in order to determine the future course of study of compounds of potential interest.[1] They may be shelved, recycled through specific tests, or moved into the next phase of testing.

Based on the comprehensive analysis of Gellhorn and Hirschberg,[5] in the initial stages of the program, screening was conducted primarily with the lymphoid leukemia L1210, adenocarcinoma 755 (Ca 755), and sarcoma 180.[6] Subsequently, in order to obtain additional perspective, a broad spectrum of tumor systems was introduced into the program, using the mouse, the rat, and the hamster as hosts. Also included were several cell-culture systems.[7] A large volume of comparative data was obtained in this fashion, which permitted a retrospective analysis of the screening systems in terms of their predictability value for the clinic.[2] It was indicated that although a number of test systems were capable of identifying compounds of clinical interest, the combination of the leukemia L1210 system plus the Walker carcinosarcoma 256 system would have detected most of the clinically active drugs. Since the greatest emphasis in the chemotherapy program is currently being placed on activity against leukemia L1210, most of the data for the alkylating agents presented in this paper were obtained in the "early" (localized) or "advanced" (systemic) leukemia L1210 system.

Early leukemia L1210 is employed in the initial screening, and the procedures have been described in detail.[3,7,8] In this system, the leukemic cells are inoculated intraperitoneally (i.p.) and intraperitoneal treatment with the test agent is initiated one day following leukemic inoculation. The survival times of untreated control animals and treated animals are determined and compared. An increase of 25% in the median survival time of test animals relative to untreated controls suggests that the test agent is of sufficient interest to warrant additional study. Active

TABLE 1

ANTITUMOR ACTIVITY OF SELECTED NEW ALKYLATING AGENTS; SCREENING AGAINST EARLY LEUKEMIA L1210 AND WALKER 256

NSC No.	Name	Structure	L1210			WM-256		
			OD	ILS	Survivors/Total	OD	TWI	Survivors/Total
79037	Urea, 1-(2-chloroethyl)-3-cyclohexyl-1-nitroso- CCNU	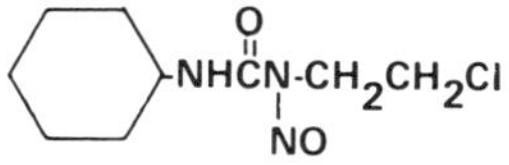	12.5	>770	9/10	--	---	---
82196	Imidazole-4(or 5)-carboxamide, 5(or 4)-[3,3-bis(2-chloroethyl)-1-triazeno]-	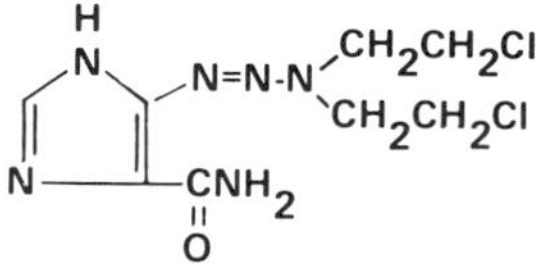	100	168	2/8	--	---	---
52695	Phosphorodiamidic acid, *N,N*-bis(2-chloroethyl)-*N′*-(3-hydroxypropyl)-comp. with cyclohexylamine (1:1) Cytoxyl alcohol	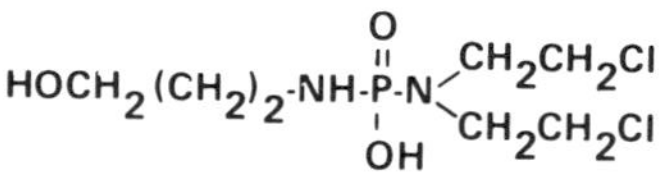	100	50	--	--	---	---
102627	1-Propanol, 3,3′-iminodi-, dimethanesulfonate, hydrochloride	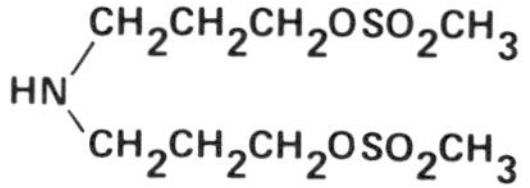	39	106	2/10	--	---	---

TABLE 1
(*Continued*)

NSC No.	Name	Structure	L1210 OD	L1210 ILS	L1210 Survivors/Total	WM-356 OD	WM-356 TWI
84641	1-Propanol, 3,3′-(methylimino)di-, dimethanesulfonate, hydrochloride	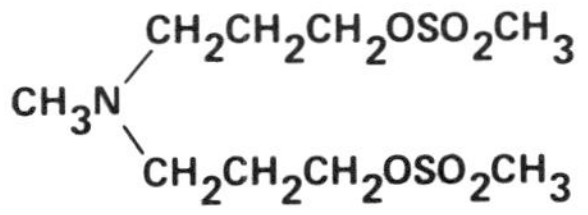	23	78	0/10	---	---
79423	Ethanol, 2,2′-[(p-nitrosophenyl) imino] di-, dimethanesulfonate	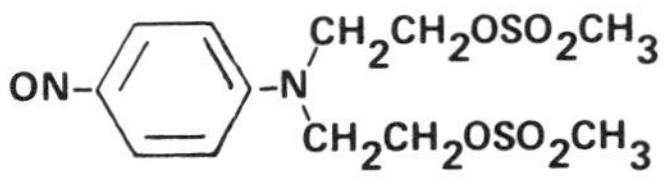	1	31	0/10	1.4	80
104800	Galactitol, 1,6-dibromo-1,-6-dideoxy, D- Dibromodulcitol	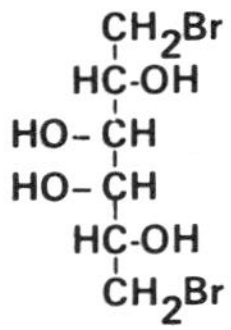	125	22	0/10	108	88

TABLE 1
(*Continued*)

94100	Mannitol, 1,6-dibromo-1,6-dideoxy, D- Dibromomannitol	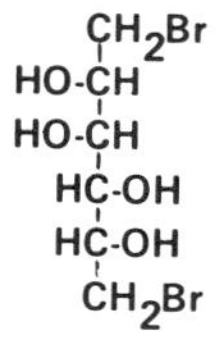	500	11	0/9	140,230	97
50741	β-D-Ribofuranoside, methyl 5-(2-chloroethylamino)-5-deoxy-2,3-0-isopropylidene-, hydrochloride	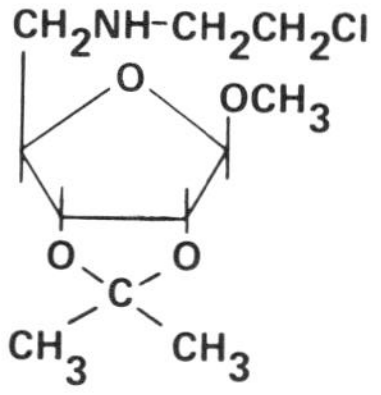	150	100	0/8		

OD = Optimal dose
ILS = Percent increase in survival time over controls
TWI = Percent tumor weight inhibition

compounds are subjected to repeat tests in the early L1210 system, and if their activity is consistent, they are then characterized with respect to the influence of schedules and routes of administration. For this purpose, precise dose-response curves are established, and the relative therapeutic efficacy of the drugs is compared. Since dose-response curves are obtained, the maximum therapeutic effect achieved at the optimal dose may be determined for each therapy.

Quantitative methodology has also been developed utilizing the advanced leukemia L1210 system, and it has been employed for the ranking of therapeutic activity of candidate agents, including alkylating agents, and for the conduct of structure-activity studies.[9–14] In the advanced leukemia L1210 system, the leukemic cells are inoculated subcutaneously (s.c.), and treatment is withheld until the disease is definitely systemic. With the inoculum level employed, this invariably occurs within five days of death, at which time a local tumor is also evident at the site of leukemic inoculation. As with the early leukemia L1210 system, the advanced leukemia L1210 system has been utilized for the determination of optimal schedules and routes of administration and for the precise comparison of the relative effectiveness of congeners of interest. In this system, each drug is tested at a series of dose levels, treatment being administered daily up to 30–60 days. The doses employed encompass toxic to nontoxic levels. Characteristically, with an effective drug as the dose of drug is increased, the survival time is increased. Then as the toxicity becomes dominant, the survival time is diminished. The median survival time of the treated animals and the control animals is determined at every dose level. This permits identification of an optimal dose, and the increase in survival time relative to the controls is determined.

In the Walker adenocarcinoma 256 test system, the tumor is inoculated intramuscularly (i.m.) in the hind leg, and following therapy, a comparison is made of the weight of the tumor in treated and control animals.[3,6,8,15] In the Walker system, the comparison of drug effectiveness is ordinarily made at the maximum tolerated dose (optimal dose).

The alkylating agents included in this report, the molecular formula, and the source are listed in Appendix I.

New Alkylating Agents

The antitumor activity of some alkylating agents of current interest selected on the basis of either early L1210 or Walker 256 activity are presented in TABLE 1. Included are the National Service Center (NSC) number, the name of the compound, and the structure. For the early L1210 system, the optimal dose, the percent increase in life-span over untreated controls, and the number of survivors out of the total number of animals are listed. For the Walker i.m. system, the optimal dose and the extent of tumor weight inhibition are listed. The wide variety of alkylating agent structure in this series is notable. The cyclohexylnitrosourea, NSC 79037, is one of a series of active compounds including BCNU (bis-β-chloroethylnitrosourea, NSC 409962) that are extremely potent in the leukemia L1210 system.[16–18] The imidazole carboxamide derivative, NSC 82196,[19,20] was also highly active. Cytoxyl alcohol, NSC 52695, is a quite active compound, and the possibility exists that it may be related to an active form of cytoxan. The two dimethanesulfonates, NSC 102627 and NSC 84641,[21,22] are quite active in the leukemia L1210 system. The other dimethanesulfonate listed, NSC 79423, was not as active in the L1210 system, but it did meet the criterion for effectiveness. It was also active in the Walker 256 system. The two sugar derivatives, dibromodulcitol (NSC 104800) and dibromomannitol (NSC 94100),[23-25] were quite active in the Walker carcinosarcoma 256 system. It is of interest that the dibromodulcitol derivative in the experiment reported here and in other experiments not listed was moderately but definitely effective in the leukemia L1210 system, whereas the dibromomannitol derivative was essentially ineffective.[26] The marked activity of the deoxyribofuranoside derivative of a one-armed mustard (NSC 50741) is notable. All of these compounds, plus others not shown here, are listed in the category of potentially interesting compounds for the clinic and are under progressive investigation.

Structure-Activity Relationshps

The structure-activity relationships are summarized in TABLES 2 to 6.[12,13,27-30] TABLE 2 shows the results of quantitative comparison of a series of nitrogen mustards against advanced leukemia L1210.

In TABLE 2(A), substitution is made on the methyl group of methyl-bis-2-chloroethylamine (nitrogen mustard, NSC 762). Nitrogen mustard itself, NSC 762, had only moderate activity in the advanced leukemia L1210 system (19% increase in life-span over controls). Nornitrogen mustard, lacking the methyl group (NSC 10873), had a somewhat higher rating (rating of 28), while the N-oxide of nitrogen mustard was inactive in the advanced leukemia L1210 system. Although glycine mustard (NSC 17661) met the criterion for activity in the L1210 system (rating of 32), alanine mustard (NSC 17663) had reduced activity (percent increase in life-span of 12). Dimethylbenzimidazole mustard, NSC 23892, was the most effective compound in this series, giving a 58% increase in life-span over controls. Benzimidazole mustard per se, NSC 23891, had a somewhat reduced rating (15% increase in life-span). It is of interest to note that the 5-chlorobenzimidazole mustard (NSC 35648) was inactive over a range of doses. The Weatherbee mustard (NSC 18321) had moderate activity (rating of 22). Pyridoxine mustard and chloroquine mustard (NSC 43146 and 3423, respectively) were essentially inactive. The tetrakis compound listed (NSC 13187), having four β-chloroethyl groups, had a rating of 30.

TABLE 2(B) shows a series of compounds in which bis-2-chloroethylamines are attached to a phenyl group. This series includes five phenylalanine mustards, all of which were active in the advanced leukemia L1210 system, the activity ratings ranging from 28 through 40. The series includes para DL, L and D phenylalanine mustard (NSC 14210, 8806, 35051). It also includes ortho-DL phenylalanine mustard (NSC 57199) and meta-DL-phenylalanine mustard (NSC 27381). The ethyl ester of p-phenylalanine mustard (NSC 62147) was also active against leukemia L1210 (rating of 47). Other derivatives, including p-benzoic acid mustard (NSC 26276), chlorambucil (NSC 3088), which is a phenylbutyric acid derivative, and the two sulfanilic acid derivatives, were ineffective against advanced leukemia L1210.

TABLE 2(C) shows bis-2-chloroethylamines linked to phosphoric acid. Cytoxan (cyclophosphamide, NSC 26271) is the notable compound in the series. It was shown to be activated *in vivo*,[31] has a broad spectrum of antitumor activity, and has been used extensively in the clinic. Whether cytoxyl alcohol (TABLE 1) is an activated form of cytoxan remains to be determined. Two additional com-

TABLE 2(A)

NITROGEN MUSTARDS: SUBSTITUTION ON THE METHYL GROUP OF METHYL-BIS(2-CHLOROETHYL)AMINE (SYSTEMIC LEUKEMIA L1210)

NSC No.	Name	Structure	Optimal dose	Percent increase in life-span over controls
10873	Diethylamine, 2,2′-dichloro-, hydrochloride Nor-nitrogen mustard	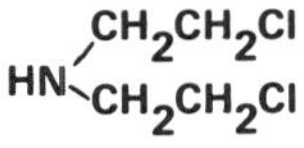	85	28
762	Diethylamine, 2,2′-dichloro-*N*-methyl-, hydrochloride Nitrogen mustard	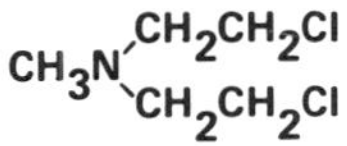	3	19
10107	Diethylamine, 2,2′-dichloro-*N*-methyl-, *N*-oxide, compd. with hydrochloride (1:1) Nitromin	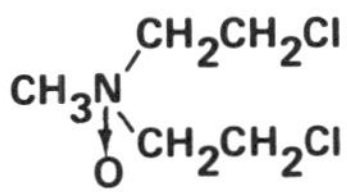	38.8	4
17661	Glycine, *N*, *N*-bis (2-chloro-ethyl)-, hydrochloride Glycine mustard	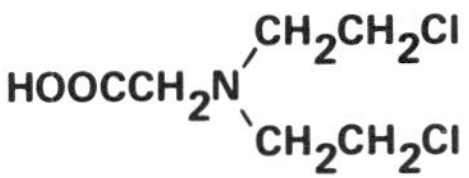	19	32
17663	Alanine, *N*,*N*-bis(2-cholro-ethyl)-, hydrochloride, DL-	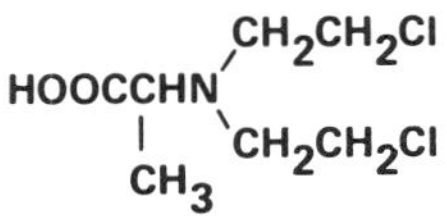	16	12

TABLE 2(A)
(*Continued*)

NSC No.	Name	Structure	Optimal dose	Percent increase in life-span over controls
23891	Benzimidazole, 2-[[bis(2-chloroethyl) amino] methyl]-, Benzimidazole mustard	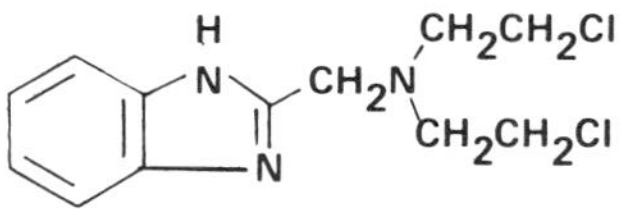	25	15
23892	Benzimidazole, 2-[[bis(2-chloroethyl)-amino] methyl]-5,6-dimethyl-, monohydro-chloride Dimethylbenzimidazole mustard	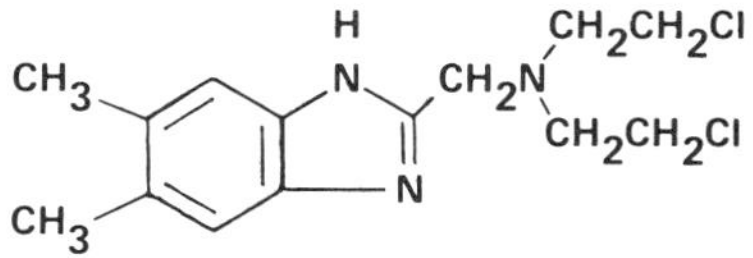	80	58
35648	Benzimidazole, 2-[[bis(2-chloroethyl)-amino] methyl]-5-chloro-,monohydrochloride 5-Chlorobenzimidazole mustard	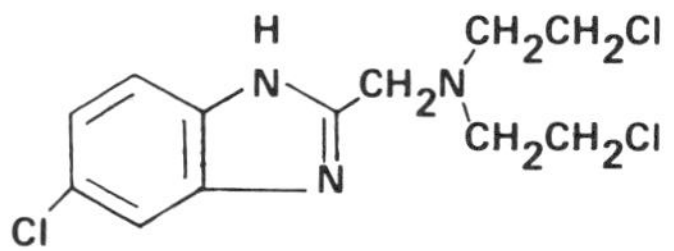	--	0
43146	3-Pyridinol, 5-[[bis(2-chloroethyl)-amino] methyl]-4-(methoxymethyl)-2-methyl-, dihydrochloride, dihydrate Pyridoxine mustard	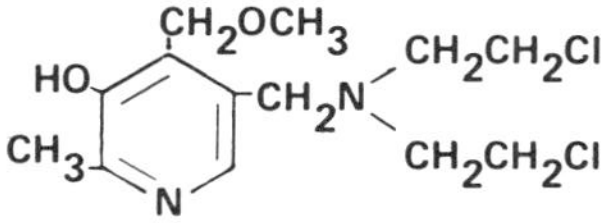	14	9

TABLE 2(A)
(*Continued*)

NSC No.	Name	Structure	Optimal dose	Percent increase in life-span over controls
18321	Hydroquinone, 2,5-bis[[bis-(2-chloroethyl) amino] methyl]-, dihydrochloride Weatherbee mustard	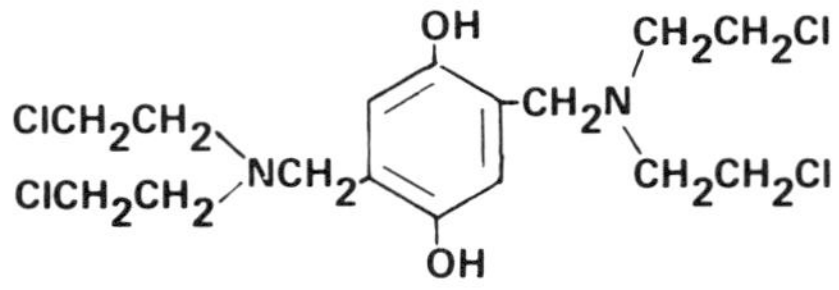	45	22
3423	2-Naphthoic acid, 4,4′-methylenebis[3-hydroxy-, compd. with 4-[[4-[bis(2-chloroethyl)amino]-1-methylbutyl]-amino]-7-chloroquinoline (1:1) Chloroquine mustard, pamoate	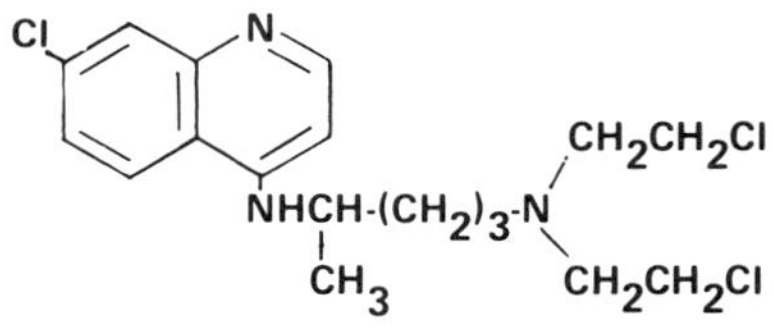 • pamoate	--	0
13187	1,3-Propanediamine, *N,N,N′*,-*N′*-tetrakis(2-chloroethyl)-, dihydrochloride	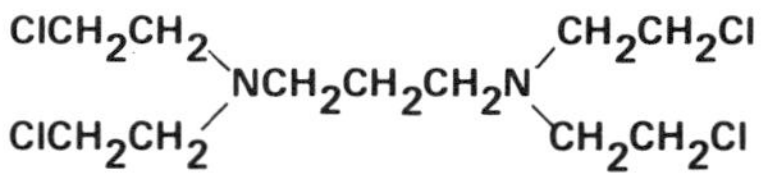	3	30

TABLE 2(B)

NITROGEN MUSTARDS: BIS(2-CHLOROETHYL)AMINES LINKED DIRECTLY TO A PHENYL GROUP (SYSTEMIC LEUKEMIA L1210)

NSC No.	Name	Structure	Optimal dose	Percent increase in life-span over controls
14210	Alanine, 3-[*p*-[bis(2-chloroethyl) amino] phenyl]-, monohydrochloride, DL- *p*-DL-Phenylalanine mustard; DL-Sarcolysin, DL-Melphalan	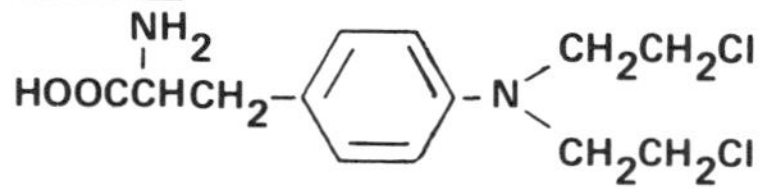	23	40
8806	Alanine, 3-[*p*-[bis(2-chloroethyl) amino] phenyl]-, monohydrochloride, L- *p*-L-Phenylalanine mustard; L-Melphalan; L-Sarcolysin	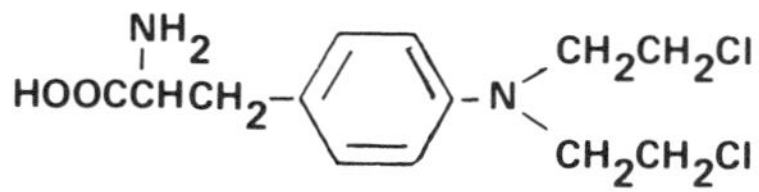	60	33
35051	Alanine, 3-[*p*-[bis(2-chloroethyl)amino] phenyl]-, D- *p*-D-Phenylalanine mustard, D-Sarcolysin, D-Melphalan	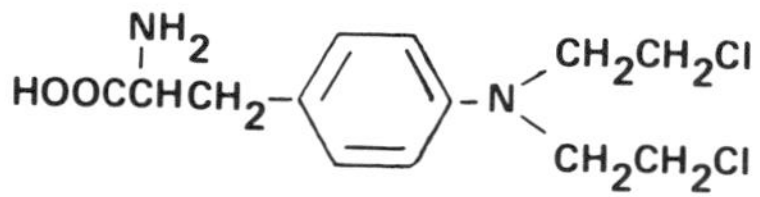	23	33
57199	Alanine, 3-[*o*-[bis(2-chloroethyl) amino] phenyl], DL *o*-DL-Phenylalanine mustard; *o*-DL-Sarcolysin	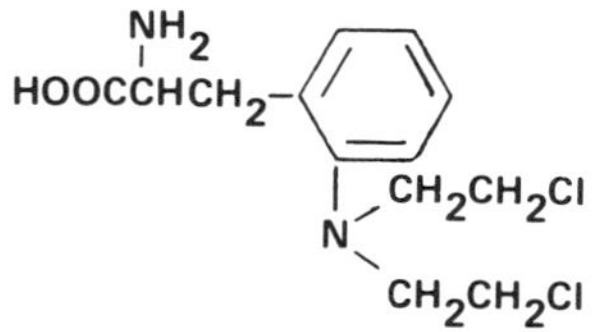	1.8	33

TABLE 2(B)
(*Continued*)

NSC No.	Name	Structure	Optimal dose	Percent increase in life-span over controls
27381	Alanine, 3-[*m*-[bis(2-chloroethyl) amino] phenyl]-, DL- *m*-DL-Phenylalanine mustard; *m*-DL-Sarcolysin	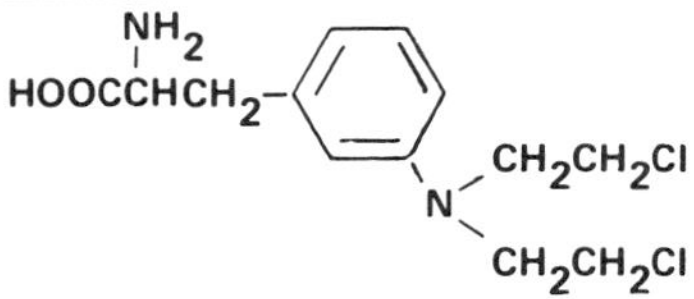	7	28
62147	Alanine, 3-(*p*-[bis(2-chloroethyl)monoamino] phenyl)-, ethyl ester, hydrochloride, *L*- *p*-Phenylalanine mustard, ethyl ester	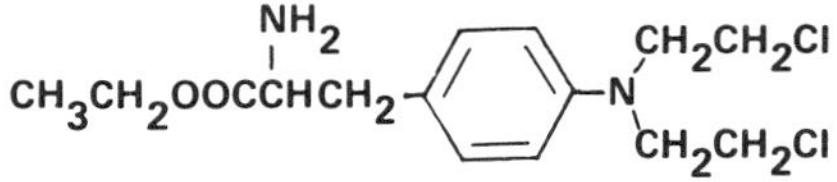	8.4	47
26276	Benzoic acid, *p*-[bis(2-chloroethyl) amino]- *p*-Benzoic acid mustard	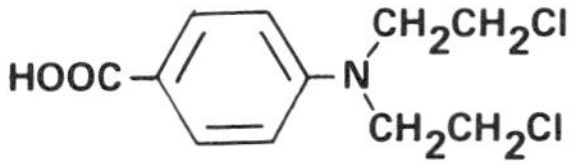	–	0
3088	Butyric acid, 4-[*p*-[bis(2-chloroethyl)amino] phenyl]- Chlorambucil	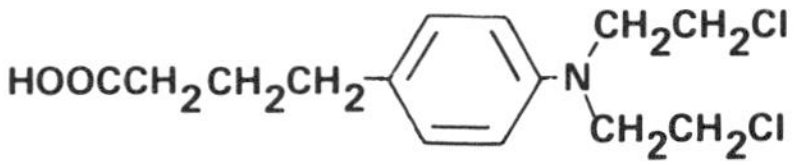	–	0

TABLE 2(B)
(Continued)

NSC No.	Name	Structure	Optimal dose	Percent increase in life-span over controls
41449	Acetic acid, [*m*-[bis(2-chloroethyl)amino] phenoxyl]-, ethyl ester *m*-Phenoxy acetic acid mustard, ethyl ester	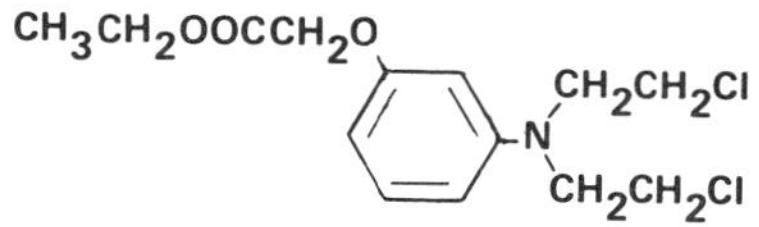	–	0
18439	Aniline, *N*,*N*-bis(2-chloroethyl)-2,3-dimethoxy-	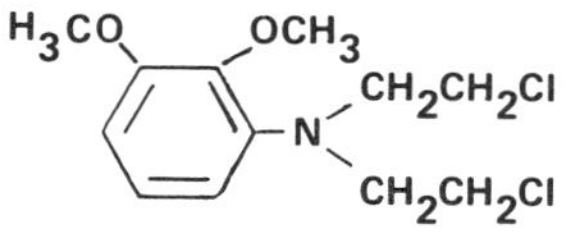	–	0
16498	Benzoic acid, *o*-[[4-[bis-(2-chloroethyl)amino]-*o*-tolyl] azo]-	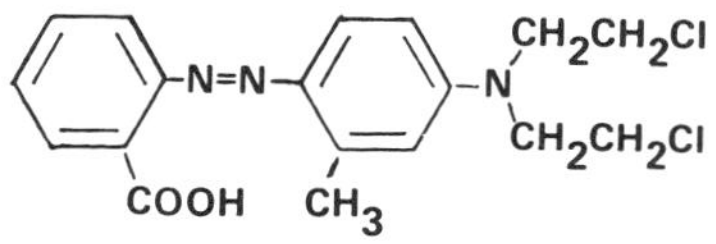	108	10
28578	Sulfanilic acid, *N*,*N*-bis-(2-chloroethyl)-, hydrazide	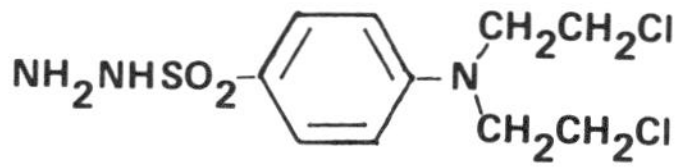	–	0
28579	Sulfanilamide, *N*4,*N*4-bis(2-chloroethyl)-*N*1-2-pyridyl-	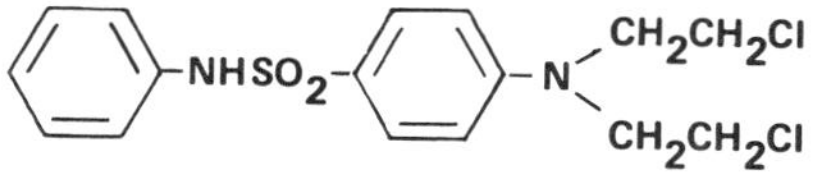	700	5

TABLE 2(C)

NITROGEN MUSTARDS: BIS(2-CHLOROETHYL)AMINES LINKED TO PHOSPHORIC ACID (SYSTEMIC LEUKEMIA L1210)

NSC No.	Name	Structure	Optimal dose	Percent increase in life-span over controls
26271	2*H*-1,3,2-Oxazaphosphorine, 2-[bis(2-chloroethyl)amino]-tetrahydro-, 2-oxide, monohydrate Cytoxan	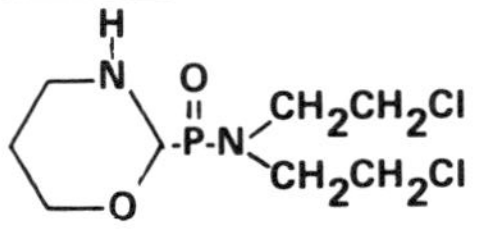	60	145
69945	Phosphorodiamidic acid, *N,N*-bis(2-chloroethyl)-, compd. with Cyclohexylamine Phosphoramide mustard	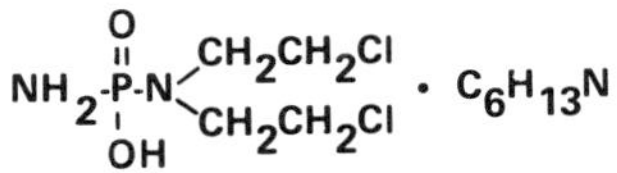	65	47
72510	Phosphonamidic acid, P-1-aziridinyl-*N,N*-bis(2-chloroethyl)-, compd. with cyclohexylamine (1:1)	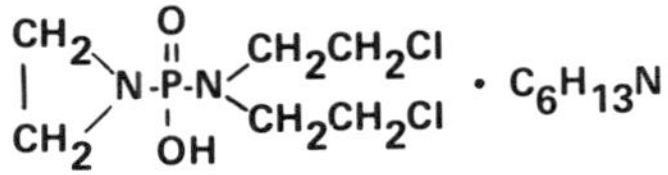	32	72
72505	Phosphoramidic acid, bis(2-chloroethyl)-, *tert*-butyl ester, compd. with cyclohexylamine (1:1)	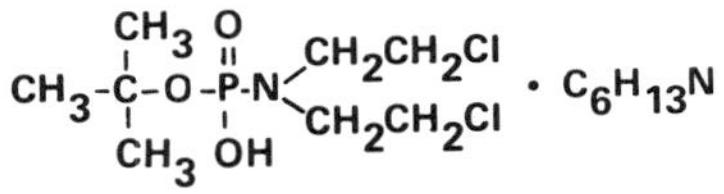	240*	11

* The optimal dose may be higher than any used.

TABLE 2(D)

NITROGEN MUSTARDS: BIS(2-CHLOROETHYL)AMINES LINKED TO A HETEROCYCLIC GROUP (SYSTEMIC LEUKEMIA L1210)

NSC No.	Name	Structure	Optimal dose	Percent increase in life-span over controls
34462	Uracil, 5-[bis(2-chloroethyl)amino]- Uracil mustard	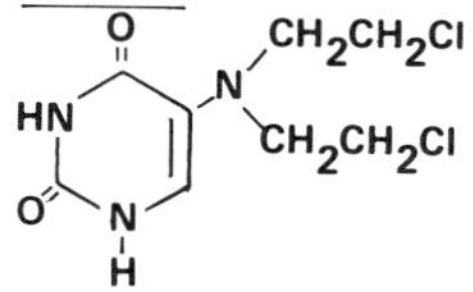	3	48
44444	Uracil, 5-[bis(2-chloroethyl)amino]-3-methyl- 3-Methyluracil mustard	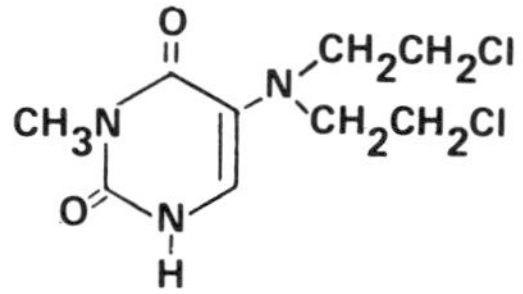	8.4	39
44629	Uracil, 5-[bis(2-chloroethyl)amino]-6-methyl- Dopan, 6-Methyluracil mustard	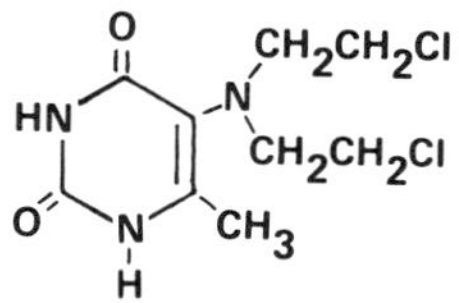	20	30
62403	Tryptophan, 5-[bis(2-chloroethyl)amino]-, DL Tryptophan mustard	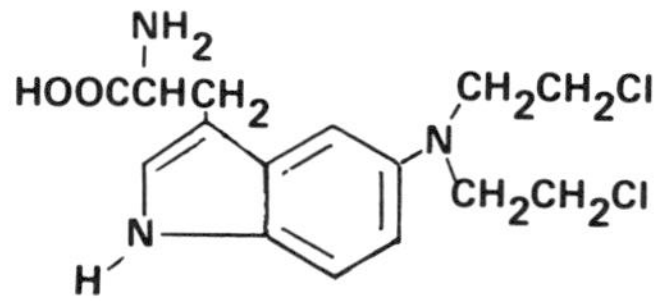	3	41

TABLE 2(E)
NITROGEN MUSTARDS: BIS(2-CHLOROETHYL)AMINES
(SYSTEMIC LEUKEMIA L1210)

NSC No.	Name	Structure	Optimal dose	Percent increase in life-span over controls
9698	Mannitol, 1,6-bis[(2-chloroethyl)amino]-1,6-dideoxy-, dihydrochloride, D- Degranol, mannitol mustard; D-mannitol mustard	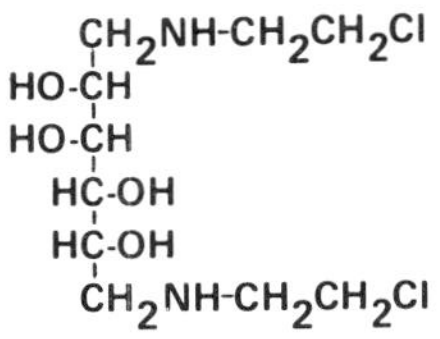	65	30
83290	2,3-Butanediol, 1,4-bis-[(2-chloroethyl)amino]-, dihydrochloride, DL- DL-Erythritol mustard	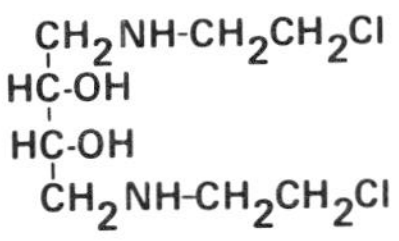	23	88
39073	2,3-Butanediol, 1,4-bis-[(2-chloroethyl)amino]-, dihydrochloride, *meso*- Meso-erythritol mustard	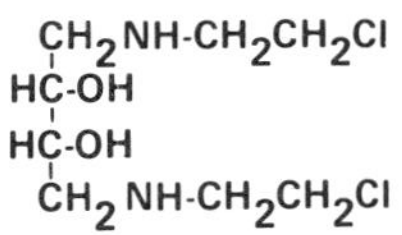	30	60
39071	2,3-Butanediol, 1,4-bis[(2-chloroethyl)amino]-, dihydrochloride, D- D-Threitol mustard	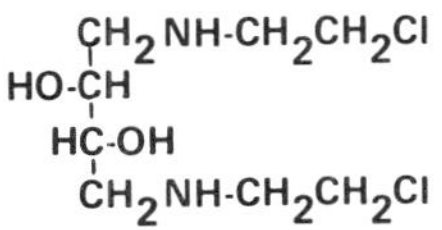	39	55

TABLE 2(E)
(*Continued*)

NSC No.	Name	Structure	Optimal dose	Percent increase in life-span over controls
39072	2,3-Butanediol, 1,4-bis[(2-chloroethyl)amino]-, dihydrochloride, L- L-Threitol mustard	$CH_2NH\text{-}CH_2CH_2Cl$ $HC\text{-}OH$ $HO\text{-}CH$ $CH_2NH\text{-}CH_2CH_2Cl$	23	63
70806	1,3-Propanediamine, *N,N′*-bis-(2-chloroethyl)-, dihydrochloride 1,3-Propanediol mustard	$CH_2NH\text{-}CH_2CH_2Cl$ CH_2 $CH_2NH\text{-}CH_2CH_2Cl$	46.7	69

TABLE 2(F)
NITROGEN MUSTARDS: ONE-ARMED MUSTARDS
(SYSTEMIC LEUKEMIA L1210)

NSC No.	Name	Structure	Optimal dose	Percent increase in life-span over controls
2059	Triethylamine, 2-chloro-, hydrochloride	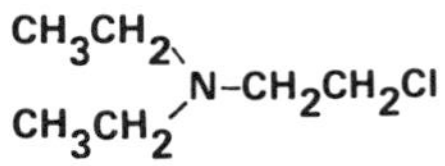	1.8	10
9995	Piperidine, 1-(2-chloro-ethyl)-, hydrochloride	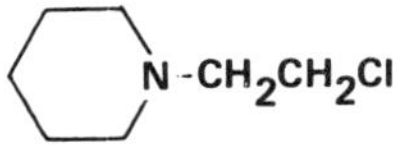		
11468	Benzylamine, *N*-(2-chloroethyl)-*N*-ethyl, hydrochloride	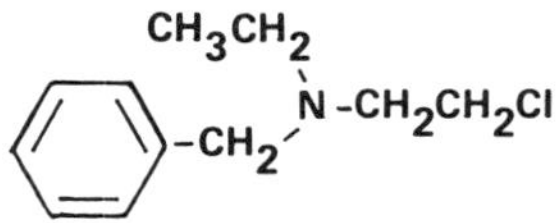	39	10
11472	Piperonylamine, *N*-(2-chloro-ethyl)-*N*-ethyl-, hydro-chloride	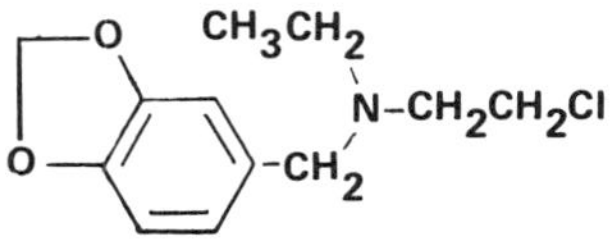	—	0

TABLE 2(F)
(*Continued*)

NCS No.	Name	Structure	Optimal dose	Percent increase in life-span over controls
11481	*p*-Cymen-7-amine, *N*-(2-chloroethy)-*N*-ethyl-, hydrochloride	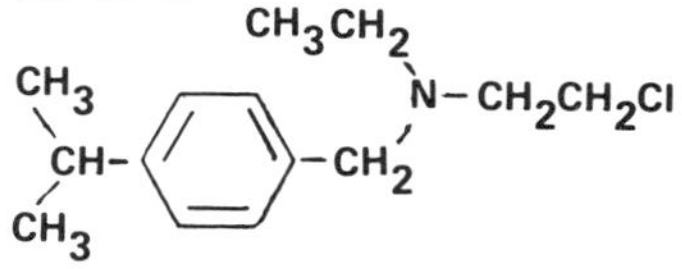	8.4	10
11486	1-Naphthalenemethylamine, *N*-(2-chloroethyl)-*N*-ethyl-, hydrochloride	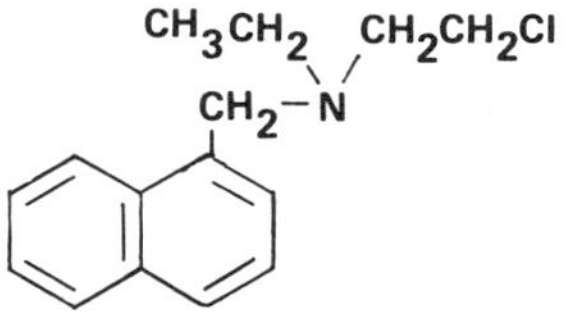	–	0

TABLE 2(G)

NITROGEN MUSTARDS: MISCELLANEOUS COMPOUNDS
(SYSTEMIC LEUKEMIA L1210)

NSC No.	Name	Structure	Optimal dose	Percent increase in life-span over controls
400721	Propylamine, 3-chloro-*N*-(2-chloroethyl)-*N*-ethyl-, hydrochloride	$CH_3CH_2N(CH_2CH_2Cl)(CH_2CH_2CH_2Cl)$	3	11
30025	Ethane, 1,2-bis[(2-chloroethyl)thio]-	$CH_2S{-}CH_2CH_2Cl$ / $CH_2S{-}CH_2CH_2Cl$	–	11
21199	Phosphonic acid, [*p*-[bis(2-iodoethyl)amino] benzyl]-, diethyl ester	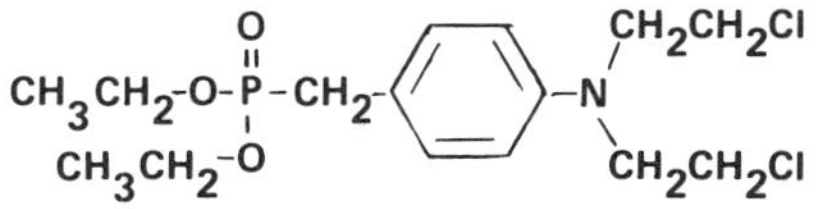	23	9

pounds (TABLE 2[C]), phosphoramide mustard (NSC 69945) and an aziridinyl phosphonamidic acid derivative (NSC 72510), were both definitely active in the advanced L1210 system. Another phosphoramidic acid derivative, NSC 72505, was inactive but was relatively nontoxic at the highest dose employed.

In TABLE 2(D) are bis-2-chloroethylamines linked to a heterocyclic group. Uracil mustard and the two derivatives, 3-methyluracil mustard and 6-methyluracil mustard (Dopan) (NSC 34462, 44444, and 44629, respectively) were all active against advanced leukemia L1210. Of the three derivatives, uracil mustard appeared to be somewhat more active. Dopan appeared to be the least toxic of the three drugs as indicated by the higher optimal dose. Tryptophan mustard (NSC 62403) was also reasonably effective, having a rating of 41.

In TABLE 2(E) are listed the bis-2-chloroethylamines separated by a three- to six-carbon chain. It is of interest that all six of the compounds listed were active in the advanced leukemia L1210 system. Included in this group is Degranol (mannitol mustard, NSC 9698), which was the least effective of the compounds listed. DL-erythritol mustard (NSC 83290) was the most active of the group, having a rating of 88. Meso-erythritol mustard (NSC 39073) had a rating of 60. Both the D and the L forms of threitol mustard (NSC 39071 and 39072) were active (ratings of 55 and 63, respectively), and 1,3-propanediol mustard (NSC 70806) had a rating of 69. This is a group of compounds worthy of additional emphasis.

In TABLE 2(F) are a number of "one-armed" mustards. Although none of the compounds was active, and it had been considered that one-armed mustards were generally ineffective against leukemia L1210, the more recently synthesized one-armed nitrosourea mustards (TABLES 1 and 6) and the one-armed deoxyribofuranoside mustard (NSC 50741 TABLE 1) were highly active.

Three additional nitrogen mustards are listed in TABLE 2(G) (miscellaneous compounds). None of them, including the bis-iodoethyl nitrogen mustard derivative (NSC 21199), was active.

In TABLE 3 a series of methanesulfonates is shown, of which nonane, 1,9-nonanediol dimethanesulfonate (NSC 3052), showed activity in the advanced L1210 system (rating of 25). Myleran® * (NSC 750) and mannitol Myleran (NSC 37538), both of which have been effective in the clinic against chronic granulocytic leukemia[23,32] were ineffective in the L1210 system. Two more recent imino-bis-methanesulfonates, as indicated in TABLE I, were quite active against leukemia L1210, but to date they have not been tested against advanced leukemia L1210.

Data on three epoxides are shown in TABLE 4. D-1,2,3,4-diepoxy butane (NSC 32605) was quite active against early leukemia L1210 (rating of 89), while the other two more complex derivatives (NSC 56308 and 56845) were active in the advanced L1210 system.

Data on a series of ethyleneimines are shown in TABLE 5. Of 11 phosphoric acid derivatives listed in TABLE 5(A), nine were definitely active against advanced leukemia L1210, yielding median survival times ranging from 44% to 86% over the controls. The first four compounds listed—TEPA (NSC 9717), thio-TEPA (NSC 6396), MEPA (NSC 745), and OPSPA (NSC 10429)—are well-known compounds,[33] as are the two carbamic acid derivatives, Uredepa (AB-100, NSC 37095) and Benzodepa (AB-103, NSC 37096).[34] The higher ratings achieved by the compounds NSC 49421 and NSC 21597, both of which have two ethyleneim-

* Busulfan; Burroughs Wellcome & Co. (U.S.A.) Inc., Tuckahoe, N. Y. 10707.

TABLE 3
METHANESULFONATES
(SYSTEMIC LEUKEMIA L1210)

NSC No.	Name	Structure	Optimal dose	Percent increase in life-span over controls
50256	Methanesulfonic acid, methyl ester	$CH_3SO_2OCH_3$	–	0
26805	Methanesulfonic acid, ethyl ester CB-1528	$CH_3SO_2OCH_2CH_3$	–	0
18016	Ethanol, 2-chloro-, methanesulfonate	$CH_3SO_2OCH_2CH_2Cl$	–	0
750	1,4-Butanediol, di-methanesulfonate Myleran	$CH_2OSO_2CH_3$ CH_2 CH_2 $CH_2OSO_2CH_3$	–	0
39069	Threitol, 1,4-di-methanesulfonate, L-	$CH_2OSO_2CH_3$ HC–OH HO–CH $CH_2OSO_2CH_3$	–	0

TABLE 3
(*Continued*)

NSC No.	Name	Structure	Optimal dose	Percent increase in life-span over controls
37538	Mannitol, 1,6-dimethane-sulfonate, D- Mannitol myleran	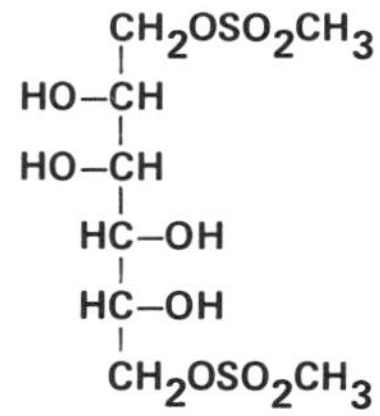	300	7
3052	1,9-Nonanediol, dimethane-sulfonate Nonane	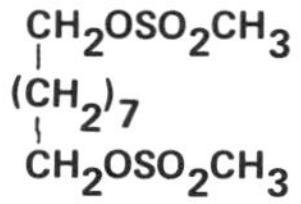	230	25
24901	Glycolamide, *N,N′*-ethylene-bis-, dimethanesulfonate	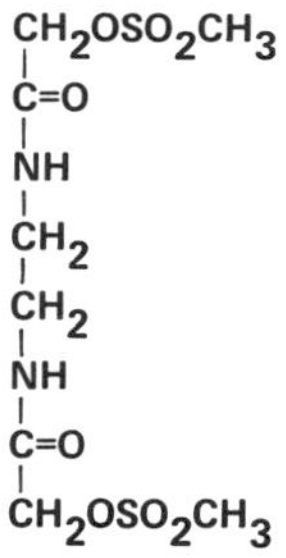	300	15

TABLE 4
EPOXIDES
(SYSTEMIC LEUKEMIA L1210)

NSC No.	Name	Structure	Optimal dose	Percent increase in life-span over controls
32605	Butane D-1,2,3,4-diepoxy	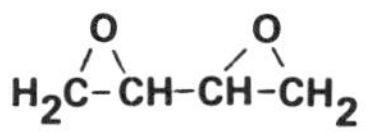	50	89*
56308	4,4′-Bipiperidine, 1,1′-bis-(2,3-epoxypropyl)-	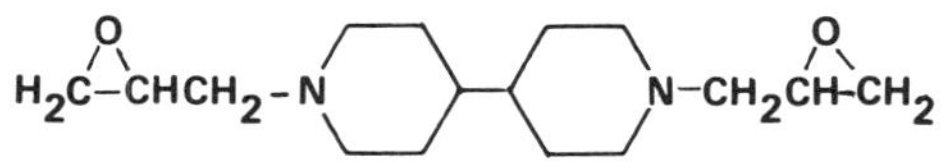	65	27
56845	Mannitol, 1,4:3,6-dianhydro-2,5-bis-*O*-(2,3-epoxypropyl)-, D-	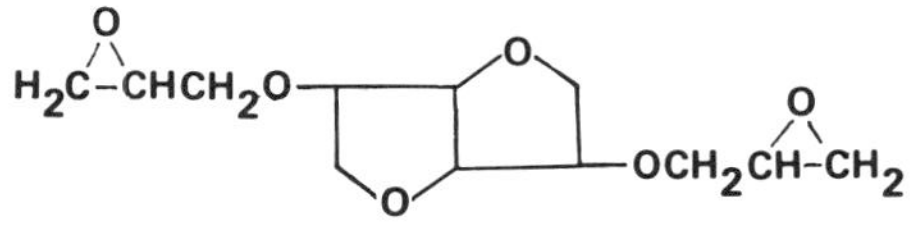	500	50

* Early L1210

TABLE 5(A)

ETHYLENEIMINES: PHOSPHORIC ACID DERIVATIVES

NSC No.	Name	Structure	Optimal dose	Percent increase in life-span over controls
9717	Phosphine oxide, tris(1-aziridinyl)- TEPA	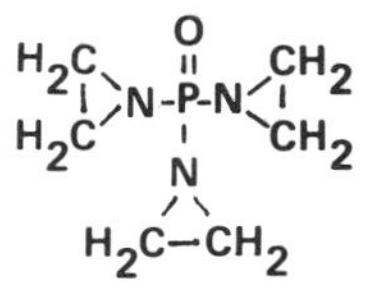	5.2	55
6396	Phosphine sulfide, tris(1-aziridinyl)- Thio-TEPA	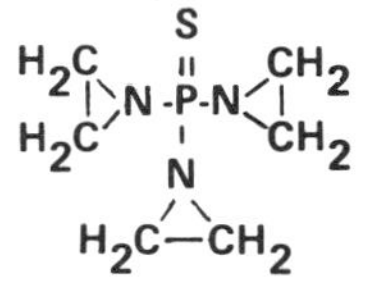	6.5	55
745	Phosphine oxide, bis(1-aziridinyl)morpholino MEPA	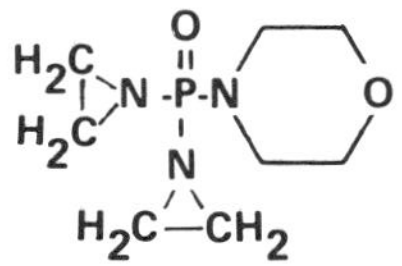	25	64
10429	Phosphine sulfide, bis(1-aziridinyl)morpholino- OPSPA	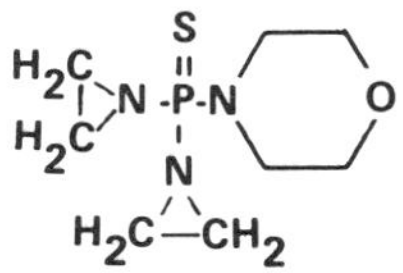	41	57

TABLE 5(A)
(*Continued*)

NSC No.	Name	Structure	Optimal dose	Percent increase in life-span over controls
37095	Carbamic acid, [bis(1-aziridinyl)phosphinyl]-, ethyl ester Uredepa AB-100	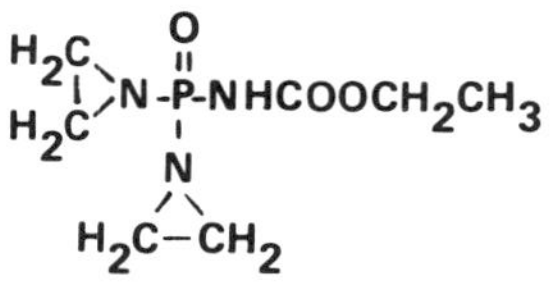	15	78
37096	Carbamic acid, [bis(1-aziridinyl)phosphinyl]-, benzyl ester Benzodepa (USAN) AB-103	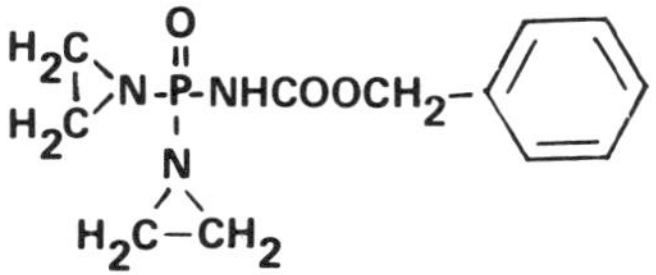	23	11
51325	Carbamic acid, [bis(2,2-dimethyl-l-aziridinyl)phosphinyl]-, ethyl ester	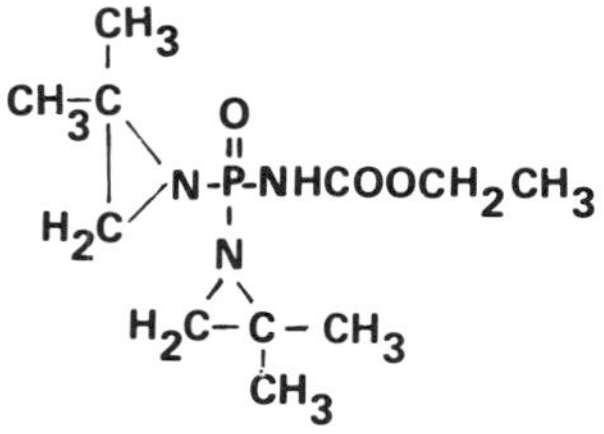	–	0

TABLE 5(A)
(*Continued*)

NSC No.	Name	Structure	Optimal dose	Percent increase in life span over controls
49421	Phosphinic amide, *P,P*-bis-(1-aziridinyl)-*N,N*-diethyl-	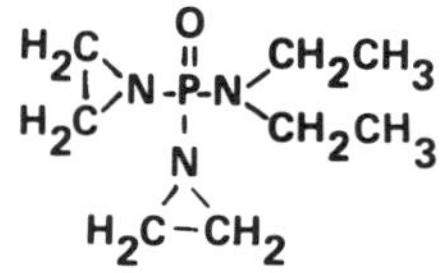	8.4	84
21596	Phosphinic amide, *P,P*-bis(1-aziridinyl)-*N,N*-dibutyl-	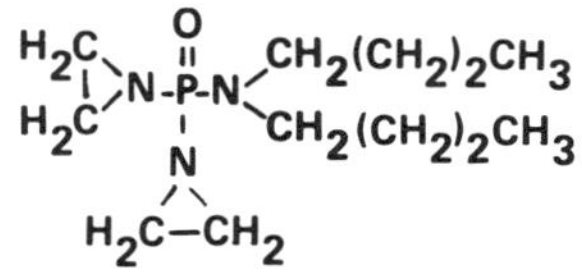	30	44
42072	Phosphine sulfide, (hexa-hydro-1-azepinyl)bis(1-aziridinyl)-1*H*-azepin-1-yl)bis(1-aziridinyl)-	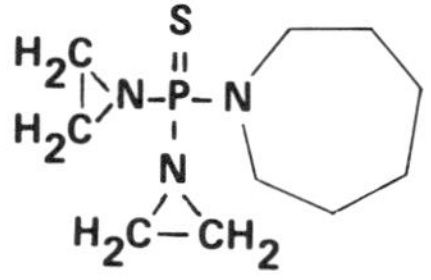	80	56
21597	Phosphinic acid, bis(1-aziridinyl)-, hexyl ester	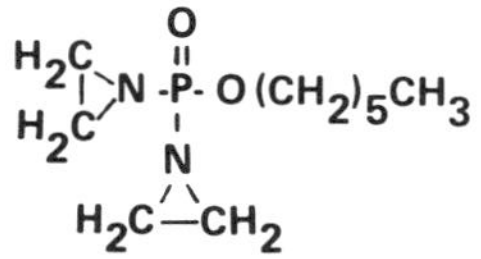	7.0	86

ine groups, indicate that additional attention could be focused on these structures.

A series of ethyleneimines containing a benzoquinone nucleus is listed in TABLE 5(B). Of the six bis aziridinyl benzoquinones listed, four were active in the L1210 system. One of these compounds, an acetamide bis aziridinyl benzoquinone, NSC 18269, had a rating of 114, which compares favorably with the activity of methotrexate and other known antitumor agents in the advanced L1210 system. The three other active bis aziridinyl benzoquinones (NSC 18270; 17262, A 139; NSC 18271) had lower ratings, while E39 (NSC 17261) had marginal activity. The tris aziridinyl listed (NSC 29215, Trenimon) also exhibited marginal activity. The rating of 50 for the tetrakis aziridinyl benzoquinone derivative (NSC 31717) is of interest.

The ethyleneimine derivative tetramin, TABLE 5(C), which is a mixture of 70% α-vinyl-1-aziridine ethanol (NSC 45726) and 30% β-vinyl-1-aziridine ethanol (NSC 45725), was active in the advanced L1210 system. The α derivative (NSC 45726) per se showed an increase in activity (rating of 73) over the mixture, while the β derivative (NSC 45725) was inactive. In a detailed investigation[14] it was indicated that the extent of effectiveness of the α component of tetramin (NSC 45726) was masked somewhat in the α-β mixture by inherent toxicity in the chemotherapeutically inactive β component, NSC 45725. Three additional ethyleneimines showed definite activity in the advanced L1210 system. These included a butanediol bis aziridine, NSC 35915 (rating of 77), a sulfonyldiethylene bis aziridine (NSC 45081) (rating of 68), and triethylene melamine, NSC 9706 (rating of 57).

Data are presented in TABLE 6 for a series of nitrosourea derivatives, a relatively new class of chemotherapeutic agents[16–18] that are highly active against leukemia L1210 and are of considerable potential interest for the clinic. It may be noted in TABLE 6 that these compounds are highly active, not only against early leukemia L1210, but also against advanced systemic disease. The compounds are capable of extensive eradication of the leukemic cells, as demonstrated previously[17] and as illustrated by the numbers of survivors listed in TABLE 6. The initial compound, 1-methyl-1-nitrosourea (NSC 23909), showed definite activity against early and advanced leukemia L1210. The introduction of one or two β-chloroethyl groups or a β-fluoroethyl group led to marked increases in chemotherapeutic activity. In addition to the extensive antileukemic properties of these compounds, the demonstrated ability of at least several of them, including BCNU (NSC 409962) and CCNU (NSC 79037), to penetrate the blood brain barrier and exert a cytolytic effect against intracranial leukemia[17,18] is of particular interest. To date, most of the attention has been focused on BCNU (NSC 409962) and CCNU (NSC 79037), but as evidenced by the data, a number of these compounds may be worthy of detailed investigation. The wide variety of structural modifications that are possible is illustrated by the retention of activity of the norbornyl (NSC 88106) and adamantyl (NSC 86056, 93161) derivatives. Delayed toxicity for the host has been manifested by this class of compounds. This toxicity may be unrelated to the chemotherapeutic effect, and congeners may be uncovered that fail to evidence this undesirable delayed toxicity.

Factors Influencing the Antileukemic Activity of Alkylating Agents

It has been well established that the therapeutic activity of a drug is not a fixed property of the drug, but may be altered by the manner in which the drug is

TABLE 5(B)

ETHYLENEIMINES: BENZOQUINONE DERIVATIVES
(SYSTEMIC LEUKEMIA L1210)

NSC No.	Name	Structure	Optimal dose	Percent increase in life-span over controls
18270	*p*-Benzoquinone, 2,5-bis(1-aziridinyl)-3,6-diethoxy-	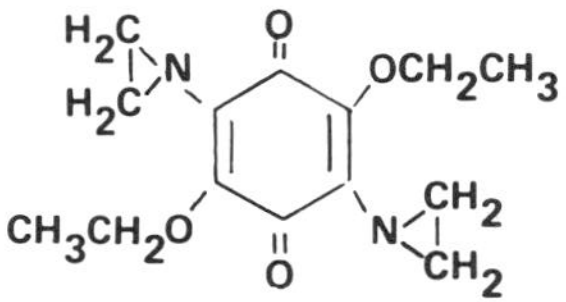	5	27
17261	*p*-Benzoquinone, 2,5-bis(1-aziridinyl)-3,6-dipropoxy- E 39	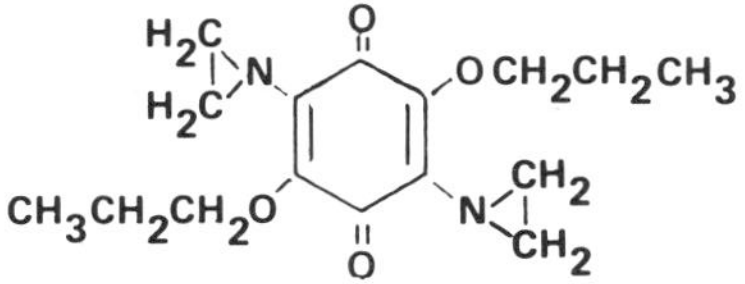	50	18
17262	*p*-Benzoquinone, 2,5-bis(1-aziridinyl)-3,6-bis(2-methoxyethoxy)- A 139	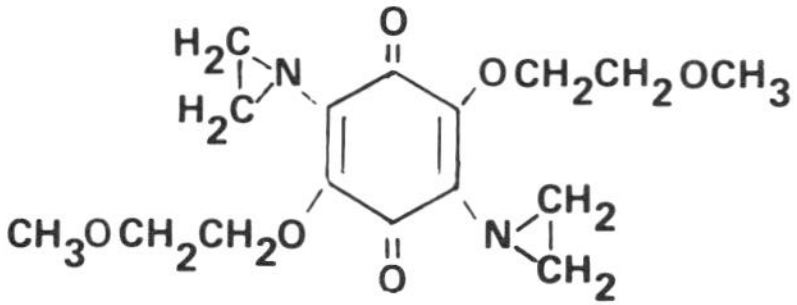	5	43
18269	Acetamide, *N,N′*-[3,6-bis-(1-aziridinyl)-*p*-benzoquinon-2,5-ylene] bis-	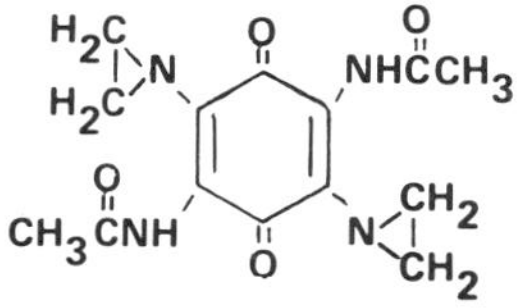	1.08	114

TABLE 5(B)
(*Continued*)

NSC No.	Name	Structure	Optimal dose	Percent increase in life-span over controls
18271	Propionamide, *N,N'*-[3,6-bis(1-aziridinyl)-*p*-benzoquinon-2,5-ylene] bis-	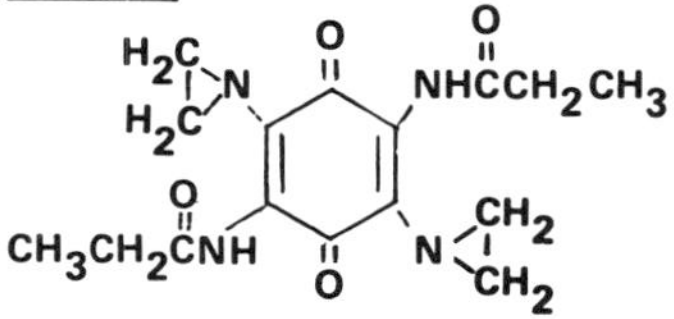	8.4	30
51915	Cyclohexanecarboxamide, *N-N'*-[3,6-bis(1-aziridinyl)-*p*-benzoquinon-2,5-ylene]-bis-	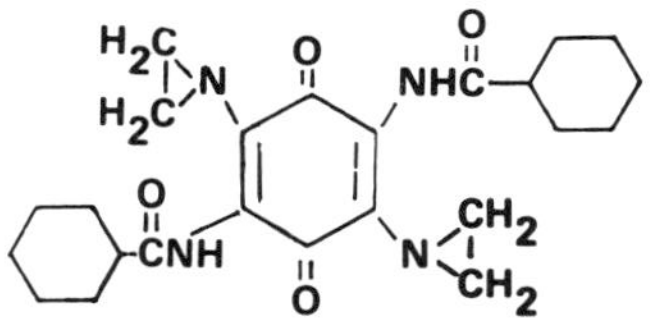	–*	0
29215	*p*-Benzoquinone, tris(1-aziridinyl)- Trenimon; Bayer 3231	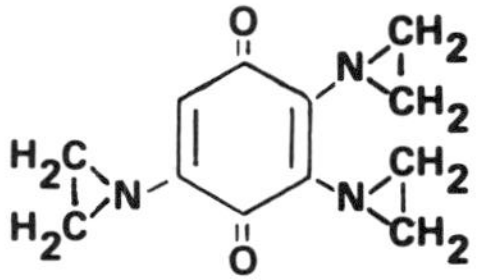	0.23	20
31717	*p*-Benzoquinone, tetrakis(1-aziridinyl)-	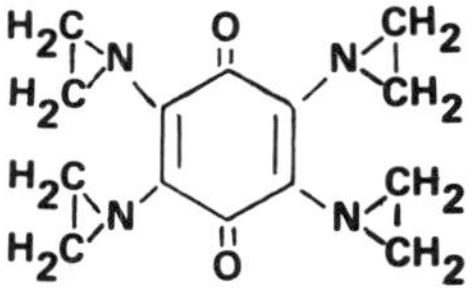	0.23	50

* The optimal dose may be higher than any employed.

TABLE 5(C)
ETHYLENEIMINES: MISCELLANEOUS COMPOUNDS
(SYSTEMIC LEUKEMIA L1210)

NSC No.	Name		Structure	Optimal dose	Percent increase in life-span over controls
26806	1-Aziridineethanol, α vinyl-, mixt. with β-vinyl-1-aziridineethanol (7:3)	70%	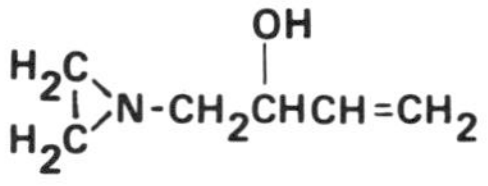	14	40
	Tetramin	30%	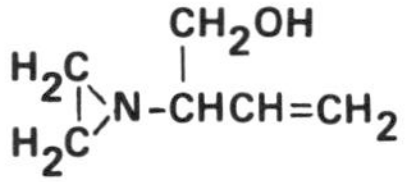		
45725	1-Aziridineethanol,- β-vinyl-		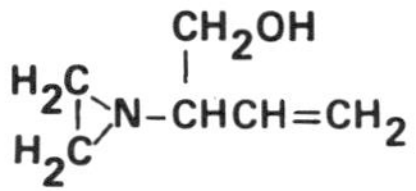	–	0
45726	1-Aziridineethanol,- α -vinyl-		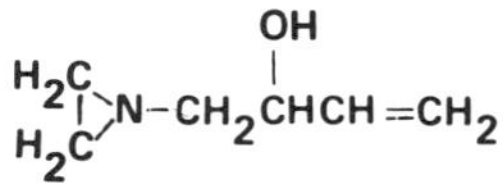	7.8	73
35915	2,3-Butanediol,- 1,4-bis(1-aziridinyl)- *meso-*		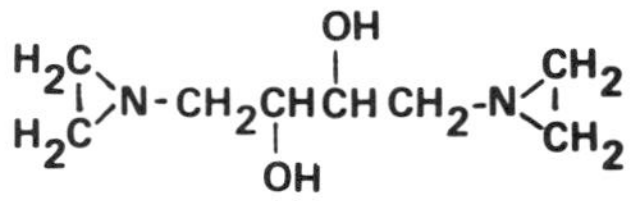	0.62	77

TABLE 5(C)
(*Continued*)

NSC No.	Name	Structure	Optimal dose	Percent increase in life-span over controls
45081	Aziridine, 1,1′-(sulfonlydiethylene)bis-[2-methyl]-	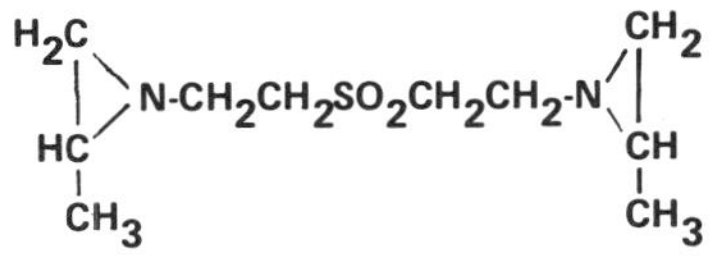	8.6	68
42399	1-Aziridinepropionic acid-, ethylene ester	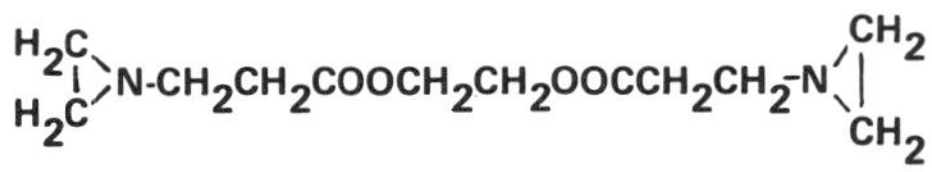	21.6	11
9706	*s*-Triazine, 2,4,6-tris(1-aziridinyl)- Triethylenemelamine; TEM	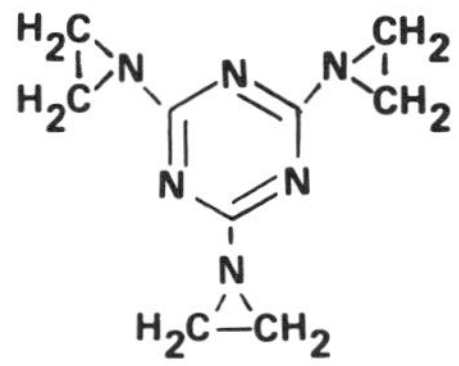	1.15	57
23436	Pyrimidine, 2,4-bis(1-aziridinyl)-6-methyl-5-nitro	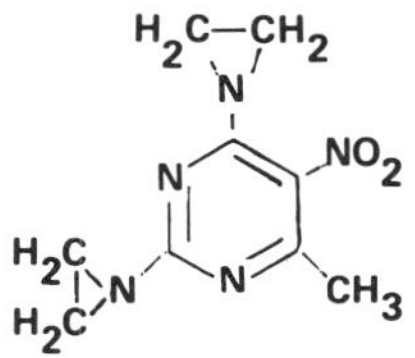		0

TABLE 6

NITROSOUREA DERIVATIVES: SCREENING DATA FOR EARLY AND SYSTEMIC LEUKEMIA L1210

NSC No.	Name	Structure	Early L1210			Systemic L1210		
			OD	ILS	Survivors	OD	ILS	Survivors
23909	Urea, 1-methyl-1-nitroso-	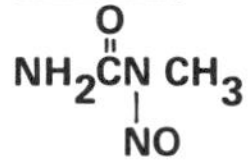	12.5	89	–	52	40	–
47547	Urea, 1-(2-chloroethyl)-1-nitroso-	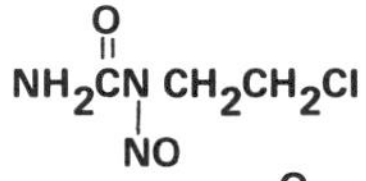	0.9	157	–	1.8	426	–
409962	Urea, 1,3-bis(2-chloroethyl)-1-nitroso- BCNU	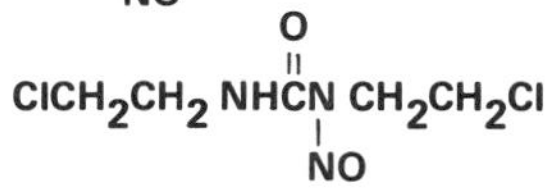	32.0 [1/]	>567	5/8	5	429	–
79037	Urea, 1-(2-chloroethyl)-3-cyclohexyl-l-nitroso- CCNU	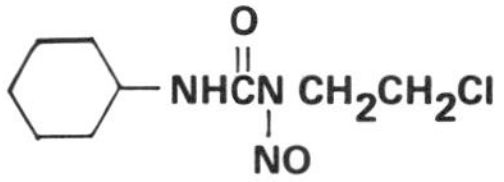	12.5	>770	7/10	8.4 14	390	–
87974	Urea, 3-cyclohexyl-1-(2-fluoroethyl)-1-nitroso-	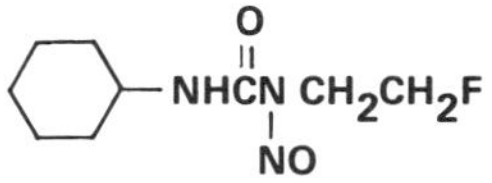	12.0	>567	9/10	14	270	–
88104	Urea, 3-(2-chlorocyclohexyl)-1-(2-chloroethyl)-1-nitroso-, *trans*	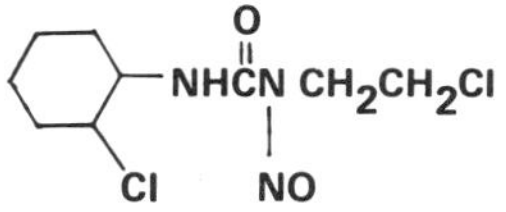	60 [1/]	>567	6/8	11 [2/]	>568	4/8

TABLE 6
(*Continued*)

NSC No.	Name	Structure	Early L1210 OD	Early L1210 ILS	Early L1210 Survivors	Systemic L1210 OD	Systemic L1210 ILS	Systemic L1210 Survivors
88106	Urea, 1-(2-chloroethyl)-3-(2-norbornyl)-1-nitroso-	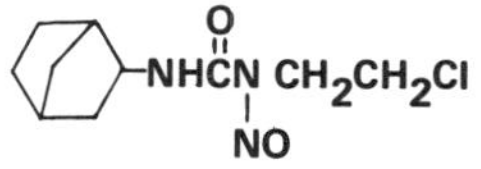	16	206	4/10	30	188	–
86056	Urea, 3-(1-adamantyl)-1-(2-chloroethyl)-1-nitroso-	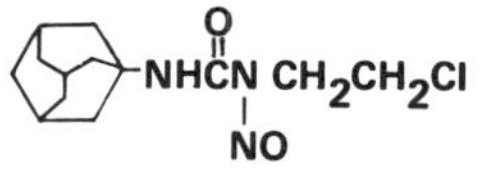	125 1/	150	5/6	50	225	–
93161	Urea, 3-(1-adamantyl)-1-(2-fluoroethyl)-1-nitroso-	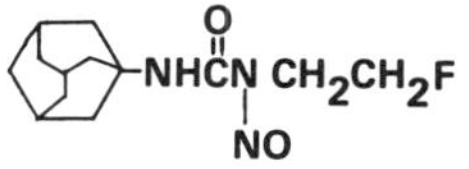	93 1/	92	1/6	65	111	2/8
89207	Urea, 3-(*p*-acetylphenyl)-1-(2-chloroethyl)-1-nitroso-	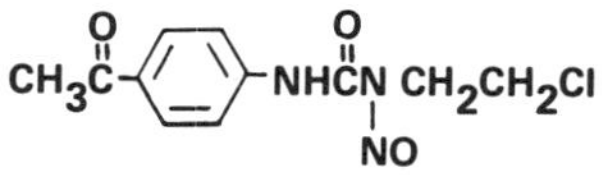	75 1/	91	1/6	65	11	–
91741	Urea, 1-(2-chloroethyl)-1-nitroso-3-(2,6-xylyl)-	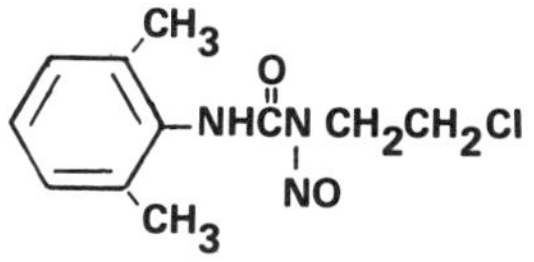	13	106	–	65	237	–

1/ Injection on day 1 only.

2/ The optimal dose may be lower than any employed.

O.D. = Optimal dose.

ILS = Percent increase in life-span over controls.

employed. Thus once it has been demonstrated that a drug is effective as a chemotherapeutic agent, the possibility exists that its effectiveness may be markedly improved by appropriate usage of the drug. Both the schedule and route of administration of a drug may be exceedingly important. A notable example was provided in studies with the antimetabolite methotrexate. Treatment with methotrexate every four days was considerably more effective than daily therapy was in increasing the survival time of mice with early leukemia L1210.[35,36] Similarly, treatment with methotrexate biweekly has shown definite improvement in remission maintenance in acute leukemia in the clinic.[37] Dichloromethotrexate, which is extremely active against leukemia L1210 when injected s.c. or i.p., is quite ineffective when administered orally.[38]

The influence of the treatment schedule and route of administration on the activity of the bis-chloroethylimidazole carboxamide derivative, NSC 82196, is illustrated in TABLE 7.[20] For the i.p. route, single injection and treatment every four or every eight days were more effective than daily treatment in increasing the survival time of the animals and in yielding a higher incidence of survivors. Oral administration was not as effective as the i.p. route. On oral administration, daily treatment appeared to be the most effective therapy and was slightly more effective than intermittent therapy. Single treatment orally was the least effective modality. Thus, not only may the route of administration influence the effectiveness of a compound, but also the optimal schedule of therapy may differ, depending upon the route of administration.

Broad experience has by now been obtained showing that therapeutic effectiveness may be enhanced by the employment of drugs in combination, and increasing emphasis is being placed on the clinical application of such combinations.[39–43] An example is provided in TABLE 8, showing that a combination of methotrexate (MTX) daily plus cyclophosphamide weekly was considerably more effective in increasing the survival time of leukemic mice than methotrexate alone daily or cyclophosphamide alone weekly were.[40] The combination of drugs elicited an approximately 100% increase in survival time over that observed with the individual drugs. As for individual drugs, the schedule of therapy may influence the effectiveness of drug combinations. When methotrexate and cyclophosphamide were employed in combination on a daily schedule (TABLE 8), they did not provide any appreciable therapeutic advantage over that observed with methotrexate alone daily or cytoxan alone daily.

Improved therapeutic effectiveness may also be obtained if drugs are employed in an appropriate sequence.[44] This is illustrated in TABLE 9, in which cyclophosphamide (Cytoxan®)† was administered as a single treatment on the fifth day following leukemic inoculation, and this was followed by treatment with cytosine arabinoside (ara-C) every three hours every fourth day from day 9.[45] It may be noted that this sequential therapy yielded a 317% increase in the median life-span of the mice, as opposed to a 139% increase with Cytoxan alone administered on day 5 only and a 144% increase with ara-C administered every three hours every fourth day from day 5. It appears that a sharp reduction in the number of leukemic cells by a single treatment with Cytoxan permitted subsequent therapy with ara-C to be more effective. The sequential therapy was also more effective than treatment with Cytoxan on a weekly schedule, which when

†Mead Johnson Laboratories, 2404 W. Pennsylvania St., Evansville, Indiana 47721.

TABLE 7

INFLUENCE OF TREATMENT SCHEDULE AND ROUTE OF ADMINISTRATION ON THE ACTIVITY OF IMIDAZOLE-4 (OR 5)- CARBOXAMIDE, 5 (OR 4)- [3,3-BIS(2-CHLOROETHYL)-1-TRIAZENO]-(NSC-82196) IN MICE WITH LEUKEMIA L1210*

Treatment Schedule†	Intraperitoneally			Orally		
	Optimal Dose (mg/kg)	‡ILS (percent)	60-Day Survivors / Total	Optimal Dose (mg/kg)	‡ILS (percent)	60-Day Survivors / Total
Daily	65.0	180	0/8	150	217	1/8
Every 4 days	180	>435	4/8	600	172	0/8
Every 8 days	300	>500	6/8	600	139	0/8
Single Injection	500	265	3/8	1,200	78	0/8

* 1 × 10^5 ascites, i.p.
† Treatment from day 5 to day 21. Oral daily treatment, days 5–13.
‡ ILS: Percent increase in life-span over controls.

TABLE 8
COMBINATION TREATMENT OF ADVANCED LEUKEMIA L1210*
(MTX PLUS CYCLOPHOSPHAMIDE)

Treatment Schedule	Optimal Dose (mg/kg)	Median Survival Time (days)	Percent ILS†
MTX alone, daily	1.08	29.0	164
Cyclophosphamide alone, daily	65.00	27.5	150
Cyclophosphamide alone, weekly	300.00	25.5	132
MTX daily +Cyclophosphamide daily	0.65 +39.00	31.0	182
MTX daily +Cyclophosphamide weekly	0.14 +180.00	42.0	382
Controls		11.0	

*Subcutaneous treatment; s.c. tumor.
†Percent increase in life-span over controls.

TABLE 9
SEQUENTIAL TREATMENT OF ADVANCED LEUKEMIA L1210 WITH CYCLOPHOSPHAMIDE AND ARA-C*

Cyclophosphamide		Ara-C		Median Survival Time (days)	Percent ILS†
Dose (mg/kg)	Treatment Schedule	Dose (mg/kg)	Treatment Schedule		
300	Weekly from day 5	0	–	32	25.5
180		0	–	20.5	195
108		0	–	18.5	106
65.0		0	–	13	44
500	Day 5 only	0	–	17	89
300		0	–	21.5	139
180		0	–	19	111
108		0	–	15	67
0	–	40.0	Every 3 hr,	16	78
0	–	20.0	every 4th day	22	144
0	–	10.0	from day 5	22	144
0	–	5.0		15.5	72
0	–	2.5		14	55
180	Day 5 only	20.0	Every 3 hr,	37.5	317
180		10.0	every 4th day	22	144
180		5.0	from day 9	25.5	184
180		2.5		24.5	172
Untreated Controls	–	–	–	9	–

*1×10^5 ascitic cells implanted s.c.; s.c. treatment; BDF_1 male mice.
†Percent increase in life-span over controls.

TABLE 10

EFFECTIVENESS OF AGENTS AGAINST THE IMIDAZOLE-CARBOXAMIDE-RESISTANT VARIANT L1210-82196/R

Agents to Which Leukemia L1210-82196/R Is Resistant				Agents to Which Leukemia L1210-82196/R Is Sensitive			
		Percent Increase over Controls				Percent Increase over Controls	
NSC No.	Compound	L1210 Sensitive	L1210 82196/R	NSC No.	Compound	L1210 Sensitive	L1210 82196/R
	Imidazole Carboxamides				Alkylating Agents		
82196	Imidazole-4(or 5)-carboxamide, 5(or 4)-[3,3-bis(2-chloroethyl)-1-triazeno]-	>300 >455 >230	18 25 9	26271	Cytoxan	344 140	>354 >291
45388	Imidazole-4(or 5)-carboxamide, 5(or 4)-(dimethyltriazeno)-	50 67	4 10	69945	Phosphorodiamidic acid, N,N-bis(2-chloroethyl)-, compd. with cyclohexylamine	75	59
	Nitrosoureas				Antimetabolites		
409962	1,3-Bis(2-chloroethyl)-1-nitrosourea (BCNU)	>455	10	740	MTX	167 100	170 86
79037	Urea, 1-(2-chloroethyl)-3-cyclohexyl-1-nitroso- (CCNU)	>330	9	63878	Ara-C	184	>360

the drug is employed individually, is usually the most effective schedule of therapy for this drug in this system.

Two of the primary limiting factors to the achievement of successful chemotherapy are the toxicity of the available drugs for the host and the origin of resistance. These limiting factors also apply to the use of alkylating agents in chemotherapy. The employment of appropriate schedules of therapy may provide a therapeutic advantage based on a slower buildup of toxicity for the host. Similarly, in certain situations the therapeutic advantage achieved by the use of a combination of drugs may also occur as the result of a delay in the appearance of limiting toxicity. Also, it has been observed that the use of a combination of drugs may result in a delay in the origin of resistance.[40] In order to prevent or delay effectively the origin of resistance and for the successful treatment of resistant tumor cells once they have appeared, it is desirable to use chemical agents that do not show cross-resistance. Data are shown in TABLE 10 on the effectiveness of a series of agents against a subline of leukemia L1210 resistant to the imidazole carboxamide derivative, NSC 82196.[46] Cross-resistance was observed for a second imidazole carboxamide derivative, NSC 45388, and for nitrosoureas. On the other hand, the imidazole-carboxamide-resistant variant was sensitive to Cytoxan, phosphoramide mustard (NSC 69945), and the antimetabolites methotrexate and cytosine arabinoside. It would be of interest, based on these studies, to determine whether the combination of the imidazole derivative (NSC 82196) with Cytoxan (NSC 26271) or with phosphoramide mustard (NSC 69945) might not be synergistic in the therapy of leukemia L1210 and whether such combinations might not also delay the origin of resistance to therapy.

Summary

From the cancer chemotherapy testing program at the National Cancer Institute as well as from other laboratories, both in the United States and abroad, new and potentially useful chemotherapeutic agents are becoming available. The active alkylating agents that are currently under development show a wide array of basic and structural modifications.

The structure-activity studies presented here indicate that an appreciable number and variety of alkylating agents, which have not received clinical attention, show significant activity in the important animal leukemia (L1210) test system. Since in general, activity in the leukemia L1210 system prognosticates well for clinical activity against leukemia and other forms of neoplasia, a number of these L1210 active alkylating agents are undoubtedly worthy of additional development and clinical testing.

In addition, many alkylating agents have been synthesized and tested in a variety of tumor systems. A very comprehensive compilation and analysis of therapeutic activity and toxicity is provided in "Comparative Pharmacology of Alkylating Agents" by L. H. Schmidt and associates.[33] The excellent recent review by Ochoa and Hirschberg[47] may be consulted for an extensive list of references pertaining to the therapeutic activity of alkylating agents. The comprehensive studies at the Chester Beatty Institute and elsewhere have resulted in tremendous contributions.[48] The strong interest in alkylating agents is reflected in the studies of Larionov.[49]

The current analysis is not intended to review the extensive list of synthesized alkylating agents,[50–53] but rather to illustrate the variety and great potential of this class of compounds for clinical use. Those compounds that have been shown to be active should be subjected to additional detailed investigation of their mechanism of action, including their actions in cell cycle kinetics,[54-58] pharmacological and biochemical activity, etc., which in turn may serve as a guide in the more effective utilization of the agents both experimentally and in the clinic.

That the various alkylating agents differ in their mode of action is indicated by their differing activity spectra in a variety of tumor systems.[59] The activity spectrum of the useful drug cyclophosphamide, for example, differs from that of a variety of alkylating agents, both in animal tumor systems and in the clinic.

This discussion emphasizes the fact that we are far from a saturated situation with respect to the alkylating agents. With close collaboration between laboratory and clinical investigators, we can look forward to the acquisition of additional chemotherapeutically useful alkylating agents.

References

1. Zubrod, C. G., S. Schepartz, J. Leiter, K. M. Endicott, L. M. Carrese & C. G. Baker. 1966. The chemotherapy program of the National Cancer Institute: history, analysis and plans. Cancer Chemother. Rep. **50:** 349–540.
2. Goldin, A., A. A. Serpick & N. Mantel. 1966. Experimental screening procedures and clinical predictability value—a commentary. Cancer Chemother. Rep. **50:** 173–218.
3. Goldin, A. 1968. Preclinical methodology for the selection of anticancer agents. *In* Methods in Cancer Research. H. Busch, Ed. **4:** 193–254. Academic Press, Inc. New York, N. Y.
4. Zubrod, C. G. 1964. Quantitative concepts in the clinical study of drugs. *In* Advances in Chemotherapy. A. Goldin & F. Hawking, Eds. **1:** 9–34. Academic Press, Inc. New York, N. Y.
5. Gellhorn, A. & E. Hirschberg, Eds. 1955. Investigation of diverse systems for cancer chemotherapy screening. Cancer Res. [Suppl.] **3:** (125 pages).
6. Leiter, J. & M. A. Schneiderman. 1959. Screening data from the Cancer Chemotherapy National Service Center screening laboratories. Cancer Res. **19** (No. 3, Part II): 31–193.
7. Leiter, J., B. J. Abbott & S. A. Schepartz. 1965. Screening data from the Cancer Chemotherapy National Service Center screening laboratories. XXVIII. Cancer Res. [Suppl.] **25** (No. 9, Part II): 1626–1769.
8. Cancer Chemotherapy National Service Center Protocols for Screening Chemical Agents and Natural Products Against Animal Tumors and Other Biologic Systems. 1962. Cancer Chemother Rep. **25:** 1–66.
9. Goldin, A., J. M. Venditti & N. Mantel. 1961. Preclinical screening and evaluation of agents for the chemotherapy of cancer: A review. Cancer Res. **21:** 1334–1351.
10. Goldin, A., J. M. Venditti, S. R. Humphreys & N. Mantel. 1956. Modification of treatment schedules in the management of advanced mouse leukemia with amethopterin. J. Nat. Cancer Inst. **17:** 203–212.
11. Goldin, A., J. M. Venditti, S. R. Humphreys & N. Mantel. 1958. Quantitative evaluation of chemotherapeutic agents against advanced leukemia in mice. J. Nat. Cancer Inst. **21:** 495–511.
12. Goldin, A., J. M. Venditti & I. Kline. 1959. Evaluation of antileukemic agents employing advanced leukemia L1210 in mice. Cancer Res. **19** (Part II): 429–466.
13. Goldin, A. & J. M. Venditti. 1962. Quantitative assessment of various classes of agents employing advanced leukemia L1210 in mice. (Part II of A Manual on Quantitative Drug Evaluation in Experimental Tumor Systems). Cancer Chemother. Rep. **17:** 145–178.
14. Venditti, J. M., A. Goldin & I. Kline. 1961. Comparison of the effectiveness of

tetramin and its components against advanced leukemia L1210 in mice. Cancer Chemother. Rep. **11:** 73–76.
15. SKIPPER, H. E. & L. H. SCHMIDT. 1962. A manual on quantitative drug evaluation in experimental tumor systems. Part I. Background description of criteria, and presentation of quantitative therapeutic data on various classes of drugs obtained in diverse experimental tumor systems. Cancer Chemother. Rep. **17:** 1–143.
16. SCHABEL, F. M., JR., T. P. JOHNSTON, G. S. MCCALEB, J. A. MONTGOMERY, W. R. LASTER & H. E. SKIPPER. 1963. Experimental evaluation of potential anticancer agents. VIII. Effects of certain nitrosoureas on intracerebral L1210 leukemia. Cancer Res. **23:** 725–733.
17. JOHNSTON, T. P., G. S. MCCALEB, P. S. OPLIGER & J. A. MONTGOMERY. 1966. The synthesis of potential anticancer agents. XXXVI. N-Nitrosoureas. II. Haloalkyl derivatives. J. Med. Chem. **9:** 892–911.
18. DEVITA, V. T., P. P. CARBONE, A. H. OWENS, JR., G. L. GOLD, M. J. KRAUT & J. EDMONSON. 1965. Clinical trials with 1,3-bis(2-chloroethyl)-1-nitrosourea, NSC-409962. Cancer Res. **25:** 1876–1881.
19. SHEALEY, Y. F. & C. A. KRAUTH. 1966. Complete inhibition of mouse leukemia L1210 by 5(or 4)-[3,3-bis(2-chloroethyl)-1-triazeno]imidazole-4-(or 5)-carboxamide (NSC 82,196). Nature **210:** 208–209.
20. HOFFMAN, G., I. KLINE, M. GANG, D. D. TYRER, J. M. VENDITTI & A. GOLDIN. 1968. Influence of treatment schedules and route of administration on the chemotherapy of murine leukemia L1210 with 5(or 4)-[3,3-bis(2-chloroethyl)-1-triazeno]-imidazole-4(or 5)-carboxamide (NSC-82196). Cancer Chemother. Reports (Part 1) **52:** 715–724.
21. EL-MERZABANI, M. M. & Y. SAKURAI. 1965. A new alkylating antitumor agent effective on experimental tumors resistant to nitrogen mustard. Gann **56:** 589–598.
22. EL-MERZABANI, M. M. & Y. SAKURAI. 1967. Anticancer activities of methane sulfonic acid esters of aminoglycols against mouse leukemia L1210. Gann **58:** 199–201.
23. SELLEI, C. 1964. Cancer control and clinical chemotherapy in Hungary. Neoplasma (Bratisl) **11:** 529–547.
24. DEWYS, W. D., S. R. HUMPHREYS & A. GOLDIN. 1968. Studies on therapeutic effectiveness of drugs with tumor weight and survival time indices of Walker 256 carcinosarcoma. Cancer Chemother. Rep. **52:** 229–242.
25. KELLNER, B., L. NEMETH, P. HORVATH & L. INSTITORIS. 1967. 1,6-Dibromo-1,6-dideoxy-dulcitol: A new antitumoral agent. Nature **213:** 402–403.
26. VENDITTI, J. M. & A. GOLDIN. To be published.
27. GOLDIN, A., J. M. VENDITTI, I. KLINE & N. MANTEL. 1960. Evaluation of antileukemic agents employing advanced leukemia L1210 in mice. II. Cancer Res. **20** (Part II): 382–448.
28. GOLDIN, A., J. M. VENDITTI, I. KLINE & N. MANTEL. 1961. Evaluation of antileukemic agents employing advanced leukemia L1210 in mice IV. Cancer Res. **21** (No. 3, Part II): 27–92.
29. GOLDIN, A., J. M. VENDITTI & I. KLINE. 1962. Evaluation of antileukemic agents employing advanced leukemia L1210 in mice. V. Cancer Res. **22** (Part II): 157–220.
30. GOLDIN, A., J. M. VENDITTI & I. KLINE. 1962. Evaluation of antileukemic agents employing advanced leukemia L1210 in mice. VI. Cancer Res. **22** (Part II): 749–835.
31. FOLEY, G. E., O. M. FRIEDMAN & B. P. DROLET. 1961. Studies on the mechanism of action of Cytoxan. Evidence of activation in vivo and in vitro. Cancer Res. **21:** 57–63.
32. GALTON, D. A. G., M. TILL & E. WILTSHAW. 1958. Busulfan (1,4-dimethanesulfonyl-oxybutane, Myleran): Summary of clinical results. Ann. N. Y. Acad. Sci. **68:** 967–973.
33. SCHMIDT, L. H., R. FRADKIN, R. SULLIVAN & A. FLOWERS. 1965. Comparative pharmacology of alkylating agents. Cancer Chemother. Rep. (Suppl. 2; Parts 1, 2, and 3): 1–1528.
34. BARDOS, T. J., Z. B. PAPANASTASSIOU, A. SEGALOFF & J. L. AMBRUS. 1959. "Dual antagonists"; alkyl N-(bis-(ethylenimido)-phosphoro)-carbamates; a new series of antitumor agents. Nature **183:** 399–400.
35. GOLDIN, A., J. M. VENDITTI, S. R. HUMPHREYS & N. MANTEL. 1956. Modification

of treatment schedules in the management of advanced mouse leukemia with amethopterin. J. Nat. Cancer Inst. **17:** 203–212.

36. Venditti, J. M., A. Goldin & I. Kline. 1960. The influence of treatment schedule on the chemotherapy of advanced leukemia L1210 in mice. Cancer Chemother. Rep. **6:** 55–57.
37. Selawry, O. S. *et al.* 1965. Cooperative study. Acute Leukemia Group B. New treatment schedule with improved survival in childhood leukemia. JAMA **194:** 75–81.
38. Venditti, J. M., A. W. Schrecker, J. A. R. Mead, I. Kline & A. Goldin. 1960. Influence of the route of administration on the relative effectiveness of 3′,5′-dichloroamethopterin and amethopterin against advanced leukemia (L1210) in mice. Cancer Res. **20:** 1451–1456.
39. Goldin, A. & N. Mantel. 1957. The employment of combinations of drugs in the chemotherapy of neoplasia: A review. Cancer Res. **17:** 635–654.
40. Venditti, J. M. & A. Goldin. 1964. Drug synergism in antineoplastic chemotherapy. *In* Advances in Chemotherapy. A. Goldin & F. Hawking, Eds. **1:** 397–498. Academic Press, Inc. New York, N. Y.
41. Frei, E., III & E. J. Freireich. 1965. Progress and perspectives in the chemotherapy of acute leukemia. *In* Advances in Chemotherapy. A. Goldin, F. Hawking & R. J. Schnitzer, Eds. **2:** 269–298. Academic Press, Inc. New York, N. Y.
42. Sullivan, M. P., E. C. Beatty, Jr., C. B. Hyman, M. L. Murphy, M. I. Pierce & N. C. Severo. 1962. A comparison of the effectiveness of standard dose 6-mercaptopurine, combination 6-mercaptopurine, and DON, and high-loading 6-mercaptopurine therapies in the treatment of acute leukemia in children: Results of a cooperative study. Cancer Chemother. Rep. **16:** 161–164.
43. Heyn, R. M., C. A. Brubaker, J. H. Burchenal, N. G. Cramblett & J. A. Wolff. 1960. The comparison of 6-mercaptopurine with the combination of 6-mercaptopurine and azaserine in the treatment of acute leukemia in children: Results of a cooperative study. Blood **15:** 350–360.
44. Venditti, J. M. & A. Goldin. 1964. Chemotherapy of advanced mouse leukemia L1210: Comparison of methotrexate alone and in sequential therapy. Cancer Res. **24:** 1457–1460.
45. Hoffman, G. S., V. S. Waravdekar, J. M. Venditti & N. Mantel. 1968. Sequential chemotherapy with Cytoxan and 1-β-D-arabinofuranosylcytosine hydrochloride (ara-C) in mice with advanced leukemia L1210. Proc. Amer. Assoc. Cancer Res. **9:** 31.
46. Tyrer, D. D., I. Kline, J. M. Venditti & A. Goldin. 1968. Effectiveness of antileukemic agents in the therapy of mice inoculated with a leukemia L1210 variant (L1210/82,196R) resistant to 5(or 4)-[3,3-bis-(2-chloroethyl)-1-triazeno] imidazole-4(or 5)-carboxamide (NSC 82,196). Proc. Amer. Assoc. Cancer Res. **9:** 72.
47. Ochoa, M., Jr. & E. Hirschberg. 1967. Alkylating agents. *In* Experimental Chemotherapy. R. J. Schnitzer & F. Hawking, Eds. **5:** 1–132. Academic Press, Inc. New York, N. Y.
48. Comparative Clinical and Biological Effects of Alkylating Agents. 1958. Ann. N. Y. Acad. Sci. **68:** 657–1266.
49. Larionov, L. F. 1965. Cancer Chemotherapy. (Translated from the Russian.): 271–338. Pergamon Press, Inc. London, England.
50. Bratzel, R. P., R. B. Ross, T. H. Goodridge, W. T. Huntress, M. T. Flather & D. E. Johnson. 1963. Survey of nitrogen mustards. Cancer Chemother. Rep. **26:** 1–322.
51. Huntress, W. T., T. H. Goodridge & R. P. Bratzel. 1963. Survey of sulfur mustards. Cancer Chemother. Rep. **26:** 323–339.
52. Goodridge, T. H., W. T. Huntress & R. P. Bratzel. 1963. Survey of aziridines. Cancer Chemother. Rep. **26:** 341–443.
53. Bratzel, R. P., T. H. Goodridge & W. T. Huntress. 1963. Survey of epoxides and episulfides. Cancer Chemother. Rep. **26:** 445–504.
54. Skipper, H. E., F. M. Schabel, Jr. & W. S. Wilcox. 1964. Experimental evaluation

of potential anticancer agents. XIII. On the criteria and kinetics associated with "curability" of experimental leukemia. Cancer Chemother. Rep. **35:** 1–111.

55. BRUCE, W. R., B. E. MEEKER & F. A. VALERIOTE. 1966. Comparison of the sensitivity of normal hematopoietic and transplanted lymphoma colony-forming cells to chemotherapeutic agents administered in vivo. J. Nat. Cancer Inst. **37:** 233–245.
56. VADLAMUDI, S., V. S. WARAVDEKAR, J. N. CHOUDRY & A. GOLDIN. 1968. Effect of treatment with 1,3-bis (2-chloroethyl)-1-nitrosourea or cyclophosphamide on spleen colony-forming units and survival time of leukemic mice. Cancer Res. **28:** 1242–1249.
57. SCHABEL, F. M., JR., H. E. SKIPPER, M. W. TRADER & W. S. WILCOX. 1965. Experimental evaluation of potential anticancer agents. XIX. Sensitivity of nondividing leukemic cell populations to certain classes of drugs in vivo. Cancer Chemother. Rep. **48:** 17–30.
58. WODINSKY, I., J. SWINIARSKI & C. J. KENSLER. 1967. Spleen colony studies of leukemia L1210. II. Differential sensitivities of normal and leukemic bone marrow colony-forming cells to single and divided dose therapy with cytosine arabinoside (NSC-63878). Cancer Chemother. Rep. **51:** 423–429.
59. ZUBROD, C. G. & A. W. PRATT. 1962. The analysis of structure-activity relationships of alkylating agents in a spectrum of rat tumors. Cancer Chemother. Rep. **16:** 29–36.

DISCUSSION OF THE PAPER

DR. T. BARDOS (*State University of New York, Buffalo, N. Y.*): At how many days after inoculation was the leukemia well established?

DR. GOLDIN: In the "advanced leukemia" L1210 system, leukemic cells are inoculated subcutaneously. We withhold therapy until palpable local tumor (8–10 mm diameter) is evident at the site of leukemic inoculation. This is usually five to eight days after leukemic inoculation, and at that time the disease is systemic. The untreated controls usually succumb in about 10 days.

DR. P. ALEXANDER (*Chester Beatty Research Institute, Institute of Cancer Research, Belmont, Sutton, Surry, England*): Do you think we ought to declare a moratorium on the preparation of further compounds?

DR. GOLDIN: I think you have in mind, and I would be inclined to agree, that we still have a lot of investigating to do with the compounds that are available. However, I do not think we ought to stop synthesizing new compounds. New and novel alkylating agents and other compounds of interest are continuing to be found in screening programs. I think we ought to continue the synthesis and testing of new agents, and at the same time, investigate the available compounds in considerable detail, at a quite basic level.

DR. BARDOS: I am very much interested in the observation that cross-resistance did not occur in all instances among the alkylating agents tested. This would suggest that there may be instances in which resistance to alkylating agents is related to structural features not connected with the alkylating ability. This offers some hope that one can increase the therapeutic effectiveness of alkylating agents by modifications in the structure of the molecule that are not involved in alkylation.

DR. GOLDIN: This is a definite and interesting possibility. I think that in the area of cross-resistance, there is much work to be done.

Appendix I: Alkylating Agents

NSC No.	Name	Molecular Formula	Source of Compound	Table No.
740	Amethopterin (MTX)	$N_8O_5C_{20}H_{22}$	Lederle Laboratories Division, American Cyanamid Co. (Dr. J. M. Ruegsegger)	8, 10
745	Phosphine oxide, bis(1-aziridinyl)-morpholino-	$N_3O_2PC_8H_{16}$	Lederle Laboratories Division, American Cyanamid Co. (Dr. J. M. Ruegsegger)	5
750	1,4-Butanediol, dimethane-sulfonate (Myleran)	$O_6S_2C_6H_{14}$	Wellcome Research Laboratories (Dr. George H. Hitchings)	3
762	Diethylamine, 2,2′-dichloro-N-methyl-, hydrochloride	$NCl_2C_5H_{11}\cdot HCl$	Merck and Company	2
2059	Triethylamine, 2-chloro-, hydrochloride	$NClC_6H_{14}\cdot HCl$	W. S. Merrell Co.	2
3052	1,9-Nonanediol, dimethane-sulfonate	$O_6S_2C_{11}H_{24}$	Eastman Kodak Company*	3
3088	Butyric acid, 4-(p-[bis(2-chloroethyl)amino]phenyl)-	$NO_2Cl_2C_{14}H_{19}$	Wellcome Research Laboratories (Dr. George H. Hitchings)*	2
3423	2-Naphthoic acid, 4,4′-methyl-enebis[3-hydroxy-, compd. with 4-[[4-[bis(2-chloroethyl)amino]-1-methylbutyl]amino]-7-chloro-quinoline (1:1) (Chloroquine mustard, pamoate)	$O_6C_{23}H_{16}\cdot N_3Cl_3C_{18}H_{24}$	John Harrison Laboratory of Chemistry, University of Pennsylvania (Prof. Charles C. Price)	2
6396	Phosphine sulfide, tris(1-aziridinyl)-	$N_3PSC_6H_{12}$	Chemical-Biological Coordination Center, National Academy of Science	5
8806	Alanine, 3-[p-[bis(2-chloroethyl)-amino]phenyl]-, monohydrochlo-ride, L- (Melpahlan)	$N_2O_2Cl_2C_{13}H_{18}\cdot HCl$	Chester Beatty Research Institute	2

9698	Mannitol, 1,6-bis[(2-chloroethyl)-amino]-1,6-dideoxy-, dihydro-chloride, D-	$N_2O_4Cl_2C_{10}H_{22}\cdot 2HCl$	Research Institute of the Pharmaceutical Industry, Budapest VII, Hungary (Prof. L. Vargha)	2
9706	s-Triazine, 2,4,6-tris(1-aziridinyl)-	$N_6C_9H_{12}$	Lederle Laboratories Division, American Cyanamide Co. (Dr. J. M. Ruegsegger)	5
9717	Phosphine oxide, tris(1-aziridinyl)-	$N_3OPC_6H_{12}$	Chemical-Biological Coordination Center, National Academy of Science	5
9995	Piperidine, 1-(2-chloroethyl)-, hydrochloride	$NClC_7H_{14}\cdot HCl$	Merck and Company	2
10107	Diethylamine, 2,2′-dichloro-N-methyl-, N-oxide, compd. with hydrochloride (1:1)	$NOCl_2C_5H_{11}\cdot HCl$	Takeda Chemical Industries, Ltd., Osaka, Japan (Sachio Himeno)	2
10429	Phosphine sulfide, bis(1-aziridinyl)morpholino-	$N_3OPSC_8H_{16}$	McArdle Memorial Laboratory, University of Wisconsin (Dr. Charles Heidelberger)	5
10873	Diethylamine, 2,2′-dichloro-, hydrochloride	$NCl_2C_4H_9\cdot HCl$	Parke, Davis and Company (Dr. John R. Dice)	2
11468	Benzylamine, N-(2-chloroethyl)-N-ethyl-, hydrochloride	$NClC_{11}H_{16}\cdot HCl$	Chemical-Biological Coordination Center, National Academy of Science	2
11472	Piperonylamine, N-(2-chloroethyl)-N-ethyl-, hydrochloride	$NO_2ClC_{12}H_{16}\cdot HCl$	Chemical-Biological Coordination Center, National Academy of Science	2
11481	p-Cymen-7-amine, N-(2-chloroethyl)-N-ethyl-, hydrochloride	$NClC_{14}H_{22}\cdot HCl$	Chemical-Biological Coordination Center, National Academy of Science	2
11486	1-Naphthalenemethylamine, N-(2-chloroethyl)-N-ethyl-, hydrochloride	$NClC_{15}H_{18}\cdot HCl$	Chemical-Biological Coordination Center, National Academy of Science	2

* Purchased by Cancer Chemotherapy National Service Center (CCNSC).

Appendix I (Continued)

NSC No.	Name	Molecular Formula	Source of Compound	Table No.
13187	1,3-Propanediamine, N,N,N′,N′-tetrakis(2-chloroethyl)-, dihydrochloride	$N_2Cl_4C_{11}H_{22}\cdot 2HCl$	Merck, Sharp and Dohme Research Labs. (Dr. A. H. Land)	2
14210	Alanine, 3-[p-[bis(2-chloroethyl)-amino]phenyl]-, monohydrochloride, DL- (Sarcolysin)	$N_2O_2Cl_2C_{13}H_{18}\cdot HCl$	Inst. Exper. Pathology and Therapy of Cancer, Acad. of Med. Sciences, USSR (rec'd through Dr. S. Farber)	2
16498	Benzoic acid, o-(4-[bis(2-chloroethyl)amino]-o-tolylazo)-	$N_3O_2Cl_2C_{18}H_{19}$	Chester Beatty Research Institute (Dr. W. C. J. Ross)	2
17261	p-Benzoquinone, 2,5-bis(1-aziridinyl)-3,6-dipropoxy-	$N_2O_4C_{16}H_{22}$	Verkauf Pharm. C., Leverkusen, Germany (Dr. Birth)	5
17262	p-Benzoquinone, 2,5-bis(1-aziridinyl)-3,6-bis(2-methoxy-ethoxy)-	$N_2O_6C_{16}H_{22}$	Verkauf Pharm. C., Leverkusen, Germany (Dr. Birth)	5
17661	Glycine, N,N-bis(2-chloroethyl)-hydrochloride (Glycine mustard)	$NO_2Cl_2C_6H_{11}\cdot HCl$	Sasaki University, Tokyo, Japan (Dr. Y. Sakurai)	2
17663	Alanine, N,N-bis(2-chloroethyl)-, hydrochloride, DL- (Alanine mustard)	$NO_2Cl_2C_7H_{13}\cdot HCl$	Sasaki University, Tokyo, Japan (Dr. Y. Sakurai)	2
18016	Ethanol, 2-chloro-, methane-sulfonate	$O_3SClC_3H_7$	Chester Beatty Research Institute (Dr. W. C. J. Ross)	3
18269	Acetamide, N,N′-[3,6-bis(1-aziridinyl)-p-benzoquinon-2,5-ylene]bis-	$N_4O_4C_{14}H_{16}$	CIBA Pharmaceutical Company (Dr. S. S. Barkulis)	5
18270	p-Benzoquinone, 2,5-bis(1-aziridinyl)-3,6-diethoxy-	$N_2O_4C_{14}H_{18}$	CIBA Pharmaceutical Company (Dr. S. S. Barkulis)	5

18271	Propionamide, N,N′-[3,6-bis(1-aziridinyl)-p-benzoquinon-2,5-ylene]bis-	$N_4O_4C_{16}H_{20}$	CIBA Pharmaceutical Company (Dr. S. S. Barkulis)	5
18321	Hydroquinone, 2,5-bis[[bis(2-chloroethyl)amine]methyl]-, dihydrochloride	$N_2O_2Cl_4C_{16}H_{24} \cdot 2HCl$	Milliken University (Dr. Carl Weatherbee)	2
18439	Aniline, N,N-bis(2-chloroethyl)-2,3-dimethoxy-	$NO_2Cl_2C_{12}H_{17}$	Abbott Laboratories (Dr. John A. Carbon)	2
21199	Phosphonic acid, (p-[bis(2-iodoethyl)amino]benzyl)-, diethyl ester	$NO_3PI_2C_{15}H_{24}$	The Upjohn Company	2
21596	Phosphinic amide, P,P-bis(1-aziridinyl)-N,N-dibutyl-	$N_3OPC_{12}H_{26}$	Minnesota Mining and Manufacturing Co.	5
21597	Phosphinic acid, bis(1-aziridinyl)-, hexyl ester	$N_2O_2PC_{10}H_{21}$	Minnesota Mining and Manufacturing Co.	5
23436	Pyrimidine, 2,4-bis(1-aziridinyl)-6-methyl-5-nitro-	$N_5O_2C_9H_{11}$	University of Michigan (Prof. Robert C. Elderfield)	5
23891	Benzimidazole, 2-([bis(2-chloroethyl)amino]methyl)-, hydrochloride	$N_3Cl_2C_{12}H_{15} \cdot HCl$	Givaudan Corporation	2
23892	Benzimidazole, 2-([bis(2-chloroethyl)-amino]methyl)-5,6-dimethyl-, hydrochloride	$N_3Cl_2C_{14}H_{19} \cdot HCl$	Givaudan Corporation	2
23909	Urea, 1-methyl-1-nitroso (Me-nitrosourea)	$N_3O_2C_2H_5$	Southern Research Institute (Dr. John A. Montgomery)	6
24901	Glycolamide, N,N′-ethylenebis-, dimethanesulfonate	$N_2O_8S_2C_8H_{16}$	Sinai Hospital of Baltimore, Inc. (Arnold M. Seligman)	3

Appendix I
(Continued)

NSC No.	Name	Molecular Formula	Source of Compound	Table No.
26271	Cyclophosphamide (Cytoxan)	$N_2O_2PCl_2$	Mead Johnson and Company (Dr. Kenneth M. Campbell)	1, 2, 8, 9, 10
26276	Benzoic acid, p-[bis(2-chloroethyl)amino]-	$NO_2Cl_2C_{11}H_{13}$	Fisk University (Samuel P. Massie)	2
26805	Methanesulfonic acid, ethyl ester	$O_3SC_3H_8$	Merck and Company*	3
26806	1-Aziridineethanol, α-vinyl-, mixt. with β-vinyl-1-aziridineethanol (7:3)	NOC_6H_{11}	Merck and Company*	5
27381	Alanine, 3-[m-[bis(2-chloroethyl)-amino]phenyl]-, DL- (DL-Metasarcolysin)	$N_2O_2Cl_2C_{13}H_{18}$	Stanford Research Institute	2
28578	Sulfanilic acid, N,N-bis(2-chloro-ethyl)-, hydrazide	$N_3O_2SCl_2C_{10}H_{15}$	Fisk University (Samuel P. Massie)	2
28579	Sulfanilamide, N4,N4-bis(2-chloro-ethyl)-N1-2-pyridyl-	$N_3O_2SCl_2C_{15}H_{17}$	Fisk University (Samuel P. Massie)	2
29215	p-Benzoquinone, tris(1-aziridinyl)-	$N_3O_2C_{12}H_{13}$	Verkauf Pharm. C., Leverkusen, Germany (Dr. Birth)	5
30025	Ethane, 1,2-bis(2-chloro-ethylthio)-	$S_2Cl_2C_6H_{12}$	Sinai Hospital of Baltimore, Inc. (Arnold M. Seligman)	2
31717	p-Benzoquinone, tetrakis(1-aziridinyl)-	$N_4O_2C_{14}H_{16}$	Verkauf Pharm. C., Leverkusen, Germany (Dr. Birth)	5
32605	Butane, D-1,2:3,4-diepoxy-	$O_2C_4H_6$	Leo Pharmaceutical Products Trading Co., Ballerup, Denmark (Dr. Erling Fredericksen)	4

34462	Uracil, 5-[bis(2-chloroethyl)-amino]-	$N_3O_2Cl_2C_8H_{11}$	The Upjohn Co.	2
35051	D-Alanine, 3-[p-[bis(2-chloroethyl)-amino]phenyl]-	$N_2O_2Cl_2C_{13}H_{18}$	Merck and Co.*	2
35648	Benzimidazole, 2-[[bis(2-chloro-ethyl)-amino]methyl]-5-chloro-, monohydrochloride	$N_3Cl_3C_{12}H_{14}\cdot HCl$	Givaudan Corp.	2
35915	*meso*-2,3-Butanediol, 1,4-bis(1-aziridinyl)-	$N_2O_2C_8H_{16}$	Stanford Research Institute	5
37095	Carbamic acid, [bis(1-aziridinyl)-phosphinyl]-, ethyl ester	$N_3O_3PC_7H_{14}$	Armour and Co. (Dr. Thomas J. Bardos)	5
37096	Carbamic acid, [bis(1-aziridinyl)-phos-phinyl]-, benzyl ester (Benzodepa)	$N_3O_3PC_{12}H_{16}$	Armour and Co. (Dr. Thomas J. Bardos)	5
37538	D-Mannitol, 1,6-dimethanesulfonate (Mannitol Myleran)	$O_{10}S_2C_8H_{18}$	Chester Beatty Research Institute (Dr. J. L. Everett)	1, 3
39069	L-Threitol, 1,4-dimethane-sulfonate	$O_8S_2C_6H_{14}$	Leo Pharmaceutical Products Trading Co., Ballerup, Denmark (Dr. Erling Fredericksen)	3
39071	D-2,3-Butanediol, 1,4-bis(2-chloro-ethylamino)-, dihydrochloride	$N_2O_2Cl_2C_8H_{18}\cdot 2HCl$	Leo Pharmaceutical Products Trading Co., Ballerup, Denmark (Dr. Erling Fredericksen)	2
39072	L-2,3-Butanediol, 1,4-bis(2-chloro-ethylamino)-, dihydrochloride	$N_2O_2Cl_2C_8H_{18}\cdot 2HCl$	Leo Pharmaceutical Products Trading Co., Ballerup, Denmark (Dr. Erling Fredericksen)	2

* Purchased by CCNSC.

Appendix I
(Continued)

NSC No.	Name	Molecular Formula	Source of Compound	Table No.
39073	2,3-Butanediol, *meso*-1,4-bis(2-chloroethylamino)-, dihydrochloride	$N_2O_2Cl_2C_8H_{18}\cdot 2HCl$	Leo Pharmaceutical Products Trading Co., Ballerup, Denmark (Dr. Erling Fredericksen)	2
41449	Acetic acid, (m-[bis(2-chloroethyl)-amino]phenoxy)-, ethyl ester	$NO_3Cl_2C_{14}H_{19}$	Stanford Research Institute	2
42072	Phosphine sulfide, (hexahydro-1-azepinyl)bis(1-aziridinyl)-	$N_3PSC_{10}H_{20}$	The Borden Co. (K. C. Tsou)	5
42399	1-Aziridinepropionic acid, ethylene ester	$N_2O_4C_{12}H_{20}$	Sterling-Winthrop Research Institute	5
43146	3-Pyridinol, 5-[bis(2-chloroethyl)-aminomethyl]-4-(methoxymethyl)-2-methyl-, dihydrochloride, dihydrate	$N_2O_2Cl_2C_{13}H_{20}\cdot 2HCl\cdot 2H_2O$	Merck and Co.*	2
44444	Uracil, 5-[bis(2-chloroethyl)-amino]-3-methyl-	$N_3O_2Cl_2C_9H_{13}$	Stanford Research Institute (Dr. B. R. Baker)	2
44629	Uracil, 5-[bis(2-chloroethyl)-amino]-6-methyl-	$N_3O_2Cl_2C_9H_{13}$	Russian compound from Larionov (Dr. Michael B. Shimkin)	2
45081	Aziridine, 1,1′-(sulfonyldi-ethylene)-bis[2-methyl-	$N_2O_2SC_{10}H_{20}$	Minnesota Mining and Manufacturing Co. (Dr. Paul R. Fram)	5
45388	Imidazole-4(or 5)-carboxamide, 5(or 4)-(dimethyltriazeno)-	$N_6OC_6H_{10}$	Southern Research Institute (Dr. John A. Montgotmery)	1, 10
45725	1-Aziridineethanol, β-vinyl-	NOC_6H_{11}	Merck and Co.*	5
45726	1-Aziridineethanol, α-vinyl-	NOC_6H_{11}	Merck and Co.*	5

47547	Urea, 1-(2-chloroethyl)-1-nitroso-	$N_3O_2ClC_3H_6$	Stanford Research Institute (Dr. B. R. Baker)	6
49421	Phosphinic amide, P,P-bis(1-aziridinyl)-N,N-diethyl-	$N_3OPC_8H_{18}$	Minnesota Mining and Manufacturing Co. (Dr. Paul R. Fram)	5
50256	Methanesulfonic acid, methyl ester	$O_3SC_2H_6$	California Corp. for Biochemical Research*	3
50741	β-D-Ribofuranoside, methyl 5-(2-chloroethylamino)-5-deoxy-2,3-0-isopropylidene-, hydrochloride	$NO_4ClC_{11}H_{20}\cdot HCl$	Stanford Research Institute (Dr. B. R. Baker)	1
51325	Carbamic acid, [bis(2,2-dimethyl-1-aziridinyl)phosphinyl]-, ethyl ester	$N_3O_3PC_{11}H_{22}$	Armour Pharmaceutical Co. (Mr. Charles Damaskus)	5
51915	Cyclohexanecarboxamide, N,N′-[3,6-bis(1-aziridinyl)-p-benzoquinon-2,5-ylene]bis-	$N_4O_4C_{24}H_{32}$	CIBA Ltd. (Dr. Prosper Loustalot)	5
52695	Phosphorodiamidic acid, N,N-bis(2-chloroethyl)-N′-(3-hydroxypropyl)-, cyclohexylamine salt (Cytoxyl alcohol)	$N_2O_3PCl_2C_7H_{17}\cdot NC_6H_{13}$	Brandeis University (Prof. Orrie Friedman)	1
56308	4,4′-Bipiperidine, 1,1′-bis(2,3-epoxpropyl)-	$N_2O_2C_{16}H_{28}$	Eli Lilly and Co. (Dr. K. Gerzon)	4
56845	D-Mannitol, 1,4:3,6-dianhydro-2,5-bis-0-(2,3-epoxypropyl)-	$O_6C_{12}H_{18}$	Atlas Powder Co. (Dr. J. W. Lemaistre)	4
57199	Alanine, 3-[o-[bis(2-chloroethyl) amino]phenyl], DL-	$N_2O_2Cl_2C_{13}H_{18}$	Chester Beatty Research Institute (Dr. W. C. J. Ross)	2
62147	L-Alanine, 3-(p-[bis(2-chloroethyl) amino]phenyl)-, ethyl ester, hydrochloride	$N_2O_2Cl_2C_{15}H_{22}\cdot HCl$	Wellcome Research Laboratories (Dr. George H. Hitchings)	2

* Purchased by CCNSC.

Appendix I
(Continued)

NSC No.	Name	Molecular Formula	Source of Compound	Table No.
62403	Tryptophan, 5-[bis(2-chloroethyl)-amino]-, DL-	$N_3O_2Cl_2C_{15}H_{19}$	Stanford Research Institute (Dr. Leon Goodman)	2
63878	Cytosine arabinoside (Ara-C)	$N_3O_5C_9H_{13}\cdot HCl$	The Upjohn Co. (Dr. W. O'Connell)	9, 10
69945	Phosphorodiamidic acid, N,N-bis(2-chloroethyl)-, compd. with cyclohexylamine (Phosphoramide mustard)	$N_2O_2PCl_2C_4H_{11}\cdot NC_6H_{13}$	Collaborative Research, Inc. (Dr. O. M. Friedman)	2, 10
70806	1,3-Propanediamine, N,N′-bis(2-chloroethyl)-, dihydrochloride	$N_2Cl_2C_7H_{16}\cdot 2HCl$	Stanford Research Institute (Dr. Leon Goodman)	2
72505	Phosphoramidic acid, bis(2-chloroethyl)-, *tert*-butyl ester, compd. with cyclohexylamine	$NO_3PCl_2C_8H_{18}\cdot NC_6H_{13}$	Collaborative Research, Inc. (Dr. O. M. Friedman)	2
72510	Phosphonamidic acid, P-1-aziridinyl-N,N-bis(2-chloroethyl)-, compd. with cyclohexylamine	$N_2O_2PCl_2C_6H_{13}\cdot NC_6H_{13}$	Collaborative Research, Inc. (Dr. O. M. Friedman)	2
79037	Urea, 1-(2-chloroethyl)-3-cyclohexyl-1-nitroso- (CCNU)	$N_3O_2ClC_9H_{16}$	Southern Research Institute (Dr. John A. Montgomery)	1, 6, 10
79423	Ethanol, 2,2′-[(p-nitrosophenyl) imino]di-, dimethanesulfonate	$N_2O_7S_2C_{12}H_{18}$	Arthur D. Little, Inc. (Dr. Zinon B. Papanastassiou)	1
82196	Imidazole-4(or 5)-carboxamide, 5(or 4)-[3,3-bis(2-chloroethyl)-1-triazeno]-	$N_6OCl_2C_8H_{12}$	Southern Research Institute (Dr. John A. Montgomery)	1, 7, 10
83290	2,3-Butanediol, DL-1,4-bis[(2-chloroethyl)amino]-, dihydrochloride	$N_2O_2Cl_2C_8H_{18}\cdot 2HCl$	Stanford Research Institute (Dr. Leon Goodman)	2

84641	1-Propanol, 3,3′-(methylimino)di-dimethanesulfonate, hydrochloride	$NO_6S_2C_9H_{21}\cdot HCl$	Sasaki University, Tokyo, Japan (Dr. Y. Sakurai)	1
86056	Urea, 3-(1-adamantyl)-1-(2-chloroethyl)-1-nitroso-	$N_3O_2ClC_{13}H_{20}$	Southern Research Institute (Dr. John A. Montgomery)	6
87974	Urea, 3-cyclohexyl-1-(2-fluoro-ethyl)-1-nitroso-	$N_3O_2FC_9H_{16}$	Southern Research Institute (Dr. John A. Montgomery)	6
88104	Urea, 3-(*trans*-2-chlorocyclohexyl)-1-(2-chloroethyl)-1-nitroso-	$N_3O_2Cl_2C_9H_{15}$	Southern Research Institute (Dr. John A. Montgomery)	6
88106	Urea, 1-(2-chloroethyl)-3-(2-norbornyl)-1-nitroso-	$N_3O_2ClC_{10}H_{16}$	Southern Research Institute (Dr. John A. Montgomery)	6
89207	Urea, 3-(p-acetylphenyl)-1-(2-chloroethyl)-1-nitroso-	$N_3O_3ClC_{11}H_{12}$	Southern Research Institute (Dr. John A. Montgomery)	6
91741	Urea, 1-(2-chloroethyl)-1-nitroso-3-(2,6-xylyl)-	$N_3O_2ClC_{11}H_{14}$	Southern Research Institute (Dr. John A. Montgomery)	6
93161	Urea, 3-(1-adamantyl)-1-(2-fluoroethyl)-1-nitroso-	$N_3O_2FC_{13}H_{20}$	Southern Research Institute (Dr. John A. Montgomery)	6
94100	D-Mannitol, 1,6-dibromo-1,6-dideoxy- (Dibromomannitol)	$O_4BR_2C_6H_{12}$	Hungarian Trading Co. for Pharm. Products (Dr. L. Hamberger)	1
102627	1-Propanol, 3,3′-iminodi-, dimethane-sulfonate (ester), hydrochloride	$NO_6S_2C_8H_{19}\cdot HCl$	Sasaki University, Tokyo, Japan (Dr. Y. Sakurai)	1
104800	Galactitol, 1,6-dibromo-, 6-dideoxy- (Dibromodulcitol)	$O_4BR_2C_6H_{12}$	Hungarian Compound from Sellei (Dr. A. Goldin, NIH)	1
400721	Propylamine, 3-chloro-N-(2-chloro-ethyl)-N-ethyl-, hydrochloride	$NCl_2C_7H_{15}\cdot HCl$	University of Michigan (Prof. B. F. Blicke)	2
409962	1,3-Bis(2-chloroethyl)-1-nitrosourea (BCNU)	$N_3O_2Cl_2C_5H_9$	Southern Research Institute (Dr. John A. Montgomery)	1, 6, 10

STRUCTURE-ACTIVITY RELATIONSHIPS OF ALKYLATING AGENTS IN CANCER CHEMOTHERAPY*

T. J. Bardos, Z. F. Chmielewicz, and P. Hebborn

Departments of Medicinal Chemistry and Biochemical Pharmacology
State University of New York at Buffalo, Buffalo, N. Y.

There seems to be a widespread feeling among clinical investigators that the usefulness of alkylating agents in cancer chemotherapy has some inherent limitations and that the selectivity and range of efficacy of these agents against human malignancies cannot be substantially improved over those of the presently used drugs. This pessimism is not shared by the medicinal chemists who view the alkylating agents as reactive chemical compounds that exert their tumor-growth inhibitory effects by undergoing typical organic reactions with certain nucleophilic groups of the functional macromolecules of the cell. This presents to the medicinal chemist a unique and fascinating challenge. In attempting to design more effective and selective agents, he can apply and extend his knowledge of the mechanism of organic chemical reactions as well as of the physicochemical interactions between small and large molecules and of the biochemical processes involved in drug metabolism and transport. By appropriate structural design, one can alter the chemical properties or biochemical behavior of the alkylating agents in many different ways, and it seems almost inconceivable that some of the more ingenious or fortunate alterations should not result in substantial (even fundamental) improvements in the efficacy and selectivity of their pharmacologic action. Rising to the challenge, and not to be discouraged by the skepticism of the clinicians (who, after all, have tested so far only a handful of alkylating agents in cancer patients), the medicinal chemists have continued to synthesize with relentless enthusiasm thousands of alkylating agents; moreover, some of the new agents appear to be based on excellent rationales. Unfortunately, many of these compounds have received only limited pharmacologic testing, using different animal tumor systems or assay techniques, which makes it difficult to compare them with the established alkylating agents on the basis of their published test results.

The problem of evaluating the chemotherapeutic potentials of the many new alkylating agents in a meaningful manner in order to select a lucky few that are to be given the chance of a clinical trial has been puzzling many investigators. This problem is discussed by Dr. Goldin (A. Goldin & H. B. Wood, Jr. Preclinical Investigation of Alkylating Agents in Cancer Chemotherapy. This monograph.), who is himself responsible for much of the progress made in this field. However, I should like to make reference at this point to a major study that was conducted several years ago by Dr. Leon Schmidt and associates under the sponsorship of the Cancer Chemotherapy National Service Center, in which the pharmacologic effects of a total of 141 alkylating agents (nitrogen mustards, ethylenimines and

*This work was supported by a US Public Health Service research grant (RO1-CA-06695-06) from the National Cancer Institute, NIH.

methane sulfonates) were compared in a qualitative and quantitative manner. The results obtained in this study were published in three volumes.[1] In order to compare their antitumor activities, the agents were screened against a selected spectrum of sensitive and relatively insensitive transplanted tumors in rodents, employing several strains of some tumors and several different assay methods. The individual compounds were then ranked according to their therapeutic indices for each of the assay systems. Many of the compounds studied had therapeutic indices of one or less, i.e., they showed little if any antitumor selectivity. Only in a few instances were therapeutic indices of 10 or higher obtained, indicating a substantial degree of selectivity against the tumor. Generally, two compounds stood out as superior to all others included in this study; these were cyclophosphamide and L-phenylalanine mustard.[2] The first is a well-known example of alkylating agents designed to be unreactive per se but to be capable of undergoing metabolic activation *in vivo* (principle of latent activity), while the second is a representative of the type of agents that was designed to be capable of active transport through cell membranes by linking the alkylating moiety to biologically significant carrying structures, i.e., in this case, a natural amino acid (carrier principle).

The relationships between the biological activity and the chemical reactivity of various alkylating agents, and the effects of structural variations on both, were first studied by W. C. J. Ross, who discussed earlier work in his well-known monograph.[3] As a measure of the chemical reactivity of nitrogen mustards, he chose their relative rates of hydrolysis as determined by measuring the ionization of the β-halogen under specified standard conditions (in 50% aqueous acetone, at 66° C, after 30 min). The percent hydrolysis values thus obtained are related to the first-order rate constants for the hydrolysis of these compounds to the corresponding β-amino alcohols and hydrogen halide.

It should be pointed out that by taking the rate of hydrolysis as the measure of the chemical reactivity of an alkylating agent one might reach false conclusions, because the mechanism of the hydrolysis of a compound is not necessarily the same as the mechanism of its reactions with different nucleophiles. The hydrolysis of a compound usually follows first-order or pseudo-first-order kinetics, regardless of the mechanism by which it reacts with different reagents under different conditions. Therefore, some of the statements in the literature that classify alkylating agents as S_N1 or S_N2 reactors[4] appear to be sometimes misleading.

In an effort to compare the chemical reactivities of various alkylating agents with respect to nucleophiles resembling the heterocyclic ring-nitrogens of nucleic acid purines and pyrimidines, we found it convenient to introduce a reaction rate parameter, k', as a measure of comparative alkylating activity.[5] The reagent of Epstein and colleagues,[6] γ-(4-nitrobenzyl)-pyridine (NBP), which had been previously used by several investigators[7–9] for the estimation of the concentration levels of a given alkylating agent in blood and animal tissues, was chosen as the model nucleophile. In order to compare the rates of the reaction of NBP with various types of alkylating agents, the reactants were employed at a standard initial concentration and heated at a given reaction temperature for various lengths of time. The absorbance readings at 600 mμ (E^{600}), measured after the addition of alkali to the reaction mixtures, were plotted versus the reaction time. It was found that throughout an initial time period (usually for 30–60 min from the beginning of the reaction) these absorbance-versus-time plots were linear for the various agents studied under the specified standard conditions.[5] It was shown that, under the limitations employed, the slopes of these linear plots are in first approximation proportional to the second-order rate constant for the nucleophilic displacement (S_N2) reactions between the alkylating agents and NBP. Thus, comparative alkylating activity was defined as $k' = E^{600}/t(\text{min})$, at the standard initial concentrations. The reaction temperature conveniently used in these measurements was 80° C for the less reactive and 50° C for the more reactive alkylating agents, and the obtained reactivity parameters were designated as k'_{80} and k'_{50} respectively.

TABLE 1 lists as illustrative examples the comparative alkylating activity (k'_{80} and/or k'_{50}) and percent hydrolysis values of 15 aromatic nitrogen mustards, taken from a larger study,[5] which led to the following conclusions:

1. As could be expected, the chemical alkylating activity of nitrogen mustards is primarily dependent on the basicity of the nitrogen. Electron-attracting substituents para to the nitrogen dramatically decrease, while electron-releasing substituents increase the reactivity of the parent phenyl nitrogen mustard with respect to nucleophilic displacement by NBP. The same relationship with respect to hydrolysis has been pointed out earlier by Ross.[3] One-arm nitrogen mustards which have a less basic secondary amino group are quite inert in both types of reactions, while methyl and, particularly, ethyl substitution on the nitrogen greatly enhance their chemical reactivities. In fact, the values for percent hydrolysis and alkylating activity show quite good parallelism through a long series of mono- and difunctional aromatic nitrogen mustards which structurally differ from each other in the nature of the para substituent, or (if monofunctional), in the N-substitution. This shows that in the case of the aromatic nitrogen mustards both types of reactions are equally dependent on the magnitude of anchimeric assistance provided by the unshared electron pair of the nitrogen atom.

2. The parallelism between the hydrolysis and the alkylation reaction breaks down, however, in the case of alkyl substitution on the β carbon. Compound 12, in which one of the alkylating side chains is a 2-bromopropyl group (i.e., a secondary instead of a primary alkyl halide), is considerably more reactive in hydrolysis and slightly less reactive in alkylation than its bis(2-bromoethyl) analog, 11. This divergence of relative reaction gives some support to the assumption that the hydrolytic reaction follows S_N1 mechanism (being promoted by the relatively greater stability of a secondary carbonium ion intermediate), in contrast to the alkylation of NBP, which we have shown[5] to be a typical S_N2 reaction (and is, in fact, adversely affected by steric hindrance).

3. Replacement of the chlorine with bromine vastly increases the chemical alkylating activity, but replacement with iodine has a more complex effect. Compared to the bromo mustards, the iodo mustards showed significantly lower hydrolysis rates (as already observed by Ross[3]), while their alkylating activities were either higher or lower than those of the corresponding bromo mustards, depending on the basicity of the nitrogen. This has been rationalized on the basis of the relative nucleophilicities and solvation energies of the Br^- and I^- ions.[5]

In order to compare the chemical reactivities of the nitrogen mustards with their *in vivo* biological activities on a quantitative molar basis, Walker carcinosarcoma 256 in rats was selected as a tumor system that is particularly sensitive to alkylating agents. In all cases, the compounds were administered in cottonseed oil, i.p., in a single injection, one day following tumor implantation; the animals were sacrificed 10 days later, and from the ratios of the mean tumor weights in the treated versus the control animals (T/C), ED_{90}, i.e., the dose corresponding to 90% inhibition (T/C = 0.1), was determined. The ratio LD_{50}/ED_{90} (therapeutic index) was used as a measure of the selective action of the agent against the

TABLE 1

COMPARATIVE CHEMICAL AND BIOLOGICAL ACTIVITIES OF AROMATIC NITROGEN MUSTARDS

No.	M	R	Hydrolysis %	Alkylating activity: $k'_{80} \times 10^3$	Alkylating activity: $k'_{50} \times 10^3$	Toxicity: LD_{50} μmole/kg	Antitumor activity: ED_{90} μmole/kg	Antitumor activity: $\frac{LD_{50}}{ED_{90}}$
1	$(ClCH_2CH_2)_2N$	H	23.2	13.0	1.0	367	400	<1.0
2	$(ClCH_2CH_2)_2N$	COOH	2.4	4.6	—	915	500	1.8
3	$(ClCH_2CH_2)_2N$	SO_2NH_2	0.0	0.1	—	1,130	1,500	<1.0
4	$(ClCH_2CH_2)_2N$	OH	60.0	48.6	21.6	74	32	2.3
5	$(ClCH_2CH_2)_2N$	NH_2	100.0	42.0	17.2	15	20	<1.0
6	$(ClCH_2CH_2)_2N$	$NHCOCH_3$	41.0	29.6	2.0	102	34	3.0
7	$ClCH_2CH_2NH$	H	3.2	1.3	—	775	>775	<1.0
8	$ClCH_2CH_2N(CH_3)$	H	11.2	4.9	0.4	3,000	>3,000	<1.0
9	$ClCH_2CH_2N(C_2H_5)$	H	58.0	32.0	5.0	1,090	>1,090	<1.0
10	$(BrCH_2CH_2)_2N$	H	71.0	123.0	18.6	39	50	<1.0
11	$(BrCH_2CH_2)_2N$	SO_2NH_2	8.0	7.5	0.4	740	205	3.6
12	$BrCH_2CH_2$, $BrCH(CH_3)CH_2$ >N	SO_2NH_2	37.0	6.1	0.67	90	24	3.8
13	$(ICH_2CH_2)_2N$	H	12.0	158.0	20.2	140	82	1.7
14	$(ICH_2CH_2)_2N$	SO_2NH_2	0.0	3.1	—	>1,650	>1,650	—
15	ICH_2CH_2, $ICH(CH_3)CH_2$ >N	SO_2NH_2	32.5	3.1	—	570	330	1.7

tumor cells. The results are shown in TABLE 1. The monofunctional mustards (7–9) were inactive, as noted earlier by Ross.[3] The biological activities of the difunctional mustards showed, in general, a better correlation with the hydrolysis rates than with the alkylating activities. This is apparent from the greater biological activities of the branched-arm mustards 12 and 15 as compared to the corresponding bis(β-haloethyl) analogs 11 and 14, and it is indicated also by the lower biological activities of *all* iodo mustards as compared to the corresponding bromo mustards. This seems to indicate that under biological conditions these compounds are to some extent stabilized in their solvated ion form.

For most of the simple difunctional mustards listed in TABLE 1, the LD_{50}/ED_{90} ratio is in the neighborhood of 1.0, except for two of the bromo mustards (11 and 12) and the p-acetylamino phenyl nitrogen mustard (6), for which this ratio is 3.0–3.8. The increased selectivity of the latter compound (6) as compared to the parent p-aminophenyl nitrogen mustard (5) is presumably due to its enzymatic deacetylation in the tumor cells to the more potent alkylating agent, 5.[10] Danielli[11] has pointed out that increased selectivity should result if the action of a drug is made dependent upon a larger number of cell variables and that this might be achieved if the release of the active nitrogen mustard requires the successive action of two or more enzymes. On the basis of his suggestion, Dr. L. N. Owen at Imperial College, London, has synthesized[12] several α-(acylamino)-acyl derivatives of the p-aminophenyl mustard, 5, which were tested in our laboratory. The results, summarized in TABLE 2, show that the four acyl derivatives 16–19 have approximately the same percent hydrolysis and k'_{80} values (i.e., the various acyl groups have similar effect in reducing the chemical reactivities of the parent p-animophenyl nitrogen mustard 5), but their *in vivo* activities are significantly different. While the general toxicity decreases (sharp increase of LD_{50}) from compounds 5 and 16 through 19, the effective therapeutic dose is lowest for compound 17, the α-acetylglycyl derivative, resulting in an optimal therapeutic index of 4.5. It has been demonstrated[13] that the LD_{50} values of these acyl derivatives are related to their rates of enzymatic hydrolysis to the active parent compound, 5, in the presence of rat tissue homogenates. While the glycyl derivative 16, having a free α-amino group, can be directly hydrolyzed to 5 by the action of aminopeptidase, the α-acylglycyl derivatives 17–19 would be expected to require sequential enzymic activation, which may be the reason for the increased selectivity of 17.

A comparative study of various esters derived from the highly toxic p-hydroxyphenyl nitrogen mustard is shown in TABLE 3. The acetate 20 and the three benzoates 21–23, although their chemical reactivities are similar, show different toxicities and antitumor activities, apparently depending on their rates of enzymatic hydrolysis to the active phenolic mustard, 4. Methyl substituents ortho to the carboxy group decrease the rate of the hydrolysis (due to steric hindrance) and increase the LD_{50} value. With respect to tumor selectivity, the optimal rate of hydrolytic activation appears to be represented by the mono-o-methylbenzoate, 23, which shows the highest therapeutic index among the four simple esters listed in TABLE 3.

The carbamate derivative 24 (IC-140) is unique in this series. It has significantly lower chemical reactivity than the simple esters, but it shows an unusually high antitumor activity and selectivity, with a therapeutic index of 17. Surprisingly, *in vitro* studies using rat tissue homogenates demonstrated little or no hydrolysis of this compound to the active phenolic mustard 4. Moreover, the slightly greater rate of hydrolysis in the presence of mouse tissue homogenates,

TABLE 2

COMPARATIVE CHEMICAL AND BIOLOGICAL ACTIVITIES OF THE P-AMINOPHENYL NITROGEN MUSTARD (5) AND ITS GLYCYL DERIVATIVES

Compound			Alkylating activity	Toxicity*	Antitumor activity†	
	$M = (ClCH_2CH_2)_2$–N– 	Hydrolysis %	$k'_{80} \times 10^3$	LD_{50} μmole/kg	ED_{90} μmole/kg	$\frac{LD_{50}}{ED_{90}}$
5	$M-NH_2 \cdot HCl$	100	42	15	20	<1.0
16	$M-NH-COCH_2NH_2 \cdot HCl$	–	10.9	34	34	1.0
17	$M-NH-COCH_2NH-COCH_3$	20	12.3	67	16	4.5
18	$M-NH-COCH_2NH-COOCH_3$	21	12.3	200	140	1.7
19	$M-NH-COCH_2NH-COCH_2Cl$	–	12.3	>1,000	–	–

* Male Holtzman rats.

† Walker carcinosarcoma 256.

TABLE 3

COMPARATIVE CHEMICAL AND BIOLOGICAL ACTIVITIES OF ESTERS DERIVED FROM THE PHENOLIC NITROGEN MUSTARD (4)

			Alk. act.	Toxicity*	Antitumor activity†	
	M = $(ClCH_2CH_2)_2N$— 	Hydrolysis %	$k'_{80} \times 10^3$	LD_{50} µmole/kg	ED_{90} µmole/kg	$\frac{LD_{50}}{ED_{90}}$
4	M - OH · HCl	60	48	82	35	2.3
20	M - $OCOCH_3$	15	...	55	26	2.1
21	M - OCO— 	15	...	94	15	6.3
22	M - OCO— 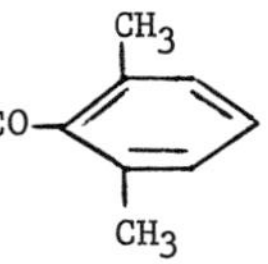	(15)	...	857	532	1.6
23	M - OCO— 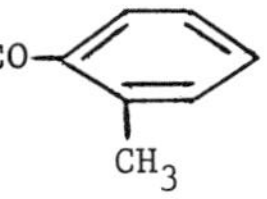	(15)	...	210	31	6.8
24	M - OCONH— 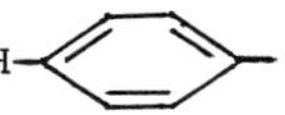 —COOH	5.2	14	151	9	17.0
25	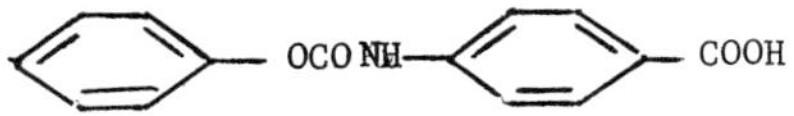	...	0	1170	> 1200	< 1.0

*Male Holtzman Rats; †Walker carcinosarcoma 256.

together with the considerably lower toxicity of compound 24 to the mouse (LD_{50} = 730 μmole/kg), argued against intracellular hydrolysis to 4 being the only prerequisite for the biological activity of this compound. Our most recent studies demonstrated that compound 24 is present in circulating blood as the intact molecule for at least 2 hr following administration. Thus, the mechanism of action of the carbamate derivative must be distinctly different from those of the simple esters of the p-hydroxyphenyl nitrogen mustard and possibly involves site-directed catalysis.

In view of the high antitumor activity and selectivity of the carbamate mustard IC-140 (24), which is now undergoing preliminary clinical trial at the Roswell Park Memorial Institute, several reverse carbamates derived from the p-aminophenyl nitrogen mustard have been studied in our laboratory recently. These compounds were kindly supplied by Dr. Owen, who also originally synthesized IC-140.

TABLE 4 shows the comparative chemical and biological activities of this new series of carbamates in which the amino group of the carbamate moiety is attached to the phenyl nitrogen mustard. It is immediately apparent that the chemical reactivities of these carbamate derivatives, while similar to each other within this series, are considerably higher than the corresponding values for IC-140. In fact, these compounds are fairly reactive alkylating agents per se, without enzymic activation. The most striking fact about this series is the unprecedented high antitumor activity and selectivity of the carboxyphenyl carbamate derivatives 28 and 29 and, particularly, of the related methyl esters 30 and 31. Compound 28 of this series, an isomer of IC-140 in which the carbamate moiety is reversed, has approximately the same toxicity to the rat as IC-140, but its activity against the Walker tumor is three times greater, thus giving a therapeutic index of 46. (It is interesting to note that this compound is considerably more toxic to the mouse than IC-140; LD_{50} = 105 μmole/kg). Its methyl ester, 30, is much less toxic and even more active against the tumor, having a therapeutic index of 137. From the structure-activity relationships shown in TABLE 4 one would predict that the methyl ester of the meta carboxylic acid 29 should have an even higher therapeutic index.

This high degree of selectivity of some of the carbamate mustards against the tumor cells is believed to be unique among the alkylating agents studied so far. Since these compounds are chemically reactive per se, selective enzymatic activation is unlikely to be a factor. Consideration of the structures of the less selective (26 and 27) and more selective (28–31) carbamates, as well as their similar chemical reactivities, leads to the conclusion that neither organic chemical nor physicochemical factors could account for the high selectivities of both the free carboxylic acids and the esters. The present data suggest that there are specific receptors in the Walker tumor cells responsible for the selective uptake of these cytotoxic agents; if this is so, then other tumors may have similar or different specific receptors. It remains to be seen whether these carbamate mustards show similar selectivities in other tumor systems and, most importantly, in human neoplasia.

Another type of alkylating agent, belonging to the general class of ethylenimines or aziridines, has been synthesized and studied in our laboratory in considerable detail during the past years, in collaboration with Dr. Ambrus and his associates at the Roswell Park Memorial Institute and with Dr. Segaloff at the Alton Ochner Medical Foundation. The first series of these agents[14] is represented by the structural formulae shown in TABLE 5. In these compounds, two aziridine rings were linked through phosphoramide bonds to a carbamate.

TABLE 4

COMPARATIVE CHEMICAL AND BIOLOGICAL ACTIVITIES OF CARBAMATES DERIVED FROM THE P-AMINOPHENYL NITROGEN MUSTARD (5)

	M = $(ClCH_2CH_2)_2N$— 	Hydrolysis %	Alk. act. $k'_{80} \times 10^3$	Toxicity* LD_{50} µmole/kg	Antitumor activity† ED_{90} µmole/kg	Antitumor activity† $\frac{LD_{50}}{ED_{90}}$
5	M - NH_2 • HCl	100	42	15	20	< 1.0
26	M - $NHCOOCH(CH_3)_2$	33	32	535	145	3.7
27	M - NHCOO— 	(30)	...	567	84	6.7
28	M - NHCOO— 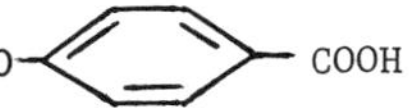	(30)	31	146	3.0	46
29	M - NHCOO— 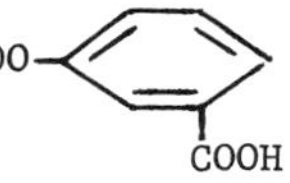	(30)	24	171	2.0	85
30	M - NHCOO— 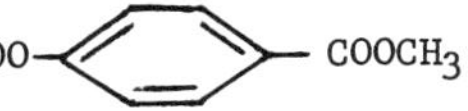	(30)	28	268	1.95	137
31	M - NHCOO— 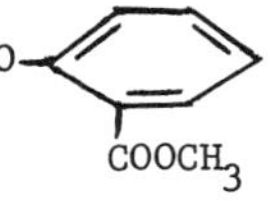	(30)	29	278	2.2	126

* Male Holtzman Rats.

† Walker carcinosarcoma 256.

TABLE 5

STRUCTURAL FORMULAE OF BIS(1-AZIRIDINYL)PHOSPHINYL CARBAMATES

Compound		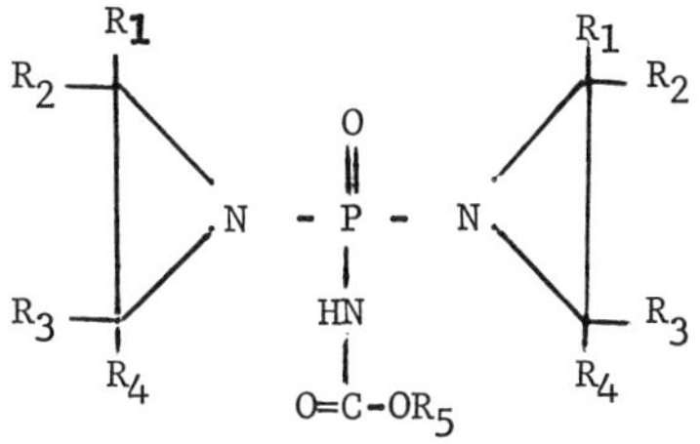
No.	Designation	
32	AB-100	$R_1 = R_2 = R_3 = R_4 = H$; $R_5 = C_2H_5$
33	AB-103	$R_1 = R_2 = R_3 = R_4 = H$; $R_5 = CH_2C_6H_5$
34	AB-143	$R_1 = R_2 = R_3 = H$; $R_4 = CH_3$; $R_5 = C_2H_5$
35	AB-132	$R_1 = R_2 = H$; $R_3 = R_4 = CH_3$; $R_5 = C_2H_5$
36	AB-144	$R_1 = R_3 = H$; $R_2 = R_4 = CH_3$; $R_5 = C_2H_5$
37	AB-145	$R_1 = R_4 = H$; $R_2 = R_3 = CH_3$; $R_5 = C_2H_5$
38	AB-140	$R_1 = H$; $R_2 = R_3 = R_4 = CH_3$; $R_5 = C_2H_5$
39	AB-148	$R_1 = R_2 = R_3 = R_4 = CH_3$; $R_5 = C_2H_5$

Our original rationale in designing these agents as potential dual antagonists was based on the reported synergism[15] between alkylating agents and urethan in animal experiments. Both Gellhorn[16] and Haddow[17] had emphasized in their concluding remarks of the conference held 11 years ago that combinations of alkylating agents and urethan should receive clinical trial. Dual antagonists are being designed in attempts to synchronize the actions of two synergistic antimetabolites by incorporating their biologically essential structural features into a single molecule.[18]

In the pharmacologic and subsequent clinical studies, AB-100 (32) and AB-103 (33) in which the aziridine ring-carbons are unsubstituted methylene groups behaved essentially like the typical ethylenimine type of alkylating agent (e.g., TEPA or thio-TEPA). Thus, their potent inhibitory activities against a spectrum of transplanted tumors in rodents,[14,19–21] their marked chemotherapeutic activities in various human malignancies,[22–29] and their dose-limiting hematologic side effects could be attributed to the alkylating aziridine function, while the carbamate portion of the molecule appeared to act mainly as a membrane transport carrier or, as a hydrophobic binding group, in a more or less selective manner. This was suggested by the fact that the benzyl carbamate analog, AB-103 (33), appeared to be more effective than the corresponding urethan analog, AB-100 (32), against several but not all animal tumor systems as well as in the clinical studies against carcinomas of the lung[25] and pancreas.[29] Chemical and nuclear magnetic resonance studies revealed that during the slow hydrolysis of the aziridine rings of AB-100 in water, at 37° C (which requires about 8 days for completion), only 13% of the urethan moiety is liberated, while most of the urethan remains attached to the phosphorus in the polymerized hydrolysis product.[30] This explains why, at the low-dose levels (limited by the toxicity of the unsubstituted aziridine function), a direct pharmacologic effect attributable to urethan could not be demonstrated.

Introduction of methyl, or ethyl, substituents into the aziridine rings generally

TABLE 6

COMPARATIVE CHEMICAL REACTIVITIES OF THE BIS(1-AZIRIDINYL)PHOSPHINYL CARBAMATES

Cpd.	Ring-CH_3	Half-Life of Aziridine Rings in: H_2O (hr)	50% aq. EtOH (hr)	Comparative Alkylating Activity $k'_{80} \times 10^3$	Toxicity (Mouse) LD_{50} μmole/kg
AB-100	–	60.0	400	3.3	216
AB-143	2	100.0	–	2.0	600
AB-132	2,2	2.5	18	2.5	1,500
AB-144	2,3 cis	125.0	–	0.8	580
AB-145	2,3 trans	35.0	–	2.1	200
AB-140	2,2,3	–	–	1.3	1,000
AB-148	2,2,3,3	–	70	0.2	750

reduced both the toxicity and the antitumor activity in most of the test systems.[31] However, the biological activities showed considerable variations with the positions of the substituents on the aziridine rings and generally did not parallel the chemical reactivities of these compounds. TABLE 6 shows the hydrolysis rates and chemical alkylating activities of AB-100 and its methyl-substituted aziridine analogs in comparison with their *in vivo* toxicities (in mice). Any correlation among these data is restricted to those relating to the cis and trans 2,3-dimethylaziridine analogs, AB-144 (36) and AB-145 (37). Within this pair of isomers, the trans compound shows three to four times higher values than the cis-isomer for hydrolysis rate, alkylating activity, and *in vivo* toxicity as well as antitumor activity (as determined in the Sarcoma 180 and Ehrlich ascites tumor systems[32]). It should be noted that the relative rates of hydrolysis of the two isomers parallel their S_N2 type reactivity with NBP. Investigation of the hydrolysis products revealed that both compounds, as well as the monomethyl aziridine analog, AB-143 (34), hydrolyze with cleavage of the phosphorus-urethan linkage, followed by an S_N2 attack of the P-O^- anion on the less hindered ring-carbon, causing ring-cleavage with Walden inversion.

By contrast, the geminally substituted aziridine derivatives were shown to undergo ring-opening hydrolysis by carbonium ion (S_N1) mechanism, followed by intramolecular cyclization and subsequent cleavage of all P-N bonds with the liberation of urethan.[33] Thus, the most interesting compound in this series, the 2,2-dimethyl analog, AB-132 (35), hydrolyzes extremely rapidly, having a half-life in water of only 2.5 hours. At the same time, it is also able to participate in alkylation reactions by S_N2 mechanism, due to its unsubstituted ring-carbon. This is indicated by its k'_{80} value, which is relatively high compared to most of the other members of this series.

Although AB-132 showed only moderate antitumor activity on screening against a spectrum of animal tumors, it was selected for clinical study because of its remarkable lack of hemopoietic toxicity. During the past six years, AB-132 has been undergoing extensive clinical trial against various forms of human malignancies, under the leadership of Dr. Ambrus at the Roswell Park Memorial Institute. In clinical pharmacologic experiments,[34–38] the relatively low hemopoietic toxicity was confirmed. However, nausea, vomiting, and gastrointestinal discomfort were found to be important side effects.[24] The compound was found to be a strong inhibitor of cholinesterases. In patients receiving 1 g of AB-132 daily i.v., plasma pseudocholinesterase level dropped to almost zero within a week's treatment, and red cell acetylcholinesterase level was close to zero.[33] Some of the CNS side effects, which appeared at about the same time, may be related to the inhibition of cholinesterase.[39,40] Some other symptoms were reminiscent of urethan intoxication.

Although some significant objective clinical results were obtained with AB-132 alone, particularly in inoperable bronchogenic carcinoma,[34,38] the remarkable radiation-potentiating effect of AB-132 appeared to be, from the therapeutic point of view, the most interesting property of this agent.[35,41,42] Due to the promising results, the clinical testing of AB-132 in combination with x-ray radiation is still being continued to date.[43]

From a chemical point of view, AB-132 is not only an alkylating agent but also a phosphorylating agent. This is due to the transient formation of a five-membered phosphoroxazine ring intermediate in the course of the hydrolysis of this compound and explains its significant inhibitory action on acetylcholinesterase.[33] Since cyclophosphamide is also theoretically capable of forming a somewhat similar cyclic intermediate,[44] it was of interest to determine whether the phos-

TABLE 7

POTENTIATION OF TOXICITY WITH SUCCINYLCHOLINE

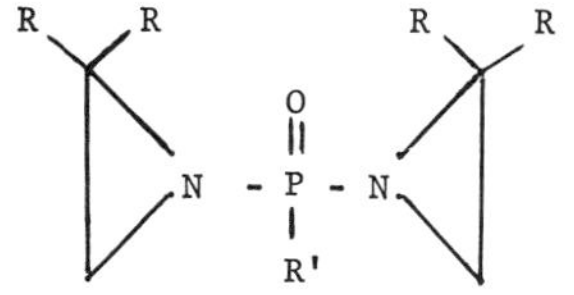

Compound No.	Compound Designation	R	R'	LD_{50} μmole/kg* Alone	LD_{50} μmole/kg* with SCh†	LD_{50} μmole/kg* Ratio
32	AB-100	H	$-NHCO_2C_2H_5$	228	>500	<1.0
35	AB-132	CH_3	$-NHCO_2C_2H_5$	1125	65	17.2
40	AB-163	CH_3	$-OCH_2CH_3$	600	290	2.1
41	AB-166	CH_3	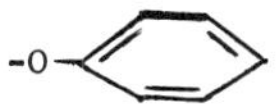	835	138	6.0
42	AB-167	CH_3		790	25	26.2
43	AB-168	H		1.7	0.124	137
44	TEPA-132	CH_3	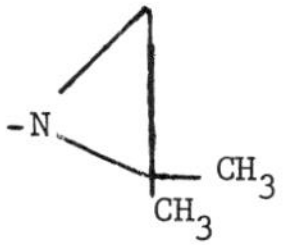	179	>200	<1.0
	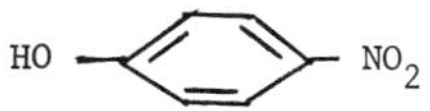			416	>430	<1.0

* Swiss mice.

†Succinyl choline, 1.0 mg/kg. In these experiments, death due to respiratory paralysis occurred within 20 min after administration of SCh. The LD_{50} values in this column are based only on the number of animals that died as a consequence of neuromuscular blockade.

phorylating activity of AB-132 contributes to the antitumor activity or only to the undesirable side effects. For this reason, we prepared the p-nitrophenyl ester analogs of both AB-132 and AB-100. Their *in vivo* phosphorylating activities with respect to cholinesterase were determined indirectly, by comparing their toxicities in the presence and in the absence of succinyl choline; synergistic potentiation of the toxicity of succinyl choline was taken as a measure of cholinesterase

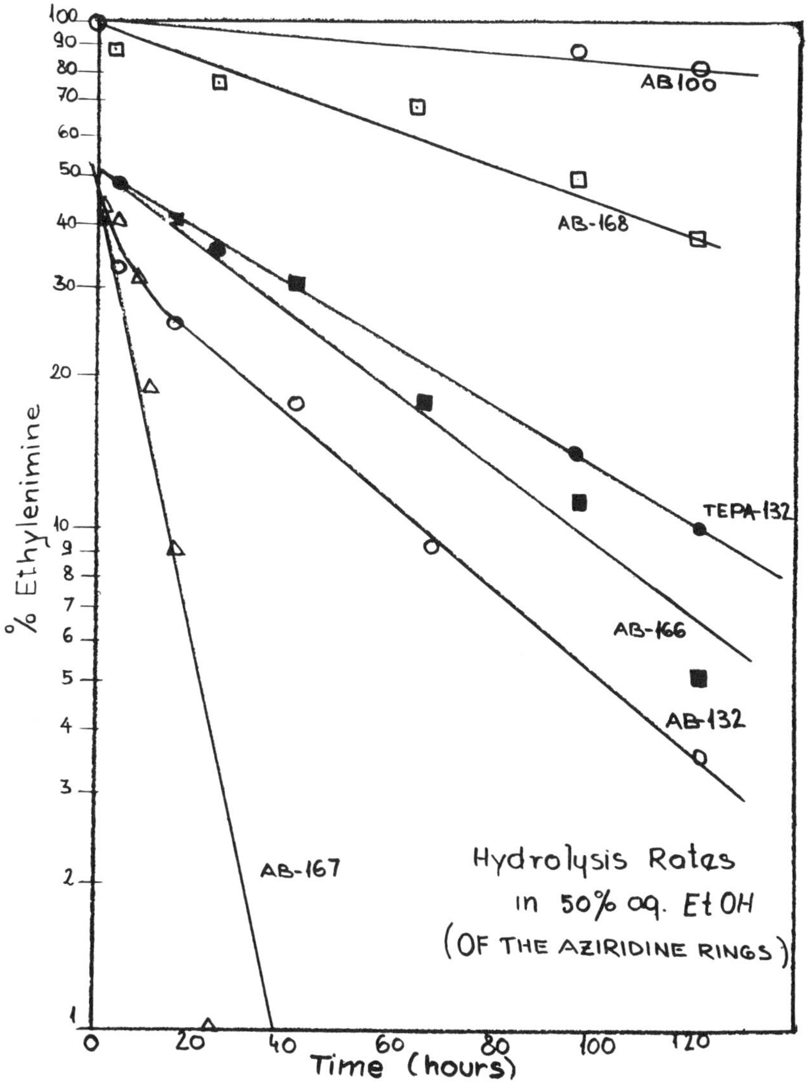

FIGURE 1. Comparative rates of hydrolysis of the aziridine rings in bis(1-aziridinyl)phosphinyl carbamates and esters listed in TABLE 7.

TABLE 8

COMPARATIVE CHEMICAL AND BIOLOGICAL ACTIVITIES OF SOME BIS(1-AZIRIDINYL)PHOSPHINYL CARBAMATES AND ESTERS

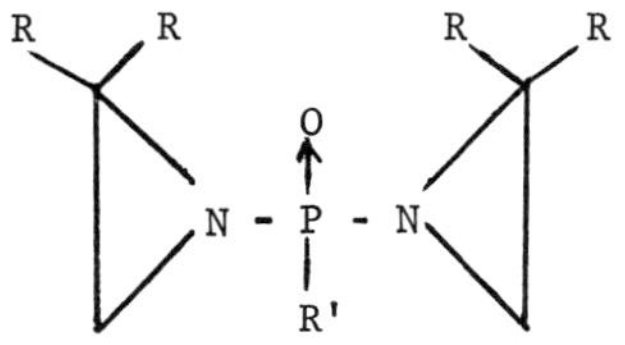

Compound		R	R′	Alkylating activity	Toxicity*	Antitumor activity†	
No.	Designation			$k' \times 10^3$	LD_{50} μmole/kg	ED_{90} μmole/kg	LD_{50}/ED_{90}
32	AB-100	H	$NHCO_2C_2H_5$	3.3	201	16	12.2
33	AB-103	H	$NHCO_2CH_2C_6H_5$	3.2	253	25	10.1
45	AB-110	H	$NHCO_2CH_2C_6H_4{-}NO_2$(p)	3.2	218	35	6.2
46	AB-111	H	$NHCO_2CH_2C_6H_4{-}NO_2$(m)	3.5	218	21	10.4
35	AB-132	CH_3	$NHCO_2C_2H_5$	2.5	1,527	509	3.0
47	AB-133	CH_3	$NHCO_2CH_2C_6H_5$	(2.5)	1,691	1,306	1.3
40	AB-163	CH_3	OCH_2CH_3	3.5	453	162	2.8
41	AB-166	CH_3	OC_6H_5	3.8	764	382	2.0
42	AB-167	CH_3	$OC_6H_4{-}NO_2$(p)	2.0	779	452	1.7
43	AB-168	H	$OC_6H_4{-}NO_2$(p)	3.5	17	13	1.2

* Male Holtzman rats.
† Walker carcinosarcoma 256.

inhibitory activity. TABLE 7 shows that AB-168 (43), the p-nitrophenyl ester analog of AB-100, which is by far the most toxic agent per se, also shows the most powerful potentiation of its toxicity by succinyl choline. This compound, in which the phosphorus-p-nitrophenolate linkage is cleaved much more rapidly than the aziridine rings, appears to be a *par excellence* phosphorylating agent and presumably owes its much higher toxicity, as compared to that of AB-100, to its phosphorylating activity. In contrast, AB-100 (32) as well as TEPA-132 (44) show no phosphorylating activity. Studies of their hydrolysis products revealed that neither of these two compounds hydrolyzes via a cyclic intermediate similar to that formed in the case of AB-132. On the other hand, such phosphorylating intermediates were found to be formed in the hydrolysis of both AB-163 (40) and AB-166 (41), but at a slower rate than was true in the case of AB-132. This may account for the weaker potentiating effect of the two esters. In the case of AB-167 (42), the p-nitrophenyl ester analog of AB-132, the hydrolysis of the P—O—P-nitrophenyl linkage accelerates the cleavage of the aziridine rings via carbonium ion and formation of the cyclic intermediate. The comparative rates of the ring-opening hydrolyses of the aziridine moieties of these compounds are shown in FIGURE 1.

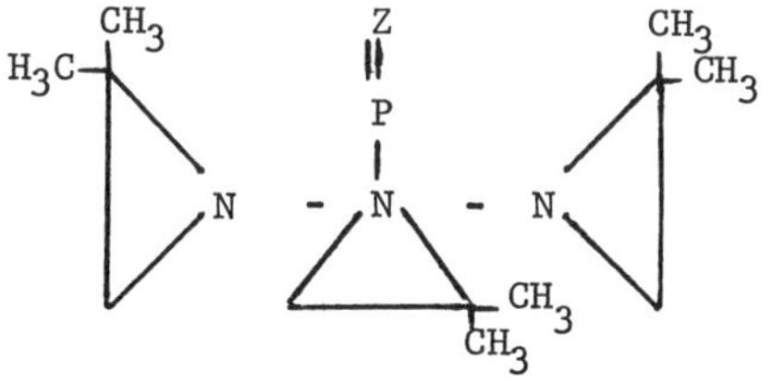

Z = O; (TEPA-132)

Z = S; (STEPA-132)

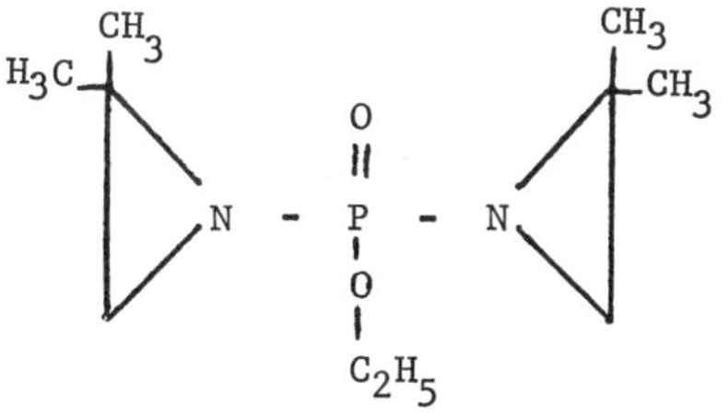

(AB-163)

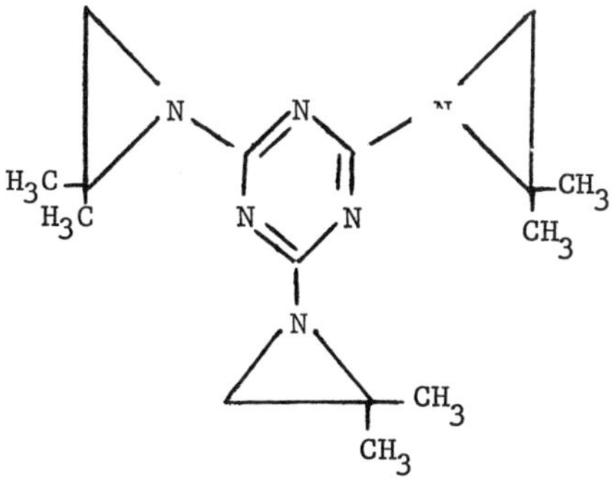

(TEM-132)

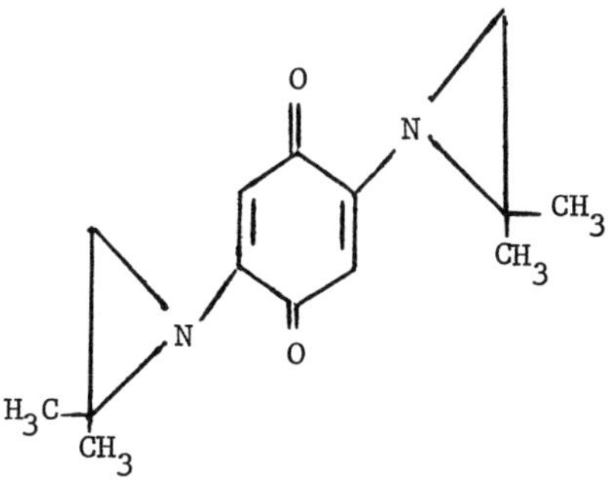

(AB-162)

FIGURE 2. Structures of some 2,2-dimethylaziridine agents.

Comparison of the antitumor activities against Walker carcinoma 256 (TABLE 8) leads to the conclusion that the phosphorylating activity contributes only to the toxicity and not to the therapeutic effect.

Another, more promising lead derived from AB-132 resulted in the synthesis of a series of compounds having diverse structures but all containing the 2,2-dimethylaziridine moiety.[45,46] The structures of these new alkylating agents are shown in FIGURE 2. Several of them are 2,2-dimethylaziridine analogs of the conventional ethylenimine type of alkylating agent. Their antitumor spectra, however, differ from the latter in a dramatic manner. While, e.g., TEPA had little or no activity against leukemia L1210, TEPA-132 (44) produced a significant number of "cures" in this tumor system and prolonged the survival time of the rest of the animals. The antitumor spectra of some of the 2,2-dimethylaziridine

TABLE 9

SUMMARY OF CHEMOTHERAPEUTIC RESULTS WITH SOME 2,2-DIMETHYLAZIRIDINES[46] *

Test System	TEPA-132	STEPA-132	TEM-132	AB-163
Leukemia L1210 (ascites):				
Percent "cures	60	20	0	30
Percent IST	75	50	0	150
Adenocarcinoma 755:				
Percent animals without tumors	100	0	–	30
Percent TI (weight)	–	50	–	50
Sarcoma 180 (solid):				
Precent animals without tumors	0	0	0	30
Percent TI (weight)	50	92	45	60
Dunning leukemia (ascites):				
Percent "cures"	50	80	0	–
Percent IST	234	236	0	–
Ehrlich ascites:				
Percent TI (cell counts)	98	–	60	96
Friend virus-induced leukemia:				
Percent Inhibition of splenomegaly	–	–	–	65
S-180 cells in tissue culture:				
μg/ml required for 50% inhibition	3.3	0.08	(0.16)†	0.5

*These *in vivo* results are those obtained at the optimal dose levels of the given compound in the given tumor system. "Cures" are defined as animals surviving 45 days or longer. Percent IST (increase of average survival time) and percent TI (average tumor inhibition) refer only to the nonsurvivors or to the animals with tumors, respectively, i.e., "cures" are not included.

†This drug did not give full inhibition at the higher concentrations.

type of alkylating agent is shown in TABLE 9. It is evident that these compounds demonstrate significant antitumor activities that are qualitatively or quantitatively different from those of the conventional alkylating agents belonging to the class of ethylenimines. Two of these new agents, TEPA-132 and AB-163, have been selected for preliminary clinical trial.

It is possible that the interesting antitumor activity spectra of the 2,2-dimethylaziridine derivative have some relationship to their unique chemical reactivity pattern, i.e., their ability to undergo S_N2 reactions with their unsubstituted ring-carbons and also S_N1 reactions through the formation of a tertiary carbonium ion. On the other hand, just as in the case of the selective carbamate mustards, it may be that there are some specific cellular receptors that are capable of selectively binding compounds containing certain structural units and thus increase the effective concentrations of these alkylating agents in the tumor cells. Such an explanation would be, of course, reminiscent of Ehrlich's original concept. In any case, the carbamate mustards and the 2,2-dimethylaziridine derivatives represent two striking examples of selective alkylating agents. Further studies of the structure-activity relationships and mode of action of these agents may throw some light on the molecular basis of their observed selectivitives against some tumors and may aid in the rational exploitation of these new leads in the design of effective drugs for cancer chemotherapy.

ACKNOWLEDGMENTS

The authors wish to thank Dr. L. N. Owen (Imperial College of Science and Technology, London University) for his cooperation in furnishing samples of the new nitrogen mustards synthesized in his laboratory. Several of the new aziridine derivatives were synthesized by Dr. Krishna C. Navada (Medicinal Chemistry Department, State University of New York at Buffalo) in the course of work toward his Ph.D. degree.

REFERENCES

1. SCHMIDT, L. H., R. FRADKIN, R. SULLIVAN & A. FLOWERS. 1965. Comparative pharmacology of alkylating agents. Cancer Chemother. Rep. Supplement 2. Part I, II, III.
2. SCHMIDT, L. H. 1963. Introductory comments on selective biological effects of alkylating agents in cancer chemotherapy. Cancer Res. **23:** 1311.
3. ROSS, W. C. J. 1962. Biological Alkylating Agents. Butterworths. London, England.
4. WARWICK, G. P. 1963. The mechanism of action of alkylating agents. Cancer Res. **23:** 1315.
5. BARDOS, T. J., N. DATTA-GUPTA, P. HEBBORN & D. J. TRIGGLE. 1965. A study of comparative chemical and biological activities of alkylating agents. J. Med. Chem. **8:** 167.
6. EPSTEIN, J., R. W. ROSENTHAL & R. J. ESS. 1955. Use of γ-(4-nitrobenzyl)pyridine as analytical reagent for ethylenimines and alkylating agents. Anal. Chem. **27:** 1435.
7. KLATT, O., A. C. GRIFFIN & J. S. STAHLEIN, JR. 1960. Method for determination of phenylalanine mustard and related alkylating agents in blood. Proc. Soc. Exp. Biol. Med. **104:** 629.
8. FRIEDMAN, O. M. & E. BOGER. 1961. Colorimetric estimation of nitrogen mustards in aqueous media. Anal. Chem. **33:** 906.

9. AUSMAN, R. K., G. E. CREVAR, H. HAGODORN, T. J. BARDOS & J. L. AMBRUS. 1961. Studies in the pharmacodynamics of mechlorethamine and AB-100. JAMA **178:** 735.
10. HEBBORN, P. & J. F. DANIELLI. 1958. The increased tumor inhibitory effect of enzyme-activated nitrogen mustards. Biochem. Pharmacol. **1:** 19.
11. DANIELLI, J. F. 1952. Cytochemical and cytological studies of drug action. Nature **170:** 863.
12. JOHNSON, B. J. & L. N. OWEN. 1964. Cytotoxic compounds. Part VI. Some N′-α(acylamino)-acyl-N,N-di-2′-chloroethyl-p-phenylenediamines. J. Chem. Soc. 3401.
13. DALTON, C. & P. HEBBORN. 1965. Sequential enzymic activation as a means of increasing therapeutic efficiency of nitrogen mustards. Biochem. Pharmacol. **14:** 1567.
14. BARDOS, T. J., Z. B. PAPANASTASSIOU, A. SEGALOFF & J. L. AMBRUS. 1959. "Dual antagonists"; alkyl N[bis(ethylenimido)phosphoro] carbamates: A new series of antitumor agents. Nature **183:** 399.
15. SKIPPER, H. E. 1949. Carbamates in the chemotherapy of leukemia. V. Observations of a possible antileukemic synergism between urethane and methyl-bis-(B-chloroethyl)amine. Cancer **2:** 475.
16. GELLHORN, A. 1958. The status of alkylating agents in clinical cancer chemotherapy. Ann. N. Y. Acad. Sci. **68:** 1254.
17. HADDOW, A. 1958. Future experimental approaches. Ann. N. Y. Acad. Sci. **68:** 1258.
18. BARDOS, T. J. 1962. Consideration of chemical reaction mechanisms in relationship to the biological action of "Dual Antagonists." Biochem. Pharmacol. **11:** 256.
19. AMBRUS, J. L., C. M. AMBRUS, N. BACK, L. STUTZMAN, J. E. SOKAL & C. A. ROSS. 1959. Pharmacology of 5-mercaptouracil (5MU), 2,4-diamino-6,7-dimethyl-2,4-deoxyalloxazine (DA), bis(ethylenemido)phosphorourethan (EPO) and its benzyl analog. Pharmacologist **1:** 80.
20. SEGALOFF, A., T. J. BARDOS, Z. B. PAPANASTASSIOU, J. L. AMBRUS & J. B. WEETH. 1959. bis(ethylenimido)phosphoro-urethan—a new type of anti-tumor agent. Proc. Amer. Assoc. Cancer Res.**3:** 62.
21. DUNNING, W. F., M. R. CURTIS, V. ARMAGHAN & D. MCKENZIE. 1961. Response of a spectrum of transplanted rat neoplasms to urethane, thioTEPA and two "Dual antagonists." Cancer Chemother. Rep. **12:** 1.
22. MCCRACKEN, S. & J. WOLF. 1960. Preliminary clinical investigation of AB-100. Cancer Chemother. Rep. **6:** 52.
23. WEETH, J. B. & A. SEGALOFF. 1961. Clinical experience with AB-100: Results of therapy in 123 patients. Southern Med. J. **54:** 39.
24. AMBRUS, J. L., J. A. SOKAL, C. M. AMBRUS, N. BACK & T. J. BARDOS. 1961. Clinical and experimental pharmacology of two ethylenimidophosphorocarbamates and preliminary clinical trial in lymphomas. Proc. Amer. Assoc. Cancer Res. **3:** 204.
25. RAZIS, D. V., J. L. AMBRUS, C. A. ROSS, L. STUTZMAN, J. E. SOKAL, A. M. REJALI & T. J. BARDOS. 1961. AB-103, A "dual antagonist" in the treatment of bronchogenic carcinoma. Cancer **14:** 853.
26. ROSS, C. A., J. E. SOKAL, J. L. AMBRUS, D. V. RAZIS & T. J. BARDOS. 1961. Benzcarbimine (AB-103) and AB-132 in the treatment of advanced bronchogenic carcinoma. Proc. Amer. Assoc. Cancer Res. **3:** 263.
27. HAYES, D. M., C. L. SPURR & J. D. HINES. 1961. Correlative studies on the chemotherapy of mouse and human myeloma with AB-100. Proc. Amer. Assoc. Cancer Res. **3:** 233.
28. PACIFIC COAST V. A. CANCER CHEMOTHERAPY GROUP. 1962. The clinical evaluation of AB-103 (NSC-37096) in various malignancies—a phase II Study. Cancer Chemother. Rep. **16:** 425.
29. PACIFIC COAST V. A. CANCER CHEMOTHERAPY GROUP. 1963. A study of benzcarbimine (AB-103; NSC-37096) in patients with various malignancies. Cancer Chemother. Rep. **33:** 15.
30. NAVADA, K. 1968. Synthesis and hydrolysis reactions of some aziridine derivatives with antineoplastic activity. Ph.D. dissertation. State University of New York at Buffalo. Buffalo, N. Y.

31. Bardos, T. J., A. K. Barua, Z. F. Chmielewicz, G. E. Crevar, J. P. Dailey, S. Divald & Z. B. Papanastassiou. 1965. Synthesis of potential dual antagonists. III. Ring substituted ethyl bis-(1-aziridinyl)-phosphinyl carbamates. J. Pharm. Sci. **54:** 187.
32. Chmielewicz, Z. F., T. J. Bardos, C. K. Navada, N. Back & J. L. Ambrus. 1967. Comparative chemical and biological properties of the stereoisomeric ethyl bis(2,3-dimethyl-1-aziridinyl)phosphinyl carbamates. Chimica Therapeutica **2:** 181.
33. Bardos, T. J. & J. L. Ambrus. 1964. AB-132, an alkylating carbamate in the chemotherapy of neoplasias. *In* Third International Congress for Chemotherapy. H. P. Kuemmerle, Ed. **II:** 1036. Hafner Publishing Co., Inc. New York, N. Y.
34. Watne, A. L., G. E. Moore, C. A. Ross & J. L. Ambrus. 1962. Clinical experience with AB-132. Cancer Chemother. Rap. **16:** 421.
35. Ross, C. A., H. A. Velasco, J. L. Ambrus, L. Stutzman, J. Webster & T. J. Bardos. 1962. Combined therapy with AB-132 and radiation in bronchogenic carcinoma. Proc. Amer. Assoc. Cancer Res. **3:** 355.
36. Ross, C. A., J. L. Ambrus, J. E. Sokal, H. A. Velasco, L. Stutzman & D. V. Razis. 1962. Chemical evaluation of AB-132 in the management of advanced bronchogenic carcinoma. Cancer Chemother. Rep. **18:** 27.
37. Stutzman, L., D. V. Razis, J. E. Sokal, J. L. Ambrus & C. A. Ross. 1962. Clinical experience with a new alkylating agent, AB-132, in the treatment of lymphomas and leukemias. Cancer Chemother. Rep. **18:** 31.
38. Delta, B. G., C. M. Ambrus, J. L. Ambrus & L. Stutzman. 1962. Ethyl bis(2,2-dimethyl-1-aziridinyl)phosphinyl carbamate (AB-132) in the treatment of children with malignant neoplasms. Cancer Chemother. Rep. **18:** 37.
39. Back, N., J. L. Ambrus, A. E. Munson & T. J. Bardos. 1962. Study on the mechanism of action of side effects produced by AB-132. Proc. Soc. Amer. Assoc. Cancer Res. **3:** 301.
40. Foldes, F. F., J. L. Ambrus, N. Back, T. J. Bardos & V. Foldes. 1962. Relationship between the anticholinesterase activity and side effect liability of AB-132 in man. Fed. Proc. **21:** 355.
41. Ross, C. A., H. A. Velasco, J. H. Webster, J. L. Ambrus & J. E. Sokal. 1963. AB-132 and radiation therapy in the treatment of intrathoracic malignancies. Proc. Amer. Assoc. Cancer Res. **4:** 59.
42. Velasco, H. V., C. A. Ross, J. H. Webster, J. E. Sokal, L. Stutzman & J. L. Ambrus, 1964. Combined use of AB-132 (Meturedepa, Turloc) and x-irradiation in the management of advanced bronchogenic carcinoma. Cancer **17:** 841.
43. Ambrus, J. L., J. H. Webster, C. A. Ross, J. E. Sokal, L. Stutzman, H. Velasco, C. M. Ambrus & T. J. Bardos. 1968. Potentiation of the therapeutic effect of radiation with AB-132 in thoracic malignancies. Proc. Amer. Soc. Clin. Oncol. **1:** 2.
44. Back, N., T. J. Bardos, Z. F. Chmielewicz, E. Achter & A. E. Munson. 1964. Studies on the mechanism of action of cyclophosphamide and AB-132 with the aid of radioprotective agents. Life Sci. **3:** 803.
45. Chmielewicz, Z. F., T. J. Bardos, N. Back, J. L. Ambrus & C. M. Ambrus. 1967. Comparative chemical and biological activities of 2,2-dimethylaziridine derivatives. Fed. Proc. **26:** 686.
46. T. J. Bardos, Z. F. Chmielewicz, J. L. Ambrus & N. Back. 1967. Effects of ring-C-methyl substituents on the chemical and biological activities of ethylenimine type alkylating agents. *In* Fifth International Congress of Chemotherapy. : 191. Vienna, Austria.

CARCINOGENESIS: FRONTIERS IN INNER SPACE*

Michael B. Shimkin

Health Sciences Center
Temple University
Philadelphia, Pa.

Sackcloth and ashes are as fashionable these days as are miniskirts and Nehru jackets—and perhaps for related reasons. Certainly as we look at the international scene and closer around us, it is difficult to be complaisant. But it is also easy to exaggerate.

We in the United States are observing the end of a golden era in biomedical research. For two decades, biomedical scientists and their institutions have enjoyed an ever-increasing flow of funds for our activities. Now we are faced by actual reductions and the resultant stresses. Biomedical research is part of our society and must share in its nausea.

For perspective, it is useful to review how we got here in the first place. How were governmental funds for biomedical research expanded from a few millions to over a billion dollars within a decade? The events are hard to reconstruct from official annual reports. We finally do have one "as-it-happened" description that is reasonably factual and fun to read. It is a piece by Mrs. Elizabeth Brenner Drew, entitled "The Health Syndicate, Washington's Noble Conspirators," which appeared in the December 1967 issue of the *Atlantic Monthly*. I commend it to your attention.

The federal developments, however, are but half of the tale. The actual research was taking place in universities. The reactions, problems, and questions that have arisen are well described in a recent compilation of the American Council in Education entitled "Sponsored Research in American Universities and Colleges." That also should be required reading for us.

The fact is that the federal cornucopia for biomedical research was not all for the good. Certainly the endless largesse had some undesirable effects on universities and related institutions. The obesity of the research budgets from outside sources produced lethargy of the institutional role and responsibility. It is during a time of relative adversity that such unpleasantnesses can be pointed out in order that remedial actions are at least considered; in flush times such alarums are considered to be almost facetious.

Early in the days of federal support of biomedical research some of our institutions of higher learning were reluctant to touch these tainted dollars. This phase soon passed, and some of the most vociferous champions against federal funds became champion recipients. Then there were the criticisms of research support because it was stated to interfere with teaching, although no institution was ever forced to accept funds, and an increasingly larger proportion of the funds were allocated to training programs and other devices for the subsidy of education.

An interesting position regarding federal research funds was successfully de-

*This paper was presented as an after-dinner address at a subscription dinner during the conference.

veloped by universities and other recipient institutions. In the matter of overhead, which grew and grew, the argument was that the funds should cover all expenses, direct and secondary, of the proposed research. This implied that the institution was doing someone a favor by accepting the funds at all and by allowing the research to proceed in its facilities, which often were also built and equipped with funds from the same sources!

This course of events was budgetarily convenient and produced an additional important source of revenue for the institution. It also identified research as a peripheral activity supported by "soft" funds, tolerated so long as such funds continued to be available. It is inevitable that under such circumstances institutions abrogated at least some of their responsibilities to the very governmental bureaus they initially purported to fear.

It is high time that universities and related institutions recapture the responsibility for biomedical research. This is possible only if the institutions truly recognize research as an essential component of their total mission, set responsible policies and priorities, and assume appropriate degrees of fiscal, personnel, and other responsibility over the endeavors. This requires administrative restructuring of research, with involvement of the faculty, of the same scope and intensity as that applied to curriculum.

It is to be hoped that the present difficulties will result in such positive reactions. These reactions include consideration of the problems of relevance, student participation and related matters that are as real in biomedical research as they are in education and other social movements. It is also hoped that it will be recognized that problem-solving orientation is academically appropriate and that interdisciplinary groupings are essential. We are all for "basic" research, but we must recognize that this is akin to patriotism—a noble concept, but also the last refuge of the scoundrel.

The immediate problem at hand is what to do about the inevitable budget cuts that have to be effected in federal research allocations. The rules toward this imposed end are being set by the government, although the scientific community is represented through various advisory groups. Is this not the time for universities and related institutions to recapture their proper leadership position by indicating how this is to be effected? I suggest that the economies should be made by reducing the overhead to the institutions and by reducing general research support subsidies. These immediate actions should be followed by a careful overall examination by the institutions of their total research role, in relation to its other missions and to national needs. Thus made lean and hungry, we might have better wind and greater longevity for the exciting days ahead.

Let me make it clear that I think that research on carcinogenesis needs no sackcloth and ashes, and miniskirts would not look good on most of us. We already have the laboratory coat as our official uniform and status symbol.

Studies on carcinogenesis have provided us with some major insights into the causation and prevention of cancer in man. Tobacco smoking, as an important type of air pollution, will some day rank historically with the discoveries of waterborne diseases. Currently, carcinogenesis research finds itself in a particularly interesting period. This is attributable to the discovery of new species of powerful chemical carcinogens, especially the alkylating agents and nitrosamines, and of the "natural" sources of carcinogens, such as aflatoxin and cycasin.

I believe it is time to direct, or redirect, our scientific attention toward endogenous sources of carcinogenic chemicals, the autocarcinogens. Estrogens must be included under this designation, as first shown with crude folliculin by Lacassagne in 1932. Five years later, Shabad published an intriguing report on the induction of sarcomas with benzene fractions of livers from patients with cancer. This lead was expanded by Steiner and Falk, but apparently came to a dead end in the cholesterol carcinogenesis studies of Hieger. I am certain there are other, more promising, avenues in the same direction.

We have a number of situations in man that seem to offer an opportunity for profitable exporation for autocarcinogens. The great susceptibility of thermal scars to neoplasms indicates one departure point. Smegma, with its relationship to penile cancer, certainly deserves more attention than it has had. Gallstones, associated with the occurrence of cancer of the gallbladder, deserve further investigation. For that matter, bile and its products are far from exhausted as legitimate materials for further research.

The studies on cycasin, and the role of bacterial flora of the intestine on its glycone, suggest the exploration of the role of bacteria in other carcinogenic situations.

A fascinating area of research, to me, is the identification and isolation of physiologically active materials from tissues—the endobiotics. Steroid hormones are the species of physiological regulators with which we are perhaps best acquainted. These chemicals should allow man to control his population and spare the earth from the human cancer that is consuming it. More recently, we have seen the discoveries of glucagon, of prostaglandin, and of thyrocalcitonin, and the end is not in sight. Salivary glands apparently contain some interesting materials. Empirical extracts of tissues have yielded several that have growth-inhibitory and growth-stimulating effects in microbial, tissue-culture, and transplanted tumor systems. I think that the most obvious tissues in which to seek growth-regulating chemicals are embryos and the placenta.

Tumors elaborate a wide variety of physiologically active materials, with an ever-growing list of bizarre syndromes resulting from so-called inappropriate secretion of hormone-like substances. Thus, tumors are certainly another type of tissue worth exploration for inhibitors and accelerators of cell growth. Years ago, Mider described the prevention of cachexia in rats bearing tumors by feeding tumor material to the animals. Subsequent publications in the area do not convince me that this interesting phenomenon has been explained.

I have been intrigued for three decades by the obverse side of the carcinogenesis coin, which could be called resistance. The model of a Wistar rat and 7,12-dimethylbenz(a)anthracene (DMBA) is an illuminating illustration. If a few milligrams of DMBA, a potent carcinogen, are instilled into the stomach, within four hours every tissue in the body will have fluorescent-detectable DMBA. Yet within a year, practically only one tissue in the female, the breast, will have undergone neoplastic transformation. This limited effect depends upon the sex, age, and nutrition of the animal. Males will develop few breast cancers, but instead, they develop cancers of the sebaceous glands and of the skin. If the animals are under two weeks old at the time of DMBA administration, there will be no breast cancers; instead, subcutaneous sarcomas arise. In females, more breast cancers are induced if the agent is given just at the time the animals reach sexual maturity, when the vagina opens. A few weeks before or after, susceptibility is much less. Take out the ovaries or the pituitary, or restrict the animal's food, and the appearance of the tumors is reduced, and many of the tumors already in evidence shrink and disappear.

Recently, we studied further the effect of dose and schedule of DMBA on the neoplastic reaction. If DMBA is given every other day for five doses, the neoplastic response is less than that to a single dose; if the same dose is given once a week, the response is accentuated. Not only that, but the subsequent *growth* of the tumors is faster if the weekly schedule is employed. And how were the intervals chosen? Tritiated thymidine determinations showed that a single dose of DMBA depressed labeling of cells in the breast ducts by up to 90% in 24 to 48 hr, and this depression was recovered in seven days. Thus, it seems that the stage of the cell cycle at which the carcinogen hits the cell population not only influences the induction of tumors, but leaves an impress upon their subsequent growth potential.

Accentuation of biochemical work upon the state of receptivity of tissues to carcinogenesis certainly seems desirable. In this, attention to tissues that do *not* respond seems as important as attention to the tissues that do. Cancer by definition is a cell population problem, in which the carcinogenic reaction initially involves but a small subpopulation group. Biochemical studies should be related to cell populations and cell dynamics; results on tissue homogenates and tissue slices may be more informative with such correlations.

We can assume that cancer is a type of disease of cell differentiation. Differentiation can be manifested only through cell divisions. Somewhere along these chains of processes, carcinogenic compounds can make their impress only if the cells possess appropriate neoreceptors. These attachment sites to carcinogenic stimuli apparently have active and inactive phases, so that they are dynamic states rather than structural characteristics.

I know of no more exciting area of biomedical research than carcinogenesis. This sense of excitement makes one impatient and, perhaps, not sufficiently cautious.

I hope that what I have said might stimulate some additional departures. My real hope, however, is that all of our combined thought and work will eventually also lead to some important arrivals.

Even in these days of Vietnam, Czechoslovakia, alienation of youth, racism, and all the diseases of opulence, scientific research will not only survive; it will prosper. The frontiers before us are limitless—interstellar space, on the one hand, and on the other, our own inner space, where lie the secrets of what we are and how we behave.